SERVICE MANAGEMENT

Operations, Strategy, and Information Technology

THIRD EDITION

James A. Fitzsimmons

William H. Seay Centennial Professor of Business
University of Texas at Austin

Mona J. Fitzsimmons

McGraw-Hill, Inc.

Boston   Burr Ridge, IL   Dubuque,   San Francisco   St. Louis
Bangkok   Bogotá   Caracas   Kuala   London   Madrid   Mexico City
Milan   Montreal   New Delhi   San   Sydney   Taipei   Toronto

McGraw-Hill Higher Education

A Division of The McGraw-Hill Companies

SERVICE MANAGEMENT
OPERATIONS, STRATEGY, AND INFORMATION TECHNOLOGY
International Edition 2001

10 09 08 07 06 05 04 03 02 01
20 09 08 07 06 05 04 03 02 01 00
CTP   SLP

"The Blue Mountain logo is a service mark of BMA Holdings, LLC, and is used with permission."
"Logo courtesy of Southwest Airlines Co."
"Logo courtesy of L.L. Bean, Inc., Freeport, ME"
"Logo courtesy of W. Atlee Burpee & Co."
"Logo courtesy of Shouldice Hospital, Ltd."
"Logo reprinted with permission of Enterprise Rent-A-Car Company."
"Logo reprinted with permission of Goodwill Industries International."
"Logo used with permission from Golfsmith, Inc."

Library of Congress Cataloging-in-Publication Data
Fitzsimmons, James A.
   Service management : operations, strategy, and information technology / James A.
Fitzsimmons, Mona J. Fitzsimmons. — 3rd ed.
   p.   cm.
   ISBN 0-07-231267-X
   Includes bibliographical references and index.
   1.   Service industries — Management. I. Fitzsimmons,. Mona J. II. Title.
HD9980.5.F549 2000
658dc—21   00026733

www.mhhe.com

When ordering this title, use ISBN 0-07-118115-6

Printed in Singapore

About the Authors

JAMES A. FITZSIMMONS received a B.S.E. in industrial engineering from the University of Michigan, an MBA from Western Michigan University, and a Ph.D. with distinction from the University of California at Los Angeles. His research in the area of emergency ambulance location won the Stan Hardy Award in 1983 for the best paper published in the field of operations management. A computer program, referred to as CALL, has been used by major cities worldwide to plan emergency ambulance systems. Consulting assignments include the RAND Corporation; the U.S. Air Force; the cities of Los Angeles, Denver, Austin, Melbourne, and Auckland; the Texas comptroller; General Motors; La Quinta Motor Inns; Greyhound; and McDonald's. Teaching experience includes faculty appointments at the University of California at Los Angeles, California State University at Northridge, the University of New Mexico, Boston University Overseas Graduate Program, California Polytechnic State University at San Luis Obispo, and the Helsinki School of Economics and Business. He is a registered professional engineer in the state of Michigan and has held industrial engineering positions at Corning Glass Works and Hughes Aircraft Company. He served in the U.S. Air Force as an officer in charge of base construction projects. He held the position of Ph.D. graduate adviser for eight years in the Department of Management at the University of Texas and was nominated for six teaching awards. With Mona Fitzsimmons he edited *New Service Development: Creating Memorable Experiences* published in 2000 by Sage Publications. He currently serves as service operations area editor for *Production and Operations Management* and member of the editorial review board of the *Journal of Service Research.*

MONA J. FITZSIMMONS, a graduate of the University of Michigan, received her undergraduate degree in journalism with major supporting work in chemistry and psychology. Her graduate work was in geology and she has taught in public and private schools and at the university level. She has done writing and editing for the Encyclopaedia Britannica Education Corporation and for various professional journals and organizations. With James Fitzsimmons she edited *New Service Development: Creating Memorable Experiences* published in 2000 by Sage Publications. Her nonprofessional activities have included volunteer work for the Red Cross aquatics program and in wildlife rehabilitation. She has particular interests in the areas of environmental issues and the responsibilities of patients and physicians in health care.

To Our Family:
Michael, Kate, and Colleen
Gary
Samantha, Darwin, and Jordan
Melba Jett

In Memory of William H. Seay

BRIEF CONTENTS

v

PART FOUR

Toward World-Class Service

CONTENTS

8. THE SERVICE ENCOUNTER

PART THREE

Managing Service Operations

PART FOUR

Toward World-Class Service

PREFACE

Services touch the lives of every person in this country every day: food services, communication services, and emergency services, to name only a few. Our welfare and the welfare of our economy are now based on services. The activities of manufacturing and agriculture will always be necessary, but we can eat only so much food and we can use only so many goods. Services, however, are largely experiential, and we will always have a limitless appetite for them.

Service operations management is firmly established as a field of study that embraces all service industries. For example, under the leadership of the senior author of this text, the discipline was recognized as an academic field and designated as a separate track by the Decision Sciences Institute (DSI) at its 1987 Boston meeting. In 1989 the *International Journal of Service Industry Management* was inaugurated. Finally, the First International Service Research Seminar in Service Management was held in France in 1990, drawing participants from the fields of operations management, marketing, and organizational behavior. This conference recognized the multidisciplinary nature of services and dropped the adjective "operations" in order to emphasize the integrative nature of service management. Following the 1996 Orlando DSI meeting, a website (http://soma.byu.edu) was established to support faculty and students who are interested in the field of service management.

In the second edition of this text, chapters on project management and managing service inventories were added to make the text appropriate for use in introductory courses in operations management. The text afforded all students of business the opportunity to study operations from the prospective of their future employment in a service economy.

This third edition recognizes the emergence of a new frontier in service management, that of an age of "experiences." We explore this exciting new experience economy in the first chapter. We also note in the first chapter that new jobs are being created primarily in services and many of those jobs are in high-tech firms offering professional salaries. Further, entrepreneurial opportunities for creative business students abound in services.

In this edition we continue to emphasize three themes that run throughout the book. First, this is a book devoted to the management of service *operations* from an open systems view, which means that the customer is a participant in the delivery process. Second, for services the "process is the product" and therefore, marketing and *strategic* issues cannot be separated from operations, which in turn cannot ignore behavioral issues associated with customer contact. Finally, we recognize that the role of *information technology (IT)* no longer is just an enabler of continuous improvement in productivity and quality in services. We have included a new chapter on Internet services to explore this new phenomenon called e-commerce. The Internet represents a new delivery channel for services that has redefined the competitive marketplace with a global reach.

This edition continues to acknowledge and emphasize the essential uniqueness of service management. These are some key features:

- The book is written in an engaging literary style, makes extensive use of examples, and is based on the research and consulting experience of the authors.
- The theme of managing services for competitive advantage is emphasized in each chapter and provides a focus for each management topic.
- The integration of marketing, operations, and human behavior is recognized as central to effective service management.
- To dispel the common belief that manufacturing management principles can be applied to services without recognition of the different operating environments, the role of services in society and the uniqueness of service delivery systems are stressed.
- The information technologies of yield management, data envelopment analysis, and computer simulation are included as illustrations of three of the strategic roles of information in managing services.
- Emphasis is placed on the need for continuous improvement in quality and productivity in order to compete effectively in a global environment.
- To motivate the reader, a vignette of a well-known company starts each chapter, illustrating the strategic nature of the topic to be covered.
- Each chapter has a preview, a closing summary, key terms and definitions, service benchmark, topics for discussion, solved problems and exercises when appropriate, and one or more cases.
- For this third edition, a CD-ROM contains PowerPoint lecture slides, ServiceModel simulation software, an Excel spreadsheet, chapter quizzes, and websites.
- The instructor's manual contains case analyses, exercise solutions, objective test banks, and lists of supplementary materials. A VHS tape library of instructive videos also accompanies the manual.

This edition includes the following pedagogical features in each chapter:

Learning objectives help students focus on the key concepts to be explored in the chapter.

Service Benchmarks illustrate outstanding examples of excellence in service.

Key Terms and Definitions at the conclusion of each chapter serves as a quick reference and reminder of the new vocabulary just presented.

Solved Problems before the exercises in selected chapters illustrate in detail the steps taken to resolve a quantitative problem.

We were very fortunate to have our manuscript reviewed by several colleagues—all people of integrity, wit, and vision. Their detailed comments, insights, and thought-provoking suggestions were gratefully received and incorporated in the text in many places. Special thanks and acknowledgment go to the following people for their valuable reviews of the first edition: Mohammad Ala, California State University, Los Angeles; Joanna R. Baker, Virginia Polytechnic Institute and State University; Mark Davis, Bentley College; Maling Ebrahimpour, University of Rhode Island; Michael Gleeson, Indiana University; Ray Haynes, California Polytechnic State University at San Luis Obispo, Art Hill, the University of Minnesota; Sheryl Kimes, Cornell University; and Richard Reid, the University of New Mexico.

The second edition benefited from the constructive comments of the following reviewers: Kimberly Bates, New York University; Avi Dechter, California State University, Northridge; Scott Dellana, East Carolina University; Sheryl Kimes, Cornell University; Larry J. LeBlanc, Vanderbilt University; Robert Lucas, Metropolitan State College of Denver; Barbara Osyk, University of Akron; Michael Showalter, Florida State University; and V. Sridharan, Clemson University.

The following reviewers contributed their experience and wisdom to this third edition: Sidhartha Das, George Mason University; Avi Dechter, California State University at Northridge; Byron Finch, Miami University of Ohio; Edward M. Hufft, Jr., Metropolitan State College of Denver; Ken Klassen, California State University at Northridge; Richard Reid, University of New Mexico, Albuquerque; Ishpal Rekki, California State University at San Marcos; and Ronald Satterfield, University of South Florida.

We wish to acknowledge two students who have assisted us. Fang Wu, Ph.D. student at the University of Texas at Austin, assisted in the development of some exercises and preparation of the PowerPoint lecture presentations for the second edition. Edmond Gonzales, an MBA student at Texas, prepared the chapter quizzes for the third edition CD-ROM. A special thanks is extended to Rob Bateman of the ProModel Corporation for the preparation of the Pronto Pizza simulation case and assistance in our adoption of the ServiceModel software for this edition. The personal computer, printer, and software provided through the generosity of William H. Seay, who endowed the senior author's professorship, made the writing of this book a great pleasure. We are also indebted to Mrs. Margaret Seay who continues her generous support.

We express special appreciation to all our friends who encouraged us and tolerated our social lapses while we produced this book. In particular, we are indebted for the support of Richard and Janice Reid, who have provided lively and stimulating conversations and activities over many years, and who generously allowed us the use of their mountain retreat. The beginning of the first edition was written in the splendid isolation of their part of the Jemez Mountains of New Mexico. No authors could want for better inspiration.

James A. Fitzsimmons
Mona J. Fitzsimmons

OVERVIEW OF THE BOOK

Part I begins with a discussion of the role of services in an economy. We first look at the evolution of societies based on economic activity, beginning with agriculture and moving to industrialization and finally to service economies. We also introduce the concept of an emerging experience economy. Next, we consider the distinctive characteristics of the service operations, which leads to an open-systems view of services. The challenge of delivering exceptional service quality is addressed in the context of a comparison of customers' perceptions and expectations. This section concludes with the formulation of the strategic service concept and a discussion of the generic competitive service strategies of overall cost leadership, differentiation, and focus. The competitive role of information is captured in the concept of the virtual value chain.

Designing the service enterprise to support the competitive strategy is the topic of Part II. The service delivery system is engineered through the use of a process flow-charting concept called blueprinting that explicitly recognizes the front office, where customer contact occurs, and the behind-the-scenes back-office operations. Questions concerning the facility design and layout next are addressed from the perspective of both customer participation and operations efficiency. Using analytical models, the critical decision of where to locate the service facility is determined. The notion of a service encounter describes the interaction between service provider and customer in the context of a service organization. Finally, a new chapter on Internet services explores the emerging area of the virtual service encounter.

Management of day-to-day operations is addressed in Part III. Forecasting service demand begins the discussion of service operations management. The question of managing waiting lines is addressed from a psychological viewpoint. A new supplement on computer simulation prepares students to use the ServiceModel animated software that is included on a CD-ROM disk packaged with the textbook. Capacity planning using queuing models next is addressed. Because the nature of services provides a challenge in matching capacity with demand, strategies are discussed including the concept of yield management. Managing facilitating goods follows. A new chapter on the topic of service chain management includes a discussion of the business-to-business purchase of services. Microsoft® Project software is the foundation for the topic on project management. Linear programming models with applications in services are illustrated with Microsoft® Excel Solver.

In Part IV, we look at strategies to achieve world-class service. The concept of continual improvement in quality and productivity is discussed in the context of the stages of service firm competitiveness. Finally, growth and expansion are explored using global service strategies.

PART ONE

UNDERSTANDING SERVICES

We begin our study of service management in Chapter 1 with an appreciation of the central role that services play in the economies of nations and in world commerce. No economy can function without the infrastructure that services provide in the form of transportation and communications and without government services such as education and health care. As an economy develops, however, services become even more important, and soon the vast majority of the population is employed in service activities.

Chapter 2 addresses the nature of service operations and identifies their distinctive characteristics. Perhaps the most important characteristic of service operations is the presence of the customer in the service delivery system. Focusing on the customer and serving his or her needs has always been an important daily activity for service providers.

Service quality, which is measured by the gap between customer expectations and perceptions of the service, is the topic of Chapter 3. We examine several approaches to managing service quality, including measurement issues, designing quality into the service, service process control, and service recovery.

An effective competitive strategy is particularly important for service firms because they compete in an environment where there are relatively low barriers to entry. Consequently, the firms are always faced with new competition. In Chapter 4 the strategic service concept is presented. The well-known generic competitive strategies—overall cost leadership, differentiation, and focus—are applied to services. The chapter concludes with a discussion of the competitive role of information in services.

CHAPTER ONE

The Role of Services in an Economy

Learning Objectives

After completing this chapter, you should be able to:

1. Describe the central role of services in an economy.
2. Discuss the evolution of an economy from an agrarian society to a service society.
3. Describe the features of preindustrial, industrial, and postindustrial societies.
4. Describe the features of the new experience economy.
5. Discuss the role of service managers with respect to innovation, social trends, and management challenges.

Services lie at the very hub of economic activity in any society. Writing about the role of the service sector in world development, Dorothy Riddle formulated the economic model shown in Figure 1.1. This model shows the flow of activity among the three principal sectors of the economy: extractive (mining and farming), manufacturing, and service, which is divided into five subgroups. All activity eventually leads to the consumer. Examples of services in each of the five subgroups are:

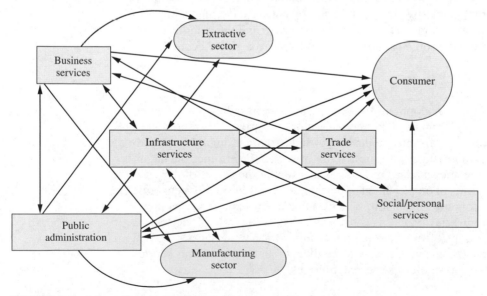

FIGURE 1.1 Interactive model of an economy.
(*Source:* After Dorothy I. Riddle, *Service-Led Growth,* Praeger, New York, 1986, p. 27.)

Business services. Consulting, finance, banking

Trade services. Retailing, maintenance, repair

Infrastructure services. Communications, transportation

Social/personal services. Restaurants, health care

Public administration. Education, government

Infrastructure services, such as transportation and communications, are the essential links among all sectors of the economy, including the final consumer. In a complex economy, both infrastructure and trade services function as intermediaries between the extractive and manufacturing sectors and as the channel of distribution to the final consumer. Infrastructure services are a prerequisite for an economy to become industrialized; therefore, no advanced society can be without these services.

In an industrialized economy, specialized firms can supply business services to manufacturing firms more cheaply and efficiently than manufacturing firms can supply these services for themselves. Thus, more and more often we find advertising, consulting, financing, testing, and other business functions being provided for the manufacturing sector by service firms.

Except for basic subsistence living, where individual households are self-sufficient, service activities are absolutely necessary for the economy to function and to enhance the quality of life. Consider, for example, the importance of a banking industry to transfer funds and a transportation industry to move food products to areas that cannot produce them. Moreover, a wide variety of social and personal services, such as restaurants, lodging, cleaning, and child care, have been created to move former household functions into the economy.

Public administration plays a critical role in providing a stable environment for investment and economic growth. Services such as public education, health care, well-maintained roads, safe drinking water, clean air, and public safety are necessary for any nation's economy to survive and people to prosper.

Thus, it is imperative to recognize that services are not peripheral activities but rather integral parts of society. They are central to a functioning and healthy economy and lie at the heart of that economy. The service sector not only facilitates but also makes possible the goods-producing activities of the extractive and the manufacturing sectors. Services are the crucial force for today's change toward a global economy.

CHAPTER PREVIEW

In a discussion of economic development, we learn that modern industrialized economies are dominated by employment in the service sector industries. This represents a natural evolution of economies from preindustrial to industrial and finally to postindustrial societies. Furthermore, the economic activity of society determines the nature of how people live and how the standard of living is measured. The nature of the service sector is explored in terms of employment opportunities, contributions to economic stability, and source of economic leadership. The idea that a new experience economy will supersede our postindustrial society is considered. Finally, the role of the service manager is discussed in terms of innovation, opportunities for new services based on demographic trends, and the many managerial challenges in an expanding service economy. We begin with a selection of service definitions.

SERVICE DEFINITIONS

Many definitions of service are available but all contain a common theme of intangibility and simultaneous consumption. The following represent a sample of service definitions:

Services are deeds, processes, and performances. (Valarie A. Zeithaml and Mary Jo Bitner, *Services Marketing,* McGraw-Hill, New York, 1996, p. 5.)

A service is an activity or series of activities of more or less intangible nature that normally, but not necessarily, take place in interactions between customer and service employees and/or physical resources or goods and/or systems of the service provider, which are provided as solutions to customer problems. (Christian Gronroos, *Service Management and Marketing,* Lexington Books, Lexington, Mass., 1990, p. 27.)

Most authorities consider the services sector to include all economic activities whose output is not a physical product or construction, is generally consumed at the time it is produced, and provides added value in forms (such as convenience, amusement, timeliness, comfort or health) that are essentially intangible concerns of its first purchaser. (James Brian Quinn, Jordan J. Baruch, and Penny Cushman Paquette, *Scientific American,* vol. 257, no. 2, December 1987, p. 50.)

A precise definition of goods and services should distinguish them on the basis of their attributes. A good is a tangible physical object or product that can be created and transferred; it has an existence over time and thus can be created and used later. A service is intangible and perishable. It is an occurrence or process that is created and used simultaneously or nearly simultaneously. While the consumer cannot retain the actual service after it is produced, the effect of the service can be retained. (Earl Sasser, R. Paul Olsen, and D. Daryl Wyckoff, *Management of Service Operations,* Allyn and Bacon, Boston, 1978, p. 8.)

A service is a time-perishable, intangible experience performed for a customer acting in the role of co-producer. (James Fitzsimmons)

ECONOMIC EVOLUTION

In the early 1900s, only 3 of every 10 workers in the United States were employed in the services sector. The remaining workers were active in agriculture and industry. By 1950, employment in services accounted for 50 percent of the workforce. Today, services employ about 8 out of every 10 workers. During the past 90 years, we have witnessed a major evolution in our society from being predominantly manufacturing-based to being predominantly service-based.

Economists studying economic growth are not surprised by these events. Colin Clark argues that as nations become industrialized, there is an inevitable shift of employment from one sector of the economy to another.[1] As productivity increases in one sector, the labor force moves into another. This observation, known as the *Clark-Fisher hypothesis,* leads to a classification of economies by noting the activity of the majority of the workforce.

Table 1.1 describes five stages of economic activity. Many economists, including Clark, limited their analyses to only three stages, of which the tertiary stage was simply services. We have taken the suggestion of Nelson N. Foote and Paul K. Hatt and subdivided the service stage into three categories.[2]

Today, an overwhelming number of countries are still in a primary stage of development. These economies are based on extracting natural resources from the land. Their productivity is low, and income is subject to fluctuations based on the prices of commodities such as sugar and copper. In much of Africa and parts of Asia, more than 70 percent of the labor force is engaged in extractive activities.

TABLE 1.1

STAGES OF ECONOMIC ACTIVITY

Primary (Extractive)
Agriculture
Mining
Fishing
Forestry

Secondary (Goods-Producing)
Manufacturing
Processing

Tertiary (Domestic Services)
Restaurants and hotels
Barber and beauty shops
Laundry and dry cleaning
Maintenance and repair

Quaternary (Trade and Commerce Services)
Transportation
Retailing
Communication
Finance and insurance
Real estate
Government

Quinary (Refining and Extending Human Capacities)
Health
Education
Research
Recreation
Arts

Based on the work activity of their populations, however, many of the so-called advanced industrial nations would be better described as service economies. Table 1.2 is a partial list of industrialized countries ranked in order of the percentage of those employed in service-producing jobs. This table contains some surprises, such as finding that Canada, known for its mining industry, is high on the list and that China's economy is becoming more sophisticated. Several observations can be made: Global economic development is progressing in unanticipated directions, successful industrial economies are built on a strong service sector, and just as it has in manufacturing, competition in services will become global. In fact, many of the largest commercial banks in the world at present are owned by the Japanese. Trade in services remains a challenge, however, because many countries erect barriers to protect domestic firms. For example, India and Mexico, among others, prohibit the sale of insurance by foreign companies.

TABLE 1.2

PERCENT EMPLOYMENT IN SERVICE JOBS FOR SELECTED INDUSTRIALIZED NATIONS, 1980–1999

Country	1980	1987	1993	1999
United States	67.1	71.0	74.3	80.4
Canada	67.2	70.8	74.8	73.9
Japan	54.5	58.1	59.9	72.4
France	56.9	63.6	66.4	70.8
Israel	63.3	66.0	68.0	70.7
Italy	48.7	57.7	60.2	61.1
China	13.1	17.8	21.2	26.4

Source:1999 Statistical Yearbook, Department of International Economic and Social Affairs Statistical Office, United Nations, New York, 1999.

FIGURE 1.2 Trends in U.S employment by sector, 1850–2000.
(From U.S. Department of Commerce, Bureau of the Census, *Historical Statistics of the United States,* 1975, p. 137, and U.S. Department of Commerce, Bureau of the Census, *Statistical Abstract of the United States,* 1995, p. 417.)

As Figure 1.2 shows, the service sector now accounts for more than 80 percent of total employment in the United States, which continues a trend that began more than one century ago. Therefore, based on employment figures, the United States can no longer be characterized as an industrial society; instead, it is a postindustrial, or service, society.

STAGES OF ECONOMIC DEVELOPMENT

Describing where our society has been, its current condition, and its most likely future is the task of social historians. Daniel Bell, a professor of sociology at Harvard University, has written extensively on this topic, and the material that follows is based on his work.[3] To place the concept of a postindustrial society in perspective, we must compare its features with those of preindustrial and industrial societies.

Preindustrial Society

The condition of most of the world's population today is one of subsistence, or a *preindustrial society.* Life is characterized as a game against nature. Working with muscle power and tradition, the labor force is engaged in agriculture, mining, and fishing. Life is conditioned by the elements, such as the weather, the quality of the soil, and the availability of water. The rhythm of life is shaped by nature, and the pace of work varies with the seasons. Productivity is low and bears little evidence of technology. Social life revolves around the extended household, and this combination of low productivity and large population results in high rates of underemployment (workers not fully utilized). Many seek positions in services, but of the personal or household variety. Preindustrial societies are agrarian and structured around tradition, routine, and authority.

Industrial Society

The predominant activity in an *industrial society* is the production of goods. The focus of attention is on making more with less. Energy and machines multiply the output per labor-hour and structure the nature of work. Division of labor is the operational "law" that creates routine tasks and the notion of the semiskilled worker. Work is accomplished in the artificial environment of the factory, and people tend the machines. Life becomes a game that is played against a fabricated nature—a world of cities, factories, and tenements. The rhythm of life is machine-paced and dominated by rigid working hours and time clocks.

An industrial society is a world of schedules and acute awareness of the value of time. The standard of living becomes measured by the quantity of goods, but note that the complexity of coordinating the production and distribution of goods results in the creation of large bureaucratic and hierarchic organizations. These organizations are designed with certain roles for their members, and their operation tends to be impersonal, with persons treated as things. The individual is the unit of social life in a society that is considered to be the sum total of all the individual decisions being made in the marketplace. Of course, the unrelenting pressure of industrial life is softened by the countervailing force of labor unions.

Postindustrial Society

While an industrial society defines the standard of living by the quantity of goods, the *postindustrial society* is concerned with the quality of life, as measured by services such as health, education, and recreation. The central figure is the professional person, because rather than energy or physical strength, information is the key resource. Life now is a game played among persons. Social life becomes more difficult because political claims and social rights multiply. Society becomes aware that the independent actions of individuals can combine to create havoc for everyone, as seen in traffic congestion and environmental pollution. The community rather than the individual becomes the social unit.

Bell suggests that the transformation from an industrial to a postindustrial society occurs in many ways. First, there is a natural development of services, such as transportation and utilities, to support industrial development. As labor-saving devices are introduced into the production process, more workers engage in nonmanufacturing activities, such as maintenance and repair. Second, growth of the population and mass consumption of goods increase wholesale and retail trade, along with banking, real estate, and insurance. Third, as income increases, the proportion spent on the necessities of food and home decreases, and the remainder creates a demand for durables and then for services.

Ernst Engel, a Prussian statistician of the 19th century, observed that as family incomes increase, the percentage spent on food and durables drops while consumption of services that reflect a desire for a more enriched life increases correspondingly. This phenomenon is analogous to the Maslow hierarchy of needs, which says that once the basic requirements of food and shelter are satisfied, people seek physical goods and, finally, personal development. However, a necessary condition for the "good life" is health and education. In our attempts to eliminate disease and increase the span of life, health services become a critical feature of modern society.

Higher education becomes the condition for entry into a postindustrial society, which requires professional and technical skills of its population. Also, claims for more services and social justice lead to a growth in government. Concerns for environmental protection require government intervention and illustrate the interdependent and even global character of postindustrial problems. Table 1.3 summarizes the features that characterize the preindustrial, industrial, and postindustrial stages of economic development.

NATURE OF THE SERVICE SECTOR

For many people, *service* is synonymous with *servitude* and brings to mind workers flipping hamburgers and waiting on tables. However, the service sector that has grown significantly over the past 30 years cannot be accurately described as composed only of low-wage or low-skill jobs in department stores and fast-food restaurants. Instead, as Table 1.4 shows, the fastest-growing jobs within the service sector are in finance, insurance, real estate, miscellaneous services (e.g., health, education, professional services), and retail trade. Note that job areas whose growth rates were less than the rate of increase in total jobs (i.e., less than 31.8 percent) lost market share, even though they showed gains in their absolute numbers. The exceptions are in mining and manufacturing, which lost in absolute numbers and thus showed negative growth rates. This trend should accelerate with the end of the cold war and the subsequent downsizing of the military and defense industry.

Changes in the pattern of employment will have implications on where and how people live, on educational requirements, and, consequently, on the kinds of

TABLE 1.3

COMPARISON OF SOCIETIES

			Features				
Society	Game	Pre-dominant activity	Use of human labor	Unit of social life	Standard of living measure	Structure	Technology
Pre-industrial	Against nature	Agriculture Mining	Raw muscle power	Extended household	Sub-sistence	Routine Traditional Authoritative	Simple hand tools
Industrial	Against fabricated nature	Goods production	Machine tending	Individual	Quantity of goods	Bureaucratic Hierarchical	Machines
Post-industrial	Among persons	Services	Artistic Creative Intellectual	Community	Quality of life in terms of health, education, recreation	Inter-dependent Global	Information

---

TABLE 1.4

RATE OF GROWTH OF U.S. NONFARM JOBS, 1989–1999

	Jobs 1989 (in 1000s)	1989 %	Jobs 1999 (in 1000s)	1999 %	Growth of jobs %
Goods-producing industries:					
Total	25,254	20.10	25,381	20.19	0.50
Construction	5,171	4.11	5,962	4.74	15.30
Manufacturing:					
Durable goods	11,394	9.07	11,210	8.92	−1.61
Nondurable goods	7,997	6.36	7,616	6.06	−4.76
Service-producing industries:					
Total	82,630	65.76	100,308	79.81	21.39
Transportation and public utilities	5,614	4.47	6,589	5.24	17.39
Wholesale trade	6,187	4.92	6,826	5.43	10.33
Retail trade	19,475	15.50	22,257	17.71	14.28
Finance, insurance, and real estate	6,668	5.31	7,400	5.89	10.98
Service	26,907	21.41	37,460	29.80	39.22
Government:					
Total	17,779	14.15	19,776	15.73	11.23
Federal	2,988	2.38	2,677	2.13	−10.41
Total nonagricultural employment	125,663		145,465		15.76

Source: Economic Indicators, prepared for the Joint Economic Committee by the Council of Economic Advisors, U.S. Government Printing Office, June 1999, p. 16. <http://www.palni.edu/gpo-1998/GPOAccess.cgi?economic_indicators/PDF/348904/3=0%20-348904%20diskb/wais/data/economic_indicators/00jn99.txt;7=%00;>.

organizations that will be important to that society. Industrialization created the need for the semiskilled worker who could be trained in a few weeks to perform the routine machine-tending tasks. The subsequent growth in the service sector has caused a shift to white-collar occupations. In the United States, the year 1956 was a turning point. For the first time in the history of industrial society, the number of white-collar workers exceeded the number of blue-collar workers, and the gap has been widening since then. The most interesting growth has been in the managerial and professional-technical fields, which are jobs that require a college education. Figure 1.3 shows the shift in employment from an industrial society of machine operators to a postindustrial society of professional and technical workers.

Today, service industries are the source of economic leadership. During the past 30 years, more than 44 million new jobs have been created in the service sector to absorb the influx of women into the workforce and to provide an alternative to the lack of job opportunities in manufacturing. The service industries now account for approximately 70 percent of the national income in the United States. Given that there is a limit to how many cars a consumer can use and how much one can eat and drink, this should not be surprising. The appetite for services, however, especially innovative ones, is insatiable. Among the services presently in demand are those that reflect an aging population, such as geriatric health care, and others that reflect a two-income family, such as day care.

The growth of the service sector has produced a less cyclic national economy. During the past four recessions in the United States, employment by service industries has actually increased, while jobs in manufacturing have been lost. This suggests that consumers are willing to postpone the purchase of products but will not sacrifice essential services like education, telephone, banking, health care, and public services such as fire and police protection.

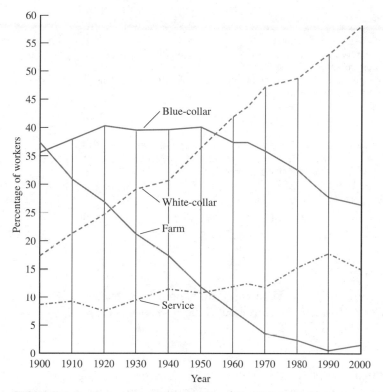

FIGURE 1.3 Occupational distribution of the U.S. labor force, 1900–2000.
(*Source:* From U.S. Department of Commerce, Bureau of the Census, *Statistical Abstract of the United States,* 1995.)

Several reasons can explain the recession resistant nature of services. First, by their nature, services cannot be inventoried, as is the case for products. Because consumption and production occur simultaneously for services, the demand for them is more stable than that for manufactured goods. When the economy falters, many services continue to survive. Hospitals keep busy as usual, and, while commissions may drop in real estate, insurance, and security businesses, employees need not be laid off.

Second, during a recession, both consumers and business firms defer capital expenditures and instead fix up and make do with existing equipment. Thus, service jobs in maintenance and repair are created.

NEW EXPERIENCE ECONOMY[4]

Services are undergoing a transformation from the traditional concept of a service transaction to one of an experience. Consider how Starbucks, Disney World, and Planet Hollywood have defined their respective services as an experience. Figure 1.4 illustrates the evolution from an agrarian to an *experience economy.*

Experiences create added value by engaging and connecting with the customer in a personal and memorable way. As businesses explicitly charge for the memorable encounters they stage, we transition from a service economy to the new experience economy. Figure 1.5 displays four types of experiences characterized by the level of customer participation and level of interaction with the environment. Entertainment

Economy	Agrarian	Industrial	Service	Experience
Function	Extract	Make	Deliver	Stage
Nature	Fungible	Tangible	Intangible	Memorable
Attribute	Natural	Standardized	Customized	Personal
Method of supply	Stored in bulk	Inventoried	Delivered on demand	Revealed over time
Seller	Trader	Manufacturer	Provider	Stager
Buyer	Market	User	Client	Guest

FIGURE 1.4 The new experience economy.
(*Source:* Reprinted by permission of *Harvard Business Review.* Exhibit adapted from "Welcome to the Experience Economy," by B. Joseph Pine II and James H. Gilmore, July-August 1998, p.98. Copyright © 1998 by the President and Fellows of Harvard College: all rights reserved.)

(e.g., watching a movie) is the least involved level of experience and escapist (e.g., skydiving) requires the most commitment from the customer.

ROLE OF THE SERVICE MANAGER

Successful growth of the service sector will depend on innovation and skilled management that will promote an ethic of continuous improvement in both quality and productivity.

Innovation

The product development model that is driven by technology and engineering could be called a *push theory of innovation.* A concept for a new product germinates in the laboratory with a new scientific discovery that becomes a solution looking for a problem. The 3M experience with Post-it notes is one example of this innovation process. The laboratory discovery was a poor adhesive, which found a creative use as a glue for notes to be attached temporarily to objects without leaving a mark when removed.

Information technology provides many examples of the push theory of service innovation. The growth of the World Wide Web as a place of commerce is changing the delivery of services. People can browse the Internet for every imaginable product or service from around the world. In fact, to stay competitive, many businesses may soon be required to offer new cost-effective and convenient services for customers who have home computers equipped with modems.

For services, the Cash Management Account introduced by Merrill Lynch is an example of the *pull theory of innovation.* During the period of high interest rates in the 1980s, a need arose to finance short-term corporate cash flows, and individual investors

		Customer participation	
		Passive	Active
Environmental relationship	Absorption	Entertainment (movie)	Education (language)
	Immersion	Estheticism (tourist)	Escapism (skydiving)

FIGURE 1.5 The four realms of an experience.
(*Source:* Reprinted by permission of *Harvard Business Review.* Exhibit adapted from "Welcome to the Experience Economy," by B. Joseph Pine II and James H. Gilmore, July-August 1998, p.102. Copyright © 1998 by the President and Fellows of Harvard College: all rights reserved.)

Scuba divers escape to an underwater world that requires special equipment for survival.
© Stephen Frink/CORBIS

were interested in obtaining an interest rate that was higher than those currently available on passbook bank deposits.

The French Revolution provides another view of service formation, this time based on changing demographics. Before the revolution, only two restaurants were in existence in Paris; shortly afterward, there were more than 500. The dispossessed nobility had been forced to give up their private chefs, who found that opening their own restaurants was a logical solution to their unemployment.

For a manufacturing firm, product innovation is often driven by engineering-based research, but in service firms, software engineers and programmers are the technocrats who develop new innovations. Customers interact directly in the service process; therefore, the focus on meeting customer needs drives service innovation and explains why marketing plays such a central role in service management.

The introduction of a new technology, however, does have an ancillary effect on service innovation. For example, the VCR has spawned a video rental business and created a renewed demand for old movies. Thus, the creation of an innovative service enterprise has many sources.

Service innovation also can arise from exploiting information available from other activities. For example, records of sales by auto parts stores can be used to identify frequent failure areas in particular models of cars. This information has value both for the manufacturer, who can accomplish engineering changes, and for the retailer, who can diagnose customer problems. In addition, the creative use of information can be a source of new services, or it can add value to existing services. For example, an annual summary statement of transactions furnished by one's financial institution has added value at income tax time.

Service innovators face a difficult problem in testing their service ideas. The process of product development includes building a laboratory prototype for testing before full-scale production is initiated. New services are seldom tested before they are launched in the marketplace, however, which provides a partial explanation for the observed high failure rate of service innovations, particularly in retailing and restaurants. At present, new service concepts usually must prove themselves in the field instead of in a "laboratory" setting. Methods to simulate service delivery systems before their introduction must be developed. One example of an effort in this direction is provided by Burger King, which acquired a warehouse in Miami to enclose a replica of its standard outlet. This mock restaurant was used to simulate changes in layout that would be required for the introduction of new features such as drive-through window service and a breakfast menu. The marketing concept of a "focus group," consisting of customers selected to review service proposals in a roundtable discussion, is another means of evaluating new service ideas. The difficulty in service prototyping is the need to evaluate the service delivery system in operation where technology, service providers, and customers are integrated.

Social Trends

Three social trends will have a major influence on services: the aging of the U.S. population, the growth of two-income families, and the increase in the number of single people. As the baby boom generation matures, the percentage of older people in America will increase greatly. The number of Americans 85 years and older is projected to be 5 million in 2005 and 11.5 million in 2035.[5] This aging of the population will create opportunities for retired people to take part-time work, in part because of fewer young people entering the workforce. In the future, companies facing a labor shortage may be forced to hire retired workers, at least on a temporary or part-time basis, and this trend is already apparent. For example, The Travelers' Insurance Company has developed a Retirement Job Bank of its retired employees that is used as a source of skilled labor to fill in during peak work times, absences, and vacations.[6] Also, elderly people are living longer and have more active lives, with consequent demands on health care, public transportation, and leisure services.

The two-income family is fast replacing the traditional family of the 1950s, which consisted of a husband, a housewife, and two children. The new two-income family unit has created demands for services such as day care, preschool, and "eating out" services. For two-income families, time is at a premium, and they are willing to pay for services that give them more free time. As a result, many new services have been created that focus exclusively on saving time for these individuals. Examples include home delivery services and personal shopping services for everything from gifts to clothing. Increased disposable income from two wage earners also may translate into increased demands for leisure, entertainment, and tourism services.

The number of single people in America is growing, and this trend is expected to continue.[7] Recreational sports and other group-oriented activities will be in demand, because they will offer the opportunity to meet other single people. Home food delivery services that now offer pizza may find a market for the delivery of gourmet meals to single people.

All of these social trends support the notion that the home will become a sanctuary for people in the future, and that sanctuary will be supported by a communication system bringing video and electronic messages from the global community into the living room.

Management Challenges

Complacency in the management of service industries, inattention to quality, disregard for customer concerns, and exclusive attention to short-term financial orientation all threaten to undermine the service sector of the economy. It is important to realize that under the pressures just mentioned, the service sector could become as vulnerable to foreign competition as the manufacturing sector has. The following discussion of the competitive challenges in services is based in part on a classic article by James Brian Quinn and Christopher E. Gagnon, in which they caution the reader that services could follow manufacturing into decline.[8]

Quinn and Gagnon point out that the economic trends in services are undeniable, and that they are similar to the recent experience in manufacturing. Since the early 1980s, the net positive trade balances in services have fallen steadily. For example, a serious loss of market share has been experienced in international airline travel as the once powerful carriers, Pan Am and TWA, declared bankruptcy in the face of foreign competitors that upgraded their fleets and emphasized quality of service.

Purely domestic services are not immune to foreign competition, either. Direct foreign investment in the U.S. service sector is substantial. Many famous names in services, such as 20th Century Fox, Stouffer's Hotels and Restaurants, Marshall Field, and Giant Foods, are now foreign-owned. In California, Japanese banks are changing the nature of competition and winning accounts by taking a much longer view in making business loans to new ventures at very competitive interest rates.

The nature of competition in services also is changing because the forces of deregulation and new technologies have restructured service industries in recent years. Deregulation has caused significant restructuring in the domestic airline industry, with successful new regional carriers appearing (e.g., Southwest and Alaska) and old giants declaring bankruptcy (e.g., Eastern and Braniff). New route networks have formed around the hub-and-spoke concept to provide service in a more cost-effective manner. The use of computer reservation systems has allowed airlines to provide a variety of competitive fares based on preselling seats at a discount; thus, they can ensure high-load factors and profitable operations. Service managers need to understand these new competitive dimensions to take advantage of opportunities to improve service quality and performance, thereby creating barriers to the entry of foreign and domestic competitors. Competing on the traditional dimensions of quality, price, and availability will always be important, but consider the following additional dimensions based on the use of information technologies, which are the source of the value added by service firms.

Economies of Scale *Economies of scale* are realized when fixed costs in new technology are allocated over increased volume; the result is reduced cost per transaction. For example, automation of the securities trading process changed the entire structure of the industry and made possible the handling of daily volumes in the millions of shares. The old system of transferring shares from seller to buyer manually has been replaced by an electronic clearinghouse. Without using a central electronic depository, Wall Street could not function as an efficient securities marketplace. New and expensive medical technologies, such as the CAT or MRI scanners, have resulted in regional treatment centers and the concentration of medical services at these large hospitals. Thus, we find that the introduction of capital-intensive technologies has resulted in the concentration of services and aggregation of demand.

Economies of Scope *Economies of scope,* a new and somewhat controversial concept, describes the benefits that are realized when entirely new service products move through established distribution networks with little added cost. For example, once the communications and information-handling technologies are in place, a much wider set of services can be distributed to a more diffuse customer base at low marginal costs. In addition, this information technology base can offer strategic benefits through more rapid product introduction and faster response to competitors' moves. Insurance companies that automated their back-office operations in the 1960s to improve billing and collections found themselves with a competitive advantage during the interest rate explosion of the 1980s. Companies had to alter their products rapidly to attract interest-sensitive new customers and to avoid the losses from current customers' borrowing against their policies at low interest rates. Only those companies with the flexibility of computer information systems could design and deploy their products quickly enough to obtain a competitive edge. Some companies added new computer-intensive financial services such as cash management accounts to attract funds. A very common example of economies of scope can be found at any local convenience store that has added self-service gasoline and microwave meal service to its original grocery stocks.

Complexity   Since deregulation, the domestic airline industry has witnessed an ever-changing fare structure so complex that fares can no longer be published in flight schedules. Computerized reservations systems allow airlines to analyze the status of flights and customer buying behavior in such detail that they can optimize margins on each type of demand and meet competitors' responses. The ability to monitor hundreds of flights and make seat allocation decisions on an hourly basis is accomplished with significant computer support and software algorithms. This special use of computer information to manage perishable capacity and to maximize revenues is called *yield management,* a topic that will be treated in detail in Chapter 13, Managing Capacity and Demand.

   Sophisticated use of information systems to manage complexity also can be found in retail stores. Bar-code scanners give instant feedback on sales and inventory movements, which results in a better match of inventory to customers' needs. This information has enabled major chains to customize the stock featured at their stores so that they can accommodate regional preferences and compete better with small specialty shops.

Boundary Crossing   Competition among services once thought to be in different industries is now becoming commonplace. Some of the most striking examples are found in the financial services. Today, many consumers use their banks and brokers almost interchangeably because neither is seriously restricted in its scope of operations. Banks, insurance companies, and brokerage houses offer a similar range of financial products and services and now compete in one market, without the traditional boundaries. As noted earlier, convenience stores now compete with fast-food restaurants as well as with service stations, and even manufacturing firms such as GM and Ford have entered the service arena by offering financing services to auto buyers. The ability of auto manufacturers to finance the sales of their cars has allowed them to offer loans at reduced interest rates as an incentive to buy their products. In fact, at present, General Motors Acceptance Corporation is the nation's largest single holder of consumer debt. Thus, we can readily see that competition in services can come from any quarter.

International Competitiveness   The worldwide service trade is growing with the help of cheaper and more flexible transportation and communication capabilities. During the 1960s, only 7 percent of the U.S. economy was exposed to foreign competition. Today, that figure is greater than 75 percent, and it is still climbing. With the world heading toward a single economy, or "global village," this trend toward greater international competition is expected to continue for both manufacturing and service firms.[9] For example, the purchase of Flying Tigers by Federal Express has enabled it to guarantee delivery anywhere in the world in two days; as a result, it joins DHL and others for a share in the growing business of global package delivery. Geographic distance is no longer a barrier between nations, and the challenges of ethnic diversity in the domestic market are multiplied by the difficulties of delivering a service in an international market with different cultural and language barriers.

SUMMARY

We have discovered that the modern industrial economies are dominated by employment in the service sector. Just as farming jobs migrated to manufacturing in the 19th century under the driving force of labor-saving technology, manufacturing jobs in due time migrated to services. Now as we begin the new millennium, an experience

---

BOX 1.1

Service Benchmark

FORTUNE ADDS SERVICE SECTOR TO ITS "500" LIST OF CORPORATIONS

After 40 years of publishing its benchmark Fortune 500 list—an annual compilation of the 500 largest industrial corporations in America—*Fortune* magazine is making a dramatic change. Having decided that its list no longer reflected the top level of American business, *Fortune* will announce Tuesday that for the first time since 1955 the 500 list will include service corporations—banks, life insurance companies, utilities, and so on—as well as industrial ones. This means that companies like J. P. Morgan, Metropolitan Life, Travelers, American Express, AT&T, and Viacom are now on the list. The new Fortune 500 issue will be dated May 15 and arrive on newsstands on May 1. The Fortune 500 rankings are a measure of standing in the business community; inclusion is considered an enormous marketing advantage and companies trumpet it in advertisements and company reports. Cities and states, in their efforts to attract industry, boast about the number of Fortune 500 companies they have.

It is hardly a secret that the industrial sector is no longer at the center of corporate America, as it was when the list was started in 1955. Indeed, few magazines have been as diligent as *Fortune* in tracking America's shift to a predominantly service economy. "If you are writing about the new economy and your list isn't reflecting it, you begin to worry," said John Huey, managing editor of the magazine. "Is Microsoft a manufacturing or a service corporation? It doesn't really matter." Not only have the lines between industrial and service companies become more blurred, but industrials have been deriving more and more of their revenue from service businesses. In 1994, for example, General Electric derived 40 percent of its revenue from service businesses.

In the first year of the new list, the number of service companies has already surpassed industrials, 291 to 209. *Fortune* ranks companies by revenue, a system that has long drawn criticism from those who say a company's market value is a better measuring rod than its sales. That aside, the inclusion of service companies on the list has strikingly raised the level of revenue represented. In the 1994 list, for example, the 500th company on the list, Texas Industries, reported revenue of $614 million. No. 500 this year, which Mr. Huey declined to name, has revenue of $2.2 billion. No. 250 last year, Quantum, had revenue of $1.7 billion. This year the 250th company has revenue of $4.65 billion.

In an interview, Mr. Huey and John Curran, assistant managing editor, who was in charge of compiling the list, disclosed little about the 1995 list and declined to give company rankings. They did say, however, that of the top 10 corporations, 7 were industrials. The highest-ranking service corporation on the list is at No. 4. A quick comparison of last year's top industrials with the 500 service companies ranked by revenue would suggest that AT&T, Wal-Mart Stores, and Sears, Roebuck are likely to be among the top 10 on the unified list.

Source: Deirdre Carmody, "*Fortune* Adds Service Sector to Its '500' List of Corporations," *New York Times*, April 24, 1995, p. C1.

economy is emerging to satisfy rising expectations for services. Chapter 2 develops new managerial skills by arguing that the distinctive characteristics of services require an approach to management that is significantly different from that found in manufacturing.

KEY TERMS AND DEFINITIONS

Clark-Fisher hypothesis a classification of economies according to the activity of the majority of the workforce.

Economies of scale allocation of the fixed costs of technology over an increased volume of sales (e.g., airline reservation system).

Economies of scope movement of new service products through established distribution networks (e.g., convenience stores adding self-serve gasoline pumps).

Experience economy a stage of economic evolution in which added value is created by engaging and connecting with the customer in a personal and memorable way.

Industrial society a society dominated by factory work in mass-production industries.

Postindustrial society a service society in which people are engaged in information, intellectual, or creative-intensive activities.

Preindustrial society an agrarian society structured around farming and subsistence living.

Pull theory of innovation service innovations that are driven by customer needs.

Push theory of innovation product innovations that originate in scientific laboratories.

TOPICS FOR DISCUSSION

1. Illustrate how the type of work he or she does influences a person's lifestyle. For example, contrast a farmer, a factory worker, and a schoolteacher.
2. Is it possible for an economy to be based entirely on services?
3. Speculate on the effect that the Internet will have on the delivery of services.
4. What is the value of self-service in an economy?
5. Comment on the role that marketing plays in the service innovation process.

SELECTED BIBLIOGRAPHY

DAVIS, STANLEY M.: *Future Perfect*, Addison-Wesley, Reading, Mass., 1987.

HESKETT, J. L., W. E. SASSER, JR., and C. W. L. HART: *Service Breakthroughs*, Free Press, New York, 1990.

NIE, WINTER, and DEBORAH L. KELLOGG: "How Professors of Operations Management View Service Operations," *Production and Operations Management*, vol. 8, no. 3, Fall 1999, pp. 339–355.

PINE, JOSEPH, and JAMES GILMORE: "Welcome to the Experience Economy," *Harvard Business Review*, July–August 1998, pp.97–105.

RIFKIN, JEREMY: *The End of Work: The Decline of the Global Labor Force and the Dawn of the Post-Market Era*, Tarcher/Putnam, New York, 1995.

ENDNOTES

1. Colin Clark, *The Conditions of Economic Progress*, 3d ed., The Macmillan Co., London, 1957.
2. N. N. Foote and P. K. Hatt, "Social Mobility and Economic Advancement," *American Economic Review*, May 1953, pp. 364–378.
3. Daniel Bell, *The Coming of Post-Industrial Society: A Venture in Social Forecasting*, Basic Books, Inc., New York, 1973.

4. Joseph Pine and James Gilmore, "Welcome to the Experience Economy*," Harvard Business Review*, July–August 1998, pp. 97–105.

5. http://www.census.gov/population/projections/nation/summary/np-t3-b
   http://www.census.gov/population/projections/nation/summary/np-t3-f.

6. Harold E. Johnson, "Older Workers Help Meet Employment Needs," *Personnel Journal*, May 1988, pp. 100–105.

7. Edward Cornish, "The Coming of the Singles Society," *The Futurist*, July–August 1987, p. 2.

8. J. B. Quinn and C. E. Gagnon, "Will Services Follow Manufacturing into Decline?" *Harvard Business Review*, November–December 1986, pp. 95–103.

9. John Greenwald, "Down and Down the Dollar Goes," *Time*, September 7, 1992, pp. 36–37.

CHAPTER TWO

The Nature of Services

Learning Objectives

After completing this chapter, you should be able to:

1. Classify a service into one of four categories using the service process matrix.
2. Describe a service using the four dimensions of the service package.
3. Discuss the managerial implications of the distinctive characteristics of a service operation.
4. Discuss the insights obtained from a strategic classification of services.
5. Discuss the role of a service manager from an open-systems view of service operations.

In this chapter, we explore the distinctive features of services. The service environment is sufficiently unique to allow us to question the direct application of traditional manufacturing-based techniques to services without some modification, although many approaches are analogous. Ignoring the differences between manufacturing and service requirements will lead to failure, but more importantly, recognition of the special features of services will provide insights for enlightened and innovative management. Advances in service management cannot occur without an appreciation of the service system environment.

The distinction between a *product* and a *service* is difficult to make, because the purchase of a product is accompanied by some facilitating service (e.g., installation) and the purchase of a service often includes facilitating goods (e.g., food at a restaurant). Each purchase includes a bundle of goods and services in varying proportions, as shown in Table 2.1.

TABLE 2.1

PROPORTION OF GOODS AND SERVICES IN TYPICAL PURCHASE BUNDLE

Goods					Services			
100% 75 50 25 0 25 50 75 100%

```
100%       75        50        25         0        25        50        75       100%
   I............Self-service gasoline...........................I
          I................Personal computer...................I
          I...............Office copier...........................I
              I..............Fast-food restaurant....................I
                 I.............Gourmet restaurant...................I
                    I...............Auto repair...........................I
                       I...............Airline flight.......................I
                          I...................Haircut.........................I
```

Source: Adapted from W. E. Sasser, R. P. Olsen, and D. D. Wyckoff, *Management of Service Operations,* Allyn and Bacon, Boston, 1978, p. 11.

Services have a clear *front-office* (e.g., bank-teller interaction with a customer) and *back-office* (e.g., a bank's check-clearing operations) dichotomy in their operations, so we would be foolish to ignore the substantial opportunities for applying manufacturing techniques to the isolated back-office operations. These opportunities will be explored in Chapter 5, in which we consider the design of the service delivery system.

CHAPTER PREVIEW

The chapter begins with a classification of services based on the degree of customer interaction or customization and the degree of labor intensiveness. This classification allows us to focus on managerial issues that are found across similar service industries. An appreciation of the nature of services begins with the realization that a service is a package of explicit and implicit benefits performed within a supporting facility and using facilitating goods. These multiple dimensions of a service are central to the design and control of a service delivery system. The distinctive characteristics of service operations are discussed, and then services are classified to obtain strategic insights.

Based on these observations, the role of the service manager is viewed from an open-system perspective. That is, the service manager must deal with an environment in which the customers are present in the delivery system. This contrasts with manufacturing operations that are isolated or "buffered" from the customer by an inventory of finished goods. Thus, manufacturing traditionally has operated as a cost center, focusing on process efficiency. Service managers, who often operate as profit centers, must be concerned with both efficient and effective delivery of services.

SERVICE CLASSIFICATION

Concepts of service management should be applicable to all service organizations. For example, hospital administrators could learn something about their own business from the restaurant and hotel trade. Professional services such as consulting, law, and medicine have special problems because the professional is trained to provide a specific clinical service (to use a medical example) but is not knowledgeable in business management. Thus, professional service firms offer attractive career opportunities for many college graduates.

A service classification scheme can help to organize our discussion of service management and break down the industry barriers to shared learning. As suggested, hospitals can learn about housekeeping from hotels. Less obviously, dry-cleaning establishments can learn from banks—cleaners can adapt the convenience of night deposits enjoyed by banking customers by providing laundry bags and after-hours drop-off boxes. For professional firms, scheduling a consulting engagement is similar to planning a legal defense or preparing a medical team for open-heart surgery.

To demonstrate that management problems are common across service industries, Roger Schmenner proposed the *service process matrix* in Figure 2.1. In this matrix, services are classified across two dimensions that significantly affect the character of the service delivery process. The vertical dimension measures the degree of labor intensity, which is defined as the ratio of labor cost to capital cost. Thus, capital-intensive services such as airlines and hospitals are found in the upper row because of their considerable investment in plant and equipment relative to labor costs. Labor-intensive services such as schools and legal assistance are found in the bottom row because their labor costs are high relative to their capital requirements.

The horizontal dimension measures the degree of customer interaction and customization, which is a marketing variable that describes the ability of the customer to

Degree of interaction and customization

	Low	High
Low	*Service factory:* • Airlines • Trucking • Hotels • Resorts and recreation	*Service shop:* • Hospitals • Auto repair • Other repair services
High	*Mass service:* • Retailing • Wholesaling • Schools • Retail aspects of commercial banking	*Professional service:* • Physicians • Lawyers • Accountants • Architects

Degree of labor intensity

FIGURE 2.1 The service process matrix.
(*Source:* From "How Can Service Businesses Survive and Prosper?" by Roger W. Schmenner, *Sloan Management Review,* vol. 27, no. 3, Spring 1986, p. 25, by permission of publisher. Copyright 1986 by the Sloan Management Review Association. All rights reserved.)

affect personally the nature of the service being delivered. Little interaction between customer and service provider is needed when the service is standardized rather than customized. For example, a meal at McDonald's, which is assembled from prepared items, is low in customization and served with little interaction occurring between the customer and the service providers. In contrast, a doctor and patient must interact fully in the diagnostic and treatment phases to achieve satisfactory results. Patients also expect to be treated as individuals and wish to receive medical care that is customized to their particular needs. It is important to note, however, that the interaction resulting from high customization creates potential problems for management of the service delivery process.

The four quadrants of the service process matrix have been given names, as defined by the two dimensions, to describe the nature of the services illustrated. *Service factories* provide a standardized service with high capital investment, much like a line-flow manufacturing plant.[1] *Service shops* permit more service customization, but they do so in a high-capital environment. Customers of a *mass service* will receive an undifferentiated service in a labor-intensive environment, but those seeking a *professional service* will be given individual attention by highly trained specialists.

Managers of services in any category, whether service factory, service shop, mass service, or professional service, share similar challenges, as noted in Figure 2.2. Services with high capital requirements (i.e., low labor intensity), such as airlines and hospitals, require close monitoring of technological advances to remain competitive. This high capital investment also requires managers to schedule demand to maintain utilization of the equipment. Alternatively, managers of highly labor-intensive services, such as medical or legal professionals, must concentrate on personnel matters.

FIGURE 2.2 Challenges for service managers.
(*Source:* From "How Can Service Businesses Survive and Prosper?" by Roger W. Schmenner, *Sloan Management Review,* vol. 27, no. 3, Spring 1986, p. 27, by permission of publishers. Copyright 1986 by the Sloan Management Review Association. All rights reserved.)

The degree of customization affects the ability to control the quality of the service being delivered and the perception of the service by the customer. Approaches to addressing each of these challenges are topics that will be discussed in later chapters.

THE SERVICE PACKAGE

Service managers have difficulty identifying their product. This problem is partly a result of the intangible nature of services, but it is the presence of the customer in the process that creates a concern for the total service experience. Consider the following examples. For a sit-down restaurant, atmosphere is just as important as the meal because many diners regard the occasion as a way to get together with friends. A customer's opinion of a bank can be formed quickly on the basis of a teller's cheerfulness or the length of the waiting line.

The *service package* is defined as a bundle of goods and services that is provided in some environment. This bundle consists of the following four features:

1. *Supporting facility.* The physical resources that must be in place before a service can be offered. Examples are a golf course, a ski lift, a hospital, and an airplane.

2. *Facilitating goods.* The material purchased or consumed by the buyer, or the items provided by the customer. Examples are golf clubs, skis, food items, replacement auto parts, legal documents, and medical supplies.
3. *Explicit services.* The benefits that are readily observable by the senses and that consist of the essential or intrinsic features of the service. Examples are the absence of pain after a tooth is repaired, a smooth-running automobile after a tune-up, and the response time of a fire department.
4. *Implicit services.* Psychological benefits that the customer may sense only vaguely, or the extrinsic features of the service. Examples are the status of a degree from an Ivy League school, the privacy of a loan office, and worry-free auto repair.

All of these features are experienced by the customer and form the basis of his or her perception of the service. It is important that the service manager offer a total experience for the customer that is consistent with the desired service package. Take, for example, a budget hotel. The supporting facility is a concrete-block building with austere furnishings. Facilitating goods are reduced to the minimum of soap and paper. The explicit service is a comfortable bed in a clean room, and implicit services might include a friendly desk clerk and the security of a well-lighted parking area. Deviations from this service package, such as adding bellhops, would destroy the bargain image. Table 2.2 lists criteria (with examples) for evaluating the service package.

The importance of facilitating goods in the service package can be used to classify services across a continuum from pure services to various degrees of mixed services. For example, psychiatric counseling with no facilitating goods would be considered a "pure" service. Automobile maintenance usually requires more facilitating goods than a haircut does.

Making general statements about service management is difficult when there are such variations in the nature of services. However, an appreciation of the unique features of the service environment is important for understanding the challenges facing service managers.

DISTINCTIVE CHARACTERISTICS
OF SERVICE OPERATIONS

In services, a distinction must be made between *inputs* and *resources*. For services, inputs are the customers themselves, and resources are the facilitating goods, employee labor, and capital at the command of the service manager. Thus, to function, the service system must interact with the customers as participants in the service process. Because customers typically arrive at their own discretion and with unique demands on the service system, matching service capacity with demand is a challenge.

For some services, such as banking, however, the focus of activity is on processing information instead of people. In these situations, information technology, such as electronic funds transfer, can be substituted for physically depositing a payroll check; thus, the presence of the customer at the bank is unnecessary. Such exceptions will be noted as we discuss the distinctive characteristics of service operations. It should be noted here that many of the unique characteristics of services, such as customer participation and perishability, are interrelated.

Customer Participation in the Service Process

The presence of the customer as a participant in the service process requires an attention to facility design that is not found in traditional manufacturing operations. That automobiles are made in a hot, dirty, noisy factory is of no concern to the eventual

---

TABLE 2.2

CRITERIA FOR EVALUATING THE SERVICE PACKAGE

Supporting facility

1. *Location:*
   Is it accessible by public transportation?
   Is it centrally located?
2. *Interior decorating:*
   Is the proper mood established?
   Quality and coordination of furniture.
3. *Supporting equipment:*
   Does the dentist use a mechanical or air drill?
   What type and age of aircraft does the charter airline use?
4. *Architectural appropriateness:*
   Renaissance architecture for university campus.
   Unique recognizable feature of a blue tile roof.
   Massive granite facade of downtown bank.
5. *Facility layout:*
   Is there a natural flow of traffic?
   Are adequate waiting areas provided?
   Is there unnecessary travel or backtracking?

Facilitating goods

1. *Consistency:*
   Crispness of french fries.
   Portion control.
2. *Quantity:*
   Small, medium, or large drink.
3. *Selection:*
   Variety of replacement mufflers.
   Number of menu items.
   Rental skis available.

Explicit services

1. *Training of service personnel:*
   Is the auto mechanic certified by the National Institute for Automotive Service Excellence (NIASE)?
   To what extent are paraprofessionals used?
   Are the physicians board certified?
2. *Comprehensiveness:*
   Discount broker compared with full service.
   General hospital compared with clinic.
3. *Consistency:*
   Airline's on-time record.
   Professional Standards Review Organization (PSRO) for doctors.
4. *Availability:*
   Twenty-four-hour ATM service.
   Is there a website?
   Is there a toll-free number?

Implicit services

1. *Attitude of service:*
   Cheerful flight attendant
   Police officer issuing traffic citation with tact.
   Surly service person in restaurant.
2. *Atmosphere:*
   Restaurant decor.
   Music in a bar.
   Sense of confusion rather than order.
3. *Waiting:*
   Joining a drive-in banking queue.
   Being placed on hold.
   Enjoying a martini in the restaurant bar.
4. *Status:*
   College degree from Ivy League school.
   Box seats at sports event.
5. *Sense of well-being:*
   Large commercial aircraft.
   Well-lighted parking lot.
6. *Privacy and security:*
   Attorney advising client in private office.
   Magnetic key card for hotel room.
7. *Convenience:*
   Use of appointments.
   Free parking.

---

buyers because they first see the product in the pleasant surroundings of a dealer's showroom. The presence of the customer on-site requires attention to the physical surroundings of the service facility that is not necessary for the factory. For the customer, service is an experience occurring in the environment of the service facility, and the quality of service is enhanced if the service facility is designed from the customer's perspective. Attention to interior decorating, furnishings, layout, noise, and even color can influence the customer's perception of the service. Compare the feelings invoked by picturing yourself in a stereotypical bus station with those produced by imagining yourself in an airline terminal. Of course, passengers are not allowed in the terminal's back office (e.g., the luggage-handling area), which is operated in a factory-like environment. However, some innovative services have opened the back office to public scrutiny to promote confidence in the service (e.g., some restaurants provide a view into the kitchen, some auto repair bays can be observed through windows in the waiting area).

An important consideration in providing a service is the realization that the customer can play an active part in the process. A few examples will illustrate that the knowledge, experience, motivation, and even honesty of the customer all directly affect the performance of the service system:

1. The popularity of supermarkets and discount stores is predicated on the idea that customers are willing to assume an active role in the retailing process.
2. The accuracy of a patient's medical record can greatly influence the effectiveness of the attending physician.
3. The education of a student is determined largely by the student's own effort and contributions.

This strategy is best illustrated by the fast-food restaurants that have significantly reduced the typical number of serving and cleaning personnel. The customer not only places the order directly from a limited menu but also is expected to clear the table after the meal. Naturally, the customer expects faster service and less expensive meals to compensate for these inputs, but the service provider benefits in many subtle ways. First, there are fewer personnel who require supervision and such things as fringe benefits. Second, and more importantly, the customer provides the labor just at the moment it is required; thus, service capacity varies more directly with demand rather than being fixed by the size of the employed staff. The customer acts like a temporary employee, arriving just when needed to perform duties to augment the work of the service staff.

This strategy has received great acceptance in a society, such as the United States, where self-reliance is valued. Instead of being a passive buyer, the customer becomes a contributor to the gross national product.

Taking the customer out of the process, however, is becoming a common practice. Consider retail banking, in which customers are encouraged to use telephone or computer transactions, direct deposit, and automatic-debit bill paying instead of actually traveling to the bank. Moreover, the advent of Internet commerce gives new meaning to the phrase "window shopping." ☺

Simultaneity

The fact that services are created and consumed simultaneously and, thus, cannot be stored is a critical feature in the management of services. This inability to inventory services precludes using the traditional manufacturing strategy of relying on inventory as a buffer to absorb fluctuations in demand. An inventory of finished goods serves as a convenient system boundary for a manufacturer, separating the internal operations of planning and control from the external environment. Thus, the manufacturing facility can be operated at a constant level of output that is most efficient. The factory is operated as a *closed system,* with inventory decoupling the productive system from customer demand. Services, however, operate as *open systems,* with the full impact of demand variations being transmitted to the system.

Inventory also can be used to decouple the stages in a manufacturing process. For services, the decoupling is achieved through customer waiting. Inventory control is a major issue in manufacturing operations, whereas in services, the corresponding problem is customer waiting, or "queuing." The problems of selecting service capacity, facility utilization, and use of idle time all are balanced against customer waiting time.

The simultaneous production and consumption in services also eliminates many opportunities for quality-control intervention. A product can be inspected before delivery, but services must rely on other measures to ensure the quality of services delivered. We address this important topic in Chapter 3.

Perishability

A service is a perishable commodity. Consider an empty airline seat, an unoccupied hospital or hotel room, or an hour without a patient in the day of a dentist. In each case, a lost opportunity has occurred. Because a service cannot be stored, it is lost forever when not used. The full utilization of service capacity becomes a management challenge, because customer demand exhibits considerable variation and building inventory to absorb these fluctuations is not an option.

Consumer demand for services typically exhibits very cyclic behavior over short periods of time, with considerable variation between the peaks and valleys. The custom of eating lunch between noon and 1 PM places a burden on restaurants to accommodate the noon rush. The practice of day-end mailing by businesses contributes to the fact that 60 percent of all letters are received at the post office between 4 and 8 P.M.[2] The demand for emergency medical service in Los Angeles was found to vary from a low of 0.5 call per hour at 6 A.M. to a peak of 3.5 calls per hour at 6 P.M.[3] This peak-to-valley ratio of 7 to 1 also was true for fire alarms during an average day in New York City.[4]

For recreational and transportation services, seasonal variation in demand creates surges in activity. As many students know, flights home are often booked months in advance of spring break and the Christmas holiday.

Faced with variable demand and a *time-perishable capacity* to provide the service, the manager has three basic options:

1. Smooth demand by:
   a. Using reservations or appointments.
   b. Using price incentives (e.g., giving telephone discounts for evening and weekend calls).
   c. Demarketing peak times (e.g., advertising to shop early and avoid the Christmas rush).
2. Adjust service capacity by:
   a. Using part-time help during peak hours.
   b. Scheduling work shifts to vary workforce needs according to demand (e.g., telephone companies staff their operators to match call demand).
   c. Increasing the customer self-service content of the service.
3. Allow customers to wait.

The last option can be viewed as a passive contribution to the service process that carries the risk of losing a dissatisfied customer to a competitor. By waiting, the customer permits greater utilization of service capacity. The airlines explicitly recognize this by offering standby passengers a reduced price for their tickets.

Intangibility

Services are ideas and concepts; products are things. Therefore, it follows that service innovations are not patentable. To secure the benefits of a novel service concept, the firm must expand extremely rapidly and preempt any competitors. Franchising has been the vehicle to secure market areas and establish a brand name. Franchising allows the parent firm to sell its idea to a local entrepreneur, thus preserving capital while retaining control and reducing risk.

The intangible nature of services also presents a problem for customers. When buying a product, the customer is able to see it, feel it, and test its performance before purchase. For a service, however, the customer must rely on the reputation of the service firm. In many service areas, the government has intervened to guarantee acceptable service performances. Through the use of registration, licensing, and regulation, the government can assure consumers that the training and test performance of some service providers meet certain standards. Thus, we find that public construction plans must be approved by a registered professional engineer, a doctor must be licensed to practice medicine, and the telephone company is a regulated utility. In its efforts to "protect" the consumer, however, the government may be stifling innovation, raising barriers to entry, and generally reducing competition.

Heterogeneity

The combination of the intangible nature of services and the customer as a participant in the service delivery system results in variation of service from customer to customer. The interaction between customer and employee in services, however, creates the possibility of a more complete human work experience. In services, work activity generally is oriented toward people rather than toward things. There are exceptions, however, for services that process information (e.g., communications) or customers' property (e.g., brokerage services). In the limited customer-contact service industries, we now see a dramatic reduction in the level of labor intensiveness through the introduction of information technology.

Even the introduction of automation may strengthen personalization by eliminating the relatively routine impersonal tasks, thereby permitting increased personal attention to the remaining work. At the same time, personal attention creates opportunities for variability in the service that is provided. This is not inherently bad, however, unless customers perceive a significant variation in quality. A customer expects to be treated fairly and to be given the same service that others receive. The development of standards and of employee training in proper procedures is the key to ensuring consistency in the service provided. It is rather impractical to monitor the output of each employee, except via customer complaints.

The direct customer–employee contact has implications for service (industrial) relations as well. Auto workers with grievances against the firm have been known to sabotage the product on the assembly line. Presumably, the final inspection will ensure that any such cars are corrected before delivery. A disgruntled service employee, however, can do irreparable harm to the organization because the employee is the firm's sole contact with customers. Therefore, the service manager must be concerned about the employees' attitudes as well as their performance. J. Willard Marriott, founder of the Marriott Hotel chain, has said, "In the service business you can't make happy guests with unhappy employees."[5] Through training and genuine concern for employee welfare, the organizational goals can be internalized.

CLASSIFYING SERVICES FOR STRATEGIC INSIGHTS[6]

A general discussion of service strategy is complicated by the diversity of service firms in the economy and their differing customer relationships. However, strategic insights that transcend industry boundaries are needed to avoid the myopic view, which is prevalent among service managers, that concepts do not translate from one industry to another. For example, competitive strategies used by banking services could find an application in laundry services because both deal with a customer's property. The new laundry drop-off and pick-up service available at commuter rail stations is similar in concept to bank automatic teller machines in supermarkets. The following classification schemes developed by Christopher Lovelock provide us with an appreciation of possible strategic dimensions that transcend industry boundaries.

Nature of the Service Act

As Figure 2.3 shows, the service act can be considered across two dimensions: who or what is the direct recipient of the service, and the tangible nature of the service. This creates four possible classifications: (1) tangible actions directed to the customer, such as passenger transportation and personal care; (2) tangible actions directed at the customer's possessions, such as laundry cleaning and janitorial services; (3) intangible actions directed at the customer's intellect, such as entertainment; and (4) intangible actions performed on the customer's assets, such as financial services.

This classification scheme raises questions about the traditional way in which services have been delivered. For example, does the customer need to be present physically throughout the service, only to initiate or terminate the transaction, or not at all? If customers must be present, then they must travel to the service facility and become part of

Direct recipient of the service

	People	Things
Tangible actions	*Services directed at people's bodies:* Health care, Passenger transportation, Beauty salons, Exercise clinics, Restaurants	*Services directed at goods and other physical possessions:* Freight transportation, Industrial equipment repair and maintenance, Laundry and dry cleaning, Landscaping/lawn care, Veterinary care
Intangible actions	*Services directed at people's minds:* Education, Broadcasting, Information services, Theaters, Museums	*Services directed at intangible assets:* Banking, Legal services, Accounting, Securities, Insurance

(Nature of the service act)

FIGURE 2.3 Understanding the nature of the service act.
(*Source:* Reprinted with permission of the American Marketing Association: Christopher H. Lovelock, "Classifying Services to Gain Strategic Marketing Insights," *Journal of Marketing,* vol. 47, Summer 1983, p. 12.)

the process, or the server must travel to the customer (e.g., ambulance service). This has significant implications for facility design and employee interaction, because the impressions that are made on the customer will influence his or her perceptions of the service. In addition, questions are raised concerning the impact of facility location and business hours on customer convenience. It is not surprising that retail banks have embraced ATMs and other electronic communication alternatives to personal interaction.

Thinking creatively about the nature of the service may identify more convenient forms of delivery or even a product that can substitute for the service. For example, videotapes of lectures and CD recordings of concerts represent a convenient substitute for physical attendance, and they also serve as permanent library records of the events.

Relationship with Customers

Service firms have the opportunity to build long-term relationships because customers conduct their transactions directly with the service provider, most often in person. In contrast, manufacturers traditionally have been isolated from the eventual end user by a distribution channel consisting of some combination of distributors, wholesalers, and/or retailers. Figure 2.4 contrasts the nature of the customer's "membership" with the nature of the service delivery. The value to the firm of customer membership is captured in this figure; however, a number of changes have occurred since it was first published in 1983. For example, car rental firms and major hotel chains have joined

Type of relationship between service organization and its customers

Nature of the service delivery		"Membership" relationship	No formal relationship
	Continuous delivery of service	Insurance Telephone subscription College enrollment Banking American Automobile Association	Radio station Police protection Lighthouse Public highway
	Discrete transactions	Long-distance phone calls Theater series subscription Commuter ticket or transit pass Sam's Wholesale Club Airline frequent flyer	Car rental Mail service Toll highway Pay phone Movie theater Public transportation Restaurant

FIGURE 2.4 Relationships with customers.
(*Source:* Reprinted with permission of the American Marketing Association: Christopher H. Lovelock, "Classifying Services to Gain Strategic Marketing Insights," *Journal of Marketing,* vol. 47, Summer 1983, p. 13.)

airlines in offering discounts through frequent flyer programs. In addition, some private toll highways offer annual passes, which can be attached to one's car. These passes electronically trigger a debit so that the driver need not stop to pay a toll.

Knowing your customers is a significant competitive advantage for a service organization. Having a data base of customers' names and addresses and their use of the service permits targeted marketing and individual treatment of customers. Customers benefit from membership because of the convenience of annual fixed fees and the knowledge that they are valued customers who will receive occasional perks (e.g., frequent flyer awards).

Customization and Judgment

Because services are created as they are consumed and the customer is often a participant in the process, an opportunity exists to tailor a service to the needs of the customer. Figure 2.5 shows that customization proceeds along two dimensions: either the character of the service permits customization, or the service personnel have the discretion to modify the service.

Selecting the quadrant of Figure 2.5 in which to position a service is a strategic choice. For example, traditional movie theaters offer only one screen; thus, they are appropriately located in the low-low quadrant. Most new movie theaters, however, are built with multiple screens, allowing some degree of customization. Among fast-food restaurants, Burger King advertises "Have it your way," permitting some customization of its "Whopper." Within a particular industry, every quadrant could be occupied by different segments of that industry, as illustrated by the various types of food service operations in Figure 2.5. A strategic choice of offering more customization and

Extent to which service characteristics are customized

Extent to which customer contact personnel exercise judgment in meeting individual customer needs	High	Low
High	Professional services Surgery Taxi service Beautician Plumber Education (tutorials) Gourmet restaurant	Education (large classes) Preventive health programs College food service
Low	Telephone service Hotel services Retail banking (excluding major loans) Family restaurant	Public transportation Routine appliance repair Movie theater Spectator sports Fast-food restaurant

FIGURE 2.5 Customization and judgment in service delivery.
(*Source:* Reprinted with permission of the American Marketing Association: Christopher H. Lovelock, "Classifying Services to Gain Strategic Marketing Insights," *Journal of Marketing,* vol. 47, Summer 1983, p. 15.)

allowing service personnel to exercise judgment, however, has implications for the service delivery system.

Nature of Demand and Supply

We have noted that the time perishability of service capacity creates a challenge for service managers because these managers lack the option of producing and storing inventory for future sale. Even so, the extent of demand and supply imbalances varies across service industries, as shown in Figure 2.6.

To determine the most appropriate strategy in each case, it is necessary to consider the following questions:

1. What is the nature of the demand fluctuation? Does it have a predictable cycle (e.g., daily meal demand at a fast-food restaurant) that can be anticipated?
2. What are the underlying causes of these fluctuations in demand? If the causes are customer habits or preference, could marketing produce a change?
3. What opportunities exist to change the level of capacity or supply? Can part-time workers be hired during peak hours?

Because managing capacity and demand is a central challenge to the success of a service firm, Chapter 13, Managing Capacity and Demand, is devoted entirely to this topic.

Extent of demand fluctuations over time

	Wide	Narrow
Peak demand can usually be met without major delay	Electricity Natural gas Telephone Hospital maternity unit Police and fire emergencies	Insurance Legal services Banking Laundry and dry cleaning
Peak demand regularly exceeds capacity	Accounting and tax preparation Passenger transportation Hotels and motels Restaurants Theaters	Services similar to those above, but with insufficient capacity for their base level of business

Extent to which supply is constrained

FIGURE 2.6 What is the nature of demand for the service relative to supply?
(*Source:* Reprinted with permission of the American Marketing Association: Christopher H. Lovelock, "Classifying Services to Gain Strategic Marketing Insights," *Journal of Marketing,* vol. 47, Summer 1983, p. 17.)

Availability of service outlets

	Single site	Multiple sites
Customer goes to service organization	Theater Barbershop	Bus service Fast-food chain
Service organization goes to customer	Lawn care service Pest control service Taxi	Mail delivery AAA emergency repairs
Customer and service organization transact at arm's length (mail or electronic communications)	Credit card company Local TV station	National TV network Telephone company

Nature of interaction between customer and service organization

FIGURE 2.7 Method of service delivery.
(*Source:* Reprinted with permission of the American Marketing Association: Christopher H. Lovelock, "Classifying Services to Gain Strategic Marketing Insights," *Journal of Marketing,* vol. 47, Summer 1983, p. 18.)

Method of Service Delivery

As Figure 2.7 shows, the method of service delivery has both a geographic component and a level-of-customer-interaction component.

Services with multiple sites have significant management implications for ensuring quality and consistency in the service offering. Detailed strategic implications of site location are discussed in Chapter 7. With advances in electronic communications, arm's-length transactions are becoming more common because they offer customer convenience and efficient service delivery. For example, use of personal computers and modems allows businesses to customize their services and to decrease the amount of physical interaction between the customer and a human service provider. The strategic implications of the design of a service delivery system and its effect on the interaction between customer and service organization are topics in Part II: Designing the Service Enterprise.

AN OPEN-SYSTEMS VIEW OF SERVICES

Service organizations are sufficiently unique in their character to require special management approaches that go beyond the simple adaptation of the management techniques found in manufacturing a product. The distinctive characteristics suggest enlarging the system view to include the customer as a participant in the service process. As Figure 2.8 shows, the customer is viewed as an input that is transformed by the service process into an output with some degree of satisfaction.

FIGURE 2.8. Open-systems view of service operations.

The role of the service operations manager includes the functions of both production and marketing in an open system with the customer as a participant. The traditional manufacturing separation of the production and marketing functions, with finished-goods inventory as the interface, is neither possible nor appropriate in services. Marketing performs two important functions in daily-service operations: (1) educating the consumer to play a role as an active participant in the service process and (2) "smoothing" demand to match service capacity. This marketing activity must be coordinated with scheduling staff levels and with both controlling and evaluating the delivery process. By necessity, the operations and marketing functions are integrated for service organizations.

For services, *the process is the product.* The presence of the customer in the service process negates the closed-system perspective that is taken in manufacturing. Techniques to control operations in an isolated factory producing a tangible good are inadequate for services. No longer is the process machine-paced and the output easily measured for compliance with specifications. Instead, customers arrive with different demands on the service; thus, multiple measures of performance are necessary. Service employees interact directly with the customer, with little opportunity for management intervention. This requires extensive training and empowerment of employees to act appropriately in the absence of direct supervision.

Further, customer impressions of service quality are based on the total service experience, not just on the explicit service that is performed. A concern for employee attitudes and training becomes a necessity to ensure that the implicit service is also appreciated by the customer. When viewed from the customer's perspective, the entire service process raises concerns ranging from the aesthetic design of the facility to pleasant diversions in waiting areas.

An open-system concept of services also allows one to view the customer as a co-producer. Permitting the customer to participate actively in the service process (e.g.,

BOX 2.1

Service Benchmark

TO COMPETE BETTER, LOOK FAR AFIELD

How can companies best compete? One excellent and relatively underused way is to seek creative insights in industries far afield from their own.

Of course, in a time of fierce global competition businesses are hardly unaware of the need to improve performance. Many have relentlessly cut costs through downsizing and other strategies, for instance. Others have scrutinized similar companies in their quest for innovative processes, technologies, and products.

But cost-cutting has its limits. And so does seeking inspiration only within one's own field. For example, many commercial real estate companies assumed during the last recession that once the economy picked up so would their business. Failing to look beyond their own realm, they could not see that more and more businesses were opting for portable and "at home" offices.

Enter the quest for creative ideas from beyond a company's own industry—from those normally unexplored regions that business strategists call "outside the box."

When Southwest Airlines wanted to improve the turnaround of its aircraft at airports, for instance, it could have examined the practices of other airlines' maintenance workers. Instead, the company went to the Indianapolis 500 to watch pit crews fuel and service race cars. The airline recognized that pit crews perform the same functions airplane maintenance crews do, just in a different industry and at much faster speed. The observations gave Southwest new ideas about equipment fittings, materials management, teamwork, and speed that, in part, enabled the airline to cut its turnaround time by 50 percent.

Or consider Granite Rock. This company wanted to improve the way it loaded gravel into trucks in its yards. Before the gravel could be loaded, drivers had to leave their trucks and fill out paperwork to indicate how much gravel they needed. But, by observing automatic teller machines in banks, Granite Rock was able to revise this expensive and time-consuming procedure. Now, the truck drivers plug their "bank" cards into a machine so they do not have to leave the truck in order to make their requests for gravel.

Focusing on processes is the key to finding useful insights in apparently unrelated places. From a process standpoint, all companies do the same things—sell to customers, buy from suppliers, hire employees.

Understanding this broad connection, a major gas utility examined how Federal Express delivers packages overnight—and discovered ways to speed the delivery of its own product, fuel. Similarly, a major telecommunications company improved its billing system by visiting a package delivery concern. The telephone company recognized that the shipper's tracking of cargo was analogous to its tracking of invoices.

The lesson for businesses? Look for insights in apparently unrelated fields. An enterprise hoping to improve its production processes, for example, might do well to examine Domino's Pizza—a company that completes its order entry, manufacturing, distribution, billing, and collection processes in 30 minutes. But the enterprise should perform this inquiry quickly. For, day by day, the global marketplace is growing more and more competitive.

Skeptical about "outside the box" thinking? Just recall Isaac Newton. The famous scientist gained his greatest insight into gravity not from learned, ancient treatises but from an apparently unlikely source: an apple.

Source: Robert Hiebeler, "To Compete Better, Look Far Afield," *New York Times,* September 18, 1994, p. 11.

providing a salad bar at a restaurant) can increase productivity, which in turn can create a competitive edge.

SUMMARY

The management of an open system requires techniques and sensitivities different from those of a closed system. Service managers are faced with nonroutine operations in which only indirect control is possible. In services, it is the human element that is central to effective operations. For example, the unavoidable interaction between service provider and consumer is a source of great opportunity, as in direct selling. However, this interaction seldom can be fully controlled; thus, service quality may suffer. For this reason, the attitude and appearance of personnel in service organizations are important considerations. For services, the presence of the customer in the process materially alters what is viewed as the product. The unique characteristics of intangibility, perishability, and simultaneous provision and consumption introduce special challenges for service management. In many respects, the service manager adopts a style of management that incorporates the functions of marketing and operations.

The important topic of service quality is examined in the next chapter. The intangible nature of services makes objective measurement of quality difficult. The consistent delivery of high-quality service is a challenge because customers evaluate quality based on a comparison of expectations with perceptions.

KEY TERMS AND DEFINITIONS

Explicit services the essential or intrinsic features readily observable by the senses (e.g., on-time departure, quality of meal).

Facilitating goods material purchased or consumed by the buyer, or items provided by the customer (e.g., food, golf clubs).

Implicit services psychologic benefits or extrinsic features the customer may sense only vaguely (e.g., security of a well-lighted parking lot, privacy of a loan office).

Service process matrix a classification of services based on the degree of interaction and customization and the degree of labor intensity that results in four categories: service factory, service shop, mass service, and professional service.

Supporting facility the physical resources that must be in place before a service can be offered (e.g., golf course, hospital building, airplane).

The service package a description of a service based on four components: supporting facility, facilitating goods, explicit service, and implicit service.

Time-perishable capacity a service that is not used during some period of time and, therefore, is lost forever (e.g., an empty seat on an airplane).

TOPICS FOR DISCUSSION

1. What are the characteristics of services that will be most appropriate for Internet delivery?
2. When does collecting information through service membership become an invasion of privacy?
3. What are some of the management problems associated with allowing service employees to exercise judgment in meeting customer needs?
4. Illustrate the "distinctive characteristics of service operations" for a service with which you are familiar.
5. What factors are important for a manager to consider when attempting to enhance a service firm's image?
6. What contributions to the management of professional service firms can a business school graduate provide?

CASE

Village Volvo

Village Volvo is the "new kid in town." It represents an effort by two former authorized Volvo dealer mechanics to provide quality repair service on out-of-warranty Volvos at a reasonable cost. On the basis of their 22 combined years of training and experience with the local Volvo dealer, they have earned a respected reputation and a following of satisfied customers, which make an independent service operation feasible. Village Volvo occupies a new Butler building (i.e., a prefabricated metal structure) that has four work bays in addition to an office, waiting area, and storage room.

The owners feel they have designed their operation to provide clients with a custom car care service that is unavailable at the local dealer. They have set aside specific times each week when clients may drive in for quick, routine services such as tune-ups and oil changes, but they encourage clients to schedule appointments for the diagnosis and repair of specific problems.

At the time of the appointment, the mechanic who will be working on the vehicle and the client discuss the problems the client has noticed. On occasion, the mechanic may take a short test drive with the client to be certain that both understand the area of concern.

Another source of information for the mechanic is the Custom Care Vehicle Dossier (CCVD). Village Volvo maintains a continuing file on each vehicle it services. This history can help the mechanic to diagnose problems and also provides a convenient record if a vehicle is returned for warranty service on an earlier repair. The owners are considering use of the CCVD as a way of "reminding" customers that routine maintenance procedures may be due.

After the mechanic has made a preliminary diagnosis, the service manager gives the vehicle owner an estimate of the cost and the approximate time when the repair will be completed if no unexpected problems arise. Company policy states that the owner will be consulted before any work other than the agreed-on job is done. Although the customer may speak with the mechanic during the repair process, the service manager is the main point of contact. It is the service manager's responsibility to be sure the customer understands the preliminary diagnosis, to advise the customer of any unexpected problems and costs, and to notify the customer when the vehicle is ready for pickup.

Village Volvo has no provisions for alternate transportation for customers at this time. A shuttle service two or three times a day is being considered, because the owners think their suburban location may deter some clients. The waiting room is equipped with a television set, comfortable chairs, coffee, a soft-drink vending machine, magazines, and the local newspaper. This facility is used almost exclusively by clients who come during the "drop-in" times (3 to 5 P.M. Wednesdays and 8 to 10 A.M. Thursdays) for quick, routine jobs such as tune-ups and buyer checks of used cars.

The owner-mechanics do no repairs between 7 and 8 A.M. and 5 and 6 P.M., because these are heavy customer contact hours. They believe it is just as important to discuss with the client the repairs that have been done as it is to discuss what problems exist before that work is done. As repairs are made, the owner-mechanic notes any other problems that might need attention in the future (e.g., fan and alternator belts show some wear and may need to be replaced in about 6,000 miles). These notes are brought to the customer's attention at pickup time and also are recorded in the CCVD for future use, perhaps in the form of a reminder postcard to the owner.

All small worn-out parts that have been replaced arc put in a clean box inside the car. More cumbersome replaced parts are identified and set aside for the client's inspection. Care is taken throughout the repair process to keep the car clean, and the inside is vacuumed as a courtesy before pickup. After the repairs are finished, the vehicle is taken for a short test drive. Then it is parked, ready for pickup.

The Village Volvo owners see their responsibility as extending beyond immediate service to their clients. The owners have developed a network of other service providers who assist in recycling used parts and waste products and to whom they can refer clients for work that is not part of Village Volvo's services (e.g., body work, alignments, and reupholstering). The owners also are considering the possibility of offering a minicourse one Saturday morning each month to teach clients what they can do to attain their 200,000-mile Volvo medals.

Questions

1. Describe Village Volvo's service package.
2. How are the distinctive characteristics of a service firm illustrated by Village Volvo?
3. How could Village Volvo manage its back office (i.e., repair operations) like a factory?
4. How can Village Volvo differentiate itself from Volvo dealers?

CASE

Xpresso Lube[7]

Charlie Green, owner of Xpresso Lube, is not your typical car repairman. A man of many talents, Charlie gained valuable knowledge of the oil-change business while working in the Special Mixtures Division of Goodyear. Charlie also learned from his father and brother while working on cars when he was growing up and later supplemented this knowledge by taking formal automotive courses. All similarities between Charlie and his fellow mechanics end there, however. Charlie also is a professional musician. He plays an upright bass and sings and owns a coffee plantation in Costa Rica.

When it's time to get your oil changed, you have only two choices—change it yourself or pay someone else (e.g., dealership, independent auto mechanic, or a "quick oil/lube" station) to do it for you. Many people choose quick oil-change stations because it is easier than doing it themselves and it is usually quicker and cheaper than going to a dealer or an independent mechanic.

Folks just want to get in and out as fast and economically as possible. Most companies that provide oil-change service are indistinguishable. They charge about the same price and are found on almost every major street. Most people pick one that is close to home and that has a short waiting line. The challenge faced by the quick-change services is to manage demand. Most customers want service during the lunch hour, after work, or on Saturdays. An oil-change business, therefore, wants to move customers in and out as quickly as possible. Speed of service is the way they try to differentiate themselves from their competitors.

Charlie remembers the last time he paid to have his car's oil changed. He was in the waiting room with several other customers when a lube technician came in to discuss a problem with an elderly lady. "Ma'am, you see this?" The technician held a PCV valve in his hand and shook it, producing a rattle. "You hear that that? That's trouble. We're gonna have to replace this PCV valve." The woman looked puzzled, but she agreed with the mechanic. Unfortunately, she didn't know that the PCV in any car is *supposed* to rattle. This event dismayed Charlie. He believed that customers deserved good service and honesty, and he was tired of seeing people get "ripped off." He decided to do something about this problem by opening his own business, Xpresso Lube, which would specialize in oil changes.

No one likes to wait a long time to have his or her oil changed, especially because the facilities usually are not very pleasant. The waiting rooms are small, dirty, and furnished with uncomfortable chairs. If a television set is available, it has a small screen and reception is poor. Any magazines are probably car related and months old. If there is coffee to drink, it has been sitting in an old pot since early that *morning!*

Charlie designed the environment for his business to be different from that of the traditional oil-change station. He chose not to compete with the other oil-change companies head to head, but instead changed "the game." When he converted an old gas/service station into Xpresso Lube, people told him that it would never work. They said he had too much waiting area and the stalls had lifts instead of the usual pits—so it would take too long to change a car's oil. Charlie used these unusual features to his advantage.

During the development phase of his business, Charlie noticed two things about the local and national economies—both the espresso bar and oil-change markets were saturated. Consumers viewed these services as commodities and based their purchase decision on price. Charlie considered that factor and the unappealing environment of existing oil-change facilities—and, in a moment of entrepreneurial revelation, decided to combine the coffee bar craze with an oil-change business.

Xpresso Lube was started with the purpose of providing a unique, pleasant, and honest experience. Charlie had thorough knowledge of both the coffee and oil-change business, so the merger of these two experiences came naturally to him. In fact, when Xpresso Lube first opened, he also drew on his musician roots and brought in bands to play in the evenings. As Xpresso Lube's success grew, Charlie had to phase out the live music because he was too busy with the other aspects of the business.

Charlie never forgot the experience of seeing others get treated dishonestly. Today, the majority of his customers are women, who frequently have been the victims of dishonest repairmen, and college students. "Little old ladies love me," Charlie says, "because we have earned their trust."

The large waiting area was transformed into a coffee bar with a number of amenities to make his customers' waits very enjoyable. He offered a variety of coffees and an atmosphere that doesn't make the customers feel as if they are in a waiting room. In fact, some customers come in just for the coffee. The floors are carpeted and there are numerous tables and chairs. An outside area is covered for use when the weather is pleasant. A stereo system provides music and the reading material is current and appealing to different interests.

Because of the atmosphere he has created, Charlie does not have to compete on speed, which allows Xpresso Lube to use lifts and only two stalls. Furthermore, using lifts gives employees an opportunity to show the customer when something is wrong with his or her car. The customer can go under the car with the technician and actually see the problem. Other oil-change stations do not have this luxury—they cannot allow their customers to go down into the pit to look at their cars. Pits are dirty and unsafe places for any customer. Consequently, a customer must take the employee's advice about extra work that needs to be done—and hope he or she is not being ripped off.

When a customer does not want to wait, Xpresso Lube provides transportation to and from work. This service helps smooth demand during the weekday afternoons, so customers will not all come after 5 P.M. during the week or on Saturdays. The transport service is provided by the automotive service center right behind Xpresso Lube, which is also owned by Charlie. University Automotive was the precursor to Xpresso Lube, which Charlie opened in 1984. University Auto provides car repair services for many makes and models of cars. A gas station was located in a lot adjacent to University Auto; when the station went out of business in the early nineties, Charlie bought the property and opened Xpresso Lube on the site in 1996. Xpresso Lube now provides 30 percent of the revenues for the joint businesses.

Austin is home to the University of Texas, a thriving high-tech business community, and arguably the nation's best live music. All of these factors give Austin a very diverse population. Xpresso Lube's location on a main street near the university attracts a broad spectrum of customers, but also it means customers can walk to many local shops while their cars are being serviced. Half-Price Bookstore, Wheatsville Coop food store, Amy's Ice Cream, and Toy Joy are all within easy walking distance. The business provides a great deal of fulfillment for Charlie. "I love coming to work because every day brings new and different customers into our shop."

Questions

1. Describe Xpresso Lube's service package?
2. How are the distinctive characteristics of a service operation illustrated by Xpresso Lube?
3. Characterize Xpresso Lube in regard to the nature of the service act, the relationship with customers, customization and judgment, the nature of demand and supply, and the method of service delivery.
4. What elements of Xpresso Lube's location contribute to its success?
5. Given the example of Xpresso Lube, what other services could be combined to "add value" for the customer?

SELECTED BIBLIOGRAPHY

CHASE, RICHARD B.: "The Mall Is My Factory: Reflections of a Service Junkie," *Production and Operations Management,* vol. 5, no. 4, Winter 1996, pp. 298–308.

COOK, DAVID, CHON-HUAT GOH, and CHEN H. CHUNG: "Service Typologies: A State of the Art Survey," *Production and Operations Management,* vol. 8, no. 3, Fall 1999, pp. 318–338.

HESKETT, JAMES L.: "Lessons in the Service Sector," *Harvard Business Review,* March–April 1987, pp. 118–129.

ENDNOTES

1. This concept of a service operated like a manufacturing factory is different from the more recent realization by manufacturing firms that operating a factory more like a service can achieve a competitive advantage. *See* R. B. Chase and D. A. Garvin, "The Service Factory," *Harvard Business Review,* vol. 67, no. 4, July–August 1989, pp. 61–69.

2. R. C. Cohen, R. McBridge, R. Thornton, and T. White, *Letter Mail System Performance Design: An Analytical Method for Evaluating Candidate Mechanization,* Report R-168, Institute for Defense Analysis, Washington, D.C., 1970.

3. James A. Fitzsimmons, "The Use of Spectral Analysis to Validate Planning Models," *Socio-Economic Planning Sciences,* vol. 8, no. 3, June 1974, pp. 123–128.

4. E. H. Blum, *Urban Fire Protection: Studies of the New York City Fire Department,* R-681, New York City Rand Institute, New York, January 1971.

5. G. M. Hostage, "Quality Control in a Service Business," *Harvard Business Review,* vol. 53, no. 4, July–August 1975, pp. 98–106.

6. Adapted from Christopher H. Lovelock, "Classifying Services to Gain Strategic Marketing Insights," *Journal of Marketing,* vol. 47, Summer 1983, p. 920.

7. Prepared by Rich Ellis, Thomas Prudhomme, and Marly Yanaza under the supervision of Professor James A. Fitzsimmons.

CHAPTER THREE

Service Quality

Learning Objectives

After completing this chapter, you should be able to:

1. Describe and illustrate the five dimensions of service quality.
2. Use the service quality gap model to diagnose quality problems for a service firm.
3. Describe how the SERVQUAL survey instrument is used to measure gaps in a service firm's quality.
4. Illustrate how Taguchi methods and poka-yoke methods are applied to quality design in services.
5. Construct a "house of quality" as part of a quality function deployment project.
6. Construct a statistical process control chart for service operation.
7. Describe the features of an unconditional service guarantee and its managerial benefits.
8. Discuss the concept of a service recovery.

Service "with a smile" used to be enough to satisfy most customers. Today, however, some service firms differentiate themselves in the marketplace by offering a "service guarantee." Unlike a product warranty, which promises to repair or replace the faulty item, service guarantees typically offer the dissatisfied customer a refund, discount, or free service. Take, for example, the First Interstate Bank of California. After interviewing its customers, the bank management discovered that they were annoyed by a number of recurring problems, such as inaccurate statements and broken automatic teller machines (ATMs). Account retention improved after the bank began to pay customers $5 for reporting each such service failure. What is surprising, however, is that the service guarantee also had a motivating effect on the employees. When an ATM failed at a branch, the employees, out of pride, decided to keep the branch open until the machine was repaired at 8:30 P.M.

Another hidden benefit of a guarantee is customer feedback. Now customers have a reason and motivation to talk to the company instead of just to their friends.

In addition to advertising the firm's commitment to quality, a service guarantee focuses employees by defining performance standards explicitly and, more important, builds a loyal customer base. The experience of Hampton Inns, an early adopter of a "100 percent satisfaction guarantee," illustrates that superior quality is a competitive advantage. In a survey of 300 guests who invoked the guarantee, more than 100 already had stayed again at a Hampton Inn. The hotel chain figures that it has received $8 in revenue for every $1 paid to a disgruntled guest.[1]

CHAPTER PREVIEW

Service quality is a complex topic, as shown by the need for a definition that includes five dimensions: reliability, responsiveness, assurance, empathy, and tangibles. We use these dimensions to introduce the concept of a service quality gap. This gap is based on the difference between a customer's expectations of a service and the perceptions of the service that is delivered. A survey instrument that measures service quality, called SERVQUAL, is based on implementing the service quality gap concept. Service quality is further defined by content, process, structure, outcome, and impact.

Quality begins with the design of the service delivery system. Thus, concepts borrowed from manufacturing such as Taguchi methods, poka-yoke, and quality function deployment are applied to the design of service delivery systems. An assessment of the cost of quality reveals the importance of preventing failure. Quality control charts illustrate the application of statistical process control to services.

However, service failures do occur and the use of an unconditional service guarantee may be offered as the equivalent of a product warranty. Because the customer is present during service delivery, service recovery strategies can be planned in anticipation of a service failure.

DEFINING SERVICE QUALITY

For services, the assessment of quality is made during the service delivery process. Each customer contact is referred to as a moment of truth, an opportunity to satisfy or dissatisfy the customer. Customer satisfaction with a service can be defined by comparing perceptions of service received with expectations of service desired. When expectations are exceeded, service is perceived to be of exceptional quality—and also to be a pleasant surprise. When expectations are not met, however, service quality is deemed unacceptable. When expectations are confirmed by perceived service, quality is satisfactory. As shown in Figure 3.1, these expectations are based on several sources, including word of mouth, personal needs, and past experience.

Dimensions of Service Quality

The dimensions of service quality as shown in Figure 3.1 were identified by marketing researchers studying several different service categories: appliance repair, retail

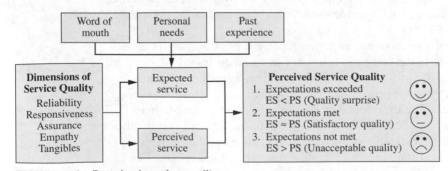

FIGURE 3.1 Perceived service quality.
(*Source:* Reprinted with permission of the American Marketing Association: adapted from A. Parasuraman, V. A. Zeithaml, and L. L. Berry, "A Conceptual Model of Service Quality and Its Implications for Future Research," *Journal of Marketing,* vol. 49, Fall 1985, p. 48.)

banking, long-distance telephone service, securities brokerage, and credit card companies. They identified five principal dimensions that customers use to judge service quality—reliability, responsiveness, assurance, empathy, and tangibles, which are listed in order of declining relative importance to customers.[2]

Reliability. The ability to perform the promised service both dependably and accurately. Reliable service performance is a customer expectation and means that the service is accomplished on time, in the same manner, and without errors every time. For example, receiving mail at approximately the same time each day is important to most people. Reliability also extends into the back office, where accuracy in billing and record keeping is expected.

Responsiveness. The willingness to help customers and to provide prompt service. Keeping customers waiting, particularly for no apparent reason, creates unnecessary negative perceptions of quality. If a service failure occurs, the ability to recover quickly and with professionalism can create very positive perceptions of quality. For example, serving complimentary drinks on a delayed flight can turn a potentially poor customer experience into one that is remembered favorably.

Assurance. The knowledge and courtesy of employees as well as their ability to convey trust and confidence. The assurance dimension includes the following features: competence to perform the service, politeness and respect for the customer, effective communication with the customer, and the general attitude that the server has the customer's best interests at heart.

Empathy. The provision of caring, individualized attention to customers. Empathy includes the following features: approachability, sensitivity, and effort to understand the customer's needs. One example of empathy is the ability of an airline gate attendant to make a customer's missed connection the attendant's own problem and to find a solution.

Tangibles. The appearance of physical facilities, equipment, personnel, and communication materials. The condition of the physical surroundings (e.g., cleanliness) is tangible evidence of the care and attention to detail that are exhibited by the service provider. This assessment dimension also can extend to the conduct of other customers in the service (e.g., a noisy guest in the next room at a hotel).

Customers use these five dimensions to form their judgments of service quality, which are based on a comparison between expected and perceived service. The gap between expected and perceived service is a measure of service quality; satisfaction is either negative or positive.

Gaps in Service Quality

Measuring the gap between expected service and perceived service is a routine customer feedback process that is practiced by leading service companies. For example, Club Med, an international hotel chain operating resort villages worldwide, uses the questionnaire shown in Figure 3.2. This questionnaire is mailed to all guests immediately after their departure from a Club Med vacation to assess the quality of their experience. Note that the first question explicitly asks the guest to evaluate the gap between his or her expectations and the actual Club Med experience.

In Figure 3.3, the gap between customer expectations and perceptions is defined as GAP 5. It is shown to depend on the size and direction of the four gaps that are associated with delivery of the service.

G.M. Questionnaire

Club Med Village: _____

Dates of your stay: From: _____ to: _____
                        Month/Day/Year   Month/Day/Year

Name: _____ Member # _____

Address: _____

City: _____ State: _____ Zip: _____

	OVERALL IMPRESSION	ORGANIZATION	TEAM OF G.O.'s	FOOD	BAR	SPORTS	DAYTIME AMBIANCE	EVENING ENTERTAINMENT	MUSIC AND DANCE	MINI CLUB	EXCURSIONS	ACCOMMODATIONS	CLUB FLIGHTS AND TRANSFERS	CLEANLINESS
EXCELLENT	6	6	6	6	6	6	6	6	6	6	6	6	6	6
VERY GOOD	5	5	5	5	5	5	5	5	5	5	5	5	5	5
GOOD	4	4	4	4	4	4	4	4	4	4	4	4	4	4
FAIR	3	3	3	3	3	3	3	3	3	3	3	3	3	3
POOR	2	2	2	2	2	2	2	2	2	2	2	2	2	2
VERY POOR	1	1	1	1	1	1	1	1	1	1	1	1	1	1

Your Comments: _____

1. Did Club Med meet your expectations?
   □ Far below expectations   □ Surpassed expectations
   □ Fell short of expectations   □ Far surpassed expectations
   □ Met expectations

2. If this was not your first Club Med, how many other times have you been to a Club Med village? _____

3. How did you make your Club Med reservations?
   □ Through a travel agent   □ Through Club Med Reservations

4. Quality of your reservations handling (pre-travel information):
   □ Very poor   □ Poor   □ Fair   □ Good   □ Excellent

5. Which one factor was most important in your choosing Club Med for your vacation?
   □ Previous stay with us   □ Advertisement   □ Editorial Article
   □ Travel Agent Recommendation   □ Friend/Relative Recommendation

6. Kindly indicate your age bracket:
   □ Under 25   □ 25-34   □ 35-44   □ 45-54   □ 55 or over

7. Kindly indicate your marital status: □ Married   □ Single

8. Would you vacation with Club Med again? □ Yes   □ No

9. If you answered yes to question 8, where would you like to go on your next Club Med vacation?
   □ U.S.A.   □ Mexico   □ French West Indies   □ Caribbean   □ Europe
   □ Other: _____

FIGURE 3.2 Customer satisfaction questionnaire.
(*Source:* After Club Med, 40 West 57th Street, New York, NY 10019.)

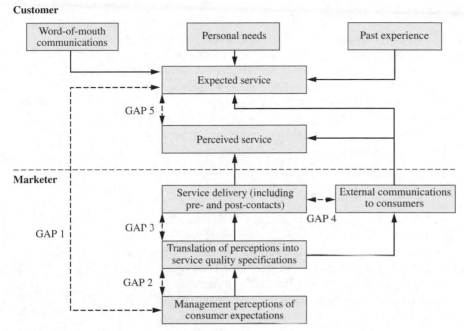

FIGURE 3.3 Service quality gap model.
(*Source:* Reprinted with permission of the American Marketing Association: V. A. Zeithaml,
L. L. Berry, and A. Parasuraman, "Communication and Control Processes in the Delivery of
Service Quality," *Journal of Marketing,* vol. 52, April 1988, p. 36.)

The first gap is the discrepancy between customer expectations and management perceptions of these expectations. GAP 1 arises from management's lack of full understanding about how customers formulate their expectations on the basis of a number of sources: advertising, past experience with the firm and its competitors, personal needs, and communications with friends. Strategies for closing this gap include improving market research, fostering better communication between management and its contact employees, and reducing the number of levels of management that distance the customer.

The second gap results from management's inability to formulate target levels of service quality to meet perceptions of customer expectations and translate these into workable specifications. GAP 2 may result from a lack of management commitment to service quality or a perception of the unfeasibility of meeting customers' expectations; however, setting goals and standardizing service delivery tasks can close this gap.

The third gap is referred to as the service performance gap because actual delivery of the service does not meet the specifications set by management. GAP 3 can arise for a number of reasons, including lack of teamwork, poor employee selection, inadequate training, and inappropriate job design.

Customer expectations of the service are formed by media advertising and other communications from the firm. GAP 4 is the discrepancy between service delivery and external communications in the form of exaggerated promises and lack of information provided to contact personnel.

The remainder of this chapter will address ways of closing these gaps in service quality. We begin by considering approaches to measuring service quality.

MEASURING SERVICE QUALITY

Measuring service quality is a challenge because customer satisfaction is determined by many intangible factors. Unlike a product with physical features that can be objectively measured (e.g., the fit and finish of a car), service quality contains many psychological features (e.g., the ambiance of a restaurant). In addition, service quality often extends beyond the immediate encounter because, as in the case of health care, it has an impact on a person's future quality of life. The multiple dimensions of service quality are captured in the SERVQUAL instrument, which is an effective tool for surveying customer satisfaction that is based on the service quality gap model.

SERVQUAL[3]

The authors of the service quality gap model shown in Figure 3.3 developed a multiple-item scale called *SERVQUAL* for measuring the five dimensions of service quality (i.e., reliability, responsiveness, assurance, empathy, and tangibles). This two-part instrument, which is shown in Table 3.1, has an initial section to record customer expectations for a class of services (e.g., budget hotels), followed by a second section to record a customer's perceptions for a particular service firm. The 22 statements in the survey describe aspects of the five dimensions of service quality.

TABLE 3.1

THE SERVQUAL INSTRUMENT*

DIRECTIONS: This survey deals with your opinions of _____ services. Please show the extent to which you think firms offering _____ services should possess the features described by each statement. Do this by picking one of the seven numbers next to each statement. If you strongly agree that these firms should possess a feature, circle the number 7. If you strongly disagree that these firms should possess a feature, circle 1. If your feelings are not strong, circle one of the numbers in the middle. There are no right or wrong answers—all we are interested in is a number that best shows your expectations about firms offering _____ services.

E1 They should have up-to-date equipment.
E2 Their physical facilities should be visually appealing.
E3 Their employees should be well dressed and appear neat.
E4 The appearance of the physical facilities of these firms should be in keeping with the type of services provided.
E5 When these firms promise to do something by a certain time, they should do so.
E6 When customers have problems, these firms should be sympathetic and reassuring.
E7 These firms should be dependable.
E8 They should provide their services at the time they promise to do so.
E9 They should keep their records accurately.
E10 They shouldn't be expected to tell customers exactly when services will be performed.(−)[†]
E11 It is not realistic for customers to expect prompt service from employees of these firms.(−)
E12 Their employees don't always have to be willing to help customers.(−)
E13 It is OK if they are too busy to respond to customer requests promptly.(−)
E14 Customers should be able to trust employees of these firms.
E15 Customers should be able to feel safe in their transactions with these firms' employees.
E16 Their employees should be polite.
E17 Their employees should get adequate support from these firms to do their jobs well.
E18 These firms should not be expected to give customers individual attention.(−)
E19 Employees of these firms cannot be expected to give customers personal attention.(−)
E20 It is unrealistic to expect employees to know what the needs of their customers are.(−)
E21 It is unrealistic to expect these firms to have their customers' best interests at heart.(−)
E22 They shouldn't be expected to have operating hours convenient to all their customers.(−)

TABLE 3.1 *(CONTINUED)*

DIRECTIONS: The following set of statements relate to your feelings about XYZ. For each statement, please show the extent to which you believe XYZ has the feature described by the statement. Once again, circling a 7 means that you strongly agree that XYZ has that feature, and circling a 1 means that you strongly disagree. You may circle any of the numbers in the middle that show how strong your feelings are. There are no right or wrong answers—all we are interested in is a number that best shows your perceptions about XYZ.

P1 XYZ has up-to-date equipment.
P2 XYZ's physical facilities are visually appealing.
P3 XYZ's employees are well dressed and appear neat.
P4 The appearance of the physical facilities of XYZ is in keeping with the type of services provided.
P5 When XYZ promises to do something by a certain time, it does so.
P6 When you have problems, XYZ is sympathetic and reassuring.
P7 XYZ is dependable.
P8 XYZ provides its services at the time it promises to do so.
P9 XYZ keeps its records accurately.
P10 XYZ does not tell customers exactly when services will be performed.(−)
P11 You do not receive prompt service from XYZ's employees.(−)
P12 Employees of XYZ are not always willing to help customers.(−)
P13 Employees of XYZ are too busy to respond to customer requests promptly.(−)
P14 You can trust employees of XYZ.
P15 You feel safe in your transactions with XYZ's employees.
P16 Employees of XYZ are polite.
P17 Employees get adequate support from XYZ to do their jobs well.
P18 XYZ does not give you individual attention.(−)
P19 Employees of XYZ do not give you personal attention.(−)
P20 Employees of XYZ do not know what your needs are.(−)
P21 XYZ does not have your best interests at heart.(−)
P22 XYZ does not have operating hours convenient to all their customers.(−)

* A seven-point scale ranging from "Strongly Agree" (7) to "Strongly Disagree" (1), with no verbal labels for the intermediate scale points (i.e., 2 through 6), accompanied each statement. Also, the statements were in random order in the questionnaire. A complete listing of the 34-item instrument used in the second stage of data collection can be obtained from the first author.
† Ratings on these statements were reverse-scored prior to data analysis.
Source: Reprinted with permission of the *Journal of Retailing* from A. Parasuraman, V. A. Zeithaml, and L. L. Berry, "SERVQUAL: A Multiple-Item Scale for Measuring Consumer Perceptions of Service Quality," *Journal of Retailing,* vol. 64, no. 1, Spring 1988, pp. 38–40.

A score for the quality of service is calculated by computing the differences between the ratings that customers assign to paired expectation and perception statements. This score is referred to as GAP 5, as was shown in Figure 3.3. Scores for the other four gaps also can be calculated in a similar manner.

This instrument has been designed and validated for use in a variety of service encounters. The authors have suggested many applications for SERVQUAL, but its most important function is tracking service quality trends through periodic customer surveys. For multisite services, SERVQUAL could be used by management to determine if any unit has poor service quality (indicated by a low score); if so, management can direct attention to correcting the source of customers' poor perceptions. SERVQUAL could be used in marketing studies to compare a service with a competitor's and again identify the dimensions of superior or inadequate service quality.

Scope of Service Quality

A comprehensive view of the service system is necessary to identify the possible measures of service quality. We will use health care delivery as our example service, and we will view quality from five perspectives: content, process, structure, outcome, and impact. For health care, the scope of service quality obviously extends beyond the quality of care that is provided for the patient; it also includes the impact on the family and community. This comprehensive view of service quality need not be limited to health care, however, as demonstrated by the negative economic impact of failed savings-and-loan institutions on their customers as well as on the community as a whole.

Content   Are standard procedures being followed? For example, is the dentist following accepted dental practices when extracting a tooth? For routine services, standard operating procedures generally are developed, and service personnel are expected to follow these established procedures. In health care, a formal peer-review system, called Professional Standards Review Organization (PSRO), has been developed as a method of self-regulation. Under this system, physicians in a community or specialty establish standards for their practices and meet regularly to review peer performance so that compliance is assured.

Process   Is the sequence of events in the service process appropriate? The primary concern here is maintaining a logical sequence of activities and a well-coordinated use of service resources. Interactions between the customer and the service personnel are monitored. Also of interest are the interactions and communications among the service workers. Check sheets such as the one shown in Table 3.2 are common measurement devices. For emergency services such as fire and ambulance, disaster drills in a realistic setting are used to test a unit's performance; problems with coordination and activity sequencing can be identified and corrected through these practice sessions.

Structure   Are the physical facilities and organizational design adequate for the service? The physical facilities and support equipment are only part of the structural dimension, however. Qualifications of the personnel and the organizational design also are important quality dimensions. For example, the quality of medical care in a group practice can be enhanced by an on-site laboratory and x-ray facilities. More important, the organization may facilitate consultations among the participating physicians. A group medical practice also provides the opportunity for peer pressure to control the quality of care that its members provide.

   Adequacy of the physical facilities and equipment can be determined by comparison with set standards for quality conformance. One well-known fast-food restaurant is recognized for its attention to cleanliness. Store managers are subjected to surprise inspections in which they are held responsible for the appearance of the parking lot, sidewalk, and restaurant interior. Personnel qualifications for hiring, promotion, and merit increases also are matters of meeting standards. University professors seldom are granted tenure unless they have published, because the ability to publish in a refereed journal is considered to be independent evidence of research quality. A measure of organizational effectiveness in controlling quality would be the presence of active self-evaluation procedures and members' knowledge of their peers' performances.

Outcome   What change in status has the service effected? The ultimate measure of service quality is a study of the end result. Is the consumer satisfied? We are all familiar with the cards on restaurant tables that request our comments on the quality of service. Complaints by consumers are one of the most effective measures of the quality outcome dimension. For public services, the assumption often is made that the status quo is acceptable unless the level of complaints begins to rise. The concept of monitoring

TABLE 3.2

QUALITY-CONTROL CHECK SHEET FOR AN EMERGENCY ROOM

Head Injuries

Date of visit: _____   MRN: _____
Nurse: _____   Physician: _____
Nurse reviewer initials: _____   Physician reviewer initials: _____

Nursing criteria	Yes	No	N/A
1. Are the patient's vital signs assessed on arrival?	☐	☐	☐
2. Does the triage note include time and mechanism of injury?	☐	☐	☐
3. Does the triage note include history of loss of consciousness and presence/absence of associated symptoms (nausea/vomiting/focal neurologic complaints)?	☐	☐	☐
4. Does the triage note include a brief neurologic assessment (Glasgow scale)?	☐	☐	☐
5. Does the triage list patient's current medications, including time of last dose recorded?	☐	☐	☐
6. Does triage note include past medical history?	☐	☐	☐
7. Is the patient's cervical spine immobilized?	☐	☐	☐
8. If history of LOC > 5 minutes or neurologic findings are present, is supplemental O_2 applied, cardiac monitor applied, i.v. line established, and physician notified immediately?	☐	☐	☐
9. Is the patient's mental status reassessed every 30 minutes?	☐	☐	☐
10. Are the discharge instructions reviewed with the patient and other responsible adult?	☐	☐	☐

Physician assessment criteria			
1. Is the chief complaint including time, mechanism of injury, and loss of consciousness recorded?	☐	☐	☐
2. Does the note include presence/absence of other injuries?	☐	☐	☐
3. Is a HEENT exam noting scalp lacerations or contusions, pupil size and reactivity, tympanic membranes, and neck exam recorded?	☐	☐	☐
4. Is Chest, Lung, Heart, and Abdominal exam recorded?	☐	☐	☐
5. Is a Neurologic exam including Glasgow scale, motor and sensory examination, and gait recorded?	☐	☐	☐

Physician action criteria			
1. Is a CAT scan obtained if there is a history of LOC or neurologic findings?	☐	☐	☐
2. Is a CAT scan obtained if there is a history of blood clotting disorder, thrombocytopenia, lethargy, or patient taking coumadin?	☐	☐	☐
3. Are X rays of the c-spine obtained?	☐	☐	☐
4. If the patient is discharged, is the mental status at the time of discharge recorded?	☐	☐	☐
5. Are discharge instructions including indications for return to the ED, aftercare plan, and referral for follow-up care given to patient and other responsible adult?	☐	☐	☐

Patient outcome criteria			
1. Do the patient and responsible adult verbalize understanding of signs and symptoms indicating need to return?	☐	☐	☐
2. If the CAT scan reveals emergent intracranial hematoma, is surgical intervention initiated within 2 hours?	☐	☐	☐
3. Did the patient require a second visit due to missed diagnosis?	☐	☐	☐

output quality by tracking some measure (e.g., the number of complaints) is widely used. For example, the performance of a hospital is monitored by comparing certain measures against industry norms. The infection rate per 1,000 surgeries might be used to identify hospitals that may be using substandard operating room procedures.

Clever approaches to measuring outcome quality often are employed. For example, the quality of trash pickup in a city can be documented by taking pictures of the city streets after the trash vehicles have made their rounds. One often-forgotten measure of outcome quality is the satisfaction of empowered service personnel with their own performance.

Impact What is the long-range effect of the service on the consumer? Are the citizens of a community able to walk the streets at night with a sense of security? The result of a poll asking that question would be a measure of the impact of police performance. The overall impact of health care often is measured by life expectancy or the infant mortality rate, and the impact of education often is measured by literacy rates and performance on nationally standardized tests.

It should be noted, however, that the impact also must include a measure of service and accessibility, which usually is quoted as the population served per unit area. Health care in the United States is criticized for the financial barriers to patient accessibility in general but especially in rural and large inner-city areas. As a result, this country's impact measures of life expectancy and infant mortality are far worse than those in all other industrial countries and even several Third World countries. In a similar fashion, the literacy rate is a measure of the impact of the education system, and again, the United States lags behind many other nations. Health care and education are perhaps the two most essential services in the United States today. Clearly, they are in great need of managers who can devise and implement excellent and innovative service operations strategies.

A commercial example of an impact measurement is the number of hamburgers sold, which once was displayed in neon lights by McDonald's. In addition, a bank's lending rate for minorities could be a measure of that institution's economic impact on a community.

Table 3.3 illustrates how this service quality perspective can be applied to measuring the quality of service delivered by a health clinic.

QUALITY SERVICE BY DESIGN

Quality can neither be inspected into a product nor somehow added on, and this same observation applies to services. A concern for quality begins with the design of the service delivery system. How can quality be designed into a service? One approach is to focus on the four dimensions of the service package that we explored in Chapter 2, The Nature of Services.

Incorporation of Quality in the Service Package

Consider the example of a budget hotel competing on overall cost leadership:

1. *Supporting facility.* Architecturally, the building is designed to be constructed of materials that are maintenance-free, such as concrete blocks. The grounds are watered by an automated underground sprinkler system. The air-conditioning and heating system is decentralized by using individual room units to confine any failure to just one room.

TABLE 3.3

MEASURING SERVICE QUALITY FOR A HEALTH CLINIC

Quality Perspective	Description	Possible Measures
Content	Evaluation of medical practice.	Review medical records for conformance with national standards of medical care.
Process	The sequence of events in the delivery of care and the interactions between patients and medical staff.	Use checklists to monitor conformance with procedures. Conduct exit interviews with patients.
Structure	The physical facilities, equipment, staffing patterns, and qualifications of health personnel.	Record times patients wait to see a doctor. Note ratio of doctors to registered nurses on duty. Record utilization of equipment.
Outcome	The change in the patient's health status as a result of care.	Record deaths as a measure of failures. Note the level of patient dissatisfaction by recording the number of complaints. Record the number of diseased organs removed in surgery.
Impact	Appropriateness, availability, accessibility, and overall effect on the community of the health clinic.	Note number of patients turned away because of lack of insurance or financial resources. Record the mode of travel and distance patients travel to reach the clinic.

2. *Facilitating goods.* Room furnishings are durable and easy to clean (e.g., bedside tables are supported from the wall to facilitate carpet cleaning). Disposable plastic cups are used instead of glass, which is more expensive, requires cleaning, and, thus, would detract from the budget image.
3. *Explicit services.* Maids are trained to clean and make up rooms in a standard manner. Every room has the same appearance, including such "trivial" matters as the opening of the drapes.
4. *Implicit services.* Individuals with a pleasant appearance and good interpersonal skills are recruited as desk clerks. Training in standard operating procedures (SOPs) ensures uniform and predictable treatment for all guests. An online computer tracks guest billing, reservations, and registration processing. This system allows guests to check out quickly and automatically notifies the cleaning staff when a room is free to be made up.

Table 3.4 illustrates how the budget hotel has taken these design features and implemented a quality system to maintain conformance to the design requirements. The approach is based on Philip Crosby's definition of quality as "conformance to requirements."[4] This example illustrates the need to define explicitly, in measurable terms, what constitutes conformance to requirements. Quality is seen as an action-oriented activity requiring corrective measures when nonconformance occurs.

TABLE 3.4

QUALITY REQUIREMENTS FOR BUDGET HOTEL

Service Package Feature	Attribute or Requirement	Measurement	Nonconformance Corrective Action
Supporting facility	Appearance of building	No flaking paint	Repaint
	Grounds	Green grass	Water grass
	Air-conditioning and heating	Temperature maintained at 68° ± 2°	Repair or replace
Facilitating goods	TV operation	Reception clear in daylight	Repair or replace
	Soap supply	Two bars per bed	Restock
	Ice	One full bucket per room	Restock from ice machine
Explicit services	Room cleanliness	Stain-free carpet	Shampoo
	Swimming-pool water purity	Marker at bottom of deep end visible	Change filter and check chemicals
	Room appearance	Drapes drawn to width of 3 ft	Instruct maid
Implicit services	Security	All perimeter lights working	Replace defective bulbs
	Pleasant atmosphere	Telling departing guests "Have a nice day"	Instruct desk clerk
	Waiting room	No customer having to wait for a room	Review room cleaning schedule

Taguchi Methods

The example above illustrates the application of *Taguchi methods,* which are named after Genichi Taguchi, who advocated "robust design" of products to ensure their proper functioning under adverse conditions.[5] The idea is that for a customer, proof of a product's quality is in its performance when abused. For example, a telephone is designed to be far more durable than necessary because more than once it will be pulled off a desk and dropped on the floor. In our budget hotel example, the building is constructed of concrete blocks and furnished with durable furniture.

Taguchi also applied the concept of robustness to the manufacturing process. For example, the recipe for caramel candy was reformulated to make plasticity, or chewiness, less sensitive to the cooking temperature. Similarly, our budget hotel uses an online computer to notify the cleaning staff automatically when a room has been vacated. Keeping the maids posted on which rooms are available for cleaning allows this task to be spread throughout the day, thus avoiding a rush in the late afternoon that could result in quality degradation.

FIGURE 3.4 Taguchi quality loss function.

Taguchi believed that product quality was achieved by consistently meeting design specifications. He measured the cost of poor quality by the square of the deviation from the target, as shown in Figure 3.4. Once again, note the attention to standard operating procedures (SOPs) used by the budget hotel to promote uniform treatment of guests and consistent preparation of the rooms.

Poka-Yoke (Failsafing)

Shigeo Shingo believed that low-cost, in-process, quality-control mechanisms and routines used by employees in their work could achieve high quality without costly inspection. He observed that errors occurred, not because employees were incompetent, but because of interruptions in routine or lapses in attention. He advocated the adoption of *poka-yoke* methods, which can be translated roughly as "foolproof" devices. The poka-yoke methods use checklists or manual devices that do not let the employee make a mistake.[6] As noted by Chase and Stewart and summarized in Table 3.5, service

TABLE 3.5

CLASSIFICATION OF SERVICE FAILURES

Server errors	Customer errors
Task:	*Preparation:*
• Doing work incorrectly	• Failure to bring necessary materials
• Doing work not required	• Failure to understand role in transaction
• Doing work in the wrong order	• Failure to engage the correct service
• Doing work too slowly	*Encounter:*
Treatment:	• Failure to remember steps in process
• Failure to acknowledge the customer	• Failure to follow system flow
• Failure to listen to the customer	• Failure to specify desires sufficiently
• Failure to react appropriately	• Failure to follow instructions
Tangible:	*Resolution:*
• Failure to clean facilities	• Failure to signal service failure
• Failure to provide clean uniforms	• Failure to learn from experience
• Failure to control environmental factors	• Failure to adjust expectations
• Failure to proofread documents	• Failure to execute post-encounter action

errors can originate from both the server and the customer. Poka-yoke methods therefore should address both sources.[7]

Service provider errors fall into three categories: tasks, treatments, and tangibles. The use of a french fry scoop at McDonald's to measure out a consistent serving of potatoes is an example of a *task* poka-yoke device that also enhances cleanliness and, hence, the aesthetic quality of the service as well. The emergency room check sheet shown in Table 3.2 is another task poka-yoke device; it reminds workers of steps often forgotten when hurrying to satisfy patients in a timely manner. A novel *treatment* poka-yoke devised by a bank for tellers to ensure customer eye contact requires them to enter the customer's eye color on a checklist at the start of the transaction. An example of a *tangible* poka-yoke is the placement of mirrors in employee break rooms to promote appropriate appearance upon returning to the customer area. The automatic spell check feature of Microsoft Outlook assures that an e-mail is not sent until it has been proofed for errors.

Because customers play an active role in the delivery of services, they also need help to avoid errors. These errors fall into three categories: preparation, encounter, and resolution. Shouldice Hospital located in Toronto, Canada, performs only inguinal hernia operations. All potential patients are required to fill out a comprehensive medical survey, that is, a *preparation* poka-yoke, to ensure that the medical condition is appropriate for treatment at Shouldice. Many *encounter* poka-yokes are unobtrusive, such as the use of height bars at amusement rides to ensure that riders exceed size limitations or frames at airport check-in counters to gauge allowable size of carry-on luggage. *Resolution* poka-yokes help mold the behavior of customers as they exit the service. Fast-food restaurants strategically locate tray-return stands and trash bins at the exits.

Using physical design to control employee and customer discretion is an important preemptive strategy to avoid mistakes. Because it is difficult for management to intervene in the service process and impose a quality appraisal system (i.e., inspection and testing), limiting discretion and incorporating poka-yoke methods facilitate mistake-free service. It is interesting to note how these unobtrusive design features channel

Airlines use this poka-yoke device to alert passengers to the size limits of carry-on luggage. © Myrleen Ferguson Cafe/PhotoEdit, Inc.

service behavior without a suggestion of coercion, such as a "beep" from our word processor to warn us that an invalid keystroke has been made.

Quality Function Deployment

To provide customer input at the product design stage, a process called *quality function deployment* (QFD) was developed in Japan and used extensively by Toyota and its suppliers. The process results in a matrix, referred to as a "house of quality," for a particular product that relates customer attributes to engineering characteristics. The central idea of QFD is the belief that products should be designed to reflect the customers' desires and tastes; thus, the functions of marketing, design engineering, and manufacturing must be coordinated. The "house of quality" provides a framework for translating customer satisfaction into identifiable and measurable conformance specifications for product or service design.[8]

Although QFD was developed for use in product planning, its application to the design of service delivery systems is very appropriate, as shown by the following example.

Example 3.1: Quality Function Deployment for Village Volvo

Recall the Village Volvo case from Chapter 2. Village Volvo is an independent auto service garage that specializes in Volvo auto maintenance and competes with Volvo dealers for customers. Village Volvo has decided to assess its service delivery system in comparison with that of the Volvo dealer to determine areas for improving its competitive position. The steps in conducting the QFD project and constructing a "house of quality" follow:

1. *Establish the aim of the project.* In this case, the objective of the project is to assess Village Volvo's competitive position. QFD also could be used when a new service delivery system is being considered for the first time.
2. *Determine customer expectations.* Based on the aim of this project, identify the customer group to be satisfied and determine their expectations. For Village Volvo, the target customer group is Volvo owners with nonroutine repairs (i.e., exclude routine maintenance for this study). Customer expectations could be solicited by interviews, focus groups, or questionnaires. In this example, we will use the five dimensions of service quality to describe customer expectations. As shown in Figure 3.5, these are the *rows* of the house of quality. In a more sophisticated QFD project, customer expectations are broken down into primary, secondary, and tertiary levels of detail; for example, the primary expectation of "reliability" could be further specified with "accuracy" at the secondary level and "correct problem diagnosed" as the tertiary level of detail.
3. *Describe the elements of the service.* The *columns* of the house of quality matrix contain the service elements that management can manipulate to satisfy customer expectations. For Village Volvo, we have selected training, attitudes, capacity, information, and equipment.
4. *Note the strength of relationship between the service elements.* The *roof* of the house of quality provides an opportunity to note the strength of correlation between pairs of service elements. We have noted three levels of strength of relationship: * = strong, • = medium, and Ø = weak. As you might expect, we note a strong relationship between training and attitudes. Noting these relationships between elements may provide useful points of leverage to improve service quality.

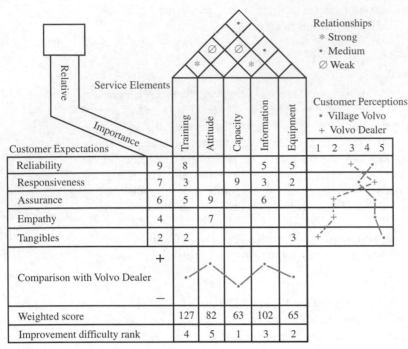

FIGURE 3.5 "House of quality" for Village Volvo.

5. *Note the association between customer expectations and service elements.* The *body* of the matrix contains numbers between 0 and 9 (9 indicating a very strong link) to indicate the strength of the link between a service element and a corresponding customer expectation. These numbers would follow a discussion by the project team about how various service elements affect the firm's capacity to satisfy the different customer expectations.

6. *Weighting the service elements.* This step is taken to measure the importance of a customer's assessment of the service element. The *chimney* of the house of quality contains a listing of the relative importance of each customer expectation. These weights on a scale of 1 to 9 indicate the importance that customers place on each of their expectations and could be determined by a customer survey. The relative importance will be multiplied by the strength of the link number in the body of the matrix under each service element to arrive at a weighted score for that element. For example, the training element would have a weighted score calculated as

$$(9)(8) + (7)(3) + (6)(5) + (4)(0) + (2)(2) = 127$$

The weighted scores are entered in the *basement* of the house of quality and represent a measure of each service element's importance to satisfying customer needs. These weighted results should be treated with caution and common sense, however, because they depend on uncertain estimates of relative importance and relationship scores.

7. *Service element improvement difficulty rank.* In the basement of the house is a ranking for the difficulty of improving each service element, with a rank of 1 being the most difficult. Capacity and equipment have a high rank because of their capital

requirements. This exercise demonstrates that even though customers may give a service element a high rank, the firm may be unable to deliver it.

8. *Assessment of competition.* A study of the Volvo dealer is made to assess customers' perceptions of service at the dealer compared with that at Village Volvo. The result of a customer survey (using customers who have experienced both providers) using a five-point scale is plotted to the *right* of the matrix. Based on knowledge of the dealer (perhaps from mechanics), a relative comparison of the level (plus or minus) of each service element is plotted at the *bottom* of the matrix. This information will be used to assess the competitive strengths and weaknesses of Village Volvo.

9. *Strategic assessment and goal setting.* Looking at the completed house of quality, Village Volvo can see some strengths and weaknesses in its strategic position relative to the Volvo dealer. Except for responsiveness, it is viewed favorably by its customers. This result must be viewed with caution, however, because these data were obtained from a survey of Village Volvo customers and, thus, were not unexpected. The comparison of service elements with the Volvo dealer and weighted scores yields some possible directions for improvement in service. In the area of attitudes and information, Village Volvo is in a superior position, but there appears to be a problem with capacity, training, and equipment. The high weighted score given to training suggests that a first-priority goal of an investment in training might be in order. In addition, leverage would be achieved because training has relationships, from strong to weak, with attitudes, capacity, and equipment. Finally, the improvement difficulty rank for training is fourth out of five.

ACHIEVING SERVICE QUALITY

Services are difficult for customers to evaluate before the fact. As we have already noted, they are intangible and consumed simultaneously with production. This presents a challenge to the service manager because quality-inspection intervention between the customer and the contact employee is not an option as in manufacturing (e.g., no slip of paper can be placed in the box by Inspector Number 12).

Cost of Quality

Caveat emptor—"let the buyer beware"—has become obsolete. As American businesses discovered in the late 1980s and early 1990s, impersonal service, faulty products, and broken promises all carry a price. A very visible example of this reality today is the prominent part that liability concerns and insurance play in almost every service imaginable. Poor quality can lead to bankruptcy. A gourmet soup company, for example, was forced out of business when its vichyssoise was found to contain poison-producing botulism organisms. Announcements of automobile recalls for correcting defects are commonplace as well.

Products can be returned, exchanged, or fixed, but what recourse does the customer of a faulty service have? Legal recourse! Medical malpractice lawsuits have been notorious for their large settlements, and although some cases of abuse by the legal system surely have occurred, the possibility of malpractice litigation does promote a physician's sense of responsibility to the patient. The threat of a negligence suit might induce a responsible doctor to take more time in an examination, seek more training, or avoid performing a procedure for which he or she is not competent. Unfortunately, as evidenced by the frequent claims of physicians that extra testing is necessary to defend against potential malpractice claims, the cost of care may increase without any improvement in quality.

No service has immunity from prosecution. For example, a Las Vegas hotel was sued for failing to provide proper security when a guest was assaulted in her room. An income tax preparer can be fined up to $500 per return if a taxpayer's liability is understated because of the preparer's negligence or disregard of Internal Revenue Service rules and regulations.

A noted quality expert, Joseph M. Juran, has advocated a cost-of-quality accounting system to convince top management of the need to address quality issues.[9] He identified four categories of costs: internal failure costs (from defects discovered before shipment), external failure costs (from defects discovered after shipment), detection costs (for inspection of purchased materials and during manufacture), and prevention costs (for keeping defects from occurring in the first place). Juran found that in most manufacturing companies, external and internal failure costs together accounted for 50 to 80 percent of the total cost of quality. Thus, to minimize this total cost, he advocated that more attention be paid to prevention. Suggestions have been made that $1 invested in prevention is worth $100 in detection costs and $10,000 in failure costs.

In Table 3.6, we have adapted Juran's cost-of-quality system for use by service firms with a banking example. In the prevention row, recruitment and selection of service personnel are viewed as ways to avoid poor quality. Identifying people with appropriate attitudes and interpersonal skills can result in hiring contact persons with the natural instincts that are needed to serve customers well.

TABLE 3.6

COSTS OF QUALITY FOR SERVICES

Cost Category	Definition	Bank Example
Prevention	Costs associated with operations or activities that keep failure from happening and minimize detection costs	Quality planning Recruitment and selection Training programs Quality improvement projects
Detection	Costs incurred to ascertain the condition of a service to determine whether it conforms to quality standards	Periodic inspection Process control Checking, balancing, verifying Collecting quality data
Internal failure	Costs incurred to correct nonconforming work prior to delivery to the customer	Scrapped forms and reports Rework Machine downtime
External failure	Costs incurred to correct nonconforming work after delivery to the customer or to correct work that did not satisfy a customer's specified needs	Payment of interest penalties Investigation time Legal judgments Negative word-of-mouth Loss of future business

Source: Adapted from C. A. Aubry and D. A. Zimbler, "The Banking Industry: Quality Costs and Improvement," *Quality Progress,* December 1983, pp. 16–20.

Inspection is included in the detection row, but it generally is impractical except in the back-office operations of a service.

Because service is an experience for the customer, any failure becomes a story for that customer to tell others. Service managers must recognize that dissatisfied customers not only will take their future business elsewhere but also will tell others about the unhappy experience, thus resulting in a significant loss of future business.

Service Process Control

The control of service quality can be viewed as a feedback control system. In a feedback system, output is compared with a standard. The deviation from that standard is communicated back to the input, and adjustments then are made to keep the output within a tolerable range. A thermostat in a home provides a common example of feedback control. Room temperature is monitored continually; when the temperature drops below some preset value, the furnace is activated and will continue to operate until the correct temperature is restored.

Figure 3.6 shows the basic control cycle as applied to service process control. The service concept establishes a basis for setting goals and defining measures of system performance. Output measures are taken and monitored for conformance to requirements. Nonconformance to requirements is studied to identify its causes and determine corrective action.

Unfortunately, it is difficult to implement an effective control cycle for service systems. Problems begin with the definition of service performance measures. The intangible nature of services makes direct measurement difficult, but it is not impossible. Many surrogate measures of service quality exist. For example, the waiting time of customers might be used. In some public services, the number of complaints that are received is used.

Monitoring service performance is frustrated by the simultaneous nature of production and consumption. This close interface between customer and provider prevents any direct intervention in the service process to observe conformance to requirements. Consequently, consumers may be asked to express their impression of service quality "after the fact" by filling out questionnaires. Monitoring only the final customer impressions of service quality, however, may be too late to avoid the loss of future sales. These difficulties in controlling service quality may be addressed by focusing on the

FIGURE 3.6 Service process control.

delivery process itself and by employing a technique borrowed from manufacturing called *statistical process control.*

Statistical Process Control

The performance of a service often is judged by key indicators. For example, the educational performance of a high school is measured by the Scholastic Aptitude Test (SAT) scores of its students. The effectiveness of a police department's crime-prevention program is judged by the crime rate, and a bank teller's performance is judged by the accuracy of his or her end-of-day balances.

What happens if the service process is not performing as expected? Generally, an investigation is conducted to identify the cause of the problem and to suggest corrective action; however, performance variations may result from random occurrences and not have a specific cause. The decision maker wants to detect true degradation in service performance and avoid the failure costs that are associated with poor service. On the other hand, making an unnecessary change in a system that is performing correctly should be avoided. Thus, two types of risks are involved in controlling quality, as shown in Table 3.7. These risks have been given names to identify the injured party. If a process is deemed to be out of control when it in fact is performing correctly, a Type I error has occurred, which is the producer's risk. If a process is deemed to be functioning properly when it in fact is out of control, a Type II error has occurred, which is the consumer's risk.

A visual display called a *control chart* is used to plot values of a measure of process performance (e.g., the time a directory assistance operator spends with a caller) to determine if the process is in control (e.g., the time is less than 30 seconds in the operator example). For example, Figure 3.7 shows a control chart that is used to monitor emergency ambulance response time. This chart is a daily plot of mean response time that permits monitoring performance for unusual deviations from the norm. When a measurement falls outside the control limits—that is, above the upper control limit (UCL) or below the lower control limit (LCL)—the process is considered to be out of control; consequently, the system is in need of attention. For our ambulance example, day 4 signaled a need for investigation by the supervisor. An excessive mean response time for that day occurred because a nearby ambulance was out of commission and our vehicle needed to travel longer distances. Since day 4, ambulance performance has remained within the control limits, so no action is required.

Constructing a control chart is similar to determining a confidence interval for the mean of a sample. Recall from statistics that sample means tend to be distributed normally according to the central-limit theorem (i.e., although the underlying statistic may be distributed in any manner, mean values drawn from this statistic have a normal distribution). We know from standard normal tables that 99.7 percent of the normal distribution falls within 3 standard deviations of the mean. Using representative historical data, both the mean and the standard deviation for some system performance measure

TABLE 3.7

RISKS IN QUALITY-CONTROL DECISIONS

True state of service	Quality-control decision	
	Take corrective action	**Do nothing**
Process in control	Type I error (producer's risk)	Correct decision
Process out of control	Correct decision	Type II error (consumer's risk)

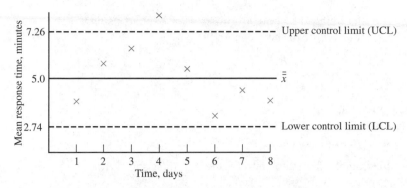

FIGURE 3.7. $\bar{X}$-chart for ambulance response.

are determined. These parameters then are used to construct a 99.7-percent confidence interval for the mean of the performance measure. We expect future sample means that are collected at random to fall within this confidence interval; if they do not, then we conclude that the process has changed and the true mean has shifted.

The steps in constructing and using a quality-control chart can be summarized as:

1. Decide on some measure of service system performance.

2. Collect representative historical data from which estimates of the population mean and variance for the system performance measure can be made.

3. Decide on a sample size, and using the estimates of population mean and variance, calculate (by convention) ± 3 standard deviation control limits.

4. Graph the control chart as a function of sample mean values versus time.

5. Plot sample means collected at random on the chart, and interpret the results as follows:
   i. Process in control (i.e., sample mean falls within control limits).
   ii. Process out of control (i.e., sample mean falls outside control limits, or a run of seven means falling either above or below the average). In this case:
      a. Evaluate the situation.
      b. Take corrective action.
      c. Check results of action.

6. Update the control chart on a periodic basis, and incorporate recent data.

Control charts for means fall into two categories based on the type of performance measure. A variable control chart (X-chart) records measurements that permit fractional values, such as length, weight, or time. An attribute control chart (p-chart) records discrete data, such as the number of defects or errors as a percentage.

Example 3.2: Control Chart for Variables ($\bar{X}$-Chart)

The quality-control chart for mean ambulance response time shown in Figure 3.7 is an example of a variable measure. It is based on taking a random sample of four ambulance calls each day to calculate a sample mean response time to monitor performance. The range of the sample values (i.e., the difference between the highest and the lowest values) will be used instead of the standard deviation to calculate the control limits. Assume that past records of ambulance system performance yield an estimated population mean response time of 5.0 minutes, with an estimated average range of 3.1

minutes. Appropriate formulas for calculating the control limits for an $\overline{X}$-chart using the $\overline{R}$ range as a substitute for the standard error of the mean are

$$\text{UCL} = \overline{\overline{X}} + A_2\overline{R} \tag{1}$$

$$\text{LCL} = \overline{\overline{X}} - A_2\overline{R} \tag{2}$$

where $\overline{\overline{X}}$ = estimate of population mean
$\overline{R}$ = estimate of population range
A_2 = value from Table 3.8 for sample size n

For the ambulance response time control chart shown in Figure 3.7, the control limits for a sample size of four are calculated as follows:

$$\text{UCL} = \overline{\overline{X}} + A_2\overline{R} = 5.0 + (0.729)(3.1) = 7.26$$

$$\text{LCL} = \overline{\overline{X}} - A_2\overline{R} = 5.0 - (0.729)(3.1) = 2.74$$

We also could monitor the variance of the ambulance response times using the range (i.e., the largest value minus the smallest value in the sample) as a measure of variance. A range or R-chart can be constructed in a manner similar to the $\overline{X}$-chart by using the following formulas:

$$\text{UCL} = D_4\overline{R} \tag{3}$$

$$\text{LCL} = D_3\overline{R} \tag{4}$$

where: $\overline{R}$ = estimate of population range

D_4 = UCL value from Table 3.8 for sample size n
D_3 = LCL value from Table 3.8 for sample size n

TABLE 3.8

VARIABLE CONTROL CHART CONSTANTS

Sample size	$\overline{X}$-chart	R-chart	
n	A_2	D_3	D_4
2	1.880	0	3.267
3	1.023	0	2.574
4	0.729	0	2.282
5	0.577	0	2.114
6	0.483	0	2.004
7	0.419	0.076	1.924
8	0.373	0.136	1.864
9	0.337	0.184	1.816
10	0.308	0.223	1.777
12	0.266	0.283	1.717
14	0.235	0.328	1.672
16	0.212	0.363	1.637
18	0.194	0.391	1.608
20	0.180	0.415	1.585
22	0.167	0.434	1.566
24	0.157	0.451	1.548

Source: Adapted from Table 27 of *ASTM Manual on Presentation of Data and Control Chart Analysis,* copyright 1976, American Society for Testing and Materials, Philadelphia.

For our ambulance case, the range control limits are calculated using the constants in Table 3.8 for a sample size of four:

$$\text{UCL} = D_4 \bar{R} = (2.282)(3.1) = 7.1$$
$$\text{LCL} = D_3 \bar{R} = (0)(3.1) = 0$$

Example 3.3: Control Chart for Attributes (p-Chart)

In some cases, system performance is classified as either "good" or "bad." Of primary concern is the percentage of bad performance. For example, consider the operator of a mechanized sorting machine in a post office. The operator must read the ZIP code on a parcel and, knowing its location in the city, divert the package by conveyor to the proper route truck. From past records, the error rate for skilled operators is about 5 percent, or a fraction defective of 0.05. Management wants to develop a control chart to monitor new operators to ensure that personnel who are unsuited for the job can be identified. Equations (5) and (6) below are used to construct a percentage or p-chart. These formulas should be familiar because they represent the $\pm$ 3 standard deviation confidence interval for a percentage.

$$\text{UCL} = \bar{p} + 3\sqrt{\frac{\bar{p}(1 - \bar{p})}{n}} \tag{5}$$

$$\text{LCL} = \bar{p} - 3\sqrt{\frac{\bar{p}(1 - \bar{p})}{n}} \tag{6}$$

where:

$$\sqrt{\frac{\bar{p}(1 - \bar{p})}{n}} = \text{standard error of percentage}$$

$$\bar{p} = \text{estimate of population percentage}$$

$$n = \text{sample size}$$

The p-chart control limits for the sorting operation are calculated using equations (5) and (6) and random samples of 100 parcels drawn from the route trucks. Note that if the calculation of an *LCL* results in a negative number, then *LCL* is set equal to zero.

$$\text{UCL} = 0.05 + 3\sqrt{\frac{(0.05)(0.95)}{100}} = 0.05 + 3(0.0218) = 0.1154 \approx 0.11$$

$$\text{LCL} = 0.05 - 3\sqrt{\frac{(0.05)(0.95)}{100}} = 0.05 - 3(0.0218) = -0.0154 \,[\text{set} = 0.0]$$

The p-chart for this operation is shown in Figure 3.8. Given this 9-day probationary experience for the new employee, would you conclude that the person is suitable for the sorting position?

FIGURE 3.8 *p*-chart for ZIP code sorting operator.

Unconditional Service Guarantee[10]

Whenever you buy a product, a warranty to guarantee its performance is expected—but to guarantee a service? Impossible! Not so, according to Christopher Hart, who writes that service guarantees such as the example shown in Figure 3.9 have five important features:

1. *Unconditional.* Customer satisfaction is unconditional, without exceptions. For example, L. L. Bean, a Maine mail-order house, accepts all returns without question and provides a replacement, refund, or credit.
2. *Easy to understand and communicate.* Customers should know precisely what to expect from a guarantee in measurable terms. For example, Bennigan's promises that if a lunch is not served within 15 minutes, the diner receives a free meal.
3. *Meaningful.* The guarantee should be important to the customer in financial as well as in service terms. Domino's Pizza guarantees that if an order is not delivered within 30 minutes, the customer gets $3 off rather than a free pizza, because its customers consider a rebate to be more desirable.
4. *Easy to invoke.* A dissatisfied customer should not be hassled with filling out forms or writing letters to invoke a guarantee. Cititravel, a service of Citibank, guarantees the lowest airfares or a refund of the difference; a toll-free call to an agent is all that is necessary to confirm a lower fare and get a refund.
5. *Easy to collect.* The best guarantees are resolved on the spot, as illustrated by Domino's Pizza and Bennigan's.

A service guarantee has obvious marketing appeal. More important, however, the service guarantee can redefine the meaning of service for an industry by setting quality standards. For example, Federal Express defined small-parcel delivery with its overnight delivery guarantee. A service guarantee promotes organizational effectiveness in several ways:

Hampton Inn

**100%
SATISFACTION
GUARANTEE**

We guarantee high quality accommodations, friendly and efficient service, and clean, comfortable surroundings.

If you're not completely satisfied, we don't expect you to pay.

FIGURE 3.9 The Hampton Inn unconditional service guarantee.

1. *Focuses on customers.* A guarantee forces a company to identify its customers' expectations. In a survey of its passengers, British Airways found that they judged its service on four dimensions: care and concern, initiative, problem solving, and—to the airline's surprise—recovery when things go wrong.
2. *Sets clear standards.* A specific, unambiguous guarantee for the customer also sets clear standards for the organization. The Federal Express guarantee of delivery "absolutely positively by 10:30 A.M." defines the responsibilities of all its employees.
3. *Guarantees feedback.* Customers invoking a guarantee provide valuable information for quality assessment. Dissatisfied customers now have an incentive to complain and to get management's attention. Manpower Inc., a temporary-worker agency, takes a proactive approach by calling the client after the first day to get feedback on customer satisfaction.
4. *Promotes an understanding of the service delivery system.* Before a guarantee is made, managers must identify the possible failure points in their system and the limits to which these can be controlled. Burger Bug Killers, Inc., a Florida exterminator, will not guarantee or accept a job unless the client adheres to recommended facility improvements such as sealing doors and windows from insect penetration. Federal Express adopted a hub-and-spoke network to ensure that all packages would be brought to Memphis in the evening for sorting and flown out that very night for delivery by 10:30 the next morning.
5. *Builds customer loyalty.* A guarantee reduces the customer's risk, makes expectations explicit, and builds market share by retaining dissatisfied customers who otherwise would leave for the competition.

SERVICE RECOVERY

As shown in Figure 3.10, a dissatisfied customer is not simply a lost future sale but potentially very damaging to a firm's reputation. Table 3.9 contains some statistics on the behavior of dissatisfied customers that suggests a quick resolution to service failure is

FIGURE 3.10 Expressing dissatisfaction.

TABLE 3.9

CUSTOMER FEEDBACK AND WORD OF MOUTH

- The average business only hears from 4 percent of its customers who are dissatisfied with the products or services. Of the 96 percent who do not bother to complain, 25 percent of them have serious problems.
- The 4 percent who complain are more likely to stay with the supplier than are the 96 percent who do not complain.
- About 60 percent of the complainers would stay as customers if their problem were resolved and 95 percent would stay if the problem were resolved quickly.
- A dissatisfied customer will tell from 10 to 20 other people about his or her problem.
- A customer who has had a problem resolved by a company will tell approximately 5 people about her or his situation.

---

an important way to create loyal customers. Because customers participate in the service delivery process, an alert employee trained in service recovery techniques can turn a potential disaster into a loyal customer.

A service failure can be turned into a service delight by empowering front-line employees with the discretion to "make things right." For example, when an airplane full of anxious passengers is delayed for some minor mechanical problem, it's time to break out complimentary drinks. More heroic efforts become legends, such as the story of a Federal Express employee who hired a helicopter to repair a downed telephone line during a snowstorm. Expenses incurred to accomplish a recovery are "pennies on the dollar" compared with the possible adverse "word-of-mouth" stories that are now turned into good stories of how an employee went the extra mile to accommodate a customer. Training employees in approaches to service recovery should be the first line of defense against defections and "poor word of mouth."

Approaches to Service Recovery[11]

There are four basic approaches to service recovery: the case-by-case, the systematic-response, the early intervention, and the substitute service recovery approaches.

1. *The case-by-case approach* addresses each customer's complaint individually. This inexpensive approach is easy to implement, but it can be haphazard. The most persistent or aggressive complainers, for example, often receive satisfactory responses while more "reasonable" complainers do not. The haphazardness of this approach can generate perceptions of unfairness.
2. *The systematic-response approach* uses a protocol to handle customer complaints. It is more reliable than the case-by-case approach because it is a planned response based on identification of critical failure points and prior determination of appropriate recovery criteria. As long as the response guidelines are continuously updated, this approach can be very beneficial because it offers a consistent and timely response.
3. *An early intervention approach* adds another component to the systematic-response approach by attempting to intervene and fix service-process problems before they affect the customer. A shipper who realizes that a shipment is being held up by a truck breakdown, for example, can choose to notify the customer immediately so the customer can develop alternative plans if necessary.
4. An alternate approach capitalizes on the failure of a rival to win the competitor's customer by providing a *substitute service recovery*. At times the rival firm may

support this approach. A desk person at an overbooked hotel, for example, may send a customer to a rival hotel. The rival hotel may be able to capitalize on such an opportunity if it can provide a timely and quality service. This approach is difficult to implement because information about a competitor's service failures is usually closely guarded.

STAGES IN QUALITY DEVELOPMENT

In this chapter we have looked at the most important issues of incorporating quality into the delivery of services. Some aspects of quality assurance in a service organization may occur simultaneously, but it is useful to look at the development in a systematic way.

The service quality ladder shown in Figure 3.11 summarizes the progressive steps in quality development. Inspection is shown as the first rung because organizations usually begin here with their first attempts to address quality problems (e.g., checking hotel rooms after cleaning). Quality function deployment is shown as the top rung because quality must finally be recognized as a basic customer requirement that must be incorporated in the design of the service delivery process.

SUMMARY

We began our study of quality issues in services by noting that customers are the ultimate judges of a service's value. Market researchers have identified five principal dimensions that customers use to judge service quality. Customers use those dimensions to make their assessments, which are based primarily on a comparison of their expectations for the service desired with their perceptions of the service delivered. We then looked at the different types of gaps that can occur when customers' expectations do not meet their perceptions of the service.

Next we turned to the problem of measuring service quality. Scope of services (that is, content, process, structure, outcome, and impact) and SERVQUAL are two useful approaches that can be used to measure quality in a variety of services.

We noted the necessity of "designing in" quality and examined the Taguchi concept of robustness, poka-yoke fail-safe strategies, and quality function deployment methods of incorporating customer requirements in design for quality.

The costs of quality are categorized as failure costs, detection costs, and prevention costs. We illustrated the application of statistical process control to avoid high failure costs in service operations.

Finally, because service failures do occur, we examined the concept of service recovery and unconditional guarantee programs.

Formulating a strategic service concept is the first topic of the next chapter. A discussion of generic competitive strategies applied to services will be examined with a look at how customers are won in the marketplace. The chapter concludes with a discussion of the competitive role of information technology in services.

KEY TERMS AND DEFINITIONS

Control chart a chart with an upper control limit and a lower control limit on which sample means are plotted periodically to show visually when a process is out of control.

Poka-yoke a "foolproof" device or checklist to assist employees in avoiding a mistake.

Quality function deployment a process in which a "house of quality" is constructed to incorporate customer needs into the design of a service process.

**QUALITY FUNCTION
DEPLOYMENT**

Define voice of the
customer in operational terms

QUALITY SERVICE BY DESIGN

Design service process for
robustness and foolproof operation

**UNCONDITIONAL SERVICE
GUARANTEE**

Focus operations and marketing
on a service performance measure

COST OF QUALITY

Quantifying the cost of poor quality

QUALITY TRAINING PROGRAMS

Employee empowerment and
responsibility for quality

STATISTICAL PROCESS CONTROL

Quality assurance during service delivery

INSPECTION

Quality checked after service delivered

FIGURE 3.11 The service quality ladder.

Service recovery converting a previously dissatisfied customer into a loyal customer.

SERVQUAL a customer survey instrument used to measure service quality gaps.

Statistical process control the use of a control chart to monitor a process performance measure that signals when intervention is needed.

Taguchi methods approaches to service process design that ensure "robustness" or an ability to function under adverse conditions.

Unconditional service guarantee a service warranty that provides a customer focus for the firm.

SOLVED PROBLEMS

1. Control Chart for Variables

Problem Statement

To become productive, Resort International is interested in setting standards for the time that telephone reservation clerks spend with vacationers making tour arrangements. Collecting data on the amount of time the reservation clerks spend with customers has been proposed to determine the mean time and average range as well as to establish a process control chart for this operation. The table below records the time in minutes that reservation clerks spent answering calls as found by observing one call each day during a typical week. The fifth row contains the $\overline{X}$ values for each day. The last row contains the range (i.e., high−low) values for each day (e.g., the high for Monday was 14 and the low was 5, yielding a range of 9).

Clerk	Mon.	Tue.	Wed.	Thur.	Fri.
Alice	5	11	12	13	10
Bill	6	5	12	10	13
Janice	14	13	10	9	9
Mike	8	6	9	12	14
$\overline{X}$	8.25	8.75	10.75	11.0	11.5
Range	9	8	3	4	5

Solution

First, we establish the population mean and range using the sample results from the five days shown above:

$$\overline{X} = \frac{8.25 + 8.75 + 10.75 + 11.0 + 11.5}{5} = 10.05$$

$$\overline{R} = \frac{9 + 8 + 3 + 4 + 5}{5} = 5.8$$

Second, we establish the control limits for an $\overline{X}$-chart using equations (1) and (2) when sampling four random calls each day for each clerk. The sample size of 4 was selected for convenience.

$$\text{UCL} = \overline{\overline{X}} + A_2\overline{R} = 10.05 + (0.729)(5.8) = 14.28$$
$$\text{LCL} = \overline{\overline{X}} - A_2\overline{R} = 10.05 - (0.729)(5.8) = 5.82$$

Third, we also establish limits for the range of call times for these samples of four calls by constructing an *R*-chart using equations (3) and (4).

$$\text{UCL} = D_4\overline{R} = (2.282)(5.8) = 13.2$$
$$\text{LCL} = D_3\overline{R} = (0)(5.8) = 0$$

Plotting the average call time, which is based on a random sample of four calls for each clerk for each day, provides a record of performance for each clerk. If the average call time for any clerk falls outside the control limits, then an explanation is in order. If the average is above the UCL, too much time is being spent taking reservations, which results in lost productivity. If the average falls below the LCL, the clerk may be too curt, which results in a customer perception of unresponsiveness.

2. Control Chart for Attributes

Problem Statement

A regional airline is concerned about its record of on-time performance. The Memphis hub experiences 20 flight operations each day of the week, with the following record of on-time departures for the previous 10 days: 17, 16, 18, 19, 16, 15, 20, 17, 18, and 16. Prepare a p-chart with a sample size consisting of 1 week's average on-time departure percentage.

Solution

First, we calculate the expected population fraction of on-time departures, which is the sum of the 10-day experience divided by a total of 200 flights:

$$\bar{p} = \frac{17 + 16 + 18 + 19 + 16 + 15 + 20 + 17 + 18 + 16}{(10)(20)} = 0.86$$

Then, the control limits are determined using equations (5) and (6) with a sample size of 7:

$$UCL = \bar{p} + 3\sqrt{\frac{\bar{p}(1-\bar{p})}{n}} = 0.86 + 3\sqrt{\frac{0.86(1-0.86)}{7}} = 0.86 + 3(0.13) = 1.25 [set = 1.00]$$

$$LCL = \bar{p} - 3\sqrt{\frac{\bar{p}(1-\bar{p})}{n}} = 0.86 - 3(0.13) = 0.47$$

As often is the case for p-charts, one limit is set equal to the extreme value (i.e., UCL = 1.00 or LCL = 0.0). In this case, an average percentage of on-time departures for the week would be calculated, and only if this is found to be less than 47 percent (or 9 out of 20 departures late) would action be taken to investigate the abnormal occurrence for cause.

TOPICS FOR DISCUSSION

1. How do the five dimensions of service quality differ from those of product quality?
2. Why is measuring service quality so difficult?
3. Illustrate the four components in the cost of quality for a service of your choice.
4. Why do service firms hesitate to offer a service guarantee?
5. How can recovery from a service failure be a blessing in disguise?

EXERCISES

3.1. In **Example 3.1,** Village Volvo wants to test the results of the QFD exercise for sensitivity to changes in the relative importance of customer expectations. Recalculate the weighted scores for the QFD exercise when customer expectations are given equal relative importance (e.g., five). Has this changed the previous recommendation to focus on training?

3.2. In **Example 3.2,** the ambulance supervisor now has decided to double the response time sample size to 8 calls per day. Calculate the new UCL and LCL for a revised $\bar{X}$-chart. For the next week, you record the following sample of daily mean response times: 5.2, 6.4, 6.2, 5.8, 5.7, 6.3, and 5.6. Would you be concerned?

3.3. The time to make beds at a motel should fall into an agreed-on range of times. A sample of four maids was selected, and the time needed to make a bed was observed on three different occasions:

	Service time, sec.		
Maid	Sample 1	Sample 2	Sample 3
Ann	120	90	150
Linda	130	110	140
Marie	200	180	175
Michael	165	155	140

a. Determine the upper and lower control limits for an $\overline{X}$-chart and an R-chart with a sample size of four.

b. After the control chart was established, a sample of four observations had the following times in seconds: 185, 150, 192, and 178. Is corrective action needed?

3.4 The management of the Diners Delight franchised restaurant chain is in the process of establishing quality-control charts for the time that its service people give to each customer. Management thinks the length of time that each customer is given should remain within certain limits to enhance service quality. A sample of six service people was selected, and the customer service they provided was observed four times. The activities that the service people were performing were identified, and the time to service one customer was recorded as noted below:

	Service time, sec.			
Service person	Sample 1	Sample 2	Sample 3	Sample 4
1	200	150	175	90
2	120	85	105	75
3	83	93	130	150
4	68	150	145	175
5	110	90	75	105
6	115	65	115	125

a. Determine the upper and lower control limits for an $\overline{X}$-chart and an R-chart with a sample size of 6.

b. After the control chart was established, a sample of six service people was observed, and the following customer service times in seconds were recorded: 180, 125, 110, 98, 156, and 190. Is corrective action called for?

3.5. After becoming familiar with their jobs, the sorting machine operators of **Example 3.3** now average only two address errors per 100 parcels sorted. Prepare a p-chart for experienced sorting operators.

3.6. Several complaints recently have been sent to the Gotham City police department regarding the increasing incidence of congestion on the city's streets. The complaints attribute the cause of these traffic tie-ups to a lack of synchronization of the traffic lights. The lights are controlled by a main computer system, and adjusting this program is costly. Therefore, the controllers are reluctant to change the situation unless a clear need is shown.

During the past year, the police department has collected data at 1,000 intersections. The data were compiled on a monthly basis as shown below:

Month	Congestion incidence
January	14
February	18
March	14
April	12
May	16
June	8
July	19
August	12
September	14
October	7
November	10
December	18

a. Construct a *p*-chart based on the above data.

b. Should the system be modified if, during the next 3 months, reports of congestion at these 1,000 intersections indicate the following:

Month	Congestion incidence
January	15
February	9
March	11

3.7. The Speedway Clinical Laboratory is a scientific blood-testing facility that receives samples from local hospitals and clinics. The blood samples are passed through several automated tests, and the results are printed through a central computer that reads and stores the information about each sample that is tested.

Management is concerned about the quality of the service it provides and wants to establish quality-control limits as a measure for the quality of its tests. Such managerial practice is viewed as significant, because incorrect analysis of a sample can lead to a wrong diagnosis by the physician, which in turn may cost the life of a patient. For this reason, 100 blood samples were collected at random each day after they had gone through testing. After retesting was performed manually on this sample, the results were:

Day	Incorrect analysis	Day	Incorrect analysis
1	8	11	4
2	3	12	6
3	1	13	5
4	0	14	10
5	4	15	2
6	2	16	1
7	9	17	0
8	6	18	6
9	3	19	3
10	1	20	2

a. Construct a *p*-chart to be used in assessing the quality of the service described above.

b. On average, what is the expected number of incorrect tests per 100 samples?

c. Later, another sample of 100 was taken. After the accuracy of the tests was established, 10 samples were found to have been analyzed incorrectly. What is your conclusion about the quality of this service?

3.8 The Long Life Insurance Company receives applications to buy insurance from its salespeople, who are specially trained in selling insurance to new customers. After the applications are received, they are processed through a computer. The computer is programmed so that it prints messages whenever it runs through an item that is not consistent with company policies. The company is concerned with the accuracy of the training that its salespeople receive, and it contemplates recalling them for more training if the quality of their performance is below certain limits. Five samples of 20 applications received from specific market areas were collected and inspected with the following results:

Sample	No. of applications with errors
1	2
2	2
3	1
4	3
5	2

a. Determine the upper and lower control limits for a *p*-chart using a sample size of 20.

b. After the control limits were established, a sample was taken and four applications were found to have mistakes. What can we conclude from this?

BOX 3.1

Service Benchmark
SERVICE WINNERS OF THE MALCOLM BALDRIGE NATIONAL QUALITY AWARD

1990
Federal Express Corporation
Memphis, Tennessee

1992
AT&T Universal Card Services
Jacksonville, Florida

The Ritz-Carlton Hotel Company
Atlanta, Georgia

1994
AT&T Consumer Communications Services
Basking Ridge, New Jersey

GTE Directories Corporation
Dallas/Ft. Worth Airport, Texas

1996
Dana Commercial Credit Corporation
Toledo, Ohio

1997
Merrill Lynch Credit Corporation
Jacksonville, Florida

Xerox Business Services
Rochester, New York

1999
The Ritz-Carlton Hotel Company
Atlanta, Georgia

Malcolm Baldrige Award winners prominently display this trophy in their headquarters lobbies.

Clean Sweep, Inc.

Clean Sweep, Inc. (CSI), is a custodial-janitorial services company specializing in contract maintenance of office space. Although not a large company compared with its primary competitors, CSI does have several major contracts to service some of the state government's offices. To enter and stay in the custodial service business, CSI adopted the strategy of having a small workforce that performs high-quality work at a reasonably rapid pace. At present, management feels that CSI has a staff that is more productive on an individual basis than those of its competition. Management recognizes that this single factor is the key to the company's success, so maintaining a high worker productivity level is critical.

Within the staff, the organizational structure is divided into four crews, each of which is composed of a crew leader and six to nine other crew members. All crews are under the direction of a single crew supervisor. Within the state building complex, there are nine buildings included in CSI's contracts, and the custodial assignments have been distributed as shown in Table 3.10 to balance the work-load distribution among the crews (on the basis of gross square feet of floor space per member).

TABLE 3.10

CUSTODIAL ASSIGNMENTS

Crew	No. of members*	Buildings assigned and gross ft^2	Total ft^2 assigned
1	6	Bldg. A, 30,000; Bldg. C, 45,000; Bldg. F, 35,000	110,000
2	8	Bldg. B East, 95,000; Bldg. H, 55,000	150,000
3	9	Bldg. B West, 95,000; Bldg. G, 85,000	180,000
4	8	Bldg. D, 40,000; Bldg. E, 75,000; Bldg. I, 42,000	157,000

* Excludes crew leader.

The responsibilities of each crew involve the following general tasks, which are listed in no order of importance: (1) vacuum carpeted floors, (2) empty trash cans and place trash in industrial waste hoppers, (3) dry-mop and buff marble floors, (4) clean rest rooms, (5) clean snack bar area(s), and (6) dust desk tops.

Each crew works an 8½-hour shift, during which it gets two 15-minute paid rest breaks and one 30-minute lunch break, which is unpaid. There is some variation among the crews in choosing break and lunch times, however, primarily because of the personalities of the crew leaders. The leaders of crews 2 and 3 are the strictest in their supervision, whereas the leaders of crews 1 and 4 are the least strict, according to the crew supervisor.

CSI's management is aware that the department of the state government overseeing the custodial service contracts makes periodic random inspections and rates the cleaning jobs that CSI does. This department also receives any complaints about the custodial service from office workers. Table 3.11 contains the monthly ratings and number of complaints received (by building) during CSI's current contracts. Because the renegotiation of CSI's contracts is several months away, company management would like to maintain a high level of quality during the remaining months to improve its competitive stance.

TABLE 3.11

COMPLAINTS ABOUT AND RATINGS OF CLEANING CREWS

Month	Building									
	A	Be	Bw	C	D	E	F	G	H	I
1	2	5	7	3	2	3	2	4	3	4
	7	5	3	6	7	5	6	5	4	5
2	1	6	8	2	1	1	2	3	2	5
	7	5	3	6	6	5	6	5	5	4
3	0	6	8	1	0	2	2	4	0	1
	8	5	4	6	8	5	6	6	6	7
4	1	5	4	1	0	1	1	4	1	3
	7	5	5	8	8	6	7	5	6	6
5	1	3	2	2	0	1	1	3	1	2
	6	6	6	7	8	6	7	5	6	6
6	2	5	3	0	1	0	0	2	1	0
	7	6	6	7	7	8	6	5	5	7
7	0	4	2	1	0	0	0	0	0	1
	8	7	7	6	6	8	8	6	7	7
8	1	2	4	2	1	0	1	2	1	1
	6	6	5	7	7	8	7	5	6	7
9	1	2	4	1	1	0	1	1	3	0
	7	7	5	6	7	8	6	5	5	8

Note: First-row numbers for each month represent total number of complaints. Second-row numbers for each month represent ratings on a 1-to-10 scale; any rating under 5 is felt to be poor, and 8 or above is good.

As with other custodial service operations, employee turnover in CSI's staff has been fairly high but is still lower than the turnover experienced by many competitors. Management attributes this to the higher pay scale that CSI offers relative to that of the competition. Even though individual staff costs are higher, the greater productivity levels of a smaller-than-average workforce have resulted in greater-than-average profits for the company. Nevertheless, problems are reported by the crew supervisor, and complaints are voiced by the crew members. These complaints fall into two general categories: (1) inequity in crew leaders' attitudes and performance expectations and (2) lack of opportunities for personal advancement. Table 3.12 shows a historical distribution of monthly complaints from each crew according to these two categories for the same period as that covered by the ratings reported in Table 3.11.

TABLE 3.12

JOB-RELATED COMPLAINTS FROM CREW MEMBERS

Month	Crew 1		Crew 2		Crew 3		Crew 4	
	Inequity	No advancement	Inequity	No advancement	Inequity	No advancement	Inequity	No advancement
1	0	1	3	3	4	3	0	2
2	0	0	2	1	1	1	0	1
3	1	0	2	1	2	2	1	2
4	0	0	1	2	3	1	0	2
5	1	1	3	1	2	1	0	2
6	1	0	1	2	2	1	0	1
7	0	1	1	1	1	3	0	1
8	0	0	2	2	1	2	1	1
9	0	0	2	1	2	2	0	2

Questions

1. Prepare an $\bar{X}$-chart for complaints, and plot the average complaints for each crew during the nine-month period. Do the same for the performance ratings. What does this analysis reveal about the service quality of CSI's crews?

2. Discuss possible ways to improve service quality.
3. Describe some potential strategies for reducing CSI's staffing problems.

The Complaint Letter

Most service problems are solved by direct communication between the server and the customer during the moment of service. Occasionally, however, a customer may be motivated to communicate some thoughtful and detailed feedback to a service provider after the encounter, as illustrated in the following letter:

THE COMPLAINT LETTER

October 13, 1986
123 Main Street
Boston, Massachusetts

Gail and Harvey Pearson
The Retreat House on Foliage Pond
Vacationland, New Hampshire

Dear Mr. and Mrs. Pearson:

This is the first time that I have ever written a letter like this, but my wife and I are so upset by the treatment afforded by your staff that we felt compelled to let you know what happened to us. We had dinner reservations at the Retreat House for a party of four under my wife's name, Dr. Elaine Loflin, for Saturday evening, October 11. We were hosting my wife's brother and his wife, visiting from Atlanta, Georgia.

We were seated at 7:00 P.M. in the dining room to the left of the front desk. There were at least four empty tables in the room when we were seated. We were immediately given menus, a wine list, ice water, dinner rolls, and butter. Then we sat for 15 minutes until the cocktail waitress asked us for our drink orders. My sister-in-law said, after being asked what she would like, "I'll have a vodka martini straight-up with an olive." The cocktail waitress responded immediately, "I'm not a stenographer." My sister-in-law repeated her drink order.

Soon after, our waiter arrived, informing us of the specials of the evening. I don't remember his name, but he had dark hair, wore glasses, was a little stocky, and had his sleeves rolled up. He returned about 10 minutes later, our drinks still not having arrived. We had not decided upon our entrees, but requested appetizers, upon which he informed us that we could not order appetizers without ordering our entrees at the same time. We decided not to order appetizers.

Our drinks arrived and the waiter returned. We ordered our entrees at 7:30. When the waiter asked my wife for her order, he addressed her as "young lady." When he served her the meal, he called her "dear."

At 10 minutes of 8 we requested that our salads be brought to us as soon as possible. I then asked the waiter's assistant to bring us more rolls (each of us had been served one when we were seated). Her response was, "Who wants a roll?" upon which, caught off guard, we went around the table saying yes or no so she would know exactly how many "extra" rolls to bring to our table.

Our salads were served at five minutes of eight. At 25 minutes past the hour we requested our entrees. They were served at 8:30, one and one-half hours after we were seated in a restaurant which was one-third empty. Let me also add that we had to make constant requests for water refills, butter replacement, and the like.

In fairness to the chef, the food was excellent, and as you already realize, the atmosphere was delightful. Despite this, the dinner was a disaster. We were extremely upset and very insulted by the experience. Your staff is not well trained. They were overtly rude, and displayed little etiquette or social grace. This was compounded by the atmosphere you are trying to present and the prices you charge in your dining room.

Perhaps we should have made our feelings known at the time, but our foremost desire was to leave as soon as possible. We had been looking forward to dining at the Retreat House for quite some time as part of our vacation weekend in New Hampshire.

We will be hard-pressed to return to your establishment. Please be sure to know that we will share our experience at the Retreat House with our family, friends, and business associates.

Sincerely,
Dr. William E. Loflin

Source: Martin R. Moser, "Answering the Customer's Complaint: A Case Study," *The Cornell HRA Quarterly,* May 1987, p. 10. © Cornell HRA Quarterly. Used by permission. All rights reserved.

Experience has shown that complaint letters receive "mixed reviews." Some letters bring immediate positive responses from the providers, whereas other letters bring no response or resolution. The restaurateur's response to the complaint letter in this case was:

THE RESTAURATEUR'S REPLY

The Retreat House on Foliage Pond
Vacationland, New Hampshire
November 15, 1986

Dr. William E. Loflin
123 Main Street
Boston, Massachusetts

Dear Dr. Loflin:
My husband and I are naturally distressed by such a negative reaction to our restaurant, but very much appreciate your taking the time and trouble to apprise us of your recent dinner here. I perfectly understand and sympathize with your feelings, and would like to tell you a little about the circumstances involved.

The Lakes Region for the past four or five years has been notorious for its extremely low unemployment rate and resulting deplorable labor pool. This year local businesses found that the situation had deteriorated to a really alarming nadir. It has been virtually impossible to get adequate help, competent or otherwise! We tried to overhire at the beginning of the season, anticipating the problems we knew would arise, but were unsuccessful. Employees in the area know the situation very well and use it to their advantage, knowing that they can get a job anywhere at any time without references, and knowing they won't be fired for incompetency because there is no one to replace them. You can imagine the prevailing attitude among workers and the frustration it causes employers, particularly those of us who try hard to maintain high standards. Unhappily, we cannot be as selective about employees as we would wish, and the turnover is high. Proper training is not only a luxury, but an impossibility at such times.

Unfortunately, the night you dined at the Retreat House, October 11, is traditionally one of the busiest nights of the year, and though there may have been empty tables at the time you sat down, I can assure you that we served 150 people that night, despite the fact that no fewer than four members of the restaurant staff did not show up for work at the last minute, and did not notify us. Had they had the courtesy to call, we could have limited reservations, thereby mitigating the damage at least to a degree, but as it was, we, our guests, and the employees who were trying to make up the slack all had to suffer delays in service far beyond the norm!

As to the treatment you received from the waitress and waiter who attended you, neither of them is any longer in our employ, and never would have been had the labor situation not been so desperate! It would have indeed been helpful to us had you spoken up at the time—it makes a more lasting impression on the employees involved than does our discussing it with them after the fact. Now that we are in a relatively quiet period we have the time to properly train a new and, we hope, better waitstaff.

Please know that we feel as strongly as you do that the service you received that night was unacceptable, and certainly not up to our normal standards.

We hope to be able to prevent such problems from arising in the future, but realistically must acknowledge that bad nights do happen, even in the finest restaurants. Believe me, it is not because we do not care or are not paying attention!

You mentioned our prices. Let me just say that were you to make a comparative survey, you would find that our prices are about one half of what you would expect to pay in most cities and resort areas for commensurate cuisine and ambience. We set our prices in order to be competitive with other restaurants in this particular local area, in spite of the fact that most of them do not offer the same quality of food and atmosphere and certainly do not have our overhead!

I hope that this explanation (which should not be misconstrued as an excuse) has shed some light, and that you will accept our deep regrets and apologies for any unpleasantness you and your party suffered. We should be very glad if someday you would pay us a return visit so that we may provide you with the happy and enjoyable dining experience that many others have come to appreciate at the Retreat House.

Sincerely,
Gail Pearson

Source: Martin R. Moser, "Answering the Customer's Complaint: A Case Study," *The Cornell HRA Quarterly,* May 1987, p. 11. © Cornell HRA Quarterly. Used by permission. All rights reserved.

Questions

1. Briefly summarize the complaints and compliments in Dr. Loflin's letter.
2. Critique the letter of Gail Pearson in reply to Dr. Loflin. What are the strengths and weaknesses of the letter?
3. Prepare an "improved" response letter from Gail Pearson.
4. What further action should Gail Pearson take in view of this incident?

SELECTED BIBLIOGRAPHY

ANDREASSEN, TOR WALLIN: "What Drives Customer Loyalty with Complaint Resolution?" *Journal of Service Research,* vol. 1, no. 4, May 1999, pp. 324–332.

BEHARA, R. S., AND R. B. CHASE: "Service Quality Deployment: Quality Service by Design," in Rakesh V. Sarin (ed.), *Perspectives in Operations Management: Essays in Honor of Elwood S. Buffa,* Kluwer Academic Publisher, Norwell, Mass., 1993.

BERRY, L. L., AND A. PARASURAMAN: "Prescriptions for a Service Quality Revolution in America," *Organizational Dynamics,* vol. 20, no. 4, 1992, pp. 5–15.

————, V. A. ZEITHAML, AND A. PARASURAMAN: "Five Imperatives for Improving Service Quality," *Sloan Management Review,* vol. 31, no. 4, Summer 1990, pp. 29–38.

BOSHOFF, CHRISTO: "An Experimental Study of Service Recovery Options," *International Journal of Service Industry Management,* vol. 8, no. 2, 1997, pp. 110–130.

————: "RECOVSAT: An Instrument to Measure Satisfaction with Transaction-Specific Service Recovery," *Journal of Service Research,* vol. 1, no. 3, February 1999, pp. 236–249.

———— and JASON LEONG: "Empowerment, Attribution, and Apologising as Dimensions of Service Recovery: An Experimental Study," *International Journal of Service Industry Management,* vol. 9, no. 1, 1998, pp. 24–47.

BOWEN, DAVID E., and ROBERT JOHNSTON: "Internal Service Recovery: Developing a New Construct," *International Journal of Service Industry Management,* vol. 10, no. 2, 1999, pp. 118–131.

BROWN, STEPHEN W., DEBORAH L. COWLES, and TRACY L. TUTEN: "Service Recovery: Its Value and Limitations as a Retail Strategy," *International Journal of Service Industry Management,* vol. 7, no. 5, 1996, pp. 32–46.

BROWN, T. J., G. A. CHURCHILL, and J. P. PETER: "Improving the Measurement of Service Quality," *Journal of Retailing,* vol. 69, no. 1, Spring 1993, pp. 127–139.

CARR, L. P.: "Applying Cost of Quality to a Service Business," *Sloan Management Review,* Summer 1992, pp. 72–77.

CHASE, R. B., and D. M. STEWART: "Make Your Service Fail-Safe," *Sloan Management Review,* Spring 1994, pp. 35–44.

CRONIN, J. J., and S. A. TAYLOR: "SERVPERF versus SERVQUAL: Reconciling Performance-Based and Perceptions-Minus-Expectations Measurement of Service Quality," *Journal of Marketing,* vol. 58, January 1994, pp. 125–131.

DUBÈ, LAURETTE, MICHAEL D. JOHNSON, and LEO MARK RENAGHAN: "Adapting the QFD Approach to Extended Service Transactions," *Production and Operations Management,* vol. 8, no. 3, Fall 1999, pp. 301–317.

DUFFY, JO ANN: "Service Recovery," in J. A. Fitzsimmons and M. J. Fitzsimmons (eds.), *New Service Development,* Sage Publications, Thousand Oaks, CA, 2000, pp. 277–290.

ESTELAMI, HOOMAN: "Competitive and Procedural Determinates of Delight and Disappointment in Consumer Complaint Outcomes," *Journal of Service Research,* vol. 2, no. 3, February 2000, pp. 285–299.

FRUCHTER, GILA, AND EITAN GERSTNER: "Selling with 'Satisfaction Guaranteed,'" *Journal of Service Research,* vol. 1, no.4, May 1999, pp. 313–323.

HALSTEAD, D.: "Five Common Myths about Customer Satisfaction," *Journal of Services Marketing,* vol. 7, no. 3, 1993, pp. 4–12.

HART, CHRISTOPHER W. L, JAMES L. HESKETT, W. EARL SASSER, JR.: "The Profitable Art of Service Recovery," *Harvard Business Review,* July–August 1990, pp. 148–156.

HARVEY, JEAN: "Service Quality: A Tutorial," *Journal of Operations Management,* vol. 16, no. 1, February 1998, pp. 583–597.

HAYS, JULIE M., and ARTHUR V. HILL: "The Market Share Impact of Service Failures," *Production and Operations Management,* vol. 8, no. 3, Fall 1999, pp. 208–220.

——— , ———, and SUSAN E. GEURS: "The Impact of Service Guarantees on Service Quality at Radisson Hotels Worldwide," in J. A. Fitzsimmons and M. J. Fitzsimmons (eds.), *New Service Development,* Sage Publications, Thousand Oaks, Calif., 2000, pp. 264–276.

HILL, ARTHUR V., JULIE M. HAYS, and EITAN NAVEH: "A Model for Optimal Delivery Time Guarantees," *Journal of Service Research,* vol. 2, no. 3, February 2000, pp. 254–264.

JOHNSON, PERRY L.: *ISO 9000: Meeting the New International Standards,* McGraw-Hill, New York, 1993.

JOHNSTON, ROBERT: "The Zone of Tolerance: Exploring the Relationship between Service Transactions and Satisfaction with the Overall Service," *International Journal of Service Industry Management,* vol. 6, no. 2, 1995, pp. 46–61.

JONES, THOMAS O., and W. EARL SASSER, JR.: "Why Satisfied Customers Defect," *Harvard Business Review,* November–December 1995, pp. 89–99.

MAYERE, ANNE: "Quality and Intellectual Services," *International Journal of Service Industry Management,* vol. 2, no. 1, 1991, pp. 61–75.

MERSHA, TIGINEH, and VEENA ADLAKHA: "Attributes of Service Quality: The Consumers' Perspective," *International Journal of Service Industry Management,* vol. 3, no. 3, 1992, pp. 34–45.

NARAYANDAS, DAS: "Measuring and Managing the Benefits of Customer Retention: An Empirical Investigation," *Journal of Service Research,* vol. 1, no. 2, November 1998, pp. 108–128.

PARASURAMAN, A., V. A. ZEITHAML, and L. L. BERRY: "More on Improving Service Quality Measurement," *Journal of Retailing,* vol. 69, no. 1, Spring 1993, pp. 140–147.

REICHHELD, FREDERICK F.: "Learning from Customer Defections," *Harvard Business Review,* March–April 1996, pp. 57–69.

————, and W. EARL SASSER: "Zero Defections: Quality Comes to Services," *Harvard Business Review,* September–October 1990, pp. 105–111.

REYNOSO, JAVIER, and BRIAN MOORES: "Towards the Measurement of Internal Service Quality," *International Journal of Service Industry Management,* vol. 6, no. 3, 1995, pp. 64–83.

SMITH, AMY K., and RUTH N. BOLTON: "An Experimental Investigation of Customer Reactions to Service Failure and Recovery Encounters: Paradox or Peril?" *Journal of Service Research,* vol. 1, no. 1, August 1998, pp. 65–81.

SOTERIOU, ANDREAS C., and GEORGE C. HADJINICOLA: "Resource Allocation to Improve Service Quality Perceptions in Multistage Service Systems," *Production and Operations Management,* vol. 8, no. 3, Fall 1999, pp. 221–239.

STAUSS, BERND, and CHRISTIAN FRIEGE: "Regaining Service Customers: Costs and Benefits of Regain Management," *Journal of Service Research,* vol. 1, no. 4, May 1999, pp. 347–361.

STEWART, DOUGLAS M., and RICHARD B. CHASE: "The Impact of Human Error on Delivering Service Quality," *Production and Operations Management,* vol. 8, no. 3, Fall 1999, pp. 240–263.

WOOD, MICHAEL: "Statistical Methods for Monitoring Service Processes," *International Journal of Service Industry Management,* vol. 5, no. 4, 1994, pp. 53–68.

YOUNGDAHL, W. E., and D. L. KELLOGG: "The Relationship between Service Customers' Quality Assurance Behaviors, Satisfaction, and Effort: A Cost of Quality Perspective," *Journal of Operations Management,* vol. 15, no. 1, February 1997, pp. 13–32.

ENDNOTES

1. Daniel Pearl, "More Firms Pledge Guaranteed Service," *The Wall Street Journal,* July 17, 1991, p. B1.
2. A. Parasuraman, V. A. Zeithaml, and L. L. Berry, "SERVQUAL: A Multiple-Item Scale for Measuring Consumer Perceptions of Service Quality," *Journal of Retailing,* vol. 64, no. 1, Spring 1988, pp. 12–40.
3. Ibid.
4. Philip B. Crosby, *Quality Is Free: The Art of Making Quality Certain,* McGraw-Hill, New York, 1979.
5. G. Taguchi and D. Clausing, "Robust Quality," *Harvard Business Review,* January–February 1990, pp. 65–75.
6. Shigeo Shingo, *Zero Quality Control: Source Inspection and the Poka-Yoke System,* Productivity Press, Stamford, Conn., 1986.
7. R. B. Chase and D. M. Stewart, "Make Your Service Fail-Safe," *Sloan Management Review,* Spring 1994, 35–44.
8. J. R. Hauser and D. Clausing, "The House of Quality," *Harvard Business Review,* May–June 1988, pp. 63–73.
9. J. M. Juran and F. M. Gryna, Jr., *Quality Planning and Analysis,* McGraw-Hill, New York, 1980.
10. From Christopher W. L. Hart, "The Power of Unconditional Service Guarantees," *Harvard Business Review,* July–August 1988, pp. 54–62.
11. T. C. Johnston and M. A. Hewa, "Fixing Service Failures," *Industrial Marketing Management,* vol. 26, 1997, pp. 467–477.

CHAPTER FOUR

Service Strategy

Learning Objectives

After completing this chapter, you should be able to:

1. Describe how a service has addressed each element in the strategic service concept.
2. Critically discuss the competitive environment of services.
3. Describe, with examples, how a service competes using the generic service strategies of overall cost leadership, differentiation, and focus.
4. Discuss the service purchase decision in the context of qualifiers, service winners, and service losers.
5. Discuss the competitive role of information in services.
6. Explain the concept of the virtual value chain and its role in service innovation.
7. Discuss the limits in the use of information.

As machine technology once changed an agricultural economy into an industrial economy, today's information technology is transforming our industrial economy into a service economy. The availability of computers and global communication technologies has created industries for collecting, processing, and communicating information. Today everyone on the globe can be in instant communication with everyone else, and this revolution is changing world society in many ways. Consider the impact of the emerging private satellite network industry, which provides uplinks and downlinks for personnel training, product introductions, credit checks, billing, financial exchanges, and overall telecommunications.

Kmart was among the first retail giants to establish a private satellite network using the new small-dish antenna VSAT (Very Small Aperture Terminal) placed on store roofs to receive and transmit masses of data. The VSAT at each Kmart is linked to the company's Troy, Michigan, data center via a satellite transponder leased from GTE Spacenet. The communication network has allowed Kmart to coordinate its multisite operations better and to realize substantial benefits, such as improved data transmission about the rate of sales, inventory status, product updates, and, most important, credit authorizations for customers. The instant accessibility of credit histories can significantly lower the risk of nonpayment that credit card companies face, thus lowering the discount rate that reverts back to the retailer. This savings alone eventually will pay for the cost of the satellite network.[1]

CHAPTER PREVIEW

The chapter begins with a discussion of the strategic service concept, which contains all elements in the design of a competitive service. The service concept is divided into four structural elements: delivery system, facility design, location, and capacity planning. It also is divided into four managerial elements: service encounter, quality, managing capacity and demand, and information. These eight elements represent the competitive dimensions of a service firm and each is allocated a separate chapter in the remainder of the book.

Three generic strategies have been found successful in formulating strategies that allow a firm to outperform competitors. The strategies of overall cost leadership, differentiation, and market focus are approaches that both manufacturing and service firms have adopted in various ways to gain competitive advantage. With each of these strategies, however, management must not lose sight of the fact that only a focus on the customers and on satisfying their needs will result in a loyal customer base.

Winning customers in the marketplace means competing on several dimensions. Customers base their purchase decisions on many variables, including price, convenience, reputation, and safety. The importance of a particular variable to a firm's success depends on the competitive marketplace and the preferences of individual customers.

A framework for viewing the contribution of information to the competitive strategy of the service firm also is presented. Using the dimensions of strategic focus, both external and internal, and competitive use of information, both online and offline, four strategic roles of information are identified: creation of barriers to entry, revenue generation, database asset, and productivity enhancement. Industry examples for each role illustrate how firms have used information effectively.

Service product innovation is driven by an appreciation of the virtual value chain based on information gathered from customer transactions. This database can be used to develop new services and create value for the customer.

The chapter concludes with a discussion of the limits in the use of information and with questions of privacy, fairness, reliability, data accuracy, and anticompetitive behavior.

THE STRATEGIC SERVICE CONCEPT

Chapter 2, The Nature of Services, introduced the idea of a *service package,* which contained four elements—supporting facility, facilitating goods, explicit service, and implicit service—as a way to describe an existing service or a vision of a new service. In this chapter, this service vision will be translated into a strategically focused *service concept* or *design* that contains eight dimensions.

Consider a building, which begins in the mind's eye of the architect and is translated onto paper in the form of engineering drawings for all the building's systems: foundation, structural, plumbing, and electrical. An analog to this design process is the strategic service concept with the system elements outlined here. These elements must be engineered to create a consistent service offering that achieves the strategic objectives. The service concept becomes a blueprint that communicates to customers and employees alike what service they should expect to give and to receive. These system elements are:

Structural:

Delivery system. Front and back office, automation, customer participation.

Facility design. Size, aesthetics, layout.

Location. Customer demographics, single or multiple sites, competition, site characteristics.

Capacity planning. Managing queues, number of servers, accommodating average or peak demand.

Managerial:

Service encounter. Service culture, motivation, selection and training, employee empowerment.

Quality. Measurement, monitoring, methods, expectations versus perceptions, service guarantee.

Managing capacity and demand. Strategies for altering demand and controlling supply, queue management.

Information. Competitive resource, data collection.

A successful hospital located in Toronto, Canada, that performs only inguinal hernia operations will be used to illustrate how each element of the service concept contributes to the strategic mission. Shouldice Hospital is privately owned and uses a special operating procedure to correct inguinal hernias that has resulted in an excellent reputation. Its success is measured by the recurrence rate, which is 12 times lower than that of its competitors.[2]

The structural elements of Shouldice's service concept that support its strategy to target customers suffering from inguinal hernias are:

- *Delivery system.* A hallmark of the Shouldice approach is patient participation in all aspects of the process. For example, patients shave themselves before the operation, walk from the operating table to the recovery area, and are encouraged the evening after surgery to discuss the experience with new patients to alleviate their preoperative fears.
- *Facility design.* The facility is intentionally designed to encourage exercise and rapid recovery within four days, providing a return-to-normal-activity time that is approximately one-half the time at traditional hospitals. Hospital rooms are devoid of amenities, such as telephones or TVs, and patients must walk to lounges, showers, and the cafeteria. The extensive hospital grounds are landscaped to encourage strolling, and the interior is carpeted and decorated to avoid any typical hospital "associations."
- *Location.* Being located in a large metropolitan community with excellent air service gives Shouldice access to a worldwide market. The large local population also provides a source of patients who can be scheduled on short notice to fill any canceled bookings.
- *Capacity planning.* Because hernia operations are elective procedures, patients can be scheduled in batches to fill the operating time available; thus, capacity is utilized to its maximum. This ease in scheduling operations allows Shouldice to operate like a fully occupied hotel; thus, the supporting activities, such as housekeeping and food service, also can be fully employed.

The managerial elements of the Shouldice service concept also support the strategy of delivering a quality medical procedure:

- *Service encounter.* All employees are trained to help counsel patients and encourage them to achieve a rapid recovery. A service culture fostering a family-type atmosphere is reinforced by communal dining for both workers and patients.
- *Quality.* The most important quality feature is the adherence of all physicians to the Shouldice method of hernia repair, which results in the low recurrence rate of inguinal hernias among these patients. In addition, patients with difficulties are referred back to the doctor who performed the procedure. Perceived quality is enhanced by the Shouldice experience, which is more like a short holiday than a typical hospital stay.

- *Managing capacity and demand.* Patients are screened by means of a mail-in questionnaire and are admitted by reservation only. Thus, the patient demand in terms of timing and appropriateness can be controlled effectively. As mentioned, walk-in patients or local residents on a waiting list are used to fill vacancies created by canceled reservations; thus, full use of hospital capacity is ensured.
- *Information.* A unique feature of the Shouldice service is the annual alumni reunion, which represents a continuing relationship of the hospital with its patients. Keeping information on patients allows Shouldice to build a loyal customer base, which is an effective word-of-mouth advertising medium. Providing free annual check-ups also allows Shouldice to build a unique database on its procedure.

UNDERSTANDING THE COMPETITIVE ENVIRONMENT OF SERVICES

In general, service firms compete in a difficult economic environment, and there are many reasons for this difficulty:

- *Relatively low overall entry barriers.* Service innovations are not patentable, and in most cases, services are not capital-intensive. Thus, innovations can easily be copied by competitors. However, other types of entry barriers exist, such as locating a resort hotel on the best beach of an island (e.g., the Club Med location on the island of Moorea in French Polynesia).
- *Minimal opportunities for economies of scale.* Recall from Chapter 2 that because of the simultaneous production and consumption of services, the customer must travel to the service facility or the service must travel to the customer. The necessity of physical travel limits the market area and results in small-scale outlets. Franchised firms can realize some economies of scale by sharing purchasing or advertising costs; in other instances, electronic communications can be substituted for physical travel (e.g., ordering from L.L. Bean by telephone).
- *Erratic sales fluctuations.* Service demand varies as a function of the time of day and the day of the week (and sometimes seasonally), with random arrivals. Can you think of some exceptions?
- *No advantage of size in dealing with buyers or suppliers.* The small size of many service firms places them at a disadvantage in bargaining with powerful buyers or suppliers. Many exceptions should come to mind, however, such as McDonald's buying beef and Marriott's buying mattresses.
- *Product substitution.* Product innovations can be a substitute for services (e.g., the home pregnancy test). Thus, service firms must not only watch other service competitors but also anticipate potential product innovations that might make their services obsolete.
- *Customer loyalty.* Established firms using personalized service create a loyal customer base, which becomes a barrier to entry by new services. For example, a hospital supply firm may place its own ordering computer terminals at customers' sites. These terminals then facilitate the placement of new orders to the extent that competitors are effectively excluded.
- *Exit barriers.* Marginal service firms may continue to operate despite low, or even nonexistent, profits. For example, a privately held firm may have employment of family members rather than maximizing profit as its goal. Other service firms, such as antique stores or scuba diving shops, have a hobby or romantic appeal that provides their owners with enough job satisfaction to offset low financial compensation. Thus, profit-motivated competitors would find it difficult to drive these privately held firms from the market.

For any particular service industry, there are firms that have overcome these competitive difficulties and prospered. For example, McDonald's has achieved a dominant position in the fast-food industry by overcoming many of the difficulties listed here. New entrants, however, must develop a service strategy that will address the important competitive features of their respective industries. Three generic strategies have been successful in providing a competitive advantage, and illustrations of how service firms have used these strategies will be our next topic.

COMPETITIVE SERVICE STRATEGIES[3]

Michael Porter has argued persuasively that three generic competitive strategies exist: overall cost leadership, differentiation, and focus.[4] Each strategy will be described in turn, with examples of how service firms use them to outperform their competition.

Overall Cost Leadership

An *overall cost leadership* strategy requires efficient-scale facilities, tight cost and overhead control, and often innovative technology as well. Having a low-cost position provides a defense against competition, because less efficient competitors will suffer first from competitive pressures. Implementing a low-cost strategy usually requires high capital investment in state-of-the-art equipment, aggressive pricing, and start-up losses to build market share. A cost leadership strategy sometimes can revolutionize an industry, as illustrated by the success of McDonald's, Wal-Mart, and Federal Express. Moreover, service firms have been able to achieve low-cost leadership using a variety of approaches.

Seeking Out Low-Cost Customers   Some customers cost less to serve than others, and they can be targeted by the service provider. For example, United Services Automobile Association (USAA) occupies a preeminent position among automobile insurers because it serves only military officers, a group that presents a lower-than-average risk of problems requiring compensation. This group also entails lower cost because its members, who are relatively nomadic, are willing to do business by telephone or mail and are accustomed to doing so. Consequently, USAA is able to conduct all of its business transactions by phone and mail, eliminating any need for the expensive sales force employed by traditional insurers. Another example of this strategy is provided by low-cost retailers such as Sam's Wholesale Club and Price Club, which target customers who are willing to buy in quantity, do without frills, and serve themselves.

Standardizing a Custom Service   Typically, income tax preparation is considered to be a customized service. H & R Block, however, has been successful in serving customers nationwide when only routine tax preparation is required. Also, storefront legal services and family health care centers are attractive means of delivering routine professional services at low cost. The key word here is *routine*.

Reducing the Personal Element in Service Delivery   The potentially high-risk strategy of reducing the personal element in service delivery can be accepted by customers if increased convenience results. For example, convenient access to ATMs has weaned customers from personal interaction with live tellers and, consequently, has reduced transaction costs for banks.

Reducing Network Costs Unusual start-up costs are encountered by service firms that require a network to knit together providers and customers. Electric utilities, which have substantial fixed costs in transmission lines, provide the most obvious example. Federal Express conceived a unique approach to reducing network costs by using a "hub-and-spoke" network. By locating a hub in Memphis with state-of-the-art sorting technology, the overnight air-package carrier was able to serve the United States with no direct routes between the cities that it served. Each time a new city is added to the network, Federal Express only needs to add one more route to and from the hub instead of adding routes between all the cities served. The efficiency of the hub-and-spoke network strategy has not been lost on passenger airline operators, either.

Taking Service Operations Offline Many services, such as haircutting and passenger transportation, are inherently "online," because they can only be performed with the customer present. For services in which the customer need not be present, the service transaction can be "decoupled," with some content performed "offline." For example, a shoe repair service could locate dispersed kiosks for customer drop-off/pick-up, thus consolidating orders for delivery to an off-site repair factory, which could even be located offshore. Performing services offline represents significant cost savings because of economies of scale from consolidation, low-cost facility location (e.g., American Airlines has one of its 800-number reservations centers located in the Caribbean), and absence of the customer in the system. In short, the decoupled service operation is run like a factory.

Differentiation

The essence of the *differentiation* strategy lies in creating a service that is perceived as being unique. Approaches to differentiation can take many forms: brand image (e.g., McDonald's golden arches), technology (e.g., Sprint's fiberoptics network), features (e.g., American Express's complete travel services), customer service (e.g., Nordstrom's reputation among department stores), dealer network (e.g., Century 21's nationwide real estate presence), and other dimensions. A differentiation strategy does not ignore costs, but its primary thrust lies in creating customer loyalty. As illustrated here, differentiation to enhance the service often is achieved at some cost that the targeted customer is willing to pay.

Making the Intangible Tangible By their very nature, services often are intangible and leave the customer with no physical reminder of the purchase. Recognizing the need to remind customers of their stay, many hotels now provide complimentary toiletry items with the hotel name prominently affixed. The Hartford Steam Boiler Inspection and Insurance Company writes insurance on industrial power plants, but this company has enhanced its service to include regular inspections and recommendations to managers for avoiding potential problems.

Customizing the Standard Product Providing a customized touch may endear a firm to its customers at very little cost. A hotel operator who is able to address a guest by name can make an impression that translates into repeat business. Hair salons have added many personalizing features (e.g., personal stylist, juice bar, relaxed surroundings, mood music) to differentiate themselves from barbershops. Burger King's efforts to promote a made-to-order policy is an attempt to differentiate itself from McDonald's classic make-to-stock approach to fast-food service.

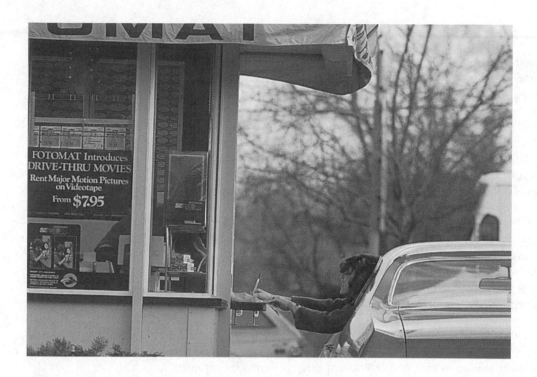

Taking operations offline allows for consolidating orders and performing the service at a low-cost factory-like location. © M. Antman/The Image Works

Reducing Perceived Risk   Lack of information about the purchase of a service creates a sense of risk-taking for many customers. Lacking knowledge or self-confidence about services such as auto repair, customers will seek out providers who take the extra time to explain the work to be done, present a clean and organized facility, and guarantee their work (e.g., Village Volvo). Customers often see the "peace of mind" that is engendered when this trusting relationship develops as being worth the extra expense.

Giving Attention to Personnel Training   Investment in personnel development and training that results in enhanced service quality is a competitive advantage that is difficult to replicate. Firms that lead their industries are known among competitors for the quality of their training programs. In some cases, these firms have established college-like training centers (e.g., Arthur Andersen's facility in St. Charles, Illinois; McDonald's Hamburger University in Oak Brook, Illinois, near Chicago).

Controlling Quality   Delivering a consistent level of service quality at multiple sites with a labor-intensive system is a significant challenge. Firms have approached this problem in a variety of ways, including personnel training, explicit procedures, technology, limits on the scope of the service, direct supervision, and peer pressure, among others. For example, to ensure consistency, the Magic Pan chain of restaurants designed a foolproof machine to produce its famous crêpes. The question of service quality is further complicated by the potential gap between customer expectations and experiences. Influencing customer quality expectations thus becomes an issue, which is explored in Chapter 3, Service Quality.

Focus

The *focus* strategy is built around the idea of serving a particular target market very well by addressing the customers' specific needs. The market segment could be a particular buyer group (e.g., USAA and military officers), service (e.g., Shouldice Hospital and patients with inguinal hernias, Motel 6 and budget travelers, Federal Express and people who need guaranteed overnight package delivery), or geographic region (e.g., Wal-Mart and rural retail buyers, Southwest Airlines and other regional airlines). The focus strategy rests on the premise that the firm can serve its narrow target market more effectively and/or efficiently than other firms trying to serve a broad market. As a result, the firm achieves differentiation in its narrow target market by meeting customer needs better and/or by lowering costs.

Davidow and Uttal argue how important customer selection is to achieving a successful focus strategy.[5] They relate how one bank in Palo Alto, California, targets wealthy individuals and discourages others by policies such as closing an account after two checks have bounced. Davidow and Uttal's three-step approach to focus includes segmenting the market to design core services, classifying customers according to the value they place on service, and setting expectations slightly below perceived performance.

The focus strategy thus is the application of overall cost leadership and/or differentiation to a particular market segment, and the relationship of the three generic strategies to market position is shown in Figure 4.1. We next discuss winning customers in the marketplace.

WINNING CUSTOMERS IN THE MARKETPLACE

Depending on the competition and personal needs, customers select a service provider using criteria listed here. This list is not intended to be complete, because the very addition of a new dimension by a firm represents an attempt to engage in a strategy of differentiation. For example, initiation of the frequent flyer program "AAdvantage" by

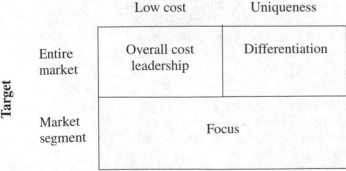

FIGURE 4.1 Market position of generic strategies.
(*Source:* Adapted with the permission of The Free Press, a Division of Simon & Schuster. from *Competitive Strategy: Techniques for Analyzing Industries and Competitors* by Michael E. Porter, Exhibit 2.1, p. 39. Copyright © 1980 by The Free Press.)

American Airlines was an attempt to add the dimension of customer loyalty to competition among airlines.

- *Availability.* How accessible is the service? The use of ATMs by banks has created 24-hour availability of some banking services (i.e., service beyond the traditional "banker's hours"). Use of 800-numbers by many service firms facilitates access after normal working hours.
- *Convenience.* The location of the service defines convenience for customers who must travel to that service. Gasoline stations, fast-food restaurants, and dry cleaners are examples of services that must select locations on busy streets if they are to succeed.
- *Dependability.* How reliable is the service? For example, once the exterminator is gone, how soon do the bugs return? A major complaint regarding automobile repair services is the failure to fix the problem on the first visit. For airlines, on-time performance is a statistic collected by the FAA.
- *Personalization.* Are you treated as an individual? For example, hotels have discovered that repeat customers respond to being greeted by their name. The degree of customization allowed in providing the service, no matter how slight, can be viewed as more personalized service.
- *Price.* Competing on price is not as effective in services as it is with products, because it often is difficult to compare the costs of services objectively. It may be easy to compare costs in the delivery of routine services such as an oil change, but in professional services, competition on price might be considered counterproductive because price often is viewed as being a surrogate for quality.
- *Quality.* Service quality is a function of the relationship between a customer's prior expectations of the service and his or her perception of the service experience both during and after the fact. Unlike product quality, service quality is judged by both the process of service delivery and the outcome of the service.
- *Reputation.* The uncertainty that is associated with the selection of a service provider often is resolved by talking with others about their experiences before a decision is made. Unlike a product, a poor service experience cannot be exchanged or returned for a different model. Positive word-of-mouth is the most effective form of advertising.
- *Safety.* Well-being and security are important considerations because in many services, such as air travel and medicine, the customers are putting their lives in the hands of the service provider.
- *Speed.* How long must I wait for service? For emergency services such as fire and police protection, response time is the major criterion of performance. In other services, waiting sometimes may be considered a trade-off for receiving more personalized services, such as reduced rates.

Writing about manufacturing strategy, Terry Hill used the term *order-winning criteria* to refer to competitive dimensions that sell products.[6] He further suggested that some criteria could be called *qualifiers,* because the presence of these dimensions is necessary for a product to enter the marketplace. Finally, Hill said that some qualifiers could be considered *order-losing sensitive.*

We will use a similar logic and the service criteria listed earlier to describe the service purchase decision. The purchase decision sequence begins with qualifying potential service firms (e.g., must the doctor be on my PPO list?), followed by making a final selection from this subset of service firms using a service winner (e.g., which of the PPO doctors has the best reputation?). After the initial service experience, a return will be based on whether a "service loser" has occurred (e.g., the doctor was cold and impersonal).

Qualifiers

Before a service firm can be taken seriously as a competitor in the market, it must attain a certain level for each service-competitive dimension, as defined by the other market players. For example, in airline service, we would name safety, as defined by the airworthiness of the aircraft and by the rating of the pilots, as an obvious qualifier. In a mature market such as fast foods, established competitors may define a level of quality, such as cleanliness, that new entrants must at least match to be viable contenders. For fast food, a dimension that once was a service winner, such as a drive-in window, over time could become a qualifier because some customers will not stop otherwise.

Service Winners

Service winners are dimensions such as price, convenience, or reputation that are used by a customer to make a choice among competitors. Depending on the needs of the customer at the time of the purchase, the service winner may vary. For example, seeking a restaurant for lunch may be based on convenience, but a dinner date could be influenced by reputation. Note that a service winner can become an industry qualifier (e.g., ATM use by banks).

Service Losers

Failure to deliver at or above the expected level for a competitive dimension can result in a dissatisfied customer who is lost forever. For various reasons, the dimensions of dependability, personalization, and speed are particularly vulnerable to becoming *service losers*. Some examples might be failure of an auto dealer to repair a mechanical problem (i.e., dependability), rude treatment by a doctor (i.e., personalization), or failure of an overnight service to deliver a package on time (i.e., speed).

THE COMPETITIVE ROLE OF INFORMATION IN SERVICES[7]

For service management, information technology is helping to define the competitive strategy of successful firms. Figure 4.2 illustrates the different roles in which information technology can support a service firm's competitive strategy. We shall explore each of these roles in turn with illustrations from successful applications.

Creation of Barriers to Entry

As noted earlier, many services exist in markets that have low entry barriers. James L. Heskett, however, has argued that barriers to entry can be created by using economies of scale, building market share, creating switching costs, investing in communications networks, and using databases and information technologies to strategic advantage.[8] We will discuss three uses of information for creating barriers to entry: reservations systems, frequent flyer or similar programs to gain customer loyalty, and development of customer relationships to increase switching costs.

Reservation Systems　A barrier to entry can be created by investing in online reservations systems that are provided to sales intermediaries such as travel agents. American Airline's SABRE System is an example of the kind of subtle barrier to entry that is created by a comprehensive information system. United and Delta have duplicated this

Competitive use of information

	Online (Real time)	Offline (Analysis)
External (Customer)	*Creation of barriers to entry:* Reservation system Frequent user club Switching costs	*Database asset:* Selling information Development of services Micromarketing
Internal (Operations)	*Revenue generation:* Yield management Point of sales Expert systems	*Productivity enhancement:* Inventory status Data envelopment analysis (DEA)

Strategic focus (vertical label on left)

FIGURE 4.2 Strategic roles of information in services.
(*Source:* Adapted from James A. Fitzsimmons, "Strategic Role of Information in Services," in Rakesh V. Sarin (ed.), *Perspectives in Operations Management: Essays in Honor of Elwood S. Buffa,* Kluwer Academic Publisher, Norwell, Mass., 1993, p. 103.)

reservations system at great cost, but most smaller carriers use these existing systems for a fee. The competitive importance of online reservations systems became evident in late 1982. At this time, the Civil Aeronautics Board (CAB) and the U.S. Department of Justice began a joint investigation of possible antitrust violations by airline reservations systems. In this investigation, Frontier Airlines filed charges accusing United of unfairly restricting competition in the use of its Apollo computerized reservations system.[9]

Frequent User Club It was a small step for American Airlines, given its massive reservations system, to add up passenger accounts to accumulate travel credit for frequent flyer awards. These programs, which award free trips and several ancillary benefits, create strong brand loyalty among travelers, particularly business travelers who are not paying their own way. Thus, the discount fares of a new competitor have no appeal to these travelers, as People Express learned. A travel consultant has been quoted as saying, "It's one of the most anticompetitive programs ever erected."[10]

Alfred Kahn, the father of deregulation, headed the CAB in the late 1970s and did not foresee how airlines would create reservations systems and frequent flyer plans to stifle competition. He is quoted as saying, "Nobody recognized all the ways in which a carrier could insulate itself from competition."[11]

Switching Costs Information technology in the form of online computer terminals has been used in the medical supplies industry to link hospitals directly to the suppliers' distribution networks. Both American Hospital Supply and McKesson, the drug distributor, have installed their online terminals in hospitals so that supplies and drugs can be purchased as the need arises. Significant switching costs are built into this arrangement, because the hospital is able to reduce inventory-carrying costs and has the convenience of online ordering for replenishments. The supplier benefits by a reduction in selling costs because it is difficult for a competitor to entice away a customer who is already co-opted into its system.[12]

Revenue Generation

Real-time information technologies with a focus on internal operations can play a competitive role in increasing revenue opportunities. The concept of *yield management* is best understood as a revenue-maximizing strategy to make full use of service capacity. Advances in microcomputers have created opportunities for innovative point-of-sale devices, and the use of expert systems tied to 800-numbers allows increased customer service.

Yield Management Through the use of its SABRE reservations system, American Airlines was the first to realize the potential of what is now called yield management. By constantly monitoring the status of both its upcoming flights and competitors' flights on the same route, American makes pricing and allocation decisions on unsold seats. Thus, the number of Supersaver fares allocated to a particular flight can be adjusted to ensure that remaining empty seats have a chance of being sold, but not at the expense of a full-fare seat. This real-time pricing strategy maximizes the revenue for each flight by ensuring that no seat goes empty for want of a bargain-seeking passenger while holding some seats in reserve for late arrivals who are willing to pay full fare.[13]

Thus, yield management is the application of information to improve the revenue that is generated by a time-perishable resource (e.g., airline seats, hotel rooms). The success of yield management for American has not gone unnoticed by other service industries; for example, Marriott Hotels has installed a nationwide yield management system to increase occupancy rates. In addition, American Airlines is capitalizing on its innovation by selling the yield management software to noncompetitive industries such as the French national railroad. The topic of yield management is covered in more detail in Chapter 13.

Point of Sale Wal-Mart has discovered a new toy for the discount shopper: the VideOcart. As the shopper pushes the VideOcart through the store, information about the department at hand flashes onto the attached video screen. The cart also helps customers find items in the store by listing hundreds of products by department and then displaying a map of the store. The company supplying the cart claims that it has increased sales by $1 per visit in trials at supermarkets.[14] For another example, consider use of the palm-sized microcomputer transmitter. With this device, a server in a restaurant can transmit an order directly to the kitchen monitor and the bill to the cashier at the same time. This saves unnecessary steps and allows more time for suggestive selling.

Expert Systems Otis Elevator Company puts an *expert system* together with laptop computers in the hands of its maintenance staff to speed repairs in the field. Collecting information on the behavior of its elevators over the years has led to a knowledge base that is incorporated into the expert system. Using a laptop computer, a repair person in the field can call up the system and receive diagnostic help in identifying the source of a problem. As a result, elevators are placed back in service quickly, and fewer repair people are needed. Some of the earlier applications of expert systems have been in the medical field, and, conceivably, these systems could be accessed by physicians for a fee. As another example, an oil exploration expert system was able to identify promising drilling sites for a major oil company.

Database Asset

James L. Heskett observed that the database a service firm possesses can be a hidden asset of strategic importance. The expense of assembling and maintaining a large database is itself a barrier to entry by competitors. More important, however, the database can be mined for profiles of customers' buying habits, and these present opportunities for developing new services.[15]

Selling Information   Dun & Bradstreet created a business by selling access to its database of business credit information. American Home Shield, a provider of service contracts for individual home heating, plumbing, and electrical systems, also discovered that it had a valuable asset in its database, accumulated over many years of repair experience; manufacturers now are invited to access this database to evaluate the performance patterns of their products. American Express has detailed information about the spending habits of its cardholders and now offers breakdowns of customer spending patterns to its retail customers.

Developing Services   Club Med, an all-inclusive resort company with locations worldwide, has evolved to reflect the maturing of its membership. Studying the database of member characteristics, Club Med realized that over time its once swinging singles members have become married with children. In order to continue capturing future vacation visits, Club Med modified some of its locations to accommodate families with young children. Now parents can enjoy the beach and water sports while their children are supervised by Club Med counselors at a children's park nearby. More recently, Club Med has added cruise ships to its vacation possibilities to attract the more senior members who are no longer interested in water sports. As this example illustrates, service firms that capture customer data at the time of the initial purchase have the opportunity to establish a lifetime relationship, with the potential for creating new or modified services for future purchase.

Rental car employees use hand-held computers to speed up the car drop-off process, allowing customers to avoid missing flights.

Micromarketing   Today, we can see a truly focused service strategy that can target customers at the micro level. Bar coding and checkout scanner technology create a wealth of consumer buying information that can be used to target customers with precision. As Table 4.1 shows, analysis of this database allows marketers to pinpoint their advertising and product distribution. To increase sales, Borden Inc. has used such information to select stores in which to feature its premium pasta sauce. Kraft USA saw its sales of cream cheese increase after targeting its flavors to the tastes of a particular store's shoppers.[16] American Express, by analyzing information about its customers and their changing spending patterns in meticulous detail, can even tell when they get married.

TABLE 4.1

EXAMPLE OF MICROMARKETING ANALYSIS

Hitting the Bull's-Eye

Micromarketers can now target a product's best customers and the stores where they're most likely to shop. Here's one company's analysis of three products' best targets in the New York area.

Brand	Heavy user profile	Lifestyle and media profile	Top three stores
Peter Pan peanut butter	Households with kids headed by 18–54-year-olds, in suburban and rural areas	• Heavy video renters • Go to theme parks • Below average TV viewers • Above average radio listeners	**Foodtown Super Market** 3350 Hempstead Turnpike Levittown, NY **Pathmark Supermarket** 3635 Hempstead Turnpike Levittown, NY **King Kullen Market** 598 Stewart Ave. Bethpage, NY
Stouffer's Red Box frozen entrees	Households headed by people 55 and older, and upscale suburban households headed by 35–54-year-olds	• Go to gambling casinos • Give parties • Involved in public activities • Travel frequently • Heavy newspaper readers • Above average TV viewers	**Dan's Supreme Super Market** 69-62 188th St. Flushing, NY **Food Emporium** Madison Ave. & 74th St. New York, NY **Waldbaum Super Market** 196-35 Horace Harding Flushing, NY
Coors light beer	Head of household 21–34 years old, middle to upper income, suburban and urban	• Belong to a health club • Buy rock music • Travel by plane • Give parties, cookouts • Rent videos • Heavy TV sports viewers	**Food Emporium** 1498 York Ave. New York, NY **Food Emporium** First Ave. & 72nd St. New York, NY **Gristede's Supermarket** 350 E. 86th St. New York, NY

Source: Michael J. McCarthy, "Marketers Zero in on Their Customers," *The Wall Street Journal,* March 18, 1991, p. B1. Reprinted with permission of *The Wall Street Journal,* © 1991 Dow Jones & Company, Inc. All Rights Reserved Worldwide.

Productivity Enhancement

New developments in the collection and analysis of information have increased our ability to manage multisite service operations. Through use of notebook computers, retail inventory can be managed on a daily basis to make better use of shelf space by matching displayed products with sales. Information collected on the performance of multisite units can be used to identify the most efficient producers, and productivity is enhanced systemwide when the sources of these successes are shared with other sites. The foundation for a learning organization is then established.

Inventory Status   Using a hand-held computer, Frito-Lay sales representatives have eliminated paper forms. They download the data collected on their routes each day via telephone to the Plano, Texas, headquarters, and the company then uses these data to keep track of inventory levels, pricing, product promotions, and stale or returned merchandise. These daily updates on sales, manufacturing, and distribution keep fresh products moving through the system, matching consumer demands. For a perishable product like potato chips, having the right product at the right place and in the proper amount is critical to Frito-Lay's success. One spokesperson said that the company saved more than $40 million in its first year because of reduced paperwork, reduced losses from stale products, and route consolidation.[17]

Data Envelopment Analysis   *Data envelopment analysis* (DEA) is a linear programming technique developed by A. Charnes, W. W. Cooper, and E. Rhodes to evaluate nonprofit and public sector organizations. Subsequently, it has found applications in for-profit service organizations. DEA compares each service delivery unit with all other service units for a multisite organization, and it computes an efficiency rating that is based on the ratio of resource inputs to outputs. Multiple inputs (e.g., labor-hours, materials) and multiple outputs (e.g., sales, referrals) are possible and desirable in measuring a unit's efficiency. Taking this information, the linear programming model determines the efficiency frontier on the basis of those few units producing at 100 percent efficiency. Areas for improvement can be identified by comparing the operating practices of efficient units with those of less efficient units. Sharing management practices of efficient units with less efficient units provides an opportunity for the latter's improvement and enhancement of total system productivity. Repeated use of DEA can establish a climate of organizational learning that fuels a competitive strategy of cost leadership.

Banker and Morey applied DEA to a 60-unit fast-food restaurant chain and found 33 units to be efficient.[18] In their analysis, three outputs (i.e., food sales for breakfast, lunch, and dinner) and six inputs (i.e., supplies and materials, labor, age of store, advertising expenditures, urban versus rural location, and existence of a drive-in window) were used. It is interesting to note that the inputs included both discretionary and uncontrollable variables (e.g., the demographic variable of urban/rural locations, whether or not the unit had a drive-in window). The topic of data envelopment analysis is covered in more detail as a supplement to Chapter 14.

THE VIRTUAL VALUE CHAIN[19]

Today, businesses compete in two worlds: a physical world of things called a *marketplace* and a virtual world of information called a *marketspace*. For example, when customers buy an answering machine to store phone messages, they are using products that are sold in the physical world. When customers contract with their telephone company for electronic answering services, however, they are purchasing information services in the virtual world.

The process of creating value has long been described as stages linked together to form a *value chain.* The traditional physical value chain, as shown at the top of Figure 4.3, consists of a sequence of stages beginning with inbound logistics (i.e., raw materials) and ending with sales to a customer. The virtual value chain, as shown at the bottom of Figure 4.3, traditionally has been treated as information supporting physical value-adding elements, but not as a source of value itself. For example, managers use information on inventory levels to monitor the process, but they rarely use information itself to create new value for the customer. This is no longer the case for breakthrough service companies. For example, FedEx now exploits its information database by allowing customers to track packages themselves using the company's website on the Internet. Now customers can locate a package in transit by entering the airbill number, and they can even identify the name of the person who signed for it when delivered. Convenient tracking of a package has added value for customers and differentiates FedEx from its competitors.

To create value with information, managers must look to the marketspace. Although the value chain of the marketspace can mirror that of the marketplace, the value-adding process first must gather raw information that is processed and finally distributed. The value-adding steps are virtual in that they are performed through and with information. Creating value in any stage of a virtual value chain involves a sequence of five

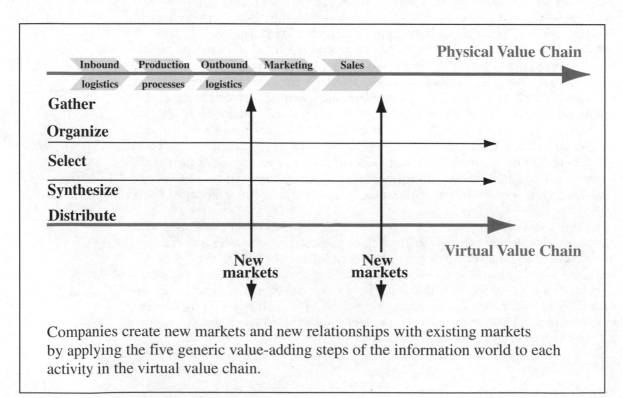

FIGURE 4.3 Exploiting the virtual value chain.
(*Source:* Reprinted from Jeffrey F, Rayport and J. J. Sviokla, "Exploiting the Virtual Value Chain," *Harvard Business Review,* November–December 1995, pp. 78, 82.)

activities: gathering, organizing, selecting, synthesizing, and distributing information. This process is captured in Figure 4.3 for a firm that has some physical product to sell; however, for many services firms, only the virtual value chain would be shown.

The United Services Automobile Association (USAA), which provides financial services to military officers, has become a world-class competitor by exploiting the virtual value chain. As the name suggests, USAA began as an automobile insurance firm. Over time, it has used its information systems—installed to automate its core business of insurance sales and underwriting—to capture significant amounts of information about its customers. Unlike a typical insurance company, USAA had no sales force. All business was conducted by telephone or mail. Consequently, USAA had a ready database and customers who were accustomed to doing business with relatively little human interaction; that is, they were predisposed to using technological innovations. As data accumulated, USAA was able to prepare customer risk profiles and customize policies. Analyzing the flow of information harvested along the virtual value chain, USAA instituted business lines targeted to specific customers' needs, such as home owners insurance and mutual funds, and eventually became a full-fledged financial services firm.

LIMITS IN THE USE OF INFORMATION

So far only the benefits of using information as a competitive strategy have been addressed. Some of these strategies, however, raise questions of fairness, invasion of privacy, and anticompetitiveness. Also, if these strategies were abused, the result could harm consumers.

Anticompetitive

To create entry barriers, the use of reservation systems and frequent user programs has been identified as potentially anticompetitive. For example, how should a frequent flyer's free-trip award be considered, particularly when the passenger has been traveling on business at corporate expense? The IRS is considering taxing the free trip as income in kind, and corporations believe that the free tickets belong to the company. The long-run implication, however, is the removal of price competition in air travel.

Fairness

Perhaps the easiest way to start a riot is asking airline passengers on a flight how much their tickets cost. Under yield management, ticket prices can change every hour; therefore, price is a moving target and the ticketing process a lottery. At the extreme, is yield management fair and equitable to the public, or has every service price always been negotiable? Are customers only now becoming aware of their buying power?

Invasion of Privacy

The concept of micromarketing has the potential to create the most violent backlash from consumers because of the perceived invasion of privacy. When a record of your every purchase at the local supermarket is shared with eager manufacturers, very manipulative sales practices, such as targeting buyers of a competitor's soft drink with enticements to buy an alternative, could result. Lotus Development Corporation felt the sting of consumer displeasure after announcing the availability of its Market-Place household database to anyone with a PC and modem. Lotus received more than 30,000 requests from irate persons wanting to be removed from this database. Lotus subsequently withdrew its offer of general availability, but it still sells access to the database to large corporations.[20]

Data Security

Allowing information to get into hands of others for inappropriate use is a significant problem for government agencies such as the IRS; however, releasing personal medical records to insurance firms or potential employers without the consent of the patient is far more common—and damaging. Some businesses market lists of people who have filed worker compensation claims or medical malpractice suits, and such databases can be used to blackball prospective employees or patients.

Reliability

Are the data accurate? Data kept on individuals can be corrupted and create havoc in people's lives. One U.S. law attempts to ameliorate such dilemmas by requiring credit-report agencies to allow individuals to review their credit records for accuracy.

SUMMARY

We first looked at the strategic service concept as a blueprint for implementing the service. Our discussion then turned to the economic nature of competition in the service sector. The fragmented nature of service industries populated with many small- to medium-sized firms suggests a rich environment for the budding entrepreneur.

The three generic competitive strategies of overall cost leadership, differentiation, and focus were used to outline examples of creative service strategies. Because of the transferability of concepts among service firms, strategies that are successful in one industry may find application in firms seeking a competitive advantage in another service industry.

Next, we looked at several dimensions of service competition and examined the concepts of service winners, qualifiers, and losers as competitive criteria. The application of the service concept to Shouldice Hospital illustrated how all eight elements support the service strategy.

The strategic role of information in service strategies is organized into four categories: creation of barriers to entry, revenue generation, database asset, and productivity enhancement. Information-based competitive strategies were illustrated for each category.

The concept of a virtual value chain provides a view of service innovation that creates value by using information gathered while serving customers. The discussion of the limits in the use of information suggests again that service managers always must be sensitive to the perceptions of their actions by the public they serve.

KEY TERMS AND DEFINITIONS

Data envelopment analysis a linear programming technique that measures the performance of service units to determine an efficiency frontier for internal benchmarking.

Differentiation a competitive strategy that creates a service that is perceived as being unique.

Expert system a computer program that can make inferences using a knowledge base and decision rules.

Focus a competitive strategy built around the concept of serving a particular target market very well by addressing the customers' specific needs.

Marketspace the virtual world of information.

Overall cost leadership a competitive strategy based on efficient operations, cost control, and innovative technology.

Qualifiers criteria used by a customer to create a subset of service firms meeting minimum performance requirements.

Service losers criteria representing failure to deliver a service at or above the expected level, resulting in a dissatisfied customer who is lost forever.

Service winners criteria used by a customer to make the final purchase decision among competitors that have been previously qualified.

Strategic service concept eight elements that define the service to be offered that are in turn grouped into structural and managerial categories.

Value chain the stages and activities, from beginning to end, that are needed to produce a service, each of which has the potential to create value for the customer.

➔ **Yield management** an information system that attempts to maximize revenue for services with time-perishable capacity (e.g., airlines, hotels).

TOPICS FOR DISCUSSION

1. Give examples of service firms that use both the strategy of focus and differentiation and the strategy of focus and overall cost leadership.
2. Apply the strategic service concept to a service of your choice, and illustrate how all eight elements support the service strategy.
3. What ethical issues are associated with micromarketing?
4. Do you agree with the travel consultant's statement about frequent flyer awards that "It's one of the most anticompetitive programs ever erected"?
5. For each of the three generic strategies (i.e., cost leadership, differentiation, and focus), which of the four competitive uses of information is most powerful?

SELECTED BIBLIOGRAPHY

EVANS, PHILIP, and THOMAS WURSTER: "Strategy and the New Economics of Information," *Harvard Business Review,* September–October 1997, pp. 71–82.

HESKETT, JAMES L., W. EARL SASSER, JR., and LEONARD A. SCHLESINGER: *The Service Profit Chain,* Free Press, New York, 1997.

HILL, TERRY: *Manufacturing Strategy,* 3rd ed., Irwin/McGraw-Hill, Burr Ridge, Ill., 2000.

KARMARKAR, U. S., and R. PITBLADDO: "Service Markets and Competition," *Journal of Operations Management,* vol. 12, nos. 3–4, June 1995, pp. 397–412.

LOVELOCK, CHRISTOPHER H.: *Principles of Service Marketing and Management,* Prentice-Hall, Upper Saddle River, N.J., 1999.

MACMILLIAN, IAN C., and RITA GUNTHER NCGRATH: "Discovering New Points of Differentiation," *Harvard Business Review,* July–August 1997, pp. 133–145.

PROKESCH, STEVEN: "Competing on Customer Service," *Harvard Business Review,* November–December 1995, pp. 101–112.

RAYPORT, JEFFREY F., and JOHN J. SVIOKLA: "Exploiting the Virtual Value Chain," *Harvard Business Review,* November–December 1995, pp. 78–85.

ROTH, ALEDA V., and MARJOLIJN VAN DER VELDE: "Operations as Marketing: A Competitive Service Strategy," *Journal of Operations Management,* vol. 10, no. 3, August 1991, pp. 303–328.

SHOSTACK, LYNN G.: "Service Positioning through Structural Change," *Journal of Marketing,* January 1987, pp. 34–43.

ZEITHAML, VALARIE A., A. PARASURAMAN, and L. L. BERRY: "Problems and Strategies in Services Marketing," *Journal of Marketing,* Spring 1985, pp. 33–46.

BOX 4.1

Service Benchmark

CENTRAL MARKET SHUNS CONVENTIONAL WISDOM AND BIG-NAME PRODUCTS

Central Market's opening in January prompted some friendly wagering among food-industry heavyweights who were left out in the cold.

The odds favored Frito-Lay's snacks appearing in the store, a specialty and fresh food supermarket, by the end of the summer. Other wagers bet that Coca-Cola and Budweiser trucks would pull up to the market's loading docks within six months. Now all bets are off.

Shunning big-name product lines is one reason why Central Market has caught the attention of the nation's $279.4 billion supermarket industry. The market—which within a year has become a flagship of the 225 Texas stores owned by parent-company H.E.B. Food Stores—has made it a practice to defy many of the standards that the country's 30,000 supermarkets embrace.

Although most supermarkets subscribe to the notion that customers want one-stop shopping, Central Market has proved that food alone sells well.

At Central Market, which carries virtually nothing except food, the average shopper spends $30 at the checkout counter, said Central Market general manager John Campbell. The national industry average, which also includes spending on general merchandise and health and beauty products, is $18.11, according to the Washington, D.C.–based Food Marketing Institute. The lower industry average results from shoppers who dash in for a few items, such as diapers or mascara, and then check out through the 10-items-or-fewer express lanes, Campbell said. "Here, they do serious shopping," he said.

Central Market also looks different from traditional stores. Its layout forces customers to walk through serpentine sections instead of straight aisles. It also houses a cooking school. There are 250 kinds of mustard, dozens of olive oils, and jams from all over the world on its shelves.

While at least half of the nation's 3.2 million supermarket workers are part-time employees, 90 percent of Central Market's 400 workers are full-time employees who receive health benefits, paid vacation time, tuition reimbursements, and profit-sharing. It's an expensive staffing decision that Campbell says pays off by generating greater enthusiasm and product knowledge among workers, two factors that he says are vital to building customer satisfaction.

At Central Market at least 20 percent of the store's sales come from its roomy produce section, which eats up almost a third of the store's 60,000 square feet of sales space. The section, kept at 65 degrees, stocks on any given day as many as 450 kinds of fruits and vegetables.

Seventy-five feet of refrigerator space display fresh fish, while the 68-foot meat counter sells more than 100 types of meat, game, and poultry. The cheese department offers 600 varieties.

In all, about two-thirds of the store's floor space is stocked with perishables. And each day, a truck from a local food bank comes by to take away the items that have failed Central Market's freshness guidelines.

Although the market risks losing money if too many of its meats and fruits aren't sold quickly, those items have higher profit margins than dry groceries. The margins for perishables are larger because those items are priced higher to make up for losses, refrigeration costs, and the increased labor expenses that result from product displays.

"The more sales you can move to perishable, the better, because the amount you can charge for Coke, Pepsi, or Tide is tight," said Kevin Coupe, executive editor of *Progressive Grocer* trade magazine in Stamford, Conn.

H.E.B. began discussing the Central Market concept in the mid-1980s when its market studies found that customers were increasingly interested in home cooking, nutrition, and better-tasting foods.

"With Central Market, we were trying to get ahead of what we see as a definite trend and one that we feel like will only continue to grow," Ozmun said.

Source: Adapted from Diana Dworin, "Central Market Proves It Can Thrive Even as It Shuns Conventional Wisdom and Big-Name Products," ©*Austin American Statesman,* October 2, 1994, p. H1.

America West Airlines

America West Airlines was established in Phoenix as an employee-owned organization and began by serving 10 cities in the southwestern United States with a fleet of new Boeing 737 aircraft. This neophyte company showed remarkable daring by entering an arena where the majors, American Airlines and Delta Air Lines, already were firmly entrenched and where Southwest Airlines was digging in. Even more daring—some would say foolhardy—was the timing: deregulation was threatening to swallow up small airlines faster than they could refuel their planes.

America West, however, came into the game prepared with a skilled and creative management team, well-trained support personnel, and an effective inside pitch. Obviously, the fledgling company did not have the resources to provide the nationwide, much less the worldwide, coverage that American and Delta provided. Its smaller region, however, allowed it to do something the majors could not: America West established a major hub in Phoenix and offered more flights per day at lower cost between its cities than the two larger competitors could. In many cases, America West offered direct routing and, consequently, relatively short flight times between destinations. "Burdened" with serving everywhere from Tallahassee to Seattle, American and Delta were able to schedule flights between America West destinations, but with longer layovers and at premium prices because they were major carriers. For example, consider travel from Austin, Texas, to Los Angeles. America West has four flights scheduled each day, with each taking approximately 4.5 hours and requiring one layover of 30 minutes in Phoenix, and its least expensive fare is $238. American Airlines offers eight flights each day, with each lasting at least 5 hours, but the traveler has a 60-minute layover in Dallas and spends $298 for American's least expensive flight.

When America West passengers have a layover, it is almost always at the Phoenix hub. (America West has a "sub-hub" in Las Vegas, where layovers usually are overnight, an appeal not lost on many travelers.) Consequently, America West's "accommodations" at the Phoenix airport are as comfortable as one could hope for in a place that hosts such a large number of people each day. The waiting areas are spacious, with banks of well-padded seats placed farther apart than in most airports. Television monitors are mounted in several places throughout the facility, and because the concessions are run by nationally known fast-food franchises, the traveler has ample reason to "feel at home."

Southwest Airlines presented a competitive challenge somewhat different from that of American and Delta. Southwest was serving the same general region as America West and also was offering frequent, low-cost flights with Boeing 737 aircraft. Thus, it would seem that these two airlines were meeting head to head and might be destined to "flight"-to-the-finish of one of them.

Southwest established its hub at Love Field in Dallas, thereby offering its passengers easier access both to and from the city, which is especially attractive to commuters. (Landing at Love Field, does, however, present a problem for those who must make connections in the Dallas–Fort Worth International Terminal.) Southwest began as the "fun airline," the one with attendants in hot pants and snappy commercials on television. Since then it has created a competitive challenge by offering its frequent, low-cost, no-frills service nationwide. It now has four fare rates including an occasional promotional fare, and there is no need to call at 1 AM "to see if fares have changed in the past ten hours." Initially, reservations for flights could be made by phone, but they had to be paid for either through a travel agent or in person at the airport desk. Passengers now have the luxury of purchasing tickets electronically over the Internet or from Southwest's version of ticketing "ATMs" located in many airports. There are no preassigned seats; seating is handled on a first-come, first-served basis according to a numbered boarding pass that is handed to the passenger at check-in time. On-board amenities usually are limited to free soft drinks, juice, and peanuts. Prepackaged cookies and crackers with cheese or peanut butter are available on long flights, and alcoholic beverages are available for a price. Except for short commuter flights, routing might involve several lengthy layovers.

Thus far, America West has managed to meet Southwest's challenge to some extent. Preassigned seating can be done by telephone, and, in contrast to Southwest's ticketing policy, travel agents can ticket passengers using the SABRE reservation system. On-board amenities include complimentary copies of *USA Today* and *The Wall Street Journal,* and, on longer trips, an uncooked snack such as a sandwich, salad, cheese, fruit, and dessert.

As the public air transport industry has matured, however, Southwest has set the "gold standard" for safety, efficiency, and satisfaction in the skies. Where Southwest leads in pricing, on-time arrivals, and "no frills" service, others still follow.

Questions

1. What generic competitive strategy has America West chosen to use in entering the air passenger market? What are the dangers of this strategy?

2. Identify the service winners, qualifiers, and service losers in America West's market.

3. How has America West addressed the eight elements in its strategic service concept?

4. Marketing analysts use market position maps to display visually the customers' perceptions of a firm in relation to its competitors regarding two attributes. Prepare a market position map for America West comparing it with American, Delta, and Southwest using the differentiation attributes of "cabin service" and "preflight service." You will need to define the endpoints on each scale to anchor the relative positioning of the airlines along the attribute (e.g., one extreme for cabin service is no amenities). The actual position is subjective, because no precise measurements are available.

CASE

The Best Little Cookie House Around[21]

A chocolate chip cookie is a pretty straightforward thing—a bit of flour, a bit of sugar, a bit of shortening, a whole lot of chocolate chips, and not much more. Given those humble beginnings, one might not expect the stir created in 1992. We refer, of course, to the national controversy over who bakes the better cookie: Barbara Bush or Hillary Clinton?

Each of those stunning ladies undoubtedly makes superb creations that would grace any schoolkid's lunchbox. But, the truth be told, there has been a major revolution in the chocolate chip cookie industry that overshadows their efforts. This revolution was brought about by a young woman, Debbi Sivyer Fields, whose chocolate chip history goes back to her early years, when she baked just for family and friends.

Mrs. Fields (yes, *that* Mrs. Fields!) opened her first cookie shop in Palo Alto, California, in 1977. By 1980, she had established shops in other cities throughout northern California and Hawaii. During this expansion, she maintained control and personal involvement in all of them, and her success was as much a tribute to the personal relationship she felt with her customers and her natural business savvy as to the quality of her cookies.

As she began her expansion to other parts of the country, however, it became apparent that conventional methods of conducting a far-flung business would not allow her to maintain the personal control and involvement in day-to-day operations that she wanted. At that time, she felt that franchising, for example, would involve transferring a degree of authority to others and a concomitant loss of control over the quality of the cookies and the service, which was unacceptable to Mrs. Fields. So, initially, the challenge became one of cooking up an organizational and operational structure to meet Mrs. Fields's requirements.

Enter Mr. Fields. (Yes, folks, there is a Mr. Fields behind the cookie dough, too.) Randy Fields is an economist, and together, the Fields have developed a business that, according to a company spokesperson, in February 1993 included 348 domestic Mrs. Fields cookie stores, 23 Mrs. Fields bakeries, 94 La Petite Boulangerie bakeries, 36 international cookie stores, and, bowing to the exigencies of the prevailing economic climate, 34 franchise operations.

The Fieldses solved the early problem of retaining direct control over their far-flung enterprises by developing a very flat organizational structure and an effective information system.

ORGANIZATIONAL STRUCTURE

Each outlet has only one administrative person, a store manager. A district store manager (DSM) supervises several store managers and reports to a regional director of operations (RDO). The RDOs report to two directors of operations, who in turn report to Mrs. Fields. The regional and district managers make marketing decisions for the stores, and store controllers at the headquarters in Park City, Utah, manage the financial affairs.

Each day, the store controllers look at the computer reports of sales at each store. They also note the trends and any problems that have occurred during that time. Within 24 hours, the controllers relay their findings to Mrs. Fields via a vice president.

OPERATIONAL SUPPORT

The MIS (Management Information Systems) people at Mrs. Fields implement and support the personal computer arrangement in each store, develop financial software, and manage telecommunications equipment and a voice-mail system. Each day, a single corporate database tracks sales in all outlets and produces reports that allow corporate management personnel to spot and resolve problems quickly.

Before a proposed system is accepted, it is subjected to a cost/benefit analysis and then justified according to one of three criteria: (1) Does it offer an economic advantage? (2) Will it promote new sales? (3) Does it have any strategic importance? Mr. Fields sees information systems as a way for the company to grow without incurring the cost of expanding staff. We also note that the original MIS for Mrs. Fields has evolved into a "spin-off" business in its own right, Fields Software Group, headed by Mr. Fields, which markets its software product ROI (Retail Operations Intelligence) to other multi-unit retail and service organizations.

MIS IN THE TRENCHES

The computer system that is installed in each store has many applications. For example, it is used to monitor the financial records, schedule operations in the store, provide marketing support, make hourly sales projections, record employee work hours, track inventory, interview applicants, and support electronic mail.

At the beginning of each workday, the store manager enters the information for that day, such as day of the week, any special event in the area that might influence sales, and weather conditions, into the computer. The computer program responds with specific questions, then uses a mathematical model to outline the day's schedule. For example, it tells the manager how many sales per hour to expect and how many cookies per hour to bake. Next, the manager enters the types of cookies to be made that day, and the system prescribes the number of batches to mix, when the batches are to be mixed, and when any unused dough must be discarded.

Sales are entered into the computer throughout the day, and the system adjusts its projections and the mixing schedules accordingly. The system also makes suggestions, such as "offer samples" or "increase suggestive selling" when sales lag. Managers, however, are not obligated to follow these suggestions. Inventory also is tracked by the system, which then generates orders for supplies.

Mrs. Fields's information system plays an integral part in the hiring of employees. The information submitted by a job applicant is entered into a program that compares that applicant's qualifications with those of Mrs. Fields's employees. The program looks for a "fit" with the corporate culture, then advises the manager whether to call the applicant back for a follow-up interview, which is conducted interactively with the computer. The program once again recommends whether to hire the applicant, but the manager may appeal the recommendation directly to the personnel department.

In addition to the Day Planner and Interview applications, the capabilities of the information system most frequently used by store managers include Form Mail, a menu-driven application used primarily for messages between the manager and staff; Labor Scheduler, an expert system that schedules the staff; Skills Test, a set of multiple-choice tests for employees being considered for raises and promotions; and Time Clock, a program that enables staff to punch in and out and that also facilitates the payroll process.

Questions

1. In what way has the management information system created a competitive advantage for Mrs. Fields?
2. How might the management information system contribute to a reported 100 percent turnover of store managers?
3. Will the management information system support or inhibit the expansion of Mrs. Fields's outlets? Why?

ENDNOTES

1. From Bernie Ward, "Microspace, Maxiprofits," *Sky,* December 1990, pp. 22–31.
2. Harvard Business School case, Shouldice Hospital Limited, ICCH no. 9-683-068, 1983, p. 3.
3. Adapted from James L. Heskett, "Positioning in Competitive Service Strategies," *Managing in the Service Economy,* Harvard Business School Press, Boston, 1986.
4. Michael E. Porter, "Generic Competitive Strategies," *Competitive Strategy,* Free Press, New York, 1980.
5. W. H. Davidow and B. Uttal, "Service Companies: Focus or Falter," *Harvard Business Review,* July–August 1989, pp. 77–85.
6. Terry Hill, *Manufacturing Strategy,* Irwin, Homewood, Ill., 1989, pp. 36–46.
7. Adapted from James A. Fitzsimmons, "Strategic Role of Information in Services," in Rakesh V. Sarin (ed.), *Perspectives in Operations Management: Essays in Honor of Elwood S. Buffa,* Kluwer Academic Publisher, Norwell, Mass., 1993.
8. James L. Heskett, "Operating Strategy Barriers to Entry," *Managing in the Service Economy,* Harvard Business School Press, Boston, 1986.
9. For specific allegations, see "Frontier Airlines, Inc. (A)," Harvard Business School Case no. 9-184-041, HBS Case Services, 1983.
10. R. L. Rose and J. Dahl, "Skies Are Deregulated, but Just Try Starting a Sizable New Airline," *The Wall Street Journal,* July 19, 1989, p. A1.
11. Ibid., p. A8.
12. From Harold S. Bott, "Information for Competitive Advantage," *Operations Management Review,* Fall 1985, p. 35.
13. Barry C. Smith, J. F. Leimkuhler, and R. M. Darrow, "Yield Management at American Airlines," *Interfaces,* vol. 22, no. 1, January–February 1992, pp. 8–31.
14. From Kevin Helliker, "Wal-Mart's Store of the Future Blends Discount Prices, Department-Store Feel," *The Wall Street Journal,* May 17, 1991, p. B1.
15. Heskett, op. cit., p. 44.
16. Michael J. McCarthy, "Marketers Zero in on Their Customers," *The Wall Street Journal,* March 18, 1991, p. B1.
17. Peter H. Lewis, "Looking beyond Innovation, an Award for Results," *New York Times,* June 23, 1991, p. 8.
18. R. D. Banker and R. C. Morey, "Efficiency Analysis for Exogenously Fixed Inputs and Outputs," *Operations Research,* vol. 34, no. 4, July–August 1986, pp. 518–519.
19. Adapted from Jeffrey F. Rayport and John J. Sviokla, "Exploiting the Virtual Value Chain," *Harvard Business Review,* November–December 1995, pp. 75–85.
20. "How Did They Get My Name?" *Newsweek,* June 3, 1991, p. 41.
21. Information for this case was gathered from several sources, including Keri Ostrofsky, "Mrs. Fields Cookies," Harvard Business School Case No. 9-189-056, 1989; Tom Richman, "Mrs. Fields' Secret Ingredient," *Inc.,* October 1987, pp. 65–69; Jack Schember, "Mrs. Fields' Secret Weapon," *Personnel Journal,* September 1991, vol. 70, no. 9, pp. 56–58; and personal communication from Nina Macheel of Fields Software Group, Inc.

PART TWO

DESIGNING THE SERVICE ENTERPRISE

Now that the service concept and competitive strategy have been articulated, our attention is directed to issues of service design. We begin with a discussion of the new service development process. A method of service process diagramming called *blueprinting* can be used to evaluate existing or proposed service delivery designs much as an engineer uses drawings of a product to showcase a design. Service design is not complete until procedures for avoiding errors are implemented, a process called *failsafing*. We explore generic approaches to service design and automation of services.

Questions of facility design, such as aesthetics, are important elements for creating the appropriate environment to support the service concept. Consideration is also given to the psychological need to avoid customer disorientation in an unfamiliar setting. The concepts of product layout and process layout used in manufacturing are adapted for service layout applications. The issue of facility location is addressed, beginning with an estimation of spatial demand, the use of appropriate location models, and final site selection considerations. The face-to-face encounter between customer and service provider is discussed in the context of the service profit chain. A chapter on delivery of services via the Internet concludes this section.

CHAPTER FIVE

New Service Development and Process Design

Learning Objectives

After completing this chapter, you should be able to:

1. Discuss the new service development process.
2. Prepare a blueprint for a service operation.
3. Describe a service process structure using the dimensions of divergence and complexity.
4. Use the taxonomy of service processes to classify a service operation.
5. Compare and contrast the generic approaches to service system design.
6. Place an example of service automation in its proper category.
7. Discuss the managerial issues associated with the adoption of new technology.

Designing a service delivery system is a creative process. It begins with a service concept and strategy to provide a service with features that differentiate it from the competition. The various alternatives for achieving these objectives must be identified and analyzed before any decisions can be made. Designing a service system involves issues such as location, facility design and layout for effective customer and work flow, procedures and job definitions for service providers, measures to ensure quality, extent of customer involvement, equipment selection, and adequate service capacity. The design process is never finished; once the service becomes operational, modifications in the delivery system are introduced as conditions warrant.

For an example of innovative service system design, consider Federal Express. The concept of guaranteed overnight air-freight delivery of packages and letters was the subject of a college term paper by the company's founder, Frederick W. Smith. As the story is told, the term paper received a C because the idea was so preposterous, but the business now is a model for the industry.

Traditionally, air freight has been slow and unreliable, an ancillary service provided by airlines that primarily are interested in passenger service. The genius of Smith, an electrical engineer, was in recognizing the analogy between freight transport and an electrical network connecting many outlets through a junction box. From this insight was born the "hub-and-spoke" network of Federal Express, with Memphis serving as the hub and sorting center for all packages. Arriving at night from cities throughout the United States, planes would unload their packages and wait approximately two hours before returning to their home cities with packages ready for delivery the next morning. Thus, a package from Los Angeles destined for San Diego would travel from Los Angeles to Memphis on one plane, then from Memphis to San Diego on another. With the exception of severe weather grounding an aircraft or a sorting error, the network design guaranteed that a package would reach its destination overnight. Thus, the design of the service delivery system itself contained the strategic advantage that differentiated Federal Express from the existing air-freight competitors. Today, Federal Express has expanded to several hubs (e.g., Newark and Los Angeles) and uses trucks to transport packages between nearby large urban centers (e.g., Boston and New York).

CHAPTER PREVIEW

The topic of new service development begins with a topology of new services. We look at a model of the new service development process that includes the elements of technology, people, and systems. We also explore the challenges of adopting new technology in services and discuss service automation. The service blueprint is an effective technique to describe the service delivery process in visual form. Using a line of visibility, we will differentiate between the front-office and back-office portions of the service delivery system. The front-office portion of the system is where customer contact occurs and is concerned with ambiance and effectiveness (e.g., a bank lobby). The back-office portion of the system is hidden from the customer and often is operated as a factory for efficiency (e.g., the check-sorting operations of a bank). The blueprint identifies fail points that are candidates for developing failsafe procedures to avoid errors during service delivery.

The analysis of structural alternatives in the system design will be considered in the context of the strategic objectives. Linking the concepts of production efficiency and sales opportunity illustrates the necessity of integrating marketing and operations in service management.

Following a taxonomy for service process design, four generic approaches for viewing service system design—the production-line approach, customer as coproducer, customer contact, and information empowerment—are presented. Each approach advocates a particular philosophy, and the features of these approaches will be examined.

NEW SERVICE DEVELOPMENT

Innovation is viewed both as the process of creating something new and also as the actual product or outcome. New service development (NSD) is analogous to research and development (R&D) found in product firms but with a "service package" description of the service as the deliverable. Service design follows the innovation process with specifications for the delivery system. Service design is analogous to engineering the product, which is the delivery system for services, because for services the product is the process. Figure 5.1 shows the NSD process cycle moving from development to analysis to design and finally to launch of the new service product.

Table 5.1 presents a classification of service innovations with two major distinctions. Radical innovations are offerings not previously available to customers or new delivery systems for existing services (e.g., the Barnes & Noble website). Incremental innovations are changes to existing services that are valued as improvements (e.g., the addition of playscapes at fast-food restaurants).

Ideas for new service innovations can originate from many sources. Customers can offer suggestions (e.g., menu additions at a restaurant). Front-line employees can be trained to listen to customers' concerns (i.e., listening posts). Customer databases can be mined for possible service extensions (e.g., additional financial services). Trends in customer demographics can suggest new services (e.g., long-term health care) and new advances in technology.

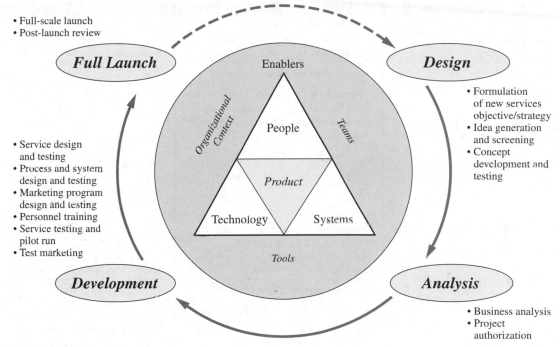

FIGURE 5.1 The NSD process cycle.
(*Source:* Reprinted with permission from S. P. Johnson, L. J. Menor, A. V. Roth, and R. B. Chase, "A Critical Evaluation of the New Service Development Process," in J. A. Fitzsimmons and M. J. Fitzsimmons (eds.) *New Service Development,* Sage Publications, Thousand Oaks, Calif., 2000, p. 18.)

Technological advances are often the basis for radical service innovation. Table 5.2 presents different technological advances that are the sources of service innovation. Thus, a service firm must include technology monitoring as an activity to protect its competitive position. As Amazon.com has illustrated, a technology first mover can build a loyal customer base and significant competitive advantage.

Figure 5.2 on page 114 presents the trajectory of new service development on a graph with dimensions of standardization and industrialization. Starting with a "face-to-face" delivery represented by low industrialization (i.e., low technology) and low standardization (i.e., customization is possible), we find three vectors. Incremental service innovation with its associated service extensions moves the service package across into a higher level of standardization owing to market segmentation. Technology-driven service innovation moves the service package down into a technology-enabled "self-service" category. Note the enlarged "technology" portion of the service package (i.e., people, systems, technology, and product). Radical service innovation is a diagonal move resulting in technology-enabled self-service with limited offerings.

TECHNOLOGICAL INNOVATION IN SERVICES

The great gains in agricultural and manufacturing productivity came from the substitution of technology for human effort. Technology need not be confined to hardware and machines, however. It also includes innovative systems, such as electronic funds transfer or automated multiphasic health testing. In manufacturing, the introduction of technological innovations goes unnoticed by consumers, but such innovations become

TABLE 5.1

LEVELS OF SERVICE INNOVATION

New service category	Descriptions	Examples
Radical innovations		
Major innovation	New services for markets as yet undefined. These innovations are usually driven by information- and computer-based technologies.	Wells Fargo® Internet banking launched in May 1995.
Start-up business	New services in a market that is already served by existing services.	Mondex USA®, a subsidiary of MasterCard International®, that designs and distributes smart cards for retail transactions.
New services for the market presently served	New service offerings to existing customers of an organization (although the services may be available from other companies).	Freestanding bank branches or kiosks in supermarkets or other retail establishments (e.g., *Wells Fargo*® kiosks in Starbuck's® coffee shops).
Incremental Innovations		
Service line extensions	Augmentations of the existing service line such as adding new menu items, new routes, and new courses.	Singapore Airlines'® first-class airport check-in in a special, exclusive lounge.
Service improvements	Changes in features of services that are currently being offered.	Delta Airlines'® use of ATM-like kiosks to distribute boarding passes to passengers.
Style changes	The most common of all "new services," these are modest forms of visible changes that have an impact on customer perceptions, emotions, and attitudes. Style changes do not change the service fundamentally, only its appearances.	Funeral homes, such as Calvary Mortuary in Los Angeles, now offer abbreviated ceremonies that celebrate life instead of mourn death, full-service flower shops, and facilities with more pastels, brighter walls, and more windows and lights.

Source: Reprinted with permission from S. P. Johnson, L. J. Menor, A. V. Roth, and R. B. Chase, "A Critical Evaluation of the New Service Development Process," in J. A. Fitzsimmons and M. J. Fitzsimmons (eds.), *New Service Development,* Sage Publications, Thousand Oaks, Calif., 2000, p. 4.

an integral part of the service that is provided. For example, many airlines have introduced automatic ticketing machines that accept credit cards and issue tickets according to a request entered by the passenger, who pushes the appropriate buttons. At many filling stations, a credit card reader located on the pump facilitates the purchase of gasoline.

Challenges of Adopting New Technology in Services

For services, "the process is the product" because customers participate directly in the service delivery. Therefore, the success of technological innovations, particularly for the front office, depends on customer acceptance. The impact on customers is not always limited to a loss of personal attention. Customers also may need to learn new skills (e.g., how to operate an automatic teller machine or pump gasoline), or they may have to forgo some benefit (e.g., loss of float through the use of electronic funds transfer). The

TABLE 5.2

TECHNOLOGY-DRIVEN SERVICE INNOVATION

Source of technology	Service example
Power/energy	Jet aircraft permitting international flights Nuclear reactors for electric generation
Physical design	Hotel atrium Enclosed sports stadiums
Materials	Environmentally friendly dry cleaning fluids Astroturf for enclosed sports stadiums
Methods	Just-in-time (JIT) Total quality management (TQM)
Information	E-commerce based on the Internet Multiple channels with cable TV

contribution of customers as active participants or coproducers in the service process must be considered when making changes in the service delivery system.

As internal customers, employees also are affected by new technology and often need retraining. The example of scanning in retail stores was minor compared with the adoption of word processing by secretaries, who were used to typewriters.

Back-office innovation that does not directly affect the customer may raise complications of a different sort. For example, consider the use of magnetic-ink-character recognition equipment in banking. This technological innovation did not affect the customer at all; instead, it made the "hidden" check-clearing process more productive. The full benefits, however, could not be realized until all banks agreed to imprint their checks using a universal character code. Without such an agreement, the checks of un-cooperative banks would need to be sorted by hand, which would limit severely the effectiveness of this technology. When all banks in the United States finally agreed on the use of the same magnetic-ink-character imprints on checks, the check-clearing process became much more efficient. The Bank of America took a leadership role in gaining acceptance for the concept, but the self-interest of banks was a principal motivation. The volume of check processing had exceeded their manual sorting capacity.

Other examples of this need to standardize occurred in retailing with the acceptance of the Universal Product Code (UPC) by manufacturers. Retailers who have adopted the UPC can use laser scanners to read a bar code (i.e., a series of vertical stripes of different widths) on products. Consequently, they can use a computer to register sales and update inventory levels simultaneously.

The incentive to innovate in services is hampered, however, because many ideas cannot be patented. One example is the idea of self-serve retailing. Much of the potential for technological and organizational progress is in this area. The prospective rewards for innovations are diminished, however, because the innovations may be freely imitated and quickly implemented by the competition.

Automation in Services

The back office has been the most logical place to introduce automation in services, because these operations often are repetitive and routine and thus amenable to labor-saving devices. Many applications have been in the hard automation category, such as

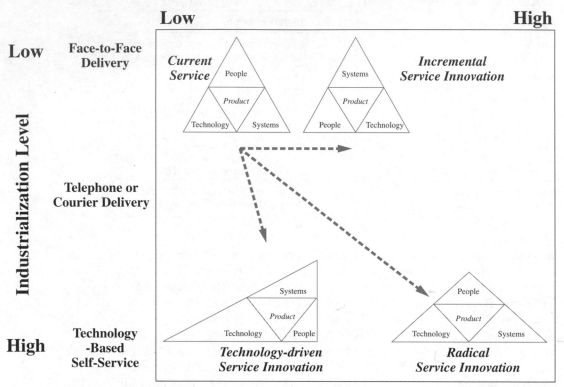

FIGURE 5.2 **The dynamics of NSD.**
(*Source:* Reprinted with permission from S. P. Johnson, L. J. Menor, A. V. Roth, and R. B. Chase, "A Critical Evaluation of the New Service Development Process," in J. A. Fitzsimmons and M. J. Fitzsimmons (eds.) *New Service Development,* Sage Publications, Thousand Oaks, Calif., 2000, p. 22.)

replacing human manual activity with a machine (e.g., an automatic lawn sprinkler system at a hotel). More advanced programmable devices also have found application in services, sometimes interacting with the customer (e.g., automated answering systems that route callers by means of Touch-Tone phones).

Thus, a classification of automation applications in services must go beyond the traditional categories that are used in manufacturing because of the opportunities for interaction with the customer. In the following automation categories, first suggested by David Collier, we include the *expert system,* which is a form of mental automation (e.g., using a computer for reasoning and problem solving):[1]

Fixed sequence (F). A machine that repetitively performs successive steps in a given operation according to a predetermined sequence, condition, and position, and whose set information cannot be changed easily. Service example: automatic parking lot gate.

Variable sequence (V). A machine that is the same as a fixed-sequence robot but whose set information can be changed easily. Service example: automated teller machine.

Playback (P). A machine that can produce operations from memory that were originally executed under human control. Service example: telephone answering machine.

Numerical controlled (N). A machine that can perform a given task according to a sequence, conditions, and a position as commanded by stored instructions that can be reprogrammed easily. Service example: animated characters at an amusement park.

Intelligent (I). A machine with sensory perception devices, such as visual or tactile receptors, that can detect changes in the work environment or task by itself and has its own decision-making abilities. Service example: autopilot for a commercial airplane.

Expert system (E). A computer program that uses an inference engine (i.e., decision rules) and a knowledge base (i.e., information on a particular subject) to diagnose problems. Service example: maintenance trouble-shooting for elevator repair.

Totally automated system (T). A system of machines and computers that performs all the physical and intellectual tasks that are required to produce a product or deliver a service. Service example: electronic funds transfer.

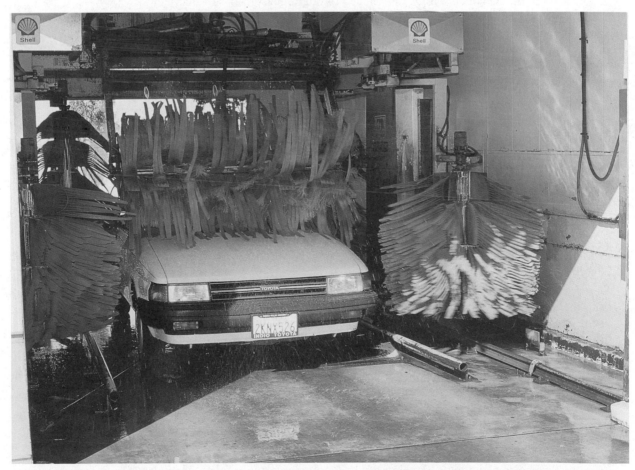

Operation of the car-washing equipment is so inexpensive that a car wash is free with a fill-up. © Tony Freeman/PhotoEdit

To illustrate the extent of automation in services, Table 5.3 provides examples of automation by service industry, with each example classified according to the preceding categories. The automation examples suggest that services are becoming more capital-intensive, and that the old notion of the service sector as being a low-skilled, labor-intensive operation must be reconsidered. Service workers will need more sophisticated skills to program, operate, and maintain the automated systems. More important, employee flexibility will be a valued attribute because the nature of work is changed by new technology. For example, consider the many changes in the office that have occurred with the introduction of personal computers and word-processing capabilities.

Managing the New Technology Adoption Process

Innovation is a destroyer of tradition; thus, it requires careful planning to ensure success. By necessity, the productivity benefits of new technology will change the nature of work. Any introduction of new technology should include employee familiarization to prepare workers for new tasks and to provide input into the technology interface design (e.g., will typing skill be required, or will employees just point and click?). For services, the impact of new technology may not be limited to the back office. It could require a change in the role that customers play in the service delivery process. Customer reaction to the new technology, determined through focus groups or interviews, also could provide input into the design to avoid future problems of acceptance (e.g., consider the need for surveillance cameras at automated teller machines).

In writing about his experiences installing computer systems, Robert Radchuk has developed a 10-step planning guide to manage the implementation process. The following modified version of these steps includes the concerns for employees and customers:[2]

Step 1: Orientation and education. Become knowledgeable about the new technology and where it is headed. Visit trade shows and other users to gain hands-on familiarity. Secure the active involvement of a senior manager to champion the technology.

Step 2: Technology opportunity analysis. Undertake a feasibility study to define opportunities, estimate costs, and identify benefits. Benchmark the use of the technology in other industries.

Step 3: Application requirements analysis. Define the requirements for the new technology, and identify the hardware and software to be purchased. Refine cost and benefit estimates.

Step 4: Functional specification. Define the operating characteristics of the application, including the inputs, outputs, operator interface, and type of equipment to be used. This working document will be used in interactions with users of the system; thus, it should be an explicit definition in nontechnical terms of how the system will work.

Step 5: Design specification. Produce a specific engineering design with inputs from users, both employees and customers, to evaluate the effectiveness of the system interfaces. For example, as noted in Chapter 1, Burger King has a mock-up of a typical store in a Miami warehouse where new technology ideas are tested in a simulated environment before their introduction into the marketplace.

Step 6: Implementation planning. Using project planning techniques, such as Microsoft® Project for Windows, develop a detailed implementation plan. This plan should account for all activities, such as personnel familiarization and training,

TABLE 5.3

CATEGORIES AND EXAMPLES OF AUTOMATION IN SERVICE INDUSTRIES

Wholesale and retail trade, 23.1%*

F	Dry cleaner's conveyor	V	Point-of-sale electronic terminal
F	Newspaper dispenser	I	Self-serve grocery checkout
V	Automatic car wash	T	Automated distribution warehouse
V	Automatic window washers	T	Automated security systems
V	Optical supermarket	T	Telemarketing

Utilities and government services, 17.9%*

F	Automated one-person garbage trucks	I	Airborne warning and control systems
V	Mail-sorting machine	I	Doppler radar
V	Optical mail scanner	T	Electric power-generating plants
N	IRS Form 1040EZ reader	T	Electronic computer-originated mail

Health care services, 7.6%*

F	Electronic beepers	I	Automated medication-delivery systems
F	Pacemakers	I	Electronic ambulance-dispatching systems
V	CAT and MRI scanners	I	Medical information systems
V	Dental chair system	E	Diagnostic expert systems
V	Fetal monitors		

Restaurants and food services, 6.0%*

F	Assembly-line and rotating-service cafeterias	F	Vending machines
		V	Automatic french fryer

Financial services, 4.9%*

F	Pneumatic delivery systems	V	MasterCard II—the electronic checkbook
V	Automated trust portfolio analysis	E	Stock trading
V	Automated teller machines	T	Electronic funds transfer systems
V	IBM 3890 encoded-check processor machine		

Transportation services, 4.9%*

F	Automatic tollbooth	I	France's TGV trains
I	Air traffic control systems	I	Ship navigation systems
I	Autopilots	T	Space shuttle
I	Bay Area Rapid Transportation system		

Communication and electronic services, 2.2%*

V	Collating copying machines	T	Teleconference phone and Picturephone
V	Two-way cable television	T	Telephone switching systems
P	Telephone answering machines		

Education services, 1.6%*

F	Audiovisual machine	P	Language translation computers
V	Electronic calculators	P	Personal and home computers
V	Speak-and-Spell, Speak-and-Read	T	Library cataloging systems

Hotel and motel services, 1.5%*

F	Automatic sprinkler systems	V	Electronic key and lock systems
F	Elevator, escalator, and conveyor	T	Electronic reservation systems

Leisure services, 1.4%*

F	Movie projectors	I	Arcade and computer games
F	Wave machines	T	Disney World (e.g., Hall of Presidents)
P	Videodisk machines		

* Percentage of total workforce as reported in *Employment and Earnings,* U.S. Department of Labor, Bureau of Labor Statistics, December 1991, Table B-2, pp. 52–62.
Source: Adapted with permission from David A. Collier, "The Service Sector Revolution: The Automation of Services," *Long Range Planning,* vol. 16, no. 6, December 1983, pp. 12–13. Copyright © Pergamon Press Ltd.

facilities planning, prototype testing, and an initial operation in parallel with the current system until the new technology is debugged.

Step 7: Equipment selection and contract commitments. Contract for equipment purchases, and schedule the equipment for delivery as per the implementation plan.

Step 8: Implementation. Execute the implementation plan, and prepare progress reports for senior management.

Step 9: Testing of technology. Before committing to full-blown operations, test the technology. If a simulation is not possible, the new technology could be introduced at one or more trial sites before the entire service network is committed. Specific tests must be defined in advance to evaluate the system's response to anticipated demands.

Step 10: Review of results. Document information that has been learned from the implementation experience by comparing original expectations with actual results. This final step may be the most important because expertise in managing the implementation of new technology can be a competitive advantage.

In the next section, we begin our discussion of service design with the topic of service blueprinting. The service blueprint captures the essence of the new service process in a flowchart format that can be used for testing the concept feasibility and documenting the service delivery system design.

SERVICE BLUEPRINTING[3]

Developing a new service based on the subjective ideas contained in the service concept can lead to costly trial-and-error efforts to translate the concept into reality. When a building is developed, the design is captured on architectural drawings called *blueprints,* because the reproduction is printed on special paper, creating blue lines. These blueprints show what the product should look like and all the specifications needed for its manufacture. G. Lynn Shostack has proposed that a service delivery system also can be captured in a visual diagram (i.e., a *service blueprint*) and used in a similar manner for the design of services.

As we explore the blueprint for a bank installment lending operation shown in Figure 5.3, many uses for this diagram will become apparent. First, the blueprint is a map or flowchart (called a *process chart* in manufacturing) of all transactions constituting the service delivery process. Some activities are processing information, others are interactions with customers, and still others are decision points. The decision points are shown as diamonds to highlight these important steps, such as providing protocols to avoid mistakes, for special consideration. Studying the blueprint could suggest opportunities for improvement and also the need for further definition of certain processes (e.g., the step "Print payment book" contains many activities, such as printing booklet, preparing check, and addressing and mailing envelope).

The *line of visibility* separates activities of the front office, where customers obtain tangible evidence of the service, from those of the back office, which is out of the customers' view. The high- and low-contact parts of the service delivery process are kept physically separate, but they remain linked by communications. This separation highlights the need to give special attention to operations above the line of visibility, where customer perceptions of the service's effectiveness are formed. A full treatment of this service encounter is the subject of Chapter 8. The physical setting, decor, employees' interpersonal skills, and even printed material all make a statement about the service,

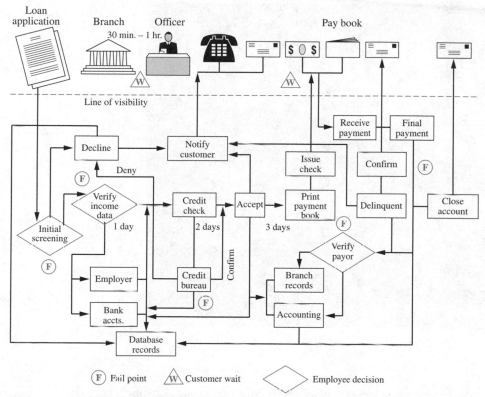

FIGURE 5.3 Blueprint for bank installment lending operation.
(*Source:* Reprinted with permission of the American Marketing Association: G. Lynn Shostack, "Service Positioning through Structural Change," *Journal of Marketing,* vol. 51, January 1987, p. 36.)

and the subject of facility design and layout is discussed in Chapter 6. Designing an efficient process is the goal of the back office, but the back-office operations have an indirect effect on the customer because of delays and errors.

The blueprinting exercise also gives managers the opportunity to identify potential *fail points* (F) and to design "foolproof" (*poka-yoke,* or failsafing, is discussed in Chapter 3) procedures to avoid their occurrence, thus ensuring the delivery of high-quality service. In the installment lending example, several verification points are included in the back-office activities. At these locations, poka-yoke devices such as checklists could be used to avoid errors. An automatic poka-yoke system could verify the mailing address by checking the compatibility of the city, state, and zip code as given by the customer with the U.S. Zip Code Registry.

For critical operations that are performance determinants of the service, we find that *standard execution times* are displayed. Some execution times will be represented as a range to account for the discretion necessary in some transactions (e.g., 30 minutes to 1 hour to apply for a loan). These standard times also will be useful in making capacity decisions and in setting expectations (e.g., loan check received six days after the application is approved).

Triangles are used to identify places in the process where customer waiting can be anticipated. Thus, customers who are waiting to see a loan officer will need a pleasant

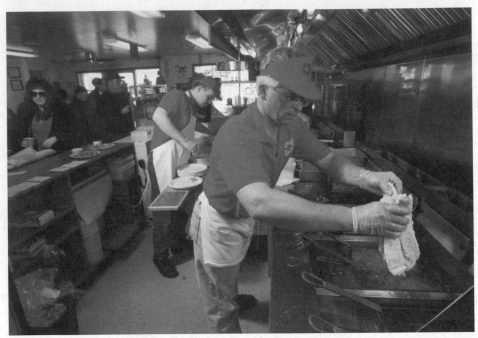

Fast-food restaurants want customers to see the cleanliness of the kitchen. © Dick Blume/The Image Works

and adequate seating area with amenities such as coffee and reading material. The subject of managing queues is discussed in Chapter 11, Managing Waiting Lines. Separating the activity of preparing the payment book from issuing the loan check could significantly reduce the time a customer must wait for that check.

In summary, a blueprint is a precise definition of the service delivery system that allows management to test the service concept on paper before any final commitments are made. The blueprint also facilitates problem solving and creative thinking by identifying potential points of failure and highlighting opportunities to enhance customers' perceptions of the service.

STRATEGIC POSITIONING THROUGH PROCESS STRUCTURE

Preparing the service blueprint is the first step in developing a service process structure that will position a firm in the competitive market. Decisions still remain on the degree of complexity and divergence desired in the service. G. Lynn Shostack defined these concepts and used them to show how a service firm can position itself on the basis of process structure.[4]

The steps and sequences in the process captured by the service blueprint and measured by the number and intricacy of the steps represent the *degree of complexity* of the service delivery structure. For example, preparation of a take-out order at a fast-food restaurant is less complex than preparation of a gourmet dinner at a fine French restaurant. The amount of discretion or freedom that the server has to customize the service is the *degree of divergence* that is allowed at each service process step. For example, the activities of an attorney, as contrasted with those of a paralegal, are highly divergent, because interaction with the client requires judgment, discretion, and situational adaptation.

The two dimensions of complexity and divergence, for example, allow us to create a market-positioning chart for the financial services industry, as shown in Figure 5.4. In all service industries, we can see movement in every direction of the process structure chart as firms position themselves in relation to their competitors.

Firms like H & R Block have sought high-volume, middle-class taxpayers by creating a *low-divergence* tax service for those seeking help in preparing standard tax returns. With low divergence, the service can be provided with narrowly skilled employees performing routine tasks, and the result is consistent quality at reduced cost.

A hair-styling salon for men represents a *high-divergence* strategy reshaping the traditional barbering industry. High divergence is characterized as a niche strategy that seeks out customers who are willing to pay extra for the personalization.

Narrowing the scope of a service by specializing is a focused strategy that results in *low complexity.* Retailing recently has seen an explosion of specialty shops selling only one product, such as ice cream, cookies, or coffee. For such a strategy to succeed, the service or product must be perceived as being unique or of very high quality.

To gain greater market penetration or maximize the revenue from each customer, a strategy of adding more services can be initiated, thereby creating a structure with *high complexity.* For example, supermarkets have evolved into superstores through the addition of banking services, pharmacies, flower shops, books, video rentals, and food preparation.

Repositioning need not be limited to changes in only one dimension of the process structure (i.e., level of divergence or complexity). For a family restaurant seeking a strategy combining changes in levels of both complexity and divergence, consider Table 5.4.

TAXONOMY FOR SERVICE PROCESS DESIGN

Service processes can be classified using the concept of divergence, the object toward which the service activity is directed, and the degree of customer contact. In Table 5.5 on page 123, services are broadly divided into low divergence (i.e., standardized service) and high divergence (i.e., customized service). Within these two categories, the object of the service process is identified as goods, information, or people. The degree

FIGURE 5.4 Structural positioning of financial services.

TABLE 5.4		
STRUCTURAL ALTERNATIVES FOR FAMILY RESTAURANT		
Lower complexity/divergence	**Current process**	**Higher complexity/divergence**
No reservations	Take reservation	Specific table selection
Self-seating; menu on blackboard	Seat guests; give menus	Recite menu; describe entrees and specials
Eliminate	Serve water and bread	Assortment of hot breads and hors d'oeuvres
Customer fills out form	Take orders	At table; taken personally by maitre d'
	Prepare orders	
Pre-prepared; no choice	Salad (4 choices)	Individually prepared at table
Limit to 4 choices	Entree (15 choices)	Expand to 20 choices; add flaming dishes; bone fish at table; prepare sauces at table
Sundae bar; self-service	Dessert (6 choices)	Expand to 12 choices
Coffee, tea, milk only	Beverage (6 choices)	Add exotic coffees, wine list, liqueurs
Serve salad and entree together; bill and beverage together	Serve orders	Separate-course service; sherbet between courses; hand-grind pepper
Cash only; pay when leaving	Collect payment	Choice of payment, including house accounts; serve mints

Source: Reprinted with permission of the American Marketing Association: G. Lynn Shostack, "Service Positioning through Structural Change," *Journal of Marketing,* vol. 51, January 1987, p. 41.

of customer contact ranges from no contact to indirect contact to direct contact (and is divided further into self-service and personal interaction with the service worker).

Degree of Divergence

A standardized service (i.e., low divergence) is designed for high volumes with a narrowly defined and focused service. The tasks are routine and require a workforce with relatively low levels of technical skills. Because of the repetitive nature of the service, opportunities to substitute automation for labor abound (e.g., use of vending machines, automatic car wash). Reducing the discretion of service workers is one approach to achieving consistent service quality, but one that also has possible negative consequences. These concepts will be referred to later as the *production-line approach* to service design.

For customized services (i.e., high divergence), more flexibility and judgment are required to perform the service tasks. In addition, more information is exchanged between the customer and the service worker. These characteristics of customized services require high levels of technical and analytic skills, because the service process is unprogrammed and not well defined (e.g., counseling, landscaping). To achieve customer satisfaction, decision making is delegated to service workers who can perform their tasks with some autonomy and discretion (i.e., the workers are empowered).

Object of the Service Process

When goods are processed, a distinction must be made between goods that belong to the customer and goods that are provided by the service firm (i.e., *facilitating goods*). For services such as dry cleaning or auto repair, the service is performed on the

TABLE 5.5

TAXONOMY OF SERVICE PROCESSES

Degree of customer contact		Low divergence (standardized service)			High divergence (customized service)		
		Processing of goods	Processing of information or images	Processing of people	Processing of goods	Processing of information or images	Processing of people
No customer contact		Dry cleaning Restocking a vending machine	Check processing Billing for a credit card		Auto repair Tailoring a suit	Computer programming Designing a building	
Indirect customer contact			Ordering groceries from a home computer Phone-based account balance verification			Supervision of a landing by an air controller Bidding at a TV auction	
Direct customer contact	No customer–service worker interaction (self-service)	Operating a vending machine Assembling premade furniture	Withdrawing cash from an auto-matic bank teller Taking pictures in a photo booth	Operating an elevator Riding an escalator	Sampling food at a buffet dinner Bagging of groceries	Documenting medical history at a clinic Searching for information in a library	Driving a rental car Using a health club facility
	Customer–service worker interaction	Food serving in a restaurant Car washing	Giving a lecture Handling routine bank transactions	Providing public transporta-tion Providing mass vaccination	Home carpet cleaning Landscaping service	Portrait painting Counseling	Haircutting Performing a surgical operation

Source: Reprinted with permission from Urban Wemmerlov, "A Taxonomy for Service Process and Its Implications for System Design," *International Journal of Service Industry Management,* vol. 1, no. 3, 1990, p. 29.

property of the customer; in this case, the property must be secured from damage or loss. Other services such as restaurants supply facilitating goods as a significant part of the service package. Therefore, appropriate stock levels and the quality of these facili-tating goods become a concern, as illustrated by McDonald's attention to the purchase of food items.

Processing information (i.e., receiving, handling, and manipulating data) occurs in all service systems. In some cases, this is a back-office activity, such as check process-ing at a bank. For other services, the information is communicated indirectly by elec-tronic means, as with telephone-based account balance verification. Service workers in these situations may spend hours before a video screen performing routine tasks, and motivation becomes a challenge. There are services such as counseling, however, in which information is processed through direct interactions between the customer and the service worker. For highly skilled employees in these services, the challenge of dealing with unstructured problems is important to job satisfaction.

Processing people involves physical changes (e.g., a haircut or a surgical operation) or geographic changes (e.g., a bus ride or a car rental). Because of the "high-touch" nature of these services, workers must possess interpersonal as well as technical skills. Attention also must be paid to service facility design and location, because the customer is physically present in the system. These topics are covered in Chapters 6 and 7.

Type of Customer Contact

Customer contact with the service delivery system can occur in three basic ways. First, the customer can be physically present and interact directly with the service providers in the creation of the service. In this instance, the customer has full sensory awareness of the service surroundings. Second, the contact may be indirect and occur via electronic media from the customer's home or office. Third, some service activities can be performed with no customer contact at all. Banking provides an example where all three options occur: making an application for an automobile loan requires an interview with a loan officer, payment on the loan can be accomplished by the electronic transfer of funds, and the financial record keeping for the loan is conducted in a back office of the bank.

Direct customer contact is subdivided into two categories: no interaction with service workers (i.e., self-service) and customer interaction with service workers. Self-service often is particularly attractive because customers provide the necessary labor at the necessary time. Many cost-effective applications of technology in services, such as direct dialing and automatic teller machines, have relied on a market segment of customers who are willing to learn how to interact with machines. When customers desire direct interaction with service providers, all the issues addressed earlier concerning the processing of people (i.e., training in interpersonal skills and facility issues of location, layout, and design) become important to ensure a successful service experience. When customers are in the service process physically, additional management problems (e.g., managing queues to avoid creating a negative image) arise. The topic of customer waiting is discussed in Chapter 11, and the related issues of managing customer demand and scheduling service capacity are discussed in Chapter 13.

Service processes with indirect customer contact or with no customer contact need not be constrained by issues that arise from the physical presence of the customer in the system. Because the customer is decoupled from the service delivery system, a more manufacturing type of approach can be taken. Decisions regarding site location, facility design, work scheduling, and training of employees all can be driven by efficiency considerations. In fact, the no-customer-contact and goods-processing combination creates a category that normally is thought of in manufacturing. For example, dry cleaning is a batch process, and auto repair is a job shop.

This taxonomy of service processes presents a way to organize the various types of processes that are encountered in service systems and helps us to understand the design and management of services. This taxonomy also serves as a strategic positioning map for service processes and, thus, as an aid in the design or redesign of service systems.

GENERIC APPROACHES TO SERVICE SYSTEM DESIGN

In Chapter 2, we defined the service package as a bundle of attributes that a customer experiences. This bundle consists of four features: supporting facility, facilitating goods, explicit services, and implicit services. With a well-designed service system, these features are harmoniously coordinated in light of the desired service package. Consequently, the definition of the service package is key to designing the service system itself. This design can be approached in several ways.

At one extreme, we can deliver services through a *production-line approach*. With this approach, routine services are provided in a controlled environment to ensure consistent quality and efficiency of operation. Another approach is to encourage active customer participation in the process. Allowing the customer to take an active role in the service process can result in many benefits to both the consumer and the provider. An intermediate approach divides the service into high- and low-customer-contact operations. This allows the low-contact operations to be designed as a technical core that is isolated from the customer.

It should be noted that combinations of these approaches also can be used. For example, banks isolate their check-processing operation, use self-serve automated tellers, and provide personalized loan service.

Production-Line Approach

We tend to see service as something personal: it is performed by individuals directly for other individuals. This humanistic perception can be overly constraining, however, and therefore can impede development of an innovative service system design. For example, we sometimes might benefit from a more technocratic service delivery system. Manufacturing systems are designed with control of the process in mind. The output often is machine-paced, and jobs are designed with explicit tasks to be performed. Special tools and machines are supplied to increase worker productivity. A service taking this production-line approach could gain a competitive advantage with a cost leadership strategy.

McDonald's provides the quintessential example of this manufacturing-in-the-field approach to service.[5] Raw materials (e.g., hamburger patties) are measured and prepackaged off-site, leaving the employees with no discretion as to size, quality, or consistency. In addition, storage facilities are designed expressly for the predetermined mix of products. No extra space is available for foods and beverages that are not called for in the service.

The production of french fries illustrates attention to design detail. The fries come precut, partially cooked, and frozen. The fryer is sized to cook a correct quantity of fries. This is an amount that will be not so large as to create an inventory of soggy fries or so small as to require making new batches very frequently. The fryer is emptied into a wide, flat tray near the service counter. This setup prevents fries from an overfilled bag from dropping to the floor, which would result in wasted food and an unclean environment. A special wide-mouthed scoop with a funnel in the handle is used to ensure a consistent measure of french fries. The thoughtful design ensures that employees never soil their hands or the fries, that the floor remains clean, and that the quantity is controlled. Further, a generous-looking portion of fries is delivered to the customer by a speedy, efficient, and cheerful employee.

This entire system is engineered from beginning to end, from prepackaged hamburgers to highly visible trash cans that encourage customers to clear their table. Every detail is accounted for through careful planning and design. The production-line approach to service system design attempts to translate a successful manufacturing concept into the service sector, and several features contribute to its success.

Limited Discretionary Action of Personnel   A worker on an automobile assembly line is given well-defined tasks to perform along with the tools to accomplish them.

Employees with discretion and latitude might produce a more personalized car, but uniformity from one car to the next would be lost. Standardization and quality (defined as consistency in meeting specifications) are the hallmarks of a production line. For standardized routine services, consistency in service performance would be valued by customers. For example, specialized services like muffler replacement and pest control are advertised as having the same high-quality service at any franchised outlet. Thus, the customer can expect identical service at any location of a particular franchise operation (e.g., one Big Mac is as desirable as another), just as one product from a manufacturer is indistinguishable from another. If more personalized service is desired, however, the concept of employee empowerment becomes appropriate. The idea of giving employees more freedom to make decisions and to assume responsibility is discussed in Chapter 8, The Service Encounter.

Division of Labor   The production-line approach suggests that the total job be broken down into groups of simple tasks. Task grouping permits the specialization of labor skills (e.g., not everyone at McDonald's needs to be a cook). Further, the division of labor allows one to pay only for the skill that is required to perform the task. Of course, this raises the criticism of many service jobs as being minimum-wage, dead-end, and low-skill employment. Consider, for example, a new concept in health care called the *automated multiphasic testing laboratory*. Patients are processed through a fixed sequence of medical tests, which are part of the diagnostic work-up. Tests are performed by medical technicians using sophisticated equipment. Because the entire process is divided into routine tasks, the examination can be accomplished without an expensive physician.

Substitution of Technology for People   The systematic substitution of equipment for people has been the source of progress in manufacturing. This approach also can be used in services, as seen by the acceptance of automated teller machines in lieu of bank tellers. A great deal can be accomplished by means of the "soft" technology of systems, however. Consider, for example, the use of mirrors placed in an airplane galley. This benign device provides a reminder and an opportunity for flight attendants to maintain a pleasant appearance in an unobtrusive manner. Another example is the greeting card display that has a built-in inventory replenishment and reordering feature; when the stock gets low, a colored card appears to signal a reorder. Using a laptop computer, insurance agents can personalize their recommendations and illustrate the accumulation of cash values.

Service Standardization   The limited menu at McDonald's guarantees a fast hamburger. Limiting service options creates opportunities for predictability and preplanning; the service becomes a routine process with well-defined tasks and an orderly flow of customers. Standardization also helps to provide uniformity in service quality, because the process is easier to control. Franchise services take advantage of standardization to build national organizations and thus overcome the problem of demand being limited only to the immediate region around a service location.

Customer as Coproducer

For most service systems, the customer is present when the service is being performed. Instead of being a passive bystander, the customer represents productive labor just at the moment it is needed, and opportunities exist for increasing productivity by shifting

To implement a demand-smoothing strategy, custome‍fers to the physical presence of the the timing of their demand to match the availability of the‍ntact can be measured by the per‑ complishing this are appointments and reservations; in ‍relative to the total service time. In pect to avoid waiting for the service. Customers also ‍n‍timing of demand and the nature of service during off-peak hours by price incentives (e.g., re‍ perceived quality of service is de‑ P.M., or midweek discounts on lift tickets at ski resorts). ‍ence. Consumers have no direct in‑

If attempts to smooth demand fail, high utilization of‍ystems, however, because they are plished by requiring customers to wait for service. Thus,‍tact category, it still may be possi‑ to productivity by permitting greater utilization of capac‍. For example, the maintenance op‑ following should be posted in waiting areas: "Your wait‍ laundry of a hospital are plants prices!"

We would expect customers to be compensated for th‍ through lower prices, but what about "free" or prepaid g‍ When service systems are sepa‑ uation, waiting is a surrogate for the price that otherwi‍area can be designed separately to The results are a rationing of the limited public service ‍tions in the design of the high- and tion of capacity. Using customers' waiting time as an inp‍te that high-contact operations re‑ ever, may be criticized on the grounds that individua‍ The service tasks and activity lev‑ differently.   mers dictate the timing of demand

The customer may need to be "trained" to assume a‍hat low-contact operations can be pendent, role as an active participant in the service pro‍ons; however, there is some need the provider is a new concept in services. Traditionally,‍ack progress of customer orders or the consumer ignorant and, thus, dependent on the serv‍ir at a distant factory). The advan‑

As services become more specialized, the customer ‍operations can be scheduled like a role. For example, does the loud noise under my car n‍ (i.e., transmission) or Midas (i.e., muffler)? Further, an‍eir operations. Airport reservation provide a quality-control check, which has been parti‍d in Paris and attend training ses‑ sional services. Thus, increased service productivity m‍age handlers seldom are seen, and self-reliant customer. A more detailed discussion of d‍ and run like a factory. Chapter 13, Managing Capacity and Demand.

The commonly held view that or‑ ‍vident when considering informa‑

Customer Contact Approach

‍g service tasks. The service design The manufacture of products is conducted in a contro‍wn in Figure 5.5, illustrates the re‑ design is totally focused on creating a continuous and‍opportunity as a function of service into products without consumer involvement. Using inv‍ is decoupled from variations in customer demand and, t‍right by increasing richness of in‑ ate at full capacity.   efficiency is related to the degree

How can service managers design their operations‍. Sales opportunity is a measure of manufacturing when customers participate in the pr‍sing the revenue that is generated argued persuasively that service delivery systems can b‍cit consideration of the trade-offs contact customer operations.[6] The low-contact, or ba‍ions when selecting the service de‑ a plant, where all the production management concep‍ are brought to bear. This separation of activities can r‍elivery option must be selected. In of personalized service while in fact achieving econo‍tiple channels of service should be processing.   - and self-service pumps, and most

The success of this approach depends on the require‍. in the creation of the service, and on the ability to isola‍ tact operations. In our taxonomy of service processes, ‍ would seem to be most appropriate for the processin‍ormation, and like it or not, we are cleaning, where the service is performed on the custom‍nger just for computer "nerds." IT

TABLE 5.6

MAJOR DESIGN CONSIDERATIONS FOR HIGH- AND LOW-CONTACT OPERATIONS

Design consideration	High-contact operation	Low-contact operation
Facility location	Operations must be near the customer.	Operations may be placed near supply, transportation, or labor.
Facility layout	Facility should accommodate the customer's physical and psychological needs and expectations.	Facility should enhance production.
Product design	Environment as well as the physical product define the nature of the service.	Customer is concerned mainly with completion dates.
Process design	Stages of production process have a direct, immediate effect on the customer.	Customer is not involved in the majority of processing steps.
Scheduling	Customer is in the production schedule and must be accommodated.	Customer is concerned mainly with completion dates.
Production planning	Orders cannot be stored, so smoothing production flow will result in loss of business.	Both backlogging and production smoothing are possible.
Worker skills	Direct workforce makes up a major part of the service product and so must be able to interact well with the public.	Direct workforce need only have technical skills.
Quality control	Quality standards are often in the eye of the beholder and hence variable.	Quality standards are generally measurable and hence fixed.
Time standards	Service time depends on customer needs, and therefore time standards are inherently loose.	Work is performed on customer surrogates (e.g., forms), and time standards can be tight.
Wage payment	Variable output requires time-based wage systems.	"Fixable" output permits output-based wage systems.
Capacity planning	To avoid lost sales, capacity must be set to match peak demand.	Storable output permits setting capacity at some average demand level.
Forecasting	Forecasts are short-term, time-oriented.	Forecasts are long-term, output-oriented.

Source: Used by permission of the *Harvard Business Review*. Exhibit II from "Where Does the Customer Fit in a Service Operation?" by Richard B. Chase (November–December 1978), p. 139. Copyright © 1978 by the President and Fellows of Harvard College; all rights reserved.

touches all of us every day. The breakfast cereal on your table represents more than puffs, flakes, or shreds of grain. You can safely assume that three funny-looking little guys named Snap, Crackle, and Pop are not actually responsible for processing and packaging your rice, nor does a little sprite cavort around putting two scoops of raisins in each box of Raisin Bran. IT can be seen all the way from the rice paddy or wheat field, where it helps to manage the planting, propagating, harvesting, and transportation of the grain, to the processing and packaging facility to your market and even to

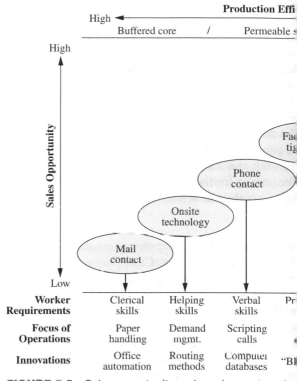

High ◄———————— **Production Effi**

Buffered core / Permeable s

FIGURE 5.5 Sales opportunity and service system des
(*Source:* Reprinted with permission from R. B. chase and N.
Marketing and Production Variables in Service System Desig
agement, 6th ed., Richard D. Irwin, Inc., Homewood, IL, 199

your table (e.g., those traffic lights you passed betwe
by an information-based technology). Essential servi
tion demand the use of IT, and the electricity and
brought to us by IT. In fact, IT is such a fundamenta
entire world that the challenge is to find some aspect

Certainly, no service today could survive withou
agers will see that IT offers much more than simp
records. Indeed, one of its most important functions i
customers.

Employee Empowerment   The earliest use of IT w
might have had a computerized database of custom
haps another database of the names and addresses fo
services. These various databases made it a little eas
the IRS—happy. They made record keeping a little fa
secretaries still just entered data, procurement clerks
front-line service people smiled a lot, and producti
their routine duties. Top management held the task o

The development of *relational databases,* howeve
or integrated, databases meant that information from
be used by anybody. A production manager could lo

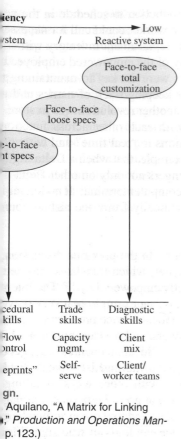

iency		
		► Low
vstem	/	Reactive system

Face-to-face
total
customization

Face-to-face
loose specs

-to-face
it specs

cedural kills	Trade skills	Diagnostic skills
Flow ontrol	Capacity mgmt.	Client mix
eprints"	Self- serve	Client/ worker teams

gn.
Aquilano, "A Matrix for Linking
," *Production and Operations Man-*
p. 123.)

n market and home are operated
es such as fire and police protec-
running water in our homes are
part of daily life throughout the
not touched by it.

use of IT, and successful man-
y a convenient way to maintain
to empower both employees and

as in record keeping. A business
r names and addresses, and per-
suppliers of essential goods and
er to keep the shareholders—and
ter and a little more accurate, but
ust ordered supplies or services,
n-floor workers still went about
juggling these diverse activities.
changed everything. Relational,
all aspects of an operation could
at sales numbers and know im-

SUMMARY

We found that service innovation can be either radical or incremental and often arises from advances in technology. Following service development, the design of the service delivery system is captured in a visual diagram called a service blueprint. The line of visibility in this diagram introduced the concept of a front-office and back-office partition of the service system. Competitive positioning of the service delivery system was accomplished using the dimensions of complexity and divergence to measure structural differentiation. We also looked at classifying services according to the concept of divergence, the object of the service, and the degree of customer contact. Four generic approaches to the design of service delivery systems were considered: production-line approach, customer participation, customer contact, and information empowerment. Because customers view the service process as the product, introduction of new technology requires attention to customer acceptance. Automation in services is widespread and has applications in both the front and back office. Our look at the structuring of services will continue in Chapter 6 with a consideration of how design and layout of the supporting facility contribute to a competitive advantage.

KEY TERMS AND DEFINITIONS

Complexity a dimension of service process structure that measures the number and intricacy of steps in the process.

Coproducer the productive role a customer can play in the service delivery process.

Customer contact a measure of the physical presence of the customer in the system as a percentage of the total service time.

Divergence a dimension of service process structure that measures the degree of customization or decision making permitted of service employees.

Line of visibility a line drawn on the service blueprint showing separation of front-office from back-office activities.

Production-line approach a service design analogous to that in a manufacturing system with tight control, use of low-skilled labor, and the offering of a standard service.

Service blueprint a diagram of the service process showing activities, flows, fail points, customer waits, and a line of visibility.

TOPICS FOR DISCUSSION

1. Shostack's "line of visibility" on a service blueprint divides the service into front-office and back-office operations. How can this be useful to managers?
2. Select a service and prepare a "blueprint" identifying fail points, decision points, customer wait points, and the line of visibility.
3. What are the limits to the production-line approach to service?
4. Give an example of a service in which isolation of the technical core would be inappropriate.
5. What are some drawbacks of increased customer participation in the service process?
6. What ethical issues are involved in the promotion of sales opportunities in a service transaction?

Service Benchmark
PACBELL'S EXPERIMENT

The project, now called Infotel, was born in September 1991, when San Francisco–based Pac-Bell sent a dozen managers to the Double Tree Inn in Santa Ana, Calif. Their familiar mission: think up ways to increase productivity.

Their leader, John Lewis, then general manager of PacBell's Los Angeles staff, wondered why the company was using traditional methods if it really wanted a quantum leap. Puzzling over the problem in the shower that first morning, he had an idea: He would "fire" his colleagues (and himself) and, unbeknownst to his bosses, change the agenda. He asked them to pretend that they had just inherited a phone company from "Uncle Herman" and found that the old man hadn't left enough money to buy a new computer system. Otherwise, they could invent a whole new phone company.

For the first few days, the participants got nowhere. They were simply too tangled in the PacBell culture, speaking in corporate acronyms and thinking old thoughts. So Mr. Lewis imposed 25-cent fines for each peep of PacBell lingo. "We had lots of cocktails" with the proceeds, he says.

Then, changes came more easily. During "I wish" sessions, the managers offered ideas beginning with those words, as in: "I wish the first person who answered . . . the phone could solve my problem." That drill developed ideas for, among other things, changing office procedures so individual workers could perform many tasks quickly. Such an office could be set up, the managers thought, if they could invent software giving workers instant access to numerous databases.

A REALITY TEST

After some four weeks of brainstorming, Mr. Lewis told his boss, Marty A. Kaplan, PacBell's executive vice president for reengineering, that the group wanted to create and run a real Infotel within the phone company. Mr. Kaplan agreed, and Infotel spent the next year developing a business plan—despite the doubts of other senior managers. The group chose Santa Clarita as the site because it is small—its population is 30,000—but has a mix of business and residential accounts. For staffing, Infotel asked the Communications Workers of America for four union volunteers, who would bring along their old work but handle it with Infotel's new procedures, plus their own innovations.

Most of Infotel's cost savings come from small changes. Because of one software glitch, for instance, PacBell computers couldn't automatically process requests for voice mail from customers served by a certain kind of phone switch. Every day, the computers across the state kicked out hundreds of orders, and employees had to spend about 10 minutes processing each one.

Sandy Coash, an Infotel worker, identified the problem and told Mr. Lewis, to whom she wouldn't normally have had access. Within three months, PacBell software engineers fixed the problem for the whole state—and eliminated all that work. That and other software fixes allowed Infotel's four union workers to cut out 85% of the work they had brought with them from their old jobs, Mr. Lewis says.

There were many other changes. A new software program for repair workers' portable computers gives them all the information they need to fix a line; no longer do they have to call other PacBell employees for help. The computers also dispatch them to their next assignment; now they don't have to call in for those, either. Cellular telephones in their vans allow them to make phone calls on the road instead of pulling over at gas stations.

And that is just the beginning. Infotel has yet to implement its crowning achievement, a software program that should make customer-service computers as easy to use as a cash register at McDonald's. Once it's in place, workers will be able to point and click at a menu of orders when a customer calls, filling the order in minutes. The same workers will have remote access to switches and also will be able to perform tests on lines.

Currently, when a customer calls regular PacBell offices to start phone service, the worker who answers must type in the name, address, billing information, and how the person wants to be listed in the directory. Then the worker fumbles through heavy manuals to look up corresponding computer codes for the whole order and type in the codes—sometimes making mistakes. The process takes an average of 22 minutes. A customer who also wants to report trouble on a line must transfer to a different department and talk to at least two more people.

BOX 5.1 (CONTINUED)

PacBell's customers in Santa Clarita are already getting better service. They can now get new features such as call-waiting in seconds, instead of hours. And repair workers have developed a sixth sense. When Cindy Pascoe's daughter shorted out a phone line by knocking over a fish tank, a repairman arrived even before she knew the line was dead. "It was wonderful!" the department-store saleswoman exclaims.

Since the Infotel group didn't have enough money to buy a new, easy-to-use computer system, they jerry-rigged the one they had by writing a new software program. So far, the software has taken more than a year and more than $10 million to develop, but that is small change compared with the $4 billion Mr. Lewis estimates as the cost of replacing all of PacBell's current computers.

The bottom line: companywide adoption of Infotel innovations, combined with other reengineering efforts, will allow PacBell to serve its existing customers with 10,000 fewer workers. Mr. Lewis is a bit sensitive about linking Infotel's success to the job cuts, which are to be completed by 1997. Infotel "is not laying them off. Competition is laying them off," he argues. Mr. Kaplan agrees: "We didn't say we're going to reengineer the business to cut 10,000 people. We said we've got to take a lot of costs out . . . and improve service."

A crucial question is how many well-paying jobs destroyed by technology will be offset by well-paying jobs created by technology. And many are being created. United Parcel Service of America Inc., for example, now has 3,000 information-technology employees, up from 90 in 1983. At many companies, more technicians will be needed to service computer networks, and more programmers to write software.

For at least a few years, however, technology-driven layoffs seem likely to dwarf new high-tech jobs. Many layoff victims will have to settle for the low-paying or part-time positions that are dominating recent job growth, because they generally aren't the ones who will get the new high-paying jobs. A telephone operator isn't qualified to install wireless communications equipment, for example. The danger is that America's workforce could evolve into an elite minority of highly paid "knowledge workers" and frustrated masses of the underemployed or unemployed.

Already, many workers are aware that technology cuts two ways. Riding in an Infotel van, Steve Symach, a repairman, marvels at how technology has made his job easier. But he realizes it could cost him his job—before he plans to retire, in 12 years. "If the result of us being efficient is me being laid off," the silver-haired 18-year phone company veteran says, "I hate to say it, but I guess that's progress."

Source: Reprinted with permission from Joan E. Rigdon, "Retooling Lives: Technological Gains Are Cutting Costs, and Jobs, in Services," *The Wall Street Journal,* February 24, 1994, p. A5. Reprinted by permission of *The Wall Street Journal,* 1994, Dow Jones & Company, Inc. All Rights Reserved Worldwide. Permission conveyed by Copyright Clearance Center, Inc.

CASE

100 Yen Sushi House[8]

Sang M. Lee tells of a meeting with two Japanese businessmen in Tokyo to plan a joint U.S.–Japanese conference to explore U.S. and Japanese management systems. As lunchtime drew near, his hosts told him with much delight that they wished to show him the "most productive operation in Japan."

Lee describes the occasion: "They took me to a sushi shop, the famous 100 Yen Sushi House, in the Shinzuku area of Tokyo. Sushi is the most popular snack in Japan. It is a simple dish, vinegared rice wrapped in different things, such as dried seaweed, raw tuna, raw salmon, raw red snapper, cooked shrimp, octopus, fried egg, etc. Sushi is usually prepared so that each piece will be about the right size to be put into the mouth with chopsticks. Arranging the sushi in an appetizing and aesthetic way with pickled ginger is almost an art in itself.

"The 100 Yen Sushi House is no ordinary sushi restaurant. It is the ultimate showcase of Japanese productivity. As we entered the shop, there was a chorus of 'Iratsai,' a welcome from everyone working in the shop—cooks, waitresses, the owner, and the owner's children. The house features an ellipsoid-shaped serving area in the middle of the room, where inside three or four cooks were busily preparing sushi. Perhaps 30 stools surrounded the serving area. We took seats at the counters and were promptly served with a cup of 'Misoshiru,' which is a bean paste soup, a pair of chopsticks, a cup of green tea, a tiny plate to make our own sauce, and a small china piece to hold the chopsticks. So far, the service was average for any sushi house. Then, I noticed something special. There was a conveyor belt going around the ellipsoid service area, like a toy train track. On it I saw a train of plates of sushi. You can find any kind of sushi that you can think of—from the cheapest seaweed or octopus kind to the expensive raw salmon or shrimp dishes. The price is uniform, however, 100 yen per plate. On closer examination, while my eyes were racing to keep up with the speed of the traveling plates, I found that a cheap seaweed plate had four pieces, while the more expensive raw salmon dish had only two pieces. I sat down and looked around at the other customers at the counters. They were all enjoying their sushi and slurping their soup while reading newspapers or magazines.

"I saw a man with eight plates all stacked up neatly. As he got up to leave, the cashier looked over and said, '800 yen, please.' The cashier had no cash register, since she can simply count the number of plates and then multiply by 100 yen. As the customer was leaving, once again we heard a chorus of 'Arigato Gosaimas' (thank you) from all the workers."

Lee continues his observations of the sushi house operations: "In the 100 Yen Sushi House, Professor Tamura [one of his hosts] explained to me how efficient this family-owned restaurant is. The owner usually has a superordinate organizational purpose such as customer service, a contribution to society, or the well-being of the community. Furthermore, the organizational purpose is achieved through a long-term effort by all the members of the organization, who are considered 'family.'

"The owner's daily operation is based on a careful analysis of information. The owner has a complete summary of demand information about different types of sushi plates, and thus he knows exactly how many of each type of sushi plates he should prepare and when. Furthermore, the whole operation is based on the repetitive manufacturing principle with appropriate 'just-in-time' and quality control systems. For example, the store has a very limited refrigerator capacity (we could see several whole fish or octopus in the glassed chambers right in front of our counter). Thus, the store uses the 'just-in-time' inventory control system. Instead of increasing the refrigeration capacity by purchasing new refrigeration systems, the company has an agreement with the fish vendor to deliver fresh fish several times a day so that materials arrive 'just-in-time' to be used for sushi making. Therefore, the inventory cost is minimum.

"... In the 100 Yen Sushi House, workers and their equipment are positioned so close that sushi making is passed on hand to hand rather than as independent operations. The absence of walls of inventory allows the owner and workers to be involved in the total operation, from greeting the customer to serving what is ordered. Their tasks are tightly interrelated and everyone rushes to a problem spot to prevent the cascading effect of the problem throughout the work process.

"The 100 Yen Sushi House is a labor-intensive operation, which is based mostly on simplicity and common sense rather than high technology, contrary to American perceptions. I was very impressed. As I finished my fifth plate, I saw the same octopus sushi plate going around for about the 30th time. Perhaps I had discovered the pitfall of the system. So I asked the owner how he takes care of the sanitary problems when a sushi plate goes around all day long, until an unfortunate customer eats it and perhaps gets food poisoning. He bowed with an apologetic smile and said, 'Well, sir, we never let our sushi plates go unsold longer than about 30 minutes.' Then he scratched his head and said, 'Whenever one of our employees takes a break, he or she can take off unsold plates of sushi and either eat them or throw them away. We are very serious about our sushi quality.'"

Questions

1. Prepare a service blueprint for the 100 Yen Sushi House operation.
2. What features of the 100 Yen Sushi House service delivery system differentiate it from the competition, and what competitive advantages do they offer?
3. How has the 100 Yen Sushi House incorporated the just-in-time system into its operation?
4. Suggest other services that could adopt the 100 Yen Sushi House service delivery concepts.

Commuter Cleaning—A New Venture Proposal[9]

The service vision of Commuter Cleaning is to provide dry cleaning services for individuals with careers or other responsibilities that make it difficult for them to find the time to go to traditional dry cleaners. The company's goals are to provide a high-quality dry cleaning service that is both reliable and convenient.

The targeted market consists of office workers who live in the suburbs of large metropolitan areas. The service will be marketed primarily to single men and women as well as dual-career couples, because this segment of the population has the greatest need for a quality dry cleaning service but does not have the time to go to the traditional dry cleaners. The targeted cities are those surrounded by suburbs from which many people commute via mass transit.

The facilities where customers will drop off and pick up their dry cleaning will be located at sites where commuters meet their trains or buses into the downtown area (i.e., park-and-ride locations and commuter train stations). For each city, it will be necessary to determine who owns these transit stations and how land can be rented from the owner. In some locations, facilities where space could be rented already exist. In other locations, there may not be any existing facilities, and the pickup and drop-off booths will need to be built.

The facilities for laundry pickup and drop-off need not be large. The building or room at the station need only be large enough to accommodate racks for hanging the finished dry cleaning.

Initially, it may be necessary to restrict the service to laundering business-wear shirts, because these are the easiest of all clothing articles to clean and also will allow the operations to be simplified. Typically, a man or woman will need a clean shirt for each workday, so a large demand exists. One drawback would be the diminished customer convenience, because dry cleaning of garments would necessitate a separate trip to a traditional dry cleaner. If dry cleaning were outsourced, however, it would be possible to offer full-service cleaning very quickly, because a plant and equipment need not be purchased.

A decision also needs to be made about providing same-day or next-day service. One factor in this decision will be whether competitors in the area offer same-day service. These cleaners represent a serious threat only if they open early enough and close late enough to be convenient and accessible to customers. Most important, same-day service should be provided only where it is feasible to deliver on this promise consistently.

All advertisements will include a phone number that potential customers can call to inquire about the service. When a customer calls, he or she can request the service. That same day, the customer will be able to pick up a Commuter Cleaning laundry bag with the customer's name and account number on it and a membership card that is coded with the account number.

The delivery system will be a hub-and-spoke system, similar to the one that FedEx uses for package handling. Customers will have the convenience of dropping off their laundry at numerous neighborhood commuter stations. All dry cleaning will be picked up and delivered to one central plant, and once the shirts are clean, they will be returned to the customer's drop-off point. Same-day service is possible with pick-ups beginning at 8:00 A.M. and returns completed by 5:00 P.M.

The customer will place the dirty shirts in the bag at home and simply leave the bag at the station on the way to work. The station worker will attach a color-coded label on the bag to identify the location where the shirts were dropped off so that they can be returned to the same station. A laundry pickup route will be established to bring bags from each location to the central cleaning plant. Once the bag reaches the central plant, the items will be counted and the number entered into the billing database. After the shirts have been cleaned, they will be put on hangers with the customer's laundry bag attached. The cleaned shirts will be segregated according to the location to which they need to be returned and then placed on a truck in reverse order of the delivery route. The customer will provide the station worker with his or her membership card, which will be used to identify and retrieve the customer's clothing and bag. Because all customers will be billed monthly, the time to pick up the laundry should be expedited and waiting lines avoided.

Initially, cleaning will be outsourced to a large dry cleaner with excess capacity. A favorable rate should be negotiated because of the predictable volume, convenience of aggregating the demand into one batch, and performing the pickup and delivery service. Contracting for the cleaning will reduce the initial capital investment required to build a plant and buy equipment, and it also will provide time for the business to build a customer base that would support a dedicated cleaning plant. Further, contracting will limit the financial risk exposure if the concept fails. If the cleaning is outsourced, there will be no need to hire and manage a workforce to perform the cleaning; therefore, management can focus on building a customer base instead of supervising back-office activities. Also, with contract cleaning, it is more feasible to offer dry cleaning services in addition to laundering business shirts.

In the long run, however, contract cleaning may limit the potential profitability, expose the business to quality problems, and prevent the opportunity to focus cleaning plant operations around the pickup-and-delivery concept. Ideally, once Commuter Cleaning has built a large client base and has access to significant capital, all cleaning will be done internally.

Most of the hiring will be targeted to area college students. Initially, two shifts of workers will be needed for the transit station facilities but just one van driver at any given time. As business expands, additional vans will be acquired and additional drivers hired. The first shift of drop-off station workers will begin at 6:00 A.M. and finish at 9:00 A.M., at which time the van driver will transport the items from the drop-off sites to the cleaning site. The number of drivers needed and the hours they work will depend on how many pickup and drop-off sites exist, their proximity to each other, the cleaning plant location, and the ability to develop efficient routing schedules. The second shift of drivers will deliver the cleaning from the plant to the transit stations from about 3:30 to 5:00 P.M. The second shift of transit-site workers will begin at 5:00 P.M. and end when the last train or bus arrives, usually about 8:30 P.M. Once cleaning is done internally, it will be possible to have plant employees also pick up the laundry and deliver it to the stations each day. This will allow Commuter Cleaning to hire some full-time workers, and it also will bring the back-office workers closer to the customers so that they can be more aware of problems and customer needs.

College students will be the best candidates for workers, because their schedules vary and classes usually are held in the middle of the day, from about 10 A.M. to 3 P.M. Also, depending on course loads, some students may only have time to work three hours a day, while others may choose to work both the first and second shifts. The starting salary will be set slightly above the wage for typical part-time service jobs available to college students to discourage turnover.

When Commuter Cleaning is first introduced into a city, additional temporary workers will be needed to manage the customer inquiries for initiating the service. The week before introduction of the service, representatives will be at the station facilities to answer questions and perform the paperwork necessary to initiate service for interested customers. Because all advertisements will include the customer service number, it will be necessary to have additional representatives manning the phones to handle the inquiries. All employees will have the title "customer service representative" to stress the function of their jobs. These workers will be encouraged to get to know their customers and reach a first-name basis with them.

When customers initiate service, they will be encouraged to open an account for monthly billing rather than to pay each time that items are picked up. At this time, the customer service representative will collect all the necessary information, including name, address, phone number, location from where they commute, and credit card number. If a customer desires, the amount owed will be charged to the credit card each month. This is the most desirable form of payment, because it is efficient and involves no worry of delayed payments. This method also is becoming more common, and people generally now are comfortable having their credit cards billed automatically. Each month, statements will be sent to all customers with transactions to verify the bill and request payment from those who do not use a credit card. If a customer is late in paying, a customer service representative will call and ask if he or she would like to begin paying with a credit card. Repeatedly delinquent customers will be required to pay at the time of pickup, a stipulation that will be included in the customer's initial agreement for service. The customer service representatives will be responsible for answering all customer inquiries, including the initiation of service, and one customer service representative will be responsible for customer billings. Each day, the laundry delivered to the plant will be entered into a database that accumulates each customer's transactions for the month.

A smooth demand throughout the week is desirable to create a stable work load; however, actions likely will be needed to control fluctuations in demand and to avoid imbalances in the work load. One method of controlling demand is through price specials and promotions. Offering a discount on certain days of the week is common practice for dry cleaners, and one approach would be to offer special prices to different customer segments to entice them to bring in their laundry on a certain day. For example, Friday may be the busiest day of the week and Monday and Tuesday the slowest. In this case, the customer base could be divided (e.g., alphabetically) and each segment offered a discount price on a particular day. Other ideas include providing a complimentary

cup of coffee to anyone bringing in laundry on Monday. These promotions can be implemented once demand fluctuations are observed. Attention also must be given to holidays, which may create temporary surges or lulls in business.

Questions
1. Prepare a service blueprint for Commuter Cleaning.
2. What generic approach to service system design is illustrated by Commuter Cleaning, and what competitive advantages does this design offer?
3. Using the data in Table 5.7, calculate a break-even price per shirt if monthly demand is expected to be 20,000 shirts and the contract with a cleaning plant stipulates a charge of $0.50 per shirt.
4. Critique the business concept, and make suggestions for improvement.

TABLE 5.7

COMMUTER CLEANING ECONOMIC ANALYSIS

Expense item	Monthly amount	Assumptions
Transit station rent	$2,800	7 locations at $400 each
Delivery van	500	1 minivan (includes lease payment and insurance)
Station customer service representatives	5,544	7 locations, 2 shifts averaging 3 hours per shift at $6 per hour
Driver	528	1 driver, 2 shifts averaging 2 hours per shift at $6 per hour
Fuel	165	30 miles per shift at 12 mpg and $1.50 per gallon
Business insurance	100	
Office customer service representatives	4,000	2 office workers each paid $24,000 a year
Laundry bags	167	Cost of 1,000 laundry bags at $2 each, amortized over one year
Total monthly expenses	$13,804	22-day month

CASE

Golfsmith

Do you like to slog for miles in dewy grass, hunt for very small objects lurking in knee-high underbrush, nurse a sore elbow, get strafed by errant dimpled objects, and get attacked by rogue sprinklers? If so, we have a game for you . . . and the business to help you enjoy it! Golfsmith International Inc., based in Austin, Texas, is the world's largest distributor of golf equipment. The company was founded in 1967 and has grown from a club-assembly operation that distributed its products only by mail-order to an operation that provides every golf-related product and service imaginable, either by mail-order or in showrooms in the U.S. and Canada. The showrooms offer "extra" services that distinguish the company from its competitors.

In recent years, golf has become a sport for everyone rather than for just the socially and financially elite. Caddies and Cadillac owners alike can aspire to the PGA. This has opened a large new and diverse market that includes do-it-yourselfers who want to make their own clubs and those who want them ready-made. All of these Tiger Woods, Jack Nicholas, Babe Didrikson Zaharias or Patty Berg "wannabes," however, want high-quality, reasonably priced equipment, and Golfsmith has the goods for them.

COMPETITION/MARKET

Golfsmith's primary direct competitors include companies such as Dynacraft Golf Products, Inc., and Ralph Maltby's GolfWorks, both located in Newark, Ohio. Direct competitors are those that compete with

Golfsmith for customers in all of the same market segments. Dynacraft is geared primarily to helping customers make their own clubs. The company offers a technical assistance hotline and sponsors a school, the Dynacraft Clubmaking Institute, that provides "hands-on training in the art of clubmaking." Dynacraft also provides "how-to" publications and videos, and a quarterly magazine for clubmakers.

GolfWorks is also dedicated to clubmaking and, like Dynacraft, offers technical assistance and publications. This company has recently acquired CAD/CAM technology and CNC machining and is noted for its innovation in component design. GolfWorks also operates a pro shop, practice golf links, and a club-repair van on the pro golf tours.

Golfsmith is subject to indirect competition from other businesses, such as golf course pro shops, sporting goods stores, and discount department stores that sell ready-made clubs and accessories.

RECENT DEVELOPMENTS AT GOLFSMITH

We noted that Golfsmith began its life about three decades ago as a supplier and assembler of golf club components. The business grew rapidly and dominated the field as a mail-order business by using state-of-the-art technology to take and assemble orders. Order-takers transcribe orders into a computerized system that creates bar-code labels. A label for a particular order is placed on a large plastic tub. The tub then makes a journey around a conveyor system where a sequence of bar-code scanners signal "robots" to retrieve the appropriate items from shelves and deposit them in the tub. When the order is complete, the items are packaged for delivery and loaded onto a waiting UPS truck, and the tub is ready for another circuit of the Golfsmith course. An order can be ready for shipment within minutes of being received from the customer. This automated and highly efficient system represents an enormous competitive advantage for Golfsmith.

Golfsmith has not rested on its early success—it has broadened its target market to include all golf enthusiasts, rather than just those who want customized clubs. The company now operates 25 stores in the United States and Canada, including "superstores" in Austin and Los Angeles and its headquarters facility. The 41-acre headquarters in Austin is home to the Golfsmith Learning and Practice Facility, which includes a 100-station practice range with sheltered hit-ting positions, a 5,000-square-foot putting green, a 2,400-square-foot chipping green, and two sand traps. The facility is home to Golfsmith's Harvey Penick Golf Academy and attracts golfers from all over the world. Ponds, waterfalls, rock escarpments, and native plants surround the links and create an award-winning environment.

GOLFSMITH TRANSITION

In recent years, Golfsmith has moved from selling only components and assembly tools to making and fixing golf clubs and marketing and selling golf accessories. The company's catalog includes everything from custom-printed golf balls to electronic distance estimators.

After 32 years of assembling golf components and shipping them to about 90 countries, Golfsmith has become the largest mail-order supplier of golf equipment and accessories in the world. Golfsmith presently employs 1,800 people, including 26 golf professionals, and processes about 8,000 web and catalog orders per day. The company has taken more than 14,000 calls in one day.

AT HOME WITH GOLFSMITH

Golfsmith's headquarters and Learning and Practice facility occupy 41 acres. The headquarters building houses the entire operation, including open office space, an area for about 250 phone-order-taking stations, the warehouse and order-assembly facility, a large retail showroom, and the Clubhouse Café, where customers can buy drinks and snacks and watch golf programming on several television screens. Visitors are enthusiastically greeted at the door by an employee wearing golf attire. Specialists are available to advise customers and assess their needs, if desired. All employees of Golfsmith, including those who take phone orders, are very knowledgeable and can "speak golfese" fluently.

A tour of the facility gives the visitor a sense of the corporate culture. The office space, even that of the officers, is open. Communication across functional boundaries in this environment is easy, and the officers are always available to all employees. Even the banks of phones where orders are received avoid conveying the feeling of anonymous minions stuck in their hidey-holes. The overriding sense is that everyone associated with Golfsmith seems to live, breathe, and talk golf. The company's strong commitment to customer service and its employees' high level of expertise and enthusiasm create a unique atmosphere.

Questions

1. Prepare a service blueprint for Golfsmith.
2. What generic approach to service system design does Golfsmith illustrate and what competitive advantages does this design offer?
3. Why is Golfsmith a good candidate for Internet sales?

SELECTED BIBLIOGRAPHY

BEHARA, RAVI S.: "Process Innovation in Knowledge-Intensive Services," in J. A. Fitzsimmons and M. J. Fitzsimmons (eds.), *New Service Development,* Sage Publications, Thousand Oaks, Calif., 2000, pp. 138–151.

BERRY, LEONARD L., AND SANDRA K. LAMPO: "Teaching an Old Service New Tricks: The Promise of Service Redesign," *Journal of Service Research,* vol. 2, no. 3, February 2000, pp. 265–275.

BOONE, TONYA: "Exploring the Link between Product and Process Innovation in Services," in J. A. Fitzsimmons and M. J. Fitzsimmons (eds.), *New Service Development,* Sage Publications, Thousand Oaks, Calif., 2000, pp. 92–110.

BOWEN, DAVID E., and WILLIAM E. YOUNGDAHL: "Lean Service: In Defense of a Production-Line Approach," *International Journal of Service Industry Management,* vol. 9, no. 3, 1998, pp. 207–225.

CLARK, GRAHAM, ROBERT JOHNSTON, and MIKE SHULVER: "Exploiting the Service Concept for Service Design and Development," in J. A. Fitzsimmons and M. J. Fitzsimmons (eds.), *New Service Development,* Sage Publications, Thousand Oaks, Calif., 2000, pp. 71–91.

EDVARDSSON, BO, LARS HAGLUND, and JAN MATTSSON: "Analysis, Planning, Improvisation and Control in the Development of New Services," *International Journal of Service Industry Management,* vol. 6, no. 2, 1995, pp. 24–35.

GILMORE, JAMES, and JOSEPH PINE: "The Four Faces of Mass Customization," *Harvard Business Review,* January–February 1997, pp. 91–101.

GUPTA, SUDHEER, and MIRJANA VAJIC: "The Contextual and Dialectical Nature of Experiences," in J. A. Fitzsimmons and M. J. Fitzsimmons (eds.), *New Service Development,* Sage Publications, Thousand Oaks, Calif., 2000, pp. 33–51.

HAYNES, RAY M., and EMIL A. THIES: "Management of Technology in Service Firms," *Journal of Operations Management,* vol. 10, no. 3, August 1991, pp. 388–397.

JOHNSON, SUSAN P., LARRY S. MENOR, ALETA V. ROTH, and RICHARD B. CHASE: "A Critical Evaluation of the New Service Development Process: Integrating Service Innovation and Service Design," in J. A. Fitzsimmons and M. J. Fitzsimmons (eds.), *New Service Development,* Sage Publications, Thousand Oaks, Calif., 2000, pp. 1–32.

KINGMAN-BRUNDAGE, JANE: "Technology, Design, and Service Quality," *International Journal of Service Industry Management,* vol. 2, no. 3, 1991, pp. 47–59.

LEONARD, DOROTHY, and JEFFREY RAYPORT: "Spark Innovation through Empathic Design," *Harvard Business Review,* November–December 1997, pp. 102–113.

MARTIN, CLAUDE R., JR. and DAVID A. HORNE: "Services Innovation: Successful versus Unsuccessful Firms," *International Journal of Service Industry Management,* vol. 4, no. 4, 1993, pp. 49–65.

PULLMAN, MADELEINE E., and WILLIAM L. MOORE: "Optimal Service Design: Integrating Marketing and Operations Perspectives," *International Journal of Service Industry Management,* vol. 10, no. 2, 1999, pp. 239–260.

RUST, ROLAND T., and RICHARD W. OLIVER: "The Real Time Service Product: Conquering Customer Time and Space," in J. A. Fitzsimmons and M. J. Fitzsimmons (eds.), *New Service Development,* Sage Publications, Thousand Oaks, Calif., 2000, pp. 52–70.

STUART, F. IAN: "The Influence of Organizational Culture and Internal Politics on New Service Design and Introduction," *International Journal of Service Industry Management,* vol. 9, no. 5, 1998, pp. 469–485.

TREACY, MICHAEL, and FRED WIERSEMA: "Customer Intimacy and Other Value Disciplines," *Harvard Business Review,* January–February 1993, pp. 84–93.

VERMA, ROHIT, GARY M. THOMPSON, and JORDAN J. LOVIERE: "Configuring Service Operations Based on Customer Needs and Preferences," *Journal of Service Research,* vol. 1, no. 3, February 1999, pp. 262–274.

WATHEN, SAMUEL, and JOHN C. ANDERSON: "Designing Services: An Information-Processing Approach," *International Journal of Service Industry Management,* vol. 6, no. 1, 1995, pp. 64–76.

ENDNOTES

1. David A. Collier, "The Service Sector Revolution: The Automation of Services," *Long Range Planning,* vol. 16, no. 6, December 1983, p. 11.

2. Adapted from Robert P. Radchuck, "Step-by-Step into High Tech," *CA Magazine*, vol. 115, no. 6, June 1982, pp. 72–73.

3. Adapted from G. Lynn Shostack, "Designing Services That Deliver," *Harvard Business Review,* January–February 1984, pp. 133–139.

4. G. Lynn Shostack, "Service Positioning through Structural Change," *Journal of Marketing,* vol. 51, January 1987, pp. 34–43.

5. Theodore Levitt, "Production-Line Approach to Service," *Harvard Business Review,* September–October 1972, pp. 41–52.

6. Richard B. Chase, "Where Does the Customer Fit in a Service Operation?" *Harvard Business Review,* November–December 1978, pp. 137–142.

7. R. B. Chase and N. J. Aquilano, "A Matrix for Linking Marketing and Production Variables in Service System Design," *Production and Operations Management,* 6th ed., Irwin, Homewood, Ill., 1992.

8. Reprinted with permission from Sang M. Lee, "Japanese Management and the 100 Yen Sushi House," *Operations Management Review,* Winter 1983, pp. 46–48.

9. Prepared by Mara Segal under the supervision of Professor James A. Fitzsimmons.

CHAPTER SIX

The Supporting Facility

Learning Objectives

After completing this chapter, you should be able to:

1. Discuss the impact of the "servicescape" on the behavior of customers and employees.
2. Describe the critical design features of a service supporting facility.
3. Identify the bottleneck operation in a product layout, and regroup activities to create new jobs that will increase the overall service capacity.
4. Use operations sequence analysis to determine the relative locations of departments in a process layout that minimize total flow-distance.
5. Prepare a process flowchart for a service operation.
6. Recommend facility design features to remove the anxiety of disorientation.

Subtle differences in facility design are important. Consider customers' perceptions of the two leading discount giants, Kmart and Wal-Mart. In several independent surveys, shoppers have said they are more satisfied with Wal-Mart and generally view Wal-Mart with higher esteem than they do Kmart.[1] These companies offer similar merchandise at almost identical prices, and they operate stores that appear to be similar. What could explain this difference in customer perceptions?

On closer scrutiny, we find subtle differences in store decor and layout. At Wal-Mart, the main aisles are wider than those at Kmart. In addition, fluorescent lighting is recessed into the ceiling, creating a softer impression than the glare from the exposed fixtures at Kmart. The apparel departments are carpeted in a warm, autumnal orange, while Kmart's are tiled in off-white. Together, such features signal consumers that Wal-Mart is more upscale and that it carries merchandise of a little better quality than at Kmart. Wal-Mart's attention to the details of facility design has helped to shape shoppers' attitudes by striking that delicate balance needed to convince customers that its prices are low without making those customers feel cheap.

Wal-Mart has successfully used facility design to differentiate itself from its competitors. Using facility design as part of a differentiation strategy is very common. For example, the A-frame structure and blue roof of IHOP (International House of Pancakes) attract travelers to a pancake breakfast just as the "golden arches" of McDonald's signal a hamburger lunch.

Using a standard, or "formula," facility is an important feature in the overall cost leadership strategy. Major gasoline retailers have perfected the design of their service stations to facilitate construction (often completed within two weeks) and lower costs, and to create a consistent image awareness that will attract customers.

For theme restaurants and bars (e.g., a western bar, an Irish pub), facility design is central to the focus strategy of targeting a particular market and creating a unique ambiance. In retail banking, however, tradition still reigns, except for an innovative bank with headquarters in Columbus, Ohio, called Banc One. Banc One has designed branches that look more like mini-shopping malls than banks, with glass atriums, "boutiques" offering special services, signs of blue neon, comfortable seating areas, and fresh coffee. With its community focus, Banc One even has branches that are open on Saturdays and Sundays.[2]

CHAPTER PREVIEW

This chapter begins with a discussion of servicescapes, the idea that the physical environment influences the behavior and perception of the service for both customers and workers. Facility design issues are addressed with respect to objectives of the service, its space requirements, flexibility, aesthetic factors, and the environment. Facility layout is discussed with attention to traffic flow, space planning, and the need to avoid unnecessary travel. The concept of process flow analysis used by industrial engineers is modified for service operations and illustrated by a restaurant study in which a new credit card processing procedure is evaluated.

The traditional product and process layouts from manufacturing are shown to have service counterparts and can be studied using the techniques of assembly-line balancing and relative location analysis. Finally, the topic of disorientation caused by poor layouts is treated from an environmental psychology viewpoint, and the importance of signage is stressed.

SERVICESCAPES[3]

The physical environment or *servicescape* of the supporting service facility influences both customer and employee behavior and should be designed with an image and feel that is congruent with the service concept. A typology of servicescapes shown in Figure 6.1 is organized according to who participates within the service environment and the degree of complexity of the servicescape.

Because of the absence of employees, the servicescape for a self-service operation plays a central role in guiding customer behavior through the use of signage (e.g., direction to the next tee) and intuitive design of interfaces (e.g., hot buttons on a website). For remote services, employee satisfaction, motivation, and operational

Who performs within servicescape	Physical complexity of the servicescape	
	Elaborate	Lean
Self-service (customer only)	Golf course Water slide park	Post office kiosk ATM E-commerce website
Interpersonal services (both customer and employee)	Luxury hotel Restaurant Disneyland Airline terminal	Budget motel Hot dog stand Roadside snake farm Bus station
Remote service (employee only)	Professional services L.L. Bean	Telemarketing Online technical support

FIGURE 6.1 Typology of servicescapes.
(*Source:* Adapted from Mary Jo Bitner, "Servicescapes: The Impact of Physical Surroundings on Customers and Employees," *Journal of Marketing,* vol. 56, April 1992, p. 59.)

efficiency are the primary physical design objectives because customers do not visit the site physically. Offices of professional services such as those of lawyers and physicians, however, should project competence and authority. Interpersonal services are the most challenging because social interaction between employees and customers and among customers should be facilitated by the servicescape. For example, the servicescape at Disneyland is famous for creating a fantasy experience for customers and a stage for employees (i.e., cast members).

Consider the photographs of two restaurant servicescapes. Note how the table settings, furniture, floor covering, and even customer attire communicate distinct expectations for customers and employees alike.

Behaviors in Servicescapes

As shown in Figure 6.2, a mix of environmental dimensions consisting of ambient conditions, space/function, and signs/symbols/artifacts describes the servicescape, which is viewed as a holistic environment by customers and employees. The internal response measured cognitively, emotionally, and physiologically is moderated by one's personal mood state (e.g., happy, depressed, anxious, or excited) and tendency to seek or avoid arousal. Arousal-seekers enjoy and look for high levels of stimulation (e.g., a bright and loud disco), whereas arousal-avoiders prefer lower levels of stimulation (e.g., a quiet museum). The servicescape is designed to invoke social interaction between and among customers and employees. A well-conceived servicescape will encourage an approach behavior for both employees (e.g., commitment and desire to remain with the firm) and customers (e.g., exploration, spending money, and returning).

Because the physical environment elicits an emotional response and influences behavior, the design of the service facility can intentionally mold the behavior of the participants to support the organization's goals. Thus, unpleasant environments that are also high in arousal (lots of stimulation, noise, confusion) are to be avoided.

Different servicescapes, from table settings to furniture and room design, create different expectations and behaviors for employees and customers.

FIGURE 6.2 Servicescape framework.
(*Source:* Mary Jo Bitner, "Servicescapes: The Impact of Physical Surroundings on Customers and Employees," *Journal of Marketing,* vol. 56, April 1992, p. 60.)

Environmental Dimensions of Servicescapes

The dimensions of the physical environment surroundings include all the objective factors that can be controlled by the firm to enhance employee and customer actions and perceptions of the service. Although these dimensions will be discussed independently, it is important to realize that people respond to their environment holistically; that is, the total combined effect on all our senses defines our perception of the servicescape.

Ambient Conditions The background of our environment, such as temperature, lighting, noise, music, and scent, affects all five of our senses. Music tempo, for example, can affect a customer's pace of shopping, length of stay, and amount of money spent. Consider a convenience store that played "elevator music" successfully to drive away teenagers who were loitering and discouraging paying customers from entering the store. Mrs. Fields' Cookies purposely leaves its doors open at its busy mall locations to invite customers with the fragrance of freshly baked cookies. All of these factors, including color of surroundings, also influence employee performance and job satisfaction.

Spatial Layout and Functionality The arrangement of furnishings and equipment and the relationships among them create a visual and functional landscape for delivery of the service. This landscape can communicate order and efficiency or chaos and uncertainty for both employees and customers. For self-service activities, the functionality or ease of use of equipment is important to allow customers to perform unattended activities. Fast-food restaurants purposely design the facility to communicate visually the appropriate activities of diners. Menus are posted over the cash registers, self-serve drink machines are positioned between the counter and the tables, and waste containers are located near exits.

Signs, Symbols, and Artifacts   Many items in the physical environment serve as explicit or implicit signals that communicate acceptable norms of behavior. Explicit signs such as "no smoking" communicate rules of behavior, whereas "recycle bins" encourage responsible acts. The quality of the floor covering, artwork, and furnishings can create an overall aesthetic impression for the visitor and a pleasant workplace for the employee. Professional services can use interior decorating to communicate competence and enhance their professional image with the client. Restaurants communicate full service and high prices with signs such as pictures of famous diners, symbols such as tablecloths, and artifacts such as antiques or pottery. Studies of faculty offices indicate that desk placement, selection of wall pictures or posters, and tidiness of the office influence students' beliefs about the person who occupies the office.

Our discussion of servicescapes suggests that the physical environment may assume a variety of strategic roles in support of the service concept. First, the servicescape provides a visual metaphor for an organization's offering. The environmental dimensions of the servicescape create a package, similar to a product's package, to convey an image suggesting the potential usage and relative quality of the service. Consider the message the servicescape of Home Depot invokes in customers.

Second, the servicescape can facilitate the delivery of the service by either aiding or hindering the ability of customers and employees to carry out their respective activities. The floorplan, layout of equipment, and equipment design impact the user friendliness of the facility and the ability to serve customers effectively. Notice how the layout of a website can facilitate the screen-to-face interaction. The servicescape can also encourage social interaction between employees and customers. The layout of a waiting room that has chairs grouped together around tables encourages social interaction and the pleasant passing of time.

Finally, the physical environment can serve as a market differentiator by signaling the intended market segment (e.g., cars parked around the perimeter of a budget motel) and conveying distinctiveness from competitors.

FACILITY DESIGN

Service operations can be directly affected by the design of the facility. For example, a restaurant with inadequate ventilation for nonsmoking diners may discourage many customers. Alternatively, a physical fitness center with easy wheelchair access may be able to enlarge its services to include a new clientele.

Design and layout represent the supporting facility component of the *service package.* Together, they influence how a service facility is used and, sometimes, if it is even used at all. Consider again Toronto's Shouldice Hospital (discussed in Chapter 4). A good portion of its success in repairing inguinal hernias results from thoughtful facility design and layout. For example, operating rooms are grouped together so that surgeons may consult with each other easily during procedures. Because early ambulation promotes faster healing, the hospital is designed to provide ample pleasant places to walk—and even to climb a few steps. Meals are served only in community dining rooms rather than in patient rooms, which requires more walking and, as an added benefit, allows patients to get together and "compare notes." While functional and comfortable, patient rooms are not equipped with "extras" such as television sets, which might encourage patients to "lie around."

Other factors of design and layout can be "urgent." Consider the generally inadequate supply of rest-room facilities for women in most public buildings, especially during mass entertainment events. During intermission at your next concert or play, observe how long it takes individual females and males to use the rest rooms. Do you see any evidence of "potty parity" being designed into the building? In addition, count the number of rest rooms for men and the number for women in your classroom building. Chances are that equal numbers exist for each gender, but this does not necessarily ensure equality of access.

Clearly, good design and layout enhance the service, from attracting customers to making them feel more comfortable to ensuring their safety (e.g., adequate lighting, fire exits, proper location of dangerous equipment). Facility design also has an impact on the implicit service component of the service package—in particular, on criteria like privacy and security, atmosphere, and sense of well-being.

Several factors influence design: (1) the nature and objectives of the service organization, (2) land availability and space requirements, (3) flexibility, (4) aesthetic factors, and (5) the community and environment.

Nature and Objectives of Service Organizations

The nature of the core service should dictate the parameters of its design. For example, a fire station must have a structure that is large enough to house its vehicles, on-duty personnel, and maintenance equipment. A bank must be designed to accommodate some type of vault. Physicians' offices come in many shapes and sizes, but all must be designed to afford patients some degree of privacy.

Beyond such fundamental requirements, however, design can contribute much more to defining the service. It can engender immediate recognition, as in the case of McDonald's arches or IHOP's blue roof. External design also can provide a clue about the nature of the service inside. One would expect to see well-manicured grounds, freshly painted or marble columns, and perhaps a fountain in front of a funeral home. A school, however, might have colorful tiles on its facade and certainly a playground or athletic field nearby.

Appropriateness of design is important as well. A gasoline service station can be constructed of brightly colored, prefabricated sheet metal; however, would you deposit money in a bank that was using a trailer on wheels for a temporary branch?

Land Availability and Space Requirements

The land that is available for a service facility often comes with many constraints, such as costs, zoning requirements, and actual area. Good design must accommodate all these constraints. In an urban setting, where land is at a premium, buildings only can be expanded upward, and organizations often must exhibit great creativity and ingenuity in their designs to use a relatively small space efficiently. For example, in some urban areas (e.g., in Copenhagen), McDonald's has incorporated a second-floor loft to provide eating space.

Suburban and rural areas frequently offer larger, more affordable parcels of land that ameliorate the space constraints of urban facilities. Many sites, however, and especially urban ones, may have strict zoning laws on land usage and ordinances governing the exterior appearance of structures. Space for off-street parking also is a requirement. In any event, space for future expansion always should be considered.

Flexibility

Successful services are dynamic organizations that can adapt to changes in the quantity and nature of demand. How well a service can adapt depends greatly on the flexibility that has been designed into it. Flexibility also might be called "designing for the future." Questions to address during the design phase might be: how can this facility be designed to allow for later expansion of present services, and how can we design this facility to accommodate new and different services in the future? For example, many of the original fast-food restaurants built for walk-in traffic have had to modify their facilities to accommodate customer demands for drive-through window service.

Several airports face facility problems today because designers failed to anticipate either the tremendous growth in the numbers of people flying or the advent of the "hub-and-spoke" airline network following deregulation. Consequently, passengers often must tote carry-on luggage through a maze of stairways and long passageways to reach the departure gate of their connecting flights. In addition, consider the frustration facing passengers trying to retrieve checked luggage from a baggage-handling operation that was designed for circa 1960s air travelers!

Designing for the future often can translate into financial savings. For example, consider a church that locates in a developing community but does not have the resources to build the sanctuary it would like plus the necessary ancillary facilities it will need. Good design might lead the congregation to build a modest structure that can be used as a temporary sanctuary but later adapted easily and economically to serve as a fellowship hall, a Sunday school, and even a day care facility to meet the needs of a growing community.

In other instances, designing for the future may require additional expenses initially, but it will save financial resources in the long run. In fact, it may provide for growth that might not be possible otherwise. For example, cities often invest in oversized water and wastewater treatment plants in anticipation of future growth.

Aesthetic Factors

Compare two shopping trips to successful, upscale clothing stores. First, we go to an upscale department store such as Nordstrom's. As we enter the women's fine dresses department, we are aware of the carpeting beneath our feet, the ample space between clothing racks, the lack of crowding of dresses on the racks, the complimentary lighting, and most certainly, the very well-groomed salesperson who is ready to serve us immediately. Fitting rooms are located in an area separate from the display area, are roomy and carpeted, and have mirrors on three sides so that you can appreciate every aspect of your appearance. Everything in the department is designed to give a sense of elegance and attention to our needs.

Our second trip takes us to an Eddie Bauer Factory Outlet store. Within just a few steps of the entrance, we are confronted by tables piled high with a vast assortment of clothing. Along the walls and among the tables are racks packed as full as possible with more clothing. Only a maze of narrow pathways is visible around the floor. Salespersons are stationed at cash-register counters and are available to help when you seek them out. Fitting rooms are small "stalls" on the showroom floor and are equipped with only one mirror. (It helps to shop here with a companion, who can give you the advantage of "hindsight.") This is a large warehouse type of store rather than a modest-sized, serene, elegant place to shop; however, the outlet store offers great bargains in exchange for sacrificing plushness and lots of personal attention.

Both stores offer attractive, quality clothing. We feel very different in each one, however, and their respective designs have played an important part in shaping our attitudes. Clearly, the aesthetic aspects of a design have a marked effect on the consumer's perceptions and behaviors, but they also affect the employees and the service they provide. Lack of attention to aesthetic factors during the design phase can lead to surly service rather than to "service with a smile."

The Community and Environment

The design of a service facility may be of greatest importance where it affects the community and its environment. Will the planned church allow enough space for parking, or will neighbors find it impossible to enter or exit their properties during church activities? Can Priscilla Price design a boarding kennel facility that will not "hound" neighboring businesses with undue noise and odor? How can a community design a detention facility that will provide adequately for the inmates' health and welfare yet still ensure the safety of the town's residents? Has the local dry cleaner designed his or her facility to keep hazardous chemicals out of the local environment?

These questions illustrate how crucial facility design can be in gaining community acceptance of a service. Zoning regulations and many public interest groups also can provide guidance in designing service facilities that are compatible with their communities and environment.

FACILITY LAYOUT

In addition to facility design, the layout, or arrangement, of the service delivery system is important for the convenience of the customer as well as the service provider. No customer should be subjected to unnecessary aggravation from a poorly planned facility. Further, a poor layout can be costly in time that is wasted when service workers are engaged in unproductive activity. Consider the following experience of a citizen attempting to secure a building permit.

Suppose you want to build the home of your dreams. You have ordered plan #1006BHG from Columbia Design Group in Portland, Oregon, for its "Cozy Cottage." You have found just the right spot of land overlooking the lake and are eager to get that hammer in your hand. Are you all set to go now? Not quite. There is just one small detail: a building permit. You make a quick phone call to the county's building inspection department and are advised that obtaining a permit is very easy: "Just come downtown to our office and pay $200, and we'll take care of you." No problem, you think; you can handle that.

You arrive at the county services building with check in hand. (You did park in a legal spot, right?) A check of the black-felt signboard in the front lobby tells you that the building inspection department is in Office 3 1. (Is that supposed to be 31, or has a little white number fallen off?) Office 31 is on this floor, so you check there first. It turns out to be a rest room. You go to the third floor and find the office across from the elevator—the building inspector's office—a small, dark, dingy, windowless room with a high counter just inside the doorway. A surly old man levers himself out of a protesting chair behind a desk piled high with pink, turquoise, beige, and yellow papers. A coffee pot and a mountain of multihued papers are strewn on a table along one wall. The old man hobbles over to the counter to help you—at least there aren't 20 people in line ahead of you—and after hearing what you want, says that you are in the wrong office, that he just assigns inspectors to issue permits for occupancy at the end of construction. You have to go to "the other wing."

"The other wing" requires a return to the lobby, a check of the black-felt board, and a ride in another elevator—assuming the elevator is working. Just inside the door of Office 333 is a sign: "Take a number and sit." Your number is 21, and there are eight chairs facing a high counter. The room is well lit and has 10 desks arranged in three rows behind the counter. There are two doors to back rooms on the east wall, and file cabinets line the west wall. Large maps are posted on the back wall. While waiting, you observe (many times) the typical interaction between an employee and a customer. They exchange pleasantries; then the employee goes to the first back room and returns with a packet of papers. The papers are shuffled back and forth between the employee and the customer, with each signing or making notations in turn. The packet is taken to the other back room and replaced by yet another packet, and the little waltz of fluttering papers and flying pens is repeated to the tune of subdued murmurs. This packet is reassembled and returned to the first office. The employee then retrieves a form from one of the file cabinets, fills it out (three pages in triplicate) on a typewriter at one of the desks, places two copies in other file cabinets, and, finally, hands the customer the treasured building permit.

After you witness 20 variations on this theme, it is your turn. You ask for your building permit. The employee goes to the first back room and returns empty-handed, saying, "I can't seem to find your other permits."

"What other permits?" you ask.

"Why, electrical connection, water connection, and sewage connection permits, of course."

You explain that you are building by the lake and will not be on a community water or sewage system; you are going to have a well and a septic tank.

"Oh, then you need to file a geologist's report, a ground percolation test report, and permits to install a septic tank and a leach field before we can issue your building permit—and you'll still need to get the electrical permit. I can tell you where to go, if you like."

This episode illustrates the effect of design and layout on service providers and consumers. Providers' attitudes and responsiveness can be influenced profoundly by their surroundings and the work patterns imposed on them by the layout of their work space.

Sometimes, solutions are relatively easy. In our example, consider your first stop, the building inspection office. With adequate lighting and rearrangement of the furniture so that applicants could approach the employee's desk, the employee might be disposed to tell the customer how to find the building permit office—and also that preliminary permits and reports are necessary before a building permit can be issued. In addition, rearrangement of the work space in the building permit office might allow more efficient service by saving steps and time. These savings would translate into employees who provide service more quickly and, consequently, with more equanimity, because they would not have to deal with applicants who have grown surly during interminable waiting. Service could be improved even further by posting signs at the front desk detailing what preliminary permits and reports must be filed before the building permit can be issued, and this simple measure would benefit the provider and the customer alike.

A larger-scale improvement in layout could be considered as well. The building inspector's office, the building permit office, and other allied permit offices could be relocated in close proximity to each other within the building. Perhaps some offices could be combined physically, allowing easier communication between employees on related matters. Here again, customers would reap the benefits of more efficient service, reduced travel time between offices, and reduced waiting time.

Many improvements can be achieved with little cost either to the service provider or the consumer. In other situations, the layout of a service organization may involve significant expense, which would necessitate a critical analysis before implementation. Along these lines, we next consider two basic layout forms, product layout and process layout, each with its own associated challenge.

Product Layout and the Line-Balancing Problem

Some standard services can be divided into an inflexible sequence of steps or operations that all customers must experience. This is an example of a *product layout* most often associated with manufacturing assembly lines, where a product is assembled in a fixed sequence of steps. The most obvious analogy is to a cafeteria, where diners push their trays along as they assemble their meal. Staffing such a service requires allocating tasks among servers to create jobs that require nearly equal time. The job requiring the most time per customer creates a *bottleneck* and defines the capacity of the service line. Any change in the capacity of the service line requires that attention be given to the bottleneck activity. Several options are available: adding another worker to the job, providing some aid to reduce the activity time, or regrouping the tasks to create a new line balance with different activity assignments. A well-balanced line would have all jobs be of nearly equal duration to avoid unnecessary idleness and inequity in work assignments. A service-line approach has the additional advantage of allowing for division of labor and use of dedicated special equipment, as illustrated by Example 6.1.

Example 6.1: Automobile Driver's License Office

The state automobile driver's license office is under pressure to increase its productivity to accommodate 120 applicants per hour with the addition of only one clerk to its present staff. The license renewal process currently is designed as a service line, with customers being processed in the fixed sequence listed in Table 6.1. Activity 1 (i.e., review application for correctness) must be performed first, and activity 6 (i.e., issue temporary license) must be the last step and, by state policy, be handled by a uniformed officer. Activity 5 (i.e., photograph applicant) requires an expensive instant camera.

The process flow diagram for the current arrangement, as shown in Figure 6.3*a*, identifies the bottleneck activity (i.e., the activity with the slowest flow rate per hour) as activity 3 (i.e., check for violations and restrictions), which limits the current capacity to 60 applicants per hour. By focusing only on the bottleneck, one might think that assigning the additional clerk to perform activity 3 would double the flow through the bottleneck and achieve the goal of 120 applicants per hour. However, the flow for

TABLE 6.1		
LICENSE RENEWAL PROCESS TIMES		
Activity	**Description**	**Time, sec.**
1	Review application for correctness	15
2	Process and record payment	30
3	Check for violations and restrictions	60
4	Conduct eye test	40
5	Photograph applicant	20
6	Issue temporary license (state trooper)	30

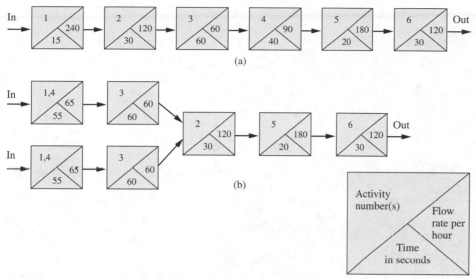

FIGURE 6.3 (*a*) Present and (*b*) proposed flow diagrams.

this system would be limited to 90 applicants per hour, because the bottleneck would shift to activity 4.

The proposed process design, as shown in Figure 6.3*b* with seven clerks, can achieve the desired capacity of 120 applicants per hour, because activities 1 and 4 have been grouped together to create a new job (i.e., review applications for correctness and conduct eye test) that better balances the work load among the staff. How did we know to group these two activities together? First, remember that a flow rate of at least 120 applicants per hour must be achieved at each step in the process. Because activities 2 and 6 already are being performed at this rate, they need not be considered further. An additional clerk is required to perform activity 3, however, because only with two clerks working in parallel can we achieve a combined flow rate of 120 applicants per hour. Next, we must ask if it is possible to combine activities requiring small amounts of time to arrive at a job that can be performed in 60 seconds or less (i.e., achieve a flow rate of at least 60 applicants per hour). By combining activity 1, which requires 15 seconds, with activity 4, which requires 40 seconds, we can achieve a combined job requiring 55 seconds per applicant (or a flow rate of 65 applicants per hour). Note that this solution requires the acquisition of one additional eye-testing machine. Another solution would be to combine activities 4 and 5 to create a job yielding a flow rate of 60 applicants per hour; however, an additional expensive camera would need to be purchased. Can you think of another process design that meets the capacity goal but could be viewed by customers and employees as offering more personalized service?

The example of the driver's license office lends itself to a radical rethinking of the product layout. If money were available to invest in computers, additional eye-testing equipment, and cameras, then the entire process could be reengineered. Consider training each clerk to perform all five activities with a combined time of 165 seconds, or an individual flow rate of approximately 22 customers per hour. Now, an arriving customer would be faced with choosing from among six clerks working in parallel, as shown in Figure 6.4. This system would be appealing to customers, however, because one clerk would handle all the transactions and, thus, customers would not be passed

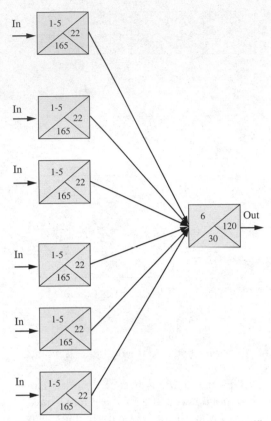

FIGURE 6.4 Reengineered driver's license office.

from one clerk to another and be required to wait in between. Further, one would expect that the total time could be shortened because information would not need to be repeated as before. Finally, staffing of the office would now be flexible because only the number of clerks required to meet anticipated demand need be on duty. This savings in labor could justify easily the investment in six work stations.

Process Layout and the Relative Location Problem

The earlier example of obtaining a building permit illustrates a *process layout,* because service personnel performing similar functions or having the same responsibility were grouped into departments. A process layout allows the customers to define the sequence of service activities to meet their needs and, thus, affords some degree of customization. The process layout also allows the service to be tailored to the customer's specifications, thereby delivering personalized services. The ability to customize service requires more highly skilled service providers, who have discretion to personalize the service to customers' needs. Professional services such as law, medicine, and consulting, which are organized into specialties, provide examples.

From the service provider's perspective, the flow of customers appears to be intermittent, so there is a need for a waiting area in each department. The variability in demand at each department results when customers choose different sequences of services and place different demands on the service provided. On arriving at a particular department, customers often will find it busy and will need to join a queue, which usually operates on a first-come, first-served basis (FCFS).

A dramatic and physical example of a service process layout is a university campus with buildings dedicated to various disciplines, giving students the flexibility of choosing classes from among them. The relative location problem can be seen in the layout of the campus. For both student and faculty convenience, we would expect selected departments such as engineering and physical sciences to be in close proximity to each other, while perhaps economics and business administration would be located together in another area. The library and administration offices would be located in a central part of the campus. One possible objective for selecting such a layout would be to minimize the total distance traveled by faculty, staff, and students between all pairs of departments. Many different layouts are possible, however. In fact, if we have identified n departments to be assigned to n locations, then n factorial layouts (i.e., 3,628,800 layouts for 10 departments) are possible. Because finding the best layout among these possibilities is beyond complete enumeration, we will use a heuristic approach to finding a good layout in Example 6.2.

Example 6.2: Ocean World Theme Park

The architect for Ocean World is beginning to formulate plans for the development of property outside Waco, Texas, for a second marine theme park after the success of its Neptune's Realm on the West Coast. Because of the hot and humid Texas weather during the summer months, ways to minimize the visitors' total travel distance between attractions are being considered. Data showing a typical day's flow of visitors between attractions at San Diego are given in Table 6.2 and will be used in the layout planning.

A heuristic called *operations sequence analysis* will be used to identify a good layout for this relative location problem.[4] This method uses as input the matrix of flows between departments and a grid showing the geographic center location for department assignments. In Table 6.2, we have created a triangularized form of the original flow matrix to sum the flows in either direction because we are interested only in the total.

The heuristic begins with an initial layout, shown on the grid in Figure 6.5a. This initial layout is arbitrary but could be based on judgment or past experience. Table 6.2 suggests that attractions with high daily flow between them should be placed adjacent

TABLE 6.2

DAILY FLOW OF VISITORS BETWEEN ATTRACTIONS, HUNDREDS*

	A	B	C	D	E	F			A	B	C	D	E	F
A	╳	7	20	0	5	6		A	╳	15	30	0	15	6
B	8	╳	6	10	0	2		B	╳	╳	12	40	10	8
C	10	6	╳	15	7	8	Net→ flow	C	╳	╳	╳	20	8	8
D	0	30	5	╳	10	3		D	╳	╳	╳	╳	30	6
E	10	10	1	20	╳	6		E	╳	╳	╳	╳	╳	10
F	0	6	0	3	4	╳		F	╳	╳	╳	╳	╳	╳

Flow matrix　　　　　　　　　　　Triangularized matrix

*Description of attractions: A = killer whale, B = sea lions, C = dolphins, D = water skiing, E = aquarium, F = water rides.

FIGURE 6.5 Ocean World site planning using operations sequence analysis.

to each other. For example, we cannot see a need to place A adjacent to D, but it would be appropriate to place A close to C.

For nonadjacent attractions, the flow between them is multiplied by the number of grids that separate the attractions. Note we have assumed that diagonal separation is approximately equal to the distance of a grid side instead of using the Pythagorean theorem. These products are summed to arrive at a total flow distance of 124 for this initial layout. Considering the large contribution made to this sum by the separation of attractions A and C, we decide to move C adjacent to A to form the revised layout shown in Figure 6.5*b*, with a total flow distance of 96. The revised layout shown in Figure 6.5*c* is the result of exchanging attractions A and C. This exchange has placed attraction C adjacent to attractions D, E, and F, thereby reducing the total flow distance to 70. The final layout, in Figure 6.5*d*, is created by exchanging attractions B and E and by moving attraction F to form a rectangular space; exchanging B and E keeps E and F adjacent as we move F to form a more compact space. By making high-flow attractions adjacent, we have reduced total nonadjacent flow distance to a value of 58 for our final site plan, which is shown in Figure 6.6.

The departmental exchange logic of operations sequence analysis was incorporated into a computer program known as *CRAFT (Computerized Relative Allocation of Facilities Technique).*[5] CRAFT requires the following inputs: an interdepartmental flow matrix, a cost matrix (i.e., cost/unit/unit distance moved), and an initial layout with exact departmental dimensions filling the space available. CRAFT can incorporate some constraints, such as fixing the location of a department. The program logic depicted in Figure 6.7 (on page 158) shows the incremental nature of the heuristic, which selects at each iteration the two departments that, if exchanged, will yield the most improvement in flow distance reduction. As can be seen in the Selected Bibliography at the end of this chapter, reports indicate the extensive use of CRAFT in service organization layout planning—for example, in insurance offices, hospitals, movie studios, and universities.

An objective other than minimization of travel distance also could be appropriate for designing the layout of a service. For example, if we had a core business with

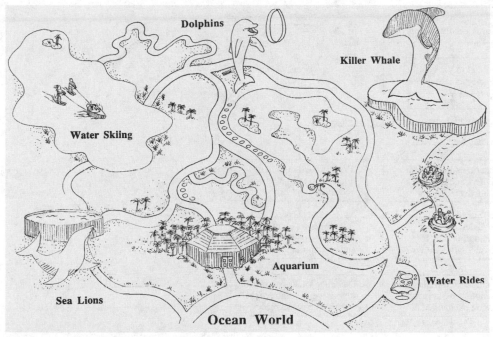

FIGURE 6.6 Final site plan for Ocean World theme park.
(Map by Kate O'Brien, Desert Tale Graphics.)

several ancillary businesses, we would want a layout that encouraged customers to browse in these other areas. Consider the layout of a gambling casino. Guests must walk through corridors lined with trendy shops and must always pass through the slot machine area to reach the front door or the restaurant.

PROCESS FLOWCHARTING

A *process flowchart* is a visual aid used by industrial engineers when analyzing production systems to identify opportunities for improvement in process efficiency. The process flowchart is similar in concept to the service blueprint (discussed in Chapter 5), except that process flowcharting focuses on employee or customer travel distance and the time associated with activities such as delays, inspections, travel, and operations. Thus, the focus is on layout efficiency as measured in time and distance traveled.

For manufacturing layout analysis, the production process is broken down into the underlying sequence of operations, with the time required for each recorded and the distance measured when material is moved between operations. Delays, inspection activity, and storage of material also are noted. A description of the process in visual form helps to identify areas where efficiency can be improved by eliminating unnecessary activities (e.g., by reducing the distance that material is moved, by combining operations).

Because the customer is part of the process in services, the traditional industrial process chart is modified for use in studying service processes by redefining the customary symbols. This is shown in Table 6.3.

Service process flowcharting begins by observing the service to identify the sequence of steps involved. Each step is classified according to the five categories in

FIGURE 6.7 **Flow diagram for CRAFT logic.**
(*Source:* Reprinted by permission of the *Harvard Business Review.* EXHIBIT from "Allocating Facilities with Craft," by E. S. Buffa, G. C. Armour, and T. E. Vollman (March–April 1964). Copyright © 1964 by the President and Fellows of Harvard College; all rights reserved.)

Table 6.3 and listed in order. The process flow is drawn by connecting the symbols and noting the time associated with each step and the distance traveled for movements.

Example 6.3: Credit Card Processing

For restaurants, credit card transactions are time-consuming for both guests and servers. A new procedure for processing such transactions has been suggested, however, and the benefits to servers and guests will be compared with the current procedure. The process flow analysis contained in Figures 6.8 and 6.9 comparing the two procedures was reported by Kimes and Mutkoski, only slightly modified here to use the service process categories as shown in Table 6.3.[6]

A close examination of the process flowcharts reveals that the last three steps of the current credit processing procedure have been eliminated in the new procedure. Thus, the proposed card processing procedure has saved the server one round-trip to the table, or 60 feet of walking. Both the server and the guest benefit from a savings of 1.75 minutes in performing the transaction.

TABLE 6.3

SERVICE PROCESS CHART CATEGORIES AND SYMBOLS

Category	Symbol	Description
Operation	○	An operation performed by the server offline or customer self-service. A possible service failure point.
Customer contact	▽	An occasion when server and customer interact. An opportunity to influence customer service perceptions.
Travel	→	The movement of customers, servers, or information between operations.
Delay	**D**	Delay resulting in a queue and a need for waiting space for customers.
Inspection	□	An activity by a customer or a server to measure service quality.

ENVIRONMENTAL PSYCHOLOGY AND ORIENTATION

Orientation is the first behavioral need of an individual on entering a place. It includes questions of place orientation (e.g., "Where am I?") as well as of function orientation (e.g., "How does this organization work, and what do I do next?"). On entering a physical setting, customers gain control when they can use spatial cues, along with previous experience, to identify where they are, where they should go, and what they need to do. Anxiety and a sense of helplessness can result if spatial cues are not present or previous experience cannot be used to avoid disorientation. Richard E. Wener argues that the causes of disorientation in service settings can be reduced by a facility design that incorporates the following: previous experience, design legibility, and orientation aids.[7]

Distance	Time					Activity
						Customer requests check
30 ft.	0.5 min.	○ →	**D**	▽	□	Server walks
	0.5 min.	○ →	**D**	▽	□	Server prepares check
30 ft.	0.5 min.	○ →	**D**	▽	□	Server walks
	0.25 min.	○ →	**D**	▽	□	Server presents check
30 ft.	0.5 min.	○ →	**D**	▽	□	Server walks
	0.5 min.	○ →	**D**	▽	□	Customer inspects, puts card out
30 ft.	0.5 min.	○ →	**D**	▽	□	Server returns to table
	0.25 min.	○ →	**D**	▽	□	Server picks up card
30 ft.	0.5 min.	○ →	**D**	▽	□	Server walks to process
	0.5 min.	○ →	**D**	▽	□	Server fills out slip
	0.5 min.	○ →	**D**	▽	□	Server processes slip
	1.0 min.	○ →	**D**	▽	□	Server obtains preauthorization
30 ft.	0.5 min.	○ →	**D**	▽	□	Server walks
	0.25 min.	○ →	**D**	▽	□	Server presents slip
30 ft.	0.5 min.	○ →	**D**	▽	□	Server walks
	0.5 min.	○ →	**D**	▽	□	Customer signs
30 ft.	0.5 min.	○ →	**D**	▽	□	Server walks
	0.25 min.	○ →	**D**	▽	□	Server picks up slip
30 ft.	0.5 min.	○ →	**D**	▽	□	(Customer leaves) Server walks
Total 270 ft.	9 min.					

FIGURE 6.8 Current credit card processing procedures.
(*Source:* S. E. Kimes and S. A Mutkoski, "The Express Guest Check: Saving Steps with Process Design," *Cornell HRA Quarterly,* vol. 30, no. 2, August 1989, p. 23. © *Cornell HRA Quarterly.* Used by permission. All rights reserved.)

Distance	Time					Activity
						Customer requests check
30 ft.	0.5 min.	O	D	▽	□	Server walks
	0.5 min.	O	D	▽	□	Server prepares check
	0.5 min.	O	D	▽	□	Server fills out slip
30 ft.	0.5 min.	O	D	▽	□	Server walks
	0.25 min.	O	D	▽	□	Server presents check and slip
30 ft.	0.5 min.	O	D	▽	□	Server walks
	0.5 min.	O	D	▽	□	Customer inspects, puts card out, signs slip
30 ft.	0.5 min.	O	D	▽	□	Server returns to table
	0.25 min.	O	D	▽	□	Server picks up card and slip
30 ft.	0.5 min.	O	D	▽	□	Server walks
	0.5 min.	O	D	▽	□	Server processes slip and card
	1.0 min.	O	D	▽	□	Server obtains authorization
30 ft.	0.5 min.	O	D	▽	□	Server walks
	0.25 min.	O	D	▽	□	Server presents card and receipt
30 ft.	0.5 min.	O	D	▽	□	Server walks
		O	D	▽	□	Customer leaves

Total 210 ft.   7.25 min.

FIGURE 6.9 Proposed credit card processing procedures.
(*Source:* S. E. Kimes and S. A. Mutkoski, "The Express Guest Check: Saving Steps with Process Design," *Cornell HRA Quarterly,* vol. 30, no. 2, August 1989, p. 23. © *Cornell HRA Quarterly.* Used by permission. All rights reserved.)

Using formula facilities, franchised services have effectively removed the anxiety of disorientation so that customers know exactly what to do. Holiday Inn took this concept a step further by advertising that a guest will find no surprises at any of its locations, capitalizing on the need for familiarity to attract repeat customers.

Orientation also can be aided by facility designs that allow customers to see both into and through the space. Layouts for banks and hotels often use an entrance atrium that allows the entire space to be viewed and conceptualized at a glance. In addition, such a layout allows customers to observe the actions of others for behavioral cues.

Orientation aids and signage such as "You Are Here" maps, if properly aligned with the user's perspective (i.e., "up" on the sign equates to straight ahead for the user) and complete with environmental landmarks, can be effective as well. Strategically located plants and artwork can act as points of reference. Color-coded subway routes with corresponding color-coded connecting arrows represent an excellent use of signage to assist in self-service and to promote smooth flow of traffic.

SUMMARY

The strategic importance of facility design and layout was demonstrated by the reported perceptions of Wal-Mart and Kmart by their customers. Facility design using aesthetics and decor must be consistent with the objectives of the service package. Analytical approaches that have been developed for product and process production systems were applied to the analysis of service facility layouts. With modification for service operations, process flowcharting was shown to be useful in analyzing service layouts to identify unnecessary activities, highlight points of potential service failure and customer contact, and identify space needs for waiting customers. The psychological implications of poor service layout were addressed, along with the need for effective signage and thoughtful facility design to avoid customer disorientation.

Chapter 7 will consider several approaches to the facility location problem and its impact on creating a competitive advantage.

KEY TERMS AND DEFINITIONS

Bottleneck the activity in a product layout that takes the most time to perform and thus defines the maximum flow rate for the entire process.

CRAFT (Computerized Relative Allocation of Facilities Technique) a computer program that uses the departmental exchange logic of operations sequence analysis to solve the relative location problem of process layouts.

Operations sequence analysis a procedure to improve the flow distance in a process layout by arranging the relative location of departments.

Process flowchart a table listing the sequence of activities for a service operation noting the type of activity with a symbol and the time and distance traveled.

Process layout a service permitting customization because customers determine their own sequence of activities (e.g., an amusement park).

Product layout a standardized service performed in a fixed sequence of steps (e.g., cafeteria).

Servicescape the physical environment of a service facility that influences the behavior and perceptions of the service for both the customers and the workers.

SOLVED PROBLEMS

1. Line-Balancing for Product Layout

Problem Statement

Arriving at JFK airport in New York from overseas requires a sequence of immigration and customs-clearing activities before a passenger can board a domestic flight for home. The table below lists the activities and their average times. Except for baggage claim, these activities must be performed in the sequence noted. What is the bottleneck activity and maximum number of passengers who can be processed per hour? What would you recommend to improve the balance of this process?

Activity	Average time, sec.
1. Deplane	20
2. Immigration	16
3. Baggage claim	40
4. Customs	24
5. Check baggage	18
6. Board domestic flight	15

Solution

First, draw the product flow diagram and identify the bottleneck activity. The slowest activity is "baggage claim," which results in a system capacity of 90 passengers per hour.

A recommendation for increasing system capacity could include doubling the capacity of the baggage claim area and combining the activities of the immigration and customs areas. This new product layout is shown in the flow diagram below, with the result of doubling the system capacity to 180 passengers per hour.

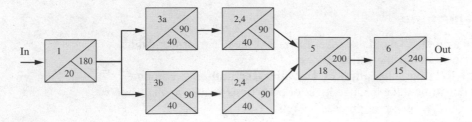

2. Relative Location for Process Layout

Problem Statement

The architect for the new undergraduate library is interested in a floor plan that would be viewed as convenient by users. Based on survey data from the old library, student movements between different areas in hundreds of trips per month are noted in the flow matrix below. Prepare a good initial rectangular layout that minimizes total flow distance between nonadjacent areas; then use operations sequence analysis to improve the layout.

Library area	A	B	C	D	E	F
A Reserve Room	—	5	9	3	7	1
B Reference Room	3	—	8	2	6	2
C Copy Room	1	1	—	7	2	3
D Stacks	2	2	10	—	2	5
E Periodical Room	1	2	6	3	—	2
F Computer Room	1	1	1	4	2	—

Solution

First, create a triangularized total flow matrix by summing flows across the diagonal.

Library area	A	B	C	D	E	F
A Reserve Room	—	8	10	5	8	2
B Reference Room	—	—	9	4	8	3
C Copy Room	—	—	—	17	8	4
D Stacks	—	—	—	—	5	9
E Periodical Room	—	—	—	—	—	4
F Computer Room	—	—	—	—	—	—

Second, locate library areas on the schematic rectangular layout shown below by placing high-flow areas adjacent to each other.

Next, calculate the total flow distance of nonadjacent pairs as shown below:

Nonadjacent area pairs	Flow		Distance		Total
AD	5	×	2	=	10
AF	2	×	2	=	4
BD	4	×	2	=	8
BF	3	×	2	=	6
					28

Finally, look for improvement by exchanging a pair of nonadjacent areas. Because no improvement is possible, accept the above layout.

TOPICS FOR DISCUSSION

1. Compare the attention to aesthetics in waiting rooms that you have visited. How did the different environments affect your mood?
2. From a customer perspective, give an example of a servicescape that supports the service concept and an example that detracts from the service concept. Explain the success and the failure in terms of the servicescape dimensions.
3. Based on your work experience, contrast a supportive servicescape with a poor servicescape in terms of job satisfaction and productivity.
4. Select a service and discuss how the design and layout of the facility meet the five factors of nature and objectives of the organization, land availability and space requirements, flexibility, aesthetics, and the community and environment.
5. For **Example 6.3,** the Ocean World theme park, make an argument for not locating popular attractions next to each other.
6. The CRAFT program is an example of a heuristic programming approach to problem solving. Why might CRAFT not find the optimal solution to a layout problem?

EXERCISES

6.1. Revisit the Automobile Driver's License Office, and assume that some of our previous recommendations for investment have been implemented. For example, "checking for violations and restrictions" will be done on a computer terminal, with that activity now taking 30 instead of 60 seconds. However, no additional eye-test machines or cameras were purchased.
   a. Assuming that one worker is assigned to each activity, what is the bottleneck activity and the maximum number of applicants who can be seen per hour?
   b. Suggest a reallocation of activities among the six workers that would result in a service capacity of 120 applicants per hour. What investment would be required to implement your layout recommendation?
6.2. Getting a physical examination at a physician's office involves a series of steps. The table below lists these activities and their average times. The activities can occur in any order, but the doctor's consultation must be the last. Three nurses are assigned to perform activities 1, 2, and 4.

Activity	Average time, min.
1. Blood pressure, wt., temp.	6
2. Medical history	20
3. Doctor's checkup	18
4. Lab work	10
5. Doctor's consultation	12

   a. What are the bottleneck activity and the maximum number of patients who can be seen per hour?
   b. Suggest a reallocation of nursing and/or doctor activities that would result in increased service capacity, and draw a product flow diagram. What is the capacity of your improved system?
6.3. A school cafeteria is operated by five persons performing the activities listed below in the average times shown.

Activity	Average time, sec.
1. Serve salad and dessert	10
2. Pour drinks	30
3. Serve entree	60
4. Serve vegetables	20
5. Tally and collect payment	40

    a. What are the bottleneck activity and the maximum service capacity per hour?

    b. Suggest a reallocation of activities that would increase capacity and use only four employees, and draw a product flow diagram. What is the capacity of your improved system?

    c. Recommend a way to maintain the serving capacity found in part b using only three employees.

6.4. Every fall, volunteers administer flu vaccine shots at a local supermarket. The process involves the following four steps:

Activity	Average time, sec.
1. Reception	30
2. Drug allergy consultation	60
3. Fill out form and sign waiver	45
4. Administer vaccination	90

    a. What are the bottleneck activity and maximum number of people who can be processed per hour?

    b. If a fifth volunteer is assigned to help administer vaccinations, what activity now becomes the bottleneck? How has this arrangement influenced the capacity of the system?

    c. Using five volunteers, suggest a reallocation of activities that would result in increased service capacity, and draw a product flow diagram. What is the capacity of your improved system?

6.5. Revisit the Ocean World Theme Park, and use the daily flow of visitors between attractions found in **Example 6.2** for a different analysis.

    a. Recommend a layout that would *maximize* the total travel distance between attractions.

    b. What benefit would such a layout have for the owners of Ocean World Theme Park?

    c. What reservations do you have about using the data from Table 6.2 for this new approach to the Ocean World Theme Park layout?

6.6. The Second Best Discount Store is considering rearranging its stockroom to improve customer service. Currently, stock pickers are given customer orders to fill from six warehouse areas. Movement between these areas is noted in the flow matrix below:

	A	B	C	D	E	F
A	—	1	4	2	0	3
B	0	—	2	0	2	1
C	2	2	—	4	5	2
D	3	0	2	—	0	2
E	1	4	3	1	—	4
F	4	3	1	2	0	—

Using the initial layout below, perform an operations sequence analysis to determine a layout that minimizes total flow between nonadjacent departments. Calculate your flow improvement.

6.7. A convenience store is considering changing its layout to encourage impulse buying. The triangular flow matrix below gives the measure of association between different product groups (e.g., beer, milk, magazines). A plus sign (+) indicates a high association, such as between beer and peanuts; a minus sign (-) indicates a repulsion, such as between beer and milk; and a zero (0) indicates no association.

	A	B	C	D	E	F
A			+	+	0	0	-
B				+	0	-	-
C					+	+	0
D						+	+
E							0
F							

Using the initial layout below, perform an operations sequence analysis to determine a layout that will encourage impulse buying by placing high-association product groups close to one another.

6.8. A community college that recently acquired a parcel of land is now preparing site plans. There is interest in locating academic departments in each of six buildings along a mall with three buildings on each side. Based on registration patterns, the daily flow of students between these six departments in hundreds is shown below.

	A	B	C	D	E	F
A. Psychology	—	6	4	8	7	1
B. English	6	—	2	3	9	5
C. Mathematics	6	1	—	12	2	4
D. Economics	3	2	10	—	3	5
E. History	7	11	2	1	—	6
F. Biology	6	2	8	10	3	—

Using the initial layout below, perform an operations sequence analysis to determine a site plan for the community college that will minimize the distance that students need to walk between classes.

Service Benchmark
WHERE, OH WHERE SHALL WE GO?

Airports are gateways to great adventures for millions of people around the world. Finding these gateways, however, can be adventures themselves.

Wall Street Journal reporter Bridget O'Brian explored the subject of signage outside airports.* She cites examples of problems such as a lack of necessary or helpful signs, ambiguous words or phrases, "inconspicuous" signs, and signs that are placed inappropriately. The consequences of poor signage can lead to bad tempers, missed flights, motor vehicle accidents, and deaths.

National standards for airport signage in the United States to cure these ills have been proposed. Such standards, if adopted, would represent an important service breakthrough.

Getting to the airport is only part of the adventure, however. Signage within airports often challenges the traveler. Consider two experienced passengers who are booked on a Delta Air Lines trip from Oakland, California, to Austin, Texas. They arrive at the Oakland International Airport and are told by the Delta agent that their Oakland–Dallas flight has been canceled. The agent gives them a voucher for an American Airlines flight and explains that they are still booked on Delta's Dallas–Austin flight, a 30-minute trip. They proceed to the American check-in counter where they receive their boarding passes. The trip is uneventful until they arrive in the Dallas–Fort Worth International Airport.

The travelers arrive at Gate 22, Concourse C, and quickly discover that the departure/arrival monitors display only American Airlines flights; the posted airport "maps" show Concourses A, B, and C—they do not indicate the existence of any other concourses. Signs for a train to the other two concourses direct the two passengers to a tram station on a lower level. They find that Concourses A and B also have gates—and monitors—for American Airlines flights only. They do not find a single sign for any airline or airport transportation service other than those for American Airlines. They finally ask for directions from an AA gate agent in Concourse A who tells them to leave the concourse opposite Gate 21A, go downstairs, and take the airport train (i.e., not the AA train) to Concourse E. Signs for a way downstairs are lacking and personnel at the concourse exit cannot speak English well enough to be helpful. Eventually they locate an elevator, descend to the lower level, and find that they must exit the building to get to the tram station. The tram station, however, is closed and a sign directs them to the next tram station to the right. They set off in that direction, although they cannot see another station. It is nighttime and the walk is deserted until a security guard comes in sight. He says the next open station is in the other direction. The transfer from an American Airlines gate to a Delta gate can be made in less than 10 minutes, but the complete absence of appropriate signs and knowledgeable personnel extends the transfer time to more than one hour.

---

* Bridget O'Brian, "Signs and Blunders: Airport Travelers Share Graphic Tales," *The Wall Street Journal,* March 28, 1995, p. B1.

Health Maintenance Organization (A)

In January 1996, Joan Taylor, the administrator of the Life-Time Insurance Company HMO in Buffalo, New York, was pleased with the Austin, Texas, location that was selected for a new ambulatory health center. (The process used to select this site is discussed in Chapter 7.) The center not only would serve as a clinic for the acutely ill but also as a center for preventive health services.

An important goal of the HMO was to offer programs that would encourage members to stay healthy. Various programs already had been planned, including those on smoking cessation, proper nutrition, diet, and exercise.

The clinic portion of the health center would be quite large; however, certain constraints in the layout would be necessary. Acutely ill patients would need to be separated from well patients. In addition, federal safety regulations prohibited the radiography department from being adjacent to the main waiting room.

It was very important to Ms. Taylor to minimize the walking distance for both the patients and the HMO personnel. The matrix below provides the expected flow between departments based on 35 patients per day.

		A	B	C	D	E	F
Reception	A	—	30	0	5	0	0
Waiting room	B	10	—	40	10	0	0
Examination	C	15	20	—	15	5	5
Laboratory	D	5	18	8	—	6	3
X-ray	E	0	4	1	2	—	4
Minor surgery	F	2	0	0	0	1	—

Questions

1. Beginning with a good initial layout, use operations sequence analysis to determine a better layout that would minimize the walking distance between different areas in the clinic.

2. Defend your final layout based on features other than minimizing walking distance.

Health Maintenance Organization (B)

The administrator of the Life-Time Insurance Company HMO, Ms. Taylor, was anxious to solve potential problems before their new clinic opened in Austin, Texas. In Buffalo, New York, where the original clinic is located, the pharmacy had been extremely busy from the beginning, and long waiting times for prescriptions to be filled presented a very real problem.

The Buffalo HMO pharmacy was modern, spacious, and well designed. The peak time for prescriptions was between 10 A.M. and 3 P.M. During this period, prescriptions would back up, and the waiting time would increase. After 5 P.M., the staff would be reduced to one pharmacist and one technician, but the two had no trouble providing very timely service throughout the evening.

Ms. Taylor became acutely aware of the long waiting times after several complaints had been lodged. Each stated that the waiting time had exceeded 1 hour. As shown in the table below, the pharmacy is staffed with five persons on duty until 5 P.M.

Ms. Taylor personally studied the tasks of all the pharmacy personnel. She noted the time required to accomplish each task, and her results are listed on page 168 as well. The prescriptions were filled in an assembly-line fashion by two technicians and three pharmacists, and each person performed only one task.

Activity	Time in seconds
Receive prescriptions	24
Type labels	120
Fill prescriptions	60
Check prescriptions	40
Dispense prescriptions	30

Note: *The activities of filling, checking, and dispensing prescriptions must be performed by a registered pharmacist.*

Questions

1. Identify the bottleneck activity, and show how capacity can be increased by using only two pharmacists and two technicians.

2. In addition to savings on personnel costs, what benefits does this arrangement have?

C A S E

Esquire Department Store

Established by Arthur Babbitt, Sr., in 1971, Esquire Department Store has shown a recent decline in sales. The store manager, young Arthur Babbitt, Jr., has noticed a decrease in the movement of customers between departments. He believes that customers are not spending enough time in the store, and that this may result from the present layout, which is based on the concept of locating related departments close to each other. Babbitt, Sr., is not convinced. He argues that he has been in business for about 20 years, and that the loyal customers are not likely to quit shopping here simply because of the layout. He believes they are losing customers to the new factory outlet mall outside town, which seems to attract them away with discount prices.

Babbitt, Jr., explains that the greater the distance the customer travels between departments, the more products the customer will see. Customers usually have something specific in mind when they go shopping, but exposure to more products may stimulate additional purchases. Thus, to Babbitt, Jr., it seems that the best answer to this problem is to change the present layout so that customers are exposed to more products. He feels the environment today is different from the environment of 1971, and that the company must display products better and encourage impulse buying.

At this point, Babbitt, Sr., interrupts to say, "Son, you may have a point here about the store layout. But before I spend money on tearing this place up, I need to see some figures. Develop a new layout, and show me how much you can increase the time customers spend in the store."

Babbitt, Jr., returns to his office and pulls out some information that he has gathered about revising the store layout. He has estimated that, on average, 57 customers enter the store per hour. The store operates 10 hours a day, 200 days a year. He has a drawing of the present layout, which is shown in Figure 6.10, and a chart depicting the flow of customers between departments, which is shown in Table 6.4.

			Loading and unloading area	
Offices			Warehouse	
(5, 7) 5	(5, 7) 9		(5, 7) 4	(5, 7) 7
(5, 7) 13	(5, 7) 6	1 (15, 2)	(5, 7) 10	(5, 7) 11
(5, 7) 12	(5, 7) 3		(5, 7) 8	(5, 7) 2
		Exit/Entrance	Display	Display
Sidewalk			Sidewalk	
Parking areas				

FIGURE 6.10 Current layout of Esquire Department Store. (Figures in parentheses refer to rows and columns.)

TABLE 6.4

FLOW OF CUSTOMERS BETWEEN DEPARTMENTS, IN THOUSANDS

	1	2	3	4	5	6	7	8	9	10	11	12	13
1	0	32	41	19	21	7	13	22	10	11	8	6	10
2	17	0	24	31	16	3	13	17	25	8	7	9	12
3	8	14	0	25	9	28	17	16	14	7	9	24	18
4	25	12	16	0	18	26	22	9	6	28	20	16	14
5	10	12	15	20	0	18	17	24	28	30	25	9	19
6	8	14	12	17	20	0	19	23	30	32	37	15	21
7	13	19	23	25	3	45	0	29	27	31	41	24	16
8	28	9	17	19	21	5	7	0	21	19	25	10	9
9	14	8	13	15	22	18	13	25	0	33	27	14	19
10	18	25	17	19	23	15	25	27	31	0	21	17	10
11	29	28	31	16	29	19	18	33	26	31	0	16	16
12	17	31	25	21	19	17	19	21	31	29	25	0	19
13	12	25	16	33	14	19	31	17	22	15	24	18	0

1. Exit-entrance
2. Appliances
3. Audio-stereo-TV
4. Jewelry
5. Housewares
6. Cosmetics
7. Ladies' ready-to-wear
8. Men's ready-to-wear
9. Boys' clothing
10. Sporting goods
11. Ladies' lingerie
12. Shoes
13. Furniture

Questions

1. Use CRAFT logic to develop a layout that will maximize customer time in the store.
2. What percentage increase in customer time spent in the store is achieved by the proposed layout?
3. What other consumer behavior concepts should be considered in the relative location of departments?

SELECTED BIBLIOGRAPHY

AUBERT-GAMET, VERONIQUE: "Twisting Servicescapes: Diversion of the Physical Environment in a Re-appropriation Process," *International Journal of Service Industry Management,* vol. 8, no. 1, 1997, pp. 26–41.

BITNER, MARY JO: "Evaluating Service Encounters: The Effects of Physical Surroundings and Employee Responses," *Journal of Marketing,* vol. 54, April 1990, pp. 69–82.

———: "Servicescapes: The Impact of Physical Surroundings on Customers and Employees," *Journal of Marketing,* vol. 58, April 1992, pp. 57–71.

FITZSIMMONS, J. A., and G. MAURER: "A Walk-Through Audit to Improve Restaurant Performance," *Cornell H.R.A. Quarterly,* vol. 31, no. 4, February 1991, pp. 94–99.

KIMES, S. E., and S. A. MUTKOSKI: "The Express Guest Check: Saving Steps with Process Design," *Cornell H.R.A. Quarterly,* vol. 30, no. 2, August 1989, pp. 21–25.

NORMAN, D. A.: *The Psychology of Everyday Things,* Basic Books, New York, 1988.

WENER, RICHARD A.: "The Environmental Psychology of Service Encounters," in J. A. Czepiel, M. R. Solomon, and C. F. Surprenant (eds.), *The Service Encounter,* Lexington Books, Lexington, Mass., 1985, pp. 101–113.

ENDNOTES

1. Francine Schwadel, "Little Touches Spur Wal-Mart's Rise," *The Wall Street Journal,* September 22, 1989, p. B1.
2. Steve Lohr, "The Best Little Bank in America," *New York Times,* July 7, 1991, sec. 3, p. 1.

3. Mary Jo Bitner, "Servicescapes: The Impact of Physical Surroundings on Customers and Employees," *Journal of Marketing,* vol. 56, April 1992, pp. 57–71.

4. Elwood S. Buffa, "Sequence Analysis for Functional Layouts," *Journal of Industrial Engineering,* vol. 6, no. 2, March–April 1955, pp. 12–13.

5. E. S. Buffa, G. C. Armour, and T. E. Vollmann, "Allocating Facilities with CRAFT," *Harvard Business Review,* vol. 42, no. 2, March–April 1964, pp. 136–159.

6. S. E. Kimes and S. A. Mutkoski, "The Express Guest Check: Saving Steps with Process Design," *Cornell HRA Quarterly,* vol. 30, no. 2, August 1989, p. 23.

7. Richard E. Wener, "The Environmental Psychology of Service Encounters," in J. A. Czepiel, M. R. Solomon, and C. F. Surprenant (eds.), *The Service Encounter,* Lexington Books, Lexington, Mass., 1985, pp. 101–113.

Service Facility Location

Learning Objectives

After completing this chapter, you should be able to:

1. Discuss how a facility location is affected by selection of the criteria for judging customer service.
2. Locate a single facility using the cross-median approach.
3. Evaluate the business viability of a retail location by estimating expected revenues and market share using the Huff model.
4. Locate multiple facilities using the set covering model.
5. Discuss the nontraditional location strategies: competitive clustering, saturation marketing, marketing intermediaries, substitution of communications for transportation, and the impact of the Internet on service location.

In addition to the traditional role of creating entry barriers and generating demand, location also affects the strategic dimensions of flexibility, competitive positioning, demand management, and focus.

Flexibility of a location is a measure of the degree to which the service can react to changing economic situations. Because location decisions are long-term commitments with capital-intensive aspects, it is essential to select locations that can be responsive to future economic, demographic, cultural, and competitive changes. For example, locating sites in a number of states could reduce the overall risk of a financial crisis resulting from regional economic downturns. This portfolio approach to multisite location could be augmented by selecting individual sites near inelastic demand (e.g., locating a hotel near a convention center).

Competitive positioning refers to methods by which the firm can establish itself relative to its competitors. Multiple locations can serve as a barrier to competition through building a firm's competitive position and establishing a market awareness. Acquiring and holding prime locations before the market has developed can keep the competition from gaining access to these desirable locations and create an artificial barrier to entry (analogous to a product patent).

Demand management is the ability to control the quantity, quality, and timing of demand. For example, hotels cannot manipulate capacity effectively because of the fixed nature of the facility; however, a hotel can control demand by locating near a diverse set of market generators that supply a steady demand regardless of the economic condition, the day of the week, or the season.

Focus can be developed by offering the same narrowly defined service at many locations. Many multisite service firms develop a standard (or formula) facility that can be duplicated at many locations. While this "cookie-cutter" approach makes expansion easier, sites that are located in close proximity could siphon business from each other.

This problem of demand cannibalization can be avoided if a firm establishes a pattern of desired growth for its multisite expansion.

Traditionally, location decisions have been based on intuition and had a considerable range of success. Although site selection often is based on opportunistic factors such as site availability and favorable leasing, a quantitative analysis can be useful to avoid a serious mistake. For example, regardless of how low the rent may be, being the only store in a deserted shopping mall offers no advantage.

CHAPTER PREVIEW

This chapter begins with an overview of the problem structure, including travel-time models, site selection, decision-making criteria, and estimation of geographic demand. Facility location models for both single- and multiple-facility systems also are explored. These models are illustrated with both public and private sector examples. The models are oriented toward selecting a site for a physical facility, but they could be used to deploy mobile units such as ambulances, police cars, and repair vehicles for field service.

Until now, we have assumed that the consumer and provider must be together physically for a service to be performed; however, alternatives exist if one is willing to substitute communication for transportation or to use marketing intermediaries. Such alternatives will be explored as possible methods of extending services beyond their immediate geographic area.

LOCATION CONSIDERATIONS

Many factors enter into the decision to locate a service facility. Figure 7.1 classifies location issues that will be used to guide our discussion throughout this chapter. The broad categories are geographic representation, number of facilities, and optimization criteria.

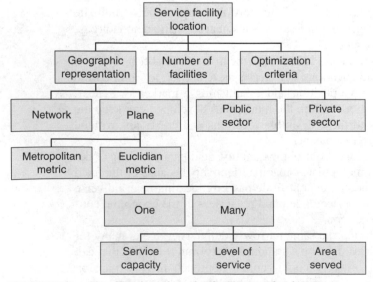

FIGURE 7.1 Classification of service facility location issues.

Geographic Representation

The traditional classification of location problems is based on how the geography is modeled. Location options and travel distance can be represented on either a plane or a network. Location on a plane (i.e., flat surface) is characterized by a solution space that has infinite possibilities. Facilities may be located anywhere on the plane and are identified by an xy cartesian coordinate (or, in a global context, by latitudes and longitudes), as shown in Figure 7.2. Distance between locations is measured at the extremes in one of two ways. One method is the *euclidian metric,* or vector, travel distance (remember the Pythagorean theorem), which is defined as

$$d_{ij} = [(x_i - x_j)^2 + (y_i - y_j)^2]^{1/2} \tag{1}$$

where d_{ij} = distance between points i and j
    x_i, y_i = coordinates of the ith point
    x_j, y_j = coordinates of the jth point

For example, if

        the origin $x_i, y_i = 2,2$ and   the destination $x_j, y_j = 4,4$

then

$$d_{ij} = [(2 - 4)^2 + (2 - 4)^2]^{1/2} = 2.83$$

The other method is the *metropolitan metric,* or rectangular displacement, travel distance (i.e., north-south and east-west travel in urban areas), which is defined as

$$d_{ij} = |x_i - x_j| + |y_i - y_j| \tag{2}$$

Using the same example from above for the metropolitan metric:

$$d_{ij} = |2 - 4| + |2 - 4| = 4.0$$

Location on a network is characterized by a solution space that is restricted to the nodes of that network. For example, a highway system could be considered a network, with major highway intersections as nodes. The arcs of the network represent travel distance (or time) between pairs of nodes, calculated using the shortest route.

The selection of geographic representation and distance metric often is dictated by the economics of the data collection effort and the problem environment. Networks can

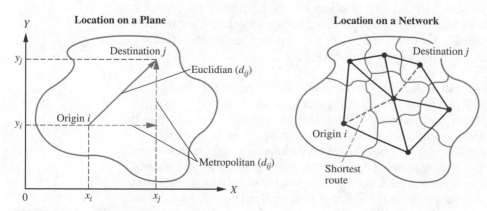

FIGURE 7.2 Geographic structure.

represent more accurately the geographic uniqueness of an area (e.g., the travel restrictions caused by a river with few bridges or by mountainous terrain). Unfortunately, the cost of gathering the travel times between nodes can be prohibitive. When locating is done on a plane that represents an urban area, the metropolitan metric often is used, because streets for some cities are arranged in an east-west and north-south pattern. Both the metropolitan and euclidian metrics require an estimate of the average speed to convert distance traveled to time.

Number of Facilities

The location of a single facility generally can be treated mathematically with little difficulty. Unfortunately, the methods used to site a single facility do not guarantee optimal results when they are modified and applied to multisite location problems. Finding a unique set of sites is complicated by assigning demand nodes to sites (i.e., defining service areas for each site), and the problem is complicated further if the capacity at each site varies. In addition, for some services such as health care, a hierarchy of service exists. Private physicians and clinics offer primary care, general hospitals provide primary care plus hospitalization, and health centers add special treatment capabilities. Thus, the selection of services provided also may be a variable in multisite location studies.

Optimization Criteria

Private and public sector location problems are similar in that they share the objective of maximizing some measure of benefit. The location criteria that are chosen differ, however, because the "ownership" is different. Within the private sector, the location decision is governed by either minimization of cost (e.g., in the case of distribution centers) or maximization of profit (e.g., in the case of retail locations). In contrast, we like to think that public facility decisions are governed by the needs of society as a whole. The objective for public decision making is to maximize a societal benefit that may be difficult to quantify.

Private Sector Criteria   Traditional private sector location analysis focuses on a trade-off between the cost of building and operating facilities and the cost of transportation. Much of the literature has addressed this problem, which is appropriate for the distribution of products (i.e., the warehouse location problem). These models may find some applications in services, however, when the services are delivered to the customers (e.g., consulting, auditing, janitorial, and lawn care services).

When the consumer travels to the facility, no direct cost is incurred by the provider. Instead, distance becomes a barrier restricting potential consumer demand and the corresponding revenue generated. Facilities such as retail shopping centers therefore are located to attract the maximum number of customers.

Public Sector Criteria   Location decisions in the public sector are complicated by the lack of agreement on goals and the difficulty of measuring benefits in dollars to make trade-offs with facility investment. Because the benefits of a public service are difficult to define or quantify directly, surrogate (or substitute) measures of utility are used.

The average distance traveled by users to reach the facility is a popular surrogate. The smaller this quantity, the more accessible the system is to its users. Thus, the problem becomes one of minimizing the total average distance traveled, with a constraint on the number of facilities. The problem is additionally constrained by some maximum travel distance for the user. Another possibility is the creation of demand. Here the user population is not considered fixed but is determined by the location, size, and number of facilities. The greater the demand created or drawn, the more efficient the system is in filling the needs of the region.

These utility surrogates are optimized with constraints on investment. Analysis of cost-effectiveness usually is performed to examine trade-offs between investment and utility. The trade-offs for the surrogates are (1) the decrease in average distance traveled per additional thousand-dollar investment and (2) the increase in demand per additional thousand-dollar investment.

Effect of Criteria on Location   The selection of optimization criteria influences service facility location. For example, William J. Abernathy and John C. Hershey studied the location of health centers for a three-city region.[1] As part of that study, they noted the effect of health-center locations with respect to the following criteria:

1. *Maximize utilization.* Maximize the total number of visits to the centers.
2. *Minimize distance per capita.* Minimize the average distance per capita to the closest center.
3. *Minimize distance per visit.* Minimize the average per-visit travel distance to the nearest center.

The problem was structured so that each city had a population with a different mix of health care consumption characteristics. These characteristics were measured along two dimensions: (1) the effect of distance as a barrier to health care use and (2) the utilization rate at immediate proximity to a health care center. Figure 7.3 shows a map of the three cities and the location of a single health care center under each of the three criteria. These criteria yield entirely different locations because of the different behavioral patterns of each city. For criterion 1 (maximize utilization), the center is located at city C, because this city contains a large number of elderly individuals for whom distance is a strong barrier. City B is selected under criterion 2 (minimize distance per capita), because this city is centrally located between the two larger cities. City A is the largest population center and has the most mobile and frequent users of health care; therefore, criterion 3 (minimize distance per visit) leads to this city being selected.

FIGURE 7.3   **Location of one health center for three different criteria.**
(*Source:* W. J. Abernathy and J. C. Hershey, "A Spatial-Allocation Model for Regional Health-Services Planning." Reprinted with permission from *Operations Research,* vol. 20, no. 3, 1972, p. 637. Operations Research Society of America. No further reproduction permitted without the consent of the copyright owner.)

ESTIMATION OF GEOGRAPHIC DEMAND

The quality of service facility location analysis rests on an accurate assessment of geographic demand for the service (i.e., demand by geographic area). This requires the selection both of some geographic unit that partitions the area to be served and of some method for predicting demand from each of these partitions. Census tracts or their smaller divisions, the block or block groups, are used. In many cases, the demand for service is collected empirically by searching past records for addresses of users and tallying these by district. The steps that define geographic demand will be illustrated by an example of a day care center.[2]

Define the Target Population

The characteristics that define the target population must be established. For example, if a system of day care centers for all families is being established, the target population might consist of families with children younger than five years and an employable adult. A private system also might include the ability to pay. In this example, the target population is defined as families that receive Aid to Families with Dependent Children (AFDC) support with children younger than five years and an employable parent.

Select a Unit of Area

For accuracy, geographic units should be as small as practicable. There are two limits: (1) the unit must be large enough to contain a sample size that is sufficient for estimating demand and (2) the number of units must not exceed the computational capacity of the computers and facility location techniques. A census tract often is selected as the unit, because demographic data on the residents are readily available on computer tapes from the U.S. Census Bureau. In this study, block groups were selected as units, because census tracts were too large and single blocks too small.

Estimate Geographic Demand

Demographic data on block-group residents were analyzed statistically using linear regression to develop equation (3), which predicts the percentage of AFDC families in each block group:

$$Y_i = 0.0043X_{1i} + 0.0248X_{2i} + 0.0092X_{3i} \qquad (3)$$

where Y_i = percentage of AFDC families in block group i

X_{1i} = percentage of persons in block group i who are under 18 and living in a housing unit with more than 1.5 persons per room

X_{2i} = percentage of families in block group i with a single male head and children younger than 18 years

X_{3i} = percentage of families in block group i with a single female head and children younger than 18 years

Once Y_i, a percentage, was estimated for each block group, it was multiplied by both the number of families in the block group and the average number of children younger than five years per family. This figure became the estimate for the number of children requiring day care service from each block group. For example, assume that 50 families live in block group 10 and they have an average of 2 children younger than 5 years per family. If Y_{10} is found to be 30 percent using equation (3), then the estimate of children from this block group who require day care would be equal to $(.30)(50)(2) = 30$.

Map Geographic Demand

The demand for each block group is plotted on a three-dimensional map to provide a visual representation of the geographic distribution of day care needs. The visual depiction of demand is useful for highlighting neighborhoods with concentrated demand that are possible candidates as sites for day care centers. Further, many facility location techniques require an initial set of locations that are improved on successively. Thus, the demand map is useful for selecting good starting locations.

FACILITY LOCATION TECHNIQUES

An understanding of the facility location problem can be gained from the results of locating a single facility on a line. For example, consider the problem of locating a beach mat concession along the beach front at Waikiki. Suppose you wish to find a location that would minimize the average walk to your concession from anywhere on the beach. Further, suppose you have data showing the density of bathers along the beachfront, which is related to the size and location of hotels. This problem is shown schematically in Figure 7.4.

The objective is

$$\text{Minimize} \qquad Z = \sum_{i=0}^{s} w_i(s - x_i) + \sum_{i-s}^{n} w_i(x_i - s) \qquad (4)$$

where w_i = relative weight of demand attached to the ith location on the beach

x_i = location of the ith demand point on the beach in feet from the origin, in this case taken to be the west end of the beach

s = site of the beach mat concession

The total-distance function Z is differentiated with respect to s and set equal to zero. This yields

$$\frac{dZ}{ds} = \sum_{i=0}^{s} w_i - \sum_{i=s}^{n} w_i = 0 \quad \text{or} \quad \sum_{i=0}^{s} w_i = \sum_{i=s}^{n} w_i \qquad (5)$$

FIGURE 7.4 Locating a single facility along a line.

This result suggests that the site should be located at the median with respect to the density distribution of bathers. That is, the site is located so that 50 percent of the potential demand is to each side (i.e., 29 in Figure 7.4). We probably should have expected this, because the median has the property of minimizing the sum of the absolute deviations from it.

The result for locating a site along a line can be generalized for locating a site on a plane if we use the metropolitan metric. Total travel distance will be minimized if the coordinates of the site correspond to the intersection of the x and y medians for their respective density distributions. We will refer to this as the *cross-median* approach.

The selection of a solution technique is determined by the characteristics of the problem, as outlined in Figure 7.1. Our discussion of location techniques is not exhaustive, but a few techniques will be discussed to illustrate various approaches to the problem. The selected techniques also represent approaches that deal with the various problem characteristics: single-facility versus multiple-facility location, location on a plane or a network, and public versus private optimization criteria.

Single Facility

Metropolitan Metric   Locating a single facility on a plane to minimize the weighted travel distances by means of the metropolitan metric is straightforward using the cross-median approach. The objective is

$$Z = \sum_{i=1}^{n} w_i\{|x_i - x_s| + |y_i - y_s|\} \tag{6}$$

where w_i = weight attached to the ith point (e.g., population)
$\quad x_i, y_i$ = coordinates of the ith demand point
$\quad x_s, y_s$ = coordinates of the service facility
$\quad\quad n$ = number of demand points served

Note that the objective function may be restated as two independent terms.

$$\text{Minimize} \qquad Z = \sum_{i=1}^{n} w_i|x_i - x_s| + \sum_{i=1}^{n} w_i|y_i - y_s| \tag{7}$$

Recall from our beach mat example that the median of a discrete set of values is such that the sum of absolute deviations from it is a minimum. Thus, our optimum site will have coordinates such that (1) x_s is at the median value for w_i ordered in the x direction and (2) y_s is at the median value for w_i ordered in the y direction. Because x_s, y_s, or both may be unique or lie within a range, the optimal location may be at a point, on a line, or within an area.

Example 7.1: Copying Service

A copying service has decided to open an office in the central business district of a city. The manager has identified four office buildings that will generate a major portion of its business, and Figure 7.5 shows the location of these demand points on an xy coordinate system. Weights are attached to each point and represent potential demand per month in hundreds of orders. The manager would like to determine a central location that will minimize the total distance per month that customers travel to the copying service.

Because of the urban location, a metropolitan metric is appropriate. A site located by the cross-median approach will be used to solve this problem. First, the median is calculated using equation (8):

FIGURE 7.5 Locating a copying service.

$$\text{Median} = \sum_{i-1}^{n} \frac{w_i}{2} \tag{8}$$

From Figure 7.5, we find that the median has a value of $(7 + 1 + 3 + 5)/2 = 8$. To identify the x-coordinate median for x_s, we sum the values of w_i in the x direction both west to east and east to west. The top half of Table 7.1 lists in descending order the demand points from west to east as they appear in Figure 7.5 (i.e., 1, 2, 3, 4). The weights attached to each demand point are summed in descending order until the median value of 8 is reached or exceeded. The median value of 8 is reached when the weight of location 2 is added to the weight of location 1: thus, the first x median is established at the value of 2 miles (i.e., the x coordinate of location 2 is circled).

TABLE 7.1		
MEDIAN VALUE FOR X_s		
Point i	Location x_i	$\sum w_i$
	Ordering west to east $\rightarrow$	
1	1	7　　= 7
2	②	7 + 1 = 8
3	3	
4	4	
	Ordering east to west $\leftarrow$	
4	4	5　　= 5
3	③	5 + 3 = 8
2	2	
1	1	

This procedure is repeated with demand points ordered from east to west, as shown in descending order in the bottom half of Table 7.1 (i.e., 4, 3, 2, 1). The second x median is established at the value of 3 miles (i.e., the x coordinate of location 3 is circled).

Table 7.2 illustrates the same procedure for identifying the y-coordinate median for y_s. The top half of Table 7.2 lists in descending order the demand points from south to north as they appear in Figure 7.5 (i.e., 4, 1, 2, 3). In this case, the median value of 8 is first exceeded at location 1 when its weight is added to that of location 4 to yield a total of 12. The y median is established at the value of 2 miles (i.e., the y coordinate of location 1 is circled). At the bottom of Table 7.2, the demand points from north to south are listed in descending order as they appear in Figure 7.5 (i.e., 3, 2, 1, 4). Again, the median value is first exceeded at location 1 when its weight is added to those of locations 3 and 2 to yield a total of 11. Thus, we are left with only one y median at 2 miles.

The cross-median approach of determining the median from all four points of the compass ensures that if a range of locations is appropriate, it will be identified readily. In this case, any location on the line segment AB minimizes total travel distance (e.g., coordinates $2 = x_s = 3$ and $y_s = 2$).

Note from Table 7.3 that the total weighted travel distance calculated for point A and point B is equal to 35 miles in both instances; thus, any location at either point A or point B or along the line between them will be acceptable. As this example illustrates, a location solution can be a line (i.e., a city street), a point (i.e., an intersection), or an area (i.e., a city block). Thus, the cross-median approach can result in some site selection flexibility.

Euclidian Metric   Changing the geographic structure to the straight-line distance between points complicates the location problem. The objective now becomes

$$\text{Minimize} \qquad Z = \sum_{i=1}^{n} w_i[(x_i - x_s)^2 + (y_i - y_s)^2]^{1/2} \tag{9}$$

Taking the partial derivatives with respect to x_s and y_s and setting them equal to zero results in two equations. Solving these equations for x_s and y_s yields the following pair of equations (10 and 11) that identify the optimal location:

TABLE 7.2

MEDIAN VALUE FOR Y_s

Point i	Location y_i	$\sum w_i$
	Ordering south to north ↑	
4	1	5 = 5
1	②	5 + 7 = 12
2	3	
3	5	
	Ordering north to south ↓	
3	5	3 = 3
2	3	3 + 1 = 4
1	②	3 + 1 + 7 = 11
4	1	

TABLE 7.3

TOTAL WEIGHTED DISTANCE FOR LOCATIONS A AND B

Location A (2,2)				Location B (3,2)			
Office	Distance	Weight	Total	Office	Distance	Weight	Total
1	1 ×	7	= 7	1	2 ×	7	= 14
2	1 ×	1	= 1	2	2 ×	1	= 2
3	4 ×	3	= 12	3	3 ×	3	= 9
4	3 ×	5	= 15	4	2 ×	5	= 10
			35				35

$$x_s = \frac{\sum_{i=1}^{n} \dfrac{w_i x_i}{d_{is}}}{\sum_{i=1}^{n} \dfrac{w_i}{d_{is}}} \qquad (10)$$

$$y_s = \frac{\sum_{i=1}^{n} \dfrac{w_i y_i}{d_{is}}}{\sum_{i=1}^{n} \dfrac{w_i}{d_{is}}} \qquad (11)$$

where $d_{is} = [(x_i - x_s)^2 + (y_i - y_s)^2]^{1/2}$

Unfortunately, these equations have no direct solution, because x_s and y_s appear on both sides of the equality (i.e., they are contained in the d_{is} term). The solution procedure begins with trial values of x_s and y_s. The formulas are used to calculate revised values of x_s and y_s, and the process is continued until the difference between successive values of x_s and y_s is negligible.

Using the copying service example shown in Figure 7.5, the calculations shown in Table 7.4 were made to find an optimal location, assuming for now that a euclidian metric is appropriate. Beginning with a trial location of ($x_s = 2, y_s = 2$) and using equation (10), we find the revised value for $x_s = 20.78/11.19 = 1.857$. Using equation (11), we find the revised value for $y_s = 23.98/11.19 = 2.143$. Time—and patience—permitting, we could continue until successive values of x_s and y_s were nearly identical and declare an optimal solution. The euclidian location always will result in a point, and only by accident will it agree with the metropolitan metric location.

In spite of the tedious mathematics, the euclidian location model is appropriate when vector travel is involved. The logic of the euclidian metric single-location model

TABLE 7.4

EUCLIDIAN METRIC CALCULATIONS FOR TRIAL LOCATION

Customer (i)	1	2	3	4
Location (x,y)	(1,2)	(2,3)	(3,5)	(4,1)
Weight (w_i)	7	1	3	5
Distance (d_{is})	1.0	1.0	3.16	2.24

was not lost on Federal Express when it selected Memphis as the hub of its air package delivery network serving the entire United States.

Locating a Retail Outlet

When locating a retail outlet such as a supermarket, the objective is to maximize profit. In this case, a discrete number of alternative locations must be evaluated to find the most profitable site.

A gravity model is used to estimate consumer demand. This model is based on the physical analog that the gravitational attraction of two bodies is directly proportional to the product of their masses and inversely proportional to the square of the distance that separates them. For a service, the attractiveness of a facility may be expressed as

$$A_{ij} = \frac{S_j}{T_{ij}^\lambda} \tag{12}$$

where A_{ij} = attraction to facility j for consumer i
S_j = size of the facility j
T_{ij} = travel time from consumer i's location to facility j
λ = parameter estimated empirically to reflect the effect of travel time on various kinds of shopping trips (e.g., where a shopping mall may have a $\lambda = 2$, convenience stores would have a $\lambda = 10$ or larger)

David L. Huff developed a retail location model using this gravity model to predict the benefit that a customer would have for a particular store size and location.[3] Knowing that customers also would be attracted to other competing stores, he proposed the ratio P_{ij}. For n stores, this ratio measures the probability of a customer from a given statistical area i traveling to a particular shopping facility j.

$$P_{ij} = \frac{A_{ij}}{\sum_{j=1}^{n} A_{ij}} \tag{13}$$

An estimate of E_{jk}, the total annual consumer expenditures for a product class k at a prospective shopping facility j, then can be calculated as

$$E_{jk} = \sum_{i=1}^{m} (P_{ij} C_i B_{ik}) \tag{14}$$

where P_{ij} = probability of a consumer from a given statistical area i traveling to a shopping facility j, calculated by means of equation (13)
C_i = number of consumers at area i
B_{ik} = average annual amount budgeted by consumer at area i for a product class k
m = number of statistical areas

An estimate of M_{jk}, the market share captured by facility j of product class k sales, can be calculated as

$$M_{jk} = \frac{E_{jk}}{\sum_{i=1}^{m} C_i B_{ik}} \tag{15}$$

An iterative procedure is used to calculate the expected annual profit of each potential site for various possible store sizes at the site. Net operating profit before taxes is calculated as a percentage of sales adjusted for the size of the store. The result is a list of potential sites with the store size at each that maximizes profit. All that remains is to negotiate a real estate deal for the site that comes closest to maximizing annual profit.

Example 7.2: Copying Service—Huff Analysis

Assume that the copying service in example 7.1 has been established at $(x = 2, y = 2)$, as shown by location A in Figure 7.5 at the far left end of the optimal line. Further, assume that each customer order represents an expenditure of approximately $10. Because convenience would be an important customer criterion, assume that $\lambda = 2$. If we wish to open a new store at location $(x = 3, y = 2)$ (i.e., at location B on the far right end of the optimal line) but with *twice* the capacity of the existing copy center, how much market share would we expect to capture? Using the travel distances in Table 7.5 as input to the Huff model, the calculations shown in Tables 7.6 to 7.8 are obtained.

This example illustrates the result of an aggressive location strategy as used by well-financed national retail chains. For example, as the name might imply, Blockbuster Video has a reputation of moving into a community with supersized stores and driving out small, locally operated video-rental establishments.

Multiple Facilities

Location Set Covering Problem The difficulty of evaluating decisions regarding public facility location has resulted in a search for surrogate, or substitute, measures of the benefit of the facility location. One such measure is the distance that the most distant customer would have to travel to reach the facility. This is known as the *maximal service distance*. We want to find the minimum number and location of facilities that will serve all demand points within some specified maximal service distance; this is known as the *location set covering* problem.

Example 7.3: Rural Medical Clinics

A state department of health is concerned about the lack of medical care in rural areas, and a group of nine communities has been selected for a pilot program in which medical clinics will be opened to serve primary health care needs. It is hoped that every community will be within 30 miles of at least one clinic. The planners would like to determine the number of clinics that are required and their locations. Any community can serve as a potential clinic site except for community 6, because facilities are unavailable there. Figure 7.6 shows a network identifying the cities as numbered circles; lines drawn between the sites show the travel distances in miles.

The problem is approached by first identifying for each community the other communities that can be reached from it within the 30-mile travel limit. Beginning with community 1, we see in Figure 7.6 that communities 2, 3, and 4 can be reached within

TABLE 7.5

TRAVEL DISTANCE IN MILES (T_{ij})
[Using Metropolitan Metric]

	Customer location (i)			
Site (j)	1	2	3	4
Proposed (3,2)	2	2	3	2
Existing (2,2)	1	1	4	3

TABLE 7.6

ATTRACTION (A_{ij})

	Customer location (i)			
Site (j)	1	2	3	4
Proposed ($S_1 = 2$)	0.5	0.5	0.2222	0.500
Existing ($S_2 = 1$)	1.0	1.0	0.0625	0.111
Total attraction	1.5	1.5	0.2847	0.611

TABLE 7.7

PROBABILITY (P_{ij})

	Customer location (i)			
Site (j)	1	2	3	4
Proposed	.33	.33	.78	.82
Existing	.67	.67	.22	.18

TABLE 7.8

MONTHLY EXPENDITURES (E_{jk}) AND MARKET SHARE (M_{jk})

	Customer expenditures					
Site (j)	1	2	3	4	Monthly total	Market share%
Proposed	$2,333	$ 333	$2,340	$4,100	$9,106	0.57
Existing	4,667	667	660	900	6.894	0.43
Totals	$7,000	$1,000	$3,000	$5,000	$16,000	1.00

TABLE 7.9

RANGE OF SERVICE FOR POTENTIAL SITES

Community	Set of communities served from site	Potential sites that could serve the community*
1	1,2,3,4	1,2,3,4
2	1,2,3	(1,2,3)†
3	1,2,3,4,5	1,2,3,4,5
4	1,3,4,5,6,7	1,3,4,5,7
5	3,4,5,6	(3,4,5)†
6	4,5,6,7,8	4,5,7,8
7	4,6,7,8	(4,7,8)†
8	6,7,8,9	7,8,9
9	8,9	(8,9)†

* Community 6 cannot serve as a clinic site.
† Subsets of potential sites.

the 30-mile distance limit. The results of similar inspections for each community are reported in the second column of Table 7.9 as the set of communities served from each site. An equivalent statement could be made that this set, less any communities that could not serve as a site, represents the set of sites that could cover the community in question for service within 30 miles. Thus, for community 5, a clinic located at site 3, 4, or 5 meets the maximal travel limit.

The third column of Table 7.9 represents the set of potential sites that could cover a given community. Several of these sets have been placed in parentheses, however, because they represent subsets of other potential locations. For example, because community 2 can only be served by sites 1, 2, and 3, one of these sites must be selected for a clinic location. Identifying these subsets reduces the problem size while ensuring that restrictions are satisfied.

Note that because of our desire to minimize the number of clinics to cover all the communities, any site common to two or more of these subsets is an excellent candidate for selection. In this case, sites 3, 4, and 8 are candidates. From inspection, we see that if sites 3 and 8 are selected, all subsets are accounted for; thus, all communities can be covered with just these two clinics. We also have identified the service region for each clinic; the clinic located at community 3 will serve communities 1 through 5, and the clinic located at community 8 will serve communities 6 through 9.

The location set covering problem often can yield more than one solution. In this example, if the maximal travel distance were set at 40 miles, the following five pairs of clinic site locations would provide coverage: (3, 8), (3, 9), (4, 7), (4, 8), and (4, 9).

Maximal Covering Location Problem   A variation of the location set covering problem is *maximal covering*. This problem is based on a very appealing objective: maximizing the population covered within a desired service distance.

A travel network such as the one shown in Figure 7.6 now would be augmented with information on the user population of each community. Richard Church and Charles ReVelle developed a *greedy adding (GA) algorithm* for solving this problem that builds on the location set covering analysis.[4] The algorithm begins with an empty solution set and then adds the best facility sites to this set one at a time. The first facility that is selected covers the largest population. Additional sites then are selected that cover the greatest amount of the remaining uncovered population until all the population is covered or the limit on the number of sites is reached.

For example, recall from Example 7.3 that sites 3, 4, and 8 were identified as candidates for the set covering problem. If we assume that each community has an equal population, then the GA algorithm would select site 4 as the first site to maximize population coverage. From Table 7.9, we see that site 4 covers communities 1, 3, 4, 5, 6, and 7. This exceeds the number of communities covered by either site 3 or site 8. Site 8 would be selected next because it covers the uncovered communities 8 and 9 whereas site 3 only would cover the uncovered community 2.

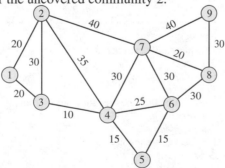

FIGURE 7.6   Travel network for a rural area.

SITE CONSIDERATIONS

Selection of the actual site requires other considerations beyond minimization of travel distance. Available real estate represents a major constraint on the final selection of a site. As indicated by Table 7.10, however, many considerations enter into the final decision.

BREAKING THE RULES

Before we leave the topic of service facility location, some caveats must be mentioned. Several creative exceptions to the assumed logic of the location models presented here need to be discussed. To this point, our location objective has been focused on customer convenience as measured in distance traveled to the planned facility. Consider, however, the success of the specialty mail-order business of L.L. Bean, located in Freeport, Maine, which calls into question the necessity of always finding a location that is convenient for customers' physical access.

In the following discussion, we will look at a marketing concept called *competitive clustering,* which is used for shopping goods, as well as a strategy called *saturation marketing* that defies the curse of cannibalization and has been successful for some urban retailers. A concept of *marketing intermediaries* is used to extend the service market well beyond the confines of geography, and, finally, the opportunity to substitute electronic communication for transportation is explored.

Competitive Clustering

Competitive clustering is a reaction to observed consumer behavior when they are choosing among competitors. When shopping for items such as new automobiles or used cars, customers like to make comparisons and, for convenience, seek out the area of town where many dealers are concentrated (i.e., the so-called motor mile).

Motel chains such as La Quinta have observed that inns located in areas with many nearby competitors experience higher occupancy rates than those located in isolation. It is surprising that locating near the competition is a strategy with profitable counter-intuitive results for some services. Further, many motels are located by an interstate highway interchange because their market is businesspeople and others traveling by car, not the local population.

TABLE 7.10

SITE SELECTION CONSIDERATIONS

1. *Access:*
   Convenient to freeway exit and entrance ramps
   Served by public transportation
2. *Visibility:*
   Set back from street
   Sign placement
3. *Traffic:*
   Traffic volume on street that may indicate potential impulse buying
   Traffic congestion that could be a hindrance (e.g., fire stations)
4. *Parking:*
   Adequate off-street parking
5. *Expansion:*
   Room for expansion
6. *Environment:*
   Immediate surroundings should complement the service
7. *Competition:*
   Location of competitors
8. *Government:*
   Zoning restrictions
   Taxes

Auto dealers that locate in clusters attract customers from afar because of the convenience of one-stop comparison shopping.

Saturation Marketing

Au Bon Pain, a cafe known for its gourmet sandwiches, French bread, and croissants, has embraced the unconventional strategy of *saturation marketing* popularized in Europe. The idea is to group outlets of the same firm tightly in urban and other high-traffic areas. Au Bon Pain has clustered 16 cafes in downtown Boston alone, with many of them fewer than 100 yards apart—in fact, one group of five shops operates on different floors of Filene's department store. Although modest cannibalization of sales has been reported, the advantages of reduced advertising, easier supervision, and customer awareness, when taken together, overwhelm the competition and far outweigh the drawbacks. This strategy works best in high-density, downtown locations, where shops can intercept impulse customers with little time to shop or eat.[5]

The success of this approach became apparent to us during a summer visit to Helsinki, Finland, where we noticed ice cream vendors from the same firm with carts on nearly every corner of the downtown walking streets. The sight of a vendor seems to plant the idea of a treat in the mind of a passerby, who then takes advantage of the next, nearby opportunity.

Marketing Intermediaries

The idea that services are created and consumed simultaneously does not seem to allow for the "channel-of-distribution" concept as developed for goods. Because services are intangible and cannot be stored or transported, the geographic area for service would seem to be restricted. However, service channels of distribution have evolved that use separate organizational entities as intermediaries between the producer and the consumer.

James H. Donnelly provides a number of examples that illustrate how some services have created unlimited geographic service areas.[6] The retailer who extends a bank's credit to its customers is an intermediary in the distribution of credit. That Bank of America is a California bank does not limit use of the VISA card, which is honored worldwide. A health maintenance organization (HMO) performs an intermediary role between the practitioner and the patient by increasing the availability and convenience of "one-stop" shopping, and group insurance written through employers and labor unions is an example of how the insurance industry uses intermediaries to distribute its service.

Substitution of Communication for Transportation

An appealing alternative to moving people from one place to another is the use of telecommunications. One proposal that has met with some success is the use of telemetry to extend health care services into remote regions. Paramedics or nurse practitioners can use communication with a distant hospital to provide health care without transporting the patient. In addition, the banking industry has been promoting direct payroll deposit, which permits employees to have their pay deposited directly into their checking accounts. By authorizing employers to deposit salaries, the employees save trips to the bank; bankers also benefit through reduced check-processing paperwork and less congestion at their drive-in teller facilities.

A study by David A. Lopez and Paul Gray illustrates how an insurance company in Los Angeles decentralized its operations by using telecommunications and strategically locating its satellite offices.[7] An examination was made of the benefits and costs to the insurance firm when work was moved to the workers rather than when workers moved to their work. Insurance companies and other information-based industries are good candidates for employer decentralization, because members of their office staff perform routine clerical tasks using the firm's computer databases. The proposed plan replaced the centralized operation in downtown Los Angeles with a network of regional satellite offices in the suburbs where the workers live.

The analysis also included a location study to determine the size, site, and number of satellites that would minimize the variable costs associated with employee travel and the fixed costs of establishing the satellite offices. The decentralization plan yielded several benefits to the company: (1) reduced staff requirements, (2) reduced employee turnover and training, (3) reduced salaries for clerical employees, (4) elimination of a lunch program, and (5) increased income from lease of the headquarters site. Employees whose travel to work was reduced by at least $5\frac{1}{2}$ miles realized a net benefit over their reduced salary and loss of subsidized lunch. This employee benefit is important in light of increasing energy expenses for transportation.

It was found that underwriting life insurance and servicing insurance policies could be performed by means of a computer terminal. Phone communications usually were sufficient for personal contacts, and few face-to-face meetings were needed. These findings substantiate those of other studies in Britain and Sweden indicating that individuals require face-to-face contacts only for initial meetings and periodic refreshing; they do not require continual face-to-face contact to reach decisions and conduct routine business.

Impact of the Internet on Service Location

With the introduction of the Internet in the mid 1990s, the potential for electronic commerce has become a reality—customers shop from a desk at home and surf the Web for interesting home pages to visit. A website has become the virtual location of pure e-commerce firms (e.g., Amazon.com) or an alternative channel of distribution for established firms, referred to as "click and mortar" retailers (e.g., Barnes and Noble). The limits of a market area were once defined by how far a customer would travel to the site, but physical travel is irrelevant in the virtual world of the Internet. Location, however, is still a concern for e-commerce retailers that must ship a product. This aspect of a business is now driven by access to overnight shippers (e.g., locating a warehouse in Memphis for access to FedEx). Internet providers of electronic services, such as brokers (e.g., Fidelity.com), are less reliant on physical offices, and the location of an auction facilitator (e.g., eBay.com) can be based on personal preference of the owners or on access to talented employees.

GEOGRAPHIC INFORMATION SYSTEM

A new use of an old technology is moving into the professional business arena. Geographic information systems (GIS) are helping to make many business decisions and solving a variety of common business problems. These systems at one time were confined to the provenances of scientists and cartographers. Now, however, the Environmental Research Institute, Inc., has introduced ArcView, a GIS for business applications.[8] This resource, available on a compact disc, can be used for tasks such as mapping customer databases, determining site locations, analyzing demand, and improving delivery service. It has applications for every area of business, including banking, health care, real estate, and management.

In very simple terms, ArcView translates data, such as demographic information, into a map. Consider, for example, a table that lists street addresses and median home values. It may be possible to discern a pattern in the list, if the data are for a community of 150 people in central Montana. If the data are for Denver, however, we cannot possibly discern a pattern that might be useful to determine a location for a new high-end specialty shop. ArcView solves our Denver problem by transferring the data to a map base and color-coding the median home values according to different zip codes. We can see immediately which areas are likely to have customers for an expensive store.

Consider another example. Suppose a state agency wants to establish a warehouse to store surplus foods for Meals on Wheels organizations in an 18-county area. Most Meals on Wheels clients are elderly and homebound, so the agency commissioner wants to identify a location that will be most convenient for the Meals on Wheels units that have the highest demand. One solution to this problem is to use ArcView to look at the distribution of the population by age groups. Figure 7.7. shows that the counties on the eastern perimeter of the area tend to have larger populations in the 55+ age group. Based on this information, the warehouse could be located to serve these counties most conveniently.

SUMMARY

Facility location plays an important role in the strategy of a service firm through its influence on the competitive dimensions of flexibility, competitive positioning, demand management, and focus. Our approach to service facility location began with a discussion of issues that must be considered, such as geographic representation, number of facilities, and optimization criteria and their effect on the location selected. The first step in the facility location analysis is estimating geographic demand. This requires a definition of the target population, selection of the unit of area, and, often, the use of regression analysis.

The discussion of facility location techniques began with the single-facility problem. Two simple models were presented that identified an optimal location for minimizing the total distance traveled by customers using the two most common travel

Population Age Groups

0–29   30–54   55+

FIGURE 7.7   **Population density by age group.**

patterns (i.e., metropolitan and euclidian). The location of a single retail outlet to maximize profit is an important decision that has been studied by David Huff using a gravity model to predict customer attractiveness to a store based on its size and location. For the multiple-facility location problem, the concept of location set covering is central to understanding the many approaches to identifying multiple-site locations.

A section on "breaking the rules" presents several location strategies that appear to be counterintuitive compared with the analytical models presented earlier. Strategies such as competitive clustering are common for shopping goods, and saturation marketing has been successful for some small retail outlets. In addition, use of marketing intermediaries can decouple the provider from the consumer. If the requirement for face-to-face interaction between server and customer is not necessary, as illustrated by Internet service providers, the substitution of electronic communication for physical transportation becomes possible. The chapter concludes with a discussion of geographic information systems that assist in making location decisions by displaying data on maps.

Service Benchmark
SATURATING CITIES WITH STORES CAN PAY

Boston commuters hurrying to work from South Station can't avoid walking past an Au Bon Pain cafe no matter how hard they try.

There's one inside the station, and one across the street at 1 Financial Center. There's another two blocks away, at 176 Federal St., another two blocks away from that at 75-101 Federal St., and still another two more blocks away, at 14 Milk St.

"We like to say you can toss a football from unit to unit," says Louis Kane, cochairman of the fast-growing chain best known for its gourmet sandwiches, freshly squeezed orange juice and freshly baked French bread, croissants and muffins.

Au Bon Pain Co. is among the latest to embrace the unconventional strategy of saturation marketing. The idea, relatively new to the U.S., is to group outlets tightly in urban and other high-traffic areas. Au Bon Pain has clustered 16 cafes in downtown Boston alone—with many less than 100 yards apart, and one group of five shops operating on different floors of Filene's department store.

The chain is so confident of the success of saturation marketing that it now plans to export the strategy to other cities, where it has only a handful of units so far. It will open more than 15 stores a year in cities 500 miles or less from here, including New York, Philadelphia and Washington, D.C. In New York, it's focusing on downtown and midtown, where there are already three Rockefeller Center outlets.

While putting too many sites too close together can cannibalize sales—as it has done modestly at some Au Bon Pain locations—proponents say the advantages outweigh the drawbacks. Clustering shops can reduce advertising expenses, make for easier supervision and attract customers from the competition.

DEVELOPING BRAND IDENTITY

"The concept of saturation marketing makes perfect sense," says Richard Winger, a vice president at Boston Consulting Group, a management consulting firm. "It's the developing of brand identity that gives [companies] that extra push. When you think of croissants [in Boston], you think Au Bon Pain."

BOX 7.1 (CONTINUED)

It's too soon to tell whether saturation marketing will catch on as the latest marketing trend. Apparently only a few other companies have tried it seriously. BayBanks Inc., a second-tier regional bank here, has nonetheless managed to become a leader in retail banking by saturating the city and suburbs with automated teller machines. In downtown alone, it has 75 machines—almost three times as many as its major competitors. "We're every place," says Donald Issachs, a spokesman for the bank. "And the public loves it."

Benetton S.p.A., the Italian clothing company, was among the first in the U.S. to adopt the strategy, using saturation marketing to become a major player in the mid 1980s. Some New York neighborhoods sprouted three or four stores carrying only Benetton clothes and promoting slightly different themes or fashions.

While good for Benetton, the strategy alienated some store owners, who operate the shops independently. Some Benetton dealers, in fact, have sued the company, charging that their sales dropped after another Benetton-only shop opened nearby.

Indeed, some merchants question the merits of saturation marketing. McDonald's Corp, for example, won't put its restaurants too close together because it doesn't want them to compete with each other. "We're not coming in, looking at 20 square blocks and saying, 'Where are we going to put the next one?' We're interested in building sales at existing restaurants. That's one of our strategies for growth," says Chuck Ebeling, a McDonald's spokesman.

LIMITATIONS OF STRATEGY

Au Bon Pain concedes that its strategy has limitations. Saturation wouldn't work for Au Bon Pain in suburban or residential areas because it's not a "destination restaurant" that people will drive to. Instead, the strategy works best in high-density, downtown locations, where shops can intercept the hordes of impulse customers with little time to shop or eat lunch. In addition, the company acknowledges that there can be too much of a good thing. While it will open some more shops here, it expects most of its growth in other cities.

Au Bon Pain was formed about a decade ago when Mr. Kane, owner of the original Au Bon Pain, merged his two stores with a cookie company owned by Ronald Shaich, now cochairman. The new closely held Au Bon Pain didn't immediately embrace saturation marketing. Like many new fast-food businesses seeking to expand rapidly, Au Bon Pain turned to franchising after opening a handful of shops here. It franchised several units along the East Coast and in the Midwest, and more in airports around the U.S.

But it found that some franchisees were a headache to deal with. At the same time, it discovered that the more company-owned shops it opened in downtown Boston, the better it did. As a result, it bought out some of the franchisees and for several years has concentrated instead on saturation marketing here. The company now has 70 stores—51 company-owned and 19 franchised—with average sales of more than $1.25 million a year and about 10,000 customers a week.

"Why do we do this craziness? We do it because we continue to make money at it," says Mr. Shaich. "In the morning, people probably don't walk more than 50 feet for breakfast and they won't walk more than a block for lunch. So if the walls of the market are a block, then we have to be in each of those mini-markets."

Cannibalization has been limited so far, the company says. The Au Bon Pain at 75-101 Federal St., for example, recently saw sales drop 5% in the two weeks after a new Au Bon Pain opened a couple of blocks away. But, even though the new store had sales of about $60,000 in its first four weeks, sales at the older shop quickly recovered to the normal $100,000 a month. Customers of that store—mostly workers at two nearby banks—apparently tried the new Au Bon Pain, but then came back to the first store because it was closer and more convenient for them, says Marianne Graziadei, general manager of the store.

Even when sales don't fully recover, the gains at new stores more than offset any marginal loss at existing stores, the company maintains. Sales at the Au Bon Pain at Summer and Hawley streets have fallen 5% since a new store opened a block away four months ago. Still, the new store's projected yearly sales of $850,000 more than offsets the $75,000 drop at the older store.

Moreover, if the new store hadn't been opened, another restaurant likely would have taken the location—and a competitor would be getting the additional sales, says Mr. Kane.

ZERO AD BUDGET

The danger of cannibalization is further offset by other benefits of saturation marketing. "We've never spent a penny on advertising," boasts Mr. Shaich. Yet the awareness level of the chain in Boston is "phenomenal," he says.

This awareness, of course, stems from the proximity of the stores, says Marc Particem, senior vice president at Booz, Allen & Hamilton Inc., a management consulting firm in New York. "It's like having outdoor billboards on every block; the stores are a substitute for advertising."

The company also benefits from close supervision. Regional managers can walk from store to store, visiting as many in one day as managers of scattered chains might visit in a week. "Our guys live in our stores," says Mr. Kane.

Source: Reprinted with permission from Suzanne Alexander, "Saturating Cities with Stores Can Pay," *The Wall Street Journal,* Monday, September 11, 1989, p. B1. Reprinted by permission of *The Wall Street Journal,* 1989, Dow Jones & Company, Inc. All Rights Reserved Worldwide.

KEY TERMS AND DEFINITIONS

Competitive clustering the grouping of competitors (e.g., automobile dealerships) in close proximity for convenience in comparative shopping by customers.

Cross-median an approach to the location of a single facility using the metropolitan metric to minimize the total weighted distance traveled.

Euclidian metric a measure of distance traveled assuming vector travel from one point to another (e.g., the flight of an airplane between two cities).

Location set covering an approach to finding the minimum number and location of facilities that will serve all demand points within a specified maximum travel distance.

Marketing intermediaries a business entity in the channel of distribution between the final customer and the service provider (e.g., a bank extending credit to a retailer through a credit card).

Metropolitan metric a measure of distance traveled assuming rectangular displacement (e.g. north-south and east-west travel in urban areas).

Saturation marketing the location of a firm's individual outlets (e.g., ice cream vendors) in close proximity to create a significant presence that attracts customer attention.

SOLVED PROBLEMS

1. Cross-Median Location Problem

Problem Statement

A health clinic is being planned to serve a rural area in west Texas. The service area consists of four communities at the following *xy* coordinate locations in miles: A(6, 2), B(8, 6), C(5, 9), D(3, 4), with populations of 2,000, 1,000, 3,000, and 2,000, respectively. Recommend a "cross-median" location for the health clinic minimizing the total weighted metropolitan distance traveled.

Solution

First, calculate the median value in thousands:

$$\text{Median} = (2 + 1 + 3 + 2)/2 = 4$$

Second, plot the four communities on the grid on page 194 with population in thousands as subscripts:

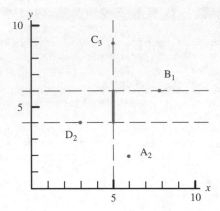

Third, draw the x-median dotted line (i.e., vertical line) on the plot by moving from left to right, adding the weights until the sum is equal to or exceeds the median (i.e., $D_2 + C_3 = 5$). The result is one vertical line at $x = 5$. Moving from right to left, add the weights until the sum is equal to or exceeds the median (i.e., $B_1 + A_2 + C_3 = 6$). The result is the same vertical line at $x = 5$.

Fourth, draw the y-median dotted line (i.e., horizontal line) on the plot by moving from top to bottom, adding the weights until the sum is equal to or exceeds the median (i.e., $C_3 + B_1 = 4$). The result is a horizontal line at $y = 6$. Moving from bottom to top, add the weights until the sum is equal to or exceeds the median (i.e., $A_2 + D_2 = 4$). The result is another horizontal line at $y = 4$. The recommended location results in a line segment shown as a dark line in the plot with xy coordinates of (5,4 to 5,6).

2. Retail Location Using the Huff Model

Problem Statement

The west Texas area in the plot above is served by a grocery store in community D. A proposed store with three times the floor space is being considered for location in community C. Assume that monthly expenditures per customer average about $100. Then, using the metropolitan metric for travel and $\lambda = 2$, use the Huff model to estimate the impact on monthly expenditures and market share for the existing store in community D if the proposed store in community C is constructed.

Solution

First, determine the travel distances using the metropolitan metric:

TRAVEL DISTANCE IN MILES (T_{ij})
[Using Metropolitan Metric]

	Community (*i*)			
Site (*j*)	A (6,2)	B (8,6)	C (5,9)	D (3,4)
Proposed C (5,9)	8	6	0	7
Existing D (3,4)	5	7	7	0

Second, using equation (12), calculate the attraction matrix with $\lambda = 2$. For example, the attraction of community A to the proposed location at C (with $S = 3$ to account for the larger floor space) would be calculated as

$$A_{ij} = \frac{S_j}{T_{ij}^\lambda} = \frac{S_1}{T_{11}^2} = \frac{3}{8^2} = \frac{3}{64} = 0.0469$$

Note that the attraction is given a value of ∞ where the store is located in the same community ($T_{ij} = 0$ in the denominator).

ATTRACTION (A_{ij})

Site (j)	Community location (i)			
	A	B	C	D
Proposed $S_1 = 3$	0.0469	0.8333	q	—
Existing $S_2 = 1$	0.0400	0.0204	—	q
Total attraction	0.0869	0.8537		

Third, using equation (13), calculate the probability using the total attraction as the denominator. For example, the probability of residents in community A traveling to the proposed grocery store location at C would be calculated as

$$P_{ij} = \frac{A_{ij}}{\sum_{j=1}^{n} A_{ij}} = \frac{A_{11}}{A_{11} + A_{12}} = \frac{0.0469}{0.0469 + 0.04} = 0.54$$

PROBABILITY (P_{ij})

Site (j)	Community location (i)			
	A	B	C	D
Proposed	.54	.98	1.0	0
Existing	.46	.02	0	1.0

Fourth, using equation (14), the monthly expenditures are calculated, and using equation (15), the market shares are determined. For example, expenditures from residents of community A at the proposed grocery store location at C would be calculated as

$$E_{jk} = \sum_{i=1}^{m} (P_{ij}C_iB_{ik}) = P_{11}C_1B_1 = (.54)(2000)(100) = \$108,000$$

MONTHLY EXPENDITURES (E_{jk}) AND MARKET SHARE (M_{jk})

Site (j)	Community expenditures				Monthly total	Market share%
	A	B	C	D		
Proposed	$108,000	$ 98,000	$300,000	$ 0	$506,000	0.63
Existing	92,000	2,000	0	200,000	294,000	0.37
Totals	$200,000	$100,000	$300,000	$200,000	$800,000	1.00

TOPICS FOR DISCUSSION

1. Pick a particular service, and identify shortcomings in its site selection.
2. How would you proceed to estimate empirically the parameter λ in the Huff retail location model for a branch bank?
3. Why do you think set covering is an attractive approach to public sector facility location?
4. What are the characteristics of a service that would make communication a good substitute for transportation?
5. What are the benefits of using intermediaries in the service distribution channel?

EXERCISES

7.1. Revisit the copying service in **Example 7.1** and assume that over the years, the monthly demand from the four customers has increased to the following weights: $w_1 = 7$, $w_2 = 9$, $w_3 = 5$, $w_4 = 7$. If we previously located the copying service at point A in Figure 7.5, should we now consider a relocation?

7.2. A temporary-help agency wants to open an office in a suburban section of a large city. It has identified five large corporate offices as potential customers. The locations of these offices in miles on an xy coordinate grid for the area are $c_1 = (4, 4)$, $c_2 = (4, 11)$, $c_3 = (7, 2)$, $c_4 = (11, 11)$, and $c_5 = (14, 7)$. The expected demand for temporary help from these customers is weighted as $w_1 = 3$, $w_2 = 2$, $w_3 = 2$, $w_4 = 4$, and $w_5 = 1$. The agency reimburses employees for travel expenses incurred by their assignments; therefore, recommend a location (i.e., xy coordinates) for the agency that will minimize the total weighted metropolitan distance for job-related travel.

7.3. Four hospitals located in one county are cooperating to establish a centralized blood-bank facility to serve them all. On an xy coordinate grid of the county, the hospitals are found at the following locations: $H_1 = (5, 10)$, $H_2 = (7, 6)$, $H_3 = (4, 2)$, and $H_4 = (16, 3)$. The expected number of deliveries per month from the blood bank to each hospital is estimated at 450, 1,200, 300, and 1,500, respectively. Using the metropolitan metric, recommend a location for the blood bank that will minimize the total distance traveled.

7.4. A pizza delivery service has decided to open a branch near off-campus student housing. The project manager has identified five student apartment complexes in the northwest area of the city, the locations of which, on an xy coordinate grid in miles, are $C_1 = (1, 2)$, $C_2 = (2, 6)$, $C_3 = (3, 3)$, $C_4 = (4, 1)$, and $C_5 = (5, 4)$. The expected demand is weighted as $w_1 = 5$, $w^2 = 4$, $w_3 = 3$, $w_4 = 1$, and $w_5 = 5$. Using the metropolitan metric, recommend a location for the pizza branch that will minimize the total distance traveled.

7.5. A small city airport is served by four airlines. The terminal is rather spread out, with boarding areas located on an xy coordinate grid at $A = (1, 4)$, $B = (5, 5)$, $C = (8, 3)$, and $D = (8, 1)$. The number of flights per day, of approximately equal capacity, is $A = 28$, $B = 22$, $C = 36$, and $D = 18$. A new central baggage claim area is under construction.

   a. Using the metropolitan metric, recommend a location for the new baggage claim area that will minimize the total weighted distance from the boarding areas.

   b. Using the euclidian metric and the result found in part **a** as an initial solution, find the optimum location assuming vector travel.

7.6. You have been asked to help locate a catering service in the central business district of a city. The locations of potential customers on an xy coordinate grid are $P_1 = (4, 4)$, $P_2 = (12, 4)$, $P_3 = (2, 7)$, $P_4 = (11, 11)$, and $P_5 = (7, 14)$. The expected demand is weighted as $w_1 = 4$, $w_2 = 3$, $w_3 = 2$, $w_4 = 4$, and $w_5 = 1$.

   a. Using the metropolitan metric, recommend a location for the catering service that will minimize the total weighted distance traveled to serve the customers.

   b. Using the euclidian metric and the result found in part **a** as an initial solution, find the optimum location assuming vector travel.

7.7. Revisit the copying service Huff analysis in **Example 7.2**. Recalculate the monthly customer expenditures and the market share for the proposed copying center at location B if the new store will be *three* times the capacity of the existing store at location A and the new demand weights from Exercise 7.1 above are used.

7.8. A locally owned department store samples two customers in each of five geographic areas to estimate consumer spending in its home appliances department. It is estimated that these customers are a good sample of the 10,000 customers the store serves. The number of customers in each area is $C_1 = 1,500$, $C_2 = 2,500$, $C_2 = 1,000$, $C_4 = 3,000$, and $C_5 = 2000$. It is found that the two consumers have the following budgets in dollars for home appliances per year: $B_{11} = 100$, $B_{12} = 150$; $B_{21} = 75$, $B_{22} = 100$; $B_{31} = 125$, $B_{32} = 125$;

$B_{41} = 100$, $B_{42} = 120$; and $B_{51} = 120$, $B_{52} = 125$. Using the Huff retail location model, estimate annual home appliance sales for the store.

7.9. Bull's-Eye, a chain department store, opens a branch in a shopping complex near the store mentioned in Exercise 7.8. The Bull's-Eye branch is three times larger than the locally owned store. The travel times in minutes from the five areas to the two stores ($j = 1$ for the locally owned store, $j = 2$ for Bull's-Eye) are $T_{11} = 20$, $T_{12} = 15$; $T_{21} = 35$, $T_{22} = 20$; $T_{31} = 30$, $T_{32} = 25$; $T_{41} = 20$, $T_{42} = 25$; and $T_{51} = 25$, $T_{52} = 25$. Use the Huff retail location model to estimate the annual consumer expenditures in the home appliance section of each store assuming that $\lambda = 1$.

7.10. A community is currently being served by a single self-serve gas station with six pumps. A competitor is opening a new facility with 12 pumps across town. Table 7.11 shows the travel times in minutes from the four different areas in the community to the sites and the number of customers in each area.

    a. Using the Huff retail location model and assuming that $\lambda = 2$, calculate the probability of a customer traveling from each area to each site.

    b. Estimate the proportion of the existing market lost to the new competitor.

TABLE 7.11

TRAVEL TIMES TO GAS STATIONS

Area	1	2	3	4
Old station	5	10	9	15
New competitor	20	8	12	6
Number of customers	100	150	80	50

7.11. Recall the rural medical clinics in **Example 7.3** and suppose that each community were required to be 25 miles at most from the nearest clinic. How many clinics would be needed, and what would their locations be? Give all possible location solutions.

7.12. A bank is planning to serve the rural communities shown in Figure 7.8 with automated teller machines (ATMs). The travel time in minutes between communities in the service area is shown on the network in Figure 7.8. The bank is interested in determining the number and location of ATMs necessary to serve the communities so that a machine will be within 20 minutes' travel time of any community.

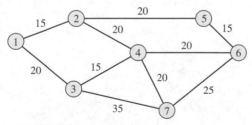

FIGURE 7.8 Service area network.

7.13. The volunteer fire department serving the communities in Figure 7.8 has just purchased two used fire engines auctioned off by a nearby city.

    a. Select all possible pairs of communities in which the fire engines could be located to ensure that all communities can be reached in 30 minutes or less.

    b. What additional consideration could be used to make the final site selection from the community pairs found in part **a**?

Health Maintenance Organization (C)

Joan Taylor, the administrator of Life-Time Insurance Company, which is based in Buffalo, New York, was charged with establishing a health maintenance organization (HMO) satellite clinic in Austin, Texas. The HMO concept would offer Austin residents an alternative to the traditional fee-for-service medical care. Individuals could enroll in the HMO voluntarily and, for a fixed fee, be eligible for health services. The fee would be paid in advance.

Ms. Taylor carefully planned the preliminary work that would be required to establish the new clinic in Austin, and when she arrived, most of the arrangements had been completed. The location of the ambulatory health center (clinic), however, had not been selected. Preliminary data on the estimated number of potential enrollees in the HMO had been determined by census tract, and these data are presented in Table 7.12. Using the cross-median approach and the census-tract map in Figure 7.9, recommend a location for the clinic.

TABLE 7.12

ESTIMATED NUMBER OF POTENTIAL ENROLLEES PER CENSUS TRACT

Census tract	Enrollees, in thousands	Census tract	Enrollees, in thousands
1	5	13.02	4
2	4	14	5
3	3	15.01	6
4	1	15.02	4
5	2	15.03	5
6	1	16.01	3
7	4	16.02	2
8	1	18.03	5
9	2	20	2
10	4	21.01	4
11	2	21.02	3
12	2	23.01	4
13.01	3		

FIGURE 7.9 Census-tract map of Austin, Texas.

CASE

Athol Furniture, Inc.[9]

Athol Furniture, Inc. (AFI), is a growing regional chain of discount furniture and large-appliance stores. Management has targeted the small city of Bluff Lake as the next location for a retail outlet. Although the total population is currently 21,000, Bluff Lake is expected to grow during the next decade because of increased mining in the surrounding hills.

AFI's marketing department did a general analysis of the potential of market expansion into Bluff Lake, but the task of locating the best site for a store has been given to Mr. Carlos Gutierrez. After obtaining the market data on Bluff Lake, Mr. Gutierrez decides

it would be very appropriate to utilize the Huff location model in developing a recommendation for the company's management. This is because there are existing competitors and several potential sites under consideration.

Figure 7.10 is a map of Bluff Lake showing major streets and highways, the railway (AFI will ship its merchandise into the city by rail from a regional warehouse 800 miles away), Crystal River, Bluff Lake, and the census block groups (numbered 1 through 12). Table 7.13 gives the number of households, average annual income per household, and average annual furniture/large-appliance expenditure per household for each census block group.

FIGURE 7.10 Bluff Lake.

TABLE 7.13

MARKET DATA

Census block group	Number of households	Avg. annual income	Avg. annual furniture/large-appliance expenditures per household
1	730	$12,000–$12,500	$180
2	1,130	8,500–9,000	125
3	1,035	19,500–20,000	280
4	635	25,000–over	350
5	160	4,500–5,000	75
6	105	4,000–4,500	50
7	125	4,000–4,500	60
8	470	8,000–8,500	115
9	305	6,000–6,500	90
10	1,755	18,500–19,000	265
11	900	15,000–15,500	215
12	290	25,000–over	370
	7640		

In Figure 7.10, the letters A and B show the locations of AFI's existing competitors, and Table 7.14 indicates the sizes of these existing stores to the nearest 5000 square feet of sales area. The letters X, Y, and Z in Figure 7.10 show the possible sites that Mr. Gutierrez feels AFI could use for a retail store. The maximum size limit (i.e., sales area) of each potential location is given in Table 7.15.

On the basis of average speeds for the main streets and highways obtained from the city's planning department, Mr. Gutierrez has developed a matrix of travel times between the existing and potential retail sites and the center of each census block group. These travel times can be found in Table 7.16.

From experience with other AFI locations, Mr. Gutierrez has developed a fairly accurate portrayal of the relationship between store size (i.e., sales area) and margin on sales, expenses, and net operating profit before taxes. This information is shown in Table 7.17.

TABLE 7.14

COMPETITORS' STORE SIZES

Store	Sales area, sq. ft.
A	10,000
B	15,000

TABLE 7.15

MAXIMUM SIZE LIMIT OF AFI SITES

Site	Maximum sales area, sq. ft.
X	15,000
Y	20,000
Z	10,000

TABLE 7.16

MINIMUM TRAVEL TIME BETWEEN POTENTIAL AND EXISTING SITES AND BLOCK GROUPS IN MINUTES

Site	Census block group											
	1	2	3	4	5	6	7	8	9	10	11	12
A	7	5	5	9	1	3	4	5	7	10	14	17
B	10	8	8	10	7	3	3	2	1	2	2	5
X	16	14	14	16	13	8	7	6	4	4	2	2
Y	12	10	10	12	9	5	4	3	2	4	2	5
Z	7	5	5	7	4	2	1	4	3	10	10	13

TABLE 7.17

RELATIONSHIP OF SIZE OF STORE TO MARGIN ON SALES, EXPENSES, AND NET OPERATING PROFIT AS A PERCENT OF SALES

Sales area, sq. ft.	Operating data		
	Margin on sales	Expenses	Net operating profit before taxes
10,000	16.2	12.3	3.9
15,000	15.6	12.0	3.6
20,000	14.7	11.8	2.9

Questions

1. Utilizing a spreadsheet version of the Huff location model (with $\lambda = 1.0$), recommend a store size and location for AFI. Assuming that AFI does not wish to consider a store that is smaller than 10,000 square feet, assess the store sizes (based on 5,000-square-foot increments) up to the maximum allowable sales area for each potential site.

2. What is the expected annual net operating profit before taxes and expected market share for the outlet you have recommended? Defend your recommendation.

3. Try two other values of λ (e.g., 0.5 and 5.0) to measure the sensitivity of customer travel propensity on your recommended location.

4. Briefly state any shortcomings you may perceive in this model.

SELECTED BIBLIOGRAPHY

CHHAJED, D., R. L. FRANCIS, and T. J. LOWE: "Contributions of Operations Research to Location Analysis," *Location Science,* vol. 1, no. 4, 1993, pp. 263–287.

CRAIG, C. S., A. GHOSH, and S. McLAFFERTY: "Models of the Retail Location Process: A Review," *Journal of Retailing,* vol. 60, no. 1, spring 1984, pp. 5–36.

FITZSIMMONS, JAMES A., and B. N. SRIKAR: "Emergency Ambulance Location Using the Contiguous Zone Search Routine," *Journal of Operations Management,* vol. 2, no. 4, August 1982, pp. 225–237.

KIMES, S. E., and FITZSIMMONS, JAMES A.: "Selecting Profitable Hotel Sites at La Quinta Motor Inns," *Interfaces,* vol. 20, no. 2, March 1990, pp. 12–20.

MANDELL, MARVIN B.: "Modeling Effectiveness-Equity Trade-offs in Public Service Delivery Systems," *Management Science,* vol. 37, no. 4, April 1991, pp. 467–482.

MIN, H.: "Location Planning of Airport Facilities Using the Analytic Hierarchy Process," *Logistics and Transportation Review,* vol. 30, no. 1, March 1995, pp. 79–94.

PRICE, W. L., and M. TURCOTTE: "Locating a Blood Bank," *Interfaces,* vol. 16, no. 5, 1986, pp. 17–26.

SCHMENNER, ROGER W.: "The Location Decisions of New Services," in J. A. Fitzsimmons and M. J. Fitzsimmons (eds.), *New Service Development,* Sage Publications, Thousand Oaks, Calif., 2000, pp. 216–238.

SWERSEY, ARTHUR J., and LAKSHMAN S. THAKUR: "An Integer Programming Model for Locating Vehicle Emissions Testing Stations," *Management Science,* vol. 41, no. 3, March 1995, pp. 496–512.

ENDNOTES

1. W. J. Abernathy and J. C. Hershey, "A Spatial-Allocation Model for Regional Health-Services Planning," *Operations Research,* vol. 20, no. 3, May–June 1972, pp. 629–642.

2. From L. A. Brown, F. B. Williams, C. Youngmann, J. Holmes, and K. Walby, "The Location of Urban Population Service Facilities: A Strategy and Its Application," *Social Science Quarterly,* vol. 54, no. 4, March 1974, pp. 784–799.

3. David L. Huff, "A Programmed Solution for Approximating an Optimum Retail Location," *Land Economics,* August 1966, pp. 293–303.

4. R. Church and C. ReVelle, "The Maximal Covering Location Problem," *Papers of the Regional Science Association,* vol. 32, Fall 1974, pp. 101–118.

5. Suzanne Alexander, "Saturating Cities with Stores Can Pay," *The Wall Street Journal,* September 11, 1989, p. B1.

6. James H. Donnelly, "Marketing Intermediaries in Channels of Distribution for Services," *Journal of Marketing,* vol. 40, January 1976, pp. 55–70.

7. D. A. Lopez and P. Gray, "The Substitution of Communication for Transportation: A Case Study," *Management Science,* vol. 23, no. 11, July 1977, pp. 1149–1160.

8. Christian Harder, *ArcView GIS Means Business,* Environmental Research Systems, Inc., Redlands, Calif., 1997, 125 pp.

9. This case was prepared by James H. Vance under the supervision of Professor James A. Fitzsimmons.

CHAPTER EIGHT

The Service Encounter

Learning Objectives

After completing this chapter, you should be able to:

1. Use the service encounter triad to describe a service firm's delivery process.
2. Identify organizational features that describe the culture of a service firm.
3. Discuss the role of information technology in employee empowerment.
4. Prepare abstract questions and write situational vignettes to screen service recruits.
5. Discuss the role of the customer as coproducer.
6. Describe how elements of the service profit chain lead to revenue growth and profitability.

Most services are characterized by an encounter between a service provider and a customer. Recall from Chapter 5, New Service Development and Process Design, that this encounter occurs above the "line of visibility" on the service blueprint. This interaction, which defines the quality of the service in the mind of the customer, has been called a "moment of truth" by Richard Normann.[1] The often brief encounter is a moment in time when the customer is evaluating the service and forming an opinion of its quality. A customer experiences many encounters with a variety of service providers, and each moment of truth is an opportunity to influence the customer's perceptions of the service quality. For example, an airline passenger experiences a series of encounters, beginning with purchasing the ticket from a telephone reservation clerk and continuing with baggage check-in at the airport, in-flight service, baggage claim on arrival, and, finally, the award of frequent flyer credit.

Realizing that such moments of truth are critical in achieving a reputation for superior quality, Jan Carlzon, the CEO of Scandinavian Airlines System (SAS), focused on these encounters in the reorganization of SAS to create a distinctive and competitive position in terms of quality of service. According to Jan Carlzon's philosophy, the organization exists to serve the front-line workers who have direct customer contact. His revolutionary thinking stood the old organization chart on its head, placing the customer-encounter personnel (formerly at the bottom) now at the top of the chart. It then became everyone else's responsibility to serve those front-line personnel, who in turn served the customer. Changing the organization chart signaled a move to refocus on satisfying the customer and managing moments of truth. It is interesting that this implementation required dividing the company into various profit centers down to the route level and allowing managers (now close to the customers) the authority to make decisions on their own.[2]

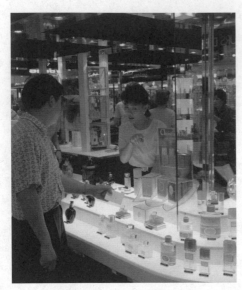

A moment of truth occurs during every customer–employee interaction. © Robert Holmes/CORBIS

CHAPTER PREVIEW

In this chapter, the service encounter is depicted as a triangle formed by the interacting interests of the customer, service organization, and contact personnel. Each participant in the service encounter attempts to exert control over the transaction, leading to the need for flexibility and the empowerment of contact personnel. A discussion of service organization culture follows, with examples of how the founders of successful service firms established a set of values and expectations encouraging their employees to focus on delivering exceptional service.

The activities of selecting and training contact personnel are addressed next. Then, the many expectations and attitudes of customers are explored, as well as the concept of the customer as coproducer. The high correlation of service quality perceptions that are shared by contact personnel and customers leads to a discussion of management's contribution to creating a customer service orientation among its employees. A chapter supplement addresses the topic of work measurement.

THE SERVICE ENCOUNTER TRIAD

One of the unique characteristics of services is the active participation of the customer in the service production process. Every moment of truth involves an interaction between a customer and a service provider; each has a role to play in an environment staged by the service organization. The *service encounter triad* shown in Figure 8.1 captures the relationships between the three parties in the service encounter and suggests possible sources of conflict.

The managers of for-profit service organizations have an interest in delivering service as efficiently as possible to protect their margins and remain competitive. Nonprofit service organizations might substitute effectiveness for efficiency, but they still must operate under the limits imposed by a budget. To control service delivery, managers

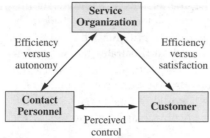

FIGURE 8.1 The service encounter triad.
(*Source:* Adapted from John E. G. Bateson, "Perceived Control and the Service Encounter," in J. A. Czepiel, M. R. Solomon, and C. F. Surprenant [eds.], *The Service Encounter,* Lexington Books, Lexington, Mass. 1985, p. 76.)

tend to impose rules and procedures on the contact personnel to limit their autonomy and discretion when serving the customer. These same rules and procedures also are intended to limit the extent of service provided for the customer and the resulting lack of customization that might result in a dissatisfied customer. Finally, the interaction between contact personnel and the customer has the element of perceived control by both parties. The contact people want to control the behavior of the customer to make their own work more manageable and less stressful; at the same time, the customer is attempting to gain control of the service encounter to derive the most benefit from it.

Ideally, the three parties gain much by working together to create a beneficial service encounter. The moment of truth can be dysfunctional, however, when one party dominates the interaction by focusing solely on his or her own control of the encounter. The following examples illustrate the conflict that arises when each party in turn dominates control of the encounter.

Encounter Dominated by the Service Organization

To be efficient and, perhaps, to follow a cost leadership strategy, an organization may standardize service delivery by imposing strict operating procedures and, thus, severely limiting the discretion of the contact personnel. Customers are presented with a few standard service options from which to choose, and personalized service is not available. Many franchise services such as McDonald's, Jiffy Lube, and H & R Block have been successful with a structural organization and environment that dominates the service encounter. Much of their success has resulted from teaching customers what *not* to expect from their service; however, much of the frustration that customers experience with other institutions, labeled pejoratively as "bureaucracies," is the result of contact personnel having no autonomy to deal with individual customer's needs. Contact personnel in such organizations may sympathize with the customer but are forced to go "by the book," and their job satisfaction is diminished in the process.

Contact Personnel–Dominated Encounter

In general, service personnel attempt to limit the scope of the service encounter to reduce their own stress in meeting demanding customers. When contact personnel are placed in an autonomous position, they may perceive themselves as having a significant degree of control over customers. The customer is expected to place considerable trust in the contact person's judgment because of the service provider's perceived expertise. The relationship between physician and patient best illustrates the shortcomings of the contact personnel–dominated encounter. The patient, who is not even referred to as a "customer," is placed in a subordinate position with no control over the encounter. Further, an allied organization, such as a hospital in this case, is subjected to tremendous demands placed on it by individual staff physicians with no regard for matters of efficiency.

Customer-Dominated Encounter

The extremes of standardized and customized services represent opportunities for customers to control the encounter. For standardized services, self-service is an option that gives customers complete control over the limited service that is provided. For example, at a self-service gasoline station that is equipped with a credit card reader, the customer need not interact with anyone. The result can be very efficient and satisfying to the customer who needs or desires very little service. For a customized service such as legal defense in a criminal case, however, all the organization's resources may be needed, at great cost in efficiency.

A satisfactory and effective service encounter should balance the need for control by all three participants. The organization's need for efficiency to remain economically viable can be satisfied when contact personnel are trained properly and the customer's expectations and role in the delivery process are communicated effectively. Our discussion of approaches to managing the service encounter begins with the service organization.

THE SERVICE ORGANIZATION

The service organization establishes the environment for the service encounter. The interaction between customer and contact personnel occurs within the context of an organization's culture as well as its physical surroundings.

Culture

Why do you choose one service over another—supermarket A over supermarket B, copying service X over copying service Y, or family practitioner M over family practitioner D? Cost, you may answer . . . or ambiance or any of several other good reasons. The bottom line, however, may be corporate *culture,* because the underlying culture helps to determine the value that customers place on the service. Several definitions of organizational culture have been proposed:

- Culture is a pattern of beliefs and expectations that is shared by the organization's members and produces norms that powerfully shape the behavior of individuals or groups in organizations.[3]
- Culture is the traditions and beliefs of an organization that distinguish it from other organizations and infuse a certain life into the skeleton of structure.[4]
- Organizational culture is a system of shared orientations that hold the unit together and give a distinctive identity.[5]

The founders and/or senior managers of a service organization establish, whether purposely or unintentionally, a climate or culture that prescribes a norm of behavior or set of values to guide employee decision making in the firm. Take, for example, ServiceMaster, a very profitable company that provides hospitals and other organizations with housekeeping services. Writing about ServiceMaster, Carol Loomis discovered that the company's name embodied its value of "Service to the Master."

> Founded by a devout Baptist, the late Marion E. Wade, the company has always described itself as driven by religious principle. The first of its corporate objectives is "to honor God in all we do." The cafeteria wall at ServiceMaster's suburban headquarters proclaims that "Joy cometh in the morning," and although there are no "Cleanliness is next to Godliness" signs around, the neatness and shine of the office project the thought.[6]

Choice of language is another approach to communicate values, as illustrated by the Walt Disney Corporation. At Disney theme parks, show business terms are used because they are in the entertainment business. Instead of Personnel there is Casting. Employees are referred to as "cast members" to instill the appropriate frame of mind. Cast members work either "onstage" or "backstage," but both kinds of employees are required to "put on the show."

The examples above illustrate how an organization's values, when consistently communicated by management, permit contact personnel to act with considerable autonomy, because their judgment is founded on a shared set of values. These values often are communicated by stories and legends about individual risk-taking on behalf of the organization and its customers. Federal Express, with a motto of "absolutely positively overnight," has many stories of extraordinary employee feats to safeguard that service guarantee. Consider, for example, the pickup driver who was faced with a collection box he was unable to open—instead of leaving it standing on the street corner until someone could come out to repair it, he wrestled the entire box into his vehicle so that the packages it contained could be liberated and delivered the next day.

The organization benefits from a shared set of values, because contact personnel are empowered to make decisions without the need for the traditional level of supervision,

The use of language and symbols communicates the culture of an organization. © The Purcell Team/CORBIS

which assumes that only management is vested with authority to act on behalf of the organization.

Empowerment

For years, McDonald's has served as the model of efficient service delivery. Incorporating the traditional mass-production philosophy of industry, McDonald's has been successful in delivering a consistent meal to billions of customers through an organization that could be described as "manufacturing in the field." The discretion of contact personnel is limited by procedures and design (e.g., the french fry scoop that guarantees portion control). Most employees are minimum-wage teenagers, and high turnover is the norm. The organization's structure is pyramid-shaped, with layers of supervision from the assistant store manager, store manager, and regional manager to corporate "consultants," to ensure consistency of service delivery across all locations.

A new model of service organization now is emerging that has a structure best described as an inverted T. In this organization, the layers of supervision are drastically reduced because contact personnel are trained, motivated, and supplied with timely, computer-based information that enables them to manage the service encounter at the point of delivery.

Jan Carlzon, the innovative president of SAS, is quoted as saying:

> Instructions only succeed in providing employees with knowledge of their own limitations. Information, on the other hand, provides them with a knowledge of their opportunities and possibilities . . . To free someone from rigorous control by instructions, policies and orders, and to give that person freedom to take responsibility for his ideas, decisions and actions, is to release hidden resources which would otherwise remain inaccessible to both the individual and the company . . . A person who has information cannot avoid taking responsibility.[7]

Perhaps it is surprising that Taco Bell has become the new service model of employee *empowerment*. Other firms adopting this new model include ServiceMaster, Marriott, and Dayton Hudson. Senior managers of these firms all share a belief that people want to do good work—and will do so if given the opportunity. Consequently, they have made the following commitments: (1) to invest in people as much as, or more than, in machines; (2) to use technology to support contact personnel rather than to monitor or replace them; (3) to consider the recruitment and training of contact personnel as critical to the firm's success; and (4) to link compensation to performance for employees at all levels. In this type of organization, a much-reduced middle management no longer has the traditional supervisory role; instead, middle managers become facilitators for the front-line or contact personnel. More important, investment in computer information systems is necessary to supply the front-line personnel with the ability to resolve problems as they arise and to ensure a quality service encounter.[8]

Empowered contact personnel must be motivated, informed, competent, committed, and well-trained. Front-line personnel should exhibit the ability to take responsibility, manage themselves, and respond to pressure from customers.

CONTACT PERSONNEL

Ideally, customer contact personnel should have personality attributes that include flexibility, tolerance for ambiguity, an ability to monitor and change behavior on the basis of situational cues, and empathy for customers. The last attribute (i.e., empathy for customers) has been found to be more important than age, education, sales-related knowledge, sales training, and intelligence.

Some individuals may find front-line service to be boring and repetitive, whereas others see the job as providing an opportunity to meet and interact with a variety of people. Those with the necessary interpersonal skills may gravitate toward high-contact service jobs, but a selection process still is required to ensure high-quality moments of truth.

Selection

No reliable tests exist to measure a person's service orientation; however, a variety of interviewing techniques have proven to be useful. Abstract questioning, the situational vignette, and role playing all have been used in evaluating potential front-line employees.

Abstract Questioning   The questions asked in the abstract interview are open-ended. They provide insights regarding an applicant's ability to relate the immediate service situation to information collected from past experience. An example of a question that assesses an applicant's attention to the environment would be "From your past work experience, what type of customer was most difficult for you to deal with and why?" To determine if an applicant actively collects information, a questioner might ask, "What was the customer's primary complaint or negative characteristic?" Some final questions to evaluate the applicant's interpersonal style could be "How did you handle the customer?" and "What would be the ideal way to deal with that type of customer?"

Abstract questioning also can be used to reveal a person's willingness to adapt. An effective employee will take notice of details in his or her personal life as well as on the job. People who consider the events around them and can describe their significance usually are able to learn more as well as faster.

Because of their nature and preparation for the interview, some applicants will be better able than others to talk extensively about their past experiences. Careful listening and probing by the interviewer for the substance of an answer to an abstract question will lessen the possibility of being deceived with "puffery." Finally, there is no assurance that the ability to reflect on past events necessarily will guarantee that such perceptiveness and flexibility will transfer to the job.

Situational Vignette   A *situational vignette* interview requires the applicant to answer questions regarding a specific situation. For example, consider the following situational vignette:

> The day after a catering service has catered a large party, a customer returns some small cakes, claiming they were stale. Although the man is demanding a refund, he is so soft-spoken and timid that you can hardly hear him across the counter. You know that your business did not make those cakes, because they don't look like your chef's work. What would you do?

Presenting a situation like this may reveal information regarding an applicant's instincts, interpersonal capabilities, common sense, and judgment. To gain more information about a candidate's adaptability, further questions about the situation can be asked: "How would you handle the man if, suddenly, he were to become irate and insistent? What steps would you take to remedy the situation?"

Situational vignettes provide an opportunity to determine whether applicants are able to "think on their feet." An applicant with good communication skills, however, still may not indicate clearly a genuine desire to serve customers or an empathic nature. Again, the interviewer must pay close attention to the substance of an applicant's response in addition to the way it is delivered.

Role Playing   Role playing is an interviewing technique that requires applicants to participate in a simulated situation and to react as if this service environment were real. Role playing often is used in the final phase of recruitment, and others in the organization are asked to cooperate by posing as "actors" for the situation.

Role playing provides a way for an interviewer to observe an applicant under stress. Interviewers using this technique may probe and change the situation as the session progresses. This method allows for more realistic responses than either the abstract questioning or situational vignette interviews; applicants are required to use their own words and react to the immediate situation instead of describing them.

Although role playing provides an excellent opportunity to observe a candidate's strengths and weaknesses in a realistic customer encounter, direct comparison of applicants is difficult. Role playing does require careful scripting, and the "actors" need to rehearse their roles before the interview.

Training

Most training manuals and employee handbooks for customer-contact personnel are devoted to explaining the technical skills that are needed to perform the jobs. For example, they often detail explicitly how to fill out guest reports, use cash registers, dress properly, and enforce safety requirements, but customer interaction skills are dismissed with a simple comment to be pleasant and smile.

Difficulties with interactions between customers and contact personnel fall into two major groups and nine categories. These are shown in Table 8.1.

Unrealistic Customer Expectations   Approximately 75 percent of the reported communication difficulties arise from causes other than a breakdown in the technical service delivery. These difficult encounters involve customers with unrealistic expectations that cannot be met by the service delivery system. Examples include passengers who

TABLE 8.1

DIFFICULTIES WITH INTERACTIONS BETWEEN CUSTOMERS AND CONTACT PERSONNEL

Unrealistic customer expectations	Unexpected service failure
1. Unreasonable demands	1. Unavailable service
2. Demands against policies	2. Slow performance
3. Unacceptable treatment of employees	3. Unacceptable service
4. Drunkenness	
5. Breaking of societal norms	
6. Special-needs customers	

Source: Adapted from J. D. Nyquist, M. J. Bitner, and B. H. Booms, "Identifying Communication Difficulties in the Service Encounter: A Critical Incident Approach," in J. A. Czepiel, M. R. Solomon, and C. F. Surprenant (eds.), *The Service Encounter*, Lexington Books, Lexington, Mass., 1985, chap. 13, pp. 195–212.

bring oversized luggage aboard an airplane or diners who snap fingers and yell at servers. Unrealistic customer expectations can be broken down into six categories:

1. *Unreasonable demands.* Services that the firm cannot offer, or customer demands that require inappropriate time and attention (e.g., "I want to carry all my luggage on board," or "Please sit with me; I'm afraid of flying").
2. *Demands against policies.* Requests that are impossible to fulfill because of safety regulations, laws, or company policies (e.g., "We've been waiting an hour for take-off, and I must have my smoke," or "Our party of 10 wants separate checks for the meal").
3. *Unacceptable treatment of employees.* Mistreatment of employees with verbal or physical abuse (e.g., "You idiot! Where is my drink?" or a diner pinching a waitress).
4. *Drunkenness.* Intoxicated customer requiring special attention (e.g., "Bring me another drink!" or an intoxicated passenger who requires assistance to get off the plane).
5. *Breaking of societal norms.* Customers breaking societal norms in general (e.g., "We can't sleep because of the loud TV in the next apartment," or guests swimming nude in the pool).
6. *Special-needs customers.* Special attention to customers with psychological, medical, or language difficulties (e.g., "My wife is hemorrhaging," or "Wieviel kostet das?").

Unexpected Service Failure   A failure in the service delivery system places a communication burden on the contact personnel. Service failures, however, provide a unique opportunity for contact personnel to demonstrate innovation and flexibility in their recovery. Three categories of service failures can be identified:

1. *Unavailable service.* Services that normally are available or expected are lacking (e.g., "I reserved a table by the window," or "Why is the ATM out of order?").
2. *Slow performance.* Service is unusually slow, creating excessive customer waiting (e.g., "Why hasn't our plane arrived?" or "We've been here for an hour, and no one has taken our order").
3. *Unacceptable service.* Service does not meet acceptable standards (e.g., "My seat doesn't recline," or "Eeegads, there's a hair in my soup!").

Unavoidable communication difficulties with customers require contact personnel whose training and interpersonal skills can prevent a bad situation from becoming worse. Programs can be developed to train contact personnel to use prescribed responses in given situations. For example, when faced with unreasonable demands—as illustrated above for category 1 difficulties—the server can appeal to the customer's sense of fairness by pointing out that the needs of other customers would be jeopardized. Actual scripts also can be developed and rehearsed for each anticipated situation. For example, in response to "I want to carry all my luggage on board," the employee need only say, "I'm very sorry, but federal safety regulations permit a passenger only two carry-on pieces small enough to be stored under the seat or overhead. May I check your larger pieces all the way to your final destination?"

Another approach involves general training in communication skills. This approach should help contact personnel to anticipate the types of exchanges they might encounter, expand their repertoire of possible responses, and develop decision rules for choosing appropriate responses to a given situation. Role playing can provide an ideal setting for gaining this communication experience. Contact personnel who are well trained will be able to control the service encounter in a professional manner, and the results will be increased satisfaction for the customer and decreased stress and frustration for the provider.

THE CUSTOMER

Every purchase is an event of some importance for the customer, whereas the same transaction usually is routine for the service provider. The emotional involvement that is associated with the routine purchase of gasoline at a self-serve station or an overnight stay at a budget hotel is minor, but consider the very personal and dramatic roles played by a customer taking an exotic vacation or seeking medical treatment. Unfortunately, it is very difficult for the bored contact personnel, who see hundreds of customers a week, to maintain a corresponding level of emotional commitment.

Expectations and Attitudes

Service customers are motivated to look for a service much as they would for a product; similarly, their expectations govern their shopping attitudes. Gregory Stone developed a now-famous topology in which shopping-goods customers were classified into four groups.[9] The definitions that follow have been modified for the service customer:

1. *The economizing customer.* This customer wants to maximize the value obtained for his or her expenditures of time, effort, and money. He or she is a demanding and sometimes fickle customer who looks for value that will test the competitive strength of the service firm in the market. Loss of these customers serves as an early warning of potential competitive threats.
2. *The ethical customer.* This customer feels a moral obligation to patronize socially responsible firms. Service firms that have developed a reputation for community service can create such a loyal customer base; for example, the Ronald McDonald House program for the families of hospitalized children has helped the image of McDonald's in just this way.
3. *The personalizing customer.* This customer wants interpersonal gratification, such as recognition and conversation, from the service experience. Greeting customers on a first-name basis always has been a staple of the neighborhood family restaurant, but computerized customer files can generate a similar personalized experience when used skillfully by front-line personnel in many other businesses.
4. *The convenience customer.* This customer has no interest in shopping for the service; convenience is the secret to attracting him or her. Convenience customers often are willing to pay extra for personalized or hassle-free service; for example, supermarkets that provide home delivery may appeal to these customers.

The attitude of customers regarding their need to control the service encounter was the subject of a study investigating customers' decision-making processes when they were confronted with the choice between a self-service option and the traditional full-service approach.[10] Customers who were interviewed appeared to be using the following dimensions in their selection: (1) amount of time involved, (2) customer's control of the situation, (3) efficiency of the process, (4) amount of human contact involved, (5) risk involved, (6) amount of effort involved, and (7) customer's need to depend on others.

It is not surprising that customers who were interested in the self-service option found the second dimension (i.e., customer's control of the situation) to be the most important factor in choosing that option. The study was conducted over a variety of

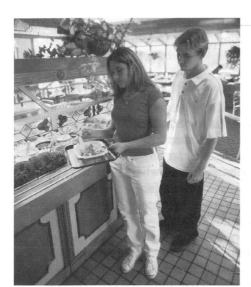

Diners who serve themselves enjoy an opportunity to build their own salads. © Spencer Grant

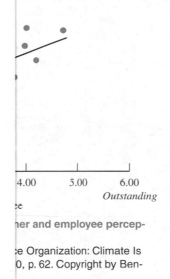

4.00   5.00   6.00
Outstanding

...er and employee percep-

...ce Organization: Climate Is
...0, p. 62. Copyright by Ben-

of your bank view the general quality of the service th...
Customers were asked: "Describe the general quality of ...
branch." Both groups graded service on the same six-poi...

Further analysis showed that customers perceived bett...ranch as one in which the manager
employees reported the following: ...y reported that service was superior

1. There is a more enthusiastic service emphasis.
2. The branch manager emphasizes service as personnel ...
3. There is an active effort to retain all customer accou...
   account holders.
4. The branch is staffed with sufficient, well-trained telle...
5. Equipment is well maintained, and supplies are plentif...

...es perceive a strong service orienta-
...customer service orientation results
...re observable by customers and, fur-
...te style for dealing with customers.
...service from different perspectives,
...re positively related.
...tomer and the employee is shown in
...ple, after a bank employee gets to
...r decreases because time is saved in
...(e.g., purchase of a certificate of de-
...sive). The loyal customer values this
...vice. Both parties enjoy the satisfac-
...for management. The way manage-
...ustomers) is reflected in how the ex-

Customer	Service Provider	
	Human	
Human	• Careful employee selection • Employees with good interpersonal skills • Easy access • Agreeable environment • Good support technology • Employees engendering trust	• Intuiti... • Custo... • Trans... • Easy... • Acce...
Machine	• Easy access • Fast response • Transaction verification • Remote monitoring	• Hard... • Track... • Autor... • Trans... • Trans... • Failsa...

FIGURE 8.2 Success factors influencing various types of ser...

FIGURE 8.4   The satisfaction mirror.
(*Source:* James L. Heskett, W. Earl Sasser, Jr., and Leonard A. Schlesinger, *The Service Profit Chain,* The Free Press, New York, 1997, p. 101.)

SERVICE PROFIT CHAIN[13]

The service profit chain proposes a relationship that links profitability, customer loyalty, and service value to employee satisfaction, capability, and productivity. Figure 8.5 shows that profitability and revenue growth are derived from loyal customers. Loyal customers, in turn, result from satisfaction that is influenced by the perceived value of the service. Satisfied, committed, capable, and productive employees create service value. Satisfied and loyal employees begin with selection and training, but require investment in information technology and other workplace support that allow decision-making latitude to serve customers.

1. *Internal quality drives employee satisfaction.* Internal service quality describes the environment in which employees work and includes employee selection and development, rewards and recognition, access to information to serve the customer, workplace technology, and job design. At USAA, a financial services company serving military officers, for example, a telephone service representative is supported by a sophisticated information system that puts complete customer information files on his or her monitor when a customer gives a membership number. The facility is located in suburban San Antonio and resembles a small college campus. Using 75 classrooms, state-of-the-art job-related training is an expected part of everyone's work experience.

2. *Employee satisfaction drives retention and productivity.* In most service jobs, the real cost of employee turnover is the loss of productivity and decreased customer satisfaction. In personalized service firms, low employee turnover is linked closely

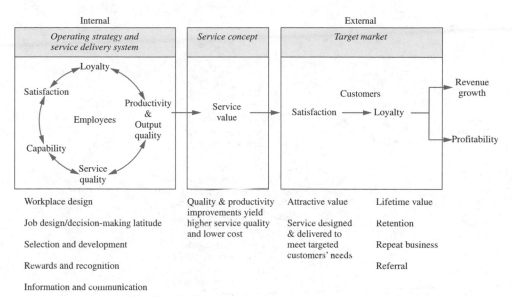

FIGURE 8.5   The service profit chain.
(*Source:* James L. Heskett, Thomas O. Jones, Gary W. Loveman, W. Earl Sasser, Jr., and Leonard A.
Schlesinger, *Harvard Business Review,* March–April 1994, Exhibit, p. 166. Copyright © 1994 by the
President and Fellows of Harvard College, all rights reserved. As adapted in James L. Heskett, W.
Earl Sasser, Jr., and Leonard A. Schlesinger, *The Service Profit Chain,* The Free Press, 1997,
Figure 2-1, p. 19.)

to high customer satisfaction. The cost of losing a valued broker at a securities firm,
for example, is measured by the loss of commissions during the time a replacement
is building relationships with customers. Employee satisfaction also can contribute
to productivity. Southwest Airlines has been the most profitable airline consistently
owing in part to its high rate of employee retention. Its turnover rate of less than 5
percent per year is the lowest in the industry.
3. *Employee retention and productivity drives service value.* At Southwest Airlines,
customer perceptions of value are very high, even though the organization does not
assign seats, offer meals, or integrate its reservation system with other airlines. Customers place high value on frequent departures, on-time service, friendly employees, and very low fares (60 to 70 percent lower than existing fares in markets it
enters). These low fares are possible in part because highly trained flexible employees can perform several jobs and because they can turn around an aircraft at the
gate in less than 15 minutes. The extent of this internal development of service employees is called "the cycle of capability" and shown in Figure 8.6.
4. *Service value drives customer satisfaction.* Customer value is measured by comparing results received to the total costs incurred in obtaining the service. Progressive Corporation, the casualty insurance company, is creating customer value by
processing and paying claims quickly and with little policyholder effort. Progressive, for example, flies a team to the scene of major catastrophes and is able to
process claims immediately, provide support services, reduce legal costs, and actually place more money in the hands of injured parties.
5. *Customer satisfaction drives customer loyalty.* When Xerox polled its customers
using a five-point scale ranging from "extremely dissatisfied" to "very satisfied," it

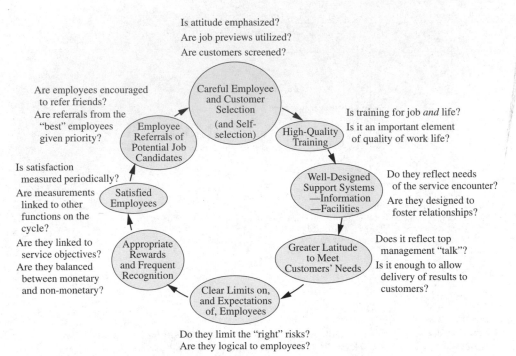

FIGURE 8.6 The cycle of capability.
(*Source:* James L. Heskett, W. Earl Sasser, Jr., and Leonard A. Schlesinger, *The Service Profit Chain,* The Free Press, New York, 1997, p. 101.)

discovered that "very satisfied" customers were six times more likely to repurchase Xerox products and services than those who were just "satisfied." Xerox called these very satisfied customers "apostles," because they would convert the uninitiated to their product. At the other extreme are the "terrorists," customers who are so unhappy that they speak out against the firm.

6. *Customer loyalty drives profitability and growth.* Because a 5 percent increase in customer loyalty can produce profit increase from 25 to 85 percent, the *quality* of market share, measured in terms of customer loyalty, deserves as much attention as the *quantity* of share. Banc One, a profitable bank based in Columbus, Ohio, for example, has developed a sophisticated system to track customer loyalty by measuring the number of services that customers use and the depth of their relationship with Banc One.

BOX 8.1

Service Benchmark
MISS MANNERS ON COMPLAINT HANDLING

In the standard exchange involving a person making a complaint and one who is receiving the complaint, usually on behalf of a commercial establishment, there are, Miss Manners has observed, two obligatory roles.

One person must say something along the lines of: "This is the most outrageous thing that ever happened. I can't imagine how anyone could be so stupid. I'm going to find out exactly how this came about, and believe me, I'm going to do something about it right away."

And the other must say: "Look, mistakes happen. This is just not all that important. There's no use getting upset, because these things happen all the time. It's not really anybody's fault."

Now here comes the peculiar part: The person at whom the complaint is directed gets to choose which role he or she wants to play, and the complainer has to take the other.

Miss Manners realizes that this is a difficult concept. It must be, because those who are obliged to receive complaints, either occasionally or as a wearisome way to earn a living, don't seem to have caught on to the possibilities of the *switcheroo*.

Here is the way the standard exchange goes:

Complainer (in more or less normal voice, with just a small edge to it): "This is an outrage."

Complainee (in bored tone): "Oh, calm down. It's nobody's fault; it just happens occasionally. It's really too late to do anything about it."

Complainer (shrieking): "You mean it's happened before? Is everyone here an idiot? I've never seen such bungling in all my life. There is no excuse for this, none whatsoever." And so on and on and on.

But here is the same situation, except that the complainee has decided not to take abuse, and so has preempted that function.

Complainee (with note of abject desperation): "It certainly is. I can't imagine how this could have happened, but you may be sure I'm going to do something about it. I can't apologize to you enough. We pride ourselves on getting things right, and this is intolerable. Please give us another chance—let me see what I can do to make it up to you."

Complainer (grudgingly at first, but warming up to the subject to counter threat of Complainee continuing in the same vein): "Oh, that's OK. We all make mistakes. It's not all that important."

The essential ingredients to pull off the switch are the apology and the promise to do something, but what makes it work is the tone. Two people can't keep up an argument in which both are carrying on like that.

Miss Manners is astonished that so few people avail themselves of this simple technique to neutralize what is otherwise a nasty exchange.

Source: Judith Martin, "Complaint-Handling Requires a Deft 'Switcheroo,'" Associated Press as printed in *Austin American Statesman,* November 1, 1992, p. E14.

SUMMARY

The service encounter is viewed as a triad, with the customer and contact personnel both exercising control over the service process in an environment defined by the service organization. The importance of flexibility in meeting customer needs has prompted many service organizations to empower their contact personnel to exercise more autonomy.

Giving employees more discretion requires a selection process that identifies applicants with the potential for adaptability in their interpersonal behaviors. Communication difficulties with customers will arise even in the best of circumstances, however. Unrealistic customer expectations and unexpected service failures must be dealt with by the contact personnel as they arise. Training to anticipate possible situations and developing "scripts" to respond to problems are two important measures that can contribute to the professionalism of the service providers.

Customers can be classified by their service expectations. Those who have a need for control are candidates for self-service options. Viewing customers as coproducers suggests the use of customer "scripts" that facilitate the service delivery and provide some behavioral predictability in the encounter.

The concept of creating a customer service orientation was discussed with reference to a study of branch banks. In this study it was discovered that customers and contact personnel share similar views of the quality of service delivered.

The chapter concludes with a discussion of the service profit chain, which provides an explanation for a firm's profitability and growth that result from the selection and development of the internal capability of the service providers and in satisfied and loyal customers.

Chapter 9 explores the service encounter in the virtual world of the Internet.

KEY TERMS AND DEFINITIONS

Abstract questioning an open-ended question used to screen potential employees by revealing a candidate's ability to adapt and use interpersonal skills.

Coproducer viewing the customer as a productive resource in the service delivery process, which requires roles to play (e.g., busing his or her lunch table) and scripts to follow (e.g., using an ATM).

Culture the shared beliefs and values of an organization that guide employee decision making and behavior in the firm.

Empowerment providing contact personnel with the training and information to make decisions for the firm without close supervision.

Service encounter triad a triangle depicting the balance of goals among the service organization, the contact personnel, and the customer.

Situational vignette a service encounter situation that can test a candidate's ability to "think on her or his feet" and to use good judgment.

TOPICS FOR DISCUSSION

1. How does the historical image of service as servitude affect today's customer expectations and service employee behavior?
2. What are the organizational and marketing implications of considering a customer as a "partial employee"?
3. Comment on the different dynamics of one-on-one service and group service in regard to perceived control of the service encounter.
4. How does use of a "service script" relate to service quality?
5. If the roles played by customers are determined by cultural norms, how can services be exported?

Amy's Ice Cream[14]

Amy's Ice Cream is a business that was founded in Austin, Texas, and has expanded to several other Texas cities. When asked about the driving force behind it, Phil Clay, the production manager, explained that "while the product is of excellent quality and does come in some unique flavors, ultimately ice cream is ice cream. One can just as easily go to Swensen's or the Marble Slab to get great ice cream. Service is what differentiates Amy's from other ice cream stores and keeps customers coming back again and again." And indeed, the service at Amy's is unique.

Amy Miller, the owner and founder, got her start in the ice cream business when she worked for Steve's Ice Cream in Boston, a store whose gimmick was mashing toppings into ice cream. She recalls how Harvard and M.I.T. graduates would work at the store—obviously for reasons other than the great salary and fringe benefits. She quickly realized that this was a business that instantly made its customers happy. Working in an ice cream store was a "feel-good" occupation, which lured such bright workers who could easily make much more money working almost anywhere else.

When she opened the first Amy's Ice Cream in October 1984, she had two philosophies: one that an employee should enjoy what he or she does, and another that the service as well as the ice cream should make the customer smile. These philosophies have provided the foundation for a business that more than one decade later is firmly established and thriving.

In the beginning, theater majors and artists often were hired as servers, because the idea of enjoying what they were doing was just as appealing to them as making money. These outgoing and creative employees were very skilled at projecting their colorful personalities across the counter. They joked and interacted with customers while filling their orders. Customers were drawn to the fun and variety of the service, which might be described as "ice cream theater," and once drawn, the customers returned again and again for repeat performances.

How does Amy's recruit employees who are up to "performing"? Originally, the employment application form was rather casual, simply handwritten and mimeographed. Mr. Clay recalls, however, that one day he was out of forms when a very large man asked for a copy. The man became somewhat belligerent at being told none was available, so Mr. Clay whipped out a white paper bag—the only writing surface under the counter—and offered it as an "alternate" form. The applicant was satisfied and carried away his form to complete! When Mr. Clay relayed this story to Amy, she said the white paper bag would work just fine, and it became the new "official" application form. In fact, it has proven to be a very good indicator of whether an applicant is willing and able to express herself or himself both easily and creatively. A person who uses the bag just to write down the usual biographical information (i.e., name, address, Social Security number, and so on) probably will not be as entertaining a scooper as one who makes it into a puppet or hot air balloon. Getting "the sack" at Amy's takes on a whole new meaning. Applicants who pass the sack test are then interviewed.

New employees go through an on-the-job training process. One part of this training concerns ice cream procedures so that servers can deliver a consistent product. The other part teaches them to express themselves from behind the counter, which includes recognizing which customers enjoy the revelry and which just want to be left alone, as well as how far the kidding can be taken with different customers. In general, employees are free to interact theatrically with those customers who want to do so.

Amy's operates on an approximate 3-percent profit margin. Consequently, the servers are minimum wage, and about 80 percent of them are part-time workers who receive no additional benefits. In fact, most managers make less than $15,000 per year, and there is a $30,000 cap for all employees—including Amy. In view of the low remuneration, how is Amy's Ice Cream always able to recruit the high-quality help that translates into satisfied customers?

Well, they do get Amy's Ice Cream T-shirts at cost and all the ice cream they can eat! Perhaps the major reason, however, is that Amy's is freedom-oriented rather than rules-oriented. The only "uniform" an employee must wear is an apron, whose primary function is to project a sense of continuity behind the counter. A hat also is de rigueur, but the employee is free to choose any hat as long as it effectively restrains the hair. In addition, the employee may wear any clothing that suits his or her mood that day as long as it is not soiled, political, or excessively revealing.

Employees can bring their own music, keeping in mind their type of clientele, to play in their stores. For example, an Amy's located in a downtown nightspot district draws a young, exuberant crowd that would appreciate lively music, whereas an Amy's located in an upscale shopping mall attracts a clientele whose musical tastes might be a bit more quiet.

The design of each store and the artwork displayed there tend to be colorful and eclectic, but again, the employees are free to make contributions. Amy's employs a local artist to decorate all stores; still, the individual managers have considerable say in what they feel is desirable for their own location. Often, the artwork is an exhibition of local artists' efforts.

Everyone does everything that needs to be done in the store. If the floor needs to be cleaned, the manager is just as likely to do it as a scooper. There is a very strong sense of teamwork and camaraderie. Employee meetings are usually held at 1 A.M., after the last Amy's Ice Cream has closed for the night. Door prizes are offered to encourage attendance.

Apparently, it is a lifestyle choice to work for Amy's. These employees are people who do not want a "real job" in which they would have to wear certain clothes, work certain hours, and not have nearly as much fun. Obviously, money is not the major motivation, and it may be that the lack of big money is one of the unifying forces among employees.

Amy's Ice Cream has created what is definitely a "nonmainstream environment," which many feel is responsible for the legions of happy customers who keep the business merrily dipping along.

Questions

1. Describe the service organization culture at Amy's Ice Cream.
2. What are the personality attributes of the employees who are sought by Amy's Ice Cream?
3. Design a personnel selection procedure for Amy's Ice Cream using abstract questioning, a situational vignette, and/or role playing.

CASE

Enterprise Rent-A-Car[15]

Enterprise Rent-A-Car (ERAC) maintains a unique selling proposition in the rental automobile industry, describing its "greatest idea [as] personal service." This proposition is built into every facet of the ERAC's operations, from point-to-point car delivery to a 427,000 rental-vehicle fleet. This is clearly seen in president Andy Taylor's welcoming message on the company's website (www.enterprise.com):

> They say the greatest ideas are the simplest ones. They're right, and our greatest idea was personal service. It was so easy because it simply required people to act like people. To treat people in a business environment the way you'd treat them if they were your neighbors. You see, our business has been shaped by this very concept. Treating our customers like good friends and neighbors has enabled us to grow to a point where our automotive operations have annual revenues in the billions, a fleet of cars and trucks numbering hundreds of thousands, and thousands of employees—each dedicated to providing personal service.[16]

BACKGROUND

Enterprise Rent-A-Car began life in 1957 as a leasing company in St. Louis, Missouri, with a fleet of 17 cars. Founder Jack Taylor soon found that his customers needed short-term rentals to cover times when their leased vehicles were in for maintenance or repairs. Although it was a relatively successful operation, it wasn't until the 1970s that the business took off. That was when a court ruling held casualty insurers liable for an insured motorist's loss from being without a car. ERAC became a major player almost overnight, and rapidly grew to a 10,000-vehicle fleet by 1977. By 1993, ERAC began serving Canada and competing internationally. At this time ERAC had more than 200,000 units covering 1,500 locations. Overseas expansion continued in the United Kingdom a year later, bringing the total operation to more than 300,000 rental units and 50,000 lease units in more than 2,500 locations. Today, ERAC operates more than 4,000 offices in the United States and 300 offices in Canada and the United Kingdom. The company has a worldwide rental fleet of more than 500,000 vehicles and annual revenues of $4.73 billion.

Now that ERAC has become the industry leader in terms of fleet size and market presence, management faces the challenge of maintaining its performance level as the company's domestic markets approach saturation.

SERVICE CONCEPT

Andrew Taylor, the current CEO and son of the founder, often says, "My father instilled his business philosophy in me, and it's very simple. When my father started the business, he said that you put customers first because if they are satisfied, they'll come back. Then come the employees. By making sure they are happy, well informed, and part of a team atmosphere, they will provide the best service possible. If you put the customers and the employees first, the bottom line will happen."[17]

Enterprise claims to offer the perfect rental package, as symbolized by its now-famous wrapped car. The focus is on three key benefits for the customer:

1. Extraordinary convenience in the form of nearby locations and picking up and dropping off customers at their homes, offices, or repair shops free of charge.
2. Excellent rates made possible by the operating strategy.
3. Exceptional selection of vehicles with something for every occasion.

From the first days of the rental business, ERAC's market focus has been on the local rental segment rather than following the "suits & shorts" emphasis on the business and holiday segment of the established players. This "hometown" rental market now includes the replacement segment (i.e., customers who need a car because of an accident, routine maintenance, or theft) and the discretionary segment (i.e., short business and leisure trips and other special occasions). ERAC relied on the pickup and drop-off components of its service to help set the company apart from the competition. This focus on convenience is now facilitated by a network of offices located within 15 minutes of 90 percent of the U.S. population.

Although ERAC has recently begun to take on the commercial market, the company maintains no on-site airport locations. Consistent with its original market focus, customers are picked up and taken back to the office to settle the paperwork and take possession of the car. Still, according to Taylor, the focus is on the customer: "After all, other companies rent, lease and sell pretty much the same cars as Enterprise. The difference is, their business is cars and ours is people, which explains why so much of our energy goes into recruiting, hiring, and training."[18]

CULTURE

A combination of unusual hiring practices and relatively strict promotion-from-within drives the company's culture. Virtually every employee is a college graduate and, according to the Cable News Network, in 1996 ERAC was one of the top four recruiters of college graduates in the United States. This factor is out of sync with the labor-intensive car-rental industry that seeks to keep employee wages of a unionized workforce low.

The recruiting itself is rather nontraditional, also. "Brainy introverts need not apply," says Donald L. Ross, ERAC's chief operating officer. "We hire from the half of the college class that makes the upper half possible," he adds wryly. "We want athletes, fraternity types—especially fraternity presidents and social directors. People people."[19] The company finds that social directors make good salespeople because they are more readily able to chat up service managers and to calm someone who has just been in a car wreck.

The focus on athletes also has a noticeable impact on the company's culture because it fosters a competitive atmosphere to go along with the emphasis on teamwork. Starting pay varies around the country, and ERAC's reward system feeds this competitive drive as employees don't receive regular pay raises. They are compensated in part according to the profit earned at their particular location. Financial results by location and region are made available for everyone to see, which further fuels the competition.

The "bottom half of the class" also tends to bring a work ethic akin to the zeal of a reformed smoker, because its alumni have been sobered by a scarcity of career opportunities. Jeffrey M. Brummett, vice president for daily rental operations and a onetime semi-pro baseball player, comments, "Nobody ever went to college planning to go into the car rental business (an often repeated comment among Enterprise employees). Then a time comes when that's the opportunity that presents itself, and you grab it."[20]

New management trainees are welcomed by long grueling hours, during which they spend most of their time cleaning cars and shuttling vehicles to customers. Still, almost every employee, including top executives, start this way. Conscious of the bond this creates, senior officers routinely get involved in the dirty work, and even CEO Andy Taylor uses a vacuum. "We were visiting an office in Berkeley and it was mobbed, so I started cleaning cars," he says. "As it was happening, I wondered if it was a good use of my time, but the effect on morale was tremendous."[21] Still, many quit after just a few weeks.

At the corporate level, Taylor leaves many of the decisions to Donald L. Ross, senior executive VP and COO, and to William F. Holekamp, executive VP. Ross and Holekamp serve as role models for new recruits, as both men started by washing cars and serving customers. In time, each decided to take the risk and open an ERAC office in a new location, and their success with these operations proved that they could help guide the company, according to the Taylor philosophy.

GROWTH

ERAC's focus on the local market continues to pay off as it takes an increasingly larger share. While the airport market has grown annually at about 3 to 5 percent, the local market has grown at 10 to 15 percent. According to Jon LeSage, managing editor of *Auto Rental News,* "The local car rental market is a lot more significant than the public would assume. The real growth in this business is going to be in the local market."[22]

ERAC will likely continue to benefit from this growth, because the company has so many rental locations spread around the country. CEO Taylor sees no sign of a slowdown. Moreover, the company has grown at an annual rate of more than 20 percent for the past several years.

Two-income families also are helping to drive the market: when both partners of a couple work, each depends on his or her car, and when one of the cars falls out, ERAC's lower price makes it a natural choice. Moreover, people are renting from ERAC even when the family car runs just fine. "We call it the Virtual Car,®" says Taylor. "Small-business people who have to pick up clients call us when they want something better than their own car. So do people who have to take a long trip and don't trust, or just don't want to use, the family car."[23]

A new office is opened usually as soon as adjacent offices have reached a 100-vehicle inventory. After a new office does open, employees move into the surrounding community to develop relationships with the service managers of every good-size repair facility in the area. ERAC knows that the recommendations of service managers carry a great deal of weight with repair customers who are busy dealing with the confusion of the moment. It has become a national Wednesday ritual for ERAC employees to bring pizza and doughnuts to workers at nearby garages. Indeed, a large portion of recent growth has come from auto dealers who offer customers a free or cheap replacement while their cars are in the shop. ERAC has agreements with many dealers to provide these replacement vehicles, but at major accounts, ERAC staffs an office on the premises for several hours a day and keeps cars parked outside. According to one Porsche, Audi, and Rover dealer in West Long Branch, New Jersey: "The Enterprise people are practically part of my staff."[24]

OPERATIONS

ERAC operations are separated along its two primary lines of business rental vehicles and corporate fleet management. Enterprise buys cars from a wide variety of American, Japanese, and European automakers. To reduce costs, it keeps its cars on the road up to six months longer than do either Hertz or Avis.

Rental Operations

ERAC's 4,000 offices are connected via an exclusive 1-800 number that links customers to the world's most advanced and most convenient office locator system. It allows customers to contact any of the North American offices via one simple number. This is supplemented by *ARMS*® (automated rental management system), which provides an electronic interface that allows major clients, such as insurance companies, to manage bookings, billings, and payments in the most efficient manner possible.

ERAC's service concepts are evident in the rental operations. Whether at home or at the repair shop, ERAC delivers the vehicle to the customer. Despite this highly personalized service, ERAC offers rates that are often 30 percent lower than those of its competitors. From Geo Metro to Cadillac DeVille, from Chevrolet Safari to Nissan Pathfinder, ERAC provides a selection from more than 60 vehicles to meet a wide range of customer needs. Variety is also a primary profit driver in the replacement market. ERAC is betting that customers who are stuck for transportation won't be in the mood to quibble about prices. While the tiny GEO Metro is available for $16 a day (i.e., the amount many insurance policies pay for replacement rentals), about 90 percent of people pay more to get a bigger car.

Fleet Management Operations

Its origin was leasing, but ERAC has expanded the scope of its fleet management services by providing complete, end-to-end fleet management, which allows client companies to outsource their entire vehicle departments. A dedicated, local Enterprise Account Services representative manages every aspect of the client's fleet including acquisition, insurance services, registration, after-market equipment, financing, fuel management and reporting, full maintenance management, corporate rental programs, and disposal.

COMPETITION

ERAC faces competition from a variety of sources, most notable of which are the traditional airport car rental companies such as Avis, Hertz, Budget, Alamo, and National. Nevertheless, ERAC focuses on a different segment of the rental car market than do these companies. Traditional companies are dedicated to short-term, on-site rental for travelers, but ERAC focuses on the "hometown" market. Consequently, its most direct competition comes from the service loaner fleets of car dealerships. When a customer brings a car in for service, many dealerships now provide a service loaner, which eliminates the opportunity for ERAC to provide service.

The shape of the competitive field is also changing with a healthy auto industry and rising car prices. Consolidation is ongoing, as the smaller players are finding themselves unable to withstand the higher capital outlays. One of the biggest threats to the independents is the cash reserve of the allied players like Hertz and Budget, both of which are owned by Ford. Still, lacking debt, outside ownership, or red ink, ERAC is one of the most secure companies in a very insecure business.

Questions

1. How has Enterprise Rent-A-Car (ERAC) defined its service differently than that of the typical national car rental company?
2. What features of its business concept allow ERAC to compete effectively with the existing national rental car companies?
3. Use the service profit chain to explain the success of ERAC.

SELECTED BIBLIOGRAPHY

ANDERSON, EUGENE W.: "Customer Satisfaction and Word of Mouth," *Journal of Service Research,* vol. 1, no. 1, August 1998, pp. 5–17.

BATESON, J.: "Perceived Control and the Service Encounter," in J. A. Czepiel, M. R. Solomon, and C. F. Surprenant (eds.), *The Service Encounter,* Lexington Books, Lexington, Mass., 1985, chap. 5, pp. 76–83.

BETTENCOURT, LANCE A., and KEVIN GWINNER: "Customization of the Service Experience: The Role of the Frontline Employee," *International Journal of Service Industry Management,* vol. 7, no. 2, 1996, pp. 3–20.

BITNER, MARY JO, B. H. BOOMS, and L. A. MOHR: "Critical Service Encounters: The Employee's Viewpoint," *Journal of Marketing,* vol. 58, October 1994, pp. 95–106.

BITRAN, GABRIEL R., and JOHANNES HOECH: "The Humanization of Service: Respect at the Moment of Truth," *Sloan Management Review,* vol. 31, no. 2, Winter 1990, pp. 89–96.

BOWEN, D. E., and E. L. LAWLER: "Empowering Service Employees," *Sloan Management Review,* Summer 1995, pp. 73–84.

BROWN, TOM J., and AMNA KIRMANI: "The Influence of Preencounter Affect on Satisfaction with an Anxiety-Provoking Service Encounter," *Journal of Service Research,* vol. 1, no. 4, May 1999, pp. 333–346.

CARLZON, JAN: *Moments of Truth,* Ballinger, Cambridge, Mass., 1987.

CHANDON, JEAN-LOUIS, PIERRE-YVES LEO, and JEAN PHILIPPE: "Service Encounter Dimensions—a Dyadic Perspective: Measuring the Dimensions of Service Encounters as Perceived by Customers and Personnel," *International Journal of Service Industry Management,* vol. 8, no. 1, 1997, pp. 65–86.

DANAHER, PETER J.: "Customer Heterogeneity in Service Management," *Journal of Service Research,* vol. 1, no. 2, November 1998, pp. 129–139.

DASU, SRIRAM, and JAY RAO: "A Dynamic Process Model of Dissatisfaction for Unfavorable, Non-routine Service Encounters," *Production and Operations Management,* vol. 8, no. 3, Fall 1999, pp. 282–300.

DE RUYTER, KO, and MARTIN WETZELS: "The Impact of Perceived Listening Behavior in Voice-to-Voice Service Encounters," *Journal of Service Research,* vol. 2, no. 3, February 2000, p. 276.

———, ———, and JOSEE BLOEMER: "On the Relationship between Perceived Service Quality, Service Loyalty, and Switching Costs," *International Journal of Service Industry Management,* vol. 9, no. 5, 1998, pp. 436–453.

EVANS, KENNETH R., TODD J. ARNOLD, and JOHN A. GRANT: "Combining Service and Sales at the Point of Customer Contact," *Journal of Service Research,* vol. 2, no. 1, August 1999, pp. 34–49.

GRAYSON, KENT: "Customer Responses to Emotional Labour in Discrete and Relational Service Exchange," *International Journal of Service Industry Management,* vol. 9, no. 2, 1998, pp. 126–154.

GREMLER, DWAYNE D., MARY JO BITNER, and KENNETH R. EVANS: "The Internal Service Encounter," *International Journal of Service Industry Management,* vol. 5, no. 2, 1994, pp. 34–56.

HALLOWELL, ROGER: "The Relationships of Customer Satisfaction, Customer Loyalty, and Profitability: An Empirical Study," *International Journal of Service Industry Management,* vol. 7, no. 4, 1996, pp. 27–42.

HANSEN, DAVID E., and PETER J. DANAHER: "Inconsistent Performance during the Service Encounter: What's a Good Start Worth?" *Journal of Service Research,* vol. 1, no. 3, February 1999, pp. 227–235.

HESKETT, JAMES L., W. EARL SASSER, JR., and LEONARD A. SCHLESINGER: *The Service Profit Chain,* The Free Press, New York, 1997.

JONES, T. O., and W. E. SASSER, JR.: "Why Satisfied Customers Defect," *Harvard Business Review,* November–December 1995, pp. 88–99.

KELLY, J., J. DONNELLY, and S. SKINNER: "Customer Participation in Serivce Production and Delivery," *Journal of Retailing,* vol. 66, no. 3, 1990, pp. 315–335.

KNOWLES, PATRICIA A., STEPHEN J. GROVE, and GREGORY M. PICKETT: "Mood versus Service Quality Effects on Customers' Responses to Service Organizations and Service Encounters," *Journal of Service Research,* vol. 2, no. 2, November 1999, pp. 187–199.

LOVEMAN, GARY W.: "Employee Satisfaction, Customer Loyalty, and Financial Performance: An Empirical Examination of the Service Profit Chain in Retail Banking," *Journal of Service Research,* vol. 1, no. 1, August 1998, pp. 18–31.

MALONE, THOMAS W.: "Is Empowerment Just a Fad?—Control, Decision Making, and IT," *Sloan Management Review,* vol. 38, no. 2, Winter 1997, pp. 23–36.

METTERS, RICHARD: "Models for Customer Selection," in J. A. Fitzsimmons and M. J. Fitzsimmons (eds.), *New Service Development,* Sage Publication, Thousand Oaks, Calif., 2000, pp. 291–304.

MILLS, PETER K., and JAMES H. MORRIS: "Some Moderating Effects of Client-Interaction Need on Perceived Technology and Structure in Service Providers' Tasks," *International Journal of Service Industry Management,* vol. 3, no. 1, 1992, pp. 4–13.

———, and DAN S. MOSHAVI: "Professional Concern: Managing Knowledge-Based Service Relationships," *International Journal of Service Industry Management,* vol. 10, no. 1, 1999, pp. 48–67.

NYQUIST, J. D., M. J. BITNER, and B. H. BOOMS: "Identifying Communication Difficulties in the Service Encounter: A Critical Incident Approach," in J. A. Czepiel, M. R. Solomon, and C. F. Surprenant (eds.), *The Service Encounter,* Lexington Books, Lexington, Mass., 1985, chap. 13, pp. 195–212.

PRICE, LINDA L., ERIC J. ARNOULD, and SHEILA L. DEIBLER: "Consumer's Emotional Responses to Service Encounters: The Influence of the Service Provider," *International Journal of Service Industry Management,* vol. 6, no. 3, 1995, pp. 34–63.

QUINN, JAMES BRIAN, PHILIP ANDERSON, and SYDNEY FINKELSTEIN: "Managing Professional Intellect: Making the Most of the Best," *Harvard Business Review,* March–April 1996, pp. 71–80.

RUST, ROLAND T., GREG I. STEWART, HEATHER MILLER, and DEBBIE PIELACK: "The Satisfaction and Retention of Frontline Employees: A Customer Satisfaction Measurement Approach," *International Journal of Service Industry Management,* vol. 7, no. 5, 1996, pp. 62–80.

SCHLESINGER, LEONARD A.: "Breaking the Cycle of Failure in Services," *Sloan Management Review,* Spring 1991, pp. 17–28.

SCHNEIDER, BENJAMIN, and DANIEL SCHECHTER: "Development of a Personnel Selection System for Service Jobs," in S. W. Brown, E. Gummesson, B. Edvardsson, and B. Gustavsson (eds.), *Service Quality: Multidisciplinary and Multinational Perspectives,* Lexington Books, Lexington, Mass., 1991.

SIMONS, ROBERT: "Control in an Age of Empowerment," *Harvard Business Review,* March–April 1996, pp. 80–88.

TANSIK, DAVID A., and WILLIAM L. SMITH: "Scripting the Service Encounter," in J. A. Fitzsimmons and M. J. Fitzsimmons (eds.), *New Service Development,* Sage Publication, Thousand Oaks, Calif., 2000, pp. 239–263.

WALKER, J. A.: "Service Encounter Satisfaction: Conceptualized," *Journal of Services Marketing,* vol. 9, no. 1, 1995, pp. 5–14.

WEATHERLY, KRISTOPHER A., and DAVID A. TANSIK: "Tactics Used by Customer-Contact Workers: Effects of Role Stress, Boundary Spanning and Control," *International Journal of Service Industry Management,* vol. 4, no. 3, 1993, pp. 4–17.

Chapter 8 Supplement: Work Measurement

Time Study

This technique of work measurement known as *time study* is used to develop standards of performance. Management can use these standard times for many purposes, such as to determine staffing needs, allocate tasks to jobs, develop standard costs, evaluate employee performance, and establish wage payment plans. (Recall the standard times attached to critical operations on the service blueprint.)

Time study involves identifying and measuring the individual work *elements* of repetitive jobs. These repetitive jobs also are called work *cycles.* For example, consider the responsibilities of the person who serves salads at your local cafeteria. A particular work cycle for this server might include the elements of retrieving a dish, filling the dish, adding a dressing, and handing the dish to the diner.

Measurements are made with a stopwatch, and the time when each element is completed is recorded on an observation sheet such as that shown in Table 8.2. The variability of the element times and the level of confidence or accuracy that is desired provide a statistical basis for determining the number of cycles to observe.

Our example worksheet contains a record of the observations of a server who wraps silverware into napkins and repeats the sequence, or cycle, 10 times. Each column represents one finished place setting. The stopwatch is started as the server begins positioning the napkin. The first reading (R), in hundredths of a minute on the watch, is noted when the server reaches for the silverware. The second reading is made after the last piece of silverware is placed on the napkin, and the third reading is noted after the napkin is rolled around the silverware. The final reading for cycle 1 is made after the rolled napkin is placed in a box. In our example, the actual readings for elements 1

TABLE 8.2

TIME STUDY OBSERVATION SHEET

Activity: _Folding silverware into napkins_

Began timing: _2:32_
Ended timing: _2:35_

Study no. _13_

Observer _C.C._

Date: _1/10/97_

Std time _0.326 min/item_

Element description		1	2	3	4	5	6	7	8	9	10	Sum	Avg. time	Rating	Normal time
							Cycles								
1 Position napkin	T	0.03	0.05	0.05	0.06	0.06	0.06	0.05	0.05	0.05	0.04	0.50	0.050	1.10	0.055
	R	3	28	65	95	25	57	85	13	42	67				
2 Group knife, fork, and spoon	T	0.05	0.08	0.09	0.08	0.08	0.07	0.08	0.09	0.06	0.08	0.76	0.076	1.00	0.076
	R	8	36	74	103	33	64	93	22	48	75				
3 Roll silverware	T	0.07	0.15	0.06	0.06	0.07	0.06	0.06	0.06	0.07	0.07	0.73	0.073	0.90	0.065
	R	15	51	80	9	40	70	99	28	55	82				
4 Place in box	T	0.08	0.09	0.09	0.10	0.11	0.10	0.09	0.09	0.08	0.09	0.92	0.092	1.05	0.097
	R	23	60	89	19	51	80	208	37	63	91				
5	T														
	R														
6	T														
	R														
7	T														
	R														
8	T														
	R														
9	T														
	R														

Foreign elements:

Normal cycle time _0.294_

÷ [1–Allowance (10%)] _0.9_

= Standard time _0.327_

Note: T = time
R = reading

through 4 in cycle 1 are noted at 3, 8, 15, and 23 one-hundredths of a minute, respectively, after the stopwatch is started. After the server is timed through nine more repetitions of the work cycle, each elapsed time (T) is calculated. For example, the time the server took between the end of the first element and the end of the second element in cycle 1 is 8 - 3 = 5 one-hundredths of a minute, which is written in the chart as 0.05.

The next step in using the time study sheet is to find the sum of the elapsed times for each element across all the cycles and then calculate the average time for each element. These average times provide information for this particular server, but if he or she is significantly faster or slower than an average server, management would not want to base decisions on such times. Therefore, the values are adjusted by means of a *performance rating* to reflect what reasonably may be expected of an "average" worker.

A performance rating represents a subjective judgment by the person who is conducting the time study. Expert analysts are trained to estimate efficiency rates by viewing films of people working at different rates. For example, a poor worker might work at what the analyst would consider to be 90 percent of normal, and the average time would be adjusted downward by a factor of 0.9. A very fast worker might be rated at 110 percent of normal, and the average time would be adjusted upward by a factor of 1.10. The adjusted times are called *normal element times* and are derived according to the following formula:

$$NT_i = R_i(OT_i) \tag{1}$$

where NT_i = normal time of the ith work element
$\quad\ OT_i$ = average observed time of the ith work element
$\quad\ R_i$ = proficiency rating of the employee in performing the ith work element, expressed as a decimal percentage (e.g., 0.90 for 90 percent of normal)

In our example, the server's normal time for the first element, position napkin, therefore is

$$NT_i = (1.10)(0.050)$$

$$= 0.055$$

Similar calculations are made to obtain normal times for the remaining elements. It should be noted, however, that because of their subjective nature, performance ratings as used in the example above can be a source of contention.

The sympathetic reader already may recognize the need to qualify the normal element times just calculated. The server cannot be expected to fold silverware into napkins in a robot-like manner for eight solid hours during a working day. Allowances must be made for breaks, personal needs, and perhaps other interruptions such as obtaining more napkins and silverware. These allowances are figured as a percentage of the job time (i.e., a 10-percent allowance would translate into six minutes every working hour). The resulting adjusted times, known as the *standard element times,* and their sum, known as the *standard cycle time,* are calculated according to the following formulas:

$$ST_i = \frac{NT_i}{1-A} \tag{2}$$

$$CT = \sum_{i=1}^{n} ST_i \tag{3}$$

where ST_i = standard time for the ith work element

      A = allowance, expressed as a decimal percentage (e.g., 0.10 for 10 percent)

     CT = standard cycle time

      n = number of work elements in the work cycle

We complete our example time study sheet by adding the normal element times to obtain a normal cycle time of 0.294. This result is adjusted by an allowance of 10 percent, or 0.10, to yield a standard cycle time of 0.327. Note that the sample time study sheet has a space to record any foreign elements observed (e.g., setting aside a dirty fork). These random occurrences are not included explicitly in the work cycle, but they are accounted for in selecting the allowance when deriving standard times. The standard cycle time now can be used by management to assign a server sufficient time to prepare enough folded silverware and napkins for the next mealtime.

Work Sampling

Time studies are used to determine how long it takes to complete a task; *work sampling* is used to determine how people allocate their time among various types of activities. Suppose we are interested in the proportion of time an employee spends at various activities that occur randomly during the workday. Tallying observations of worker activity that are noted at random times during the day would lead to our desired proportions.

Consider, for example, a server at a Red Lobster restaurant. This server must take drink and food orders, serve drinks, dish up and serve salads, grind fresh pepper on the salads, serve biscuits, serve entrees, take dessert orders, serve desserts, and present the check as well as clear away dirty dishes and refill drinks as required throughout. Obviously, there is much variation in the server's duties: one diner may require information on how particular foods are prepared before the order can be taken, another may drink his or her water as fast as the glass is filled, some may eat quickly and require little attention beyond the basic service, and still others may request much extra service.

To study worker activity that is as complex and seemingly random as we have just described, we can use the work sampling method, which is concerned with the proportion of time that a worker is engaged in different activities rather than with the actual time that is spent performing an activity. This technique is most useful in the design and redesign of contact personnel jobs because of the nonprogrammed nature of direct customer contact activities.

As described by Sheryl E. Kimes and Stephen A. Mutkoski, work sampling involves seven steps:[25]

1. *Define the activities.* Divide the work into as few categories as possible that do not overlap.
2. *Design the observation form.* The form should be designed with ease of use and ease of future analysis in mind.
3. *Determine the length of the study.* The study must be long enough to provide a random sample of activities.
4. *Test the form.* Try the form in actual practice to see if the categories are well defined and if it is easy to use and accurate. Does the test application suggest any changes that should be made in the definition of the categories or the design of the form?
5. *Determine the sample size and observation pattern.* Common statistical methods can be used to select the size of the sample to study and an observation schedule. In general, the larger the sample size, the more accurate and representative the sample

will be. A formula can be used to determine how many observations must be made to achieve the desired level of confidence or accuracy, and a schedule for making those observations must be devised. Details of the statistical methods involved are described later in this supplement in the section called "Sample Size."

6. *Conduct the study.* Observers must be trained to use the form properly. Kimes and Mutkoski also point out the importance of considering the effect the study can have on the behavior of those who are being observed, and they suggest two approaches to mediate any adverse effect on the subjects: to inform and assure them that they are not being evaluated and to make very discreet, unobtrusive observations without informing them. In addition, data for the first day or two could be discarded to allow the workers to feel more at ease with the data collection process.

7. *Analyze the data.* Again, common statistical methods can be used to calculate the information required by management. In simplest terms, it is necessary only to total the number of observations in each category and calculate the percentage of time spent on that activity.

Kimes and Mutkoski describe an application of work sampling in a study of servers working in two different types of restaurants: family and "mid-scale." The major difference between these two restaurant types for the purposes of their study is in the nature and amount of customer-server interaction: they hypothesized that the emphasis in the family restaurants "would be on efficiency with an eye toward increasing table turnover, while in a mid-scale restaurant, the emphasis would be more on guest service with the idea of increasing 'add-on' sales and guest satisfaction."

Above all, their sampling plan needed to provide "a good random representative sample" of servers' activities. Therefore, they selected six different family restaurants and six different mid-scale restaurants and conducted their studies during the peak lunch and dinner times. They observed two servers at each restaurant for at least 1½ hours.

For this study, the servers' activities were divided into the following eight categories:

1. *Guest contact.* Any interaction with the customer.
2. *Walk—empty.* Walking without carrying anything.
3. *Walk—full.* Walking while carrying food, beverages, or dirty dishes.
4. *Bus.* Clearing a vacated table.
5. *Prepare.* Preparing food and beverages before service.
6. *Can't see.* Server is out of sight.
7. *Check.* Delivering or processing the check.
8. *Rest.* Server's break time.

These categories are listed on the form shown in Table 8.3, which was to be used by the student observers who visited each restaurant anonymously to minimize any effect they might have on the subjects. Observations were recorded at one-minute intervals: one server was checked on the minute, and the other server was checked on the half minute. Because observations made at such regular intervals are not random, the researchers compensated by drawing a random sample of the student observations at each restaurant for their final analysis.

Kimes and Mutkoski suggest ways that management can use the information from their study. If servers are spending more or less time with customers than desired, perhaps the jobs can be redesigned to increase or decrease the customer contact time. If servers are spending too much time on busing tables, perhaps more bus help could be

---

TABLE 8.3

WORK SAMPLING FORM FOR RESTAURANT STUDY

Restaurant _____ Lunch _____ Dinner _____
Date _____ Time _____

Key OB#	Guest Contact	Walk—Empty	Walk—Full	Bus	Prepare	Can't See	Check	Rest	Key OB#
1		√							1
2	√								2
3	√								3
4		√							4
5						√			5
6						√			6
34						√			34
35						√			35
36						√			36
37			√						37
38	√								38
39		√							39
40							√		40
Sum									Sum

By noting what the server is doing once each minute, an observer can obtain a sampling of which tasks occupy the server's time. The 40 observation points indicated in the above form would not constitute a sufficient sample by themselves, but would be part of a lengthier study.

Source: S. E. Kimes and S. A. Mutkoski, "Customer Contact in Restaurants: An Application of Work Sampling," *Cornell HRA Quarterly,* May 1991, p. 86. © Cornell HRA Quarterly. Used by permission. All rights reserved.

---

employed. If servers are off the floor too much, perhaps a type of "front-waiter, back-waiter" system would be helpful.

Sample Size

Consider the following situation: The nursing supervisor at a major hospital must make up a new work schedule for her staff and needs information on which to base her decisions. Therefore, she is interested in determining the actual proportion of time that nurses (RNs) spend in direct patient care. She believes the RNs spend approximately 20 percent of their time in direct patient care but wants to conduct a work sampling study to validate her estimate. For this study, she wants to be 95 percent confident that the resulting estimate will be within 5 percent of the true proportion.

Given the desired confidence level defined above, we can calculate the size of the sample that would be required for the study. The size of the sample (or the number of observations) depends on both an estimate of the proportion of time spent in a particular activity and the accuracy that is desired. The formula for calculating the sample size is

$$N = \frac{Z^2 P(1 - P)}{E^2} \tag{4}$$

where N = sample size

Z = standard normal deviate for desired level of confidence

P = assumed proportion, expressed as a decimal percentage

E = maximum error allowed, expressed as a decimal percentage

In actual practice, an estimate of the proportion of time spent on a particular activity (P) can be made by conducting small initial studies or by assigning a conservative value of 50 percent, or 0.5 (which will guarantee that the sample size is large enough to achieve the desired level of confidence). A third way of estimating P is to make a reasonable assumption based on experience, as the supervisor did in our hospital example when she set P equal to 0.2 (i.e., 20 percent). For this example, E = 0.05 and Z = 1.96 (for a two-tailed 0.95 confidence level as found in the end-of-book Appendix A table, "Areas of a Standard Normal Distribution"). Substituting these values in equation (4) yields

$$N = \frac{(1.96)^2 (0.2)(1 - 0.2)}{(0.05)^2} = 246 \text{ observations}$$

The supervisor now needs to construct a schedule of random observations made over a period of time that is long enough to ensure adequate representation of all activities. For this example, assume that the study will be conducted for 20 weekdays. This means that 13 observations per day (246/20 = 12.3) are required. These observations should be made at random times during each workday, and the hour and minute for each observation can be determined using a random-number table.

Work Methods Charts

The flow of work activities and the interactions between customers and workers can be represented graphically. The most commonly used graphical tools are *worker-customer charts* and *activity charts*.

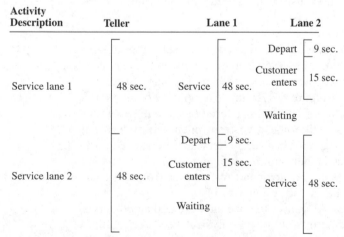

Total cycle time: 96 seconds   Idle-lane time per cycle: 48 seconds
Idle-teller time per cycle: 0   Working-lane time per cycle: 144 seconds
Working-teller time per cycle: 96 seconds

FIGURE 8.7 Worker-customer chart: teller serving two lanes of a drive-in bank.

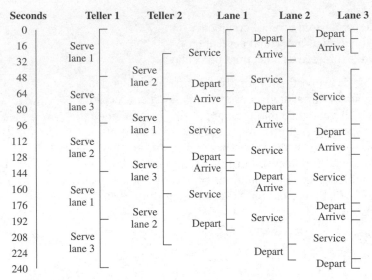

FIGURE 8.8   Activity chart: two tellers serving three lanes of a drive-in bank.

Worker-Customer Charts   When the server's work cycle time is shorter than that required by the supply of customers, the interaction can be shown on a time scale. The resulting worker-customer chart can be used to schedule work activities so that one employee can serve more than one customer at a time.

Figure 8.7 shows a worker-customer chart for a bank in which one drive-in teller serves two lanes. We simplify this example by using average times and ignoring randomness. On the average, a customer takes 15 seconds to approach the service area, 48 seconds to be served, and 9 seconds to depart. Note that the customer's average cycle time is 72 seconds, but the teller's average cycle time is 48 seconds. You also can see that while the teller is occupied with the first customer, a second customer has entered the system and is waiting for service in the second lane.

Activity Charts   The worker-customer chart described above is a useful tool in simple situations, but a situation involving multiple servers and many customers may benefit from use of a more complex graphical depiction called an activity chart. An activity chart also uses a time scale, as shown in Figure 8.8. In this example, two tellers at a drive-in bank are located in a single station. The bank has three lanes, one served directly from the teller station window and the other two from pneumatic tubes that transfer materials to and from the teller station. The average service time at each position is 48 seconds per customer. Each customer requires an average of 15 seconds to enter the service area and an average of 9 seconds to depart. We can see from this chart that the system is operating efficiently; that is, the system quickly adapts to avoid waiting by customers and idle time for tellers. Also, note that we have created a two-server queuing system with a single waiting line in spite of the physical need for multiple lanes. (For a discussion of queuing systems, see Chapter 11.)

SOLVED PROBLEMS

1. Time Study

Problem Statement

A discount tire dealer is interested in determining the optimal staffing level for his mechanics during busy hours to avoid excessive customer waiting. Using a stopwatch during one afternoon, he observed a mechanic taking an average of 18 minutes to spin balance and mount four tires on a car. He judged that this experienced mechanic had a proficiency rating of about 110 percent. What is the normal time for this activity? If the allowance for fatigue and personal time is 15 percent, what should the standard time for this activity be? For planning purposes, how many cars can one mechanic service per hour?

Solution

Using equation (1), we calculate the normal time as

$$NT_i = R_i\,(OT_i) = (1.10)(18) = 19.8 \text{ minutes}$$

Using equation (2), we calculate the standard time as

$$ST_i = \frac{NT_i}{1 - A} = 19.8/(1 - 0.15) = 23.3 \text{ minutes}$$

Therefore, the number of cars a mechanic can service in one hour = $60/23.3 \cong 2.5$ cars per hour.

2. Work Sampling

Problem Statement

The discount tire owner is concerned about the excessive waiting of customers and wants to determine the percentage of time that his mechanics are idle. He wants an estimate within a $\pm$ 5 percent degree of accuracy at a 95-percent confidence level.

Solution

A work sampling study over a 10-day period is suggested. Because no estimate of the percentage of idle time is given, we will use 0.5 to guarantee a conservative sample size, which is calculated using equation (4):

$$N = \frac{Z^2\,P(1 - P)}{E^2} = \frac{(1.96)^2\,(0.5)(1 - 0.5)}{(0.05)^2} = 384$$

Thus, 38 random observations of the work area should be made during each day, or approximately one every 12 minutes assuming an 8-hour workday.

EXERCISES

8.1. We want to estimate the proportion of time when a car wash facility is unused. It is known that the facility is busy for at least 80 percent of the day, and a study is conducted for 1 week. If we need an estimate within $\pm$ 5 percent at a 90-percent confidence level, how many observations are required each day?

8.2. If a team of workers takes 14 minutes on average to wash and handwipe a typical car, how many cars per hour can be serviced if an allowance of 10 percent is allowed for fatigue and personal needs?

8.3. One of the cleaning staff at the Last Resort Motel was observed making beds at an average rate of 8 minutes per bed. The proficiency rating of the staff person is estimated to be 90 percent.

    a. What is the normal time for this task?

    b. If the allowance for fatigue and personal needs is 10 percent, what is the standard time for this task?

8.4. A restaurant manager has noticed that tables are not cleared fast enough and diners are kept waiting during the busy lunch period. To justify hiring a part-time person to clear tables, she has decided to conduct a time study to determine how many tables one person can clear per hour. After observing tables being cleared for 1 week, an average of 3 minutes per table has been observed.

    a. What is the normal time for clearing a table if the proficiency rating of the person observed was 85 percent?

    b. If the allowance for fatigue and personal needs is 10 percent, what is the expected number of tables that can be cleared per hour?

8.5. A check-out line at a supermarket consists of two activities in sequence, one performed by a cashier and the other by a grocery packer. The cashier was observed taking 4 minutes on average to process a shopper, whereas the packer was able to finish bagging the groceries in 3 minutes. The proficiency ratings of the cashier and packer are estimated to be 80 percent and 90 percent, respectively.

    a. What is the normal time for the check-out process?

    b. If the allowance for fatigue and personal needs is 15 percent, how many shoppers can be processed per hour?

8.6. The cleaning staff at the Last Resort Motel has complained of being overworked. Management has decided to conduct a work sampling study to verify its contention that the staff is busy only about 60 percent of the time. The study should yield an estimate of idle time with a ± 5 percent degree of accuracy at a 95-percent confidence level.

    a. How many random observations should be made?

    b. Explain how you would select each observation time during a typical 8-hour day (the study will be conducted for 10 days).

8.7. The telephone company is considering taking public telephones out of service if their utilization rate is less than 20 percent. A 10-day work sampling study is conducted. The estimate of utilization should be within a ± 5-percent degree of accuracy at a 95-percent confidence level.

    a. How many random observations should be made per day?

    b. If the telephone is located in a restaurant, explain how you could enlist a waitperson to conduct the study using a fixed observation interval of 15 minutes.

8.8. One station attendant serves a full-service gas station that has a total of three pumps. On the average, a car takes 10 seconds to pull up to a pump; the attendant takes 15 seconds to find out customer needs and to begin pumping gas. It takes 40 seconds for the gas to be pumped (the attendant is free during this time), and cleaning the windshield takes 15 seconds. Finally, it takes 30 seconds to replace the nozzle on the pump and for payment to be made. Customers enter the station every 60 seconds (deterministic). Assume a customer goes to an empty pump if available or to any pump otherwise. Draw a worker-customer chart for a five-minute observation of this scenario.

County General Hospital[26]

County General is a large public hospital serving a major metropolitan area in the growing Sunbelt region of the United States. A significant portion of the hospital's budget is consumed by labor costs, and the total number of employees can be broken down as follows:

Administrative and management	18
Professional	
MDs	67
RNs	145
LVNs	196
Support	<u>368</u>
Total	794

The hospital's top management has been concerned for some time that the labor costs for professional staff, particularly the registered nurses, have not been kept under control as closely as the annual operating plan envisioned at its inception. In attempting to see how the nursing staff could be utilized better, management has decided to undertake a work sampling study of the registered nurses to see what proportions of their time actually are spent on various tasks.

In designing the study, management established eight general categories of activities for defining the registered nurse's typical workday: (1) direct patient care, (2) indirect patient care (i.e., preparation of medicine, equipment, and so on), (3) paperwork, (4) communication and teaching, (5) escorting and errands, (6) housekeeping, (7) travel, and (8) nonproductive (i.e., idle time, mealtime, and so on).

Observers who perform the actual sampling will be given lists of specific duties that would define each category and also would ensure that the study has a high degree of consistency in the allocation of a nurse's daily duties to the correct categories. On the basis of a pilot study, County General's management estimates that the proportions of time spent in each of the above categories are 15, 12, 10, 40, 5, 3, 5, and 10 percent, respectively. The study will be conducted during a 14-day period from each of three workshifts, and management wants to ensure that the estimates come within ±2 percent of the true proportions with a 98-percent confidence level.

Questions

1. How many observations will be required to ensure that all categories have enough data collected to meet the established parameters for accuracy? Assume there is a normal distribution.

2. The study was accomplished as designed, and the hospital management team was given the following summary data:

Category	% of time	Category	% of time
1	13.8	5	3.1
2	12.3	6	4.5
3	11.9	7	3.1
4	39.7	8	11.6

On the basis of your knowledge of hospital functions and the general goal of providing a high level of service to patients, suggest at least one or two strategies management might apply to utilize better the time of the registered nursing staff. Describe the effects that your strategies might have on the time requirements for other staff groups and on the general level of health care in County General.

ENDNOTES

1. Richard Normann, *Service Management,* John Wiley & Sons, New York, 1984, p. 89.
2. Jan Carlzon, *Moments of Truth,* Ballinger, Cambridge, Mass., 1987.
3. H. M. Schwartz and S. M. Davis, "Matching Corporate Culture and Business Strategy," *Organizational Dynamics,* vol. 59, 1981, p. 33.
4. Henry Mintzberg, *Mintzberg on Management: Inside Our Strange World of Organizations,* The Free Press, New York, 1989, p. 98.
5. Wayne K. Hoy, C. John Tarter, and Robert B. Kottkamp, *Open Schools/Healthy Schools,* Sage Publications, London, 1991, p. 5.
6. Carol J. Loomis, "How the Service Stars Managed to Sparkle," *Fortune,* June 11, 1984, p. 117.
7. W. E. Sasser, Jr., C. W. L. Hart, and J. L. Heskett, *The Service Management Course,* The Free Press, New York, 1991, p. 97.
8. L. A. Schlesinger and J. L. Heskett, "The Service-Driven Service Company," *Harvard Business Review,* September–October 1991, p. 72.
9. Gregory P. Stone, "City Shoppers and Urban Identification: Observations on the Social Psychology of City Life," *American Journal of Sociology,* July 1954, pp. 36–43.
10. John E. G. Bateson, "The Self-Service Consumer: Empirical Findings," in L. Berry, L. Shostack, and G. Upah (eds.), *Marketing of Services,* American Marketing Association, Chicago, 1983, pp. 76–83.
11. Adapted from M. R. Solomon, C. F. Surprenant, J. A. Czepiel, and E. G. Gutman, "A Role Theory Perspective on Dyadic Interactions: The Service Encounter," *Journal of Marketing,* vol. 49, Winter 1985, pp. 99–111.
12. Adapted from Benjamin Schneider, "The Service Organization: Climate Is Crucial," *Organizational Dynamics,* Autumn 1980, pp. 52–65.
13. Adapted from J. L. Heskett, T. O. Jones, G. W. Loveman, W. E. Sasser, Jr., and L. A. Schlesinger, "Putting the Service-Profit Chain to Work," *Harvard Business Review,* March–April 1994, pp. 164–174.
14. Prepared by Bridgett Gagne, Sandhya Shardanand, and Laura Urquidi under the supervision of Professor James A. Fitzsimmons.
15. Prepared by Yair Almagor, Jason Hearnsberger, Gijun Kim, and Michael Sebold under the supervision of Professor James A. Fitzsimmons.
16. Andrew C. Taylor, "Welcome Message," http://www.enterprise.com, accessed on March 20, 1998.
17. "Enterprising Growth with a Hometown Flavor," *St. Louis Commerce,* June 1996.
18. Dan Callahan, "Enterprise's Strategy of Local Domination," *Auto Rental News,* December/January 1994.
19. Brian O'Reilly, "The Rent-A-Car Jocks Who Made Enterprise #1," *Fortune,* October 28, 1996.
20. Ibid.
21. Ibid.
22. Ibid.
23. Ibid.
24. Ibid.
25. S. E. Kimes and S. A. Mutkoski, "Customer Contact in Restaurants: An Application of Work Sampling," *Cornell HRA Quarterly,* May 1991, pp. 82–88.
26. Prepared by James Vance under the supervision of Professor James A. Fitzsimmons.

CHAPTER NINE

Internet Service

After completing this chapter, you should be able to:

1. Describe different Internet business models.
2. Contrast an electronic and a traditional service.
3. Describe the relationship between the product and the process structure of electronic services.
4. Locate an Internet service on the electronic services product-process matrix.

Preparing a chapter on electronic services is much like trying to hit a moving target, so it seems prudent to issue a disclaimer of sorts. We can report on a practice that is common at a traditional bricks-and-mortar business with some confidence that the information will hold true at least for several months, if not for the life of the new edition of a textbook. The world of e-commerce, however, evolves on a scale of minutes and hours, so the information we present today on specific services might be out-of-date before the period ends this sentence. Today's information, even if outdated tomorrow, presents principles that are instructive.

The world's largest garage sale is not around the corner—it's on the Internet. In one place, Web surfers can pick through more than 3.5 million listings for toys, china, software, computers, and sports memorabilia—you name it. It's no wonder that eBay.com has become a hot spot for collectors and bargain seekers. eBay uses the Internet to reach people and has created a virtual auction for exchange of items between individuals. A seller can list an item on the eBay site and, if it sells, then pay a commission of 5 percent of the sale price up to $25, and 2.5 percent of the amount over $25, as long as the price doesn't exceed $1,000.

To place a bid, a buyer enters a user ID, a password, and the amount of the bid. A moment later the website reports the status of the bid. Often it says, "You've been outbid," because someone has put in a higher bid. The bidder can then submit a higher offer. Auctions typically remain open for up to a week and bidders receive daily e-mails notifying them that their bid is still the highest or that they have been outbid. Sellers, meanwhile, can set a minimum price called the "reserve," but that figure is not disclosed at the start.

The eBay virtual auction does have some drawbacks. Unlike in a real-world auction, the actual merchandise cannot be touched. The opportunity for face-to-face haggling with the seller, common at a flea market, is lost. Furthermore, a bidder must submit a maximum bid up-front, and he or she is obliged to pay that amount if bidding gets that high and doesn't go higher, even if he or she has lost interest in the item during the course of the auction. A final drawback involves paying for the item before it is shipped. The seller has three days to contact the high bidder and ask for payment, usually by a cashier's check. The seller must receive payment before the item is sent. If the item was misrepresented, the buyer's only recourse is to try to get his or her money back from the seller. If that fails, eBay will post a feedback report on the seller for future buyers to consider. eBay can also refuse the seller future access to the site. Despite these drawbacks, eBay is one of the most successful Web-based innovations and has attracted imitation from other Internet businesses, such as Yahoo! and Amazon.com.

CHAPTER PREVIEW

We begin with a discussion of the nature of Internet services. Internet business models and different uses of websites by businesses are explored. Electronic services are contrasted with traditional services to highlight the differences between the dimensions of products and processes. We also use an electronic service matrix as a framework for understanding the strategic fit between the level of service product offered and the appropriate electronic service delivery process.

INTERNET SERVICES

What do saddles, chocolate chip cookies, a new Toyota Sienna, 40 shares of Dell Computers stock, a begonia, and this textbook have in common? As recently as five years ago, we could say "absolutely nothing." Today, however, they do have something in common—all of them are available over the Internet. E-commerce allows us to obtain effortlessly every item imaginable from Allegra (http://www.rx.com) to zebras (http://www.alumni.caltech.edu/~kantner/zebras/), all kinds of services from maids (http://www.maids.com) to grocery shopping (http://homer.natural.com), and even to scheduling physicians' appointments (http://www.adclinic.com).

Most companies that do business in the "real world" now have websites. In addition to those real-world companies, there are other companies that were "born" on the Internet and exist only in the virtual world of dot-com.

The ease and speed with which we can shop online may lead us to think that the days of storefront businesses are numbered. Experts think otherwise. Predictions indicate that online shopping will account for only 7 percent of total retail shopping by the year 2004. The total U.S. revenues from online shopping, however, are predicted to rise dramatically from an estimated $20 billion in 1999 to almost $200 billion in 2004.[1]

Formalized e-learning is a recent phenomenon on the Internet. According to Robert Ramers, CEO of Learnabililty, Inc. (http://www.learnability.com), e-learning has grown to be a $6 billion industry in the United States in just two years, 1998 and 1999.[2] Ramers is in the business of teaching adults and provides training and instruction for businesses worldwide. He points out that a business can "train 3,000 people in one week much cheaper online" than in conventional training sessions, and that quality and retention of material also are much better. The Internet provides powerful tools for many educators, including those who home-school their children. Home-schooled children were once constrained by the walls of their homes. They had pencils, paper, textbooks, and little else, except, perhaps, for an occasional local field trip. The Internet has put the world at the fingertips of these youngsters—they can take virtual tours of foreign lands, interact with other people, and access the latest information on advances in any field of study or interest. Their Internet-assisted home-schooling, combined with some weight training and swimming, can provide a rich educational experience!

Coming of Age for the Internet and Websites

The Internet is an "invention" of the United States military. The idea was to link all military computer communications so that if any part of the system were destroyed, military operations could continue. Today's Internet, however, has more stars and stripes than a generation of generals and sergeants. It is still used by the military and many local, state, and national governments. U.S. president Bill Clinton, for example, has proposed that the U.S. Center for Disease Control establish a nationwide surveillance system that will track outbreaks of communicable diseases and notify physicians of the best way to treat them. The United States already uses the Internet to provide information directly to the public (e.g., http://www.faa.gov). The most "visible" use of the Internet today, however, is by businesses selling services or products and by people seeking services, products, information, or just communication with other people. Use of the Internet is so widespread, in fact, that the term "website" conveys all the aid and comfort of mom and apple pie.

A website can serve different purposes for different businesses. Some organizations use the Internet solely to communicate with employees, suppliers of raw materials, or suppliers of supporting services, such as bookkeeping, legal advice, or research materials. Local and national governments around the world maintain websites that are of interest to both tourists and businesses. Other organizations use websites to sell products and services directly to the customer. Clearly, websites can be used in many different ways:

As a Channel to Sell a Product or Service   Some retailers, such as amazon.com and wine.com, do not have physical stores. These firms sell exclusively through the Internet, and either distribute goods locally or deliver by mail or shipping service.

As a Supplemental Channel   "Click-and-mortar" firms represent traditional retailers, such as Barnes & Noble, that have extended their market reach by adding a website. Delivery of items can be made from a regional warehouse by mail or within urban areas by truck from the local store. Purchasers in an area served by a "bricks-and-mortar" Barnes & Noble store, for example, can order a book, either by phone or online, and the local store will deliver it that day. Home Depot has plans to offer a similar service.

For Technical Support   Product firms that offer after-sales technical support find the Internet to be an inexpensive avenue to help customers solve common problems. Answers to questions about setting up a new computer, for example, can be found on the Dell Computer website (http://www.dell.com).

To Embellish Existing Service   Services that traditionally have been offered by mail can be augmented by using a website. Harvard Business School Press, for example, uses a website to distribute business cases that faculty can review prior to adoption. The publisher also offers archival services for past issues of the *Harvard Business Review.*

To Process Orders   A website can be a convenient link for customers to order services. Airlines quickly made use of websites to allow customers to order electronic tickets. This service bypasses travel agents as a distribution channel and saves the airlines the cost of commissions. The airline websites also give customers access to schedules and a way to comparison shop for the lowest fare. This direct connection with customers also allows airlines to "advertise" discounted fares (i.e., unsold seats) for the coming weekend via e-mail.

To Convey Information   Many companies use their websites to convey information about the organization (e.g., names of officers, addresses, phone numbers, and technical assistance). Other websites serve as information repositories. The Dr. Koop site, for example, provides a source of information for people interested in health issues.

Internet Business Models

The Internet has created the opportunity for an entirely new class of business models for the delivery of services. Consider the following categories of Internet service models.

Internet Access Providers   Firms, such as America Online and CompuServe, provide access to the World Wide Web and e-mail services. Monthly fees provide a certain number of hours of online access and storage space on a server for e-mail files.

Portal   Descendants of the original Internet access providers now provide a variety of services that include information searching, news, white- and yellow-page directories, e-mail boxes, discussion and newsgroups, and links to online shopping. Yahoo!, for example, allows visitors to search for information on everything from bananas in the Bahamas to today's weather in Washington. It also maintains message boards so subscribers can "chat" with each other about a broad range of subjects, and it provides e-mail service.

Information Content   Some traditional information providers, such as the *New York Times,* use the Internet to distribute the news. Others, such as Hoover's.com, provide online business information for a fee.

Online Retailers   The most widely advertised use of the Internet has come from online retailers that sell everything from books (e.g., amazon.com) to gardening products (e.g., garden.com).

Transaction Enablers   Stock trading is a natural Internet business because of the electronic nature of the transactions. E*Trade has been so successful in reducing the transaction cost of buying or selling stocks and bonds that Merrill Lynch is now considering abandoning its practice of charging a commission for a stock trade and moving to account management fees instead.

Market Makers   The online auction takes advantage of the power of the Internet to reach extensive markets without the constraints of geography. The success of eBay is due to its ability to create a market for items that would be difficult to sell locally.

Electronic and Traditional Services

A comparison of electronic and traditional services is shown in Table 9.1. The features represent general characteristics that vividly differentiate the alternative delivery systems.

Table 9.2 displays the advantages and disadvantages of online and traditional grocery shopping, an activity in which almost everyone participates.

Service Product Dimensions

Electronic services share many of the characteristics of traditional services. Electronic services are intangible, because the service transactions and experiences delivered via

TABLE 9.1

COMPARISON OF ELECTRONIC AND TRADITIONAL SERVICES

Features	Electronic service	Traditional service
Service encounter	Screen-to-face	Face-to-face
Availability	Anytime	Standard working hours
Access	From home	Travel to location
Market area	Worldwide	Local
Ambiance	Electronic interface	Physical environment
Competitive differentiation	Convenience	Personalization
Privacy	Anonymity	Social interaction

TABLE 9.2

COMPARISON OF ONLINE AND TRADITIONAL GROCERY

	Online shopping	Traditional shopping
Advantages	Convenience	Five senses influence buying
	Saves time	Memory trigger
	Reduces impulse buying	Product sampling
		Exposure to new items
		Social interaction
Disadvantages	Less price and selection control	Time consuming
	Forget items	Waiting lines and parking
	Reliance on computer	Carrying groceries home
	Delivery fee	Impulse buying
		Safety

electronic channels are difficult to measure, inventory, or describe fully. The differing needs, expectations, self-service capabilities, willingness to interact, and perceptions of customers contribute to the heterogeneity of electronic services. A customer's modem capability or type of other connection to the electronic service provider, for example, contributes to the heterogeneity in speed of delivery. Finally, the consumption and delivery of electronic services are simultaneous and, thus, inseparable in both traditional and electronic services.

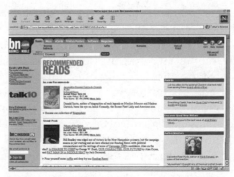

The dual life of Barnes & Noble—one business, two storefronts. © Jacques M. Chenet/CORBIS
© The Image Works

Traditional and electronic services both have core and auxiliary elements. Core elements of a service are central to the product, but auxiliary elements provide less important service dimensions. Electronic services can include both core and auxiliary dimensions, which may occur as both online offerings, such as multiplayer-gaming services, and offline offerings, such as delivery of food items from a local supermarket.

Service Process Dimensions

Service processes include front-office processes that involve direct interaction with customers and back-office processes that have little customer contact. Service processes can be characterized according to degree of contact and interaction, degree of labor intensity, and degree of labor customization. In addition, service processes include customer participation in the service delivery.

Electronic services differ in the extent to which customer contact, customization, interaction, labor intensity, service inputs, and technology can be used to differentiate between operations. Electronic-service offerings are composed of online interactive service dimensions and offline noninteractive service dimensions. The online service dimensions involve continuous customer contact with the service system, and offline elements involve little customer contact.

Customization can occur during online customer interactions with the electronic service and through offline back-office processes that are separated from the customer. Online customization might use technologies, such as video-conferencing systems and others that connect customizable technologies directly to online service operations. Labor and technology in traditional back-office service operations can be used to accomplish offline customization.

DESIGN AND DELIVERY OF ELECTRONIC SERVICES

A successful electronic service does not just happen. The software available today makes it easy for anyone who can find the "on" button on a computer to set up a website. A vast leap exists, however, between the first click and a competitive and profitable online operation.

Heim and Sinha studied the electronic food industry and adapted the product-process matrix used in manufacturing to argue that a strategic fit between the delivery process and the market exists for electronic services.[3] In the electronic services matrix, the *product structure* is defined in terms of service content and target-market segments. The *process structure* is defined along the dimension of delivery technology flexibility.

Electronic Service Product Structure

Heim and Sinha describe a product structure matrix, shown in Figure 9.1, that is defined by the content of the website, either *static* or *dynamic,* and by the targeted market segment, either *unique* or *broad.* Static content refers to a fixed presentation of the service. Such a website might have drawings or photos, but information content is fixed and noninteractive. Static pages usually offer a fixed order form, but some give only a phone number or address for placing orders. Dynamic content often involves feedback, music, action graphics, and very detailed descriptions of products or services, and it usually is interactive. Dynamic pages on a website allow customers to customize their orders and submit them electronically.

The product structure matrix describes the type of market that is found within each category according to five dimensions:

1. Scale and scope of the services.
2. Level of demand.

Market Segment	Electronic Service Content	
	Static	Dynamic
	Niche markets	**Customized markets**
Unique	One or a few services Low demand Low online customization High offline customization No joint branding	Many services High demand High online customization Low offline customization High joint branding
	Extender markets	**Mass markets**
Broad	Several services Low/medium demand Medium online customization Medium offline customization Low joint branding	Many services Medium/high demand Medium/high online customization Low offline customization Medium joint branding

FIGURE 9.1 Categories of electronic service product structure.
(Reprinted with permission from Gregory R. Heim and Kingshuk K. Sinha, "Design and Delivery of Electronic Services: Implications for Customer Value in Electronic Food Retailing," in James A. Fitzsimmons and Mona J. Fitzsimmons, *New Service Development: Creating Memorable Experiences,* eds. Sage Publications, Thousand Oaks, Calif., 2000, p. 160.)

3. Degree of online customization.
4. Degree of offline customization.
5. Nature of joint branding.

Niche Markets *Niche-market* (i.e., unique static) electronic-service products are targeted at a local or niche market that offers a small number of services and has relatively low demand. Most niche-market services offer only static online elements. If any customization is offered, it is done offline, because online customization is expensive to design and deliver, and the business must have a high volume of sales to cover those costs. Niche-market providers are "solo acts"; that is, they do not engage in joint branding with other organizations.

Beka (http://www.bekainc.com) and Jockey International (http://www.jockey.com) are examples of niche-market companies. Both of these companies offer online static pages that include product lists and photos. Beka, a manufacturer of specialty wood products such as weaving looms and children's easels, also lists prices on its website, but the customer must place an order by phone or e-mail. Jockey (yes, the underwear folks) does not give prices on its website or make any other provision for purchasing its clothing online to protect the stores that carry its products. Beka's products are carried in some stores, so Beka charges a little more for online orders to avoid taking sales away from dealers. Some niche-market providers also include other information, such as recipes and nutritional information. Offline customization for niche and local markets takes different forms including gift-wrapping, local transportation to the buyer, and creation of personalized labels.

Extender Markets *Extender markets* (i.e., broad static) have slightly higher demand but lower offline customization than niche markets have. These broader markets also include some online customization, and they might have joint branding with other organizations.

Golfsmith, based in Austin, Texas, began in the niche market of supplying and assembling components for golf clubs. In recent years it has moved into the extender market by offering a much broader selection of products and services. The Golfsmith website has dynamic pages and a shopping cart capability. Customers can order clubs assembled from components, readymade clubs, and a broad spectrum of golf accessories. Visitors to the site also can receive tips from pros, although no absolute guarantee to lower handicaps is implied!

Mass Markets   *Mass-market* (i.e., broad dynamic) electronic services target a large number of customers who have a broad spectrum of needs. This type of demand is difficult to satisfy solely with offline customization. Consequently, mass markets provide dynamic pages or a combination of static and dynamic pages that help customers to tailor their orders online. For example, etoys (http://www.etoys.com) provides an initial menu that includes categories such as toys for different age groups, toys by manufacturer, and books. This menu allows a customer who is shopping for a toy for a two-year-old toddler to go directly to a list of appropriate toys instead of having to sort through a list of every toy offered. The online service includes a wealth of information to help the customer. The first list displays pictures and a brief description of several toys for toddlers. The shopper then can click on a particular item, perhaps Pound A Ball, to see a larger picture of the item, a detailed description, and information that "kids who like Pound A Ball also like Roll Around Tower."

Mass-market e-services can be imitated easily, so they can gain a competitive advantage by incorporating joint branding. Joint branding in a mass market usually consists of links between the different services. Amazon.com (http://www.amazon.com), for example, practices joint branding by "selling" virtual shelf space to other dot-com providers. Such a portfolio of jointly branded services is difficult to duplicate.

The broad scope of online customization for mass markets does not eliminate a need for some offline customization. Ancillary services such as gift-wrapping or personalizing labels are commonly available.

Customized Markets   *Customized-market* (i.e., unique dynamic) electronic services are hybrids of niche-market services and mass-market services. They are focused on a specialized market, just as niche-market services are, but they seek the high level of demand that mass-market services have. We noted that a few static pages of product lists and descriptions are sufficient for the low levels of demand of niche markets, but high demand requires dynamic pages that allow a high level of online customization. We also noted that duplication of high-demand services by competitors is easy and appealing, so many mass-market and customized-market services offer a portfolio of joint services to discourage imitation. Mass-market joint offerings usually include a broad scope of services, whereas customized-market offerings usually include only services related to the primary provider's focus. Visit the Epicurious website (http://www.epicurious.com), for example. Epicurious's dynamic pages include links to Bon Appétit and Gourmet magazines, Williams-Sonoma stores, and a site to buy or sell vintage cookbooks. Other pages allow visitors to swap or search for recipes and to get advice for everything from choosing wines to how to use each of the four forks on the left side of the dinner plate.

Electronic Service Process Structure

Heim and Sinha identify the electronic service process structure as the "second building block" of their product-process matrix. This structure consists of four stages that are defined according to the ability of the electronic service process technology to adapt to the complex and changing needs of customers.[4] The four stages—service kiosk, service mart, mass-service customization, and joint-alliance service customization—involve different types and levels of technologies that range from those with little flexibility to those that are highly flexible (see Figure 9.2). Technologies used in an earlier stage of the electronic-service operations often are still required for delivery in later stages.

Heim and Sinha chose names for the stages of the electronic service-process structure that relate to operations already found in the bricks-and-mortar marketplace:

> *Service kiosk,* for example, evokes the notion of small stands set up in shopping malls or airports for individual operators to deliver services. *Service mart* evokes the notion of a store that can deliver a relatively varied but small number of options to customers. *Mass-service customization* describes a provider that delivers a large number of services to meet dynamically changing customer preferences. Finally, *joint-alliance service customization* evokes the notion of several service firms that attempt to surpass what they can deliver individually

FIGURE 9.2 Stages in the electronic service process structure: technologies and technical support staff.
(Adapted with permission from Gregory R. Heim and Kingshuk K. Sinha, "Design and Delivery of Electronic Services: Implications for Customer Value in Electronic Food Retailing," in *New Service Development: Creating Memorable Experiences,* eds. James A. Fitzsimmons and Mona J. Fitzsimmons, Sage Publications, Thousand Oaks, Calif., 2000, p. 164.)

by using mass customization to deliver portfolios of services that are designed to meet the preferences of individual customers.[5]

Service Kiosk   The *service-kiosk* online service employs electronic technology that has little or no flexibility. The online pages are written with static-scripting language, such as HyperText Markup Language (HTML), and images also are static. Although these are elementary technologies, they are expensive to maintain and operate. Therefore, many service kiosks outsource this aspect of their businesses by leasing the necessary technology, such as servers, security systems, and access to telecommunication infrastructure. They might also employ services to maintain and operate the systems.

Service kiosks can compensate for the lack of flexibility in their online systems by incorporating a flexible offline component into their service. Heim and Sinha characterize service kiosks as "storefronts that allow the customer to specify and order offline services." The Enrico Biscotti Company (http://www.enricobiscotti.com) is an example of a service kiosk that acts as a storefront. Enrico Biscotti is a small bakery in Pittsburgh, Pennsylvania, that specializes in Italian dipping pastries called biscotti. The website consists of two static pages: One page describes the company, its products, and the all-natural ingredients it uses. The second page is an order form that allows customers to choose from 18 varieties of biscotti and to choose if the biscotti should be drizzled with a white or dark chocolate. Enricobiscotti.com's technology does include a security protocol and a shopping cart system that allows visitors to order more than one type of biscotti at a time. The only dynamic feature of its website is a flying biscotti! Other service kiosks exist only as virtual services without any bricks-and-mortar store behind them.

Visit the Oldphones website (oldphones.com). Oldphones has been up and running since 1998 and sells working antique telephones, which have been restored by the company owner. The company also repairs old phones, provides information on wiring, and offers advice on the care of old phones. The website has static pages that include photographs and information on available items, a security protocol, and an order form.

Service Mart   The *service-mart* process stage uses modified service-kiosk technologies. Service-mart technologies are more flexible than their service-kiosk analogs, and technical staff support them. The increased flexibility and technical support allow some online customization. Pages of a service-mart website have a dynamic component that can track a customer's preferences and purchases. A return customer, for example, can be greeted by his or her name and told of new or sale items that fall within the preference profile that the customer filled out during his or her initial visit. When billing information, such as mailing address and telephone number, is a permanent part of the customer's profile, the customer will not have to spend time filling out the form for each visit.

Heim and Sinha point out a need for robust server and telecommunication capacity at the service-mart stage. Skilled technicians, sophisticated hardware, and experienced design personnel are required to set up and manage a service-mart business. Security of transactions becomes very important at this stage, because customers can relay payment information online.

Burpee Gardens (http://www.burpee.com), a large producer of seeds and plants, is an example of a service-mart operation. The Burpee website has dynamic pages and a shopping cart system for its online catalog. The site also lets visitors take a 3-D tour of a garden, submit questions, search an extensive archive of questions and answers, get recipes for preparing homegrown produce, and join Club Burpee. Club Burpee members are e-mailed special offers, and they get online discounts and new catalog releases.

Mass-Service Customization According to Heim and Sinha, *mass-service customization* uses the most flexible electronic service technologies and requires the greatest scope of technologies and technical support. Companies in this category need systems of multiple servers that can handle high levels of demand, and many have redundant backup systems that can be used if part of the first-line system goes down. The technical support system may include film directors, musicians, and other creative people in addition to highly skilled professional computer programmers.

Blue Mountain Arts (http://bluemountain.com) is an excellent example of an electronic service operating at the level of mass-service customization. The company, based in Boulder, Colorado, publishes greeting cards, note cards, and fine poetry books, and its website might offer the best value of all electronic services online. Bluemountain.com has cards for every conceivable occasion—or nonoccasion—you name it! A small sample list includes Feast of the Radishes, Celebrate Beethoven's Birthday, Make Up Your Mind Day, and the ever-popular Underdog Day. Most cards are animated, many include music, and some are interactive. An interactive Easter card, for example, allows a child to go on an Easter egg hunt. The Endangered Species and Planet Earth series for Earth Day includes some stereogram cards—recipients who have "agile" eyes can see hidden images. Any card can be personalized with the sender's name, the recipient's name, and a personal message, and, often, the sender has a choice in the music that accompanies the card. Now here's the value part—the cards are free. Bluemountain.com conveys happiness, sympathy, beauty, encouragement, and wisdom at no cost to the sender or recipient. The company does sell ancillary services and products, however. A sender may order flowers or chocolates, for example, to accompany a card. Blue Mountain Arts publishes cards, notecards, and books that also are sold online.

Bluemountain.com's success has required some business changes. In order to finance the rapidly growing operation, the formerly private organization went public and is merging with Excite@Home Network. Blue Mountain Arts retains editorial and creative control, and Excite@Home manages the technical side of the operation that is becoming increasingly complex.

Heim and Sinha note that much of the usefulness of mass-service customization technologies results from the ability to deliver value-added services, such as customer registration, storage of payment information, product-search systems, and flexible-payment systems. These technologies also can include decision-support systems, capacity management capabilities, data warehouse and mining systems, and enhanced security systems.

Joint-Alliance Service Customization *Joint-alliance services customization* has the most flexible technology of all the process structures. The technology crosses organizational and geographical boundaries. Databases of participating services, for example, are linked, creating huge data warehouses. Skilled managers must be in place to oversee these operations.

Consider drkoop.com (http://www.drkoop.com). This health care service was launched in 1998 and, within one year, became the leading source of health care information on the Internet. Drkoop.com has entered into strategic partnerships with various Web access providers, leading search engines, online news sites, health care organizations, health care information "libraries," and suppliers of medicines and other health care goods. Visitors to the drkoop.com website can get the latest health care news, nutritional advice, and general health and wellness information. The site also includes interactive health assessment tools and a "MyHealth" feature that allows a visitor to create his or her own personalized version of the site.

ELECTRONIC SERVICE STRATEGY AND THE PRODUCT-PROCESS MATRIX

The product-process matrix for electronic services, shown in Figure 9.3, is a strategic framework that is useful in planning a service. The horizontal side of the matrix includes the four categories of the service-product structure, and the vertical side includes the four categories of the service-process structure.

An arrow traveling diagonally down the matrix represents a "center of gravity" for aligning the product and process structures. As we move along the arrow from upper left to lower right, we see increasing flexibility in technologies, wider scope of services, and a shift from little or no online customization and a high level of offline customization to high online customization and low offline customization.

Heim and Sinha offer three propositions about services and their positions in the matrix:[6]

Electronic Service-Product Structure

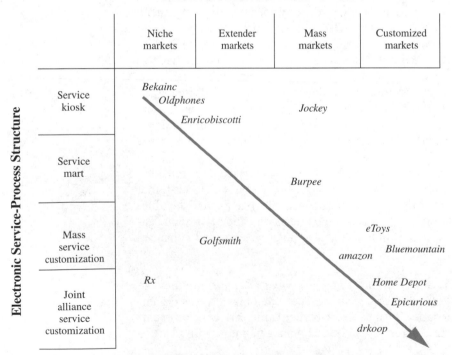

FIGURE 9.3 Electronic services product-process matrix.
(Adapted with permission from Gregory R. Heim and Kingshuk K. Sinha, "Design and Delivery of Electronic Services: Implications for Customer Value in Electronic Food Retailing," in *New Service Development: Creating Memorable Experiences,* eds. James A. Fitzsimmons and Mona J. Fitzsimmons, Sage Publications, Thousand Oaks, Calif., 2000, p. 170.)

1. Services located along the diagonal offer greater customer value than do those in the upper-right or lower-left corners.
2. Services located in the lower one-half of the matrix offer greater customer value than do those in the upper one-half.
3. Services located in the right one-half of the matrix offer greater customer value than do those in the left one-half, except when the value is derived primarily from offline processes.

These attributes of the matrix can be used as guidelines when designing an electronic service by pointing to the attributes the service must have to occupy a desired position in the e-commerce market. A customer's perceived value of a service might be the most important factor in the customer's choice of a service provider. Heim and Sinha suggest, therefore, that "the delivery of customer value will determine the rate and the extent to which customers will switch from conventional services to electronic services."[7]

SUMMARY

In this chapter we have explored the nature of electronic services. Electronic service products were divided into four categories: niche markets, extender markets, mass markets, and customized markets. Electronic service processes, in order of increasing flexibility, were categorized as service kiosk, service mart, mass-service customization, and joint-alliance service customization. A product-process matrix, adapted from manufacturing, is used to align service-product structure with service-process structure to position an Internet service provider strategically.

KEY TERMS AND DEFINITIONS

Customized markets are a hybrid of niche-market and mass-market services that focus on a specialized market but that also seek a high level of demand.

Extender markets offer several services to a broad market with some customization and joint branding.

Joint-alliance service customization has the most flexible technology and crosses organizational boundaries to link databases.

Mass markets target a large number of customers with a broad spectrum of needs.

Mass-service customization uses very flexible electronic technology with extensive technical support to deliver value-added services, such as product search, customer registration, and enhanced security systems.

Niche markets offer products or services that have a specific area of interest and low demand.

Service kiosk is a storefront technology that has little or no online flexibility but that allows customers to specify and order offline services.

Service mart uses an electronic process that is supported by technical staff and that allows some online customization, such as tracking a customer's preferences and purchases.

TOPICS FOR DISCUSSION

1. Can an Internet service encounter be a memorable experience?
2. What is the "front office" of an Internet service?
3. What is the contribution to gross national product (GNP) of "self-service" activities?
4. Visit the following websites and position them on the electronic services product-process matrix: cookingpost.com, chocoholic.com, peapod.com, raisinrack.com, and wine.com.

BOX 9.1

Service Benchmark

MICROSOFT, FORD DRIVE WEB DEAL

Ford Motor Company, the world's second largest automaker, and Microsoft Corporation are forming a venture to let Ford sell built-to-order vehicles through the software company's MSN CarPoint online car-buying service.

Currently, shoppers use CarPoint to research cars, measure resale value, and contact dealers for no-hassle pricing. The new service will go further, allowing consumers to pick a car the way they buy computers directly from companies such as Dell Computer Corporation or Compaq Computer Corporation. Instead of choosing the size of a hard drive and processor speed, shoppers will select among standard car options, such as color, number of doors, and whether or not they want a compact-disc player.

Using Microsoft software, Ford will locate an existing car on a dealer lot or order a custom-built vehicle and deliver it to the buyer's closest dealership, which will handle negotiations for price and payment options. "Ford benefits because it will no longer build 50,000 red Tauruses that nobody wants," said Sheldon Sandler, chief executive of Bel Air Partners, a Princeton, New Jersey, company that advises publicly traded dealers. "It's very exciting and very scary. The manufacturers are dead serious about eliminating the middle man." Industry executives say that 20 to 25 percent of the cost of a new vehicle is added between the assembly plant and delivery to the customer.

In a news conference announcing the agreement, Ford Chief Executive Jacques Nasser and Microsoft President Steve Ballmer stressed that dealers will be involved in all sales conducted through CarPoint, including Volvo, Jaguar and Aston Martin. By keeping final sales and pricing in the hands of the dealers, Ford may avoid traversing the tricky path that Compaq struggled with when it began selling online—becoming a competitor with retailers that sell its products.

"I don't think this is going to negatively affect us," said Tommy Perez, general sales manager at Covert Ford on Research Boulevard in Austin, who said Ford told dealers very little beyond the contents of its press release. "I don't think it will remove the dealer. It will just supply leads to dealerships and help change the ordering process."

Competitor CarsDirect.com has already moved to eliminate dealerships from the car-buying equation. With CarsDirect—partly owned by Dell CEO Michael Dell—consumers can enter on a Web site what kind of car and what options they want, and the company will deliver that vehicle directly to their home or office.

Other car manufacturers are trying tactics similar to Ford's new arrangement. General Motors Corporation said last month it will work with Sun Microsystems Inc. to expand its current GM Buy-Power service. Toyota Motor Corporation in August said it would be able to deliver custom-ordered Camry Solaras within five days from its Cambridge, Ontario, assembly plant.

Besides leading to more efficient manufacturing and quicker delivery, Ford hopes letting users configure cars online will provide valuable market research for car companies, according to Nasser. "Today that information is very difficult to get," Nasser said. While Ford owns a stake in the venture, it will still have to pay Microsoft for the information about consumer preferences involved in the car purchases. Ford could also get the information from its dealers.

CarPoint is seeking investments from other automakers. Monday's announcement also revealed that Honda Motor Company will pay an unspecified amount to license CarPoint's DealerPoint technology for use by its 1,000 Honda and 250 Acura dealers. DealerPoint helps manage sales leads that come into CarPoint.

Other automakers, including GM and Isuzu, have links on CarPoint. None have an equity stake such as Ford is taking.

Source: "Microsoft, Ford Drive Web Deal," *Austin American Statesman,* September 21, 1999, p. D1.

Amazon.com[8]

Amazon.com opened its virtual doors in July 1995. Since then, the retailer has served 8 million customers in 160 countries and grosses more than $20 in sales per second on its website.[9] Many people regard amazon.com as the "golden child" of the Internet.

The company is the concept of Jeffrey Bezos. The young CEO started Amazon with the intention of establishing a strong brand name that he could leverage into other products. He marketed books first, because he believed they are ideal cyberspace products. Customers do not need much physical interaction with the product or with a salesperson to purchase books. Books, therefore, are well suited to marketing over the Web.

A key success factor for Amazon.com is that it captures market share and fosters brand loyalty by focusing on customer needs. Bezos believes that paying too much attention to short-term gains means forgetting about long-term customer satisfactions. This long-term customer focus comes at a price. Despite impressive sales growth, Amazon has yet to turn a profit, but this hasn't stopped Amazon from becoming a dominant force in online retailing. The Amazon website now includes products and services such as music, software, toys, and online auctions.

AMAZON'S GUIDING FORCE—
THE CUSTOMER

Amazon's guiding philosophy is to provide superior service to its customers. Bezos and his management team spent one year creating the website and database programs that drive Amazon.com. They sought to create a friendly site that would not demand a high level of computer literacy.

Bezos recognized that Internet commerce would shift the balance of power toward consumers. Consequently, Amazon.com builds customer relationships by customizing its service, involving its website visitors in the service, and creating a communal spirit. Focus on the consumer is the cornerstone for developing customer loyalty.

Customer as Coproducer and Service Customization

Amazon.com integrates customers into the service delivery process in several ways. Customers may participate in the Discussion Board service. This service presents an opportunity to read comments from readers about books of interest to the customer. The customer also can chat with other Discussion Board participants. The "wish list" is another service that Amazon.com offers. A customer can enter titles of books he or she would like to have in a personal wish list. Someone who wants to give a friend a book as a gift, for example, can make a selection from the friend's wish list.

Amazon also makes personalized recommendations to individual customers. Some of these recommendations are based on the customer's past purchases, and other recommendations are based on the behavior of past customers who have made purchases similar to those of the customer. If a consumer purchases a book on Amish quilts, for example, amazon.com's software will search for all the people who purchased this same book. Using a mathematical process called collaborative filtering, the software determines what other books are popular with people who read the Amish quilt book. It then develops a list of proposed titles for the customer to read based on this information. Amazon.com uses this technique to provide the same friendly and personalized reading advice that a local bricks-and-mortar bookstore operation can, but it achieves greater accuracy and convenience at a fraction of the cost.

One flaw of early collaborative filtering was its inability to distinguish gift purchases. Someone buying his or her mother a book on quilting, for example, would receive recommendations on this topic despite a lack of personal interest. Recently, amazon.com solved this problem by including a check box on the order page so the customer can indicate if the item is a gift. Another problem can arise because the power of collaborative filtering is based on the customer's history. If a person changes e-mail addresses frequently and uses a new Amazon.com identification, all of the data are lost.

In addition to collaborative filtering, the company uses other strategies to achieve its mission. When repeat customers log on to the website, a personalized web page greets the customer by name and allows him or her to view the new recommendations made by the collaborative filtering tool. Bezos compares this personalized front page with "walking into your favorite store and finding only items that you want on the shelves near the door." Amazon also allows customers to store information on the company's secure server. Customers can authorize Amazon.com to keep a record of their credit cards and mailing addresses, for example. This technology, called 1-Click, streamlines the service so that customers don't have to reenter the information every time they make purchases.

Amazon.com doesn't wait for customers to come to its site to provide its service. If a customer doesn't visit the site in a certain length of time, Amazon sends an e-mail encouraging him or her to visit Amazon.com, and giving a list of recommendations on books to check out on the next visit.

Other Unique Uses of Technology for the Customer

Amazon.com not only has used technology to personalize the customer experience, but it also has designed its site with customers in mind. The pages are easy to understand and use. The website avoids large graphics, which can take a long time to load. According to Keynote systems, Amazon is one of the fastest and most accessible sites on the Internet.[10]

A powerful search engine is another unique feature of Amazon.com. The company employs a "do what I mean" (DWIM) search function. The site recognizes the misspellings that customers frequently make and changes the search function to account for these mistakes. If a customer misspells Fitzsimmons as Fitsimmons, for example, Amazon.com displays the book *Service Management*.

More Than Just Friendly Technology

Amazon's technology has helped to create loyal customers who not only visit the site, but, as we have noted, also interact with it. Amazon.com is an active virtual community that involves the customer.

Another feature of its Discussion Board service is the Author's Corner, which sometimes allows readers to engage in question-and-answer sessions with their favorite writers. The company also encourages visitors and customers to post reviews of any book on the site. This review process involves the customers in developing the content on the website, and also creates an information tool for other website visitors. Amazon also allows users to form reading groups where customers can post comments to one another about specific books. The library of reviews is an important barrier to entry in a digital environment where entrepreneurs can easily copy this business model in a week.

Amazon.com employees go to great lengths for the customers and consider them as part of a community. One customer reported with joy that a copy of his father's book, 20 years out of print, had been located for him by Amazon. Associates Program expands this "community" beyond the websites under Amazon's direct control. Amazon.com allows registered websites, such as Yahoo!, to recommend specific books, CDs, videos, and other Amazon products to their visitors using a hyperlink. If customers follow the hyperlink and purchase the product on Amazon.com, these associates receive a commission. A 15 percent commission is given on more than 400,000 titles and 5 percent on more than 1.1 million additional Amazon products. Amazon claims "tens of thousands" of associates are participating in the program, which expands Amazon's presence and publicity on the Web, but it also means that Amazon could lose some control of its brand and image.

Amazon has encountered some other problems. A reporter revealed that Amazon was selling space to publishers on a list of favorite books. Amazon also has been accused of selling authors extra e-mail support on the website for various titles.[11] The company was flooded with outraged e-mails and has since stopped all paid promotions. This incident raises the question, Will the loyal customer base of Amazon.com or any other electronic service tolerate being used for financial gain?

AS AMAZON LOOKS TO THE FUTURE— WILL IT BECOME THE WAL-MART OF THE INTERNET?

Although it is not yet profitable, Amazon.com has been very successful. Amazon's personalized customer service and online community strategy work well. The company claims 85 percent of online book sales, and it is the largest seller of videos and music on the Web. An impressive 64 percent of Amazon .com's business is from repeat customers.[12] Retention rate is crucial to any business, but especially to Internet retailers. Early skeptics suggested that price-sensitive buyers would constantly search the net for the lowest prices and leave companies without any pricing power or brand loyalty. Amazon has not observed this predicted pattern.

Amazon.com has aggressive plans to duplicate this community for other products. It already has expanded into the online auction business by launching Amazon.com Auctions in March of 1999. The firm has acquired interests in other online retailers also. For example, Amazon.com purchased a 50 percent ownership stake in Pets.com and has a minority stake in Drugstore.com.

Fast expansion into other retailing areas reinforces Amazon's goal to be a one-stop shopping site on the Internet. This Wal-Mart strategy has its dangers, however. Amazon runs the risk of expanding too rapidly, which could damage or dilute its brand image. Time will tell if this long-term growth strategy will be successful.

Questions

1. How would you contrast Amazon's business design with that of Barnes & Noble before Barnes & Noble went online? From a customer's perspective, what are the advantages and disadvantages of each design?
2. Why has Amazon.com not turned a profit yet and what needs to be done to achieve profitability?
3. Will Amazon continue to be successful against "click and mortar" competitors, such as Barnes & Noble, which go online?
4. Is Amazon.com a model for the future of retailing?

CASE

TheGift.com[13]

TheGift.com was founded in Grapevine, Texas, a community adjacent to Dallas/Ft.Worth airport, in June 1997 and began operations on March 1, 1998. Customers who access TheGift's website (www.thegift.com) can purchase gifts for any occasion, including special occasions such as weddings, Father's Day, graduations, and births.

Jeff Swearingen and Robert Bingham, TheGift's co-founders, are no strangers to sales and marketing in the high-tech world. Both men have business backgrounds and they saw the potential for an Internet-based gift service. They established their operations in Dallas for several reasons. First, Texas offers an easily accessible location that is close to the distributors with whom TheGift has electronic commerce and order-processing arrangements. Second, Dallas has an excellent source of technical workers and programmers who are required for rapid expansion and Internet service development. Finally, unlike other airport-tangent communities, Grapevine offers reasonably priced, easily accessible, and aesthetically pleasing office parks.

When the founders conceived the idea for TheGift, they realized that they would need to distinguish their service package from other similar gift services. They saw an opportunity to differentiate themselves from their competitors by offering a broad range of products and services. Other Internet-based gift services offered relatively homogeneous product lines (i.e., flowers only or chocolates only). Swearingen and Bingham agreed upon nine major service areas:

Wedding and Baby Registry Couples can register all of their wedding or baby gifts online with TheGift.com. With the help of online work screens, couples could create a wedding or baby registry just as they would at Dillard's or any other store. Couples could register at one site, TheGift, rather than at multiple stores. This registry creates a tremendous convenience for the couple and the buyers by eliminating the need to travel to Bloomingdale's or Babies 'R' Us.

Shipping Unlike many other gift services, TheGift can ship multiple gifts to multiple locations throughout the United States within the same transaction. Competitors often do not allow shipping to locations other than the billing address.

Satisfaction and Lowest Price Guarantee TheGift .com will not be undersold by any authorized retailer. This guarantee is valid for the day of the transaction and 29 days after, but does not apply to liquidation sales at retailer sites. The guarantee even applies to items that a retailer does not have in stock, but TheGift must be able to verify the price. Products are guaranteed or your money back. If a buyer is unhappy with any item for any reason, he or she has two options: the gift can be returned in its original condition within 30 days of purchase for a prompt refund to the originating credit card or TheGift can issue store credit for the full product purchase price.

Recommendation Services For any special event, TheGift offers a list of recommended products. Furthermore, customers can contact the firm online to ask for gift ideas and recommendations.

Reminder Service Customers can set up a personalized catalog of special-event reminders (e.g., a spouse's birthday or an anniversary). Customers can use this service to indicate when they would like to receive automated e-mail reminders, thereby allowing them enough time to plan for gift purchases.

Gift Wrapping and Personalized Cards Customers can select from a wide variety of personalized gift-wrappings and even create their own card designs and messages.

Online Address Book As part of facilitating the gift experience for customers, TheGift anticipates that some customers might welcome an easy way to organize their gift giving. Consequently, TheGift allows customers to create a contact book that is linked to the reminder service.

Transaction Security TheGift assures that the buyer's financial information is transmitted safely and confidentially. The online transaction system is integrated with Secure Sockets Layer (SSL) technology, the best secure transaction technology available. This technology allows buyers to select "secured" or "unsecured" shopping at TheGift.com. All sensitive information is encrypted before being sent over the Internet.

Historical Anecdotes TheGift includes pleasant short stories, such as the history of Father's Day, to make the visit to TheGift's website more enjoyable.

Beyond these service offerings, however, TheGift has another unique attraction owing to its wide range of product offerings. TheGift's products include items, such as small appliances, cookware, books, flowers, electronics, cutlery, home accents, chocolates, wines, and gardening accessories. Furthermore, TheGift offers products from many manufacturers within any given product category. A buyer purchasing flatware, for example, can select from products made by Dansk, Lenox, Mikasa, Gorham, Noritake, Oneida, Reed & Barton, and Yamazaki.

Unlike TheGift, the majority of Internet-based gift services are specialized. For example, TheKnot.com is a wedding registry only. Couples can register all of their gifts on this website, and buyers can purchase and ship gifts much like the process involved with TheGift.com. TheKnot, however, offers nothing for special occasions, such as Father's Day or graduations. There are numerous other online services, such as Amazon.com (i.e., books, music, and auctions), 911Gift.com (i.e., some special occasions only), and Gifttree.com (i.e., cookies, chocolates, teddy bears only). All of these Internet-based gift companies lack the wide selection of gift categories that TheGift offers.

TheGift is able to offer such a wide spectrum of gifts because of its unique delivery system. Stocking only the most popular items in a small inventory warehouse, the firm conducts almost all order processing, filling, wrapping, and shipping through electronic means and prearranged service agreements with distributors and manufacturers. Much like Calyx and Corolla (i.e., flowers), distributors are equipped with special order-processing and wrapping capabilities to fulfill orders originating from TheGift's customers. Unlike Amazon.com, TheGift never receives the product as an intermediary. Orders are dropshipped from either the distributor or the manufacturer to the shipping address. The are five steps in the sequence of receiving and filling orders:

1. Orders arrive at the TheGift's website.
2. E-mail notification is sent to the distributor, the manufacturer, or TheGift's warehouse (i.e., for popular items).
3. An order processor at the distributor or the manufacturer's warehouse checks the order details, ships the product, and updates TheGift's database in real-time.

4. The order is shown as "shipped" and includes UPS or FedEx tracking identification numbers.
5. The customer receives the gift.

The owners work with seven employees and have only one year's worth of information, so they are confronted with critical decisions. They began with $500,000 in startup capital, and they estimate that they need another $3–$5 million to hire new employees and acquire capital equipment. TheGift is growing rapidly and having trouble keeping up with orders. As a privately held firm that has not yet become profitable, the owners must consider how to raise capital and gain awareness in the marketspace in order to take full advantage of the exuberant Internet climate.

Questions

1. Visit TheGift.com website and critique the home page.
2. Does TheGift.com have a compelling competitive advantage over the category sites such as Amazon.com or Gifttree.com?
3. How can TheGift.com be profitable?
4. What is TheGift.com really selling?

SELECTED BIBLIOGRAPHY

BENJAMIN, ROBERT, and ROLF WIGAND: "Electronic Markets and Virtual Value Chains on the Information Superhighway," *Sloan Management Review,* vol. 36, no. 2, Winter 1995, pp. 62–72.

FINCH, BYRON J.: "Internet Discussions as a Source for Consumer Product Customer Involvement and Quality Information: An Exploratory Study," *Journal of Operations Management,* vol. 17, no. 5, August 1999, pp. 535–556.

GHOSH, SHIKHAR: "Making Business Sense of the Internet," *Harvard Business Review,* March–April 1998, pp. 126–135.

GREENSPUN, PHILIP: *Philip and Alex's Guide to Web Publishing,* Morgan Kaufmann Publishers, San Francisco, 1999.

HEIM, GREGORY R., and KINGSHUK K. SINHA: "Design and Delivery of Electronic Services: Implications for Customer Value in Electronic Food Retailing," in J. A. Fitzsimmons and M. J. Fitzsimmons (eds.), *New Service Development,* Sage Publications, Thousand Oaks, Calif., 2000, pp. 152–182.

ENDNOTES

1. Steve Lohr, "In E-Commerce Frenzy, Brave New World Meets Old," *New York Times,* October 10, 1999, p. 5.
2. Robert Ramers, personal communication, January 14, 2000.
3. Gregory R. Heim and Kingshuk K. Sinha, "Design and Delivery of Electronic Services," in J. A. Fitzsimmons and M. J. Fitzsimmons (eds.), *New Service Development,* Sage Publications, Thousand Oaks, Calif., 2000, Chapter 8.
4. Ibid., p. 163
5. Ibid., p. 165.
6. Ibid., pp. 171–173.
7. Ibid., p. 170.
8. Prepared by Laura Bennett, Sarah Bird, and Matt Rhone under the supervision of Professor James A. Fitzsimmons.
9. "Where a Fingertip Click Meets the Elbow Grease," *New York Times,* December 23, 1998.
10. "Amazon.com Amazing Online Gamble Pays Off with Rocketing Success," *USA Today,* December 24, 1998.
11. Peter DeJonge, "Riding the Perilous Waters of Amazon.com," *New York Times Magazine,* March 14, 1999.
12. "Amazon.com: The Wild World of E-Commerce," *Business Week,* December 14, 1998.
13. Prepared by Matthew Duke, James Ecker, and Edmond Gonzales under the supervision of Professor James A. Fitzsimmons.

PART THREE

MANAGING SERVICE OPERATIONS

The day-to-day operation of a service is a constant challenge because the objectives of the organization, the needs of the customer, and the attention to service providers all must be managed simultaneously in an ever-changing environment. We begin by exploring how to forecast the expected demand for services, which can vary by month, day, and hour. This discussion leads naturally to capacity planning and the queuing models that are used to account for the trade-off between the cost of service capacity and customer waiting time. ServiceModel, an animated simulation software package found on the CD-ROM attached to the back cover of the text, can be used to make capacity planning decisions.

The inability of services to inventory output challenges management to match customer demand and service capacity. This challenge illustrates the inseparability of marketing and operations in service management. Marketing approaches that can influence customer demand are explored, including a continuation of our earlier discussion of the concept of yield management pioneered by American Airlines. Adjusting service capacity to match demand uses linear programming models to schedule workshifts. A perfect match is seldom possible, however, and the result is waiting customers. Thus, the management of waiting lines to avoid customer perceptions of a poor service experience is an important skill.

The final chapters of Part Three discuss inventory systems to manage the facilitating goods found in service organizations, service supply chain management including a supplement on the routing of service delivery vehicles, managing service projects, and conclude with linear programming applications.

CHAPTER TEN

Forecasting Demand for Services

Learning Objectives

After completing this chapter, you should be able to:

1. Recommend the appropriate forecasting model for a given situation.
2. Conduct a Delphi forecasting exercise.
3. Describe the features of exponential smoothing that make it an attractive model for time series forecasting.
4. Conduct time series forecasting using the exponential smoothing model with trend and seasonal adjustments.

Forecasting techniques allow us to translate the multitude of information available from databases into strategies that can give a service a competitive advantage. The particular techniques we will describe are classified into three basic models: subjective, causal, and time series. It must be noted, however, that whereas some services may use only one or another of these models, others will use two or more depending on the application. For example, a fast-food restaurant may be interested in using a time series model to forecast the daily demand for menu items. The demand for hotel services, however, has both temporal and spatial characteristics, which will require the use of both time series and causal models. On occasion, service firms may use subjective models to assess the future impact of changing demographics, such as the aging of the general population. Overall, as we move from subjective to causal to time series models, the forecast time horizon becomes shorter. The models, their characteristics, and their possible applications are shown in Table 10.1.

CHAPTER PREVIEW

This chapter begins with subjective models, because these methods are useful at the initial planning stage for service delivery systems when a long-term horizon is being considered. The Delphi technique is illustrated with an application to government policy planning for nuclear power. Causal models use regression analysis to form a linear relationship between independent variables and a dependent variable of interest. The site-selection problem facing motel chains is used to illustrate the causal modeling approach to forecasting future occupancy of alternative sites.

The discussion of time series models begins with the common N-period moving average. A more sophisticated time series model, called *exponential smoothing,* then is introduced and shown to accommodate trends and seasonal data.

TABLE 10.1

CHARACTERISTICS OF FORECASTING METHODS

Method	Data required	Relative cost	Forecast horizon	Application
Subjective models:				
Delphi method	Survey results	High	Long term	Technological forecasting
Cross-impact analysis	Correlations between events	High	Long term	Technological forecasting
Historical analogy	Several years of data for a similar situation	High	Medium to long term	Life cycle demand projection
Causal models:				
Regression	All past data for all variables	Moderate	Medium term	Demand forecasting
Econometric	All past data for all variables	Moderate to high	Medium to long term	Economic conditions
Time series models:				
Moving average	*N* most recent observations	Very low	Short term	Demand forecasting
Exponential smoothing	Previous smoothed value and most recent observation	Very low	Short term	Demand forecasting

---

SUBJECTIVE MODELS

Most forecasting techniques, such as time series and causal models, are based on data whose pattern is relatively stable over time, so we can expect to make reasonably useful forecasts. In some cases, however, we may have few or no data with which to work, or we may have data that exhibit patterns and relationships only over the short run and, therefore, are not useful for long-range forecasts.

When we lack sufficient or appropriate data, we must resort to forecast methods that are subjective or qualitative in nature. These include the Delphi method, cross-impact analysis, and historical analogy.

Delphi Method

Developed at the Rand Corporation by Olaf Helmer, the *Delphi method* is based on expert opinion. In its simplest form, persons with expertise in a given area are asked questions, and these individuals are not permitted to interact with each other. Typically, the participants are asked to make numerical estimates. For example, they might be asked to predict the highest Dow Jones average for the coming year.

The test administrator tabulates the results into quartiles and supplies these findings to the experts, who then are asked to reconsider their answers in light of the new information. Additionally, those whose opinions fall in the two outside quartiles are asked to justify their opinions. All the information from this round of questioning is tabulated and once again returned to the participants. On this occasion, each participant who remains outside the middle two quartiles (i.e., the interquartile range) may be asked to provide an argument as to why he or she believes those at the opposite extreme are incorrect.

The process may continue through several more iterations, with the intent of eventually having the experts arrive at a consensus that can be used for future planning. This method is very labor-intensive and requires input from persons with expert knowledge. Obviously, Delphi is a very expensive, time-consuming method and is practical only for long-term forecasting.

An example of the Delphi method can be seen in a study of the nuclear power industry.[1] Ninety-eight persons agreed to participate in this study. These people occupied key upper-level positions with architect-engineering firms, reactor manufacturers, and utility companies in the industrial sector concerned with nuclear power as well as with state regulatory agencies, state energy commissions, congressional staffs, and nuclear regulatory agencies in the public sector.

The round 1 questionnaire contained 37 questions, 11 concerning the past evolution of the nuclear industry and 26 concerning the future. These questions were to be answered on a seven-point Likert scale, ranging from "strongly agree" to "uncertain" to "strongly disagree," as shown below:

It is desirable *that utilities be permitted to integrate capital investment costs more aggressively into rate structures.*

No jdgmt.	Strong disagr.	Disagr.	Disagr. somewh.	Uncert.	Agree somewh.	Agree	Strong. agree

The questionnaire also asked for open-ended comments.

For round 2 of this study, the administrator provided a comprehensive summary of the first-round responses to the 11 questions concerning the past and a summary of the open-ended comments concerning the future. The number of responses to the question above are noted below, with the median (M) and interquartile range (designated by the vertical bars) shown below the responses:

1	6	5	6	15	35	8
No jdgmt.	Strong disagr.	Disagr.	Disagr. somewh.	Uncert.	Agree somewh.	Agree	Strong. agree

|---M---|

The 11 questions concerning the past were dropped from the round 2 questionnaire, and 11 new questions prompted by the open-ended comments from round 1 were added. The participants were invited to "defend" their positions with supporting comments if their opinions fell outside the interquartile range.

For round 3, which was the final round in this study, the administrator once again supplied the participants with feedback, this time from round 2, and invited the participants to "vote" again on the same questions. The following illustration of the resulting median and interquartile range after each round of voting demonstrates how the opinions shifted and finally arrived at a consensus for this particular question:

No jdgmt.	Strong disagr.	Disagr.	Disagr. somewh.	Uncert.	Agree somewh.	Agree	Strong. agree
Round 1				---M---	
Round 2					--------------------M--------------------	
Round 3					--------------------M---	

As noted, some of the questions asked for assessments of where the industry has been and where it stands today. Other questions not only asked the experts where they thought it should be headed but also to address issues such as resource allocation and the political realities affecting the future of nuclear power. As shown, the Delphi method is a useful tool in addressing situations for which quantifiable data are not available.

Cross-Impact Analysis

Cross-impact analysis assumes that some future event is related to the occurrence of an earlier event. As in the Delphi method, a panel of experts studies a set of correlations between events presented in a matrix. These correlations form the basis for estimating the likelihood of a future event occurring.

For example, consider a forecast conducted in 1997 that assumes $3-per-gallon gasoline prices by 2000 (event A) and the corresponding doubling of ridership on mass transit by 2005 (event B). By initial consensus, it might be determined that given A, the conditional probability of B is .7, and that given B, the conditional probability of A is .6. These probabilities are shown in the matrix below:

	Probability of event	
Given event	A	B
A	—	.7
B	.6	—

Assume that the forecasted unconditional probability for doubling mass transit ridership by 2005 is 1.0 and that the forecasted unconditional probability of $3 per gallon for gasoline by 2000 is .8. These new values are statistically inconsistent with the values in the matrix. The inconsistencies would be pointed out to the experts on the panel, who then would revise their estimates in a series of iterations. As with the Delphi method, an experienced administrator is needed to arrive at a satisfactory conditional probability matrix that can be used for generating a forecast.

Historical Analogy

Historical analogy assumes that the introduction and growth pattern of a new service will mimic the pattern of a similar concept for which data are available. Historical analogy frequently is used to forecast the market penetration or life cycle of a new service. The concept of a product life cycle as used in marketing involves stages, such as introduction, growth, maturity, and decline.

A famous use of historical analogy was the prediction of the market penetration by color television based on the experience with black-and-white television only a few years earlier. Of course, the appropriate analogy is not always so obvious. For example, growth in the demand for housekeeping services could follow the growth curve for child-care services. Because the pattern of previous data can have many interpretations and the analogy can be questioned, the credibility of any forecast using this method often is suspect. The acceptance of historical analogy forecasts depends on making a convincing analogy.

CAUSAL MODELS

It is fairly easy to make short-term forecasts when we are presented with uncomplicated data. On occasion, however, a competitive service organization must deal with a wealth of statistical information, some of which may be relevant to making profitable forecasts and some of which may be extraneous. In these situations, it also is more likely that the forecasts must be made for the next year—or for the next decade—rather than just for the next day, week, or month. Obviously, a long-term forecast has the potential of spelling success or devastation for the organization. Therefore, we need a way of separating out the critical information and processing it to help us make an appropriate forecast.

Causal models make assumptions that are similar to those of time series models (which we will consider later): that the data follow an identifiable pattern over time and that an identifiable relationship exists between the information we wish to forecast and other factors. These models range from very simple ones, in which the forecast is based on a technique called *regression analysis,* to those known as *econometric models,* which use a system of equations.

Regression Models

A regression model is a relationship between the factor being forecasted, which is designated as the *dependent variable* (or Y), and the factors that determine the value of Y, which are designated as the *independent variables* or (X_i). If there are n independent variables, then the relationship between the dependent variable Y and the independent variables X_i is expressed as

$$Y = a_0 + a_1X_1 + a_2X_2 + \cdots + a_nX_n \tag{1}$$

The values $a_0, a_1, a_2, \cdots, a_n$ are coefficients that are determined by the computer program being used. If calculations are done by hand, values are determined by using regression equations found in elementary statistics texts.

As an example, the management of La Quinta Motor Inns, a national chain of hotels, commissioned a study to determine the direction of its expansion efforts.[2] It wanted to know which factors determined a profitable hotel location and, thus, would allow management to screen available real estate for new hotel sites. Investigators collected data on many factors at existing locations, such as traffic count, number of competitive rooms nearby, visibility of signs, local airport traffic, types of neighboring businesses, and distance to the central business district. In all, 35 factors, or independent variables, were considered, as shown in Table 10.2.

A preliminary statistical evaluation of the data for all those variables then allowed the investigators to identify four critical factors—STATE, PRICE, INCOME, and COLLEGE—to be used in the forecast model.

The firm's operating margin, obtained by adding depreciation and interest expenses to the profit and then dividing by the total revenue, was chosen as the most reliable measure, or dependent variable Y, on which to base a forecast. For this case, the coefficients were calculated as $a_0 = 39.05$, $a_1 = -5.41$, $a_2 = +5.86$, $a_3 = -3.09$, and $a_4 = +1.75$. Substituting these coefficient values and the independent variables into equation (1) yields the following regression forecasting model:

Operating margin $Y = 39.05 + (-5.41)$STATE $+ (5.86)$PRICE $+$
(-3.09)INCOME$+ (1.75)$COLLEGE

By investigators' collecting data on the independent variables at a proposed hotel site and making appropriate transformations as needed, the operating margin can be forecasted. The results of this study proved the model to be very good in predicting the likelihood of success for a new inn at a proposed location.

As shown, development of a regression model requires an extensive data collection effort to meet the needs of the individual organization, which often involves considerable time and expense. It also requires expertise in the selection of independent and dependent variables to ensure a relationship that has a logical and meaningful interpretation. For these reasons, regression models are appropriate for making medium- and long-term forecasts.

TABLE 10.2

INDEPENDENT VARIABLES FOR HOTEL LOCATION

Name	Description
Competitive factors	
INNRATE	Inn price
PRICE	Room rate for the inn
RATE	Average competitive room rate
RMS1	Hotel rooms within 1 mile
RMSTOTAL	Hotel rooms within 3 miles
ROOMSINN	Inn rooms
Demand generators	
CIVILIAN	Civilian personnel on base
COLLEGE	College enrollment
HOSP1	Hospital beds within 1 mile
HOSPTOTL	Hospital beds within 4 miles
HVYIND	Heavy industrial employment
LGTIND	Light industrial acreage
MALLS	Shopping mall square footage
MILBLKD	Military base blocked
MILITARY	Military personnel
MILTOT	MILITARY + CIVILIAN
OFC1	Office space within 1 mile
OFCTOTAL	Office space within 4 miles
OFCCBD	Office space in central business district
PASSENGER	Airport passengers enplaned
RETAIL	Scale ranking of retail activity
TOURISTS	Annual tourists
TRAFFIC	Traffic count
VAN	Airport van
Area demographics	
EMPLYPCT	Unemployment percentage
INCOME	Average family income
POPULACE	Residential population
Market awareness	
AGE	Years inn has been open
NEAREST	Distance to nearest inn
STATE	State population per inn
URBAN	Urban population per inn
Physical attributes	
ACCESS	Accessibility
ARTERY	Major traffic artery
DISTCBD	Distance to downtown
SIGNVIS	Sign visibility

Source: Reprinted by permission, S. E. Kimes and J. A. Fitzsimmons, "Selecting Profitable Hotel Sites at La Quinta Motor Inns," *Interfaces,* vol. 20, no. 2, March–April 1990, p. 14. Copyright © 1990, the Operations Research Society of America and The Institute of Management Sciences, 290 Westminster Street, Providence, RI 02903.

Econometric Models

Econometric models are versions of regression models that involve a system of equations. The equations are related to each other, and the coefficients are determined as in the simpler regression models. An econometric model consists of a set of simultaneous equations expressing a dependent variable in terms of several different independent variables. Econometric models require extensive data collection and sophisticated analysis to create; thus, they generally are used for long-range forecasts.

TIME SERIES MODELS

Time series models are applicable for making short-term forecasts when the values of observations occur in an identifiable pattern over time. These models range from the simple *N-period moving average* model to the more sophisticated and useful *exponential smoothing* models.

N-Period Moving Average

Sometimes, observations that are made over a period of time appear to have a random pattern; consequently, we do not feel confident in basing forecasts on them. Consider the data in Table 10.3 for a 100-room hotel in a college town. We have decided to forecast only Saturday occupancy because the demand for each day of the week is influenced by different forces. For example, on weekdays, demand is generated by business travelers, but weekend guests often are people on vacation or visiting friends. Selection of the forecasting period is an important consideration and should be based on the nature of the demand and the ability to use that information. For example, fast-food restaurants forecast demand by the hour of the day.

The hotel owner has noted increased occupancy for the last two Saturdays and wishes to prepare for the coming weekend (i.e., September 12), perhaps by discontinuing the practice of offering discount rates. Do the higher occupancy figures indicate a change in the underlying average occupancy? To answer this question, we need a way of taking out the "noise" of occasional blips in the pattern so that we do not overreact to a change that is random rather than permanent and significant.

The *N*-period moving-average method may be used in this simple example to smooth out random variations and produce a reliable estimate of the underlying average occupancy. The method calculates a moving average MA_t for period t on the basis of selecting N of the most recent actual observations A_t, as shown in equation (2):

$$MA_t = \frac{A_t + A_{t-1} + A_{t-2} + \cdots + A_{t-N+1}}{N} \qquad (2)$$

TABLE 10.3

SATURDAY OCCUPANCY AT A 100-ROOM HOTEL

Saturday	Period	Occupancy	Three-period moving average	Forecast
Aug. 1	1	79		
8	2	84		
15	3	83	82	
22	4	81	83	82
29	5	98	87	83
Sept. 5	6	100	93	87
12	7			93

If we select N equal to 3, then we cannot begin our calculation until period 3 (i.e., August 15), at which time we add the occupancy figures for the three most recent Saturdays (i.e., August 1, 8, and 15) and divide the sum by 3 to arrive at a three-period moving average of $[(83 + 84 + 79)/3] = 82$. We use this value to forecast occupancy for the following Saturday (i.e., August 22). The moving-average forecast has smoothed out the random fluctuations to track better the average occupancy, which then is used to forecast the next period. Each three-period *moving-average forecast* thus involves simply adding the three most recent occupancy values and dividing by 3. For example, to arrive at the moving average for August 22, we drop the value for August 1, add the value for August 22, and recalculate the average, getting 83. Continuing this iterative process for the remaining data, we see how the moving-average occupancy of approximately 82 percent for Saturdays in August has increased recently, reflecting the near-capacity occupancy of the past two weekends. If the local college football team, after playing two consecutive home games, is scheduled for an away game on September 12, how confident are you in forecasting next Saturday's occupancy at 93 percent?

Although our N-period moving average has identified a change in the underlying average occupancy, this method is slow to react because old data are given the same weight (i.e., $1/N$) as new data in calculating the averages. More recent data may be better indicators of change; therefore, we may wish to assign more weight to recent observations. Rather than arbitrarily assigning weights to our moving-average data to fix this shortcoming, we instead will use a more sophisticated forecasting method that systematically ages the data. Our next topic, exponential smoothing, also can accommodate trends and seasonality in the data.

Simple Exponential Smoothing

Simple exponential smoothing is the time series method most frequently used for demand forecasting. Simple exponential smoothing also "smooths out" blips in the data, but its power over the N-period moving average is threefold: (1) old data are never dropped or lost, (2) older data are given progressively less weight, and (3) the calculation is simple and requires only the most recent data.

Simple exponential smoothing is based on the concept of feeding back the *forecast error* to correct the previous smoothed value. In equation (3) below, S_t is the smoothed value for period t, A_t is the actual observed value for period t, and α is a smoothing constant that usually is assigned a value between 0.1 and 0.5.

$$S_t = S_{t-1} + \alpha(A_t - S_{t-1}) \tag{3}$$

The term $(A_t - S_{t-1})$ represents the forecast error because it is the difference between the actual observation and the smoothed value that was calculated in the prior period. A fraction α of this forecast error is added to the previous smoothed value to obtain the new smoothed value S_t. Note how self-correcting this method is when you consider that forecast errors can be either positive or negative.

Our moving-average analysis of the occupancy data in Table 10.3 indicated an actual increase in average occupancy over the two most recent Saturdays. These same occupancy data are repeated in Table 10.4, with the actual value for each period (A_t) shown in the third column. Using simple exponential smoothing, we will demonstrate again that a significant change in the mean occupancy has occurred.

Because we must start somewhere, let the first observed, or actual, value A_t in a series of data equal the first smoothed value S_t. Therefore, as Table 10.4 shows, S_1 for August 1 equals A_1 for August 1, or 79.00. The smoothed value for August 8 (S_2) then may

TABLE 10.4

SIMPLE EXPONENTIAL SMOOTHING

Saturday Hotel Occupancy ($\alpha = 0.5$)

Saturday	Period t	Actual occupancy A_t	Smoothed value S_t	Forecast F_t	Forecast error $\|A_t - F_t\|$
Aug. 1	1	79	79.00		
8	2	84	81.50	79	5
15	3	83	82.25	82	1
22	4	81	81.63	82	1
29	5	98	89.81	82	16
Sept. 5	6	100	94.91	90	10

be derived from the actual value for August 8 (A_2) and the previous smoothed value for August 1 (S_1) according to equation (3). We have selected an α equal to 0.5 because, as will be shown later, this results in a forecast that is similar to the one obtained using a three-period moving average. For August 8:

$$S_2 = S_1 + \alpha(A_2 - S_1)$$

$$= 79.00 + 0.5(84 - 79.00)$$

$$= 81.50$$

Similar calculations then are made to determine the smoothed values (S_3, S_4, S_5, S_6) for successive periods.

Simple exponential smoothing assumes that the pattern of data is distributed about a constant mean. Thus, the smoothed value calculated in period t is used as the forecast for period ($t + 1$) rounded to an integer, as shown below:

$$F_{t+1} = S_t \tag{4}$$

Our best estimate for August 15 occupancy will be 81.50, the most recent smoothed value at the end of August 8. Note that the forecast error ($84 - 79$) was a positive 5 (i.e., we underestimated demand by 5), and that one-half of this error was added to the previous smoothed value to increase the new estimate of average occupancy. This concept of error feedback to correct an earlier estimate is an idea borrowed from control theory.

The smoothed values shown in Table 10.4 were calculated using an α value of 0.5. As noted, however, if we wish to make the smoothed values less responsive to the latest data, we can assign a smaller value to α. Figure 10.1 demonstrates graphically how an α of 0.1 and of 0.5 smooth the curve of the actual values. It is easily seen in this figure that the smoothed curve, particularly with an α of 0.5, has reduced the extremes (i.e., the dips and peak) and responded to the increased occupancy in the last two Saturdays. Therefore, basing forecasts on smoothed data helps to prevent overreacting to the extremes in the actual observed values.

Equation (3) may be rewritten as follows:

$$S_t = \alpha(A_t) + (1 - \alpha)S_{t-1} \tag{5}$$

The basis for the name "exponential smoothing" can be observed in the weights that are given past data in equation (5). We see that A_t is given a weight α in determining S_t,

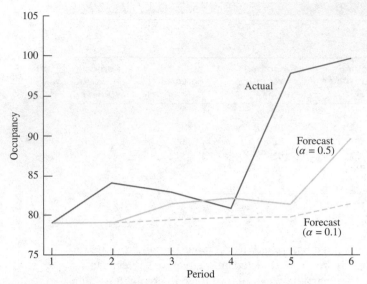

FIGURE 10.1 Simple exponential smoothing: Saturday hotel occupancy ($\alpha = 0.1$ and $\alpha = 0.5$).

and we easily can show by substitution that A_{t-1} is given a weight $\alpha(1 - \alpha)$. In general, actual value A_{t-n} is given a weight $\alpha(1 - \alpha)^n$, as Figure 10.2 shows by graphing the exponential decay of weights given a series of observations over time. Note that older observations never disappear entirely from the calculation of S_t as they would when the N-period moving average is used, but they do assume progressively decreasing importance.

Relationship between α and N

Selecting the value for α is a matter of judgment, often based on the pattern of historical data, with large values giving much weight to recent data in anticipation of changes. To help select α, a relationship can be made between the number of periods N in the moving-average method and the exponential smoothing constant α. If we assume that the two methods are similar when the average ages of past data are equal, then the following relationship results:

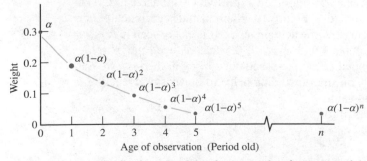

FIGURE 10.2 Distribution of weight given past data in exponential smoothing ($\alpha = 0.3$).

Moving average:

$$\text{Average age} = \frac{(0 + 1 + 2 + \cdots + N - 1)}{N}$$

$$= \frac{(N - 1)(N/2)}{N}$$

$$= \frac{N - 1}{2}$$

Exponential smoothing:

$$\text{Average age} = 0(\alpha) + 1(\alpha)(1 - \alpha) + 2(\alpha)(1 - \alpha)^2 + \cdots$$

$$= \frac{(1 - \alpha)}{\alpha}$$

The average age above is a geometric series with the sum equal to

$$\frac{ar}{(1 - r)^2} \quad \text{for } a = \alpha \quad \text{and} \quad r = 1 - \alpha$$

When the average ages are equated, the result is

$$\alpha = \frac{2}{(N + 1)} \quad \text{or} \quad N = \frac{(2 - \alpha)}{\alpha}$$

Using this relationship results in the following sample values for equating α and N:

As shown, the usual assignment of a smoothing value between 0.1 and 0.5 is reasonable when compared with the number of periods in an equivalent moving-average

α	0.05	0.1	0.2	0.3	0.4	0.5	0.667
N	39	19	9	5.7	4	3	2

forecast. The particular value assigned to α is a trade-off between overreacting to random fluctuations about a constant mean and detecting a change in the mean value. Higher values of α are more responsive to change because of the greater weight that is given to recent data. In practice, the value of α often is selected on the basis of minimizing the forecast error as measured by the mean absolute deviation (MAD).

Forecast Error

Although it is obvious in Figure 10.1 that the smoothed curves have evened out the peaks and valleys of the actual curve, how do we measure the accuracy of forecasts? One common method is calculating the *mean absolute deviation (MAD)*. This is the calculation of the average value for the *absolute* values of forecast errors $|A_t - F_t|$ shown in Table 10.4. To calculate the MAD for this example, total the absolute differences and then divide by the number of observations. For this case, MAD = (5 + 1 + 1 + 16 + 10)/5 = 6.6.

Recall that the forecast values in this example were derived from smoothed values calculated with $\alpha = 0.5$, because this method is similar to a three-period moving-average method. For the three-period moving-average forecast developed earlier, the MAD value is 9.7. In this case, simple exponential smoothing resulted in more accurate forecasts than the corresponding three-period moving-average method. If an α of 0.1 is used, however, the MAD value is 8.8, reflecting the unresponsiveness to change of a small smoothing constant. It should be noted that selecting an α to minimize MAD for a set of data can be accomplished using Excel Solver.

In any event, we desire an unbiased forecast with respect to its tracking of the actual mean for the data. Thus, the sum of the forecast errors should tend toward zero, taking into account both positive and negative differences. If it does not, then we should look for underlying trends or seasonality and account for them explicitly. For the results shown in Table 10.4, the sum of forecast errors is calculated as

$$\Sigma(A_t + F_t) = 5 + 1 - 1 + 16 + 10 = 31$$

This high positive sum suggests that an upward trend exists in the data, and that our simple exponential smoothing forecasts are falling short of actual hotel occupancy. Thus, we must incorporate a trend adjustment into our forecast.

Exponential Smoothing with Trend Adjustment

The *trend* in a set of data is the average rate at which the observed values change from one period to the next over time. The changes created by the trend can be treated using an extension of simple exponential smoothing.

Table 10.5 follows the experience of a new commuter airline during its first eight weeks of business. The average weekly load factors (i.e., percentages of seats sold) show a steady increase, from approximately 30 percent for week 1 to approximately 70 percent for week 8. In this example, the smoothed value S_t is calculated using equation (6), which is equation (5) modified by the addition of a trend value T_{t-1} to the previous smoothed value S_{t-1} to account for the weekly rate of increase in the load factor.

$$S_t = \alpha(A_t) + (1 - \alpha)(S_{t-1} + T_{t-1}) \tag{6}$$

To incorporate a trend adjustment in our calculation, we will use β as a smoothing constant. This constant usually is assigned a value between 0.1 and 0.5 and may be the same as, or different from, α. The trend for a given period t is defined by $(S_t - S_{t-1})$, the rate of change in smoothed value from one period to the next (i.e., the slope of the demand curve). The smoothed trend T_t then is calculated at period t using equation (7),

---

TABLE 10.5

EXPONENTIAL SMOOTHING WITH TREND ADJUSTMENT

Commuter Airline Load Factor ($\alpha = 0.5$, $\beta = 0.3$)

Week t	Actual load factor A_t	Smoothed value S_t	Smoothed trend T_t	Forecast F_t	Forecast error $\lvert A_t - F_t \rvert$
1	31	31.00	0.00		
2	40	35.50	1.35	31	9
3	43	39.93	2.27	37	6
4	52	47.10	3.74	42	10
5	49	49.92	3.47	51	2
6	64	58.69	5.06	53	11
7	58	60.88	4.20	64	6
8	68	66.54	4.63	65	3
				MAD	6.7

which is a modification of the basic exponential smoothing equation—equation (5)—with the observed trend $(S_t - S_{t-1})$ used in place of A_t.

$$T_t = \beta\,(S_t - S_{t-1}) + (1 - \beta)\,T_{t-1} \tag{7}$$

To anticipate cash flows during the business startup period, the commuter airline owners are interested in forecasting future weekly load factors. After observing the first two weeks of activity, you are asked to provide a forecast for week 3. The smoothed values, trend figures, and forecasts in Table 10.5 are calculated in a stepwise manner. For the first observation in a series, week 1 in this instance, the smoothed value S_1 is equal to the actual value A_1, and the trend T_1 is set equal to 0.00. The forecast for week 2 is calculated using equation (8). In this case, $F_2 = 31 + 0.00 = 31$ rounded to an integer.

$$F_{t+1} = S_t + T_t \tag{8}$$

To compute the smoothed values for week 2 and a forecast for week 3, we will use $\alpha = 0.5$ and $\beta = 0.3$. First, the smoothed value S_2 for week 2 is calculated using equation (6):

$$S_2 = (0.5)(40) + (1 - 0.5)(31 + 0.00)$$
$$= 35.50$$

Now, we calculate the trend for week 2 with equation (7):

$$T_2 = (0.3)(35.50 - 31.00) + (1 - 0.3)0.00$$
$$= 1.35$$

The final step is to make a forecast for week 3 according to equation (8):

$$F_3 = 35.5 + 1.35 = 36.85 \cong 37$$

When the actual data for the following weeks are received, similar calculations can be made for the smoothed value, the trend, the forecast, and the forecast error. For all the forecasts shown in Table 10.5, the MAD is 6.7.

The sum of the forecast error values (both positive and negative) is a measure of forecast bias. For this example $\Sigma\,(A_t - F_t) = 9 + 6 + 10 - 2 + 11 - 6 + 3 = 31$. The sum of the forecast errors for an unbiased forecast should approach zero (i.e., the positive and negative errors cancel out each other).

In Figure 10.3, the actual load factors are plotted against the forecasts to illustrate the tracking ability of exponential smoothing with a trend adjustment.

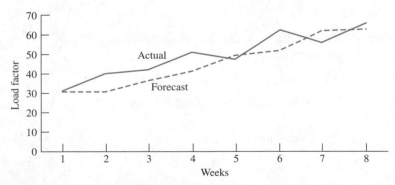

FIGURE 10.3 Exponential smoothing with trend adjustment: commuter airline load factors ($\alpha = 0.5$, $\beta = 0.3$).

Exponential Smoothing with Seasonal Adjustment

To account for seasonal effects on a set of data, we can use another extension of simple exponential smoothing. In simplest terms, we first remove the seasonality from the data and then smooth those data as we already have learned; finally, we put the seasonality back in to determine a forecast.

We will apply this seasonal adjustment to the data in Table 10.6, which reports the number of passengers per month taking a ferry to a resort island in the Caribbean for the years 1995 and 1996. In general, we denote a cycle L as the length of one season. L may be any length of time, even the 24 hours of a day, but frequently, as in this case, it is 12 months. Note that we must have actual data for at least one full season before we can begin smoothing and forecasting calculations.

A *seasonality index I_t* is used to deseasonalize the data in a given cycle L. Initially, I_t is estimated by calculating a ratio of the actual value for period t, A_t, divided by the average value $\overline{A}$ for all periods in cycle L as shown in equation (9):

$$I_t = \frac{A_t}{\overline{A}} \qquad (9)$$

where $\overline{A} = (A_1 + A_2 + \cdots + A_L)/L$

In our passenger ferry example, $\overline{A} = 1971.83$, and by substituting this value into equation (9), we can calculate the index I_t for each period in the first season of L periods. The resulting indices for the months of 1995, which are shown in column 5 of Table 10.6, then are used to deseasonalize the data for the corresponding months in 1996 according to equation (10), which is a minor modification of our basic exponential smoothing equation—equation (5)—with A_t adjusted to account for seasonality using index I_{t-L}:

$$S_t = \alpha \frac{A_t}{I_{t-L}} + (1 - \alpha)S_{t-1} \qquad (10)$$

For this example, data for the 12 months in 1995 are used to give initial estimates of the seasonality indices. Therefore, we cannot begin to calculate new smoothed data until period 13 (i.e., January 1996). To begin the process, we assume that S_{12} equals A_{12}, as shown in Table 10.6 with a value of 1794.00. The smoothed value for January 1996 now can be calculated using equation (10), with $I_{t-L} = 0.837$ (i.e., the index I_t of 12 months ago for January 1995) and $\alpha = 0.2$:

$$S_{13} = (0.2)\frac{1806}{0.837} + (1 - 0.2)1794.00$$

$$= 1866.74$$

The forecast for February (period $t + 1$) then is made by seasonalizing the smoothed value for January according to the following formula:

$$F_{t+1} = (S_t)(I_{t-L+1}) \qquad (11)$$

Note that the seasonalizing factor I_{t-L+1} in this case is the index I_t for February 1995. Therefore, our forecast for February 1996 is

$$F_{14} = (1866.74)(0.662)$$

$$= 1235.78 \cong 1236$$

TABLE 10.6

EXPONENTIAL SMOOTHING WITH SEASONAL ADJUSTMENT

Ferry Passengers Taken to a Resort Island ($\alpha = 0.2$, $\gamma = 0.3$)

Period	t	Actual passengers A_t	Smoothed value S_t	Index I_t	Forecast F_t	Forecast error $|A_t - F_t|$
			1995			
January	1	1651	—	0.837	—	
February	2	1305	—	0.662	—	
March	3	1617	—	0.820	—	
April	4	1721	—	0.873	—	
May	5	2015	—	1.022	—	
June	6	2297	—	1.165	—	
July	7	2606	—	1.322	—	
August	8	2687	—	1.363	—	
September	9	2292	—	1.162	—	
October	10	1981	—	1.005	—	
November	11	1696	—	0.860	—	
December	12	1794	1794.00	0.910	—	
			1996			
January	13	1806	1866.74	0.876	—	—
February	14	1731	2016.35	0.721	1236	495
March	15	1733	2035.76	0.829	1653	80
April	16	1904	2064.81	0.888	1777	127
May	17	2036	2050.28	1.013	2110	74
June	18	2560	2079.71	1.185	2389	171
July	19	2679	2069.06	1.314	2749	70
August	20	2821	2069.19	1.363	2820	1
September	21	2359	2061.38	1.157	2404	45
October	22	2160	2078.95	1.015	2072	88
November	23	1802	2082.23	0.862	1788	14
December	24	1853	2073.04	0.905	1895	42
					MAD	110

If the seasonality indices are stable, forecasts that are based on only one cycle, L, will be reliable. If, however, the indices are not stable, they can be adjusted, or smoothed, as new data become available. After calculating the smoothed value S_t for an actual value A_t at the most recent period t, we can denote a new observation for a seasonality index at period t as (A_t/S_t). To apply the concept of exponential smoothing to the index, we use a new constant γ, which usually is assigned a value between 0.1 and 0.5. The smoothed estimate of the seasonality index then is calculated from the following formula:

$$I_t = \gamma \frac{A_t}{S_t} + (1 - \gamma)I_{t-L} \qquad (12)$$

Now, we can continue the calculations for 1996 in Table 10.6 by using equation (12) to update the seasonality indices for each month for future use. Remember, however, that in actual practice, smoothed values, indices, and forecasts for each period (i.e., month) in this new season of L periods would be calculated on a month-to-month basis as the most recent actual values became available. Here, according to equation (12), the new smoothed seasonality index for January 1996, I_{13}, using $\gamma = 0.3$ is

$$I_{13} = 0.3\frac{1806}{1866.74} + (1 - 0.3)0.837$$

$$= 0.876$$

The MAD for February through December 1996 is 110, which indicates a very good fit of forecasts to actual data that exhibit a definite seasonality. Is it possible, however, to make even more accurate forecasts?

Exponential Smoothing with Trend and Seasonal Adjustments

The answer to the earlier question—Is it possible to make even more accurate forecasts?—is yes (sometimes). In some cases, adjusting only for trend or seasonality will provide the current best estimate of the average; at others, the forecast can be improved by considering all factors together. We can include *both* trend and seasonal adjustments in exponential smoothing by weighting a *base* smoothed value with trend and seasonal indices to forecast the following period. The appropriate equations are

$$S_t = \alpha \frac{A_t}{I_{t-L}} + (1 - \alpha)(S_{t-1} + T_{t-1}) \tag{13}$$

$$T_t = \beta (S_t - S_{t-1}) + (1 - \beta)T_{t-1} \tag{14}$$

$$I_t = \gamma \frac{A_t}{S_t} + (1 - \gamma)I_{t-L} \tag{15}$$

$$F_{t+1} = (S_t + T_t)I_{t-L+1} \tag{16}$$

These equations can be applied to the data in Table 10.7, and the resulting MAD of 160 for February through December 1996 tells us that, in this case, we have not gained anything by adding a trend adjustment to the seasonal adjustment. Figure 10.4 demonstrates graphically the results of treating the actual data with a seasonal adjustment only and with both seasonal and trend adjustments.

Summary of Exponential Smoothing

Exponential smoothing is a relatively easy and straightforward way to make short-term forecasts. It has many attributes, including:

- All past data are considered in the smoothing process.
- Recent data are assigned more weight than older data.
- Only the most recent data are required to update a forecast.
- The model is easy to implement on a personal computer using spreadsheet software.
- Smoothing constants allows us to alter the rate at which the model responds to changes in the underlying pattern in the data.

TABLE 10.7

EXPONENTIAL SMOOTHING WITH SEASONAL AND TREND ADJUSTMENTS

Ferry Passengers Taken to a Resort Island ($\alpha = 0.2$, $\beta = 0.2$, $\gamma = 0.3$)

Period	t	Actual passengers A_t	Smoothed value S_t	Trend T_t	Index I_t	Forecast F_t	Forecast error $\lvert A_t - F_t \rvert$
			1995				
January	1	1651	—	—	0.837	—	
February	2	1305	—	—	0.662	—	
March	3	1617	—	—	0.820	—	
April	4	1721	—	—	0.873	—	
May	5	2015	—	—	1.022	—	
June	6	2297	—	—	1.165	—	
July	7	2606	—	—	1.322	—	
August	8	2687	—	—	1.363	—	
September	9	2292	—	—	1.162	—	
October	10	1981	—	—	1.005	—	
November	11	1696	—	—	0.860	—	
December	12	1794	1794.00	0.00	0.910	—	
			1996				
January	13	1806	1866.59	14.52	0.876	—	
February	14	1731	2027.99	43.89	0.719	1245	486
March	15	1733	2080.17	45.55	0.824	1699	34
April	16	1904	2136.87	47.78	0.878	1855	49
May	17	2036	2146.20	40.09	1.000	2232	196
June	18	2560	2188.55	40.54	1.166	2547	13
July	19	2679	2188.69	32.46	1.292	2946	267
August	20	2821	2190.96	26.42	1.340	3027	206
September	21	2359	2179.80	18.91	1.138	2577	218
October	22	2160	2188.97	16.96	0.999	2209	49
November	23	1802	2183.75	12.53	0.850	1897	95
December	24	1853	2164.36	6.14	0.894	1998	145
						MAD	160

SUMMARY

Decisions to embark on a new service concept often require subjective judgments about the future needs of customers. Subjective models like the Delphi method allow a panel of experts to defend their positions concerning the future, and through a number of iterations, these experts approach a consensus. Regression models have found application in service location analysis because of the need to account for several independent variables that contribute to demand generation. We ended our discussion of forecasting with an examination of time series models. Although the moving-average method is straightforward, we discovered that exponential smoothing has many superior qualities and has found wide acceptance in practice. Accounting for trends and seasonality is an important feature in forecasting service demand and is accommodated easily by means of exponential smoothing.

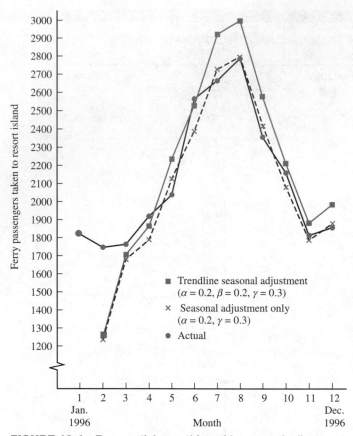

FIGURE 10.4 Exponential smoothing with seasonal adjustment.

KEY TERMS AND DEFINITIONS

Cross-impact analysis a technological forecasting method that assumes some future event is related to an earlier event with an estimated probability.

Delphi method a technological forecasting method that uses a group of experts to arrive at a consensus about the future.

Exponential smoothing a time series forecast based on the concept of adjusting a previous forecast by feeding back a percentage of the forecast error.

Forecast error the difference between the actual observation and the forecasted value.

Mean absolute deviation (MAD) a measure of forecasting accuracy calculated as the average absolute forecast error.

Moving-average forecast a simple time series forecast formed by adding together the most recent data and dividing by the number of observations.

BOX 10.1

Service Benchmark

L. L. BEAN IMPROVES CALL-CENTER FORECASTING

Two forecasting models are developed for use at L. L. Bean, Inc., a widely known retailer of high-quality outdoor goods and apparel. The models forecast customer telephone call volumes incoming to L. L. Bean's call-center that are used to produce weekly staffing schedules. The majority of L. L. Bean's sales are generated through telephone orders via 800-service, which was introduced in 1986. Ten percent of the $870 million in 1993 sales was derived through store transactions and 18 percent ordered through the mail. However, 72 percent of the total sales volume was generated through orders taken at the company's call center.

Calls to L. L. Bean's call center fit into two major classifications, telemarketing (TM) and telephone-inquiry (TI), each with its own 800-number. TM calls are primarily the order-placing calls that generate the vast majority of the company's sales. TI callers are mainly customers who ask about the status of their orders, report problems regarding orders they have received, or inquire about a number of other issues.

The volume and average duration are quite different for these two classes of incoming calls. Annual call volumes for TM are many times higher than those of TI, but the average length of a TM call is much less than that of a TI call. TI agents are responsible for customer inquiries in a variety of areas, including order information, back orders, catalog requests, returns and exchanges, product questions, address corrections, and billing. Not surprisingly, with all this added complexity, TI agents require special training. Thus, it is important to forecast accurately the incoming call volumes for TI and TM separately to properly schedule these two distinct server groups.

Schedulers use the two forecasting models to predict daily call volumes for the next three weeks so that they can create week-long staffing schedules. However, with a two-week scheduling lead time, the real focus of these predictions is on the third week ahead. That is, every Monday, on the first day of the 21-day planning horizon, the TI and TM schedules each loads a seven-day forecast of daily call volumes for Monday (the 15th day) through Sunday (the 21st day) into their automated staff scheduling system. This allows them to post agent work schedules for work weeks (Monday–Sunday) two weeks in advance.

Inaccurate forecasts are very costly to L. L. Bean because they result in a mismatch of supply and demand. Understaffing of TM agents increases opportunity costs due to diminished revenues from lost orders—since a percentage of the customers who do not get through immediately will abandon and never return. Understaffing of TI agents decreases overall customer satisfaction, which erodes patron loyalty and the likelihood of repeat business. Furthermore, understaffing in either server group leads to excessive queue times, which cause telephone-connect charges to increase dramatically. On the other hand, overstaffing of TI or TM agents incurs the obvious penalty of excessive direct labor costs for the underutilized pool of telephone agents on duty.

These staffing decisions would be quite routine were it not for the erratic nature and extreme seasonality of L. L. Bean's business as shown in the figure. The three-week peak period just before Christmas can make or break the year: the company accepts nearly 20 percent of its annual calls during these three weeks. For the peak season, L. L. Bean typically will more than double the number of agents and almost quadruple the quantity of the telephone lines. Following this rapid build up for the peak season, management must shift its focus to the opposite extreme—the build-down process.

The forecasting models used the autoregressive/integrated/moving average (ARIMA) methodology put forth by Box and Jenkins.[1] Autoregressive (AR) terms, which are lagged values of the dependent variable, serve as independent variables in the model. Moving-average (MA) terms are lagged values of the errors between past actual values and their predicted values and also serve as independent variables. Integrated (I) refers to the practice of differencing, which transforms a time series by subtracting past values of itself.

---

[1] G. E. P. Box and G. M. Jenkins, *Time Series Models for Forecasting and Control,* Holden Day, San Francisco, Calif., 1976.

BOX 10.1 (CONTINUED)

DATA DESCRIPTION

As seen in the accompanying exhibits, plots of these daily call data reveal the presence of strong day-of-week patterns. Monday generally has the highest call volume, with each successive day decreasing monotonically to the weekly low on Sunday. As noted, TI and TM both exhibit strong seasonal patterns for the year. Call volumes are reasonably stable through the second and third quarters of each year. TI and TM volumes begin to steadily ramp up during the fourth quarter and then virtually explode in the last month of the year. Then they drop down to their stable level during the first quarter of the next year. Weekly TI call volumes usually rise and fall without a break in the uptrend or downtrend until they reach a trend turning point, while weekly TM volumes seem much more volatile. Also, TM ramps more steeply up to and down from its Christmas peak than does TI. Lastly, TI consistently peaks two to three weeks later than TM.

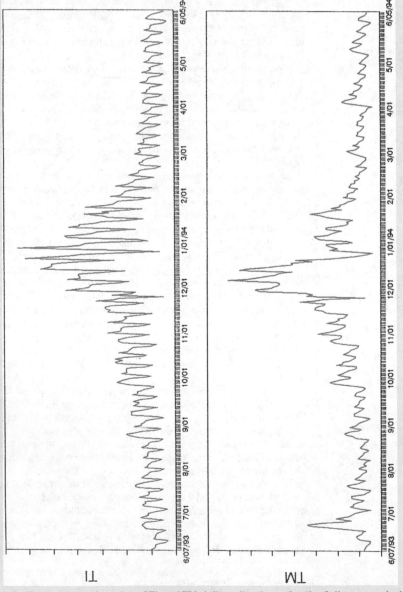

L. L. Bean time series plot of TI and TM daily call volume for the full-year period from June 7, 1993, to June 5, 1994.

BOX 10.1 (CONTINUED)

Two four-year time series plots show that these seasonal patterns recur from year to year for both TI and TM. Unfortunately, the repetition is not exact. Although call volumes do not show an overwhelming pattern for Bean's off-season, the busy-season peaks and total annual volumes generally have been increasing each year for both TI and TM. Coinciding with this, it appears that their within-year variability has been increasing in recent years.

TM and TI call volumes are both driven by orders, but in different ways. For TM, the relationship is direct and immediate. That is, today's order calls produce today's orders. The connection for TI is more complicated. When an order is taken on a TI 800-line, the relationship is immediate here too. More often, however, the response is lagged and occurs when a customer subsequently calls to inquire about the status of an outstanding order or to report a problem with a recently received order. To further complicate matters, some TI calls are for such purposes as address corrections, which are not related to orders at all.

In many weeks, the normal, declining day-of-week pattern does not hold. Most of these disruptions coincide with the occurrence of holidays or catalog mailings. Call volumes are generally much lower on holidays than would otherwise be expected. Usually, one or two days before a holiday call volumes decrease. After a holiday, call volumes increase over normal levels as customers make up for the lack of ordering over the previous days. The magnitudes of these decreases and increases and the number of days affected depend upon the importance of the holiday. For example, the Fourth of July causes a larger and longer decrease than President's Day.

Catalogs are the primary medium through which L. L. Bean advertises and stimulates customer calling. The company mails out millions of copies of 20 to 25 different catalogs a year, each offering different merchandise depending upon the season and the target customers. L. L. Bean times most catalog mailings, or "drops," so that the bulk of the catalogs arrive around Tuesday. Many eager customers order immediately from their new catalogs. This results in high weekly order and call volumes, and it also causes the day-of-week pattern to deviate greatly from what occurs in a week without a catalog drop. For example, many catalogs cause the TM call volumes for Tuesday, Wednesday, and Thursday to rise above Monday's level. Other catalogs yield less dramatic shifts from the normal daily distribution. On the TI side, catalogs also can distort the usual pattern as heavy congestion on the TM lines encourages customers to "backdoor" their way through the TI lines to place orders.

MODEL RESULTS

The TI and TM models were built using SAS's Economic Time Series package on a mainframe IBM 3090/200J-VF. The conditional least squares option was used to estimate more than 100 coefficients in each model. The extensive exploratory efforts during the model-construction phase and subsequent ex-post forecasting evaluations led to hundreds of SAS runs, each averaging about three minutes of CPU time.

The TM model fit over five years of historical daily data with a mean absolute percent error (MAPE) of 7.4 percent, and the TI model fit its time series with a MAPE of 11.4 percent. We produced a year of ex-post forecasts for each model to measure their ability to predict the third week ahead (days 15–21). The TM model forecasted third-week-ahead volumes, from June 7, 1993, to June 3, 1994, with a MAPE of 9.8 percent. The TI model forecasted the same period with a MAPE of 12.0 percent. We are encouraged by these results since they are not significantly higher than the MAPEs for the historical fitting ranges.

On average, our TM model produces slightly more accurate estimates than our TI model. This is true for historical fits as well as ex-post forecasts. This derives from the fact that, although TM volumes are more variable, they can be better explained because of their direct and stable relationship with independent variables, especially orders. Since the composition of TI call volumes is much more complex, the independent variables in its model are less able to predict their behavior accurately.

Source: Adapted from Bruce H. Andrews and Shawn M. Cunningham, "L. L. Bean Improves Call-Center Forecasting," *Interfaces,* vol. 25, no. 6, November–December 1995, pp. 1–13.

SOLVED PROBLEMS

1. Simple Exponential Smoothing

Problem Statement

The first-week demand for a new barbecue burger is

Day	Demand, burgers
Monday	22
Tuesday	27
Wednesday	38
Thursday	32
Friday	34

What is the forecast demand for next Monday using a smoothing constant $\alpha = 0.3$?

Solution

Using equation (5) with $\alpha = 0.3$ yields the simple exponential smoothing model $S_t = 0.3(A_t) + 0.7(S_{t-1})$ with $F_{t+1} = S_t$. The calculations are shown in the worktable below:

Day	Period t	Actual A_t	Smoothed S_t	Forecast F_t	Error $|A_t - F_t|$
Mon.	1	22	22	—	—
Tues.	2	27	23.5	22	5
Wed.	3	38	27.85	24	14
Thurs.	4	32	29.095	28	4
Fri.	5	34	29.9665	29	5
Mon.				30	MAD = 7.0

2. Exponential Smoothing with Trend

Problem Statement

Recalculate the forecast for next Monday using a trend adjustment with $\beta = 0.2$. Using the MAD measure, compare the quality of this trend-adjusted forecast with the simple exponential smoothing in problem 1.

Solution

Using equations (6), (7), and (8) with $\alpha = 0.3$ and $\beta = 0.2$, we get the following exponential smoothing model with trend adjustment. The calculations are shown in the worktable below.

$$S_t = 0.3(A_t) + 0.7(S_{t-1} + T_{t-1})$$

$$T_t = 0.2(S_t - S_{t-1}) + 0.8(T_{t-1})$$

$$F_{t+1} = S_t + T_t$$

Day	Period t	Actual A_t	Smoothed S_t	Trend T_t	Forecast F_t	Error $|A_t - F_t|$
Mon.	1	22	22	0	—	—
Tues.	2	27	23.5	0.3	22	5
Wed.	3	38	28.06	1.15	23.8 ≅ 24	14
Thurs.	4	32	30.047	1.3174	29.21 ≅ 29	3
Fri.	5	34	31.55508	1.355536	31.3644 ≅ 31	3
Mon.					32.9106 ≅ 33	MAD = 6.25

3. Exponential Smoothing with Seasonal Adjustment

Problem Statement

Given the data below from the second week, there appears to be a cycle during the week peaking on Wednesday. Recalculate the forecast for Monday of the following week using a seasonal adjustment with $\gamma = 0.3$.

Day	Demand, burgers
Monday	25
Tuesday	31
Wednesday	42
Thursday	34
Friday	32

Solution

Using Equations (9), (10), (11), and (12) with $\alpha = 0.3$ and $\gamma = 0.2$ yields the following exponential smoothing model with seasonal adjustment. Results are shown in the worktable below.

$$I_t = \frac{A_t}{\overline{A}}$$

$$S_t = 0.3\frac{A_t}{I_{t-L}} + 0.7(S_{t-1})$$

$$F_{t+1} = (S_t)(I_{t-L+1})$$

$$I_t = 0.2\frac{A_t}{S_t} + 0.8(I_{t-L})$$

First, the average value $\overline{A}$ for the first week is calculated and then used in formula (9) to calculate the initial seasonality indexes.

$$\overline{A} = (22 + 27 + 38 + 32 + 34)/5 = 30.6$$

Second, using formula (9), the initial seasonality indexes are calculated as shown in the worktable below for the first week:

Day	Period t	Actual A_t	Smoothed S_t	Index I_t
Mon.	1	22	—	0.72
Tues.	2	27	—	0.88
Wed.	3	38	—	1.24
Thurs.	4	32	—	1.05
Fri.	5	34	34	1.11

Third, the smoothed values, undated seasonal index, and forecast are made using formulas (10), (11), and (12) as shown in the worktable below:

Day	Period t	Actual A_t	Smoothed S_t	Index I_t	Forecast F_t	Error $|A_t - F_t|$
Mon.	6	25	34.217	0.74	—	—
Tues.	7	31	34.520	0.88	$30.11 \cong 30$	1
Wed.	8	42	34.325	1.24	$42.80 \cong 43$	1
Thurs.	9	34	33.742	1.04	$36.04 \cong 36$	2
Fri.	10	32	32.268	1.09	$37.45 \cong 37$	5
Mon.	11				$23.88 \cong 24$	MAD = 2.25

TOPICS FOR DISCUSSION

1. What characteristics of service organizations make forecast accuracy important?
2. For each of the three forecasting methods (i.e., time series, causal, and subjective), what costs are associated with the development and use of the forecast model? What costs are associated with forecast error?
3. The number of customers at a bank likely will vary by the hour of the day and by the day of the month. What are the implications of this for choosing a forecasting model?
4. Compare N-period moving-average models with exponential smoothing models.
5. Suggest a number of independent variables for a regression model to predict the potential sales volume of a given location for a retail store (e.g., a video rental store).
6. Suggest how the Delphi method can be incorporated into a cross-impact analysis.

EXERCISES

10.1. In September 1996, there were 1,035 checking-account customers at a neighborhood bank. The forecast for September, which was made in August, was for 1,065 checking-account customers. Use an α of 0.1 to update the forecast for October.
10.2. During the noon hour this past Wednesday at a fast-food restaurant, 72 hamburgers were sold. The smoothed value calculated the week before was 67. Update the forecast for next Wednesday using simple exponential smoothing and an α of 0.1.
10.3. For the data in exercise 10.2, update the fast-food restaurant forecast if a trend value of 1.4 was calculated for the previous week. Use a β of 0.3 to update the trend for this week, and determine the forecast for next Wednesday using exponential smoothing with trend adjustment.
10.4. The demand for a certain drug in a hospital has been increasing. For the past six months, the following demand has been observed:

Month	Demand, units
January	15
February	18
March	22
April	23
May	27
June	26

Use a three-month moving average to make a forecast for July.
10.5. For the data in exercise 10.4, use an α of 0.1 to make a forecast for July.
10.6. For the data in exercise 10.4, use an α of 0.1 and a β of 0.2 to make a forecast for July and August. Calculate the MAD for your January through June forecasts.
10.7. Prepare a spreadsheet model for the Saturday hotel occupancy data in Table 10.4, and recalculate the forecasts using an α of 0.3. What is the new MAD?
10.8. Prepare a spreadsheet model for the commuter airline's weekly load factor data in Table 10.5, and recalculate the forecasts using an α of 0.2 and a β of 0.2. Have you improved on the original MAD?
10.9. Prepare a spreadsheet model for the ferry passenger data in Table 10.6, and recalculate the forecasts using an α of 0.3 and a γ of 0.2. Has this change in the smoothing constants improved the MAD?
10.10. Prepare a spreadsheet model for the ferry passenger data in Table 10.7, and recalculate the forecasts using an α of 0.3, a β of 0.1, and a γ of 0.2. Has this change in the smoothing constants improved the MAD?

Oak Hollow Medical Evaluation Center[3]

Oak Hollow Medical Evaluation Center is a nonprofit agency offering multidisciplinary diagnostic services to study children with disabilities or developmental delays. The center can test each patient for physical, psychological, or social problems. Fees for services are based on an ability-to-pay schedule.

The evaluation center exists in a highly competitive environment. Many public-spirited organizations are competing for shrinking funds (i.e., Proposition 13 syndrome), and many groups such as private physicians, private and school psychologists, and social service organizations also are "competing" for the same patients. As a result of this situation, the center finds itself in an increasingly vulnerable financial position.

Mr. Abel, the director of the center, is becoming increasingly concerned with the center's ability to attract adequate funding and serve community needs. Mr. Abel now must develop an accurate estimate of the future patient load, staffing requirements, and operating expenses as part of his effort to attract funding. To this end, the director has approached an operations management professor at the local university for assistance in preparing a patient, staffing, and budget forecast for the coming year. The professor has asked you to aid her in this project. Tables 10.8 through 10.11 give you some pertinent information.

TABLE 10.8

ANNUAL NUMBER OF PATIENT TESTS PERFORMED*

Test	1992	1993	1994	1995	1996
Physical exam	390	468	509	490	582
Speech and hearing screening	102	124	180	148	204
Psychological testing	168	312	376	386	437
Social-worker interview	106	188	184	222	244

*All entering patients are given a physical examination. Patients then are scheduled for additional testing deemed appropriate.

TABLE 10.9

ANNUAL EXPENSES

Area	1992	1993	1994	1995	1996
Physical and neurological exams	$18,200	$24,960	$32,760	$31,500	$41,600
Speech and hearing tests	2,040	2,074	3,960	3,950	4,850
Psychological testing	6,720	12,480	16,450	16,870	20,202
Social-worker interview	3,320	3,948	4,416	5,550	7,592
Subtotal	$30,280	$43,462	$57,586	$57,870	$74,244
Other expenses	46,559	48,887	51,820	55,447	59,883
Total	$76,839	$92,349	$109,406	$113,317	$134,127

TABLE 10.10

MONTHLY PATIENT DEMAND, SEPTEMBER 1995–DECEMBER 1996

	Physical exam	Speech and hearing tests	Psychological testing	Social-worker interview
1995				
September	54	16	42	24
October	67	21	54	31
November	74	22	48	33
December	29	9	23	13
1996				
January	58	20	44	24
February	52	18	39	22
March	47	16	35	20
April	41	14	31	17
May	35	12	26	15
June	29	10	22	12
July	23	8	17	10
August	29	10	22	12
September	65	24	48	27
October	81	29	61	34
November	87	31	66	37
December	35	12	26	14

TABLE 10.11

CURRENT STAFFING LEVELS*

Physicians	2 part-time, 18 hours per week
Speech and hearing clinician	1 part-time, 20 hours per week
Psychologists	1 full-time, 38 hours per week
	1 part-time, 16 hours per week
Social worker	1 full-time, 40 hours per week

*The Oak Hollow Medical Evaluation Center operates on a 50-week year.

Assignments

1. Given the information available and your knowledge of different forecasting techniques, recommend a specific forecasting technique for this study. Consider the advantages and disadvantages of your preferred technique, and identify what additional information, if any, Mr. Abel would need.

2. Develop forecasts for patient, staffing, and budget levels for next year.

CASE

Gnomial Functions, Inc.[4]

Gnomial Functions, Inc. (GFI), is a medium-sized consulting firm in San Francisco that specializes in developing various forecasts of product demand, sales, consumption, or other information for its clients. To a lesser degree, it also has developed ongoing models for internal use by its clients. When contacted by a potential client, GFI usually establishes a basic work agreement with the firm's top management that sets out the general goals of the end product, primary contact personnel in both firms, and an outline of the project's overall scope (including any necessary time constraints for intermediate and final completion and a rough price estimate for the contract). Following this step, a team of GFI personnel is assembled to determine the most appropriate forecasting technique and develop a more detailed work program to be used as the basis for final contract negotiations. This team, which may vary in size according to the scope of the project and the client's needs, will perform the tasks that are established by the work program in conjunction with any personnel from the client firm who would be included in the team.

Recently, GFI was contacted by a rapidly growing regional firm that manufactures, sells, and installs active solar water-heating equipment for commercial and residential applications. DynaSol Industries has seen its sales increase by more than 200 percent during the past 18 months, and it wishes to obtain a reliable estimate of its sales during the next 18 months. The company management expects that sales should increase substantially because of competing energy costs, tax-credit availability, and fundamental shifts in the attitudes of the regional population toward so-called exotic solar systems. The company also faces increasing competition within this burgeoning market. This situation requires major strategic decisions concerning the company's future. When GFI was contacted, DynaSol had almost reached the manufacturing capacity of its present facility, and if it wishes to continue growing with the market, it must expand either by relocating to a new facility entirely or by developing a second manufacturing location. Each involves certain known costs, and each has its advantages and disadvantages. The major unknown factors as far as management is concerned are growth of the overall market for this type of product and how large a market share the company would be able to capture.

Table 10.12 contains the preliminary information available to GFI on DynaSol's past sales.

TABLE 10.12

DYNASOL MONTHLY SALES FOR PERIOD SEPTEMBER 1994–FEBRUARY 1996

Month	DynaSol Industries sales, units	Sales	Regional market sales, units	Sales
1994				
September	24	$ 44,736	223	$ 396,048
October	28	52,192	228	404,928
November	31	59,517	230	408,480
December	32	61,437	231	422,564
1995				
January	30	57,998	229	418,905
February	35	67,197	235	429,881
March	39	78,621	240	439,027
April	40	80,637	265	484,759
May	43	86,684	281	529,449
June	47	94,748	298	561,479
July	51	110,009	314	680,332
August	54	116,480	354	747,596
September	59	127,265	389	809,095
October	62	137,748	421	931,401
November	67	148,857	466	1,001,356
December	69	153,300	501	1,057,320
1996				
January	74	161,121	529	1,057,320
February	79	172,007	573	1,145,264

Assignments

1. Given the information available and your knowledge of different forecasting techniques, develop a recommendation for utilizing a specific forecasting technique in the subsequent study. The final contract negotiations are pending, and so it is essential that you account for the advantages and disadvantages of your preferred technique as they would apply to the problem at hand and point out any additional information you would like to have.

2. Assume that you are a member of DynaSol's small marketing department and that the contract negotiations with GFI have fallen through irrevocably. The company's top management has decided to use your expertise to develop a forecast for the next six months (and, perhaps, for the six-month period following that one as well), because it must have some information on which to base a decision about expanding its operations. Develop such a forecast, and for the benefit of top management, note any reservations or qualifications you feel are vital to its understanding and use of the information.

SELECTED BIBLIOGRAPHY

DAVIS, C. H., and J. A. FITZSIMMONS: "The Future of Nuclear Power in the United States," *Technological Forecasting and Social Change,* Elsevier Science Publishing Co., Inc., New York, vol. 40, no. 2, September 1991, pp. 151–164.

KIMES, S. E., and J. A. FITZSIMMONS: "Selecting Profitable Hotel Sites at La Quinta Motor Inns," *Interfaces,* vol. 20, no. 2, March–April 1990, pp. 12–20.

NETER, JOHN, WILLIAM WASSERMAN, and MICHAEL H. KUTNER: *Applied Linear Regression Models,* Irwin, Homewood, Ill., 1989.

WILSON, J. HOLTON, and BARRY KEATING: *Business Forecasting,* Irwin, Homewood, Ill., 1990.

ENDNOTES

1. C. H. Davis and J. A. Fitzsimmons, "The Future of Nuclear Power in the United States," *Technological Forecasting and Social Change,* vol. 40, no. 2, September 1991, pp. 151–164.
2. S. E. Kimes and J. A. Fitzsimmons, "Selecting Profitable Hotel Sites at La Quinta Motor Inns," *Interfaces,* vol. 20, no. 2, March–April 1990, pp. 12–20.
3. Prepared by Frank Krafka under the supervision of Professor James A. Fitzsimmons.
4. Prepared by Frank Krafka under the supervision of Professor James A. Fitzsimmons.

Managing Waiting Lines

Learning Objectives

After completing this chapter, you should be able to:

1. Describe how queues form.
2. Apply Maister's two "laws of service."
3. Describe the psychology of waiting components, and suggest management strategies to deal with each.
4. Describe the essential features of a queuing system.
5. Explain why the negative exponential distribution of time between arrivals is equivalent to the Poisson distribution of arrival rates.
6. Conduct a simulation study of a service system.

The management of queues at Burger King represents an evolving process of refinement. When these stores first opened, a "conventional" lineup was used that required customers to arrange themselves in single file behind a single cash register, where orders were taken. Assemblers prepared the orders and presented them to customers at the far end of the counter. This conventional style of line-up often is called the "snake," as mentioned in the following *Wall Street Journal* article.[1]

Louis Kane hates snakes.

The restaurant executive means the single lines that feed customers one at a time to a group of cashiers. He thinks snakes are much too "institutional." Besides, he says, he would rather try to guess which line will move the fastest. But surveys show that customers prefer snakes to multiple lines because they hate "getting stuck behind some guy ordering nine cappuccinos, each with something different on top," says Mr. Kane, co-chairman of the Boston-based Au Bon Pain soup-and-sandwich chain.

The customers have won. Over the past couple of years, Au Bon Pain has instituted snakes at every restaurant that has enough room. But the debate lives on. "We talk about this a great deal," Mr. Kane says.

The issue is queues. Experts suggest that no aspect of customer service is more important than the wait in line to be served. The act of waiting—either in person or on the phone—"has a disproportionately high impact" on customers, says David Maister, a Boston consultant who has studied the psychology of waiting. "The wait can destroy an otherwise perfect service experience."

A customer waiting in line is potentially a lost customer. According to one study, up to 27% of customers who can't get through on the telephone will either buy elsewhere or skip the transaction altogether, says Rudy Oetting, a senior partner at Oetting & Co., a New York company that consults on telephone use. Adds Russell James, an official at Avis Rent a Car Inc.: "You can't be out-lined by a competitor or you will lose business."

Today's customers are also more demanding than ever. "The dramatic difference between 1980 and 1990 can be described in one word: speed," says N. Powell Taylor, manager of GE Answer Center, a General Electric Co. operation that fields three million calls a year. "People expect quicker answers. No one has the time any more."

In the past few years particularly, many companies have stepped up efforts to shorten waits—or at least make them more tolerable. Here are some of the methods they are trying:

Animate

Some contend that a wait isn't a wait if it's fun. At Macy's in New York now, the line to see Santa Claus wends its way through displays of dancing teddy bears, elves and electric trains. "It's part of the adventure of going to see Santa Claus," says Jean McFaddin, a vice president at the big department store, where 300,000 people see Santa in 30 days.

At Disneyland and Walt Disney World, the waits—which can be up to 90 minutes long—are planned along with the attractions themselves. Visitors waiting for rides that board continuously pass animated displays that are designed to be viewed as people walk along. Waits for theater shows include such attractions as singers and handicraft displays aimed at audiences that will be waiting in one place as long as 30 minutes. Indeed, the waits themselves are called "preshows." Says Norman Doerges, executive vice president of Disneyland, "that's what makes the time pass, is the entertainment."

At the Omni Park Central Hotel in New York, when a line exceeds six people, assistant managers are dispatched to the hotel restaurant to bring out orange and grapefruit juice to serve to the people in line. "We are trying to tell the guest 'we know you are here,'" says Philip Georgas, general manager and regional vice president.

Still, not all diversions are suitable. Many callers don't like listening to recordings while they're on hold. GE plays its corporate theme for customers while they wait, but it draws the line at playing recorded advertising. "We tend to stay away from commercials," says Mr. Taylor, because of the fear that customers will think company employees "are probably sitting there doing nothing," making customers wait so they will have to listen to the commercials.

Discriminate

"The key thing is not just moving people out of the line," says Mr. James at Avis. "The key is who you move out of the line." For the past two years, high-volume renters at Avis have been able to sign a permanent rental agreement in advance and be driven directly to their cars when they arrive at many Avis locations. Somewhat less-frequent renters check in at a kiosk near the car park. Other car rental concerns are offering similar preferential services.

Such service is increasingly common in the travel, banking and credit-card industries. But "one needs a great deal of creativity in this area" lest less-favored customers be offended, says Mr. Maister. "Those businesses that want to serve priority customers faster are best advised to do it out of sight of the regular customers." He cites some airlines that locate first-class check-in counters away from the economy counters. "You don't want to rub the noses of the economy passengers in it."

Automate

While assembly-line techniques can accelerate manufacturing operations, they often slow the delivery of services. When callers must speak to several different people to get a complete answer, "crew interference" sets in, says Warren Blanding, editor of Customer Service Newsletter in Silver Spring, Md. "The most efficient way to do a job is to have one person do it." So Employers Health Insurance, Green Bay, Wis., has assembled a complex computer database of scripts that employees can read to customers on the telephone. The employee keys in the caller's name, location and type of health insurance question. The computer then pops up a question-and-answer format that can be read verbatim.

"We know that 75% of the calls we get in are standard questions," says Sterling L. Phaklides, an assistant vice president in the claims division. "Because people are sticking to the scripts, they are giving up-to-date information" without consulting technicians, he says. But callers who ask questions that aren't covered in the scripts can be referred to specialists at any point. "It does save telephone time," the official says. The claims area handles 3,700 calls a day; only about 1% of callers hang up before they are connected—which is better than average, he says.

Obfuscate

Mr. Maister says the perceived wait is often more important than the actual wait. In a paper on the psychology of waiting, he notes that some restaurants deliberately announce longer waiting times, thus pleasing customers when the wait is actually shorter. At Disneyland in Anaheim, Calif., lines snake around corners, Mr. Maister says. Thus people focus more on how fast the line is moving than on how long the line is.

Disneyland says its aim isn't to deceive. It posts waiting times at the start of each line. "A big danger in disguising a line is that people don't know what they are getting into," says Mr. Doerges. "If you do it without proper preparation, people get frustrated."

Still, some think that even that information will be too depressing. Technology is available that will announce a caller's place in line, but Penny Rhode, vice president, customer service, at First Gibralter Bank in Dallas, chose not to use it. "I felt like . . . focusing on the positive, rather than perhaps saying that there are 14 callers ahead of you."

Under First Gibralter's system, after $1\frac{1}{2}$ minutes a phone voice offers the caller the option of continuing to wait or leaving a message. Since it started the system in October, the bank has averaged about 100 messages a day out of between 3,000 and 3,200 calls.

Dissatisfaction with the slowness of a single-line arrangement led Burger King to try the "hospitality" line-up, in which cash registers are evenly spaced along the counter and customers select a line (in effect betting on which of several will move the fastest). In this arrangement, the cashier who takes an order also assembles the order. Although the hospitality line-up proves to be very flexible in meeting peak-period demand, it does tend to be more labor-intensive than the conventional line-up. Consequently, Burger King made yet another change, this time to what is called a "multi-conventional" line-up, which is a hybrid of both earlier systems. The restaurant returned to a single line, but a new cash register now allows up to six orders to be recorded at the same time. Assemblers prepare the orders and distribute them at the end of the counter. Returning to a single line has guaranteed fairness, because customers are served in the order of their arrival. In addition, customers have enough time to make their meal selection without slowing the entire order-taking process.

Burger King's concern with reducing customer waiting time represents a trend toward providing faster service. In many cases, speed of delivery is viewed as a competitive advantage in the marketplace. For example, many hotels today will total your bill and slide it under your room door during the last night of your stay, thereby achieving "zero waiting time" at the check-out counter.

Fluctuations in demand for service are difficult to cope with because the consumption and production of services occur simultaneously. Customers typically arrive at random and place immediate demands on the available service. If service capacity is fully utilized at the time of his or her arrival, then the customer is expected to wait patiently in line. Varying arrival rates and service time requirements result in the formation of queues (i.e., lines of customers waiting their turn for service). The management of queues is a continuing challenge for service managers.

CHAPTER PREVIEW

Our understanding of waiting lines begins with a definition of queuing systems and the inevitability of waiting, and then the implications of asking people to wait are studied further from a psychological perspective. We shall discover that the perception of waiting often is more important to the consumer than the actual time spent waiting, suggesting that innovative ways should be found to reduce the negative aspects of waiting. The economic value of waiting as a cost for the provider and currency for the consumer also is considered. Finally, the essential features of a service system are discussed in terms of a schematic queuing model, and queuing terminology is defined.

QUEUING SYSTEMS

A *queue* is a line of waiting customers who require service from one or more servers. The queue need not be a physical line of individuals in front of a server, however. It might be students sitting at computer terminals that are scattered around a college campus, or a person being placed on "hold" by a telephone operator. Servers typically are considered to be individual stations where customers receive service. The stereotypical queue—people waiting in a formal line for service—is seen at the check-out counters of a supermarket and the teller windows in a bank, yet queuing systems occur in a variety of forms. Consider the following variations:

1. Servers need not be limited to serving one customer at a time. Transportation systems such as buses, airplanes, and elevators are bulk services.
2. The consumer need not always travel to the service facility; in some systems, the server actually comes to the consumer. This approach is illustrated by urban services such as fire and police protection as well as by ambulance service.
3. The service may consist of stages of queues in a series or of a more complex network of queues. For example, consider the haunted-house attraction at amusement parks like Disneyland, where queues are staged in sequence so that visitors can be processed in batches and entertained during the waiting periods (e.g., first outside on the walk, then in the vestibule, and finally on the ride itself).

In any service system, a queue forms whenever current demand exceeds the existing capacity to serve. This occurs when servers are so busy that arriving consumers cannot receive immediate service. Such a situation is bound to occur in any system for which arrivals occur at varying times and service times also vary.

THE INEVITABILITY OF WAITING

As Figure 11.1 shows, waiting is part of everyone's life, and it can involve an incredible amount of time. For example, a typical day might include waiting at several stoplights, waiting for someone to answer the telephone, waiting for your meal to be served, waiting for the elevator, waiting to be checked out at the supermarket—the list goes on and on.

In the old Soviet Union and even the newly independent countries that have formed since its break-up, we find dramatic examples of the role that queuing can play in people's daily lives. A noted Russian scholar, Hedrick Smith, observed that the queue in that country is a national pastime:

> Personally, I have known of people who stood in line 90 minutes to buy four pineapples, three hours for a two-minute roller coaster ride, three and a half hours to buy three large heads of cabbage only to find the cabbages were gone as they approached the front of the line, 18 hours to sign up to purchase a rug at some later date, all through a freezing December night to register on a list for buying a car, and then waiting 18 more months for actual delivery, and terribly lucky at that. Lines can run from a few yards long to half a block to nearly a mile, and usually they move at an excruciating creep.[2]

He also found that there was a matter of line etiquette. Line jumping by serious shoppers was accepted for ordinary items but not for scarce ones. Smith observed:

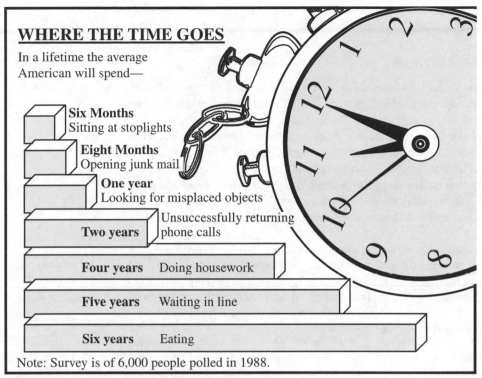

WHERE THE TIME GOES

In a lifetime the average
American will spend—

Six Months
Sitting at stoplights

Eight Months
Opening junk mail

One year
Looking for misplaced objects

Two years
Unsuccessfully returning
phone calls

Four years   Doing housework

Five years   Waiting in line

Six years   Eating

Note: Survey is of 6,000 people polled in 1988.

FIGURE 11.1   Where the time goes.
(*Source:* Copyright, 1989, *U.S. News & World Report,* January 30, 1989, p. 81.)

"People know from experience that things actually run out while they are standing in line," advised one young [woman]. "So if the line is for something really good and you leave it for very long, people get very upset. They fly off the handle and curse you and try to keep you from getting back in when you return. It's up to the person behind you to defend your place in line. So it's serious business asking someone to hold your place. They take on a moral obligation not only to let you in front of them later on but to defend you. You have to be stubborn yourself and stand your ground in spite of the insults and the stares. And when you get to the front of the line, if the sales clerks are not limiting the amount, you can hear people, maybe six or eight places back, shouting at you not to take so much, that you are a person with no scruples or that you have no consideration for other people. It can be rather unpleasant."[3]

Since Smith made his observations, *perestroika* has brought about many changes in the former Soviet Union, but it has yet to affect the queues that still are so much a part of daily life in that region. The Russian queuing experience is far more severe than that found in the United States; however, in any service system, waiting is bound to occur. A complete absence of waiting only would be possible in a situation where consumers are asked to arrive at fixed intervals and service times are deterministic (e.g., a psychiatrist schedules patients every hour for 50-minute sessions). Later, we will demonstrate that waiting is caused by both the fluctuations in arrival rates and the variability in service times. Thus, as long as service times vary, delays can be encountered even when arrivals are scheduled by appointment. This is a common experience for patients waiting in a physician's office. Waiting also occurs at fast-food restaurants, where the variability of service times has been reduced by offering a short menu but customers arrive at random. Therefore, waiting is inevitable, and service operations managers must consider how customers in queue are to be treated.

THE PSYCHOLOGY OF WAITING[4]

If, as noted above, waiting is such an integral and ordinary part of our lives, why does it cause us so much grief? David H. Maister offers some interesting perspectives on this subject.

He suggests two "Laws of Service." The first deals with the customer's expectations versus his or her perceptions. If a customer receives better service than he or she expects, then the customer departs a happy, satisfied person, and the service may benefit from a trickle-down effect (i.e., the happy customer will tell friends about the good service). Note, however, that the trickle-down effect can work both ways: a service can earn a bad reputation in the same manner (and create more interesting stories for the customer to pass along).

Maister's second law states that it is hard to play "catch-up ball." By this, he means that first impressions can influence the rest of the service experience; thus, a service that requires its customers to wait would be advised to make that period a pleasant experience. To do the "impossible"—to make waiting at least tolerable and, at best, pleasant and productive—a creative and competitive service management must consider the following aspects of the psychology of waiting.

That Old Empty Feeling

Just as "nature abhors a vacuum," people dislike "empty time." Empty, or unoccupied, time feels awful. It keeps us from other productive activities; frequently is physically uncomfortable; makes us feel powerless and at the mercy of servers, whom we may perceive as uncaring about us; and, perhaps worst of all, seems to last forever. The challenge to the service organization is obvious: fill this time in a positive way. It may require no more than comfortable chairs and a fresh coat of paint to cheer up the environment. Furnishings in a waiting area can affect indirectly the perception of waiting. The fixed, bench-like seating in bus and rail terminals discourages conversation. The light, movable table-and-chair arrangement of a European sidewalk cafe brings people together and provides opportunities for socializing. In another situation, a music recording may be enough to occupy a telephone caller who is on hold and, at the same time, reassure the caller that he or she has not been disconnected.

Perhaps the strategy most widely noted in the literature is that of installing mirrors near elevators. Hotels, for example, record fewer complaints about excessive waits for elevators that are surrounded by mirrors. The mirrors allow people to occupy their time by checking their grooming and surreptitiously observing others who are waiting.

Services often can make waiting times productive as well as pleasurable. Instead of treating the telephone caller mentioned above to the strains of Mozart or Madonna, the service can air some commercials. Such a practice involves risk, however, because some people resent being subjected to this tactic when they are being held captive. At The Olive Garden restaurants, diners who are waiting for tables can spend their time in the bar, which benefits the restaurant with added sales, or can wait in the lobby and watch a chef prepare fresh pastas, which certainly stimulates appetites. No need to play "catch-up ball" here. Each diner reaches the table happily anticipating an agreeable experience rather than sourly grumbling, "It's about time!"

Services that consist of several stages, such as one might find at a diagnostic clinic, can conceal waiting by asking people to walk between successive stages. There are innumerable other ways to fill time: reading matter, television monitors, live entertainment, posters, artwork, toys to occupy children, and cookies and pots of coffee. The diversions are limited only by management's imagination and desire to serve the customer effectively.

A Foot in the Door

As noted above, some diversions merely fill time so that waiting doesn't seem so long, and others also can provide the service organization with some ancillary benefits. Happy customers are more likely than unhappy customers to be profitable customers. Another aspect of diversions is important, however.

Maister points out that "service-related" diversions themselves, such as handing out menus to waiting diners or medical history forms (and paper cups) to waiting patients, "convey a sense that service has started." One's level of anxiety subsides considerably once service has started. In fact, people generally can tolerate longer waits, within reason, if they feel service has begun better than they can tolerate such waits if service has not even started. Another view is that customers become dissatisfied more quickly with an initial wait than with subsequent waits after the service has begun.

The Light at the End of the Tunnel

There are many anxieties at work before service begins. Have I been forgotten? Did you get my order? This line doesn't seem to be moving; will I ever get served? If I run to the rest room, will I lose my turn? When will the plumber get here? Will the plumber get here at all? Whether rational or not, anxieties may be the single biggest factor influencing the waiting customer.

Managers must recognize these anxieties and develop strategies to alleviate them. In some cases, this may be a simple matter of having an employee acknowledge the customer's presence. At other times, telling the customer how long he or she will have to wait is sufficient reassurance that the wait at some point will end. Signs can serve this purpose as well. As you approach the Port Aransas, Texas, ferry landing, for example, you see signs posted along the road noting the number of minutes you have left to wait if you are stopped in line at that point.

When appropriate, scheduling appointments is one strategy to reduce waiting time, but it is not foolproof. Unforeseen events might interfere, or prior appointments may require more time than expected. If the appointed time comes and goes, the anxiety of not knowing how long the wait will be sets in—along with some measure of irritation at the "insult" of being stood up. A simple explanation and apology for the delays, however, usually will go a long way in reestablishing goodwill.

Excuse Me, but I Was Next

Uncertain and unexplained waits create anxieties and, as noted above, occasionally some resentment in customers. The moment a customer sees a later arrival being served first, however, anxiety about how long the wait will be is transformed into anger about the unfairness of it all. This can lead to a testy—if not explosive—situation, and the service provider is just as likely as the usurper to be the target of the anger.

A simple strategy for avoiding violations of the first-come, first-served (FCFS) queuing policy is the take-a-number arrangement. For example, customers entering a meat market take a number from a dispenser and wait for it to be called. The number currently being served may be displayed so that the new customer can see how long the wait will be. With this simple measure, management has relieved the customer's anxiety over the length of the wait—and the possibility of being treated unfairly. As an ancillary benefit, it also encourages "impulse buying" through allowing the customer to wander about the shop instead of needing to protect a place in line. As equitable as it is, however, this system is not totally free from producing anxiety; it does require the customer to stay alert for the numbers being called or risk losing his or her place in line.

Another simple strategy for fostering FCFS service when there are multiple servers is use of a single queue. Banks, post offices, and airline check-in counters commonly employ this technique. A customer who enters one of these facilities joins the back of the line; the first person in line is served by the next available server. Anxiety is relieved, because there is no fear that later arrivals will "slip" ahead of their rightful place.[5] Often, customers who have been "guaranteed" their place in this way will relax and enjoy a few pleasantries with others in the line. Note that such camaraderie also occupies the customer's empty time and makes the waiting time seem shorter. Queue configurations are examined in more detail later in this chapter.

Not all services lend themselves to such a straightforward prioritization, however. Police service is one example; for obvious reasons, an officer on the way to a call about a "noisy dog next door" will change priorities when told to respond to a "robbery-in-progress." In this case, the dispatcher can ameliorate the "noisy-dog" caller's wait anxiety by explaining the department's response policy and providing the caller with a reasonable expectation of when an officer will arrive.

Other services may wish to give preferential treatment to special customers. Consider the express check-in for "high rollers" at Las Vegas hotels, or for first-class passengers at airline check-in counters. Keep in mind, however, that such special "perks" also can engender irritation among the unfavored who are standing in long lines nearby. A management sensitive to the concerns of all its customers will take measures to avoid an image of obvious discrimination. In the example just mentioned, one solution might be to "conceal" the preferential treatment by locating it in an area that is separate from the regular service line.

They Also Serve, Who Sit and Wait

Management must remember that one of the most important parts of its service package is attention to the needs of its customers during the waiting process. The customer who is subjected to unnecessary anxiety or aggravation during this period likely will be a demanding and difficult customer—or, worse, a former customer.

THE ECONOMICS OF WAITING

The economic cost of waiting can be viewed from two perspectives. For a firm, the cost of keeping an employee (i.e., an internal customer) waiting may be measured by unproductive wages. For external customers, the cost of waiting is the forgone alternative use of that time. Added to this are the costs of boredom, anxiety, and other psychological distresses.

In a competitive market, excessive waiting—or even the expectation of long waits—can lead to lost sales. How often have you driven by a filling station, observed many cars lined up at the pumps, and then decided not to stop? One strategy to avoid lost sales is to conceal the queue from arriving customers. In the case of restaurants, this often is achieved by diverting people into the bar, a tactic that frequently results in increased sales. Amusement parks such as Disneyland require people to pay for their tickets outside the park, where they are unable to observe the waiting lines inside. Casinos "snake" the waiting line for nightclub acts through the slot-machine area both to hide its true length and to foster impulsive gambling.

The consumer can be considered a resource with the potential to participate in the service process. For example, a patient who is waiting for a doctor can be asked to complete a medical history record and thereby save valuable physician time (i.e., service capacity). The waiting period also can be used to educate the person about good health habits, which can be achieved by making health publications or filmstrips available. As another example, restaurants are quite innovative in their approaches to engaging the customer directly in providing the service. After giving your order to a waiter in many restaurants, you are asked to go to the salad bar and prepare your own salad, which you eat while the cook prepares your meal.

Consumer waiting may be viewed as a contribution to productivity by permitting greater utilization of limited capacity. The situation of customers waiting in line for a service is analogous to the work-in-process inventory for a manufacturing firm. The service firm actually is inventorying customers to increase the overall efficiency of the process. In service systems, higher utilization of facilities is purchased at the price of customer waiting. Prominent examples can be found in public services such as post offices, medical clinics, and welfare offices, where high utilization is achieved with long queues. Yoram Barzel reports the following event to illustrate the economic value of waiting:[6]

> On June 14, 1972, the United States of America Bank (of Chicago) launched an anniversary sale. The commodity on sale was money, and each of the first 35 persons could "buy" a $100 bill for $80 in cash. Those farther down the queue could each obtain similar but declining bonuses: the next 50 could gain $10 each; 75, $4 each; 100, $2 each; and the following 100, $1 each. Each of the next 100 persons could get a $2 bill for $1.60 and, finally, 800 (subsequently, it seems, expanded to 1800) persons could gain $0.50 each. The expected waiting time in such an unusual event was unpredictable; on the other hand, it was easy to assess the money value of the commodity being distributed.
>
> First in line were four brothers aged 16, 17, 19, and 24. Because the smallest was 6'2", their priority was assured. "I figured," said Carl, the youngest brother, "that we spent 17 hours to make a $20 profit. That's about $1.29 an hour."
>
> "You can make better than that washing dishes," added another of the brothers. Had they been better informed they could have waited less time. The 35th person to join the line arrived around midnight, had to wait just 9 hours, and was the last to earn $20—$2.22 per hour. To confirm her right, she made a list of all those ahead of her in the line.
>
> "Why am I here?" she asked. "Well, that $20 is the same as a day's pay to me. And I don't even have to declare it on my income tax. It's a gift, isn't it?"

The experience described above demonstrates that those in line considered their waiting time as the cost of securing a "free" good. While waiting can have a number of economic interpretations, its true cost is always difficult to determine. For this reason, the trade-off between the cost of waiting and the cost of providing service seldom is made explicit, yet service providers must consider the physical, behavioral, and economic aspects of the consumer waiting experience in their decision making.

ESSENTIAL FEATURES OF QUEUING SYSTEMS

Figure 11.2 depicts the essential features of queuing systems. These are (1) calling population, (2) arrival process, (3) queue configuration, (4) queue discipline, and (5) service process.

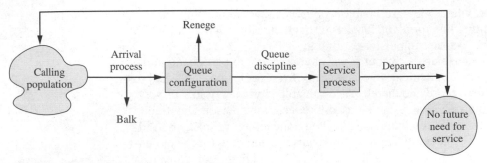

FIGURE 11.2 Queuing system schematic.

Services obtain customers from a *calling population.* The rate at which they arrive is determined by the *arrival process.* If servers are idle, then the customer is immediately attended; otherwise, the customer is diverted to a queue, which can have various configurations. At this point, some customers may *balk* when confronted with a long or slow-moving waiting line and seek service elsewhere. Other customers, after joining the queue, may consider the delay to be intolerable, and so they *renege,* which means that they leave the line before service is rendered. When a server does become available, a customer then is selected from the queue, and service begins. The policy governing the selection is known as the *queue discipline.* The service facility may consist of no servers (i.e., self-service), one or more servers, or complex arrangements of servers in series or in parallel. After the service has been rendered, the customer departs the facility. At that time, the customer may either rejoin the calling population for future return or exit with no intention of returning.

We shall now discuss in more detail each of these five essential features of queuing systems.

Calling Population

The calling population need not be homogeneous; it may consist of several subpopulations. For example, arrivals at an outpatient clinic can be divided into walk-in patients, patients with appointments, and emergency patients. Each class of patient will place different demands on services, but more important, the waiting expectations of each will differ significantly.

In some queuing systems, the source of calls may be limited to a finite number of people. For example, consider the demands on an office copier by a staff of three secretaries. In this case, the probability of future arrivals depends on the number of persons who currently are in the system seeking service. For instance, the probability of a future arrival becomes zero once the third secretary joins the copier queue. Unless the population is quite small, however, an assumption of independent arrivals or infinite population usually suffices. Figure 11.3 shows a classification of the calling population.

Arrival Process

Any analysis of a service system must begin with a complete understanding of the temporal and spatial distribution of the demand for that service. Typically, data are

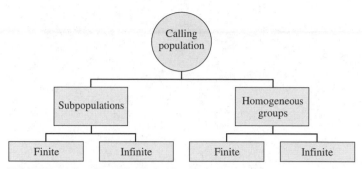

FIGURE 11.3 Classification of calling population.

collected by recording the actual times of arrivals. These data then are used to calculate interarrival times. Many empirical studies indicate that the distribution of interarrival times will be exponential, and the shape of the curve in Figure 11.4 is typical of the *exponential distribution.* Note the high frequency at the origin and the long tail that tapers off to the right. The exponential distribution also can be recognized by noting that both the mean and the standard deviation are theoretically equal ($\mu = 2.4$ and $\sigma = 2.6$ for Figure 11.4).

The exponential distribution has a continuous probability density function of the form

$$f(t) = \lambda e^{-\lambda t} \qquad t \geq 0 \tag{1}$$

where λ = average arrival rate within a given interval of time (e.g., minutes, hours, days)

$\quad t$ = time between arrivals

$\quad e$ = base of natural logarithms (2.718 . . .)

$\quad$ mean = $1/\lambda$

variance = $1/\lambda^2$

The cumulative distribution function is

$$F(t) = 1 - e^{-\lambda t} \qquad t \geq 0 \tag{2}$$

Equation (2) gives the probability that the time between arrivals will be t or less. Note that λ is the inverse of the mean time between arrivals. Thus, for Figure 11.4, the mean time between arrivals is 2.4 minutes, which implies that λ is $1/2.4 = 0.4167$ arrival per minute (i.e., an average rate of 25 patients per hour). Substituting 0.4167 for λ, the exponential distribution for the data displayed in Figure 11.4 is

$$f(t) = 0.4167\, e^{-0.4167t} \qquad t \geq 0 \tag{3}$$

$$F(t) = 1 - e^{-0.4167t} \qquad t \geq 0 \tag{4}$$

Equation (4) now can be used to find the probability that if a patient has already arrived, another will arrive in the next 5 minutes. We simply substitute 5 for t, and so

$$F(5) = 1 - e^{-0.4167(5)}$$

$$= 1 - 0.124$$

$$= 0.876$$

FIGURE 11.4 Distribution of patient interarrival times for a university health clinic.
(*Source:* E. J. Rising, R. Baron, and B. Averill, "A Systems Analysis of a University Health-Service Outpatient Clinic." Reprinted with permission from *Operations Research,* vol. 21, no. 5, September–October 1973, p. 1038, Operations Society of America. No further reproduction permitted without the consent of the copyrighted owner.)

Thus, there is an 87.6 percent chance that another patient will arrive in the next 5-minute interval. Test this phenomenon the next time you are waiting in a physician's office.

Another distribution, known as the *Poisson distribution,* has a unique relationship to the exponential distribution. The Poisson distribution is a discrete probability function of the form

$$f(n) = \frac{(\lambda t)^n e^{-\lambda t}}{n!} \qquad n = 0, 1, 2, 3, \ldots \tag{5}$$

where λ = average arrival rate within a given interval of time (e.g., minutes, hours, days)

t = number of time periods of interest (usually $t = 1$)

n = number of arrivals (0, 1, 2, . . .)

e = base of natural logarithms (2.718 . . .)

mean = λt

variance = λt

The Poisson distribution gives the probability of n arrivals during the time interval t. For the data of Figure 11.4, substituting for $\lambda = 25$, an equivalent description of the arrival process is

Poisson distribution of number of arrivals per hour (top view)

Exponential distribution of time between arrivals in minutes (bottom view)

FIGURE 11.5 Poisson and exponential equivalence.

$$f(n) = \frac{(25)^n e^{-25}}{n!} \qquad n = 0, 1, 2, 3, \ldots \qquad (6)$$

This gives the probability of 0, 1, 2, . . . patients arriving during any 1-hour interval. Note that we have taken the option of converting $\lambda = 0.4167$ arrival per minute to $\lambda = 25$ arrivals per hour. Equation (6) can be used to calculate the interesting probability that no patients will arrive during a 1-hour interval by substituting 0 for n as shown below:

$$f(0) = \frac{(25)^0 e^{-25}}{0!} = e^{-25} = 1.4 \times 10^{-11}, \text{a very small probability}$$

Figure 11.5 shows the relationship between the Poisson distribution (i.e., arrivals per hour) and the exponential distribution (i.e., minutes between arrivals). As can be seen, they represent alternative views of the same process. Thus, an exponential distribution of interarrival times with a mean of 2.4 minutes is equivalent to a Poisson distribution of the number of arrivals per hour with a mean of 25 (i.e., 60/2.4).

Service demand data often are collected automatically (e.g., by trip wires on highways), and the number of arrivals over a period of time is divided by the number of time intervals to arrive at an average rate per unit of time. The demand rate during the unit of time should be stationary with respect to time (i.e., lambda [λ] is a constant); otherwise, the underlying fluctuations in demand rate as a function of time will not be accounted for. This dynamic feature of demand is illustrated in Figure 11.6 for hours in a day, in Figure 11.7 for days of the week, and in Figure 11.8 for months of the year.

Variation in demand intensity directly affects the requirements for service capacity. When possible, service capacity is adjusted to match changes in demand, perhaps by varying the staffing levels. Another strategy is to smooth demand by asking customers to make appointments or reservations. Differential pricing is used by the telephone company to encourage callers to use off-peak hours, and movie theaters provide ticket discounts for patrons arriving before 6 P.M. Smoothing demand and adjusting supply are important topics, which are covered in depth in Chapter 13, "Managing Capacity and Demand." Figure 11.9 presents a classification of arrival processes.

Our discussion has focused on the frequency of demand as a function of time, but the spatial distribution of demand also may vary. This is particularly true of emergency ambulance demand in an urban area, which has a spatial shift in demand resulting from the temporary movements of population from residential areas to commercial and industrial areas during working hours.

FIGURE 11.6 **Ambulance calls by hour of day.**
(*Source:* Reprinted with permission from James A.
Fitzsimmons, "The Use of Spectral Analysis to Validate
Planning Models," *Socio-Economic Planning,* vol. 8, no. 3,
June 1974, p. 127. Copyright © 1974, Pergamon Press Ltd.)

FIGURE 11.7 **Patient arrivals at health
clinic by day of week.**
(*Source:* E. J. Rising, R. Baron, and B. Averill, "A
Systems Analysis of a University Health-Service
Outpatient Clinic." Reprinted with permission
from *Operations Research,* vol. 21, no. 5, September–October 1973, p. 1035, Operations
society of America. No further reproduction
permitted without the consent of the copyrighted
owner.)

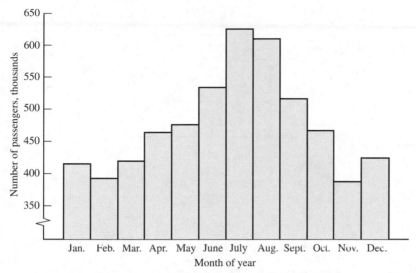

FIGURE 11.8 International airline passengers by month of year. (*Source: FAA Statistical Handbook of Civil Aviation,* 1960.)

FIGURE 11.9 Classification of arrival process.

Queue Configuration

Queue configuration refers to the number of queues, their locations, their spatial requirements, and their effects on customer behavior. Figure 11.10 illustrates three alternative waiting configurations for a service, such as a bank, a post office, or an airline counter, where multiple servers are available.

For the multiple-queue alternative shown in Figure 11.10*a,* the arriving customer must decide which queue to join. The decision need not be irrevocable, however, because one may switch to the end of another line. This line-switching activity is called *jockeying.* In any event, watching the line next to you moving faster than your own is a source of aggravation, but the multiple-queue configuration does have the following advantages:

FIGURE 11.10 Alternative waiting-area configurations.

1. The service provided can be differentiated. The use of express lanes in supermarkets is an example. Shoppers with small demands on service can be isolated and processed quickly, thereby avoiding long waits for little service.
2. Division of labor is possible. For example, drive-in banks assign the more experienced teller to the commercial lane.
3. The customer has the option of selecting a particular server of preference.
4. Balking behavior may be deterred. When arriving customers see a long, single queue snaked in front of a service, they often interpret this as evidence of a long wait and decide not to join that line.

Figure 11.10*b* depicts the common arrangement of brass posts with red velvet ropes strung between them, forcing arrivals to join one sinuous queue. Whenever a server becomes available, the first person in line moves over to the service counter. This is a popular arrangement in bank lobbies, post offices, and amusement parks. Its advantages are:

1. The arrangement guarantees fairness by ensuring that a first-come, first-served rule (FCFS) applies to all arrivals.
2. There is a single queue; thus, no anxiety is associated with waiting to see if one selected the fastest line.
3. With only one entrance at the rear of the queue, the problem of cutting-in is resolved and reneging made difficult.
4. Privacy is enhanced because the transaction is conducted with no one standing immediately behind the person being served.
5. This arrangement is more efficient in terms of reducing the average time that customers spend waiting in line.

Figure 11.10*c* illustrates a variation on the single queue in which the arriving customer takes a number to indicate his or her place in line. When using such numbers to indicate positions in a queue, there is no need for a formal line. Customers are free to wander about, strike up a conversation, relax in a chair, or pursue some other diversion. Unfortunately, as noted earlier, customers must remain alert to hear their numbers being called or risk missing their turns for service. Bakeries make subtle use of the "take-a-number" system to increase impulse sales. Customers who are given the chance to browse among the tantalizing pastries often find that they purchase more than just the loaf of fresh bread for which they came.

If the waiting area is inadequate to accommodate all customers desiring service, then they are turned away. This condition is referred to as a *finite queue.* Restaurants with limited parking may experience this problem to a certain extent. A public parking garage is a classic example because, once the last stall is taken, future arrivals are rejected with the word *FULL* until a car is retrieved.

Finally, concealment of the waiting line itself may deter customers from balking. Amusement parks often process waiting customers by stages. The first stage is a line outside the concession entrance, the second is the wait in an inside vestibule area, and the final stage is the wait for an empty vehicle to convey a party through the attraction. Figure 11.11 shows a classification of queue configurations.

Queue Discipline

The *queue discipline* is a policy established by management to select the next customer from the queue for service. The most popular service discipline is the first-come, first-served (FCFS) rule. This represents an egalitarian approach to serving waiting customers, because all customers are treated alike. The rule is considered to be static because no information other than position in line is used to identify the next customer for service.

Dynamic queue disciplines are based on some attribute of the customer or status of the waiting line. For example, computer installations typically give first priority to waiting jobs with very short processing times. This shortest-processing-time (SPT) rule has the important feature of minimizing the average time that a customer spends in the system.[7] This rule is seldom used in its pure form, however, because jobs with long operation times would continually be set aside for more recent arrivals with shorter times. By selecting next the job with the shortest service time, excessive delays result for jobs with long service times. Typically, arrivals are placed in priority classes on the basis of some attribute, and the FCFS rule is used within each class. An example is the express check-out counter at supermarkets, where orders of 10 or fewer items

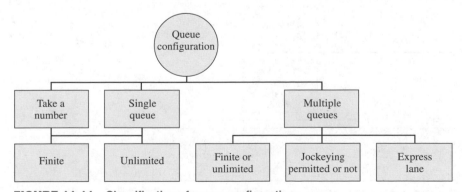

FIGURE 11.11 Classification of queue configurations.

are processed. This allows large stores to segment their customers and, thereby, compete with the neighborhood convenience stores that provide prompt service. In a medical setting, the procedure known as *triage* is used to give priority to those who would benefit most from immediate treatment.

The most responsive queue discipline is the preemptive priority rule. Under this rule, the service currently in process for a person is interrupted to serve a newly arrived customer with higher priority. This rule usually is reserved for emergency services, such as fire or ambulance service. An ambulance that is on the way to a hospital to pick up a patient for routine transfer will interrupt this mission to respond to a suspected-cardiac-arrest call.

The queue discipline can have an important effect on the likelihood that a waiting customer will renege. For this reason, information on the expected waiting time might be made available to the arriving customer, and updated periodically for each waiting customer. This information usually is available to computer-center users who are interested in the status of their jobs waiting in queue to be processed.

Some fast-food chains (e.g., Wendy's) take a more direct approach to avoid customer reneging. When long lines begin to form, a service person begins to take orders while customers are waiting in line. Taking this idea further is the concept of round-robin service as used by time-shared computer systems. In these systems, a customer is given partial service, and then the server moves on to the next waiting customer. Thus, customers alternate between waiting and being served. Figure 11.12 shows a classification of queue disciplines.

Service Process

The distribution of service times, arrangement of servers, management policies, and server behavior all contribute to service performance. Figure 11.13 contains histograms of several service time distributions in an outpatient clinic, and as the figure shows, the distribution of service times may be of any form. Conceivably, the service

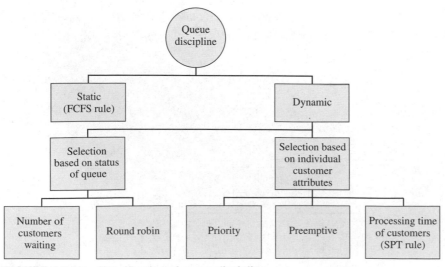

FIGURE 11.12 Classification of queue discipline.

FIGURE 11.13 Histograms of outpatient-clinic service times.
(*Source:* E. J. Rising, R. Baron, and B. Averill, "A Systems Analysis of a University Health-Service Outpatient Clinic." Reprinted with permission from *Operations Research,* vol. 21, no. 5, September–October 1973, p. 1039, Operations Society of America. No further reproduction permitted without the consent of the copyrighted owner.)

TABLE 11.1

SERVICE FACILITY ARRANGEMENTS

Service facility	Server arrangement
Parking lot	Self-service
Cafeteria	Servers in series
Toll booths	Servers in parallel
Supermarket	Self-serve, first stage; parallel servers, second stage
Hospital	Many service centers in parallel and series, not all used by each patient

time could be a constant, such as the time to process a car through an automated car wash; however, when the service is brief and simple to perform (e.g., preparing orders at a fast-food restaurant, collecting tolls at a bridge, or checking out items at a supermarket), the distribution of service times frequently is exponential (*see* Figure 11.4). The histogram for second-service times, Figure 11.13c, most closely approximates an exponential distribution. The second-service times represent those brief encounters in which, for example, the physician prescribes a medication or goes over your test results with you. The distribution of service times is a reflection of the variations in customer needs and server performances.

Table 11.1 illustrates the variety of service facility arrangements that are possible. With servers in parallel, management gains flexibility in meeting the variations in demand for service. Management can vary the service capacity effectively by opening and closing service lines to meet changes in demand. At a bank, additional teller windows are opened when the length of queues becomes excessive. Cross-training employees also adds to this flexibility. For example, at supermarkets, stockers often are used as cashiers when lines become long at the check-out counters. A final advantage of parallel servers is that they provide redundancy in case of equipment failures.

The behavior of service personnel toward customers is critical to the success of the organization. Under the pressure of long waiting lines, a server may speed up and spend less time with each customer; unfortunately, a gracious and leisurely manner then becomes curt and impersonal. Sustained pressure to hurry may increase the rate of customer processing, but it also sacrifices quality. This behavior on the part of a pressured server also can have a detrimental effect on other servers in the system. For example, a busy emergency telephone operator may dispatch yet another patrol car before properly screening the call for its critical nature; in this situation, the operator should have spent more time than usual to ensure that the limited resources of patrol cars were being dispatched to the most critical cases. Figure 11.14 suggests a classification of service processes.

SUMMARY

An understanding of the queuing phenomenon is necessary before creative approaches to the management of service systems can be considered. An appreciation of the behavioral implications of keeping customers waiting reveals that the perception of waiting often is more important than the actual delay. Waiting also has economic implications for both the service firm and its customers.

A schematic queuing model identified the essential features of queuing systems: calling population, arrival process, queue configuration, queue discipline, and service process. An understanding of each feature provides insights and identifies management options for improving customer service.

In Chapter 12, "Queuing Models and Capacity Planning," we will explore applications of several analytical queuing models that are useful for predicting customer waiting times. These models will suggest further insights that will be helpful in capacity planning and scheduling decisions.

FIGURE 11.14 Classification of service processes.

BOX 11.1

Service Benchmark
CONQUERING THOSE KILLER QUEUES

Five o'clock at a Grand Union market in Greenwich Village. One line swelled to five people, then fell back to three. Another hit four, whereupon the woman at the end maneuvered her cart to the next lane just in time to beat out a less dexterous man. Two express lanes stayed steady at two or three deep. It was pretty much what the computer said should happen. Supermarkets have found from research that customers will put up with a line of seven people before getting fed up enough to leave, so many use computers to schedule cashiers.

Grand Union tries to keep lines at no more than three. At its 300-store chain, it has determined three peak periods: 8:30 to 10 A.M., 11:30 to 1 P.M., and 4:30 to 7 P.M. To deal with these bursts, Grand Union, like some others in the business, relies heavily on part-timers. As many as 65 percent of its cashiers are elderly, housewives, or high school students who work four hours a day.

Additional help has come from electronic scanners, which Grand Union has installed in about half its stores. All large stores also have at least one express checkout. In May, Grand Union opened a 65,000-square-foot expanse in Kingston, N.Y. It boasts 20 checkouts, six of them express lanes. Two of them are a new concept being tested: the super-express lane, which takes six items or less and only cash. "Our goal is to get people through the cash registers in about five to seven minutes," the Grand Union spokesman said. "That's what we assume is tolerable."

One way to take some of the sting out of waiting is to entertain customers. Since 1959, the Manhattan Savings Bank has offered live entertainment during the frenzied noontime hours. In 13 branches, a pianist performs and one branch has an organ player (Willard Denton, the former Chemical chairman who dreamed up the idea, liked organs, though present management thinks they are a trifle loud for a bank). Occasionally, to make line-waiting even more wonderful, Manhattan Savings has scheduled events such as a fancy-cat exhibit, a purebred dog show, and a boat show.

Because of all this, Manhattan Savings believes customers endure long waits better than those who go to banks where the only music is the person in front of you grinding his teeth. "At very hectic times, we get very few complaints," said Jean Madsen, a senior vice president.

At hotels and office buildings, mirrors affixed to elevator doors make people less maniacal during waits. Instead of deciding whom to kill, they can comb their hair. A study done by Russel Ackoff showed that hotels that had mirrors received far less grumbling about elevator delays than ones without mirrors.

Just telling people how long they have to wait often cheers them up. Disneyland is sensitive to waiting, since the line for a hot attraction like Star Tours can run to 1,800 people. Like many amusement parks, Disney employs entertainment for waiters, but it is also big on feedback. At various spots along lines, signs give estimated delays from those points. Queuing experts say nothing is worse than the blind waiting familiar to people at bus stops, who don't know if the next bus is one minute or 15 minutes away. Disney's feedback permits parents to weigh odd options: Is it wiser to wait 25 minutes for Mr. Toad's Wild Ride or 30 minutes for Dumbo?

There are lots more tricks to be tried. The Port Authority of New York and New Jersey once figured out that the best way to move cars through the Holland Tunnel was to have stoplights space the cars into clusters of 14. Last year, when PATH train fares rose to $1 from 75 cents, the Port Authority found that lines moved quickest when quarters-only machines collected fares.

Peter Kolesar, a professor of operations research at the Columbia University Business School, thinks there ought to be more efforts to shift demand by altering pricing. Some rail lines, for example, charge less for off-peak trains and restaurants offer early-bird discounts.

During a whimsical moment, Dick Larson speculated that if the average American waited half an hour a day in one line or another, then the population expended 37 billion hours a year in lines. It strikes him, he said, that businesses ought to consider merchandising products to idle waiters to take their minds off pulling out their hair. "Like those flower peddlers outside tunnels and bridges," he said. "They're very shrewd."

Source: N. R. Kleinfield, "Conquering Those Killer Queues," *New York Times,* September 25, 1988, p. 1.

KEY TERMS AND DEFINITIONS

Balk occurs when an arriving customer sees a long queue and decides not to seek service.

Calling population source of service customers from a market area.

Exponential distribution the continuous distribution that describes the time between arrivals or service times.

Jockeying the practice of customers in a multiple-queue system leaving one queue to join another.

Poisson distribution the discrete distribution that describes random arrivals or departures from a busy server per time interval (e.g., hour).

Queue discipline a rule for selecting the next customer in line to be served (e.g., FCFS).

Reneging occurs when a customer in queue departs before obtaining service.

TOPICS FOR DISCUSSION

1. Suggest some strategies for controlling the variability in service times.
2. Suggest diversions that could make waiting less painful.
3. Select a bad and a good waiting experience, and contrast the situations with respect to the aesthetics of the surroundings, diversions, people waiting, and attitude of servers.
4. Suggest ways that service management can influence the arrival times of customers.
5. When the line becomes long at some fast-food restaurants, an employee will walk along the line taking orders. What are the benefits of this policy?

Thrifty Car Rental

Thrifty Car Rental has become one of the U.S. southwest's major rental agencies, even though it competes with several national firms. It definitely is the largest regional company, with offices and outlets in 19 cities and five states, and it primarily operates off-site from the airport terminals of those major cities. Thrifty's rental fleet consists almost entirely of fuel-efficient compact and subcompact automobiles. Its clientele utilizes these vehicles for tourism and business purposes, obtaining service at any location with or without prior arrangements. Thrifty does lose customers on occasion when the desired vehicles are unavailable at a given location, but this "stockout" situation occurs less than 10 percent of the time.

The service counter where customers are processed by Thrifty's personnel has a simple design. In the "old days," it varied only in the number of cubbyholes that keep various forms within easy reach of the servers. Today, the cubbies and forms have given way to computer terminals for more streamlined service. The number of servers varies with the size of the local market and the level of demand at specific times. In smaller markets, Thrifty may need three people at one time behind the counter, but in the largest markets, this number could be as high as eight when demand is heaviest. Usually, these peak-demand times reflect the airport's inbound-outbound flight schedule; as they occur, one or more attendants may deal exclusively with clients who have made prior arrangements to pick up a vehicle or with those who are returning vehicles. When this situation exists, these attendants hang appropriate messages above their chosen stations to indicate their special service functions to clientele. Because the speed of customer service is an important factor in maintaining Thrifty's competitive edge, management and service personnel have worked very hard to ensure that each client is processed without unnecessary delay.

Another important factor in Thrifty's competitive stance is the ability to turn incoming vehicles around and quickly prepare them for new clients. The following steps are necessary to process a vehicle from incoming delivery to outgoing delivery: (1) confirmation of odometer reading, (2) refueling and confirmation of fuel charge, (3) visual damage inspection, (4) priority assessment, (5) interior cleaning, (6) maintenance assessment, (7) maintenance and check-out, (8) exterior cleaning and polishing, (9) refueling and lot storage, and (10) delivery to customer.

When a client returns a vehicle to any location, one of Thrifty's crew will confirm the odometer reading, drive about 200 meters to the service lot, and confirm any fuel charge necessary to refill the car's tank. In some cases, the crew member may be able to process all this information on a hand-held computer, and the customer can be on her or his way without having to queue up in the office. In less streamlined locations, the crew member will relay the information to all attendants immediately so that the client may complete payment inside and be released as soon as possible. (If the crew member notices any interior or exterior damage to the vehicle, the attendant will notify the manager on duty; the client must clarify his or her responsibility in the circumstances and may be delayed while this is occurring.) After the damage-inspection step, the fleet supervisor assigns a priority status to incoming cars on the basis of the company's known (i.e., certain) demand and reserve policy (for walk-up clients): high-priority treatment for cars that are needed within the next six-hour period, and normal treatment for everything else. High-priority vehicles get preferential treatment for servicing.

After the vehicle's interior is cleaned thoroughly and sprayed with a mild air freshener, a mechanic examines the vehicle's maintenance record, gives the vehicle a test drive, and notes on a form any maintenance actions he or she deems necessary. Thrifty has certain policies covering periodic normal maintenance, such as oil and filter changes, tire rotation and balancing, lubrication, coolant replacement, and engine tune-ups. Major special maintenance actions, such as brake repair, transmission repair or adjustment, or air-conditioning and heating repair, are performed as needed.

Typically, a garage in Thrifty's system has a standard side-by-side, three-bay design: two bays always are used for normal maintenance, and the third is used for either normal or special maintenance. About 20 percent of the time is spent on special maintenance in this third bay. In general, Thrifty uses a team of five mechanics for its garages: one master mechanic (who is the garage manager), two journeymen mechanics, and two apprentices. The apprentices who are responsible for all normal maintenance tasks except the engine tune-up are stationed to service every vehicle in each outside bay, and alternate on vehicles in the middle bay. The journeyman mechanics are responsible for all other maintenance, and they also alternate on servicing vehicles in the middle bay.

After servicing, the vehicle is moved outside to the car wash area, and a team of two people washes, rinses, and buffs the exterior to ensure a good appearance. Because part of the rinse cycle contains a wax-type liquid compound, the vehicle usually does not require a time-consuming wax job. From this point, the vehicle's fuel tank again is topped off, and the vehicle is placed in the lot for storage. When the vehicle is called for by an attendant, a driver will take it to the rental area for the client.

Assignment   On the basis of your experience and the description of Thrifty's operations, describe the five essential features of the queuing systems at the customer counter, the garage, and the car wash.

Eye'll Be Seeing You[8]

Mrs. F arrives 15 minutes early for a 1:30 P.M. appointment with her Austin, Texas, ophthalmologist, Dr. X. The waiting room is empty and all the prior names on the sign-in sheet are crossed out. The receptionist looks up but does not acknowledge her presence. Mrs. F, unaware of the drama about to unfold, happily anticipates that she may not have to wait long beyond her scheduled time and settles into a chair to read the book she has brought with her. Large windows completely surround three sides of the waiting room. The receptionist sits behind a large opening in the remaining wall. Attractive artwork decorates the available wall space, and trailing plants rest on a shelf above the receptionist's opening. It is an appealing, comfortable waiting room.

At 1:25 P.M., another patient, Jack, arrives. Mrs. F knows his name must be Jack, because the receptionist addresses him by first name and the two share some light-hearted pleasantries. Jack takes a seat and starts looking through a magazine.

At 1:40 P.M., a very agitated woman enters and approaches the receptionist. She explains that she is very sorry she missed her 1 o'clock appointment and asks if it would be possible for Dr. X to see her anyway. The receptionist replies very coldly, "You're wrong. Your appointment was for 11."

"But I have 1 o'clock written down!" responds the patient, whose agitation now has changed to distress.

"Well, you're wrong."

"Oh dear, is there any way I can be worked in?" pleads the patient.

"We'll see. Sit down."

Mrs. F and her two "companions" wait until 1:50 P.M., when staff person number 2 (SP2) opens the door between the waiting room and the hallway leading to the various treatment areas. She summons Jack, and they laugh together as she leads him to the back. Mrs. F thinks to herself, "I was here first, but maybe he just arrived late for an earlier appointment," then goes back to her book. Five minutes later, Ms. SP2 appears at the door and summons the distressed patient. At this point, Mrs. F walks to the back area (she's a long-time patient and knows the territory), seeks out Ms. SP2, and says, "I wonder if I've been forgotten. I was here before those two people who have just been taken in ahead of me."

Ms. SP2 replies very brusquely, "Your file's been pulled. Go sit down."

Once again occupying an empty waiting room, Mrs. F returns to her reading. At 2:15 P.M. (no patient has yet emerged from a treatment area), Ms. SP2 finally summons Mrs. F and takes her to room 1, where she uses two instruments to make some preliminary measurements of Mrs. F's eyes. This is standard procedure in Dr. X's practice. Also standard is measuring the patient's present eyeglass prescription on a third instrument in room 1. Mrs. F extends her eyeglasses to Ms. SP2, but Ms. SP2 brushes past her and says curtly, "This way." Mrs. F then is led to a seat in the "dilating area," although no drops have been put in her eyes to start dilation.

The light in the dilating area is dimmed to protect dilating eyes, but Mrs. F is able to continue reading her book. No one else is seated in the dilating area. At 2:45 P.M., Ms. SP2 reappears, says, "this way" (a woman of very few words, our Ms. SP2), and marches off to examining room 3. "Wait here," she commands, leaving Mrs. F to seat herself in the darkened room.

Mrs. F can hear Dr. X and Jack laughing in the next examining room. At 2:55 P.M., she hears the two men say good-bye and leave the room. Mrs. F expects Dr. X to enter her room shortly. At 3:15 P.M., however, when he still has not appeared, she walks forward and interrupts Ms. SP2, the receptionist, the bookkeeper, and Ms. SP3, who are socializing. "Excuse me, but have I been forgotten?" she asks. Ms. SP2 turns her head from her companions and replies, "No, he's in the line. Go sit down."

Mrs. F wonders what that means but returns to her assigned place. She is here, after all, for a particular visual problem, not just for a routine check-up.

All good things, however, including Mrs. F's patience and endurance of abusive treatment, eventually end. At 4:00 P.M., Mrs. F does some marching of her own—to the front desk, where she announces to the assembled Mss. SP1 through SP4 that she has been waiting since 1:30 P.M., that she has been sitting in the back for 2½ hours, and that not once during that time has one member of the staff come to let her know what the problem is, how much longer she can expect to wait, or, indeed, that she has not been forgotten. She adds that she will wait no longer, and she feels forced to seek the services of a physician who chooses to deliver health care. There are several patients seated in the waiting room at the time.

There is an epilogue to this case. Mrs. F went directly home and wrote the following letter to Dr. X informing him of the treatment she had (not) received at his office and stating that she and her family would seek care elsewhere:

———————

———————

January 5, 1989

————————, M.D.
Austin, Texas
Dear Dr. ————:

It is with very real regret that I am transferring our eye care to another physician, and I want you to know the reason for my decision.

It is 4:22 P.M., and I have just returned home from a 1:30 P.M. appointment with(out) you. The appointment was made because I had received an adverse report from Seton Hospital's recent home vision test. I was kept waiting in the dilation area and in examining room 3 for more than two-and-one-half hours, during which time not one single member of your staff gave me any explanation for the delay or assured me I had not been forgotten. When I finally asked if I were forgotten, I was treated with a very bad attitude ("how dare I even ask!") and still was given no reason for the delay or any estimate of how much longer I would have to wait. Consequently, I left without seeing you.

As I stated above, I make this change with very real regret, because I value your expertise and the treatment you personally have given the four of us during these past many years. But I will not tolerate the callous treatment of your staff.

Sincerely yours,
Mrs. ——————

Questions

1. In this chapter, we referred to Maister's First and Second Laws of Service. How do they relate to this case?
2. What features of a good waiting process are evident in Dr. X's practice? List the shortcomings that you see.
3. Do you think that Mrs. F is typical of most people waiting for a service? How so? How not?
4. If Dr. X were concerned with keeping the F family as patients, how could he have responded to Mrs. F's letter? Write a letter on Dr. X's behalf to Mrs. F.
5. How could Dr. X prevent such incidents in the future?
6. List constructive ways in which customers can respond when services fall seriously short of their requirements or expectations.

Chapter 11 Supplement
Computer Simulation

Computer simulation provides management an experimental laboratory in which to study a model of a real system and to determine how the system might respond to changes in policies, resource levels, or customer demand. A system, for our purposes, is defined as a combination of elements that interact to accomplish an objective. Systems simulation can be used to answer "what-if" questions about existing or proposed systems. For example, what if another teller is added in a bank lobby? What if some tellers handle only depositors? What if an ATM is placed outside the lobby? The response of the system to these changes can be "observed" over an extended period by means of a simulation. Without having to change the real system, a simulation model generates estimates of system performance, such as average customer waiting time, for each scenario of interest. An animated simulation running on a personal computer allows decision makers to view the activity of the system (e.g., flow of customers) in accelerated time.

Service delivery systems are both dynamic and stochastic in their nature. A *dynamic* system is one that is influenced by actions over time. The queue behavior at an airline terminal, for example, is subject to arrival of passengers, staffing of attendants, and airline schedules. *Stochastic* refers to the underlying probabilistic nature of a system with events occurring at random from a probability distribution. Recall that the Poisson distribution of customer arrivals is a random process, because the arrival of any future customer is unpredictable even though the average number of arrivals during an hour may be known. Table 11.2 shows examples of simulation applications in services.

TABLE 11.2

EXAMPLES OF SIMULATION APPLICATIONS IN SERVICES

Application	Simulation objective
Staffing bank tellers	Consider the waiting time of customers when determining the number of tellers to staff a workshift
Emergency ambulance location	Analyze the response time implications of location options
Hospital patient flows	Develop procedures to manage patient flows and resource utilization
Order processing	Analyze order processing procedures to support just-in-time shipments
Aircraft maintenance	Determine the impact on downtime of preventive maintenance schedules
Hazardous waste handling	Analyze capacity of recycling facilities and transportation needs
Scheduling of police patrols	Investigate the impact of targeting crime areas on crime prevention
Project management	Determine the project completion time distribution when activity times are uncertain
Recreational facilities	Predict the impact upon facilities under different operating policies

PROCESS OF SYSTEMS SIMULATION

Basically, simulation is a tool for evaluating ideas. The process of developing a systems simulation is a substantial undertaking that has been made easier with the availability of modeling software such as ServiceModel, to be discussed later. The experimental nature of systems simulation is shown in Figure 11.15.

Simulation Methodology

Developing an accurate and concise problem definition is important because this activity involves the client in the process and facilitates implementation of the results. The statement of objectives follows naturally and provides a framework for the scope of the model and system performance measures. A problem, for example, might involve improving customer service in a bank lobby with the objective of reducing waiting times.

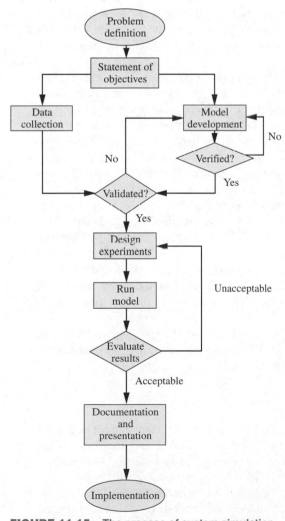

FIGURE 11.15 The process of system simulation.

Data collection and model development are often accomplished concurrently to save time. For ongoing systems, historical data such as the distribution of customer arrivals might be available or the data can be collected on-site. For systems that do not yet exist, data, of course, are not available, but other data may be available from similar systems. The model development begins with a conceptual abstraction of the system, perhaps in the form of a process flowchart. As event processing and relationships between events are defined, the conceptual model becomes a logic model.

After a preliminary model has been developed, it is checked or *verified* to ascertain that it works in the way intended. Verification is accomplished by running the model step by step to be sure that the intended logic is being followed. Another method is to perform a few hand calculations to see if they agree with the computer output. Most complex models will require some "debugging" to fix shortcomings in the logic.

Validation makes sure the model reflects the operations of the real system under study in sufficient detail to address the problem. Data collected on the real system are compared with results generated by the model. In the validation of an emergency ambulance model, for example, the historical distribution of response times is compared to the model's prediction of this distribution. The prediction of response times is important, because the study is interested in how different ambulance deployments would affect response times. The validation stage is also an excellent time to involve the client because of his or her familiarity with the system and the need to be convinced of the model's credibility.

Simulation experiments are then designed using the preliminary ideas about alternatives to be evaluated. Procedures and tests for analyzing and comparing alternatives are formulated. Studies involving stochastic elements need to be controlled to ensure that each experiment is subjected to the same randomness by designating a common stream of random numbers that produces an identical sequence of events. This control of inputs to the simulation will guarantee that the results observed are due to the "treatment" and not confounded by variations in the environment. The model is run for a certain number of replications and the warm-up time is considered before statistics are recorded. Results of the simulation run often suggest additional experiments. In the case of the emergency ambulance study, the identification of which hospitals would receive patients was found to be important, in addition to staffing levels, to match demand fluctuations during the day and night.

Each configuration of the model and its associated output results should be documented for future reference. Graphic presentation capabilities found in simulation software produce an effective visual representation of model results that can be self-explanatory.

Implementation of the results should be assured when the client is involved from the beginning and during the simulation process. Finally, a post-mortem of the simulation study could generate ideas for improving the next project.

Monte Carlo Simulation

Typically, systems simulation is used to analyze complex models that cannot be solved practically by means of analytical methods. These models often are stochastic to account for the realities of the system. Monte Carlo simulation is a method that enables us to model random variables with their associated probability distributions.

Monte Carlo simulation relies upon sampling values from the probability distributions associated with the random variables. Values of the random variables are selected at random from the appropriate distributions and then are used in the simulation. These observations of the random variables are made repetitively to imitate the behavior of the variables.

There are several methods that can be used to select observations of random variables from their probability distributions, but all are based on the use of *random numbers*. A random number (*RN*) is a special random variable that is uniformly distributed between 0 and 1. This means that all values in the interval [0, 1] have equal likelihood of being selected.

Computer-based simulations actually use *pseudo-random* numbers. These are values that behave like random numbers, although they are generated using a mathematical function. While pseudo-random numbers are not truly random, they have the appearance of being random. Pseudo-random numbers have the advantage of not requiring large amounts of file space in the computer. More important, they permit the exact replication of experimental conditions by allowing the same stream of numbers to be realized from a "seed" value. Table 11.3 gives a sample of some pseudo-random numbers generated by a computer.

Generating Random Variables

How are random numbers used to obtain observations of random variables? First we need to realize that random variables can be either *discrete* (e.g., number of customers arriving during an hour) or *continuous* (e.g., the time a customer spends being served). The process of generating observations in both cases makes use of the unique feature of any random variable—its cumulative distribution always sums to 1.0.

Discrete Random Variable   Consider the distribution of airline passengers waiting to board a rental car shuttle shown in the first column of Table 11.4. The third column of Table 11.4 contains the cumulative distribution of passengers, which is determined by the successive summing of the probabilities from top to bottom [e.g., $F(2) = p(1) + p(2) = 0.02 + 0.03 = 0.05$]. The cumulative distribution gives the likelihood that the number of passengers is fewer than or equal to the specific value. The probabilities must range from 0 to 1. Recall that the random number *RN* is uniformly distributed in the interval [0, 1]. This relationship between the cumulative distribution and *RN* is the basis for generating observations of random variables.

Now we can make some observations of passengers boarding the shuttle by using the cumulative distribution and the random numbers. This approach for generating observations of random variables, known as the *inverse transformation method,* is straightforward:

TABLE 11.3

UNIFORMLY DISTRIBUTED RANDOM NUMBERS [0, 1]

0.65481	0.32533	0.60527	0.73407
0.90124	0.04805	0.59466	0.41994
0.74350	0.68953	0.45973	0.25298
0.09893	0.02529	0.46670	0.20539
0.61196	0.99970	0.82512	0.61427
0.15474	0.74717	0.12472	0.58021
0.94557	0.10805	0.29529	0.19255
0.42481	0.77602	0.39333	0.33440
0.23523	0.32135	0.20106	0.57546
0.04493	0.45753	0.42941	0.21615

TABLE 11.4

PROBABILITY DISTRIBUTION OF PASSENGERS AND RANDOM-NUMBER ASSIGNMENT

Passengers x	Probability p(x)	Cumulative distribution F(x)	Random-number assignment
1	0.02	0.02	$0.00 \leq RN < 0.02$
2	0.03	0.05	$0.02 \leq RN < 0.05$
3	0.15	0.20	$0.05 \leq RN < 0.20$
4	0.30	0.50	$0.20 \leq RN < 0.50$
5	0.20	0.70	$0.50 \leq RN < 0.70$
6	0.15	0.85	$0.70 \leq RN < 0.85$
7	0.08	0.93	$0.85 \leq RN < 0.93$
8	0.05	0.98	$0.93 \leq RN < 0.98$
9	0.02	1.00	$0.98 \leq RN < 1.00$

1. Select any random number RN from Table 11.3.
2. Equate the cumulative distribution to the random number. In Table 11.4, for example, use the last column to find the interval within which RN lies.
3. Read across to the first column for the number of passengers boarding that equates the cumulative distribution to the random number. This value is the observation used in the simulation.

As an example, begin in the upper left corner of Table 11.3 and select the first random number as $RN = 0.65481$. Using Table 11.4, note that our RN falls into the range $[0.50 \leq RN < 0.70]$ and that this range is associated with 5 passengers. The process is illustrated graphically in Figure 11.16 where the cumulative distribution is displayed by a bar graph. Note that the portion of each bar exposed to the vertical axis is equal to the probability of the associated random variable. To make another observation, we move down the column in Table 11.3 to the next random number $RN = 0.90124$. Reading across Table 11.4 from the RN assignment range $[0.85 \leq RN < 0.93]$ we find 7 boarding passengers as the second observation. If we repeat this process many times, 2 percent of the observations of service time will be 1 passenger, 3 percent will be 2 passengers, and so on, mimicking the actual distribution.

Continuous Random Variable   The approach for selecting random variables from continuous distributions will equate RN to the cumulative distribution function and solve for the random variable value. We illustrate this approach for three common continuous random variable distributions: uniform, negative exponential, and normal.

1. Uniform Distribution   For a random variable uniformly distributed between values a and b ($b > a$), the function that returns a value x given RN is

$$x = a + RN(b - a) \tag{7}$$

Assume, for example, that the distribution of shuttle travel time from remote parking to the airport terminal is uniform over the range of 10 to 20 minutes. For this case, our random variable function is

$$x = 10 + RN(20 - 10)$$

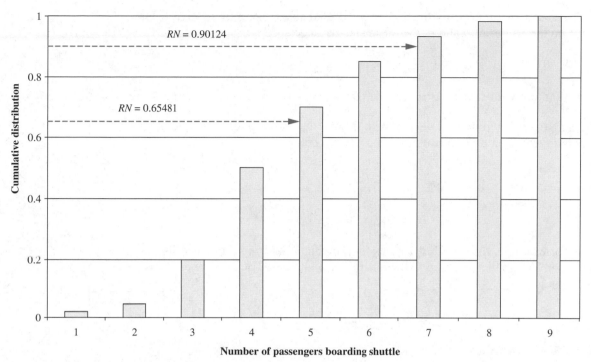

FIGURE 11.16   Cumulative distribution of passengers.

2. Negative Exponential Distribution   Recall that the cumulative distribution for the negative exponential distribution is given by equation (2) as:

$$F(x) = 1 - e^{-\lambda x}$$

Set $RN = F(x) = 1 - e^{-\lambda x}$ and solve to get $e^{-\lambda x} = 1 \quad RN$.

Taking logs to the base e and solving for x, we obtain the following function that returns a negative exponentially distributed random variable x given an RN:

$$x = -\frac{1}{\lambda}\log_e(1 - RN) \qquad \text{or, more simply,} \qquad x = -\frac{1}{\lambda}\log_e RN \qquad (8)$$

Assume, for example, that the distribution of customer arrivals at the shuttle stop is Poisson with a mean of 15 arrivals per hour. If we are interested in generating the time between arrivals, the negative exponential distribution is appropriate. Thus, the time between arrivals measured in hours is obtained from the random variable function:

$$x = -\frac{1}{15}\log_e RN$$

3. Normal Distribution   Because the normal distribution does not have a closed form expression for the cumulative distribution, we use a property of the Central Limit Theorem to devise a method for generating a standard normal deviate z with $\mu = 0$ and $\sigma = 1$. We begin with two considerations. First, recall from the Central Limit Theorem that the distribution of means from any source has a normal distribution. Second, the random number *RN* is uniformly distributed between 0 and 1. For a uniform distribution between the values of *a* and *b*, the mean and variance are

$$\mu = a + \frac{(b-a)}{2} \quad \text{and} \quad \sigma^2 = \frac{(b-a)^2}{12}$$

Thus, the random number *RN* has $\mu = \frac{1}{2}$ and $\sigma^2 = \frac{1}{12}$.

To generate a random normal deviate with mean 0 and variance of 1, therefore, we simply add together 12 *RNs* and subtract 6, as shown below:

$$\frac{x-\mu}{\sigma} = \sum_{i=1}^{12} RN_i - 6 \quad \text{or}$$

$$x = \mu + \sigma \left[\sum_{i=1}^{12} RN_i - 6 \right] \quad (9)$$

Suppose, for example, that the travel times for our shuttle have a normal distribution with mean of 15 minutes and standard deviation of 2 minutes. Then the random variable function is

$$x = 15 + 2 \left[\sum_{i=1}^{12} RN_i - 6 \right]$$

Discrete Event Simulation

A discrete-event simulation is driven by events that occur at certain points in time such as the arrival of a customer or completion of a service. When an event occurs, the state of the system changes. A customer arrival increases the number of customers in the system, for example, while a customer departure (i.e., service completion) reduces the number in the system. The computer maintains a timing device known as the simulation clock, which advances with each event taking place. After each event occurs, descriptors of the state of the system are recorded.

Figure 11.17 shows the flowchart of a discrete-event simulation for an airline ticket counter. First, the arrival time of the next customer is generated based upon an interarrival time distribution using the inverse transformation method. The simulation clock that begins at time 0 is set equal to the next chronological event time. If the next event is an arrival, then the consumer will either enter service or wait in line, depending upon the status of the server. If the next event is a departure (i.e., service completion), then either another consumer will enter service or the server will become idle, depending on the status of the waiting line. The state of the system is updated in response to the event, and the clock time is compared with a prespecified maximum time. If the clock time is greater than or equal to the maximum time, then summary statistics describing the system are calculated and printed, and the simulation is stopped. Otherwise, the clock moves to the next event time.

Example 11.1: Airline Ticket Counter Simulation

A discrete-event simulation will be used to observe the activities at an airline ticket counter. The system has a single ticket agent and customers are served on a first-come, first-served basis. In this simulation we are concerned with the number of customers waiting, their waiting time, and the status of the ticket agent (i.e., busy or idle).

Table 11.5 gives the service times and interarrival times (i.e., time between arrivals) of the first 10 customers. The service times and interarrival times were generated from appropriate probability distributions using the inverse transformation method.

The simulation clock begins at time 0. Table 11.6 gives the times that each customer arrives, enters service, and departs service. For example, the first customer arrives at

FIGURE 11.17 Flowchart of airline ticket counter discrete-event simulation.

time 5, immediately enters service, and departs at time 9. Customer 4, however, arrives at time 18 and finds the server busy. This customer enters service at time 19 and departs at time 23. The total time waiting in line for the 10 customers is 8 minutes. This gives an average waiting time of 0.8 minute per customer. We see that the ticket agent was idle for a total of 7 minutes out of the 50-minute simulation, or 14 percent idleness.

SERVICEMODEL SIMULATION SOFTWARE[9]

The Windows operating environment has allowed the development of point-and-click, menu-driven, nonprogramming, graphic simulation models. Using a personal

TABLE 11.5

INTERARRIVAL TIMES AND SERVICE TIMES FOR FIRST 10 CUSTOMERS

Customer	Interarrival time, min.	Service time, min.
1	5	4
2	4	3
3	4	6
4	5	4
5	3	2
6	4	5
7	5	4
8	5	6
9	4	4
10	3	5

computer, complex systems can be simulated with graphic animation of the process activity. The layout of a benefits planning office is shown in Figure 11.8. This model can be found in the Training file of ServiceModel and is used in a tutorial for learning how to build animated simulation models.

Models are defined by completing the necessary modules contained in the Build menu. These modules consist of edit tables and dialog boxes used to structure the parameters that are required for the model. The Build menu contains eleven elements, but only Locations, Entities, Processing, and Arrivals are mandatory. The office layout shown in Figure 11.18 is used to illustrate the elements that follow.

Locations   Fixed points, such as a reception desk or couches in the waiting area, are defined as locations. The number of entities that can be at the location at one time is defined as its capacity. The queue discipline for waiting areas, such as FCFS, is specified here. Graphics used to represent locations may be sized and positioned on the layout display (e.g., note arrangement of desks and chairs).

Entities   Customers, paperwork, and anything else that requires system resources and that is processed through the system are entities. Each entity (e.g., client) may have several graphic icons to represent different states of processing such as sitting while waiting or standing while walking. A speed is defined for people moving through the process.

TABLE 11.6

SIMULATION OF FIRST 10 CUSTOMERS
(Time in Minutes)

Customer	Arrival time	Time service begins	Time service ends	Time in line	Time in system	Time agent idle
1	5	5	9	0	4	5
2	9	9	12	0	3	0
3	13	13	19	0	6	1
4	18	19	23	1	5	0
5	21	23	25	2	4	0
6	25	25	30	0	5	0
7	30	30	34	0	4	0
8	35	35	41	0	6	1
9	39	41	45	2	6	0
10	42	45	50	3	8	0

FIGURE 11.18 Layout of benefits planning office.

Path Networks The paths from location to location are defined as path networks (i.e., lines on the layout between locations). Self-transporting entities such as clients follow these paths on their own. Travel may be defined in terms of time or by inclusion of speed and distance parameters. Several entities and resources can share a common path network.

Resources A delivery vehicle that is required to perform some action but does not remain at a fixed location, for example, is defined as a resource. A receptionist is considered a resource because he or she accompanies walk-in clients to the appropriate office. Resources move along predetermined paths. Alternate graphics can be used to represent the state of a resource, such as sitting or walking.

Processing Processing is defined for each type of entity at each location where it either undergoes some action or waits to be processed. Logic is provided to define the operations performed, and includes time distribution and onward routing with the name of the next location to which the entity will travel. Upon entering, entities go to the reception desk; sit in the waiting area; and then move either to the auditor, the loan office, or the service office, and finally depart.

Arrivals Arrivals (e.g., new clients appearing at the Enter point) are the introduction of entities into the system. The interarrival time is usually defined as a negative exponential probability distribution. A schedule of arrivals, however, could be read in from an external spreadsheet. Cyclical arrivals, such as the hourly variation in customer arrivals, can be defined using an arrival cycle.

Shifts   Resources and locations may be assigned to specific work shift schedules, and breaks during the shift also can be specified.

More Elements   Optional elements, such as variables, attributes, and arrival cycles, are found here.

General Information   For animation purposes, such as the movement of customers in the graphic layout, default settings for time and distance units are assigned. Several libraries containing graphic icons (e.g., desks, chairs, and people) are provided. Notes about the particular simulation, such as scenario parameters, revision date, and other relevant details, can be entered in this module.

Costs   Objects such as locations, resources, and entities are assigned an operating rate per time unit.

Background Graphics   In order to create a more realistic animation, background designs or drawings of the facility can be imported and are assigned in front of or behind the grid. In Figure 11.18, we see the floor layout for the benefits planning office as the background graphic.

The ServiceModel tool bar also includes the following modules: View, to show model features; Simulation, where the model is run; Output, to view simulation run statistics; Tools, where Stat:Fit is found; and Help, to use when trouble arises.

SOLVED PROBLEMS

1. Monte Carlo Simulation

Problem Statement

A textbook publishing company is considering the release of three books next year. Because of a cash flow problem, the company is interested in predicting the expected revenue and its range from sales of these books. Using the Monte Carlo method, simulate 10 realizations of the first year's sales experience.

Book	Expected sales in first year	Selling price
A	200	$25
B	1,000	10
C	3,000	5

Deviation from expected sales, %	Probability
80	0.1
90	0.2
100	0.4
110	0.2
120	0.1

Solution

Step 1: Prepare a cumulative distribution for sales deviations and random number assignment table.

Sales deviation, %	Probability	Cumulative probability	Random number assignment
80	.1	.1	$0 \leq RN < .1$
90	.2	.3	$.1 \leq RN < .3$
100	.4	.7	$.3 \leq RN < .7$
110	.2	.9	$.7 \leq RN < .9$
120	.1	1.0	$.9 \leq RN < 1.0$

Step 2: Prepare a Monte Carlo simulation table with RN selected from Appendix B beginning at the top of the first column and working down in sequence.

Sales revenue realization	RN	Book A $5,000 expected	RN	Book B $10,000 expected	RN	Book C $15,000 expected	Total sales revenue $
1	.06785	4,000	.81075	11,000	.98544	18,000	33,000
2	.31479	5,000	.12484	9,000	.23882	13,500	27,500
3	.23897	4,500	.40374	10,000	.73622	16,500	31,000
4	.36952	5,000	.14510	9,000	.12719	13,500	27,500
5	.99407	6,000	.32694	10,000	.42780	15,000	31,000
6	.00633	4,000	.38490	10,000	.22363	13,500	27,500
7	.54105	5,000	.31786	10,000	.47556	15,000	30,000
8	.70850	5,500	.64791	10,000	.21424	13,500	29,000
9	.77524	5,500	.39867	10,000	.87641	16,500	32,000
10	.51653	5,000	.75057	11,000	.88287	16,500	32,500

The expected sales revenue is $30,100, with a range of $27,500 to $33,000.

2. Discrete Event Simulation

Problem Statement

Dr. Swift, a veterinarian, has the following appointment schedule for Saturday morning:

Patient	Appointment time	Expected duration, min.
A	9:00	10
B	9:15	20
C	9:30	30
D	10:00	10
E	10:15	30
Γ	10:45	20
G	11:00	10
H	11:15	30

His secretary has researched past records and determined the following distributions:

Arrival time	Frequency	Appointment duration, % of expected time	Frequency
20 min. early	10	80	5
10 min. early	20	90	25
Just on time	50	100	30
10 min. late	10	110	25
Not show up (NS)	10	120	15
	100		100

Two days ago, Dr. Swift received a telegram from New York advising him that his mother is seriously ill. He is scheduled to fly east at 2 P.M. Saturday. In order to get to the airport on time, he knows that he must leave the office by noon. Develop a discrete event simulation model to assist Dr. Swift in determining the probability of completing his morning appointments in time to make the flight. Test the model with the simulation of one Saturday's experience.

Solution

Step 1: Prepare a simulation flowchart.

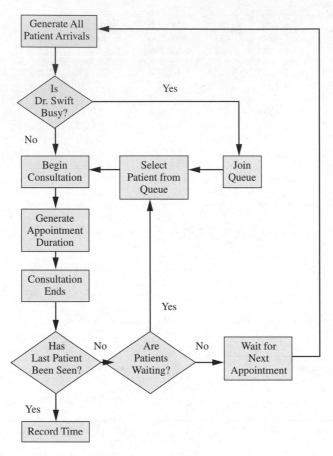

Step 2: Prepare random number assignment tables.

Patient arrival	Cumulative probability	*RN* assignment	Appointment duration %	Cumulative probability	*RN* Assignment
−20	.1	$.0 \leq RN < .1$	80	.05	$.00 \leq RN < .05$
−10	.3	$.1 \leq RN < .3$	90	.30	$.05 \leq RN < .30$
On time	.8	$.3 \leq RN < .8$	100	.60	$.30 \leq RN < .60$
+10	.9	$.8 \leq RN < .9$	110	.85	$.60 \leq RN < .85$
NS	1.0	$.9 \leq RN < 1.0$	120	1.00	$.85 \leq RN < 1.0$

Step 3: Prepare realization table and conduct simulation.

Patient	*RN*	Arrival time	*RN*	Appointment duration	Time begins	Time ends
A	.06785	8:40	.73622	11	8:40	8:51
B	.81075	9:25	.36952	20	9:25	9:45
C	.98544	NS	.14510	27	—	—
D	.31479	10:00	.12719	9	10:00	10:09
E	.12484	10:05	.99407	36	10:09	10:45
F	.23882	10:35	.32694	20	10:45	11:05
G	.23897	10:50	.42780	10	11:05	11:15
H	.40374	11:15	.00633	24	11:15	11:39

For this realization of the Saturday morning, Dr. Swift can leave the office at 11:39. Many more replications, however, would be needed to obtain a distribution of office departures in order to assess the probability of leaving by noon.

EXERCISES

11.1. You have been asked by a retail association to develop an inventory control program for use on a PC. The program development requires the completion of the following three activities in sequence. You are concerned about the likelihood of finishing the project in the promised 10 days.

Activity	Description	Expected time, days	Deviation from expected time, days	Probability
A	Write program	5	+2	0.1
B	Debug program	2	+1	0.2
C	Write user manual	3	0	0.3
			−1	0.4

Using the Monte Carlo method, simulate 10 program development experiences. On the basis of your simulation results, what is the probability of finishing the project in 10 days?

11.2. Constructing a distribution of demand during reorder lead time is complicated if the lead time itself is variable. Consider the following distribution for a reorder point inventory system.

Daily demand		Lead time	
Demand	Probability	Days	Probability
0	0.1	1	0.1
1	0.2	2	0.5
2	0.3	3	0.4
3	0.4		

a. What is the range of possible demands during the variable lead time?

b. Using the Monte Carlo method and random numbers from Appendix B, simulate 10 demands during lead time that could be used to form a histogram.

11.3. The Dell Factory Outlet has the following daily demand distribution for laptop computer carrying cases.

Demand	Probability
0	.1
1	.2
2	.3
3	.25
4	.15
5 or more	0

Simulate 5 days of retail sales using the following inventory policy. If the ending inventory of cases is 0 or 1, order enough units such that the starting inventory on the next day will be 5 cases. Ordered units arrive the next morning and are stocked before the store opens for business. If a stock-out occurs, the sale is lost.

The cost structure is as follows:

Storage cost = $0.10/unit/day

Shortage cost = $5/unit

Order cost = $3/order

Fill in the following simulation table using the random numbers provided.

Day	Starting inventory	Random number	Daily demand	Ending inventory	Storage cost	Shortage cost	Order cost	Total daily cost
1	4	.153						
2		.379						
3		.821						
4		.962						
5		.731						

11.4. The Coast Guard maintains a lighted buoy in the harbor entrance to warn ships of a dangerous reef. The flashing beacon contains two high-intensity quartz halogen bulbs. The supplier has provided the following data on bulb life:

Life, months	Probability
1	0.05
2	0.15
3	0.20
4	0.30
5	0.20
6	0.10

The estimated cost of dispatching a motor launch with a crew to the buoy to remove and replace the weatherproof cover over the bulbs is $50, and the bulbs cost $10 each. The time involved in replacing a bulb is negligible. Coast Guard regulations require that both bulbs work all the time.

a. Develop a Monte Carlo simulation model that will help the Coast Guard to decide between the following replacement policies: (1) Replace only the bulb that burns out or (2) replace both bulbs when one burns out.

b. Simulate five years of activity using the table of random numbers in Appendix B. Discuss some questions of experimental design that this problem poses.

c. Can you think of other bulb replacement policies to test?

11.5. The project network for building a garage is shown in Figure 11.19 and includes data on activity times and their deviations.

a. Develop a Monte Carlo simulation model that can be used to generate a distribution of project completion times.

b. Simulate 5 project completion experiences using Appendix B. What is the expected project duration time?

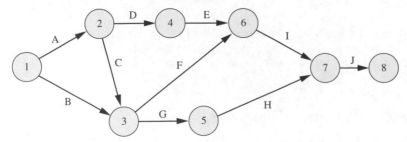

FIGURE 11.19 Project network for new computer installation.

Activity	Expected time, days	Deviation from expected activity time, days	Probability
A	3	+2	0.2
B	5	+1	0.3
C	2	0	0.4
D	4	−1	0.1
E	3		
F	4		
G	2		
H	4		
I	3		
J	2		

11.6. Consider the travel network shown in Figure 11.20 in which the probabilities of selecting a route from each node are shown in parentheses.
   a. Develop a Monte Carlo simulation model to determine the expected trip time from node 1 to node 7.
   b. Simulate 10 trips and calculate the expected trip time.
11.7. The number of fires occurring during a 24-hour day follows a Poisson distribution with a mean of 4 fires per day as shown in the accompanying table. In examining past records, the fire chief finds that 75 percent of all fires require only one truck and the amount of time required to extinguish a fire is normally distributed with a mean of 3 hours and a standard deviation of 0.5 hour. The other 25 percent of reported fires required 2 trucks and the time to put them out is normally distributed with a mean of 4 hours and a standard deviation of 1 hour. Assume the district has 10 trucks and use a simulation sample of 10 days to determine the average daily utilization of trucks.

Fires per day	0	1	2	3	4	5	6	7	8	9
Probability	.02	.07	.15	.20	.20	.16	.10	.06	.03	.01

11.8. Electronic Car-diogram (ECG), a firm specializing in the diagnosis of automobile engine problems, is planning to open a new service center with two diagnostic bays. Based on the experience at other ECG facilities, it has been found that the diagnostic service time is a uniform distribution between 40 and 60 minutes. Based on its historical experience and the demographics of the new location, ECG believes the average time between customer arrivals will be 60 minutes with a negative exponential distribution. Simulate eight hours (480 minutes) of operations with a two-bay facility, recording the waiting time of customers. ECG expects customers will wait while their cars are being diagnosed and plans to promote an unconditional guarantee that customers who wait more than 60 minutes will receive a gift certificate. From your simulation, how many gift certificates are given out per day?

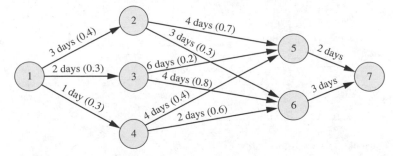

FIGURE 11.20 Travel network.

CASE

Pronto Pizza

Pronto Pizza is a delivery-only pizza service that promises delivery within 40 minutes of receiving a call for an order or the customer gets $2 off the price. Pronto employs a single pizza maker, paid $10 per hour, who can make, on the average, one pizza every three minutes. This service time has a negative exponential distribution. Pizzas are placed in a large oven with a capacity for 10 pizzas to bake for approximately 12 minutes. The one-way travel time to deliver a pizza in the market area averages 10 minutes, with negative exponential distribution. Calls for pizza average one every five minutes, with negative exponential distribution. Drivers who use their own cars are paid $8 per hour to deliver pizzas to one customer at a time.

Assignments

1. Draw a process flow diagram and identify the bottleneck operation.
2. Use the ServiceModel computer simulation software and the Pronto.pkg file to determine the number of drivers that minimizes the total cost of salaries and guarantee discounts.
3. Based on your simulation recommended staffing level, what is the probability of paying off on the guarantee?
4. What do you think of this service guarantee policy?
5. What other design or operating suggestions could improve Pronto Pizza's performance and customer service?

CASE

Renaissance Clinic (A)

On a hillside in Rollingwood, a community just southwest of Austin, Texas, the Renaissance Clinic provides dedicated obstetric and gynecological services. The medical treatment at this facility is wrapped in an exclusive-feeling physical environment that is distinctly unique in Austin. The practice of Dr. Margaret Thompson is one of supporting care within an efficient and friendly facility. Attention to the ambiance is reflected in a brightly colored interior that makes patients feel better just entering. A relaxed atmosphere prevails in the birthing rooms that are large enough to hold several family members in a homelike atmosphere of wood floors and quilts on the beds. The practice is intimate—only a receptionist and a nurse clinician assist Dr. Thompson. The receptionist has been trained to screen patients and directs them either to the nurse clinician waiting area or to Dr. Thompson's waiting area. Some patients, following a preliminary examination by the nurse clinician, will be asked to join the queue to see Dr. Thompson. Figure 11.21 shows the flow of patients during routine office visits. The arrival rate per hour was found to be Poisson distributed [E(interarrival time in minutes)], and the service times in minutes were uniformly distributed [U(range)] for the receptionist and normally distributed [N(μ, σ)] for the nurse and physician. The data in Table 11.7 were collected over several days of typical activity.

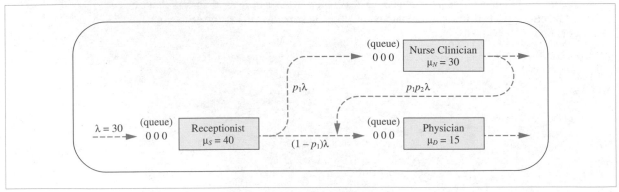

FIGURE 11.21 Flow of patients for routine office visits.

TABLE 11.7

PROCESSING DATA AT RENAISSANCE CLINIC

Model Parameter	Description	Expectations
λ	Arrival rate of patients	30 per hour or E(2)
p_1	Fraction of patients who go to nurse clinician	2/3
p_2	Fraction of nurse clinician patients who also see physician	0.15
μ_S	Service rate of receptionist	40 per hour or U(1,2)
μ_N	Service rate of nurse clinician	30 per hour or N(2,1)
μ_D	Service rate of physician	15 per hour or N(4,2)

Assignments

1. Assume the waiting lines at the receptionist, the nurse clinician, and the doctor are managed independently with a FCFS priority. Model this system using Service-Model to determine the utilization of each resource (receptionist, nurse clinician, and physician) and the distribution of time in the system for an arriving patient. Begin by selecting the Build menu - Background Graphic - Behind Grid. Then select the Edit menu - Import Graphic - Pracmod. This will give you an office floor plan on which you can arrange furniture.

2. If you could hire one more person to augment the staff, what position would be your choice (receptionist, nurse clinician, or physician)? How would the clinic performance measures that you determined above change?

3. What further advice would you give Dr. Thompson on the operation of her clinic?

SELECTED BIBLIOGRAPHY

BATEMAN, R. E., R. G. BOWDEN, T. J. GOGG, C. R. HARRELL, and J. R. A. MOTT: *System Improvement Using Simulation,* 5th ed., PROMODEL Corporation, Orem, Utah, 1997.

BRENNAN, JOHN F., BRUCE L. GOLDEN, and HAROLD K. RAPPOPORT: "Go with the Flow: Improving Red Cross Bloodmobiles Using Simulation Analysis, " *Interfaces,* vol. 22, no. 5, September–October 1992, pp 1–13.

DAVIS, MARK M., and JANELLE HEINEKE: "How Disconfirmation, Perception and Actual Waiting Times Impact Customer Satisfaction," *International Journal of Service Industry Management,* vol. 9, no. 1, 1998, pp. 64–73.

DAVIS, MARK M., and MICHAEL J. MAGGARD: "An Analysis of Customer Satisfaction with Waiting Times in a Two-Stage Service Process," *Journal of Operations Management,* vol. 9, no. 3, August 1990, pp. 324–334.

DECISION SCIENCE, INC., *SimRunner: Powerful Simulation Made Easy,* Version 1.0, Ypsilanti, Mich., 1996.

DURRANDE-MOREAU, AGNES: "Waiting for Service: Ten Years of Empirical Research," *International Journal of Service Industry Management,* vol. 10, no. 2, 1999, pp. 171–189.

———, and JEAN-CLAUDE USUNIER: "Time Styles and the Waiting Experience: An Exploratory Study," *Journal of Service Research,* vol. 2, no. 2, November 1999, pp. 173–186.

JONES, PETER, and EMMA PEPPIATT: "Managing Perceptions of Waiting Times in Service Queues," *International Journal of Service Industry Management,* vol. 7, no. 5, 1996, pp. 47–61.

KATZ, K. L., B. M. LARSON, and R. C. LARSON: "Prescription for the Waiting-in-Line Blues: Entertain, Enlighten, and Engage," *Sloan Management Review,* vol. 32, no. 2, Winter 1991, pp. 44–53.

LARSON, RICHARD C.: "Perspectives on Queues: Social Justice and the Psychology of Queuing," *Operations Research,* vol. 35, no. 6, November–December 1987, pp. 895–905.

———: "There's More to a Line Than Its Wait," *Technology Review,* July 1988, pp. 61–67.

LAW, A. M., and KELTON, W. D., *Simulation Modeling and Analysis,* McGraw-Hill, New York, 1991.

MAISTER, D. H.: "The Psychology of Waiting Lines," in J. A. Czepiel, M. R. Solomon, and C. F. Surprenant (eds.), *The Service Encounter,* Lexington Press, Lexington, Mass., 1985, pp. 113–123.

PROMODEL CORPORATION: *ServiceModel,* Version 4.2, Orem, UT, 1999.

TANSIK, DAVID A., and ROBERT ROUTHIEAUZ: "Customer Stress-Relaxation: The Impact of Music in a Hospital Waiting Room," *International Journal of Service Industry Management,* vol. 10, no. 1, 1999, pp. 68–81.

TAYLOR, SHIRLEY.: "Waiting for Service: The Relationship between Delays and Evaluations of Services," *Journal of Marketing,* vol. 58, April 1994, pp. 56–69.

ENDNOTES

1. Amanda Bennett, "Their Business Is on the Line," *The Wall Street Journal,* December 7, 1990, p. B1. Reprinted by permission of *The Wall Street Journal,* © 1989, Dow Jones & Company, Inc. All Rights Reserved Worldwide.
2. Hedrick Smith, *The Russians,* Quadrangle Press, New York, 1975, pp. 64–65.
3. Ibid., p. 67.
4. Adapted from David H. Maister, "The Psychology of Waiting Lines," in J. A. Czepiel, M. R. Solomon, and C. F. Surprenant (eds.), *The Service Encounter,* Lexington Press, Lexington, Mass., 1985, chap. 8, pp. 113–123.
5. For a discussion of slips and skips, see Richard C. Larson, "Perspectives on Queues: Social Justice and the Psychology of Queuing," *Operations Research,* vol. 35, no. 6, November–December 1987, pp. 895–905.
6. Yoram Barzel, "A Theory of Rationing by Waiting," *Journal of Law and Economics,* vol. 17, no. 1, April 1974, p. 74.
7. R. W. Conway, W. L. Maxwell, and L. W. Miller, *Theory of Scheduling,* Addison-Wesley Publishing Company, Reading, Mass., 1967, p. 27.
8. This case, sad to say, is true in its entirety. The names of the physician and his staff have been omitted, not to protect them but because this kind of treatment of patients is so pervasive in the American health care system that it serves no purpose to identify them. We offer the case for two reasons: first, because it is very instructive regarding important material in this chapter, and second, because it points out that customers and providers must work together in our evolving service society. Service providers must be sensitive to the needs of customers and customers must demand and reward good service.
9. From R. E. Bateman, R. G. Bowden, T. J. Gogg, C. R. Harrell, and J. R. A. Mott, *System Improvement Using Simulation,* 5th ed., PROMODEL Corporation, Orem, Utah, 1997.

CHAPTER TWELVE

Queuing Models and Capacity Planning

Learning Objectives

After completing this chapter, you should be able to:

1. Discuss the strategic role of capacity planning.
2. Describe a queuing model using the *A/B/C* notation.
3. Use queuing models to calculate system performance measures.
4. Describe the relationships between queuing system characteristics.
5. Use queuing models and various decision criteria for capacity planning.

The capacity planning decision involves a trade-off between the cost of providing a service and the cost or inconvenience of customer waiting. The cost of service capacity is determined by the number of servers on duty, whereas customer inconvenience is measured by waiting time. Figure 12.1 illustrates this trade-off, assuming that a monetary cost can be attributed to waiting. Increasing service capacity typically results in lower waiting costs and higher service costs. If the combined cost to the firm constitutes our planning criterion, then an optimal service capacity minimizes these service-versus-waiting costs.

Xerox Corporation faced precisely this dilemma when it introduced the Model 9200 Duplicating System.[1] Its existing service and maintenance operation, which consisted of individual technical representatives serving individual territories, no longer was able to provide the level of service that gave the company its decisive competitive advantage. Compromising the level of service meant that customers would have to wait, which would translate in this case into lost revenue for the customer (and, indirectly, for Xerox). Consequently, Xerox performed a queuing analysis to determine the best

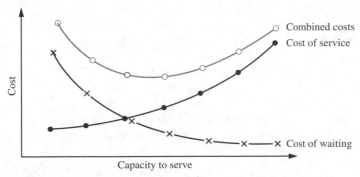

FIGURE 12.1 Economic trade-off in capacity planning.

333

way to resolve its dilemma. Initial constraints, primarily involving human factors such as some loss of autonomy by the technical representatives and perceptions by the customer of less "personal" attention, led the company to consider establishing miniteams of service people who could provide faster service for more customers.

The cost to the Xerox customer was straightforward, because the Model 9200 was being used to replace a printer's previous offset system. Thus, a Xerox machine that was "down" meant lost income. The problem Xerox faced at this point was to determine the appropriate number of members to assign to each team. The company used queuing analysis to minimize both the customer waiting cost and the Xerox service cost, and they arrived at an optimum result of three representatives per team. The monetary cost of delaying a customer usually is more difficult to calculate than in this example, and it sometimes is impossible to determine. In a hospital, the cost of keeping a surgical team waiting for a pathologist's report could be the combined salaries of the team members plus the operating room cost. The cost of keeping a patient waiting in the reception room for a physician, however, is not easily calculated. Further, as noted in Chapter 11, "Managing Waiting Lines," circumstances affect the customer's perception of waiting.

The trade-off between customer waiting and service capacity can be seen daily. For example, an emergency ambulance seldom is busy more than 30 percent of the time. Such low utilization is required in exchange for the ability to provide assistance on a moment's notice. Excess ambulance capacity is necessary, because the implicit cost of waiting for this particular service may be exorbitant in terms of human lives. The usual scene at a post office, however, is lines of impatient people waiting for service. Here, a judgment has been made that the implicit cost of waiting is not critical—and certainly not life-threatening—and besides, customers have few alternatives. Another result of this strategy is harried postal employees, who may not be able to provide the best possible service under the pressure of demanding customers! The desire of customers to avoid waiting has not been lost on the Travis County, Texas, Tax Collector/Assessor's office; for an extra dollar, an automobile owner has the option of renewing his or her annual auto registration by mail, thus avoiding the necessity of appearing in person.

CHAPTER PREVIEW

The chapter begins with a discussion of the strategic role of capacity planning for service firms. The lack of control over customer demands for service and the presence of the customer in the process complicate capacity planning. For services, it is necessary to predict the degree of customer waiting associated with different levels of capacity. This chapter presents a number of analytical queuing models for use in making these waiting time predictions. The models are analytical and equations have been derived for each case. Given a minimal amount of data—in particular, the mean arrival rate and the mean service rate—the equations can generate characteristics of the system, such as the average time a customer should expect to wait. From these calculations, capacity planning decisions, such as determining the size of a parking lot, can be made, using different criteria. In addition, the queuing models help explain the queuing phenomenon. The models, for example, can predict the results of adding servers to a multiple-server system, as shown in the Xerox case, or they can show the effect of reducing service time variation on waiting time.

CAPACITY PLANNING

Capacity is the ability to deliver service over a particular time period. For services, the time horizon can vary from decades (e.g., the decision to build a resort hotel) to hours (e.g., staffing a fast-food restaurant during the lunch hour). Capacity is determined by the resources available to the organization in the form of facilities, equipment, and labor. Capacity planning is the process of determining the types and amounts of resources that are required to implement an organization's strategic business plan. The objective of strategic capacity planning is to determine the appropriate level of service capacity by specifying the proper mix of facilities, equipment, and labor that is required to meet anticipated demand.

Capacity planning is a challenge for service firms because of the open system nature of service operations and, thus, the inability to create a steady flow of activity to use capacity fully. For service systems idle capacity (e.g., service providers waiting for customers) is always a reality. As noted in Chapter 11, customer arrivals can fluctuate from one minute to the next (e.g., a call center) and the time customers spend being served also varies (e.g., diners at a gourmet restaurant). Because of the inability of services to control the demands placed upon them, capacity is usually measured in terms of inputs (e.g., number of hotel rooms) rather than outputs (e.g., guest nights).

The capacity decision is further complicated because customers are participants in the service process and the level of congestion has an impact on the quality of the service experience. The recent increase in customer complaints about flying experiences is directly related to the success of airlines in filling their planes to capacity (e.g., consider your anxiety hoping no one will sit in the center seat next to you). On the other hand, however, people seek out the excitement of a crowded discotheque.

Strategic Role of Capacity Decisions

Capacity decisions in services have strategic importance based on the time horizon in question. The decision to build a luxury hotel in a city can be a preemptive strike against a competitor, because the market demand for guests is so limited that only one hotel can survive. This occurs because capacity of fixed facilities comes in economically feasible sizes (e.g., a 500-room luxury hotel versus a 100-room budget motel). Thus, if a luxury hotel can be feasible with a 60 percent average occupancy, a market of 300 guest nights only will support one hotel. For this reason we seldom find both a Ritz Carlton and a Four Seasons hotel in midsized cities.

Failure to plan for short-term capacity needs, such as staffing for the lunch hour, can generate customers for the competition. This is particularly true when customers can gauge the expected waiting time by observing the length of the queue and then renege or balk, seeking service elsewhere.

Significant and irreversible financial investment (e.g., building a hotel) results from a capacity decision that must be balanced against the costs of lost sales if capacity is inadequate or against operating losses if demand does not reach expectations. Because physical capacity (i.e., facilities and equipment) is added in discrete units (e.g., adding another aircraft to a fleet), the ability to match capacity with demand is fruitless and a strategy of building ahead of demand is often taken to avoid losing customers. Communication providers such as America Online, for example, have learned that a successful marketing campaign can lead to hostile customers if capacity is not in place to handle the growing demand.

Example 12.1: Capacity Planning for Cookies and Cream—Naive Approach

An enterprising student is considering opening a "Cookies and Ice Cream" shop in space that has become available in a food court. Observations of traffic during the lunch hour suggest a potential peak demand of 50 customers, each ordering on average one ice cream sundae, six baked-to-order cookies, and a 12-ounce self-serve soft drink and spending 20 minutes at a table.

A cookie sheet can accommodate a dozen cookies and baking time is 10 minutes. One server requires on average 6 minutes to take an order, mix a batch of cookies, make change, prepare the sundae, and assemble the order. Capacity requirements are determined by calculating the units of facility, equipment, and labor needed to accommodate the anticipated peak demand.

Facility requirements include the seats necessary to accommodate diners. We will use a relationship called "Little's Law" discussed later in the chapter to calculate the seats required. Little's Law states that the average number of customers in a system (L) is equal to the arrival rate (λ) times the average waiting time (W) or $L = \lambda W$. With 50 customers arriving during the peak hour and each staying approximately 20 minutes, or one-third of an hour, we need $(50)(20/60) = 16.7$ chairs.

Equipment requirements include the calculation of the number of cookie sheets needed. This is determined by dividing the total number of cookies ordered for the hour by the capability of one cookie sheet that is used for only 10 minutes per batch (i.e., reused 6 times per hour). Assume that orders can be combined to fill a sheet.

$$\text{Number of cookie sheets needed} = \frac{(50 \text{ customers/hour})(6 \text{ cookies/order})}{(12 \text{ cookies/sheet})(6 \text{ cycles/hour})} = 4.16$$

Labor requirement is focused on calculating the number of servers required. As in the equipment calculations, we divide the total minutes of server time demanded for the hour by one unit of service capability (i.e., 60 minutes available for the hour).

$$\text{Number of servers needed} = \frac{(50 \text{ customers/hour})(6 \text{ minutes each})}{(60 \text{ minutes/hour})} = 5.0$$

Caution needs to be exercised in implementing the results of such a naive capacity planning exercise. Excess capacity is required in a service system because variability in customer arrivals and service times is the expectation and creates idle capacity that is lost. As we shall see in the queuing model section, the capacity to serve must *exceed* the arrival rate to avoid out-of-control waiting lines. Because the calculations for capacity needs are based on averages, the results represent an infeasible solution to our capacity requirements. Our capacity planning analysis of Cookies and Cream will be revisited with a more sophisticated queuing analysis after our discussion of queuing models.

ANALYTICAL QUEUING MODELS

On the basis of our discussion of queues in Chapter 11, "Managing Waiting Lines," it is evident that many different queuing models exist. A popular system classifies parallel-server queuing models using the following notation in which three features are identified: *A/B/C*. *A* represents the distribution of time between arrivals, *B* the distribution of service times, and *C* the number of parallel servers. The descriptive symbols used for the arrival and service distributions include

M = exponential interarrival or service time distribution (or the equivalent Poisson distribution of arrival or service rate)

D = deterministic or constant interarrival or service time

E_k = Erlang distribution with shape parameter k (if $k = 1$, then Erlang is equivalent to exponential; if $k = \infty$, then Erlang is equivalent to deterministic)

G = general distribution with mean and variance (e.g., normal, uniform, or any empirical distribution)

Thus, $M/M/1$ designates a single-server queuing model with Poisson arrival rate and exponential service time distribution. The $A/B/C$ notation will be used here to define the class to which a queuing model belongs. Further considerations that are particular to the model in question, such as if the queue length is finite because of little space (e.g., a parking lot) or a small number of potential customers (e.g., an office cafeteria), will be noted. Figure 12.2 classifies the six analytical queuing models that we will study in this chapter according to these features using the $A/B/C$ notation. Each queuing model (e.g., $M/M/1$) also is given a roman numeral (e.g., I, II, III) to designate a set of equations for that model. These equations are repeated in Appendix D.

A final consideration involves the concepts of *transient state* and *steady state*. In a transient state, the values of the operating characteristics of a system depend on time. In a steady state, the system characteristics are independent of time, and the system is considered to be in statistical equilibrium. Because of their dependence on initial conditions, system characteristics usually are transient during the early stages of operation. For example, compare the initial conditions for a department store at opening time on a normal business day and on an end-of-year-sale day, when crowds overwhelm the clerks. The number in queue initially will be quite large, but given a long enough period of time, the system eventually will settle down. Once normal conditions have been reached, a statistical equilibrium is achieved in which the number in queue assumes a distribution that is independent of the starting condition. All the queuing model equations found in Appendix D assume that a steady state has been reached. As noted in Chapter 11, most service systems operate in a dynamic environment, with arrival rates sometimes changing every hour; thus, a steady state seldom is achieved.

FIGURE 12.2 Classification of queuing models.

However, steady-state models can provide useful system performance projections for long-range capacity planning decisions.

For each queuing model, the assumptions underlying its derivation are noted. The usefulness of an analytical model for a particular situation is limited by these assumptions. If the assumptions are invalid for a particular application, then one typically resorts to a computer-simulation approach. Applications of these queuing models to decision-making situations use the equations found in Appendix D, "Equations for Selected Queuing Models." The symbols used in these models and their definitions are

n = number of customers in the system

λ = [lambda] mean arrival rate (e.g., customer arrivals per hour)

μ = [mu] mean service rate per busy server (e.g., service capacity in customers per hour)

ρ = [rho] traffic intensity (λ/μ)

N = maximum number of customers allowed in the system

c = number of servers

P_n = probability of exactly n customers in the system

L_s = mean number of customers in the system

L_q = mean number of customers in queue

L_b = mean number of customers in queue for a busy system

W_s = mean time customer spends in the system

W_q = mean time customer spends in queue

W_b = mean time customer spends in queue for a busy system

Standard *M/M/*1 Model

Every queuing model requires specific assumptions regarding the queuing system features as discussed in Chapter 11 (i.e., calling population, arrival process, queue configuration, queue discipline, and service process). The application of any queuing model, therefore, should include validation with respect to these assumptions. The derivation of the standard *M/M/*1 model requires the following set of assumptions about the queuing system:

1. *Calling population.* An infinite or very large population of callers arriving. The callers are independent of each other and not influenced by the queuing system (e.g., an appointment is not required).
2. *Arrival process.* Negative exponential distribution of interarrival times or Poisson distribution of arrival rate.
3. *Queue configuration.* Single waiting line with no restrictions on length and no balking or reneging.
4. *Queue discipline.* First-come, first-served (FCFS).
5. *Service process.* One server with negative exponential distribution of service times.

The selected equations found in Appendix D can be used to calculate performance characteristics on the basis of only the mean arrival rate λ and the mean service rate per server μ. These equations clearly indicate why the mean arrival rate λ always must be *less* than the mean service rate μ for a single-server model. If this condition were not true and λ were equal to μ, the mean values for the operating characteristics would be undefined, because all the equations for mean values have the denominator $(\mu - \lambda)$. Theoretically, the system would never reach a steady state. In general, the system's capacity to serve, which is represented by $c\mu$ (i.e., number of servers times service rate per server), always must exceed the demand rate λ.

Example 12.2: Boat Ramp

Lake Travis has one launching ramp near the dam for people who trailer their small boats to the recreational site. A study of cars arriving with boats in tow indicates a Poisson distribution with a mean rate of $\lambda = 6$ boats per hour during the morning launch. A test of the data collected on launch times suggests that an exponential distribution with a mean of 6 minutes per boat (equivalent service rate $\mu = 10$ boats launched per hour) is a good fit. If the other assumptions for an *M/M/*1 model apply (i.e., infinite calling population, no queue length restrictions, no balking or reneging, and FCFS queue discipline), then the equations found in Appendix D (and repeated here) may be used to calculate the system characteristics.

(Note: $\rho = \lambda/\mu = 6/10 = 0.6$.)

Probability that an arriving customer waits (i.e., $k = 1$):

$$P(n \geq 1) = \rho^1 = 0.6^1 = 0.6 \qquad (\text{I.2})$$

Probability of finding the ramp idle:

$$P_0 = 1 - \rho = 0.4 \qquad (\text{I.1})$$

Mean number of boats in the system:

$$L_s = \frac{\lambda}{\mu - \lambda} = \frac{6}{10 - 6} = 1.5 \text{ boats} \qquad (\text{I.4})$$

Mean number of boats in queue:

$$L_q = \frac{\rho\lambda}{\mu - \lambda} = \frac{(0.6)(6)}{10 - 6} = 0.9 \text{ boat} \qquad (\text{I.5})$$

Mean time in the system:

$$W_s = \frac{1}{\mu - \lambda} = \frac{1}{10 - 6} = 0.25 \text{ hour (15 min.)} \qquad (\text{I.7})$$

Mean time in queue:

$$W_q = \frac{\rho}{\mu - \lambda} = \frac{0.6}{10 - 6} = 0.15 \text{ hour (9 min.)} \qquad (\text{I.8})$$

From our calculations, we find that the boat ramp is busy 60 percent of the time. Thus, arrivals can expect immediate access to the ramp without delay 40 percent of the time (i.e., when the ramp is idle). The calculations are internally consistent, because the mean time in the system (W_s) of 15 minutes is the sum of the mean time in queue (W_q) of 9 minutes and the mean service time of 6 minutes. Arrivals can expect to find the number in the system (L_s) to be 1.5 boats and the expected number in queue (L_q) to be 0.9 boat. The expected number of boats in queue plus the expected number being launched should sum to the expected number of boats in the system. The expected number of boats being launched is not 1, the number of servers, however, but instead is calculated as:

$$\begin{aligned}
\text{Expected number} &= \text{expected number} + \text{expected number} \\
\text{being served} &\quad\ \text{when idle} \qquad\quad\ \text{when busy} \\
&= P_0(0) \qquad\qquad\ + P(n > 0)(1) \\
&= (1 - \rho)(0) \qquad\ + \rho(1) \\
&= \rho
\end{aligned}$$

Adding $\rho = 0.6$ person in the process of launching a boat and 0.9 boat on the average in queue, we get the expected 1.5 boats in the system.

Note that the number of customers in the system, n, is a random variable with a probability distribution given by equation (I.3), which is found in Appendix D and repeated here in different form:

$$P_n = (1 - \rho)\rho^n \tag{I.3}$$

The number of customers in the system also can be used to identify system states. For example, when $n = 0$, the system is idle. When $n = 1$, the server is busy but no queue exists; when $n = 2$, the server is busy and a queue of 1 has formed. The probability distribution for n can be very useful in determining the proper size of a waiting room (i.e., the number of chairs) to accommodate arriving customers with a certain probability of assurance that each will find a vacant chair.

For the boat ramp example, determine the number of parking spaces needed to ensure that 90 percent of the time, a person arriving at the boat ramp will find a space to park while waiting to launch. Repeatedly using the probability distribution for system states for increasing values of n, we accumulate the system-state probabilities until 90 percent assurance is exceeded. Table 12.1 contains these calculations and indicates that a system state of $n = 4$ or less will occur 92 percent of the time. This suggests that room for four boat trailers should be provided because 92 percent of the time arrivals will find three (i.e., four minus the one being served) or fewer people waiting in queue to launch.

Finite-Queue M/M/1 Model

A modification of the standard *M/M/*1 model can be made by introducing a restriction on the allowable number of customers in the system. Suppose that N represents the maximum number of customers allowed, or, in a single-server model, that $N - 1$ indicates the maximum number of customers in the queue. Thus, if a customer arrives at a point in time when N customers already are in the system, then the arrival departs without seeking service. An example of this type of *finite queue* is a telephone exchange in which callers are put on hold until all the trunk lines are in use; then, any further callers receive a busy signal. Except for this one characteristic of finite capacity, all the assumptions of the standard *M/M/*1 model still hold. Note that the traffic intensity ρ now may exceed unity. Further, P_N represents the probability of not joining the system, and λP_N is the expected number of customers who are lost.

TABLE 12.1		
DETERMINING REQUIRED NUMBER OF PARKING SPACES		
n	**P_n**	**P(number of customers $\leq n$)**
0	$(0.4)(0.6)^0 = 0.4$	0.4
1	$(0.4)(0.6)^1 = 0.24$	0.64
2	$(0.4)(0.6)^2 = 0.144$	0.784
3	$(0.4)(0.6)^3 = 0.0864$	0.8704
4	$(0.4)(0.6)^4 = 0.05184$	0.92224

This particular model is very useful in estimating lost sales to be expected from an inadequate waiting area or excessive queue length. In the boat ramp example, assume that the waiting area can accommodate only two boat trailers; thus, $N = 3$ for the system. Using equations (V.1) and (V.3) found in Appendix D and repeated here, we can calculate the probabilities of 0, 1, 2, and 3 customers being in the system when $N = 3$ and $\rho = 0.6$:

$$P_0 = \frac{1 - \rho}{1 - \rho^{N+1}} \qquad \text{for } \lambda \neq \mu \qquad \text{(V.1)}$$

$$P_n = P_0\rho^n \qquad \text{for } n \leq N \qquad \text{(V.3)}$$

n	Calculation	P_n
0	$\dfrac{1 - 0.6}{1 - 0.6^4}(0.6)^0$	0.46
1	$(0.46)(0.6)^1$	0.27
2	$(0.46)(0.6)^2$	0.17
3	$(0.46)(0.6)^3$	0.10
		1.00

Note that this distribution totals 1.00, which indicates that we have accounted for all possible system states. System state $n = 3$ occurs 10 percent of the time. With an arrival rate of 6 people per hour, 0.6 person per hour (6×0.10) will find inadequate waiting space and look elsewhere for a launching site. Using equation (V.4), which is repeated here, we can calculate the expected number in the system (L_s): 0.9. This figure is much smaller than that in the unlimited-queue case, because on average, only 90 percent of the arrivals are processed.

$$L_s = \frac{\rho}{1 - \rho} - \frac{(N + 1)\rho^{N+1}}{1 - \rho^{N+1}} \qquad \text{for } \lambda \neq \mu \qquad \text{(V.4)}$$

$$= \frac{0.6}{1 - 0.6} - \frac{4(0.6)^4}{1 - (0.6)^4}$$

$$= 1.5 - 0.6$$

$$= 0.9$$

M/G/1 Model

For the *M/G*/1 model, any general service time distribution with mean $E(t)$ and variance $V(t)$ may be used. The condition that ρ be less than 1 still applies for the steady state, where ρ now equals $2E(t)$. Except for the generality of the service time distribution, all the assumptions for the standard *M/M*/1 model apply. Unfortunately, an equation does not exist for determining the system-state probabilities; however, the list of equations in Appendix D does contain equations for L_s, L_q, W_s, and W_q. Equation (III.2) is repeated here, because the appearance of the service time variance term $V(t)$ provides some interesting insights:

$$L_q = \frac{\rho^2 + \lambda^2 V(t)}{2(1 - \rho)} \qquad \text{(III.2)}$$

Clearly, the expected number of customers waiting for service directly relates to the variability of service times. This suggests that customer waiting can be reduced by controlling the variability in service times. For example, the limited menu of fast-food restaurants contributes to their success, because such reduction in the variety of offered meals allows for standardization of service.

Recall from Chapter 11, "Managing Waiting Lines," that the variance of the exponential distribution is $1/\mu^2$, and note that substituting this value for $V(t)$ in equation (III.2) yields $L_q = \rho^2/(1 - \rho)$, which is equivalent to equation (I.5) for the standard $M/M/1$ model. Now consider the $M/D/1$ model, with a deterministic service time and zero variance. Again, according to equation (III.2), when $V(t) = 0$, then $L_q = \rho^2/[2(1 - \rho)]$. Thus, one-half the congestion measured by L_q is explained by the variation in service times. This implies that the variability in time between arrivals accounts for the remaining congestion. Thus, considerable potential exists for reducing congestion simply by using appointments or reservations to control the variability in arrivals. Congestion in a queuing system is caused equally by variability in service times and interarrival times; therefore, strategies for controlling congestion should address both sources.

Standard *M/M/c* Model

The assumptions for the standard $M/M/c$ model are the same as those for the standard $M/M/1$ model, with the stipulation that service rates across channels be independent and equal (i.e., all servers are considered to be identical). As before, $\rho = \lambda/\mu$; however, ρ now must be less than c, the number of servers, for steady-state results to occur. If we define the system utilization factor as $\lambda/c\mu$, then for any steady-state system, the utilization factor must range between 0 and 1. Figure 12.3 illustrates the characteristic curves for L_s as a function of the utilization factor and c, the number of parallel servers. These curves graphically demonstrate the excessive congestion that occurs as one attempts to gain full utilization of service capacity.

The curves also can be used to demonstrate the disproportional gain that occurs when congestion is reduced by adding parallel servers. For example, consider a single-server system ($c = 1$) with a utilization factor of 0.8. From Figure 12.3, the value of L_s is 4. By adding another identical server, a two-channel system is created, and the utilization factor is reduced by one-half to 0.4. Figure 12.3 gives $L_s \approx 1$, and a 400-percent reduction in congestion is achieved just by doubling the number of servers.

Now, instead of creating a two-channel system, double the service rate of the single-server system and, thus, reduce the utilization factor to 0.4. Figure 12.3 gives $L_s \approx 0.67$

FIGURE 12.3 *M/M/c* model curves for L_s.

for this superserver system; however, this additional gain in reducing L_s is obtained at the cost of increasing the expected number in queue (from $L_q = 0.15$ to 0.27), as seen in Table 12.2. This is not surprising, because a single-server system would require more people to wait in line. In a multiple-server system of equal capacity, more people are able to be in service; thus, fewer wait in line. Therefore, the decision to use one superserver or the equivalent capacity with several servers in parallel depends on concern for the expected waiting time in queue (L_q/λ) or the expected time in the system (L_s/λ). As noted in Chapter 11, a concern for reducing the waiting time in queue usually is advisable, particularly if people must physically wait in line. Further, once service begins, the customer's attitude toward time changes, because now the customer is the center of attention. The concept of using one large computer system to serve an entire university community often is justified, however, because short turnaround time (i.e., time in the system) and large memory are of primary importance.

Consolidating the entire service capacity into a single superserver is one approach to achieving economies of scale in services. Another is the concept of pooling services, which is accomplished by gathering together independent servers at one central location to form a single service facility with multiple servers.

Example 12.3: The Secretarial Pool

A small business school has assigned a secretary to each of its four departments: accounting, finance, marketing, and management. Each secretary word-processes class materials and correspondence only for her or his own departmental faculty. The dean has received complaints from the faculty, however, and particularly from the accounting faculty, about delays in getting work accomplished. The dean assigns an assistant to collect data on arrival rates and service times. After analyzing these data, the assistant reports that secretarial work arrives with a Poisson distribution at an average rate of $\lambda = 2$ requests per hour for all departments except accounting, which has an average rate of $\lambda = 3$ requests per hour. The average time to complete a piece of work is 15 minutes regardless of its source, and the service times are distributed exponentially.

Because of budget limitations, no additional secretaries can be hired. The dean believes, however, that service could be improved if all the secretaries were pooled and instructed to receive work from the entire business school faculty. All work requests would be received at one central location and processed on a first-come, first-served basis by the first secretary who became available, regardless of his or her departmental affiliation. Before proposing the plan to the faculty, the dean asks the assistant who collected the data to analyze the performance of the existing system and compare it with the pooling alternative.

TABLE 12.2

EFFECTS OF DOUBLING SERVICE CAPACITY

System characteristic	Single-server baseline system	Two-server system	Single-superserver system
ρ	0.8	0.8	0.4
$(\lambda / c\mu)^*$	0.8	0.4	0.4
L_s	4.0	0.95	0.67
L_q	3.2	0.15	0.27

*Utilization factor.

The present system is essentially four $M/M/1$ independent, single-channel queuing systems, each with a service rate of $\mu = 4$ requests per hour. The appropriate measure of system performance is the expected time in the system—or turnaround time, from the faculty viewpoint. The difference in arrival rates should explain why the accounting faculty are particularly concerned about delays. Using the $M/M/1$ equation $W_s = 1/(\mu - \lambda)$, we find for the present system of independent departmental secretaries that accounting faculty members experience an average turnaround time of $W_s = 1/(4 - 3) = 1.0$ hour, or 60 minutes, and the faculty members in the other departments experience an average turnaround time of $W_s = 1/(4 - 2) = 0.5$ hour, or 30 minutes.

The proposal to pool the secretarial staff creates a multiple-channel, single-queue system, or an $M/M/4$ system in this case. The arrival rate is the combined arrivals ($2 + 2 + 2 + 3$) from all departments, or $\lambda = 9$ requests per hour. Equation (II.1), which is repeated here with $c = 4$ and $\rho = 9/4$, is used to calculate the value of P_0:

$$P_0 = \cfrac{1}{\left(\sum_{i=0}^{c-1} \cfrac{\rho^i}{i!}\right) + \cfrac{\rho^c}{c!(1 - \rho/c)}} \tag{II.1}$$

$$P_0 = \cfrac{1}{\cfrac{(9/4)^0}{0!} + \cfrac{(9/4)^1}{1!} + \cfrac{(9/4)^2}{2!} + \cfrac{(9/4)^3}{3!} + \cfrac{(9/4)^4}{4!(1 - 9/16)}}$$

$$= \cfrac{1}{1 + 9/4 + \cfrac{81/16}{2} + \cfrac{729/64}{6} + \cfrac{6561/256}{24(7/16)}}$$

$$= \cfrac{1}{7.68 + 2.44}$$

$$= 0.098$$

Equation (II.4), repeated below, is used to calculate the value of L_s:

$$L_s = \cfrac{\rho^{c+1}}{(c - 1)!(c - \rho)^2} P_0 + \rho \tag{II.4}$$

$$= \cfrac{(9/4)^5}{(4 - 1)!(4 - 9/4)^2}(0.098) + 9/4$$

$$= \cfrac{59,049/1024}{6(1.75)^2}(0.098) + 2.25$$

$$= 0.31 + 2.25$$

$$= 2.56$$

$$W_s = \cfrac{L_s}{\lambda} = \cfrac{2.56}{9} = 0.28 \text{ hour, or 17 minutes}$$

The substantial reduction in expected turnaround time from 30 minutes (60 minutes for the accounting faculty) to 17 minutes should easily win faculty approval.

The benefits from pooling are achieved through better utilization of idle secretaries. Under the departmental system, four independent queues existed, which allowed situations to develop in which a secretary in one department could be burdened with a long waiting line of work whereas a secretary in another department was idle. If a waiting request could be transferred to the idle secretary, then it would be processed immediately. Switching to a single queue avoids the utilization problem by not allowing a secretary to become idle until the waiting line of requests is empty.

Because calculations for the $M/M/c$ model are so tedious, we tyically use Appendix C, "Values of L_q for the $M/M/c$ Queuing Model," to solve for L_q. For this problem, in which $c = 4$ and $\rho = 2.25$, we find $L_q = 0.31$ by interpolation and, thus, $L_s = L_q + \rho = 2.56$.

The success of pooling service resources comes from realizing that congestion results from variation in the rate of arrivals and service times. If a total systems perspective of the process is taken, temporary idleness at one location can be used to reduce congestion at another that has been caused by a temporary surge in demand or time-consuming requests. Further, server idleness that can be put to use but is not represents lost service capacity and results in a deterioration of service quality as measured by customer waiting. The concept of pooling need not apply only to servers who are at different locations. The common practice in banks and post offices of having customers form a single queue rather than line up in front of the individual windows represents an application of the pooling concept. Theoretically, the average waiting time is reduced from that of multiple queues; however, the single long line may give arriving customers the impression of long waits. This is the reason McDonald's gave for abandoning the idea: it was feared that customers would balk on seeing a long line.

Pooling service resources at onc location should be undertaken with some caution if customers must travel to that facility. In this case, the expected travel time to the facility should be included with the expected waiting time in queue when the proposal is evaluated. For emergency services, dispersing servers throughout the service area generally is preferred to assigning all services to one central location. An emergency ambulance system is a particularly good example of this need for physically dispersed servers to minimize response time.

Finite-Queue M/M/c Model

This finite-queuc $M/M/c$ model is similar to the finite-queue $M/M/1$ model, with the exception that N, thc maximum number in the system, must be equal to or greater than c, the number of servers. An arriving customer is rejected if the number in the system equals N or the length of the queue is $N - c$. All other assumptions for the standard $M/M/c$ model hold, except that ρ now can exceed c. Because excess customers are rejected, the system can reach a steady state even when the capacity is inadequate to meet the total demand (i.e., $\lambda = c\mu$).

An interesting variation on this model is the no-queue situation, which occurs when no possibility exists for a customer to wait—because a waiting area is not provided. This situation can be modeled as a finite-queue system with $N = c$. A parking lot is an illustration of this no-queue situation. If we consider each parking space as a server, then when the parking lot is completely full, an opportunity for further service no longer exists and future arrivals must be rejected. If c equals the number of parking spaces, then the parking lot system can be modeled as a no-queue variation of the finite-queue $M/M/c$ model.

General Self-Service M/G/∞ Model

If a multiple-server system has an infinite number of servers or arrivals serve themselves, then no arriving customer must wait for service. This, of course, describes exactly the concept that has made the modern supermarket so popular. At least during the shopping portion (excluding checkout), customers do not experience waiting. The number of customers in the process of shopping does vary because of random arrivals and differing service times, and the probability distribution of the number of customers in the system can be calculated by means of equation (IV.1), which is repeated here. Note that this distribution for P_n in fact is Poisson, with the mean, or L_s, being equal to ρ. Further, this model is not restricted to an exponential distribution of service times.

$$P_n = \frac{e^{-\rho}}{n!} \rho^n \qquad \text{where} \qquad L_s = \rho \qquad \text{(IV.1)}$$

This model also is useful as an approximation to describe circumstances in which waiting only rarely may occur (e.g., emergency ambulance services). Using the Poisson distribution of the number of customers in the system, we can calculate the number of servers that are required to ensure that the probability of someone waiting is quite small.

Example 12.4: Supermarket

The typical supermarket can be viewed as two queuing systems in tandem. The arriving customer secures a shopping cart and proceeds to serve himself or herself by picking items from the shelves. On completing this task, the shopper joins a single queue (a new idea to reduce waiting caused by multiple queues) behind the checkout registers.

The checker tallies the bill, makes change, and sacks the groceries. The shopper then exits this system, perhaps with the assistance of a carryout person. Because departures from the standard $M/M/c$ queuing system also are Poisson-distributed, the supermarket system can be analyzed as two independent systems in series. The first is a self-service shopping, or $M/M/\infty$, system, and the second (at the cash registers) is an $M/M/c$ system. Observation of customer behavior indicates that arrivals are Poisson-distributed, with a rate of 30 per hour, and that shopping is completed in 20 minutes on the average, with exponential distribution. Shoppers then join the single queue behind the three checkout registers and wait until a register becomes available. The checkout process requires 5 minutes on average, with exponential distribution.

For the shopping experience, the $M/M/\infty$ model applies, with $\rho = 30/3$, resulting in $L_s = 10$ customers on the average being engaged in the shopping activity. To study the checkout system, we use Appendix C with $c = 3$ and $\rho = 30/12 = 2.5$, and find that $L_q = 3.5$. The average number of customers in the checkout area $L_s = L_q + \rho = 6$ customers. Together, we find on average a total of 16 shoppers in the store. The expected time that a customer spends in the supermarket is 20 minutes shopping plus 12 minutes (i.e., $L_s/\lambda = 6/30 = 0.2$ hour) checking out, for a total of 32 minutes.

GENERAL RELATIONSHIPS BETWEEN SYSTEM CHARACTERISTICS

In concluding the discussion of queuing models, it is necessary to point out some general relationships between the average system characteristics that exist across all models. The first two relationships are definitional in nature.

First, the expected number in the system should equal the expected number in queue plus the expected number in service, or

$$L_s = L_q + E \qquad \text{(number in service)} \qquad \text{(1)}$$

Note that E (number in service) is not the number of servers. It equals ρ for all models except the finite-queue case.

Second, the expected time in the system should equal the expected time in queue plus the expected time in service, or

$$W_s = W_q + \frac{1}{\mu} \tag{2}$$

where $1/\mu$ is the reciprocal of the service rate.

The characteristics for a busy system are conditional values that are based on the probability that the system is busy, or $P(n \geq c)$. Thus, the expected number in queue for a busy system simply is the expected number under all system states divided by the probability of the system being busy, or

$$L_b = \frac{L_q}{P(n \geq c)} \tag{3}$$

Similarly, the expected waiting time in queue for a busy system is

$$W_b = \frac{W_q}{P(n \geq c)} \tag{4}$$

Further, the following relationship exists between the expected number in the system and the expected time in the system:

$$W_s = \frac{1}{\lambda} L_s \tag{5}$$

This relationship, referred to as Little's Law, when restated as $L = \lambda W$ also holds true for expected number in queue and the expected waiting time:[2]

$$W_q = \frac{1}{\lambda} L_q \tag{6}$$

When equations (5) and (6) are applied for systems with a finite queue, an effective arrival rate must be used for λ. For a system with a finite queue, the effective arrival rate is $\lambda(1 - P_N)$.

These relationships are very useful because they permit derivation of all the average characteristics of a system from the knowledge of one characteristic obtained by analysis or by the collection of data on actual system performance.

CAPACITY PLANNING CRITERIA

Queuing theory indicates that, in the long run, capacity to serve must exceed the demand. If this criterion is not met, at least one of the following adjustments must occur:

1. Excessive waiting by customers will result in some reneging (i.e., a customer leaves the queue before being served) and, thus, in some reduction of demand.
2. Excessive waiting, if known or observed by potential customers, will cause them to reconsider their need for service and, thus, will reduce demand.
3. Under the pressure of long waiting lines, servers may speed up, spending less time with each customer, and, thus, increase service capacity. A gracious and leisurely manner, however, now becomes curt and impersonal.
4. Sustained pressure to hurry may result in eliminating time-consuming features and performing the bare minimum and, thus, service capacity is increased.

These uncontrolled situations result from inadequate service capacity, which can be avoided through rational capacity planning.

Several approaches to capacity planning are explored on the basis of different criteria for evaluating service system performance. Determining the desired level of service capacity implies a trade-off between the cost of service and the cost of customer waiting, as suggested by Figure 12.1. Thus, capacity analysis will utilize the queuing models to predict customer waiting for various levels of service.

Average Customer Waiting Time

The criterion of average customer waiting time for capacity planning can be appropriate in several circumstances. For example, a restaurant owner may wish to promote liquor sales in the bar and, therefore, stipulates that customers be kept waiting 5 minutes on average for a table. It has been suggested that because the face of a watch typically is divided into 5-minute increments, people who are waiting in line may not realize how long they have been waiting until at least 5 minutes have passed. Therefore, in designing a drive-in bank facility, it may be advisable to have customers wait no more than 5 minutes on average for service. In these cases, use of the *M/M/c* model would be appropriate to identify the service capacity in terms of the number of servers that would guarantee the desired expected customer waiting time.

Example 12.5: Drive-in Bank

Excessive congestion is a problem during the weekday noon hour at a downtown drive-in bank facility. Bank officials fear customers may take their accounts elsewhere unless service is improved. A study of customer arrivals during the noon hour indicates an average arrival rate of 30 per hour, with Poisson distribution. Banking transactions take 3 minutes on average, with exponential distribution. Because of the layout of the drive-in facility, arriving customers must select one of three lanes for service. Once a customer is in a lane, it is impossible for him or her to renege or jockey between lanes because of separating medians. Assuming that arriving customers select lanes at random, we can treat the system as parallel, independent, single-channel queuing systems with the arrival rate divided evenly among the tellers. If the bank officers agree to a criterion that customers should wait no more than 5 minutes on average, how many drive-in tellers are required? Because we are concerned only with customers who actually wait, equation (I.9), which is repeated here, is appropriate:

$$W_b = \frac{1}{\mu - \lambda} \tag{I.9}$$

For the current three-teller system, arrivals per teller $\lambda = 30/3 = 10$ per hour. Thus, $W_b = 1/(20-10) = 0.1$ hour, or 6 minutes. Table 12.3 indicates that one additional teller is required to meet the service criterion.

TABLE 12.3

EXPECTED TIME IN QUEUE FOR BANK TELLER ALTERNATIVES

Number of tellers	λ per teller	μ	W_b, min.
3	10	20	6
4	7.5	20	4.8

Example 12.6: Capacity Planning for Cookies and Cream—Queuing Analysis

In the naive capacity planning for Example 12.1, we used averages to determine that a need existed for 16.7 chairs, 4.16 cookie sheets, and 5 servers. We pointed out that these values would be inadequate because of the nature of services that require capacity in excess of expected demand. Suppose our criterion for acceptable service is an expected customer waiting time in queue of one minute (i.e., $W_Q = 1/60$ hour) for each resource (i.e., chairs, cookie sheets, and servers). Using Little's Law, a one-minute wait time given an arrival rate of $\lambda = 50$ per hour translates into $L_Q = \lambda W_Q = 50/60 = 0.833$. Table 12.4 contains the queuing analysis using Appendix C to find the value for L_Q where possible (i.e. $\rho < 8$) and in the case of determining the number of chairs, reverting to the tedious equations for the *M/M/c* model found in Appendix D.

As the queuing analysis indicates, we need many more resources than the naive analysis indicated. This becomes obvious when we realize that the naive analysis was only an exercise in determining the value for $\rho = \lambda/\mu$. But for queuing systems to be feasible, the number of servers must exceed the value of ρ.

Probability of Excessive Waiting

For public services that have difficulty identifying the economic cost of waiting, a service level often is specified. This service level is stated in a manner such that P or more percent of all customers should experience a delay of less than T time units. For example, a federal guideline states that the response time for 95 percent of all ambulance calls should be less than 10 minutes for urban and less than 30 minutes for rural systems. The Public Utilities Commission gives a similar performance criterion for telephone service, directing that telephone service must be provided at a resource level such that 89 percent of the time, an incoming call can be answered within 10 seconds. A probability distribution of delays is required to identify service levels that will meet these probabilities of not exceeding a certain excessive delay, and equations for these delay probabilities are available for the standard *M/M/c* model. For the case when no delay is desired ($T = 0$), equation (II.3) can be used to find a value for c such that the probability of immediate service is at least P percent.

Example 12.7: Self-Serve Gas Station

A retail gasoline distributor plans to construct a cash only self-service filling station on vacant property leading into a new housing development. On the basis of the traffic in

---

TABLE 12.4

QUEUING ANALYSIS FOR COOKIES AND CREAM

Resource	μ in customers/hour	$\rho = 50/\mu$	Number Required for $L_Q < 0.833$
Chairs	$\dfrac{60 \text{ min./hr.}}{20 \text{ min./customer}} = 3$	16.7	22*
Cookie sheets	$\dfrac{(60 \text{ min./hr.})(12 \text{ cookies})}{(10 \text{ min./customer})(6 \text{ cookies})} = 12$	4.16	6
Servers	$\dfrac{60 \text{ min./hr.}}{6 \text{ min./customer}} = 10$	5.0	7

* $LQ = 0.582$ using equations (II.1), (II.4), and (II.5).

that area, the distributor forecasts a demand of 24 cars on average per hour. Time studies that have been conducted at other sites reveal an average self-service time of 5 minutes for a driver to fill the tank, pay the cashier, and drive away. The service times are distributed exponentially, and past experience justifies assuming an arrival rate with a Poisson distribution. The distributor believes that the success of self-service stations results from competitive gasoline prices and the customers' desires for fast service. Therefore, the distributor would like to install enough pumps to guarantee that arriving customers will find a free pump at least 95 percent of the time. We use equation (II.3) to calculate the probability that a customer waits for various values of c, and results for up to six pumps are summarized in Table 12.5. When $c = 6$, the $P(n \geq c)$ reaches a value of 0.02 and, thus, meets the criterion that fewer than 5 percent of arriving customers have to wait. This result suggests that six pumps should be installed.

Minimizing the Sum of Customer Waiting Costs and Service Costs

If both customers and servers are members of the same organization, then the costs of providing service and employee waiting are equally important to the organization's effectiveness. This situation arises, for example, when organizations rely on a captive service, such as a secretarial pool or a computer facility. In these cases, the cost of employees' waiting time is at least equal to their average salary, and in fact, this cost could be considerably more if all the implications of waiting, such as the frustration of not completing a task or the effect of delays on others in the organization, are assessed.

The economic trade-off depicted in Figure 12.1 best describes this situation in which the capacity to serve may be increased by adding servers. As servers are added, the cost of service increases, but this cost is offset by a corresponding decrease in the cost of waiting. Adding both costs results in a convex total-cost curve for the organization that identifies a service capacity with minimum combined costs. The queuing models are used to predict the expected waiting time of employees for different levels of capacity, and the values are substituted in the total-cost function here.

Assuming linear cost functions for service and waiting and comparing alternatives based on steady-state performance, we calculate the total cost per unit of time (hour) as:

$$\text{Total cost per hour} = \text{Hourly cost of service} + \text{Hourly waiting cost}$$

$$TC = C_s C + C_w \lambda W_s$$

$$= C_s C + C_w L_s \text{ (from Little's Law)} \tag{7}$$

where C = number of servers
  C_s = hourly cost per server
  C_w = hourly cost of waiting customer

TABLE 12.5

PROBABILITY OF FINDING ALL GAS PUMPS IN USE

c	P_0	$P(n \geq c)$
3	0.11	0.44
4	0.13	0.27
5	0.134	0.06
6	0.135	0.02

For equation (7), waiting is defined as time in the system; however, if waiting in queue is more appropriate, then L_q is substituted for L_s. In situations in which service is self-service, such as using a copying or a fax machine, waiting in queue might be justified.

Example 12.8: Work Station Rental

The director of a large engineering staff is considering the rental of several work stations that will permit the staff to analyze structural design problems. On the basis of a survey of the staff, the director finds that the department will generate, on average, eight requests per hour for structural analysis, and the engineers estimate that the average analysis will require 15 minutes. A work station that is adequate for these needs rents for $10 per hour. When the average salary of the engineering staff is considered, the cost of keeping an engineer idle is $30 per hour. For a "quick and dirty" analysis, the director assumes that requests for service are Poisson distributed and that user times are exponentially distributed. Further, the engineering staff is large enough to assume an infinite calling population. Using the *M/M/c* model with $\rho = 8/4 = 2$ and Appendix C to calculate L_q, the director obtains the results shown in Table 12.6.

Note that L_q is used instead of L_s in the calculations, because the engineer is productive while using the work station. The results indicate that four work stations will minimize the combined costs of rent for the work stations and salary for the waiting engineers.

Our assumption of waiting costs being linear with time, as shown in equation (7), is suspect because, as the delay increases, a larger percentage of customers become dissatisfied and vocal, possibly creating a mass exodus. Taguchi's concept of a quadratic quality loss function as described in Chapter 3, "Service Quality," seems to be more appropriate, particularly when alternative service is available from a competitor. First, the longer the wait, the more irritated customers become and the greater the probability that they will take their future business elsewhere. In addition, they will tell friends and relatives of their bad experiences, which also will affect future sales. Finally, the loss of an immediate sale is small compared with the future stream of lost revenues when a customer is lost forever. In practice, however, the linear assumption usually is made because of the difficulty of determining a customer waiting cost function.

Probability of Sales Lost Because of Inadequate Waiting Area

This planning criterion concerns capacity of the waiting area rather than capacity to serve. An inadequate waiting area may cause potential customers to balk and seek service elsewhere. This problem is of particular concern where arriving customers can see the waiting area, such as the parking lot at a restaurant or the driveway at a drive-in bank. Analysis of these systems uses the finite-queue *M/M/c* model to estimate the number of balking customers.

TABLE 12.6

TOTAL COST OF WORK STATION RENTAL ALTERNATIVES

C	L_q	C_sC	C_wL_q	TC
3	0.88	$30	$26.4	$56.4
4	0.17	40	5.1	45.1
5	0.04	50	1.2	51.2
6	0.01	60	0.3	60.3

If N is the maximum number of customers allowed in the system, then P_N is the probability of a customer arriving and finding the system to be full. Thus, P_N represents the probability of sales lost because of an inadequate waiting area, and λP_N represents the expected number of sales lost per unit of time. The cost of sales lost because of an inadequate waiting area now can be compared with the possible investment in additional space.

Example 12.9: Downtown Parking Lot

A parking lot is a multiple-server queuing system without a queue; that is, the lot can be considered a service system in which each parking space is a server. After the lot is full, subsequent arrivals are rejected, because the system has no provision for a queue. Thus, a parking lot is a finite-queuing system with a queue capacity of zero, because $N = c$.

With this model in mind, an enterprising student notes the availability of a vacant lot in the central business district. The student learns from a real estate agent that the owner is willing to rent the property as a parking lot for $50 a day until a buyer is found. After making some observations of traffic in the area, the student finds that approximately 10 cars per hour have difficulty finding space in the parking garage of the department store across the street from the vacant lot. The garage attendant reports that customers spend approximately 1 hour shopping in the store. To calculate the feasibility of this venture, the student assumes that arrivals are Poisson distributed and that shopping times are exponentially distributed. The student is interested in what potential business is lost because the lot has room for only 6 cars.

This parking lot can be considered an *M/M/c* finite-queuing system with no provision for a queue. Therefore, equations for the finite-queue *M/M/c* model are calculated with $c = N$. Substituting for $c = N$ in equations (VI.1), (VI.2), (VI.4), and (VI.7) yields the following results for the no-queue case (i.e., $L_Q = W_Q = 0$). No other equations are applicable.

$$P_0 = \frac{1}{\displaystyle\sum_{i=0}^{N} \frac{\rho^i}{i!}} \tag{8}$$

$$P_n = \frac{\rho^n}{n!} P_0 \tag{9}$$

$$L_s = \rho(1 - P_N) \tag{10}$$

$$W_s = \frac{1}{\mu} \tag{11}$$

With $\lambda = 10$, $N = 6$, and $\mu = 1$, we calculate $P_0 = 0.000349$ using equation (8) and calculate $P_6 = 0.48$ using equation (9). Thus, of the 10 arriving customers per hour, approximately one-half ($10 \times 0.48 = 4.8$) find the lot full. Therefore, this lot with a capacity of 6 cars serves approximately one-half the demand.

Requirement That Expected Profit on Last Unit of Capacity Should Just Exceed Expected Loss

This capacity planning criterion does not rely on use of queuing models; rather, it relies on an economic principle called *marginal analysis,* which is discussed in Chapter 14, "Managing Facilitating Goods." This approach is useful when a capacity decision must be made in which losses are associated with both inadequate and excess capacity. This capacity problem typically arises during the facility design phase, such as when decisions are made concerning the seating capacity of a restaurant or movie theater. In addition to an estimate of the unit profit per customer and possible loss, the analysis requires a probability distribution for the service demand.

The *critical fractile,* which is derived in Chapter 14, is shown here. It requires the expected revenue on the last sale to exceed the expected loss on the last sale.

$$P(d < x) \leq \frac{C_u}{C_u + C_o} \qquad (12)$$

where C_u = unit contribution from potential sale, cost of *under*estimating demand (inadequate capacity)

C_o = unit loss from idle capacity, cost of *over*estimating demand (excess capacity)

d = demand

x = capacity (e.g., airline seats, hotel rooms)

Example 12.10: Paradise Tours

For the past several years, Paradise Tours has offered a Hawaiian adventure package each summer that has attracted a good though variable-sized group of vacationers from the local university. A review of past records suggests that demand for this tour is distributed normally, with a mean of 50, standard deviation of 10, and no trend indicated. Paradise Tours reserves seats with a regularly scheduled airline at a special, reduced, affinity-group rate. This policy enables the airline to attract small groups that are not large enough to charter an entire plane. The airline also allows the travel agent to charge a $30 service fee in addition to the ticket price; however, a major concern of Paradise is the $10 charge by the airline for each unsold reserved seat. The airline is concerned about tying up seats during the peak season and also wants to prevent oversubscription by travel agents. Paradise has been reserving 50 seats and finds that it has no record of ever paying the $10 overbooking charge. Should it continue this reservation policy?

Using equation (12), we calculate the following critical fractile:

$$P(d < x) \leq \frac{30}{30 + 10} \leq 0.75$$

From Appendix A, "Areas of a Standard Normal Distribution," the z value for 0.75 is 0.68. Thus, the number of seats to reserve is determined as

Reserved seats $= \mu + z\sigma$

$= 50 + (0.68)(10)$

$= 56 \qquad$ (rounded down because of inequality)

BOX 12.1

Service Benchmark

SIMULATION MODELING FOR PROCESS REENGINEERING IN THE TELECOMMUNICATIONS INDUSTRY

Traditionally, firms have used simulation modeling to analyze manufacturing processes and to evaluate production management strategies. More recently, they have used it to analyze various service processes. U S WEST Communications has used a service process model to analyze the installation (provisioning) process of a high-capacity fiber-optic telecommunications service. This process is a sequence of tasks that includes interaction with the customer, verification of available facilities, changes to billing information, and testing equipment. Managers who need to design and improve the process frequently make decisions based on intuition, historical patterns, or descriptive statistics drawn from insurmountable amounts of raw data. We developed a process simulation model to support the managers in designing and reengineering the service process. The model enables managers to gain insight that will help them control the current complex service flow. This insight and an analysis of the process help them to identify areas that need reengineering and to predict the quantitative impact of reengineering efforts.

Business process reengineering, a term coined by Hammer and Champy,[1] is the managerial paradigm that many businesses need to radically change the organizational structure of a business process and the policies and methods by which the process operates in order to achieve significant improvements. It is an alternative to "continuous improvement," which aims to incrementally improve existing outdated structures within the process, leaving the fundamental framework of the process intact. Process reengineering, in contrast, emphasizes the overall improvement of a process with respect to its quality, cost, and efficiency. Process simulation modeling allows us to observe the work flows within a service process in their entirety. We thus can easily identify key service functions and subsequently improve, consolidate, or dissolve them through process reengineering.

The modeling group used simulation modeling to reflect the current status of a service process and to quantify the impact of changes imposed on the process by tracking performance measures. By reflecting the dynamics of a service process, our simulation model has helped managers determine why and where they should reengineer processes. It also helps them to establish tangible management goals. For example, it can help them determine when and how much to increase the workforce to maintain or to improve current service cycle times. It also can help them determine how much to spend for improvements to information systems that automate or simplify tasks within the process. Simulation modeling provides us with quantitative service performance measures, such as queue length, total cycle time, and idle time at each service center, that help managers allocate their resources.

DS1 (digital signal level 1) networks are high-capacity, high-speed (1.5 Mb/sec) data transfer pathways used primarily by long distance carriers, large businesses, and government agencies. As shown in Exhibit 12.1, the DS1 service process originates with the arrival of a service request from a long-distance carrier at the interexchange carrier service center (ICSC) or from a business or government customer at the market unit (MU) service center. The ICSC (or the MU) confirms the request and issues a service order to a high-capacity provisioning center (HCPC) that generates an engineering specification "work order record details" (WORD). However, if the customer or the service representative at the ICSC or the MU made errors in receiving or issuing the service order, the HCPC issues a "supplement order" and sends it back to the ICSC or the MU for correction. At the HCPC, we have three pathways for the WORD.

First, if the necessary facilities are already in place to handle the request (a preprovisioned request), we send the WORD directly to the digital services operations center (DSOC) for execution. Second, we may send the WORD to the interoffice facilities current planning center (IFCPC), which orders the materials necessary to fill the request. Third, we may send the WORD to the construction management center (CMC), which is responsible for building new conduits or for attaching new facilities to existing conduits. Once the IFCPC has ordered the materials or the CMC has completed, we notify the DSOC to execute the work order to install the service. However, if the DSOC discovers errors made by the HCPC, it sends "re-WORD" to the HCPC for

---

[1] Michael Hammer and James Champy, *Reengineering the Corporation,* Harper Business, New York, 1994.

BOX 12.1 (CONTINUED)

modification. Because this provisioning process includes both forward flows and backward flows, we conceptualized it as a stochastic queuing network model. In the model, we assumed that handling an error takes 50 percent of the time it takes to handle a normal order at each processing center. We also experimented with several sequencing rules, including the shortest-processing-time rule, to assign priorities to service requests at each processing center. That is, we assigned the highest priority to preprovisioned requests because their processing time is shortest. We did this to test whether we could reduce overall average cycle time and improve the percentage of customer-requested due date commitments. Below, we discuss five key steps of process simulation modeling in turn.

Our first step in constructing the model was to determine its primary objective and scope. We talked to the managers supervising the process to gather the modeling requirements and agreed that the primary focus of the model should be analyzing the impact of changes in demand, workforce, or error rate on the cycle time of connecting a DS1 line, from the service request to the final physical installation. The scope is the Minneapolis/St. Paul region, because this region represents U S WEST fairly well in terms of demand pattern and service quality. Also, we decided to model only the centers

Our second crucial step in developing the model was gathering the data we needed to develop a stochastic queuing model. This step was closely tied in with determining the objective of the model, because the lack of detailed data forced us to reevaluate the scope of the model. We found that the lack of relevant data prevented us from modeling the true service process. Collecting data was one of the most challenging steps in our project. We initially had difficulty obtaining data in a timely manner because many managers did not consider gathering data important until they were pressured by their supervisors. Also, getting those working in the service centers to agree on common definitions was challenging and time-consuming. For example, we spent a lot of time coming to an agreement on exactly what a "supplement order" is or on the precise meaning of the "processing time" of a task.

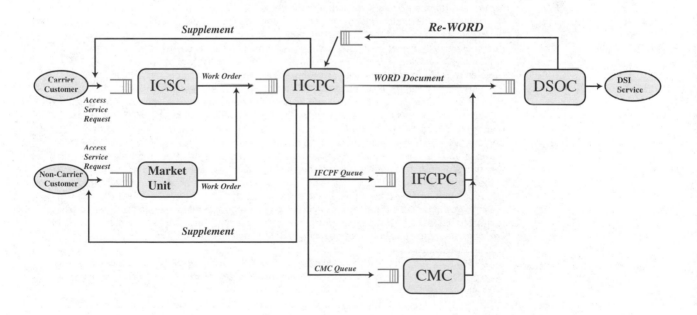

EXHIBIT 12.1 U S WEST high-capacity digital signal queuing network.
(*Source:* Youngho Lee and Amie Elcan, "Simulation Modeling for Process Reengineering in the Telecommunications Industry," *Interfaces,* vol. 26, no. 3, May–June 1996, p. 3.)

BOX 12.1 (CONTINUED)

In our model, we established several key parameters, such as the distribution of service processing times, the error rate, the scheduling rules, the preprovision rate, and the staffing level at each process center as well as the arrival pattern of service requests. By varying these parameters, we performed various what-if scenario analyses. However, since the complete input data set either was inaccessible or would require an unreasonable amount of resources to collect, we adjusted the scale of the model to accommodate the available data sets. As an example, because arrival data were collected on a daily basis, we were forced to make the time unit of the request arrival pattern daily, though we would have preferred arrival data collected hourly. After collecting suitable data sets, we fit the distribution of daily arrivals with a Weibull distribution and made assumptions about the distribution of task-processing times since the only available data were estimates for the minimum, the maximum, and the mean times based on interviews with people working within the centers. We experimented with exponential distributions to represent the distribution of processing times but later found that the Erlang II distribution was a better representation because it had a smaller right tail and less mass distributed at times close to zero.

Building and implementing the simulation model was the third key step. We implemented the conceptual queuing model on the PC with SIMPROCESS, developed by CACI.[2] We selected this discrete event simulation programming tool because its animation feature helped us to communicate with the managers. From the beginning, we recognized that good communication was a critical factor. SIMPROCESS is an object-based modeling tool containing preconstructed building blocks that represent work centers, queues, and item generators. These blocks may be attached to represent work flows, and descriptive statistical results may be collected easily. Its animation capabilities let the user observe items moving from work center to work center within the process. It also allows the user to attach queues to blocks to capture work-center delay times. The fourth key step in implementing our simulation model was to maintain close contact with the managers at the process centers to verify that the model's intermediate results were valid. This required several visits to interview people working in the centers. Their feedback during the preliminary stages of model development was crucial in verifying that the model accurately represented work flow through the centers.

The fifth and final step was to analyze the model results and present recommendations to managers. Once we had verified that the model output closely reflected previously known estimates of cycle times, we conducted what-if experiments by varying key process parameters. This analysis enabled us to predict the quantitative impact of the process parameters on the cycle time. To do the analysis, we had to develop an appropriate experimental design. We ran the model 5 to 10 times under each scenario and computed 95-percent confidence intervals for average cycle times, utilization rates, and work-center delay times under steady-state conditions.

We ran the models using a set of five what-if scenarios provided by U S WEST process managers. We carried out these five scenarios under three different error rates, 5, 20, and 50 percent. We ran the simulation model for a period of six months using daily time intervals, while we observed the total average cycle time as a key performance measure. A primary observation was that a decrease in error rate diminishes the impact of increases in demand and decreases in the workforce. Also, we measured the performance of the process centers by tracking their queue lengths and utilization rates. These observations led us to believe that the error rate is a driving force in process improvement. Accordingly, we recommended that process reengineering teams should focus on decreasing error rates and on mechanizing certain manual processes to compensate for the increase in cycle times under various scenarios.

2. CACI Products Company, *Reference Manual for SIMFACTORY II.5 and SIMPROCESS,* La Jolla, Calif., 1992.
Source: Adapted from Youngho Lee and Amie Elcan, "Simulation Modeling for Process Reengineering in the Telecommunications Industry," *Interfaces,* vol. 26, no. 3, May–June 1996, pp. 1–9.

SUMMARY

When their assumptions are met, analytical queuing models can help service system managers to evaluate possible alternative courses of action by predicting waiting time statistics. The models also provide insights that help to explain such queuing phenomena as pooling, the effect of finite queues on realized demand, the nonproportional effects of adding servers on waiting time, and the importance of controlling demand as seen by reducing service time variance. The approach to capacity planning depends on the criterion of system performance being used. Further, queuing models are useful in the analysis because of their ability to predict system performance. If the queuing model assumptions are not met or the system is too complex, however, then computer-simulation modeling (found in the Chapter 11 supplement) is required.

KEY TERMS AND DEFINITIONS

A/B/C **classification of queuing models** where *A* stands for the arrival distribution, *B* for the service time distribution, and *C* for the number of servers in a parallel-server queuing system.

Critical fractile a cumulative probability of customer demand that will be accommodated by an optimal level of capacity.

Finite queue a queue that is limited physically (e.g., a limited number of parking spaces).

Steady state the condition of a system when distribution of its characteristics, such as the number of customers in the queue, becomes stationary regarding time (i.e., the system has moved out of an initial transient state and reached statistical equilibrium).

SOLVED PROBLEMS

1. Calculating System Characteristics

Problem Statement

Sunset Airlines is reviewing its check-in procedures in anticipation of its "two for the price of one" fare promotion. Presently, a single clerk spends an average of 3 minutes per passenger checking luggage and issuing boarding passes. Service times have a negative exponential distribution, and passenger arrivals are Poisson distributed, with an anticipated mean of 15 per hour during flight operations.

a. What is the probability that an arriving passenger will be served immediately without waiting?

Solution

Note that we have an *M/M/*1 system with $\lambda = 15$ per hour and $\mu = 60/3 = 20$ per hour. Using equation (I.1):

$$P(\text{system idle}) = P_0 = 1 - \rho$$
$$= 1 - (15/20)$$
$$= 0.25$$

b. The area immediately in front of the Sunset counter can accommodate only three passengers, including the one being served. What percentage of time will this area be inadequate for waiting passengers?

Solution

Using equation (I.2):

$$P(inadequate\ waiting\ space) = P(n \geq 4) = \rho^4 = (15/20)^4 = 0.316$$

Thus, the waiting area is inadequate 32 percent of the time.

c. Anticipating an increase in demand, Sunset has decided to add another clerk when passengers begin to experience an average wait time in queue of 17 minutes. Since arrival rates are monitored at the check-in counter, determine what arrival rate per hour would indicate the need for another clerk.

Solution

Set equation (I.8) equal to 17/60 hour, substitute $\mu = 20$, and solve for λ:

$$W_q = \frac{\rho}{\mu - \lambda} = \frac{\lambda}{20}\left[\frac{1}{20 - \lambda}\right] = \frac{\lambda}{400 - 20\lambda} = \frac{17}{60}$$

Therefore,

$$\lambda = 17\ \text{per hour}$$

2. Capacity Planning

Problem Statement

The average arrival rate of customers has reached 20 per hour, and Sunset Airlines must increase the capacity of its check-in system with the addition of one clerk. Based on a customer survey, $15 per hour is considered to be the opportunity cost of waiting in queue. Clerks are paid $10 per hour and still process a passenger in 3 minutes. Evaluate the following check-in system alternatives to find the least expensive arrangement using total hourly costs of clerks and customers waiting in queue.

a. Consider a multiple-queue configuration with separate waiting lines and no customer jockeying. Assuming demand is divided equally among the two clerks, what is the total hourly cost of this arrangement?

Solution

Treat each line as independent $M/M/1$ queues, with total system cost being twice the single-line cost. Calculate the value for L_q using equation (I.5) and substitute in equation (7) to determine the line cost:

$$L_q = \frac{\rho\lambda}{\mu - \lambda}$$

$$= \frac{10}{20}\left[\frac{10}{20 - 10}\right]$$

$$= 0.5$$

Therefore, total system cost $= 2[10 + 15(0.5)] = \$35$ per hour.

b. Consider adding one self-serve automatic ticketing machine (ATM) with a constant service time of 3 minutes to help the single clerk. Assume demand is divided equally between the single live clerk and the ATM. What is the total hourly cost of this arrangement if the ATM operating costs are negligible?

Solution

Treat each line as independent, with one being an $M/M/1$ as in part **a,** with $L_q = 0.5$, and the other being an $M/D/1$ (constant service of ATM). First, calculate the L_q for the ATM line using equation (III.2) with $V(t) = 0$:

$$L_q = \frac{\rho^2 + \lambda^2 V(t)}{2(1 - \rho)}$$

$$= \frac{0.5^2 + 10^2(0)}{2(1 - 0.5)}$$

$$= 0.25$$

Therefore, total system cost = single clerk + ATM = 10 + 15(0.5) + 0 + 15(0.25) = $21.25 per hour.

c. Consider a single-queue arrangement with two live tellers. What is the total hourly cost of this arrangement?

Solution

From Appendix C, with $c = 2$ and $\rho - 20/20 = 1$, we find $L_q = 0.333$, so the total system cost = 10(2) + 15(0.333) = $25 per hour.

TOPICS FOR DISCUSSION

1. Example 12.1 presented a naive capacity planning exercise and was criticized for using averages. Recall the concept of a "bottleneck" from Chapter 6, "The Supporting Facility," and suggest other reservations about this planning exercise.
2. For a queuing system with a finite queue, the arrival rate can exceed the capacity to serve. Use an example to explain how this is possible.
3. What are some disadvantages associated with the concept of pooling service resources?
4. Discuss how the $M/G/\infty$ model could be used to determine the number of emergency medical vehicles required to serve a community.
5. Discuss how one could determine the economic cost of keeping customers waiting.

EXERCISES

12.1. A general-purpose auto repair garage has one mechanic who specializes in muffler installations. Customers seeking service arrive at an average rate of 2 per hour, with a Poisson distribution. The average time to install a muffler is 20 minutes, with negative exponential distribution.

    a. On arrival at the garage, how many customers should one expect to find in the system?

    b. The management is interested in adding another mechanic when the customer's average time in the system exceeds 90 minutes. If business continues to increase, at what arrival rate per hour will an additional mechanic be needed?

12.2. A business school is considering replacing its old minicomputer with a faster model. Past records show that the average student arrival rate is 24 per hour, Poisson distributed, and that the service times are distributed exponentially. The computer selection committee has been instructed to consider only machines that will yield an average turnaround time (i.e., expected time in the system) of 5 minutes or less. What is the smallest computer-processing rate per hour that can be considered?

12.3. The Lower Colorado River Authority (LCRA) has been studying congestion at the boat-launching ramp near Mansfield Dam. On weekends, the arrival rate averages 5 boaters per hour, Poisson distributed. The average time to launch or retrieve a boat is 10 minutes, with negative exponential distribution. Assume that only one boat can be launched or retrieved at a time.

    a. The LCRA plans to add another ramp when the average turnaround time (i.e., time in the system) exceeds 90 minutes. At what average arrival rate per hour should the LCRA begin to consider adding another ramp?

    b. If there were room to park only 2 boats at the top of the ramp in preparation for launching, how often would an arrival find insufficient parking space?

12.4. On average, 4 customers per hour use the public telephone in the sheriff's detention area, and this use has a Poisson distribution. The length of a phone call varies according to a negative exponential distribution, with a mean of 5 minutes. The sheriff will install a second telephone booth when an arrival can expect to wait 3 minutes or longer for the phone.

   a. By how much must the arrival rate per hour increase to justify a second telephone booth?

   b. Suppose the criterion for justifying a second booth is changed to the following: install a second booth when the probability of having to wait at all exceeds 0.6. Under this criterion, by how much must the arrival rate per hour increase to justify a second booth?

12.5. A company has a central document-copying service. Arrivals are assumed to follow the Poisson probability distribution, with a mean rate of 15 per hour. Service times are assumed to follow the exponential distribution. With the present copying equipment, the average service time is 3 minutes. A new machine is available that will have a mean service time of 2 minutes. The average wage of the people who bring the documents to be copied is $3 an hour.

   a. If the new machine can be rented for $4 per hour more than the old machine, should the company rent the new machine? Consider lost productive time of employees as time spent waiting in queue only because the copying machine is a self-serve device.

   b. For the old copying machine, what is the probability when a person arrives that he or she will encounter people already waiting in line for service? (Be careful to identify properly the number of customers who might be present for this situation to arise.)

   c. Suppose the new copying machine is rented. How many chairs should be provided for those waiting in line if we are satisfied when there will be enough chairs at least 90 percent of the time?

12.6. Sea Dock, a private firm, operates an unloading facility in the Gulf of Mexico for supertankers delivering crude oil for refineries in the Port Arthur area of Texas. Records show that, on average, 2 tankers arrive per day, with a Poisson distribution. Supertankers are unloaded one at a time on a first-come, first-served (FCFS) basis. Unloading requires approximately 8 hours of a 24-hour working day, and unloading times have a negative exponential distribution.

   a. Sea Dock has provided mooring space for 3 tankers. Is this sufficient to meet the U.S. Coast Guard requirement that at least 19 of 20 arrivals should find mooring space available?

   b. Sea Dock can increase its unloading capacity to a rate of 4 ships per day through additional labor at a cost of $480 per day. Considering the $1,000-per-day demurrage fee charged to Sea Dock for keeping a supertanker idle (this includes unloading time as well as time spent waiting in queue), should management consider this expansion opportunity?

12.7. Last National Bank is concerned about the level of service at its single drive-in window. A study of customer arrivals during the window's busy period revealed that, on average, 20 customers per hour arrive, with a Poisson distribution, and they are given FCFS service, requiring an average of 2 minutes, with service times having a negative exponential distribution.

   a. What is the expected number of customers waiting in queue?

   b. If Last National were using an automated teller machine with a constant service time of 2 minutes, what would be the expected number of drive-in customers in the system?

   c. There is space in the drive for 3 cars (including the one being served). What is the probability of traffic on the street being blocked by cars waiting to turn into the bank driveway?

   d. Last National is considering adding tellers at the current drive-in facility. It has decided on $5 per hour as the imputed cost of customer waiting time in the system. The hourly cost of a teller is $10. The average arrival rate of customers has reached 30 per hour. On the basis of the total hourly cost of tellers and customer waiting, how many tellers do you recommend? Assume that with use of pneumatic tubes, tellers can serve customers as though there were a single queue.

12.8. Green Valley Airport has been in operation for several years and is beginning to experience flight congestion. A study of airport operations revealed that planes arrive at an average rate of 12 per hour, with a Poisson distribution. On the single runway, a plane can land and be cleared every 4 minutes on average, and service times have a negative exponential distribution. Planes are processed on an FCFS basis, with takeoffs occurring between landings. Planes waiting to land are asked to circle the airport.

    a. What is the expected number of airplanes circling the airport, waiting in queue for clearance to land?

    b. A new ground-approach radar system approved by the Federal Aviation Administration is being considered as a means of reducing congestion. Under this system, planes can be processed at a constant rate of 15 per hour (i.e., the variance is zero). What would be the expected number of airplanes circling the airport, waiting in queue for clearance to land, if this system were to be used?

    c. Assume that the cost of keeping an airplane in the air is approximately $70 per hour. If the cost of the proposed radar system were $100 per hour, would you recommend its adoption?

12.9. Community Bank is planning to expand its drive-in facility. Observations of the existing single-teller window reveal that customers arrive at an average rate of 10 per hour, with a Poisson distribution, and that they are given FCFS service, with an average transaction time of 5 minutes. Transaction times have a negative exponential distribution. Community Bank has decided to add another teller and to install four remote stations with pneumatic tubes running from the stations to the tellers, who are located in a glassed-in building. The cost of keeping a customer waiting in the system is represented as a $5-per-hour loss of goodwill. The hourly cost of a teller is $10.

    a. Assume that each teller is assigned two stations exclusively, that demand is divided equally among the stations, and that no customer jockeying is permitted. What is the average number of customers waiting in the entire system?

    b. If, instead, both tellers work all the stations and the customer waiting the longest is served by the next available teller, what is the average number of customers in the system?

    c. What hourly savings are achieved by pooling the tellers?

12.10. Consider a one-pump gas station that satisfies the assumptions for the $M/M/1$ model. It is estimated that, on average, customers arrive to buy gas when their tanks are one-eighth full. The mean time to service a customer is 4 minutes, and the arrival rate is 6 customers per hour.

    a. Determine the expected length of the queue and the expected time in the system.

    b. Suppose that customers perceive a gas shortage (when there is none) and respond by changing the fill-up criterion to more than one-eighth full on average. Assuming that changes in λ are inversely proportional to changes in the fill-up criterion, compare results when the fill-up criterion is one-quarter full with the results in part **a.**

    c. Making the same assumption as in part **b,** compare the results obtained if the fill-up criterion is one-half full. Do we have the makings of a behaviorally induced gasoline panic?

    d. It is reasonable to assume that the time to service a customer will decrease as the fill-up criterion increases. Under "normal" conditions, it takes, on average, 2 minutes to pump the gasoline and 2 minutes to clean the windshield, check the oil, and collect the money. Rework parts **b** and **c** if the time to pump the gasoline changes proportionally to changes in the fill-up criterion.

Houston Port Authority

The Houston Port Authority has engaged you as a consultant to advise it on possible changes in the handling of wheat exports. At present, a crew of dockworkers using conventional belt conveyors unloads hopper cars containing wheat into cargo ships bound overseas. The crew is known to take an average of 30 minutes to unload a car. The crew is paid a total wage of $10 per hour. Hopper car arrivals have averaged 12 per 8-hour shift. The railroad assesses a demurrage charge from time of arrival to release at a rate of $4 per hour on rolling stock not in service. Partially unloaded cars from one shift are first in line for the following shift.

A chi-square "goodness-of-fit" analysis of arrival rates for the past months indicates a Poisson distribution. Data on unloading times for this period may be assumed to follow a negative exponential distribution.

Because of excessive demurrage charges, adding another work crew has been proposed. A visit to the work area indicates that both crews will be unable to work together on the same car because of congestion; however, two cars may be unloaded simultaneously with one crew per car.

During your deliberations, the industrial engineering staff reports that a pneumatic handling system has become available. This system can transfer wheat from cars to cargo ships at a constant rate of three cars per hour, 24 hours per day, with the assistance of a skilled operator earning $8 per hour. Such a system would cost $400,000 installed. The Port Authority uses a 10-percent discount rate for capital improvement projects. The port is in operation 24 hours per day, 365 days per year. For this analysis, assume a 10-year planning horizon, and prepare a recommendation for the Port Authority.

Freedom Express

Freedom Express (FreeEx), affectionately known as the Filibuster Fly, is a small commuter airline based in Washington, D.C., that serves the U.S. East coast. It runs nonstop flights between several cities and Reagan National Airport (DCA).

DCA frequently is congested, and at such times, planes are required to fly in a "stack" over the field. In other words, planes in the process of landing and those waiting for permission to land are deployed above the field.

FreeEx management is interested in determining how long its planes will have to wait so that an adequate amount of fuel can be loaded before departure from the outlying city to cover both the intercity flying time and the time in the stack. Excess fuel represents an unnecessary cost, however, because it reduces the payload capacity. Equally important is the

present cost of aviation fuel, $1.80 per gallon, and an average consumption rate of 20 gallons per minute.

The rate of arrival for all planes at DCA varies by the hour. The arrival rate and time in the stack are greatest each weekday between 4 and 5 P.M. and so FreeEx selected this time period for an initial study.

The study indicated that the mean arrival rate is 20 planes per hour, or one every 3 minutes. The variance about this mean, resulting from flight cancellations as well as charter and private flights, is characterized by a Poisson distribution.

During clear weather, the DCA control tower can land 1 plane per minute, or 60 planes per hour. Landings cannot exceed this rate in the interest of air safety. When the weather is bad, the landing rate is 30 per hour. Both good- and bad-weather landing rates are mean rates with a Poisson distribution. FreeEx's flights are short enough that management usually can tell before takeoff in an outlying city whether or not the rate of landings in DCA will be reduced because of weather considerations.

When a plane runs short of fuel while in the stack, it is given priority to land out of order. DCA rules, however, make clear that the airport will not tolerate abuse of this consideration. Therefore, FreeEx ensures that its planes carry enough fuel so that it will take advantage of the policy no more than 1 time in 20.

Questions

1. During periods of bad weather, as compared with periods of clear weather, how many additional gallons of fuel on average should FreeEx expect its planes to consume because of airport congestion?
2. Given FreeEx's policy of ensuring that its planes do not run out of fuel more than 1 in 20 times while waiting to land, how many reserve gallons (i.e., gallons over and above expected usage) should be provided for clear-weather flights? For bad-weather flights?
3. During bad weather, FreeEx has the option of instructing the Washington air controller to place its planes in a holding pattern from which planes are directed to land either at Washington National or at Dulles International, whichever becomes available first. Assume that the Dulles landing rate in bad weather also is 30 per hour, Poisson distributed, and that the combined arrival rate for both airports is 40 per hour. If FreeEx must pay $100 per flight to charter a bus to transport its passengers from Dulles to Washington National, should it exercise the option of permitting its aircraft to land at Dulles during bad weather? Assume that if the option is used, FreeEx's aircraft will be diverted to Dulles about one-half the time.

CASE

Renaissance Clinic (B)

Renaissance Clinic is a hospital dedicated to the health care of women. It is located in the hill country surrounding Austin, Texas, and offers an environment that is unique in Austin. At the time of a visit, a patient of Dr. Margaret Thompson's practice is directed by the receptionist either to a nurse clinician or to Dr. Thompson. On some occasions, a patient might see both the nurse and the doctor. In the case of Renaissance Clinic (A) in Chapter 11, we used a computer simulation model to determine resource allocation.

For this case, we want to apply queuing theory to Dr. Thompson's practice. The data in Table 12.7 were collected over several days of typical activity and the histograms indicate that arrival rates and service rates fit a Poisson distribution. Figure 12.4 shows the flow of patients during routine office visits.

TABLE 12.7

ARRIVAL AND SERVICE RATES AT RENAISSANCE CLINIC

Model parameter	Description	Expectations
λ	Arrival rate of patients	30 per hour
p_1	Fraction of patients who go to nurse clinician	⅔
p_2	Fraction of nurse clinician patients who also see physician	0.15
μ_S	Service rate of receptionist	40 per hour
μ_N	Service rate of nurse clinician	30 per hour
μ_D	Service rate of physician	15 per hour

Assignments

1. Assume the waiting line at the receptionist, the nurse clinician, and the doctor are managed independently with an FCFS priority. Using queuing formulas and the assumption that patients exiting from an activity follow a Poisson distribution, estimate the following statistics:

   a. Average waiting time in each of the queues (i.e., receptionist, nurse clinician, and physician).

   b. Average time in the entire system for each of the three patient paths.

   c. Overall average time in the system (i.e., expected time for an arriving patient).

   d. Average idle time in minutes per hour of work for the receptionist, the nurse clinician, and the doctor.

2. What are the key assumptions involved in your analysis above? Discuss the appropriateness of each in this situation.

3. What would be the impact on the above calculations of adding a second doctor to the clinic and sharing the doctor queue between them on a "first MD available" basis?

4. The clinic is considering adopting a queue priority system that is determined by the time of entry into the system at the receptionist. How might patients waiting for the doctor react to this policy?

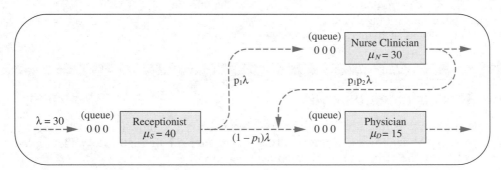

FIGURE 12.4 **Patient flow at Renaissance Clinic.**

SELECTED BIBLIOGRAPHY

GRASSMAN, W. K.: "Finding the Right Number of Servers in Real-World Queuing Systems," *Interfaces,* vol. 18, no. 2, 1988, pp. 94–104.

KOLESAR, PETER J., and LINDA V. GREEN: "Insights on Service System Design from a Normal Approximation to Erlang's Delay Formula," *Production and Operations Management,* vol. 7, no. 3, Fall 1998, pp. 282–293.

PULLMAN, MADELEINE E., JOHN C. GOODALE, and ROHIT VERMA: "Service Capacity Design with an Integrated Market Utility-Based Method," in J. A. Fitzsimmons and M. J. Fitzsimmons (eds.), *New Service Development,* Sage Publications, Thousand Oaks, Calif., 2000, pp. 111–137.

ROTHKOPF, M. H., and P. RECH: "Perspectives on Queues: Combining Queues Is Not Always Beneficial," *Operations Research,* vol. 35, no. 6, November–December 1987, pp. 906–909.

ENDNOTES

1. W. H. Bleuel, "Management Science's Impact on Service Strategy," *Interfaces,* vol. 6, no. 1, November 1975, part 2, pp. 4–12.

2. J. D. C. Little, "A Proof of the Queuing Formula: $L = \lambda W$," *Operations Research,* vol. 9, no. 3, May–June 1961, pp. 383–387. Also W. S. Jewell, "A Simple Proof of $L = \lambda W$," *Operations Research,* vol. 15, no. 6, November–December 1967, pp. 1109–1116; S. Stidham, Jr., "A Last Word on $L = \lambda W$," *Operations Research,* vol. 22, no. 2, March–April 1974, pp. 417–421.

CHAPTER THIRTEEN

Managing Capacity and Demand

Learning Objectives

After completing this chapter, you should be able to:

1. Describe the strategies for matching supply and demand for services.
2. Determine the overbooking strategy for a service that minimizes expected loss.
3. Use a Linear Programming model to prepare a weekly workshift schedule with two consecutive days off for each employee.
4. Prepare a work schedule for part-time employees.
5. Use yield management to establish the inventory level of a perishable resource to reserve for customers who are willing to pay a premium.

After fixed capacity investment decisions have been made (e.g., number of hotel rooms to be built or aircraft to be purchased) using the approaches described in Chapter 12, "Queuing Models and Capacity Planning," the hotel beds must be filled or the airline seats sold to make the daily operations profitable. The subject of this chapter is the challenge that is faced by managers of matching service supply with customer demand on a daily basis in a dynamic environment.

Service capacity is a perishable commodity. For example, a plane flying with empty seats has lost forever the revenue opportunity of carrying those additional passengers. American Airlines was the first in its industry to address this problem and to realize the potential of using what now is called *yield management,* which was discussed briefly in Chapter 4 and will be addressed in more detail here. Use of information technology to support yield management was not lost on Mr. Donald Burr, CEO of People Express, whose failing airline was bought by Texas Air in 1986. He is quoted as saying, "I'm the world's leading example of a guy killed by a computer chip."[1]

Unlike products that are stored in warehouses for future consumption, a service is an intangible personal experience that cannot be transferred from one person to another. Instead, a service is produced and consumed simultaneously. Whenever demand for a service falls short of the capacity to serve, the results are idle servers and facilities. Further, the variability in service demand is quite pronounced, and, in fact, our culture and habits contribute to these fluctuations. For example, most of us eat our meals at the same hours and take our vacations in July and August, and studies of hospitals indicate low utilization in the summer and fall months. These natural variations in service demand create periods of idle service at some times and of consumer waiting at others.

CHAPTER PREVIEW

In this chapter, we shall explore operating strategies that can increase capacity utilization by better matching the supply of and demand for services. We begin with a discussion of marketing-oriented strategies that can alter and smooth customer demand, such as using price incentives and promotion to stimulate off-peak utilization. Another common strategy is creating complementary services to balance the total demand among several services. In addition, the controversial practice of *overbooking* is examined in the context of making better use of perishable service capacity.

We also will look at operations-oriented strategies to control the level of service supply, such as scheduling workshifts, using part-time employees, and cross-training customer contact personnel to be more flexible in response to changes in customer demand. In conclusion, the new concept of yield management as pioneered by the airline industry will be explored as a comprehensive approach using many of these strategies in a sophisticated online information system.

STRATEGIES FOR MANAGING DEMAND

Excessive fluctuations in demand for service need not be accepted as inevitable. Service systems can smooth their demand by using both active and passive measures. With *smoothed demand,* the cyclical variation has been reduced. While the arrival of consumers will continue to occur at random intervals, the average rate of arrivals will be more stable over time. We shall discuss several strategies for smoothing demand, and Figure 13.1 summarizes those that commonly are used to manage service capacity.

FIGURE 13.1   Strategies for matching supply of and demand for services.

Partitioning Demand

Demand for a service seldom derives from a homogeneous source. For example, airlines differentiate between weekday business travelers and weekend pleasure travelers. Demand often is grouped into random arrivals and planned arrivals. For example, a drive-in bank can expect visits from its commercial account holders on a regular, daily basis and at approximately the same time; it also can expect visits from its personal account holders on a random basis.

An analysis of health clinic demand by E. J. Rising, R. Baron, and B. Averill showed that the greatest number of walk-in patients arrived on Monday and fewer during the remaining weekdays.[2] While walk-in demand is not controllable, appointments are. Therefore, why not make appointments in the latter part of the week to level demand? Using data for the same week in the previous year, these researchers noted the number of walk-in patients for each weekday. Subtracting these walk-in patients from daily physician capacity gives the number of appointment patients who are needed each day to smooth demand. For the sample week shown in Figure 13.2, this procedure yielded the number of appointment periods per day shown in Table 13.1.

The daily smoothing of demand was refined further by scheduling appointments at appropriate times during the day. After a two-month shakedown period, smoothing demand yielded the following benefits:

1. The number of patients seen increased by 13.4 percent.
2. This increase in patient demand was met, even though 5.1 percent fewer physician hours were scheduled.
3. The overall time physicians spent with patients increased 5.0 percent because of the increased number of appointments.

FIGURE 13.2 Effect of smoothing physician visits.
(*Source:* E. J. Rising, R. Baron, and B. Averill, "A Systems Analysis of a University Health-Service Outpatient Clinic." Reprinted with permission from *Operations Research,* vol. 21, no. 5, September–October 1973, p. 1035, Operations Research Society of America. No further reproduction permitted without the consent of the copyright owner.)

TABLE 13.1

SMOOTHING DEMAND BY APPOINTMENT SCHEDULING

Day	Appointments
Monday	84
Tuesday	89
Wednesday	124
Thursday	129
Friday	114

4. The average waiting time for patients remained the same.

5. A team of sociologists concluded that physician morale increased.

Offering Price Incentives

There are many examples of differential pricing. Consider the following:

1. Weekend and night rates for long-distance telephone calls.

2. Matinee or reduced prices before 6 P.M. at movie theaters.

3. Off-season hotel rates at resort locations.

4. Peak-load pricing by utility companies.

Differential pricing has been suggested for federal campsites to encourage better use of this scarce resource. For example, J. C. Nautiyal and R. L. Chowdhary developed a discriminatory pricing system to ensure that camping fees accurately reflect the marginal benefit of the last campsite on any given day.[3]

They identified four different camping experiences on the basis of days and weeks of the camping season. Table 13.2 contains a schedule of daily fees by experience type.

These experience groupings were made on the basis of total daily occupancy in the park under the assumption that occupancy is directly affected by available leisure time and climate. Campers in each experience group were interviewed to determine their travel costs. The marginal visitor was assumed to be the camper who incurred the highest cost in coming to the recreation site. This information was used to develop a demand curve for each experience type, and given the available number of campsites, the campsite fee was determined by means of these demand curves. Table 13.3 compares revenues generated under the existing system with those estimated when using discriminatory fees. Note that under the proposal, more campers are attracted, but with a corresponding reduction in total revenue. During the 78 days of free camping, how-

TABLE 13.2

SUGGESTED DISCRIMINATORY FEE SCHEDULE

Experience type	Days and weeks of camping season	Number of days	Daily fee
1	Saturdays and Sundays of weeks 10 to 15, plus Dominion Day and civic holidays	14	$6.00
2	Saturdays and Sundays of weeks 3 to 9 and 15 to 19, plus Victoria Day	23	2.50
3	Fridays of weeks 3 to 15, plus all other days of weeks 9 to 15 that are not in experience type 1 or 2	43	0.50
4	Rest of camping season	78	Free

TABLE 13.3

COMPARISON OF EXISTING REVENUE AND PROJECTED REVENUE FROM DISCRIMINATORY PRICING

Experience type	Existing fee of $2.50		Discriminatory fee	
	Campsites occupied	Revenue	Campsites occupied (est.)	Revenue
1	5,891	$14,727	5,000	$30,000
2	8,978	22,445	8,500	21,250
3	6,129	15,322	15,500	7,750
4	4,979	12,447	—	—
Total	25,977	$64,941	29,000	$59,000

ever, a savings in labor cost is possible, because no ranger is needed to collect fees at the campsite. Even so, for the arrangement to work effectively in altering demand, it must be well advertised and include an advance booking system for campsites.

Note the projected increase in demand for experience type 3 because of the substantially reduced fee. The result of off-peak pricing is to tap a latent demand for campsites instead of redistributing peak demand to off-peak times. Thus, discriminatory pricing fills in the valleys (i.e., periods of low demand) instead of leveling off the peaks. The result is better overall utilization of a scarce resource and, for a private-sector firm, the potential for increased profit (assuming that fees cover variable costs). Private firms, however, also would want to avoid directing high-paying customers to low-rate schedules. For example, airlines exclude the business traveler from discount fares through restrictions such as requiring passengers to remain at their destination over a weekend.

Promoting Off-Peak Demand

Creative use of off-peak capacity results from seeking different sources of demand. One example is use of a resort hotel during the off-season as a retreat location for business or professional groups. Another is a mountain ski resort that becomes a staging area for backpacking during the summer. Telephone companies offer lower rates to encourage long-distance dialing at night or on weekends, when switching equipment is underutilized. Figure 13.3 shows such a schedule for one such long-distance carrier.

	Monday	Tuesday	Wednesday	Thursday	Friday	Saturday	Sunday
8 AM–5 PM							
5 PM–11 PM							
11 PM–8 AM							

Day Rate Plus additional volume discounts of 10%	**Evening Rate** Plus additional volume discounts of 20%–30%	**Night/Weekend Rate** Plus additional volume discounts of 20%–30%

FIGURE 13.3 Rate schedule for Sprint PLUS.

Creative use of a ski resort during the summer avoids the cost of idle facilities.
© Karl Weatherly/CORBIS

The strategy of promoting off-peak demand can be used to discourage overtaxing the facility at other times. A department store's appeal to "shop early and avoid the Christmas rush" as well as a supermarket's offer of double coupons on Wednesdays are examples.

Developing Complementary Services

Restaurants have discovered the benefits of complementary services by adding a bar. Diverting waiting customers into the lounge during busy periods can be profitable for the restaurant as well as soothing to anxious consumers. Movie theaters traditionally have sold popcorn and soft drinks, but now they also include video games in their lobbies. These examples illustrate complementary services being offered to occupy waiting consumers.

Convenience stores have expanded their services to include self-service gas pumps and fast-food meals. The concept of holistic medicine, which combines traditional medical attention with nutritional and psychiatric care, is a further example. Developing complementary services is a natural way to expand one's market, and it is particularly attractive if the new demands for service are contracyclical and result in a more uniform aggregate demand (i.e., when the new service demand is high, the original service demand is low). This explains why nearly all heating contractors also perform air-conditioning services.

Using Reservation Systems and Handling the Overbooking Problem

Taking reservations presells the potential service. As reservations are made, additional demand is deflected to other time slots at the same facility or to other facilities within the same organization. Hotel chains with national reservation systems regularly book customers in nearby hotels owned by their chain when the customer's first choice is not available.

Reservations also benefit consumers by reducing waiting and guaranteeing service availability. Problems do arise, however, when customers fail to honor their reservations. (These customers are referred to as *no-shows*.) Usually, customers are not held financially liable for their unkept reservations. This can lead to undesirable behavior, such as when passengers make several flight reservations to cover contingencies. This was a common practice of business passengers who did not know exactly when they would be able to depart; with multiple reservations, they would be assured of a flight out as soon as they were able to leave. All unused reservations result in empty seats, however, unless the airline is notified of the cancellations in advance. To control no-shows among discount flyers, airlines now issue nonrefundable tickets.

Faced with flying empty seats because of the no-shows, airlines adopted a strategy of *overbooking*. By accepting reservations for more than the available seats, airlines hedge against significant numbers of no-shows; however, the airlines risk turning away passengers with reservations if they overbook too many seats. Because of overbooking abuses, the U.S. Federal Aviation Administration instituted regulations requiring airlines to reimburse overbooked passengers and to find them space on the next available flight. Similarly, many hotels place their overbooked guests in a nearby hotel of equal quality at no expense to the guests. A good overbooking strategy should minimize the expected opportunity cost of idle service capacity as well as the expected cost of turning away reservations. Thus, adopting an overbooking strategy requires training front-line personnel (e.g., front-desk clerks at a hotel) to handle graciously guests whose reservations cannot be honored. At a minimum, a courtesy van should be available to transport the customer to a competitor's hotel after making arrangements for an equivalent room.

Example 13.1: Surfside Hotel

During the past tourist season, Surfside Hotel did not achieve very high occupancy despite a reservation system that was designed to keep the hotel fully booked. Apparently, prospective guests were making reservations that, for one reason or another, they failed to honor. A review of front-desk records during the current peak period, when the hotel was fully booked, revealed the record of no-shows given in Table 13.4.

TABLE 13.4

SURFSIDE HOTEL NO-SHOW EXPERIENCE

No-shows d	Probability P(d)	Reservations overbooked x	Cumulative probability P(d < x)
0	.07	0	0
1	.19	1	.07
2	.22	2	.26
3	.16	3	.48
4	.12	4	.64
5	.10	5	.76
6	.07	6	.86
7	.04	7	.93
8	.02	8	.97
9	.01	9	.99

A room that remains vacant because of a no-show results in an opportunity loss of the $40 room contribution. The expected number of no-shows is calculated from Table 13.4 as

$$0(.07) + 1(.19) + 2(.22) + \cdots + 8(.02) + 9(.01) = 3.04$$

This yields an expected opportunity loss of 3.04 × $40, or $121.60, per night. To avoid some of this loss, management is considering an overbooking policy; however, if a guest holding a reservation is turned away owing to overbooking, then other costs are incurred. Surfside has made arrangements with a nearby hotel to pay for the rooms of guests whom it cannot accommodate. Further, a penalty is associated with the loss of customer goodwill and the impact this has on future business. Management estimates this total loss to be approximately $100 per guest "walked" (a term used by the hotel industry). A good overbooking strategy should strike a balance between the opportunity cost of a vacant room and the cost of not honoring a reservation; the best overbooking strategy should minimize the expected cost in the long run.

Table 13.5 displays the loss that is associated with each possible overbooking alternative. Note that no costs are incurred along the diagonal of the table, because in each case, the number of reservations that were overbooked exactly matched the no-shows for that day (e.g., if 4 reservations were overbooked and 4 guests failed to arrive, then every guest who did arrive would be accommodated and, further, the hotel is fully occupied, which is a win-win situation). The values above the diagonal are determined by moving across each row and increasing the cost by a multiple of $100 for each reservation that could not be honored, because fewer no-shows occurred than anticipated. For example, consider the first row, which is associated with zero no-shows occurring, and note that a $100 loss is associated with overbooking by one reservation. The values below the diagonal are shown as increasing by multiples of $40 as we move down each column, because more no-shows occurred than expected, which resulted in vacant rooms for the night. For example, consider the first column that is associated with not implementing an overbooking strategy, and note the increasing cost implications of trusting guests to honor their reservations.

For each overbooking reservation strategy, the expected loss is calculated by multiplying the loss for each no-show possibility by its probability of occurrence and then

TABLE 13.5

OVERBOOKING LOSS TABLE

		Reservations overbooked									
No-shows	Probability	0	1	2	3	4	5	6	7	8	9
0	.07	0	100	200	300	400	500	600	700	800	900
1	.19	40	0	100	200	300	400	500	600	700	800
2	.22	80	40	0	100	200	300	400	500	600	700
3	.16	120	80	40	0	100	200	300	400	500	600
4	.12	160	120	80	40	0	100	200	300	400	500
5	.10	200	160	120	80	40	0	100	200	300	400
6	.07	240	200	160	120	80	40	0	100	200	300
7	.04	280	240	200	160	120	80	40	0	100	200
8	.02	320	280	240	200	160	120	80	40	0	100
9	.01	360	320	280	240	200	160	120	80	40	0
Expected loss($)	—	121.60	91.40	87.80	115.00	164.60	231.00	311.40	401.60	497.40	560.00

adding the products. For example, the expected loss of overbooking by two reservations is calculated by multiplying the probabilities in column 2 (i.e., Probability) by the losses in column 5 (i.e., 2 Reservations overbooked) as follows:

$$.07(\$200) + .19(\$100) + .22(\$0) + .16(\$40) + .12(\$80) + .10(\$120)$$

$$+ .07(\$160) + .04(\$200) + .02(\$240) + .01(\$280) = \$87.80$$

Table 13.5 indicates that a policy of overbooking by two rooms will minimize the expected loss in the long run. If this policy is adopted, we can realize a gain of $33.80 per night from overbooking. That is the difference in the expected loss between not overbooking of $121.60 and the expected loss from overbooking by two rooms of $87.80. This substantial amount explains why overbooking is a popular strategy for capacity-constrained service firms such as airlines and hotels.

In Chapter 14, "Managing Facilitating Goods," the *critical fractile* criterion is derived for perishable goods, which we apply to our inventory of rooms:

$$P(d < x) \le \frac{C_u}{C_u + C_o} \tag{1}$$

where

C_u = the $40 room contribution that is lost when a reservation is not honored (i.e., the number of no-shows is *under*estimated)

C_o = the $100 opportunity loss associated with not having a room available for an overbooked guest (i.e., the number of no-shows is *over*estimated

d = the number of no-shows based on past experience

x = the number of rooms overbooked

This critical probability, which is based on marginal analysis, also can be used to identify the best overbooking strategy. Thus, the number of rooms overbooked should just cover the cumulative probability of no-shows and no more, as calculated below:

$$P(d < x) \le \frac{\$40}{\$40 + \$100} \le 0.286$$

From Table 13.4, a strategy of overbooking by two rooms satisfies the critical fractile criterion, because the cumulative probability $P(d<x) = 0.26$ and, thus, confirms the earlier decision based on minimizing the expected overbooking loss.

STRATEGIES FOR MANAGING SUPPLY

For many services, demand cannot be smoothed very effectively. Consider, for example, the demand for telephone operators as shown in Figure 13.4. These data are the half-hourly call rates during a typical 24-hour day for a metropolitan telephone company. We see that the peak volume (2,500 calls) occurs at 10:30 A.M. and the minimum volume (20 calls) occurs at 5:30 A.M. The peak-to-valley variation is 125 to 1. No inducements are likely to change this demand pattern substantially; therefore, control must come from adjusting service supply to match demand. Several strategies can be used to achieve this goal.

Using Daily Workshift Scheduling

By scheduling workshifts carefully during the day, the profile of service supply can be made to approximate demand. Workshift scheduling is an important staffing problem

FIGURE 13.4 **Daily demand for telephone operators.**
(*Source:* E. S. Buffa, M. J. Cosgrove, and B. J. Luce, "An Integrated Work
Shift Scheduling System," *Decision Sciences,* vol. 7, no. 4, October 1976,
p. 622. Reprinted with permission from Decision Sciences Institute,
Georgia State University.)

for many service organizations that face cyclical demand, such as telephone companies, hospitals, banks, and police departments.

The general approach begins with a forecast of demand by hour, which is converted to hourly service staffing requirements. The time interval could be less than an hour; for example, 15-minute intervals are used by fast-food restaurants to schedule work during meal periods. Next, a schedule of tours, or shifts, is developed to match the staffing requirements profile as closely as possible. Finally, specific service personnel are assigned to tours, or shifts. The telephone-operator staffing problem will be used to demonstrate the analysis required for each step; however, the approach can be generalized to any service organization.

Forecast Demand   Daily demand is forecast in half-hour intervals, as shown in Figure 13.4, and must account for both weekday and weekend variations as well as seasonal adjustments. The Saturday and Sunday call load was found to be approximately 55 percent of the typical weekday load. Summer months were found to be generally lower in demand. Special high-demand days, such as Mother's Day and Christmas, were taken into account.

Convert to Operator Requirements   A profile of half-hour operator requirements is developed on the basis of the forecast daily demand and call distribution. A standard service level, which is defined by the Public Utilities Commission, requires that 89 percent of the time, an incoming call must be answered within 10 seconds. The half-hour operator requirements are determined using a conventional queuing model to ensure that the service level is achieved for each half hour.[4] The result is a topline profile of operators required by the half hour, as shown in Figure 13.5.

Schedule Shifts   Tours, representing various start and end times of work, need to be assigned so that they aggregate to the topline profile, shown in Figure 13.5. Each tour consists of two working sessions separated by a rest pause or meal period (e.g., 9 A.M.–1 P.M., lunch break, 2 P.M.–6 P.M.). The set of possible tours is defined by state and federal laws, union agreements, and company policy. A heuristic computer program

FIGURE 13.5 Profile of operator requirements and tour assignments.
(*Source:* E. S. Buffa, M. J. Cosgrove, and B. J. Luce, "An Integrated Work Shift Scheduling System," *Decision Sciences,* vol. 7, no. 4, October 1976, p. 626. Reprinted with permission from Decision Sciences Institute, Georgia State University.)

prepared especially for this problem chooses tours from the permissible set such that the absolute difference between operator requirements and operators assigned is minimized when summed over all "n" half-hour periods. If R_i is the number of operators required in period i and W_i is the number of operators assigned in period i, then the objective can be stated as follows:

$$\text{Minimize} \qquad \sum_{i=1}^{n} |R_i - W_i| \qquad (2)$$

The schedule-building process is shown schematically in Figure 13.6. At each iteration, one tour at a time is selected from all possible tours. The tour selected at each step is the one that best meets the criterion stated in equation (2). Because this procedure favors shorter tours, the different shift lengths are weighted in the calculation to avoid this bias. The result is a list of tours required to meet the forecast demand, as well as a schedule of lunch and rest periods during those tours.

Assign Operators to Shifts   Given the set of tours required, the assignment of operators to these tours is complicated because of the 24-hour, 7-days-per-week operation. Questions of equity arise regarding the timing of days off and the assignment of overtime work, which involves extra pay. Another computer program makes operator assignments according to policies such as "give at least 1 day off per week and maximize consecutive days off." The actual assignment of operators to shifts also accounts for employee shift preferences. The result of this final step is a feasible schedule of employees assigned to tours.

Using Weekly Workshift Scheduling with Days-Off Constraint

As noted, developing tours to match the profile of daily demand is only part of the problem. Many public services such as police, fire protection, and emergency hospital care must be available 24 hours a day, every day of the week. For these organizations, a typical employee works 5 days a week with 2 consecutive days off each week, but not

FIGURE 13.6   **The schedule-building process.**
(*Source:* E. S. Buffa, M. J. Cosgrove, and B. J. Luce, "An Integrated Work Shift Scheduling System," *Decision Sciences,* vol. 7, no. 4, October 1976, p. 622. Reprinted with permission from Decision Sciences Institute, Georgia State University.)

necessarily Saturday and Sunday. Management is interested in developing work schedules and meeting the varying employee requirements for weekdays and weekends with the smallest number of staff members possible.

This problem can be formulated as an integer linear programming (ILP) model. To begin, the desired staffing levels are determined for each day in the week. The problem then becomes one of determining the minimum number of employees required for assignment to each of seven possible tours. Each tour consists of 5 days on and 2 consecutive days off; each will begin on a different day of the week and last for 5 consecutive working days. Consider the following general formulation of this problem as an ILP model.

Variable definitions:

x_i = number of employees assigned to tour i, where day i begins 2 consecutive days off [e.g., employees assigned to x_i have Sunday and Monday off]

b_j = desired staffing level for day j

Objective function:

Minimize $x_1 + x_2 + x_3 + x_4 + x_5 + x_6 + x_7$

Constraints:

Sunday $x_2 + x_3 + x_4 + x_5 + x_6 \geq b_1$

Monday $x_3 + x_4 + x_5 + x_6 + x_7 \geq b_2$

Tuesday $x_1 \quad\quad + x_4 + x_5 + x_6 + x_7 \geq b_3$

Wednesday $x_1 + x_2 \quad\quad + x_5 + x_6 + x_7 \geq b_4$

Thursday $x_1 + x_2 + x_3 \quad\quad + x_6 + x_7 \geq b_5$

Friday $x_1 + x_2 + x_3 + x_4 \quad\quad + x_7 \geq b_6$

Saturday $x_1 + x_2 + x_3 + x_4 + x_5 \quad\quad \geq b_7$

$x_i \geq 0$ and integer

Example 13.2: Hospital Emergency Room

The emergency room is operated on a 24-hour, 7-days-per-week schedule. The day is divided into three eight-hour shifts. The total number of nurses required during the day shift is:

Day	Su	M	Tu	W	Th	F	Sa
Nurses	3	6	5	6	5	5	5

The emergency room director is interested in developing a workforce schedule that will minimize the number of nurses required to staff the facility. Nurses work 5 days a week and are entitled to 2 consecutive days off each week.

The ILP model above is formulated with the appropriate right-hand-side constraint values (i.e., $b_1 = 3$, $b_2 = 6, \cdots, b_6 = 5$, $b_7 = 5$), and the solution yields the following results: $x_1 = 1$, $x_2 = 1$, $x_3 = 2$, $x_4 = 0$, $x_5 = 3$, $x_6 = 0$, $x_7 = 1$. This means we have one tour with Sunday and Monday off, one tour with Monday and Tuesday off, two tours with Tuesday and Wednesday off, three tours with Thursday and Friday off, and one tour with Saturday and Sunday off. The corresponding staffing schedule is shown in Table 13.6 with excess staff occurring only on Sunday and Saturday.

These scheduling problems typically result in multiple optimal solutions. For example, in this case, the solution $x_1 = 1$, $x_2 = 1$, $x_3 = 1$, $x_4 = 1$, $x_5 = 1$, $x_6 = 1$, $x_7 = 2$ is feasible and also requires eight nurses. Why might this second solution be preferred to the schedule shown in Table 13.6?

Increasing Customer Participation

The strategy of increasing customer participation is illustrated best by the fast-food restaurants that have eliminated personnel who serve food and clear tables. The customer (now a coproducer) not only places the order directly from a limited menu but also clears the table after the meal. Naturally, the customer expects faster service and

TABLE 13.6

WEEKLY NURSE STAFFING SCHEDULE, × = WORKDAY

Nurse	Su	M	Tu	W	Th	F	Sa
A	···	···	×	×	×	×	×
B	×	···	···	×	×	×	×
C	×	×	···	···	×	×	×
D	×	×	···	···	×	×	×
E	×	×	×	×	···	···	×
F	×	×	×	×	···	···	×
G	×	×	×	×	···	···	×
H	···	×	×	×	×	×	···
Total	6	6	5	6	5	5	7
Required	3	6	5	6	5	5	5
Excess	3	0	0	0	0	0	2

less-expensive meals to compensate for this help; however, the service provider benefits in many subtle ways. Of course, there are fewer personnel to supervise and to pay, but more important, the customer as a coproducer provides labor just at the moment it is required. Thus, capacity to serve varies more directly with demand rather than being fixed.

Some drawbacks to self-service do exist, because the quality of labor is not completely under the service manager's control. A self-service gas customer may fail to check the tire pressure and oil level regularly, which eventually can lead to problems. Self-service of "bulk" foods (e.g., cereals, grains, honey, peanut butter) in markets can lead both to contamination of the product in the bulk container and to waste because of spillage.

Creating Adjustable Capacity

Through design, a portion of capacity can be made variable. Airlines routinely move the partition between first class and coach to meet the changing mix of passengers. An innovative restaurant, Benihana of Tokyo, arranged its floor plan to accommodate eating areas serving two tables of eight diners each. Chefs are assigned to each area, and they prepare the meal at the table in a theatrical manner, with flashing knives and animated movements. Thus, the restaurant can adjust its capacity effectively by having only the number of chefs on duty that is needed.

Capacity at peak periods can be expanded by the effective use of slack times. Performing supportive tasks during slower periods of demand allows employees to concentrate on essential tasks during rush periods. This strategy requires some cross-training of employees to allow performance of noncustomer-contact tasks during slow-demand periods. For example, servers at a restaurant can wrap silverware in napkins or clean the premises when demand is low; thus, they are free of these tasks during the rush period.

Sharing Capacity

A service delivery system often requires a large investment in equipment and facilities. During periods of underutilization, it may be possible to find other uses for this capacity. Airlines have cooperated in this manner for years. At small airports, airlines share the same gates, ramps, baggage-handling equipment, and ground personnel. It also is common for some airlines to lease their aircraft to others during the off-season; the lease agreement includes painting on the appropriate insignia and refurbishing the interior.

Cross-Training Employees

Some service systems are made up of several operations. When one operation is busy, another operation sometimes may be idle. Cross-training employees to perform tasks in several operations creates flexible capacity to meet localized peaks in demand.

The gains from cross-training employees can be seen at supermarkets. When queues develop at the cash registers, the manager calls on stockers to operate registers until the surge is over. Likewise, during slow periods, some of the cashiers are busy stocking shelves. This approach also can help to build an esprit de corps and give employees relief from monotony. In fast-food restaurants, cross-trained employees create capacity flexibility, because tasks can be reassigned to fewer employees during slow periods (temporarily enlarging the job) and become more specialized during busy periods (division of labor).

Using Part-Time Employees

When peaks of activity are persistent and predictable, such as at mealtimes in restaurants or paydays in banks, part-time help can supplement regular employees. If the required skills and training are minimal, then a ready part-time labor pool is available from high school and college students as well as others who are interested in supplementing their primary source of income.

Another source of part-time help is off-duty personnel who are placed on standby. Airlines and hospitals often pay their personnel some nominal fee to restrict their activities and be ready for work if they are needed.

Scheduling Part-Time Tellers at a Drive-In Bank[5]

Drive-in banks experience predictable variations in activity on different days of the week. Figure 13.7 shows the teller requirements for a typical week based on customer demand variations. This bank usually employed enough tellers to meet peak demands on Friday; however, the policy created considerable idle teller time on the low-demand days, particularly Tuesday and Thursday. To reduce teller costs, management decided to employ part-time tellers and to reduce their full-time staff to a level that just meets the demand for Tuesday. Further, to provide equity in hours worked, it was decided that a part-time teller should work at least 2, but no more than 3, days in a week.

A primary objective of scheduling part-time workers is to meet the requirements with the minimum number of teller-days. A secondary objective is to have a minimum number of part-time tellers. This approach is illustrated here using bank tellers, but the same procedure can be used for scheduling part-time employees in many other services.

Determine the Minimum Number of Part-Time Tellers Needed Figure 13.7 shows that with two full-time tellers, 12 teller-days remain to be covered during the week. Using 3-day schedules, we see that five tellers on Friday determines the feasible minimum in this case.

Develop a Decreasing-Demand Histogram From Figure 13.7, note the daily part-time teller requirements. Resequence the days in order of decreasing demand, as shown in Figure 13.8.

FIGURE 13.7 Teller requirements.

FIGURE 13.8 Histogram of decreasing part-time teller demand.

Assign Tellers to the Histogram Starting with the first part-time teller, assign that individual in Figure 13.8 to the first block on Friday, the second teller to block two, and so forth. Repeat the sequence with Monday, and carry over the remaining tellers into Wednesday. Table 13.7 summarizes the resulting daily part-time work schedule, which consists of two three-day work assignments for Tellers 1 and 2 and three two-day work assignments for Tellers 3, 4, and 5.

YIELD MANAGEMENT[6]

Since deregulation permitted airlines to set their own prices, a new approach to revenue maximization—called *yield management*—has emerged. Yield management actually is a comprehensive system that incorporates many of the strategies discussed earlier in this chapter (e.g., using reservation systems, overbooking, and partitioning demand).

Because of the perishable nature of airline seats (i.e., once a flight has departed, the potential revenue from an empty seat is lost forever), offering a discount on fares to fill the aircraft became attractive. Selling all seats at a discount, however, would preclude the possibility of selling some at full price. Yield management attempts to allocate the fixed capacity of seats on a flight to match the potential demand in various market segments (e.g., coach, tourist, and supersaver) in the most profitable manner. Although airlines were the first to develop yield management, other capacity-constrained service industries (e.g., hotels, rental-car firms, and cruise lines) also are adopting this practice.

Yield management is most appropriate for service firms that exhibit the following characteristics:

Relatively fixed capacity. Service firms with a substantial investment in facilities (e.g., hotels and airlines) can be considered as being capacity-constrained. Once all the seats on a flight are sold, further demand can be met only by booking passengers on a later flight. Motel chains with multiple inns in the same city, however, have some capacity flexibility, because guests attempting to find room at one site can be diverted to another location within the same company.

TABLE 13.7

DAILY PART-TIME WORK SCHEDULE, × = WORKDAY

Teller	Mon.	Tues.	Wed.	Thurs.	Fri.
1	×	⋯	×	⋯	×
2	×	⋯	⋯	×	×
3, 4	×	⋯	⋯	⋯	×
5	⋯	⋯	×	⋯	×

Ability to segment markets. For yield management to be effective, the service firm must be able to segment its market into different customer classes. By requiring a Saturday-night stay for a discounted fare, airlines can discriminate between a time-sensitive business traveler and a price-sensitive customer. Developing various price-sensitive classes of service is a major marketing challenge for a firm using yield management. Figure 13.9 shows how a resort hotel might segment its market into three customer classes and adjust the allocation of available rooms to each class on the basis of the seasons of the year.

Perishable inventory. For capacity-constrained service firms, each room or seat is referred to as a *unit* of inventory to be sold (actually, to be rented). As noted for the airlines, revenue from an unsold seat is lost forever. Airlines attempt to minimize this spoiled inventory by encouraging standby passengers. Given this time-perishable nature of an airline seat, what is the cost to the airline when a passenger is awarded a free ticket on a flight that has at least one empty seat?

Product sold in advance. Reservation systems are adopted by service firms to sell capacity in advance of use; however, managers are faced with the uncertainty of whether to accept an early reservation at a discount price or to wait and hope to sell the inventory unit to a higher-paying customer. In Figure 13.10, a demand-control chart (recall quality-control charts from Chapter 3) is drawn for a hotel on the basis of past bookings for a particular day of the week and season of the year. Because some variation in demand is expected, an acceptable range (in this case, ± 2 standard deviations) is drawn around the expected reservation accumulation curve. If demand is higher than expected, budget-rate classes are closed and only reservations at standard rates accepted. If the accumulation of reservations falls below the acceptable range, then reservations for rooms at budget rates are accepted.

Fluctuating demand. Using demand forecasting, yield management allows managers to increase utilization during periods of slow demand and to increase revenue during periods of high demand. By controlling the availability of budget rates, managers can maximize total revenue for the constrained service. Yield management is implemented in real time by opening and/or closing reserved sections—even on an hourly basis if desired.

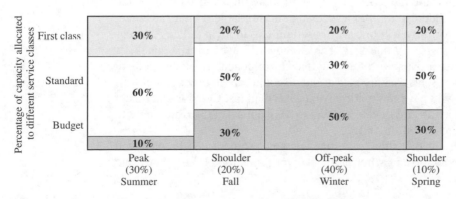

FIGURE 13.9 Seasonal allocation of rooms by service class for a resort hotel. (*Source:* After Christopher H. Lovelock, "Strategies for Managing Demand in Capacity-Constrained Service Organizations," *Service Industries Journal,* vol. 4, no. 3, November 1984, p. 23.)

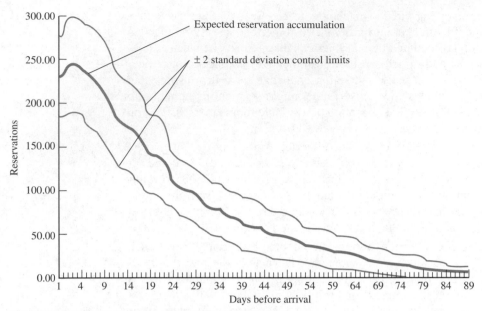

FIGURE 13.10 Demand control chart for a hotel.
(*Source:* Adapted from Sheryl E. Kimes, "Yield Management: A Tool for Capacity-Constrained Service Firms," *Journal of Operations Management,* vol. 8, no. 4, October 1989, p. 359. Reprinted with permission, The American Production and Inventory Society.)

Low marginal sales costs and high marginal capacity change costs. The cost of selling an additional unit of inventory must be low, such as the negligible cost of a snack for an airline passenger. The marginal cost of capacity additions is large, however, because of the necessary lumpy facility investment (i.e., a hotel addition must be at least an increment of 100 rooms).

Example 13.3: Blackjack Airline

During the recent economic slump, Blackjack Airline discovered that airplanes on its Los Angeles–to–Las Vegas route have been flying with more empty seats than usual. To stimulate demand, it has decided to offer a special, nonrefundable, 14-day advance-purchase "gamblers fare" for only $49 one way based on a round-trip ticket. The regular full-fare coach ticket costs $69 one way. The Boeing 737 used by Blackjack, as shown in Figure 13.11, has a capacity of 95 passengers in coach, and management wants to limit the number of seats that are sold at the discount fare in order to sell full-fare tickets to passengers who have not made advance travel plans. Considering recent experience, the demand for full-fare tickets appears to have a normal distribution, with a mean of 60 and a standard deviation of 15.

Phillip E. Pfeifer observed that this yield management problem can be analyzed with the critical fractile model used earlier in the chapter [equation (1)] for analyzing the overbooking problem.[7]

$$P(d < x) \leq \frac{C_u}{C_u + C_o}$$

where x = seats reserved for full-fare passengers
d = demand for full-fare tickets

FIGURE 13.11 The Boeing 737 cabin.

C_u = lost revenue associated with reserving too few seats at full fare (underestimated demand). The lost opportunity is the difference between the fares ($69 − $49 = $20) because we assume that the nonshopper passenger, willing to pay full fare, purchased a seat at the discount price.

C_o = cost of reserving one too many seats for sale at full fare (overestimated demand). We assume that the empty full-fare seat could have been sold at the discount price. However, C_o takes on two values, depending on the buying behavior of the passenger who would have purchased the seat if not reserved for full fare.

$$C_o = \begin{cases} \$49 & \text{if passenger is a shopper} \\ -(\$69 - \$49) & \text{if passenger is a nonshopper} \end{cases}$$

For the nonshopper case, the cost is reduced by the difference between the fares, because the airline profits from the nonshopper, who did not make the purchase, paying the full rather than the discount fare. To establish an expected value for C_o, however, we need the proportion p of passengers who are shoppers. In this case, market research determined that approximately 90 percent of passengers are discount seekers; thus, the expected value for the cost of overage becomes

$$C_o = (0.9)(\$49) - (1 - 0.9)(\$69 - \$49) = \$42.10$$

The critical fractile value $P(d < x) = \$20/(\$20 + \$42.10) = 0.32$ (see Figure 13.12). From Appendix A, "Areas of a Standard Normal Distribution," the z value for a cumulative probability of 0.32 is -0.47. Thus, the number of full-fare seats to reserve is found as follows:

$$\text{Reserved full} = \text{fare seats} = \mu + z\sigma$$

$$= 60 + (-0.47)(15)$$

$$= 53$$

Substituting symbols for the values used in the example above, we can derive a simple expression for determining the number of full-fare seats to reserve.

$$P(d < x) \leq \frac{(F - D)}{p \cdot F} \tag{3}$$

where x = seats reserved for full-fare passengers
$\quad d$ = demand for full-fare tickets
$\quad F$ = price of full fare
$\quad D$ = price of discount fare
$\quad p$ = probability that a passenger is a shopper

Yield Management Applications[8]

The following discussion provides a sampling of how yield management is used by other companies that face high fixed costs/low variable costs, spoilage, and temporary

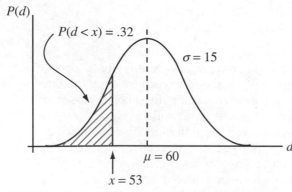

FIGURE 13.12 Critical fractile for Blackjack Airline.

demand imbalances to accomplish the same goals that airline pricing and yield management systems achieve.

Holiday Inn Reservation Optimization (HIRO)[9]   The hotel industry is similar to the airline industry, because hotels have extremely high costs invested in real estate and maintenance, temporary capacity, and demand imbalances. Imbalances such as varying, peak and low seasons, spoilage, and rooms not rented out for a night all represent lost revenue opportunities. Holiday Inn has recognized these classic management problems and uses both demand and capacity management to maximize revenues.

To achieve Holiday Inn's corporate objectives of ensuring that maximum occupancy and revenue are realized in each hotel and that guests, franchises, and internal staff are experiencing the highest level of customer satisfaction, Holiday Inn installed HIRO. The goal of maximizing occupancy and revenue means renting as many rooms as possible for the best price that the market will bear. With more than 500,000 rooms in the equation, a yield management optimization system could increase revenue tremendously.

HIRO, which is similar to American Airlines' SABRE, uses historical and current booking behavior to analyze room requests for each hotel. The yield management optimization equation includes seasonal occupancy patterns, local events, weekly cycles, and current trends to develop a hurdle price (i.e., the lowest point at which rooms should be booked at that particular hotel). The system predicts full occupancy at hotels and "filters out" discounted requests. HIRO even uses overbooking to account for cancellations and no-shows. As with any yield management system in the service industry, HIRO helps the hotel manager balance the ability to charge full price for a room and still maintain satisfaction from its loyal customer base.

Ryder's RyderFirst[10]   Ryder must manage the same logistical problems that are faced by any transportation company, and the shipping and trucking industry can use yield management to maximize revenue very effectively. Again, we see the classic business problem of high fixed costs/low variable costs with an expansive fleet of trucks, temporary capacity, and demand imbalances resulting from the seasonality of shipping (i.e., holidays and other peak inventory stocking periods), the threat of spoilage, and valuable unused capacity.

With the help of the American Airlines Decision Technology Group (AADT), Ryder implemented a yield management, pricing, and logistics system that helps it react quickly to competition and take advantage of the price elasticities of its different customer segments. The yield management system allows Ryder to move its truck capacity from areas of surplus to areas of demand by modeling the historical utilization patterns in each market.

Restaurant Catering Software[11]   Yield management techniques are being incorporated into software for use in the restaurant catering industry to ensure efficient utilization of expensive kitchens. Yield management software alerts operators to the potential for increased off-premise or catering bookings during anticipated low in-store demand days, thus enhancing overall profitability. Computer modeling also includes the manipulation of prices based on demand fluctuations. For example, a restaurant may reduce its menu item prices to increase customer count and overall revenue. Similarly, in peak demand periods, item prices may be increased to increase the average check revenue. Yield management helps to smooth the fluctuating demand patterns in the catering industry by anticipating when temporary demand and capacity imbalances will occur.

Amtrak[12]   As far back as 1988, Amtrak introduced a pricing and yield management system identical to that of airlines. This yield management system utilizes a tiered-fare structure, overbooking, discount allocation, and traffic management to maximize yields and capacity utilization. Like the airlines, Amtrak uses the yield management market information to decide what routes to enter and how much capacity is necessary to satisfy demand. Amtrak's flexible capacity allows it to make last-minute capacity adjustments much more easily than in the airline industry by attaching and detaching different classes of rail cars.

SUMMARY

The inherent variability of demand creates a challenge for managers trying to make the best use of service capacity. The problem can be approached from two perspectives. One focuses on smoothing consumer demand, permitting fuller utilization of a fixed service capacity. Various alternatives for managing demand are available, such as partitioning demand, offering price incentives, promoting off-peak use, and developing complementary services and reservation systems.

Another strategy considers the problem from the supply side, and many alternatives have been proposed to adjust service capacity to match demand. Elaborate procedures for workshift scheduling have been developed to adjust capacity to demand. When possible, part-time employees can be used to create variable capacity. Increasing consumer participation in the service process shifts some tasks to the consumer and reduces part of the burden during peak-demand periods. Other possibilities include sharing capacity with others, as airlines do by leasing aircraft during off-season periods. Occasionally, capacity can be adjusted—for example, by opening and closing dining areas in a restaurant. Cross-training employees also can provide flexible capacity by enabling employees to assist one another during busy periods.

The strategies are presented as two separate views of the same problem, one from the demand side and the other from the supply side. Of course, this should not preclude the use of mixed strategies to mediate the problem from both perspectives. Yield management as practiced by American Airlines is considered just such a mixed strategy, because the company integrates supply and demand management using the power of information contained in its computer reservation system. The result is the real-time ability to sell a class of service to the right customer at the appropriate time and the most competitive price.

KEY TERMS AND DEFINITIONS

Critical fractile the cumulative probability of demand formed by the ratio of the cost of *under*estimating demand divided by the sum of the costs of *under*estimating demand and *over*estimating demand.

Overbooking taking reservations in excess of available capacity in anticipation of customer no-shows.

Yield management a comprehensive system to maximize revenue for capacity-constrained services using reservation systems, overbooking, and partitioning demand.

BOX 9.1

Service Benchmark
YIELD MANAGEMENT AT AMERICAN AIRLINES

In its 1987 annual report, American Airlines broadly described the function of yield management as "selling the right seats to the right customers at the right prices." While this statement over-simplified yield management, it does capture the basic motivation behind the strategy. A better description of yield management as it applies to airlines is the control and management of reservations inventory in a way that increases (maximizes, if possible) company profitability, given the flight schedule and fare structure.

The role of yield management at American is analogous to the inventory control function for a manufacturing company. Planning departments determine the airline's flight schedule and fares. The combination of schedule and fares defines the products to be offered to the public. Yield management then determines how much of each product to put on the shelf (make available for sale). American's "store front" is the computerized reservations system, SABRE* (semi-automated business research environment). All sale and cancellation transactions, whether from American Airlines reservations agents or travel agents, pass through SABRE, updating reservations inventory for all affected flights. New reservations are accepted only if yield management controls permit.

Although there is some interaction, the American Airlines yield management system is typically divided into three major functions:

1. *Overbooking* is the practice of intentionally selling more reservations for a flight than there are actual seats on the aircraft. Airlines use overbooking to offset the effects of passenger cancellations and no-shows. Without overbooking, about 15 percent of seats would be unused on flights sold out at departure. Even more seats would be unused for flights sold out prior to departure.
2. *Discount allocation* is the process of determining the number of discount fares to offer on a flight. Airlines offer discount fares to stimulate demand and fill seats that would otherwise be empty. The availability of discount fares must be limited on popular flights to preserve space for late-booking, higher-revenue passengers. Therefore, airlines treat reservation space as a scarce resource that must be intelligently allocated to various discount fares.
3. *Traffic management* is the process of controlling reservations by passenger origin and destination to provide the mix of markets (multiple-flight connecting markets versus single-flight markets) that maximizes revenue. A passenger flying into Dallas/Fort Worth can connect and continue on to any of several final destinations on a second flight. Therefore, to maximize revenue across the entire system of flights, reservation inventory controls for one flight must consider the passenger demand on connecting flights.

The nature of today's marketplace in the airline industry makes yield management absolutely essential to profitable operations. At large airlines, such as American, the number of inventory controls and the frequency of updates require an automated decision-making system. American's current yield management system, DINAMO (dynamic inventory and maintenance optimizer), was fully implemented in 1988. DINAMO is the latest step of a development process that spans the last 25 years, responding to changes in the airline industry and taking advantage of innovations in computer technology. Three major changes motivated and shaped yield management development:

- The implementation of a computer reservations system (SABRE) in 1966, which had the capability of controlling reservations inventory.
- The introduction of supersaver discount fares in 1977.
- The deregulation of airline schedules and prices in 1979.

---

*Since the original publication of this article, American Airlines, Inc., and the SABRE Group have become separate subsidiaries of AMR, Inc.
Source: Barry C. Smith, John F. Leimkuhler, and Ross M. Darrow, "Yield Management at American Airlines," *Interfaces,* vol. 22, no. 1, January–February 1992, pp. 8–31.

BOX 9.1 (CONTINUED)

Prior to the implementation of SABRE, American had no centralized methods for reviewing or controlling reservation activity. Reservation offices, established in major cities, acted independently in making inventory decisions. Without the data on passenger behavior needed to do more sophisticated yield management, reservations control was limited to rudimentary overbooking.

SABRE provided a central point from which to collect data. SABRE also provided the centralized control needed to coordinate and enforce these new decisions. In 1968, American Airlines implemented an automated overbooking process, the flight load predictor, which determined overbooking levels based on management-specified service levels. In 1976, this system was replaced by a different approach to overbooking. The new system, RIPACS (reservations inventory planning and control system), attempted to maximize overbooking profitability by explicitly accounting for the revenue and costs associated with the decision. The current overbooking model, implemented in 1987, makes better use of information on costs and benefits.

With the introduction of supersaver discount fares in 1977, the role of yield management expanded to include allocating reservations inventory to different classes of passengers who compete for space on the same flights. Supersaver fares introduced new pricing controls to the industry and enabled airlines to effectively divide passengers into business travelers and personal and pleasure travelers. Turning supersaver availability on and off resulted in an early form of demand-responsive pricing. The objective of this type of pricing is to adjust the demand to match the supply of seats. American offered cheaper fares to stimulate demand in a controlled manner on low demand flights while maintaining higher profits on popular flights by limiting the number of supersaver fares offered. Allowing the sale of too many discount fares causes the displacement of higher revenue passengers, while allowing too few discount sales results in empty seats on the plane. In 1982, Decision Technologies developed an optimization model to determine the appropriate number of reservations to allocate to each fare type.

Airline deregulation in 1979 led to additional complexity in the practice of yield management. Two major changes took place. First, the number and variety of discount fares increased. Second, airlines began offering connecting service, using centrally located airports as hubs, to serve more of the traveling public and provide national service. For example, a single American Airlines flight from Dallas/Fort Worth to Denver may serve passengers from over 40 different eastern cities who are connecting to the Denver flight. The resulting airline environment is very complex. Many different passenger itineraries are possible, all with many different fares. Also, prices change rapidly, with up to 50,000 fare changes made daily.

Yield management has played a key role in allowing American Airlines to compete and succeed in an environment of stiff price competition. Some of the benefits are difficult to measure, such as increasing American Airlines' ability to survive price wars. Overall, yield management has provided quantifiable benefits of over $1.4 billion for the last three years. To put these increased revenues in perspective, AMR (the holding company for American Airlines) had a net profit (after all expenses and taxes) of $892 million for the same three-year period. As the airline grows and yield-management models become more sophisticated, the annual revenue benefit will increase.

SOLVED PROBLEMS

1. Overbooking Problem

Problem Statement

A family-run inn is considering the use of overbooking, because the frequency of no-shows listed below has left many rooms vacant during the past summer season. An empty room represents an opportunity cost of $69, which is the average room rate. Accommodating an overbooked guest is expensive, however, because the nearby resort rooms average $119 and the inn must pay the difference. What would be the expected gain per night from overbooking?

No-shows	0	1	2	3
Frequency	4	3	2	1

Solution

First, create an overbooking loss table using $69 as the cost of an empty room and $119−$69 = $50 as the cost of "walking" a guest.

No-shows	Probability	Reservations overbooked			
		0	**1**	**2**	**3**
0	.4	0	50	100	150
1	.3	69	0	50	100
2	.2	138	69	0	50
3	.1	207	138	69	0
Expected loss		$69.00	$47.60	$61.90	$100.00

Second, calculate the expected loss by multiplying each overbooking column by the corresponding probability of no-shows and then adding each term. For 0 reservations overbooked, this yields

$$(0)(.4) + (69)(.3) + (138)(.2) + (207)(.1) = 69$$

Looking across the expected-loss row, we find that overbooking by one reservation will minimize the expected loss and result in an expected nightly gain from overbooking of $69.00 − $47.60 = $21.40.

2. Weekly Workshift Scheduling

Problem Statement

The telephone reservation department for a major car-rental firm has the daily shift requirements for operators below:

Day	Su	M	Tu	W	Th	F	Sa
Operators	4	8	8	7	7	6	5

Prepare a weekly workshift schedule with two consecutive days off.

Solution

Formulate the problem as an integer linear programming model, and solve using Excel Solver.

Objective function:

Minimize $x_1 + x_2 + x_3 + x_4 + x_5 + x_6 + x_7$

Constraints:

Sunday $\quad\quad x_2 + x_3 + x_4 + x_5 + x_6 \quad\quad \geq 4$

Monday $\quad\quad\quad x_3 + x_4 + x_5 + x_6 + x_7 \geq 8$

Tuesday $\quad x_1 \quad\quad\quad + x_4 + x_5 + x_6 + x_7 \geq 8$

Wednesday $\quad x_1 + x_2 \quad\quad\quad + x_5 + x_6 + x_7 \geq 7$

Thursday $\quad x_1 + x_2 + x_3 \quad\quad\quad + x_6 + x_7 \geq 7$

Friday $\quad\quad x_1 + x_2 + x_3 + x_4 \quad\quad\quad + x_7 \geq 6$

Saturday $\quad x_1 + x_2 + x_3 + x_4 + x_5 \quad\quad\quad \geq 5$

$\quad\quad\quad\quad x_i \geq 0$ and integer

Using Excel Solver yields the following: $x_1 = 2$, $x_2 = 0$, $x_3 = 0$, $x_4 = 0$, $x_5 = 3$, $x_6 = 1$, $x_7 = 4$.

The corresponding weekly workshift schedule is

Operator	Schedule matrix, × = workday						
	Su	**M**	**Tu**	**W**	**Th**	**F**	**Sa**
A	...	...	×	×	×	×	×
B	...	...	×	×	×	×	×
C	×	×	×	×	...	...	×
D	×	×	×	×	...	...	×
E	×	×	×	×	...	...	×
F	×	×	×	×	×	...	...
G	...	×	×	×	×	×	...
H	...	×	×	×	×	×	...
I	...	×	×	×	×	×	...
J	...	×	×	×	×	×	...
Total	4	8	10	10	7	6	5
Required	4	8	8	7	7	6	5
Excess	0	0	2	3	0	0	0

3. Yield Management

Problem Statement

A ski resort is planning a year-end promotion by offering a weekend special for $159 per person based on double occupancy. The high season rate for these rooms, which includes lift tickets, normally is $299. Management wants to hold some rooms for late arrivals who are willing to pay the season rate. If the proportion of skiers who are willing to pay full rate is approximately 20 percent and their average weekend demand has a normal distribution with a mean of 50 and a standard deviation of 10, how many rooms should be set aside for full-paying skiers?

Solution

Using equation (3), we can determine the critical fractile as follows:

$$P(d < x) \leq \frac{(F - D)}{p \cdot F} = \frac{(299 - 159)}{(0.8)(299)} \leq 0.58$$

Turning to areas of a standard normal distribution in Appendix A, the z value for a cumulative probability of 0.58 is 0.02. Thus, the number of rooms to protect for full-paying skiers is

$$\mu + z\sigma = 50 + (0.02)(10)$$

$$= 52 \text{ rooms}$$

TOPICS FOR DISCUSSION

1. What organizational problems can arise from the use of part-time employees?
2. How can computer-based reservation systems increase service capacity utilization?
3. Illustrate how a particular service has implemented successful strategies for managing both demand and supply.
4. What possible dangers are associated with developing complementary services?
5. Will the widespread use of yield management eventually erode the concept of fixed prices for any service?
6. What possible negative effects can yield management have on customer relations?

EXERCISES

13.1. An outpatient clinic has kept a record of walk-in patients during the past year. The table below shows the expected number of walk-ins by day of the week:

Day	Mon.	Tues.	Wed.	Thurs.	Fri.
Walk-ins	50	30	40	35	40

The clinic has a staff of five physicians, and each can examine 15 patients a day on average.
  a. What is the maximum number of appointments that should be scheduled for each day if it is desirable to smooth out the demand for the week?
  b. Why would you recommend against scheduling appointments at their maximum level?
  c. If most walk-ins arrive in the morning, when should the appointments be made to avoid excessive waiting?
13.2. Reconsider **Example 13.1** (Surfside Hotel), because rising costs now have resulted in a $100 opportunity loss from a no-show. Assume that the no-show experience has not significantly changed and that the resulting loss when a guest is overbooked still is $100. Should Surfside revise its no-show policy?
13.3. A commuter airline overbooks all its flights by one passenger (i.e., the ticket agent will take seven reservations for an airplane that only has six seats). The no-show experience for the past 20 days is shown below:

No-shows	0	1	2	3	4
Frequency	6	5	4	3	2

Using the critical fractile $P(d < x) \leq C_u/(C_u + C_o)$, find the maximum implied overbooking opportunity loss C_o if the revenue C_u from a passenger is $20.
13.4. Crazy Joe operates a canoe rental service on the Guadalupe River. He currently leases 15 canoes from a dealer in a nearby city at a cost of $10 per day. On weekends, when the water is high, he picks up the canoes and drives to a launching point on the river, where he rents canoes to white-water enthusiasts for $30 per day. Lately, canoeists have complained about the unavailability of canoes, so Crazy Joe has recorded the demand for canoes and found the experience below for the past 20 days:

Daily demand	10	11	12	13	14	15	16	17	18	19	20
Frequency	1	1	2	2	2	3	3	2	2	1	1

Recommend an appropriate number of canoes to lease.
13.5. An airline serving Denver's Stapleton Airport and Steamboat Springs, Colorado, is considering overbooking its flights to avoid flying with empty seats. For example, the ticket agent is thinking of taking seven reservations for an airplane that has only six seats. During the past month, the no-show experience has been

No-shows	0	1	2	3	4
Percentage	30	25	20	15	10

The operating costs associated with each flight are pilot, $150; first officer, $100; fuel, $30; and landing fee, $20.
  What would be your recommendation for overbooking if a one-way ticket sells for $80 and the cost of not honoring a reservation is a free lift ticket worth $50 plus a seat on the next flight? What is the expected profit per flight for your overbooking choice?

13.6. Reconsider **Example 13.2** (Hospital Emergency Room) to determine if additional nurses will be required to staff the revised daily shift requirements shown below:

Day	Sun.	Mon.	Tues.	Wed.	Thurs.	Fri.	Sat.
Nurses	3	6	5	6	6	6	5

Develop a weekly workshift schedule providing 2 consecutive days off per week for each nurse. Formulate the problem as an integer linear programming model to minimize the number of nurses needed, and solve using Excel Solver. If more nurses are required than the existing staff of eight, suggest an alternative to hiring full-time nurses.

13.7. The sheriff has been asked by the county commissioners to increase weekend patrols in the lake region during the summer months. The sheriff has proposed the following weekly schedule, shifting deputies from weekday assignments to weekends:

Day	Sun.	Mon.	Tues.	Wed.	Thurs.	Fri.	Sat.
Assignments	6	4	4	4	5	5	6

Develop a weekly workshift schedule of duty tours, providing 2 consecutive days off per week for each officer. Formulate the problem as an integer linear programming model to minimize the number of officers needed, and solve using Excel Solver.

13.8. Reconsider **Example 13.3** (Blackjack Airline). After initial success with the Los Angeles–to–Las Vegas route, Blackjack Airline's demand for full-fare tickets has increased to an average of 75, with the standard deviation remaining at 15. This early experience has allowed Blackjack to make a better estimate of the percentage of discount-seeking passengers, which appears to be 80 percent. Consequently, Blackjack has decided to raise all ticket prices by $10. Under these new conditions, how many full-fare seats should Blackjack reserve?

13.9. Town and Country has experienced a substantial increase in business volume because of recent fare wars between the major air carriers. Town and Country operates a single office at a major international airport, with a fleet of 60 compact and 30 midsize cars. Recent developments have prompted management to rethink the company's reservation policy. The table below contains data on the rental experience of Town and Country:

Car	Rental rate	Discount rate	Discount seekers, %	Daily demand	Standard deviation
Compact	$30	$20	80	50	15
Midsize	$40	$30	60	30	10

The daily demand appears to follow a normal distribution; however, it has been observed that midsize-car customers do not choose to rent a compact when no midsize car is available. The discount rate is available to persons who are willing to reserve a car at least 14 days in advance and agree to pick up that car within 2 hours after their flight arrives. Otherwise, a nonrefundable deposit against their credit card will be forfeited. The current reservation policy is that 40 compact cars are held for customers who are willing to pay the full rate and 25 midsize cars are held for full rate–paying customers.

   a. Using yield management, determine the optimal number of compact and midsize cars to be held for customers paying the full rate.

   b. Given your optimal reservation policy determined here, would you consider a fleet expansion?

CASE

River City National Bank

River City National Bank has been in business for 10 years and is a fast-growing community bank. Its president, Gary Miller, took over his position 5 years ago in an effort to get the bank on its feet. He is one of the youngest bank presidents in the southwest, and his energy and enthusiasm explain his rapid advancement. Mr. Miller has been the key factor behind the bank's increased status and maintenance of high standards. One reason for this is that the customers come first in Mr. Miller's eyes; to him, one of the bank's main objectives is to serve its customers better.

The main bank lobby has one commercial teller and three paying-and-receiving teller booths. The lobby is designed to have room for long lines should they occur. Attached to the main bank are six drive-in lanes (one is commercial only) and one walk-up window to the side of the drive-in. Because of the bank's rapid growth, the drive-in lanes and lobby have been constantly overcrowded, although the bank has some of the longest hours in town. The lobby is open from 9 A.M. until 2 P.M., Monday through Saturday, and re-opens from 4 to 6 P.M. on Friday. The drive-in is open from 7 A.M. until midnight, Monday through Friday, and on Saturday from 7 A.M. until 7 P.M. Several old and good customers have complained, however. They did not like the long wait in line and also felt that the tellers were becoming quite surly.

This was very disheartening to Mr. Miller, despite the cause of the problem being the increased business. Thus, it was with his strong recommendation that the board of directors finally approved the building of a remote drive-in bank just down the street. As Figure 13.13 shows, this drive-in can be approached from two directions and has four lanes on either side. The first lane on either side is commercial only, and the last lane on each side has been built but is not yet operational. Hours for this facility are 7 A.M. to 7 P.M., Monday through Saturday.

The bank employs both full-time and part-time tellers. The lobby tellers and the morning tellers (7 A.M. to 2 P.M.) are considered to be full-time employees, whereas the drive-in tellers on the afternoon shift (2 P.M. to 7 P.M.) and the night-owl shift (7 P.M. to midnight) are considered to be part-time. The tellers perform normal banking services: cashing checks, receiving deposits, verifying deposit balances, selling money orders and traveler's checks, and cashing government savings bonds.

At present, overcrowding for the most part has been eliminated. The hardest problem in resolving the situation was making customers aware of the new facility. After six months, tellers at the remote drive-in still hear customers say, "I didn't realize ya'll were over here. I'm going to start coming here more often!"

Now, instead of facing an overcrowding situation, the bank is finding problems with fluctuating demand. River City National rarely experienced this problem until the extra capacity of tellers and drive-in lanes was added in the new remote facility.

Two full- and four part-time tellers are employed at the remote drive-in Monday through Friday. Scheduling on Saturdays is no problem, because all six tellers take turns rotating, with most working every other Saturday. On paydays and Fridays, the lanes at the remote drive-in have cars lined up out to the street. A high demand for money and service from

FIGURE 13.13 Layout of remote drive-in.

the bank is the main reason for this dilemma, but certainly not the only one. Many customers are not ready when they get to the bank. They need a pen or a deposit slip, or they do not have their check filled out or endorsed yet. Of course, this creates idle time for the tellers. There also are other problems with customers that take time, such as explaining that their accounts are overdrawn and their payroll checks therefore must be deposited instead of cashed. In addition, there usually is a handful of noncustomers who are trying to cash payroll or personal checks. These people can become quite obstinate and take up a lot of time when they find that their checks cannot be cashed. Transactions take 30 seconds on average; transaction times range from 10 seconds for a straight deposit to 90 seconds for cashing a bond to about 3

minutes for making out traveler's checks. (The latter occurs very rarely.)

Compared with the peak banking days, the rest of the week is very quiet. The main bank stays busy but is not crowded. On the other hand, business at the remote drive-in is unusually slow. Mr. Miller's drive-in supervisor, Ms. Shang-ling Chen, studied the number of transactions that tellers at the remote facility made on the average. The figures for a typical month are shown in Table 13.8.

Once again, customers are complaining. When tellers at the remote drive-in close out at 7 P.M. on Fridays, they are always turning people away while they are in the process of balancing. These customers have asked Mr. Miller to keep the new drive-in open at least until 9 P.M. on Friday. The tellers are very much

---

TABLE 13.8

TRANSACTIONS FOR TYPICAL MONTH AT REMOTE DRIVE-IN

Day of week	First week		Second week	
	Morning shift	Afternoon shift	Morning shift	Afternoon shift
Monday	. . .	. . .	175	133
Tuesday	. . .	. . .	120	85
Wednesday	200	195	122	115
Thursday	156	113	111	100
Friday	223*	210	236*	225
Saturday	142	127	103	98

Day of week	Third week		Fourth week	
	Morning shift	Afternoon shift	Morning shift	Afternoon shift
Monday	149	120	182	171
Tuesday	136	77	159	137
Wednesday	182	186	143	103
Thursday	172	152	118	99
Friday	215*	230	206*	197
Saturday	147	150	170	156

Day of week	Fifth week	
	Morning shift	Afternoon shift
Monday	169	111
Tuesday	112	89
Wednesday	92	95
Thursday	147	163
Friday	259*	298

*Most of these transactions occurred after 10 A.M.

against the idea, but the board of directors is beginning to favor it. Mr. Miller wants to keep his customers happy but feels there must be some other way to resolve the situation. Therefore, he calls in Ms. Chen and requests that she look into the problem and make some recommendations for a solution.

Assignment As Ms. Chen's top aide, you are assigned the task of analyzing the situation and recommending a solution. This is your opportunity to serve your company and community as well as to make yourself "look good" and earn points toward your raise and promotion.

C A S E

Gateway International Airport[13]

Gateway International Airport (GIA) has experienced substantial growth in both commercial and general aviation operations during the past several years. (An *operation* is a landing or takeoff.) Because of the initiation of new commercial service at the airport, which is scheduled for several months in the future, the Federal Aviation Administration (FAA) has concluded that the increased operations and associated change in the hourly distribution of takeoffs and landings will require an entirely new work schedule for the current air traffic control (ATC) staff. The FAA feels that GIA may need to hire additional ATC personnel, because the present staff of five probably will not be enough to handle the expected demand.

After examining the various service plans that each commercial airline submitted for the next 6-month period, the FAA developed an average hourly demand forecast of total operations (Figure 13.14) and a weekly forecast of variation from the average daily demand (Figure 13.15). An assistant to the manager for operations has been delegated the task of developing workforce requirements and schedules for the ATC staff to maintain an adequate level of operational safety with a minimum of excess ATC "capacity."

The various constraints are:

1. Each controller will work a continuous, 8-hour shift (ignoring any lunch break), which always will begin at the start of an hour at any time during the day (i.e., any and all shifts begin at X:00), and the controller must have at least 16 hours off before resuming duty.

FIGURE 13.14 Hourly demand for operations.

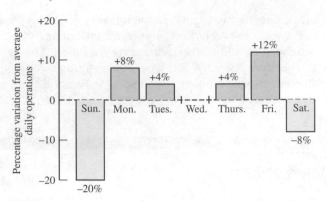

FIGURE 13.15 Daily demand variation from average.

2. Each controller will work exactly 5 days per week.

3. Each controller is entitled to 2 consecutive days off, with any consecutive pair of days being eligible.

4. FAA guidelines will govern GIA's workforce requirements so that the ratio of total operations to the number of available controllers in any hourly period cannot exceed 16.

Questions

1. Assume that you are the assistant to the manager for operations at the FAA. Use the techniques of workshift scheduling to analyze the total workforce requirements and days-off schedule. For the primary analysis, you may assume that:

a. Operator requirements will be based on a shift profile of demand (i.e., 8 hours).

b. There will be exactly three separate shifts each day, with no overlapping of shifts.

c. The distribution of hourly demand in Figure 13.14 is constant for each day of the week, but the levels of hourly demand vary during the week as shown in Figure 13.15.

2. On the basis of your primary analysis, discuss the potential implications for workforce requirements and days-off scheduling if assumptions **a** and **b** above are relaxed so that the analysis can be based on hourly demand without the constraints of a preset number of shifts and no overlapping of shifts. In other words, discuss the effects of analyzing hourly demand requirements on the basis of each ATC position essentially having its own shift, which can overlap with any other ATC shift to meet that demand.

3. Do you feel this would result in a larger or smaller degree of difficulty in meeting the four general constraints? Why?

4. What additional suggestions could you make to the manager of operations to minimize the workforce requirements level and days-off scheduling difficulty?

C A S E

The Yield Management Analyst[14]

On the morning of November 10, 1992, Jon Thomas, market analyst for the Mexico leisure markets, canceled more than 300 seats "illegally" reserved on two flights to Acapulco. All the seats on Jon's Acapulco flights were booked by the same sales representative under a corporate name, Uniden Corporation. Jon could tell that the sales representative reserved space one passenger at a time using the relevant available fare; some seats were reserved at round-trip fares of more than $2,000

per person. By using a special corporate name field, the sales representative used a common gaming technique to suspend auto-cancellation and instant purchase payment programs that are required for all individual bookings by SABRE (Semi-Automated Business Research Environment), American Airlines' (AA's) customer reservation system. Jon felt justified in canceling this space, because he previously had denied the group-space request and the sales representative subsequently violated established rules regarding the reservation of space for large groups.

No more than 24 hours after Jon canceled the Uniden Corporation's space, he received an irate phone call from Patty Dial, the Dallas–Fort Worth area regional sales manager. Uniden, a local Fort Worth–based company, needed more than 300 seats to Acapulco for its annual sales incentive trip. Jon faces the conflict of whether to accept or deny large groups each day, and he realizes that his market judgment is all part of managing yield for each flight. The Uniden group issue escalated to higher levels of management when Uniden, a major corporate customer for AA, found out that space promised by AA's sales representative had been canceled. With the customer relations issue in mind, Jon entered a negotiation process with Patty to reallocate space.

Normal group reservation procedure requires the sales representative to send an electronic message to the yield management analyst to request a block of space on a flight. It is the yield management analyst's prerogative to approve the request and block space for the group or to deny that request. The yield management analyst uses a variety of decision support systems based on historical market activity to make this decision. From the sales representatives' perspectives, capturing this group is a clear victory, because it drives market share through increased sales volume for their regions. From the yield manager's perspective, filling the plane with one group at the same fare on a peak-period flight is a wasted opportunity to use excess demand and the market's limited capacity to maximize revenue per passenger. Unfortunately, sales representatives can fool SABRE into accepting group reservations without the yield manager's approval. As in Jon's case, a sales representative may book seats in blocks of fewer than 10 passengers, set up a corporate name field in the reservation that suspends all auto-cancellation programs, establish a sales contract, and negotiate a special off-tariff price for the group regardless of the fares listed in each reservation.

Conflicting corporate objectives for sales representatives and yield managers is a major source of frustration for a yield management analyst. AA's sales representatives establish monthly revenue and passenger goals to meet progressively higher market share objectives. Sales representatives maintain relationships with large corporate clients and travel agencies, and they implement volume- and revenue-based discount programs for large corporate accounts and travel agencies. AA's yield management analyst attempts to maximize aircraft utilization (revenue per passenger and load factor at the same time) to improve overall market revenue. The yield management analyst has very little contact with the end customer and uses decision support systems to manipulate pricing and inventory allocation programs. The sales representative's goal is stimulation of sales, while the yield management analyst's goal is sales optimization. Jon and Patty's conflict highlights a situation in which yield management and sales objectives come in direct conflict and the system breaks down.

Yield management is an ideal operating strategy for companies that face temporary imbalances between capacity and demand, spoilage (i.e., a product that must be used immediately), and high fixed costs/low variable costs. Yield management enables companies to maximize use of constrained productive capacity with a discriminating eye on product yield. Each day, Jon faces the decision of whether to fill a plane early with lower fares or to save space for higher-revenue passengers.

YIELD MANAGEMENT IN THE AIRLINE INDUSTRY

Passenger demand often outpaces capacity during peak seasons, days, or other times, as in Jon's Acapulco market. In essence, airlines face temporary imbalances between capacity and demand on a daily basis. In the situation that Jon faces, only Aeromexico, Mexicana, and AA have direct flights to Mexico from Dallas. During low-season periods, it is difficult to fill these planes, whereas in high season, there is more demand than the total market capacity can handle. Clearly, AA faces high fixed costs and low variable costs, because adding one more passenger to a flight costs very little compared with the fixed costs of providing and maintaining the scheduled aircraft service. Finally, once the airplane pulls away from the gate, all the empty seats can never be sold, and this results in spoilage. When faced with excess demand and limited capacity, the yield management analyst may "choose" what traffic is most desirable to optimize the total revenue on each flight. The different levels of yield management sophistication between airlines is the source of a competitive advantage in some highly competitive markets.

From mid-November through the end of May, Jon's Mexico leisure market enters its peak season and provides an excellent opportunity for textbook yield management strategies. During the time that this case covers, AA has a total of nine daily round-trip flights to Acapulco, Cancun, and Puerto Vallarta. Jon is in charge of setting all the fares connecting Mexico with the rest of the world as well as managing the inventory control. Each origin–destination market, such as Dallas–Cancun, has more than 30 fares to maintain. In general, all airlines use price discrimination and yield management to maximize revenue. By maintaining a tiered-fare structure, the yield management analyst can force passengers to pay higher prices in times of greater demand.

Jon helps AA to maintain a tiered, market-based fare structure that leverages the price sensitivities and flexibility of its business and leisure customer segments. Fare rules and prices are differentiated based on the time and date of the flight, origin of the passenger, and historical demand patterns in that market. Table 13.9 outlines the different behavior of the two passenger segments.

Facing spoilage, high fixed costs/low variable costs, and temporary demand imbalances, airlines use *both* demand and capacity management to maximize revenue. Airlines use three yield management tools to maximize revenue and sell the "right" fares to the "right" passengers: "overbooking, discount allocation, and traffic management."[15] To execute price discrimination with a tiered-fare structure, the airplane capacity is divided into different sections, regardless of where the passenger sits (unless the passenger is in business or first class). The yield management analyst spreads the available fares over the sections (i.e., discount allocation) and uses overbooking and traffic management strategies to maximize revenue.

Taking passenger reservations beyond the true capacity of the airplane to ensure a full flight is referred to as *overbooking*. This strategy, based on seasonally adjusted historical data, accounts for expected no-shows, last-minute cancellations, and missed connections. Overbooking generates a tremendous amount of incremental revenue for the airline, and it provides airline travelers with greater choice. More flights and fares are made available to a greater number of passengers. In Jon's Mexico leisure markets, levels of overbooking average approximately 25 percent more than capacity and can reach as high as 50 percent. The overbooking level typically starts off high 6 months before departure of a flight and slowly declines as bookings turn over, restricts excess sales, and forces "selling up" during periods closer to departure.

Discount allocation works together with traffic management to spread the tiered-fare structure over the different inventory sections of a plane. Discount allocation attempts to save seats for higher-valued, last-minute business customers who are willing to pay more than the discounted price. AA's Boeing 727, which is the aircraft used in Jon's Mexico markets, holds 150 passengers: 12 in first class and 138 in coach. On a typical flight, Jon may have two or three separate fares for first-class passengers and 25 different fares for coach passengers. AA's traffic management or indexing system automatically spreads Jon's fares over the plane's inventory sections to provide

TABLE 13.9

BEHAVIOR OF AIRLINE PASSENGER SEGMENTS

Leisure Passenger	Business Passenger
Price-sensitive	Price-insensitive
Advance booking	Last minute booking
Flexible day and time	Inflexible on day and time
Long trips	Short trips
Discretionary travel	Time-dependent travel
Consults travel agents	Frequent flyer and knows destination
Travels over weekends	Weekday travel only
Seasonal travel	Less seasonal
Little loyalty	Loyalty based on frequent flyer credit

more inventory for higher-paying and less inventory for lower-paying passengers when faced with excess demand. Traffic management or AA's indexing system also values long-haul, higher-paying passengers more than short-haul passengers, and it provides increased inventory availability for the higher fares.

Overbooking and discount allocation levels are set differently based on historical demand patterns for the particular flight's departure time, day of week, days until departure, and season of departure. The levels change daily for each flight in AA's expansive system based on fluctuating demand. Jon is responsible for overriding system decisions and implementing different and new discount allocation and traffic management strategies to improve the average revenue per passenger and the load factor of his market. Specifically, Jon decides what fares to file for each passenger group, what restrictions to apply to each fare, how many seats to save between higher- and lower-valued fares, increased availability for longer-haul and high-demand markets, and inventory restriction for lower-valued fares.

SABRE opens flights for sale more than 300 days before departure. Maintaining yield in a volatile market, such as Jon's Mexico leisure markets, adds increased uncertainty because of the large fluctuation and less predictable nature of the historical demand patterns. Jon's Mexico leisure markets are especially unpredictable, because frequent yet dispersed group movements distort decision support system inventory projections, average demand, overbooking levels, and discounted seat allocation.

Assignment Read the following instructions for the Yield Management Game. Your instructor will supply passenger data and a tally sheet for a class exercise on "game day."

Yield Management Game and Instructions

The yield management game illustrates the trade-off between overbooking (selling more than capacity) and spoilage (having idle capacity), with the objective of maximizing revenue when faced with excess demand in the form of various revenues per passenger and different passenger volumes. This particular game focuses on airline capacity management, but is applicable to all fixed capacity services (e.g., hotels and cruise ships).

When allocating seats to prospective passengers, the yield management analyst confronts a problem of maximizing total revenue for each flight. This includes capturing, the ideal mix of discount and premium passengers at full capacity utilization without overselling too many customers. The objective of revenue maximization is simple (fill the airplane with the highest paying passengers), but uncertainty makes it a challenge.

Specifically, historical booking trends in the airline industry indicate that the more flexible discount or leisure traveler makes reservations far in advance of departure, while the inflexible premium or business traveler waits until the last minute, often walking up to the plane at the time of departure. To capitalize on this passenger behavior, the airlines have exercised price discrimination to differentiate the passengers with advance purchase, time-of-day, and duration of stay requirements. While price discrimination helps the airline manage its capacity constrained resource, it does not address how many seats to sell each customer segment—business or leisure passengers.

To further complicate the yield management analyst's task of maximizing total revenue, last minute cancellations, passengers missing connections (misconnect), and no-shows threaten to "spoil" (empty seats) seats and lose potential revenue. You will be using the strategies of *discount allocation* and *overbooking* to address this problem.

Discount allocation is necessary because a plane can be filled long before departure with discount passengers—clearly not a revenue maximizing strategy. Therefore, the yield management analyst attempts to "save" seats for the last-minute premium demand by allocating only a certain amount of seats to early-booking leisure passengers. While overbooking helps overcome spoilage, it opens the possibility for oversales. The yield management analyst attempts to weigh the cost of an oversale against the cost of "spoiling" seats or losing potential revenue from an additional sale. The analyst prefers to oversell the flight up to the point where the oversale cost equals the additional revenue of adding a passenger.

In this game, you will act as the yield management analyst in charge of a pseudo-flight. Based on the historical booking pattern for your flight, leisure passenger demand, typically large groups, appears as far out as 100 days before departure up until 14 days before departure. Business passenger demand enters the market closer to departure at approximately nine days prior to departure up until the time of departure.

Other historical market statistics for your plane show that the average misconnect, no-show, and cancellation rate for this peak season flight is 20 percent and the average revenue per passenger is $400.

Both oversales and spoilage cost the airline revenue: oversales are a direct expense, while spoilage is lost potential revenue. The higher the number of oversales, the more money gate agents must pay to get passengers off the plane. Your objective is to maximize total revenue generated on this flight.

GAME FACTS

Airplane Capacity: 100 seats

Historical Market Information:

Average no-show, misconnect, and cancellation rate: 20 percent

Average revenue per passenger: $400

Spoilage penalty: $200 for each empty seat

Oversale penalty:

1–5 oversales	$200 per passenger
6–10	$500
10–15	$800
16+	$1,000

Game Phases

The game will be played in three phases reflecting the different time periods prior to departure. *Phase I* is total passenger demand received outside of 13 days prior to departure. *Phase II* is total passenger demand between 13 days prior to departure and the day of departure. Historical market trends suggest that large groups and families make reservations during Phase I, while individuals and business passengers make reservations during Phase II. *Phase III* shows you the number of passengers who actually show up for the flight and their resulting revenue contribution.

Objective: Maximize Total Revenue!

SELECTED BIBLIOGRAPHY

ANTLE, D. W., and R. A. REID: "Managing Service Capacity in an Ambulatory Care Clinic," *Hospital & Health Services Administration,* vol. 33, no. 2, Summer 1988, pp. 201–211.

ARMISTEAD, COLIN G., and GRAHAM CLARK: "The 'Coping' Capacity Management Strategy in Services and the Influence on Quality Performance," *International Journal of Service Industry Management,* vol. 5, no. 2, 1994, pp. 5–22.

BELOBABA, PETER P.: "Application of a Probabilistic Decision Model to Airline Seat Inventory Control," *Operations Research,* vol. 37, no. 2, March–April 1989, pp. 183–197.

BITRAN, G. R., and S. V. MONDSCHEIN: "An Application of Yield Mangement to the Hotel Industry Considering Multiple Day Stays," *Operations Research,* vol. 43, no. 3, May–June 1995, pp. 427–443.

CARROLL, WILLIAM J., and RICHARD C. GRIMES: "Evolutionary Change in Product Management: Experiences in the Car Rental Industry," *Interfaces,* vol. 25, no. 5, September–October 1995, pp. 84–104.

CRANDALL, RICHARD E., and ROBERT E. MARKLAND: "Demand Management—Today's Challenge for Service Industries," *Production and Operations Management,* vol. 5, no. 2, Summer 1996, pp. 106–120.

EASTON, FRED F., DONALD F. ROSSIN, and WILLIAM S. BORDERS: "Analysis of Alternative Scheduling Policies for Hospital Nurses," *Production and Operations Management,* vol. 1, no. 2, Spring 1992, pp. 159–174.

GOODALE, JOHN C., and ENAR TUNC: "Tour Scheduling with Dynamic Service Rates," *International Journal of Service Industry Management,* vol. 9, no. 3, 1998, pp. 226–247.

KIMES, SHERYL E.: "Yield Management: A Tool for Capacity-Constrained Service Firms," *Journal of Operations Management,* vol. 8, no. 4, October 1989, pp. 348–363.

———: "The Basics of Yield Management," *Cornell H.R.A. Quarterly,* November 1989, pp. 14–19.

———: "The Relationship between Product Quality and Revenue per Available Room at Holiday Inn," *Journal of Service Research,* vol. 2, no. 2, November 1999, pp. 138–144.

————, and Richard B. Chase: "The Strategic Levers of Yield Management," *Journal of Service Research,* vol. 1, no. 2, November 1998, pp. 156–166.

Mabert, Vincent A., and Michael J. Showalter: "Measuring the Impact of Part-Time Workers in Service Organizations," *Journal of Operations Management,* vol. 9, no. 2, April 1990, pp. 209–229.

Malhotra, Manoj K., and Larry P. Ritzman: "Scheduling Flexibility in the Service Sector: A Postal Case Study," *Production and Operations Management,* vol. 3, no. 2, Spring 1994, pp. 100–117.

Metters, Richard, and Vicente Vargas: "Yield Management for the Nonprofit Sector," *Journal of Service Research,* vol. 1, no. 3, February 1999, pp. 215–226.

Ng, Irene C. I., Jochen Wirtz, and Khai Sheang Lee: "The Strategic Role of Unused Service Capacity," *International Journal of Service Industry Management,* vol. 10, no. 2, 1999, pp. 211–238.

Pfeifer, Phillip E.: "The Airline Discount Fare Allocation Problem," *Decision Sciences,* vol. 20, Winter 1989, pp. 149–157.

Radas, Sonja, and Steven M. Shugan: "Managing Service Demand: Shifting and Bundling," *Journal of Service Research,* vol. 1, no. 1, August 1998, pp. 47–64.

Relihan, Walter J., III: "The Yield-Management Approach to Hotel-Room Pricing," *Cornell H.R.A. Quarterly,* May 1989, pp. 40–45.

Shemwell, D. J., and J. J. Cronin: "Services Marketing Strategies for Coping with Demand/Supply Imbalances," *Journal of Services Marketing,* vol. 8, no. 4, 1994, pp. 14–24.

Smith, Barry C., John F. Leimkuhler, and Ross M. Darrow: "Yield Management at American Airlines," *Interfaces,* vol. 22, no. 1, January–February 1992, pp. 8–31.

Thompson, Gary M.: "Optimal Scheduling of Shifts and Breaks Using Employees Having Limited Time-Availability," *International Journal of Service Industry Management,* vol. 7, no. 1, 1996, pp. 56–73.

ENDNOTES

1. R. L. Rose and J. Dahl, "Skies Are Deregulated, but Just Try Starting a Sizable New Airline," *The Wall Street Journal,* July 19, 1989, p. 1.
2. E. J. Rising, R. Baron, and B. Averill, "A Systems Analysis of a University Health-Service Outpatient Clinic," *Operations Research,* vol. 21, no. 5, September 1973, pp. 1030–1047.
3. J. C. Nautiyal and R. L. Chowdhary, "A Suggested Basis for Pricing Campsites: Demand Estimation in an Ontario Park," *Journal of Leisure Research,* vol. 7, no. 2, 1975, pp. 95–107.
4. The $M/M/c$ queuing model as described in Chapter 12 is used. This model permits the calculation of probabilities for having a telephone caller wait for different numbers of operators.
5. From V. A. Mabert and A. R. Raedels, "The Detail Scheduling of a Part-Time Work Force: A Case Study of Teller Staffing," *Decision Sciences,* vol. 8, no. 1, January 1977, pp. 109–120.
6. From Sheryl E. Kimes, "Yield Management: A Tool for Capacity-Constrained Service Firms," *Journal of Operations Management,* vol. 8, no. 4, October 1989, pp. 348–363.
7. Phillip E. Pfeifer, "The Airline Discount Fare Allocation Problem," *Decision Sciences,* vol. 20, Winter 1989, p. 155.
8. Adapted with permission from Kevin Baker and Robert B. Freund, "The Yield Management Analyst," University of Texas at Austin, 1994.
9. Lenny Leibmann, "Holiday Inn Maximizes Profitability with a Complex Network Infrastructure," *LAN Magazine,* June 1995, vol. 10, no. 6, p. 123.
10. "On the Road to Rebound," *Information Week,* September 3, 1991, p. 32.
11. Michael Kasavana, "Catering Software: Problems for Off-Premise Bookings Can Greatly Increase Operational Efficiency," *Restaurant Business,* vol. 90, no. 13, September 1, 1991, p. 90.

12. "Travel Advisory: Amtrak Adopts Fare System of Airlines," *New York Times,* December 4, 1989, Section 3, p. 3.

13. Prepared by James H. Vance under the supervision of Professor James A. Fitzsimmons.

14. Adapted with permission from Kevin Baker and Robert B. Freund, "The Yield Management Analyst," University of Texas at Austin, 1994.

15. Quoted from Barbara Amster, former vice president of the American Airlines Pricing and Yield Management department and current vice president of Canadian Pacific Airlines Pricing and Yield Management department.

CHAPTER FOURTEEN

Managing Facilitating Goods

Learning Objectives

After completing this chapter, you should be able to:

1. Discuss the role of information technology in the management of inventory.
2. Describe the function, characteristics, and costs of an inventory system.
3. Determine the order quantity for various inventory applications.
4. Determine the reorder point and safety stock for inventory systems with uncertain demand.
5. Design a continuous or periodic review inventory-control system.
6. Conduct an ABC analysis of inventory items.
7. Use either expected value or incremental analysis to determine the order quantity for the single-period inventory model.
8. Describe the rationale behind the retail discounting model.

All agree that well-stocked shelves make happy customers, but do well-stocked shelves make providers happy as well? Consider a pharmacy with a shelf-full of a particular prescription medicine. If all of that medicine does not sell quickly, the pharmacy may have a shelf-full of medication that has passed its expiration date and no longer can be sold. The obvious dilemma is to match "stores-on-hand" to demand. The pharmacy certainly does not want to turn away sick customers because it is out of the requested medicine; on the other hand, it also does not want to incur the losses that result from an inventory of out-of-date medicine.

In the "old" days, inventory management required workers to monitor sales and stock-on-hand, then to mail or phone orders for new supplies when it "seemed" to be advisable. This system frequently resulted in excess inventories or stockouts (i.e., the empty-shelf syndrome). Information management, however, has transformed inventory management into a process allowing the service to meet customer demands without incurring the expense of excess inventory. Use of computer-based information systems in inventory management represents one of the earliest and most successful applications of information technology. All of us are familiar with the bar codes, as shown in Figure 14.1, that are found on nearly every inventory item purchased in retail stores. The bar code supplies information that allows management to track where inventory is located and how fast it is moving. For example, most supermarkets use computerized inventory systems to maintain automatically records of inventory balances based on point-of-sale (POS) scanning of the bar codes on items. When stock levels are depleted (or reach a predetermined reorder point), a purchase order to a preapproved

Bar code printed on a 20 ounce can of
Hunt's Big John's Beans 'n Fixin's

Bar code stapled to an eight foot length of $1'' \times 2''$

FIGURE 14.1   Bar code applications.

vendor is initiated automatically using electronic data interchange (EDI). When the order is received, the inventory balance is adjusted accordingly. Such use of information
technology saves costs by avoiding paperwork, facilitating cash management, and creating a system that responds quickly to inventory needs among suppliers, service
providers, and customers.

Clearly, few service enterprises can eliminate inventories of goods and supplies entirely. Auto parts stores must have a reserve of motor oil and commonly used parts to
meet daily demand. A Pizza Hut restaurant must have a reserve of cheese and other
food items. A document-copying business must have stores of paper, printer ink, and
toner, and your community's fire department must have a ready supply of fuel for its
trucks. Because such inventories of goods often represent large capital investments, we

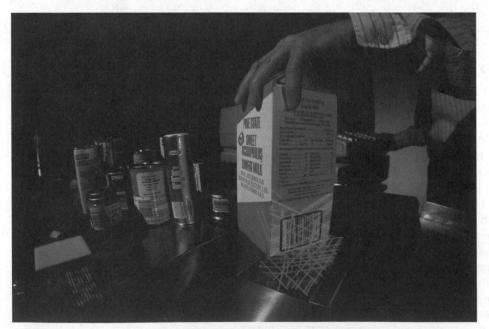

As items are scanned, the bar code identifies the price and records the new inventory
level. Replenishment orders are triggered automatically when the inventory level falls
below a predetermined point. © Charles O'Rear/CORBIS

must have effective ways of managing them. Keeping track of a wide variety of items (i.e., stock-keeping units [SKUs]), both those on hand and those that should be ordered, as well as when they should be ordered is a significant challenge for management, and it requires a knowledge of inventory theory.

CHAPTER PREVIEW

Managing the facilitating goods component of a service package involves cost trade-offs, customer service, and information systems. This chapter begins with a discussion of the role of inventory in services, its characteristics, and costs. A fundamental inventory management question concerns what quantity to order, and order quantity models are developed for various inventory applications.

When to place an order (called a *reorder point*) is another inventory management question. This decision is complicated when services are faced with uncertain demand and, thus, the need for safety stocks to protect against stockouts. The continuous review system and the periodic review system are computer information systems for implementing these decisions. Design parameters for each of these systems are developed with illustrations. The ABC classification of inventory items is used to identify which computer inventory system to install.

The chapter concludes with a discussion of two special inventory situations. For perishable goods, a model is developed to identify the optimal order quantity to balance the opportunity cost of underestimating demand with the lost investment in inventory resulting from overestimating demand. Finally, a retail discounting model is proposed to determine the discount price for items that are not selling to generate cash to buy more popular goods.

INVENTORY THEORY

Inventory theory covers several aspects of the inventory of goods and supplies, including the role that inventory plays in the operation of a service, the characteristics of various inventory systems, and the costs that are involved in maintaining inventories.

Role of Inventory in Services

Inventories serve a variety of functions in service organizations, such as decoupling the stages in the distribution cycle, accommodating a heavy seasonal demand, and maintaining a supply of materials as a hedge against anticipated increases in their cost. We will look at these and other functions in more detail later; first, we will examine the inventory distribution system.

- *Decoupling inventories.* Consider the physical goods distribution system depicted in Figure 14.2. Two types of flow exist within the system. One is the flow of information beginning with the customer and proceeding back to the original source(s) of the goods or service, and the other is the actual movement of goods—in this case, from the producer to the customer—by way of inventory reserves at each stage of the system.

Following the diagram, we see that the customer makes a demand, and for the purposes of our analysis, we will consider this demand to be a random variable with an associated probability distribution. When, for example, demand for a box of cereal occurs at a grocery retailer, the item is withdrawn from the available stock (either on the shelf or in the retailer's inventory). As the demand continues, the stock must be

Replenishment order   Replenishment order   Replenishment order   Customer order

Factory   Wholesaler   Distributor   Retailer   Customer

Production delay

Shipping delay   Shipping delay   Item withdrawn

Wholesaler inventory   Distributor inventory   Retailer inventory

‹– – – – – Information

——————▶ Physical product

FIGURE 14.2   Physical goods distribution system.

replenished, and an order is placed with the distributor. From the time the order is made until it is received, however, the available stock continues to decline. This interval is called the *replenishment lead time,* and it may vary from a day to a week or even more. It also may vary from one order period to another. This flow of information originating with the customer's demand is directed in turn along the distribution channel to the producer.

If we follow the movement of the item itself, we see that it makes its way through the distribution channel with stops at the various inventory sites where it is held in readiness for the next leg of its journey to the customer. Each of these inventory stages serves as a buffer, allowing each organization in the interdependent system to operate somewhat independently and without interruption. Here, we can see the *decoupling function* of inventory systems. The retailer, distributor, wholesaler, and factory are stages in the system, and a stockout at any stage would have immediate and drastic consequences for the others. Inventories, however, decouple these stages and help to avoid expensive interruptions of service.

- *Seasonal inventories.* Some services involve significant seasonal demands. Consider toy stores and the year-end holidays, camping-gear retailers and summer vacation time, or garden-supply stores and spring planting time. Services that experience such ~~al~~ high-demand times may accumulate large inventories in advance of the ~~emand~~ season to accommodate their customers.

  ~~l~~ative inventories. A service that anticipates a significant increase in the cost of ~~l~~ in which it deals may find it more economical to accumulate and maintain a ~~n~~ventory at present prices rather than to replenish its supplies after the in-~~. The strategy of maintaining a speculative inventory is known as *forward buy-*~~he~~ reverse of this strategy occurred in the spring of 1996, when U.S. oil ~~nies~~ anticipated the reentry of Iraq into the international petroleum market, ~~would~~ decrease the market value of the resource. These companies did not ~~o~~ have huge reserves of "pre-Iraq" expensive oil when the world price ~~d~~; therefore, they allowed their reserves (i.e., their inventory) to decline dras-~~—*forward hedging!*

- *Cyclical inventories.* The term *cyclical inventory* refers to normal variations in the level of inventories. In other words, the level of stock in inventory is at its highest just after an order is received, and it declines to its lowest point just before a new order is received.
- *In-transit inventories.* The term *in-transit inventories* is used for stock that has been ordered but has not yet arrived.
- *Safety stocks.* An effective service maintains an inventory of stock that will meet expected demand. Services operate in a dynamic environment, however, which means that uncertainties in replenishment lead time and demand always exist. To deal with such unexpected fluctuations, many services maintain inventory in excess of the inventory that is kept to meet the expected demand. This excess inventory is referred to as *safety stock.*

Inventory management is concerned with three basic questions:

1. What should be the *order quantity?*
2. When should an order be placed (called a *reorder point*)?
3. How much *safety stock* should be maintained?

Later, we will see that determining the reorder point is related to determining the safety stock. Both are influenced by the *service level,* which is the probability that all demand during the replenishment lead time is met (e.g., if the probability of a stockout is 5 percent, then the service level is 95 percent).

Characteristics of Inventory Systems

To design, implement, and manage an inventory system, we must consider the characteristics of the stocks that are to be stored and understand the attributes of the various inventory systems that are available.

- *Type of customer demand.* When evaluating the type of demand, we first look for any trends, cycles, or seasonality. Has demand been increasing steadily during the observation period without significant drops, or do we see a monthly cycle in which demand begins high and then tapers off by the end of the month? As noted earlier, demand also may be seasonal.

  Other attributes of demand also are important to consider. Demand may occur in discrete units, such as the number of scuba-diving masks sold per day. It also may be continuous, such as gallons of water consumed, or bulk, such as passengers on an airline flight. If final customer demand can be described as a probability distribution, it is referred to as *independent demand,* and we then can forecast future demand. In other cases, the demand for one type of inventory item may be related to the demand for another; for example, the demand for catsup at McDonald's restaurant is dependent on the number of hamburgers and french fries that are sold. This type of demand is called *dependent demand.*
- *Planning time horizon.* Management must consider whether it will stock an inventory of a particular item indefinitely or if the need for the item is temporary. For example, a hospital will always need tanks of oxygen, but a sports clothing retailer will not need an endless supply of Atlanta Olympics sweatshirts.
- *Replenishment lead time.* The replenishment lead time has an obvious impact on inventory needs. If we expect a relatively long time between placing an order and receiving it, we must carry a larger inventory than if we anticipate a short lead time, especially when critical items are involved. If lead time is stochastic with an associated probability distribution, we may be able to use this information to determine our inventory needs during the lead time.

- *Constraints and relevant inventory costs.* Some constraints are straightforward. For example, available storage space determines the maximum amount of goods that can be stored, and the "shelf life" of a good likewise may limit the number of perishable items that can be held in inventory. Other constraints are more complex, such as the costs of maintaining an inventory, and there are obvious costs such as the capital expenditures for the storage facility, be it a warehouse or a walk-in refrigerator. Items held in inventory also represent a capital expenditure (i.e., they represent an opportunity cost of capital). Other costs include those of personnel and the maintenance required to manage the inventory as well as "incidentals" such as insurance and taxes on the inventoried assets. Yet another cost to consider is that of overcoming existing constraints (e.g., what would it cost to expand the size of the warehouse or refrigerator?).

Relevant Costs of an Inventory System

The performance of an inventory system usually is gauged by its average annual cost. Relevant costs to be considered include holding costs, ordering costs, stockout costs, and the purchase cost of the items; Table 14.1 provides a detailed listing of the sources of these costs. The inventory holding cost is the cost that varies directly with the number of items held in stock. The opportunity cost associated with capital tied up in inventory is a major component of the holding cost. Other components are insurance cost, obsolescence cost, deterioration cost, and direct handling cost. The ordering cost is the cost that varies directly with the number of orders that are placed. Order preparation, transportation, receiving, and inspection on arrival are major contributors to the ordering cost of purchases from suppliers. The stockout cost varies directly with the number of units out of stock, and this cost includes the margin on a lost sale and the potential loss of future sales. The purchase cost of the item can be a function of the order size when quantity discounts are offered by the supplier.

In the following section, we will develop models that determine the appropriate size of the order quantity based on minimizing the total annual cost of the inventory system.

ORDER QUANTITY MODELS

Many different models have been developed to answer the question: How much do we order? All these models use relevant inventory costs as the criteria for gauging performance; however, each is based on a particular inventory situation that is best described by a plot of inventory level versus time. Figure 14.3 shows the actual stock record (i.e., inventory behavior) during a year for an item at an auto parts store. As shown, the demand rate can be considered to be approximately constant; thus, replenishment orders (40 units in this case) can be placed to arrive when units on hand approach zero but still are sufficient to avoid a stockout.

The inventory stock behavior over time is modeled to account for the costs both of holding and of ordering inventory over a typical year. Using calculus, the functional form of the inventory costs is differentiated to arrive at an optimal value for the order quantity, which is referred to as Q^*. The best-known inventory model is a simple formula to determine an economic order quantity for purchased lots.

Economic Order Quantity

The simple *economic order quantity (EOQ)* model, which assumes a constant rate of demand and no stockouts, is a surprisingly accurate model for retail grocery items such as sugar, flour, and other staples. In this situation, demand appears to be constant, because a large number of customers make periodic purchases in small amounts and stockouts of these necessities are not permitted. Figure 14.4 depicts the inventory bal-

TABLE 14.1

INVENTORY MANAGEMENT COSTS

Ordering costs
- Preparing specifications for items to be purchased
- Locating or identifying potential suppliers and soliciting bids
- Evaluating bids and selecting suppliers
- Negotiating prices
- Preparing purchase orders
- Issuing or transmitting purchase orders to outside suppliers
- Following up to ensure that purchase orders are received by suppliers

Receiving and inspection costs
- Transportation, shipping, and pickup
- Preparing and handling records of receipts and other paperwork
- Examining packages for visible damage
- Unpacking items
- Counting or weighing items to ensure that the correct amount has been delivered
- Withdrawing samples and transmitting them to inspection and testing organizations
- Inspecting or testing items to ensure that they conform to purchase specifications
- Transferring items into storage areas

Holding or carrying costs
- Interest charges on money invested in inventories
- Opportunity cost of capital tied up in inventory items, warehouses, and other parts of the inventory system
- Taxes and insurance
- Moving items into and out of inventory stores and keeping records of the movements
- Theft or pilferage
- Providing security systems for protecting inventories
- Breakage, damage, and spoilage
- Obsolescence of parts and disposal of out-of-date materials
- Depreciation
- Storage space and facilities (size is usually based upon maximum inventories rather than average)
- Providing controlled environments of temperature, humidity, dust, etc.
- Managing (tasks such as supervising stores personnel, taking physical inventory periodically, verifying and correcting records, etc.)

Shortage costs
- Lost sales and profits
- Customer dissatisfaction and ill-will; lost customers
- Penalties for late delivery or nondelivery
- Expediting orders to replenish exhausted stock

---

ances over time for this simple system, with a cycle being repeated every Q/D fraction (i.e., order quantity/annual demand) of a year. For example, if Q is 100 units and the annual demand D is 1200, then the cycle will be repeated each month. We want to determine Q^*, the quantity that minimizes relevant costs. There are no costs associated with stockouts because they do not occur. Also, we will exclude the annual cost of purchasing the item because we assume that the unit cost is constant and, therefore, not affected by the size of the order quantity. This leaves two incremental costs (i.e., costs that vary with the order quantity): the ordering cost and inventory holding cost. The *total cost purchase lot* (TC_p) function for an *EOQ* inventory system for one year is:

$$TC_p = \text{ordering cost } plus \text{ average holding cost} \qquad (1)$$

We can express equation (1) in a more usable form. First, we define some notation:

FIGURE 14.3   Actual stock record for an auto part.

D = demand in units per year
H = holding cost in dollars per unit per year
 S = cost of placing an order in dollars per order
Q = order quantity in units

Note that D and H must be in the same time units (e.g., months, years).

   The annual ordering cost is easy to derive. Because all demand D must be satisfied with orders of size Q, then D/Q orders are placed annually. Each time an order is

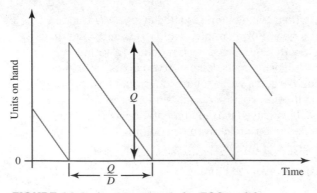

FIGURE 14.4   Inventory levels for *EOQ* model.

placed, it costs S dollars, and this results in an annual ordering cost of $S(D/Q)$. The annual cost to hold inventory also is straightforward. If one unit is kept in inventory for 1 year, the holding cost is H dollars. From Figure 14.4, the maximum inventory balance is Q, whereas the minimum balance is zero. This gives an average inventory level of $Q/2$ units. Thus, the annual inventory holding cost becomes $H(Q/2)$.

We now can rewrite the relevant annual cost of the inventory system with purchase lots as

$$TC_p = S(D/Q) + H(Q/2) \tag{2}$$

As Figure 14.5 shows, both the holding cost and the ordering cost change with different values of Q, and the total cost curve is shaped as a shallow bowl. Thus, there is a unique value of Q that gives a minimum total annual cost for the inventory system. This value, of course, is the EOQ; however, other nearby values of Q are only slightly more costly.

There are several ways to determine EOQ. For example, we can take the derivative of equation (2) with respect to Q, set the derivative equal to zero, and solve for EOQ.[1] There is another, easier way to solve for EOQ, however. Observe that the minimum of TC_p occurs where the ordering cost equals the inventory holding cost. Therefore, we can equate the two costs and solve for EOQ.

$$S(D/Q) = H(Q/2)$$

$$Q^2 = 2DS/H$$

$$EOQ = \sqrt{\frac{2DS}{H}} \tag{3}$$

Example 14.1. Rocky Mountain Power—*EOQ*

Rocky Mountain Power (RMP) maintains an inventory of spare parts that is valued at nearly $8 million. This inventory is composed of thousands of different stock-keeping units (SKUs) used for power generation and utility line maintenance, and the inventory balances are updated on a computerized information system.

Glass insulators (i.e., SKU 1341) have a relatively stable usage rate, averaging 1000 items per year. RMP purchases these insulators from the manufacturer at a cost of $20 per unit delivered to the Denver warehouse. An order for replenishment is placed whenever the inventory balance reaches a predetermined reorder point. The cost that is associated with placing an order is estimated to be $30. This includes the cost of order processing, receiving, and distribution to outlying substations.

FIGURE 14.5 Relevant annual costs for *EOQ* model.

An estimate of the annual inventory holding cost for SKU 1341 is $6 per unit. This holding cost represents a 30 percent opportunity cost of capital. SKU 1341 is essential, and RMP must avoid depleting its stock of this item. We want to determine the replenishment order size for SKU 1341 that minimizes the relevant inventory costs.

From the problem description, we know the following:

D = 1000 units per year
S = $30 per order
H = $6 per unit per year

We can substitute values of Q into equation (2) to see what happens to the total annual cost. From Table 14.2, we see that as Q increases from 70 units, TC_p decreases, until it reaches a minimum at $600. From this point on, TC_p increases. When plotted in Figure 14.5, these values demonstrate the bowl-shaped total annual cost curve. Of course, we can calculate the EOQ directly by using equation (3), which gives

$$EOQ = \sqrt{\frac{2DS}{H}}$$

$$EOQ = \sqrt{\frac{2(1000)(30)}{6}} = 100 \text{ units}$$

The annual relevant cost when $Q^* = 100$ units, as shown in Table 14.2, is $600 equally divided between ordering cost and holding cost. Nearby values of Q could be considered as being more appropriate, however. For example, an order of 120 units (10 boxes of a dozen each) has a TC_p exceeding the EOQ by only $10 per year.

Inventory Model with Quantity Discounts

Suppliers have their own interest in the size of the order quantity. Production runs cost money to set up and often result in an economical batch size. For example, the time and effort that are necessary to make a batch of four dozen chocolate chip cookies is not much more than for baking a batch of one dozen. Similarly, manufacturing firms have an interest in encouraging customers to buy in full batch sizes. Further, savings in transportation costs are available to shippers who require a full truckload instead of a less-than-full truckload. Offering a per-unit price discount to customers who order in large quantities permits the savings in manufacture and transportation to be shared between both parties. Very often, the price break occurs at an order quantity much larger than the customer's EOQ. Thus, a trade-off occurs between a savings on the cost of purchasing the inventory and the expense of holding a larger-than-desired quantity. To study this trade-off, we must recognize that the price of the item now is a variable and must be included in the total annual cost function. Thus, our TC_p equation (2) is

TABLE 14.2

TABULATION OF INVENTORY COSTS

Order quantity Q	Order cost, $30	Inventory holding cost, $6	Total cost TC_p
70	428.57	210.00	638.57
80	375.00	240.00	615.00
90	333.33	270.00	603.33
100	300.00	300.00	600.00
110	272.73	330.00	602.73
120	250.00	360.00	610.00
130	230.77	390.00	620.77

modified by adding the purchase cost, and this new equation is called *total cost with quantity discounts* (TC_{qd}).

Total cost = Purchase cost + Ordering cost + Holding cost

$$TC_{qd} = CD + S(D/Q) + I(CQ/2) \qquad (4)$$

where C = unit cost of item in dollars

I = annual inventory holding cost expressed as a percentage of the cost of the item (note: $IC = H$)

To demonstrate the trade-off analysis in the evaluation of a quantity discount offer, we return to the Rocky Mountain Power example.

Example 14.2. Rocky Mountain Power—Quantity Discount Problem

The supplier of the glass insulators, SKU 1341, is negotiating with RMP to place replenishment order quantities in lots greater than the current 100-unit size. The following quantity discount schedule has been proposed:

Order quantity	Unit price
1–239	$20.00
240–599	19.50
≥600	18.75

How should RMP respond? Because the price of the item now varies with the order quantity, the appropriate inventory cost model now becomes equation (4), using $I = 30$ percent. How does one proceed, however, to use equation (4) to determine the order quantity that minimizes the total annual inventory cost, which now includes the purchase cost as well as the ordering and holding costs? Figure 14.6 illustrates one option,

FIGURE 14.6 Annual costs for the quantity discount model.

which is plotting the total cost as a function of order quantity and noting the lowest point of the resulting *discontinuous* curve (in this case, at the price break of 240 units).

We can arrive at this same conclusion, however, using the following analytical steps:

1. Compute EOQ for the *lowest* price per unit, substituting $IC = H$ in equation (3):

$$EOQ = \sqrt{\frac{2DS}{IC}}$$

$$EOQ = \sqrt{\frac{2(1000)(30)}{(0.30)(18.75)}}$$

$$= 103, \text{ but the price of \$18.75 is appropriate only for } EOQ \geq 600.$$

2. If the *EOQ* falls outside the appropriate price range (as occurred in the last paragraph), then we recalculate *EOQ* for the next lowest price and proceed until the *EOQ* is found in the appropriate price range. Therefore, we recalculate the *EOQ* for a price of $19.50 (i.e., substitute 19.50 for *C*) and obtain a revised *EOQ* of 101. This result is not useful, however, because the *EOQ* of 101 is outside the appropriate range of 240 to 599 for a unit price of $19.50. Next, we calculate the *EOQ* with *C* = $20 and obtain a value of 100, which is appropriate because it falls within the range of 1 to 239 for a unit price of $20. The table below summarizes the series of calculations we make to arrive at an appropriate *EOQ*:

Order quantity	Unit price	*EOQ*
$\geq$ 600	$18.75	103
240–599	19.50	101
1–239	20.00	100 (appropriate *EOQ*)

3. Calculate TC_{qd} using equation (4) for the *EOQ* found in step 2 and compare with TC_{qd} when substituting for the *Q*'s that just obtain all higher price discounts (the discontinuity points in the TC_{qd} function as shown in Figure 14.6). Select the *Q* that minimizes TC_{qd}.

$$TC_{qd}(EOQ = 100) = 20(1,000) + 30(1,000)/100 + 0.30(20)(100)/2$$

$$(C = 20)$$

$$= 20,000 + 300 + 300$$

$$= 20,600$$

$$TC_{qd}(Q = 240) = 19.50(1,000) + 30(1,000)/240 + 0.30(19.50)(240)/2$$

$$(C = 19.50)$$

$$= 19,500 + 125 + 702$$

$$= 20,327$$

$$TC_{qd}(Q = 600) = 18.75(1,000) + 30(1,000)/600 + 0.30(18.75)(600)/2$$

$$(C = 18.75)$$

$$= 18,750 + 50 + 1687.5$$

$$= 20,487.5$$

Total annual costs are minimized with an order quantity of 240 units.

Inventory Model with Planned Shortages

When customers are willing to tolerate stockouts, an inventory system with planned shortages is possible. For example, a tire store may not stock all sizes of high-performance tires, knowing that a customer is willing to wait a day or two if the particular tire is out of stock. For this strategy to be acceptable to customers, however, the promised delivery date must be adhered to, and it must be within a reasonable length of time. Otherwise, customers would fault the retailer for being unreliable.

Using *electronic data interchange (EDI)* and predictable delivery from suppliers, a strategy of minimal inventory stocking can be implemented. The benefits of such a system are captured by the trade-off between the cost of holding inventory and the cost that is associated with a stockout that can be *backordered*. An item is considered to be backordered when a customer is willing to wait for delivery; thus, the sale is not lost. Some subjective cost should be associated with customer inconvenience, however. Software manufacturers have taken this tolerance of stockouts to the extreme by creating "vaporware," which is software that is planned but not yet available. Such a company would advertise this software to gauge the level of demand; however, excessive use of this strategy risks the credibility of the firm in the mind of customers. For retailers, this strategy can attract customers when the inventory cost savings are passed along as everyday low prices.

Figure 14.7 illustrates the idealized behavior of a planned shortage inventory system assuming a constant rate of demand and customers who will wait until the next order quantity Q is received to satisfy backorders that have accumulated to a maximum of K units. A new total inventory cost equation, which is called *total costs with backorders* (TC_b), now is required:

$$TC_b = \text{ordering cost } plus \text{ holding cost } plus \text{ backorder cost}$$

$$= S\frac{D}{Q} + H\frac{(Q-K)^2}{2Q} + B\frac{K^2}{2Q} \tag{5}$$

where K = number of stockouts backordered when order quantity arrives
  B = backorder cost in dollars per unit per year

Using the similar-triangles argument from geometry (i.e., the sides and heights of right triangles are proportional) and noting that inventory is held physically only for a fraction of the inventory cycle, the expression for average inventory can be derived as follows:

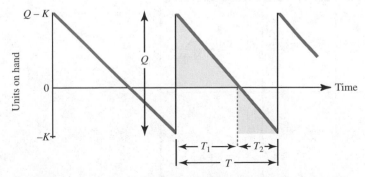

FIGURE 14.7 Inventory levels for the planned shortages model.

Average inventory held during the inventory cycle $= \left(\dfrac{Q - K}{2}\right)\left(\dfrac{T_1}{T}\right)$ but, by similar triangles, $T_1/T = (Q - K)/Q$ and, by substitution, we obtain $(Q - K)^2/2Q$.

In a similar manner, we can derive the expression for average backorders as follows:

Average number of backorders held during the inventory cycle $= \left(\dfrac{K}{2}\right)\left(\dfrac{T_2}{T}\right)$ but, by similar triangles, $T_2/T = K/Q$ and, by substitution, we obtain $K^2/2Q$.

Because the total inventory cost expression shown in equation (5) contains two decision variables, Q and K, we must take partial derivatives and solve for each variable to obtain the following values for order quantity and size of backorders:[2]

$$Q^* = \sqrt{\frac{2DS}{H}\left(\frac{H + B}{B}\right)} \tag{6}$$

$$K^* = Q^*\left(\frac{H}{H + B}\right) \tag{7}$$

The planned shortages model and the resulting equations (6) and (7) provide considerable insight into inventory systems when the backorder cost B is permitted to take on values from 0 to ∞ as shown in Table 14.3. Substituting ∞ for B in equation (6) reduces the equation to the classic EOQ equation (3). Thus, when a business uses the classic EOQ, the implication is that backorder cost is infinitely large and no stockout should occur. Because the cost of a backorder has a finite value, however, using the EOQ equation results in an inventory system that is more costly than necessary.

Letting the backorder cost decrease to zero results in an undefined value for EOQ because we have division by zero. However, inventory models that fit this situation do exist. For example, consider patients waiting for heart transplants. Because the donors

TABLE 14.3

VALUES FOR Q^* AND K^* AS A FUNCTION OF BACKORDER COST

B	Q^*	K^*	Inventory levels
$B \longrightarrow \infty$	$\sqrt{\dfrac{2DS}{H}}$	0	
$0 < B < \infty$	$\sqrt{\dfrac{2DS}{H}\left(\dfrac{H + B}{B}\right)}$	$Q^*\left[\dfrac{H}{H + B}\right]$	
$B \longrightarrow 0$	Undefined	Q^*	

cannot be inventoried, we have a queue or inventory of recipients in backorder status who are waiting for an available donor.

Example 14.3. Rocky Mountain Power—Planned Shortages Problem

Assume that the cost of a backorder for the glass insulator is the price of a $50 overnight FedEx package. Using equations (6) and (7), calculate a new order quantity and maximum backorder accumulation. Has a savings in total annual costs been realized compared with the classic *EOQ* approach?

$$Q^* = \sqrt{\frac{2DS}{H}\left(\frac{H+B}{B}\right)} = \sqrt{\frac{2(1000)(30)}{6}\left(\frac{6+50}{50}\right)} = 106$$

$$K^* = Q^*\left(\frac{H}{H+B}\right) = 106\left(\frac{6}{6+50}\right) = 11$$

$$TC_b = S\frac{D}{Q} + H\frac{(Q-K)^2}{2Q} + B\frac{K^2}{2Q}$$

$$= 30\frac{1000}{106} + 6\frac{(106-11)^2}{2(106)} + 50\frac{11^2}{2(106)}$$

$$= 283 + 255 + 29 = 567$$

Recall that the TC_p for the *EOQ* of 100 was $600, a value $33 in excess of the TC_b calculated above. Thus, using the simple *EOQ* model can be costly because of the implied assumption that stockouts cannot occur. Note that on an annual basis, both ordering and holding costs have been reduced significantly below the $300 value for the *EOQ* model at the small cost of $29 for backordering.

INVENTORY MANAGEMENT UNDER UNCERTAINTY

The simple *EOQ* formula does not consider uncertainties in demand rate or in replenishment lead time. Each time an order is placed, these uncertainties pose a risk of stockouts occurring before the replenishment order arrives. To reduce the risk of stockouts during this time, extra inventory can be held in excess of expected demand during the lead time. A trade-off exists between the cost of investing in and holding excess inventory and the cost of stockouts, however. In any event, except by good luck, either some stock remains in inventory or stockouts have occurred and the shelves are bare when the replenishment order arrives.

The key to inventory management under uncertainty is the concept of a *service level*. This is a customer-oriented term and is defined as the percentage of demand occurring during the lead time that can be satisfied from inventory. Some analytical approaches for determining the optimal service level have been suggested, but in practice, selecting a service level is a policy decision. Consider, for example, a convenience store. Depending on competition and the patience of customers, cold beer might require a 99-percent service level, but a 95-percent service level might be appropriate for fresh bread.

The service level is used to determine a *reorder point* (*ROP*), which is the level of inventory on hand when a replenishment order is initiated. The reorder point is set to achieve a prespecified service level. This, of course, requires information on the frequency distribution of demand during the replenishment lead time (*LT*). When we set the reorder point, we also are determining the *safety stock* level (*SS*), which is the excess inventory that is held during the reorder lead time to achieve the desired service level. The reorder point equals the safety stock level plus the *average demand during the lead time* (d_L). That is,

$$ROP = SS + d_L \tag{8}$$

The demand during lead time distribution now can be described in the following general manner, where the daily demand has a mean μ and standard deviation σ:

$$d_L = \mu(LT) \tag{9}$$

$$\sigma_L = \sigma \sqrt{LT} \tag{10}$$

The Central Limit Theorem allows us to assume that the demand during lead time distribution has a normal distribution no matter what the daily demand distribution is. The safety stock now can be calculated using the following equation, where z_r is the standard normal deviate for r-percent service level:

$$SS = z_r \sigma \sqrt{LT} \tag{11}$$

Figure 14.8 illustrates the concept of establishing a demand during lead time distribution for the case in which daily demand has a mean of 3 and standard deviation of 1.5 and the lead time is 4 days. Note that the *ROP* is the stock level that is on hand when an order is placed and, thus, should be sufficient to satisfy r percent of demand during the lead time. We assume that daily demand is an independent variable. The independence assumption permits the summation of individual daily demand means and variances to arrive at a total demand during the lead time, which has a normal distribution based on the Central Limit Theorem.

Example 14.4. Rocky Mountain Power—Reorder Point

Recall inventory item SKU 1341, the glass insulator. RMP's computerized information system has tracked the daily demand rate for this item. Daily demand appears to be distributed normally with mean $\mu = 3$ and standard deviation $\sigma = 1.5$. The replenishment lead time has been a constant 4 days. Because SKU 1341 is an important item for utility line maintenance, it is company policy to achieve a 95-percent service level for such items. What reorder point and safety stock should be recommended?

Using equations (9) and (10), the demand during lead time for RMP becomes

$$d_L = \mu(LT) = 3(4) = 12$$
$$\sigma_L = \sigma\sqrt{LT} = 1.5\sqrt{4} = 3$$

Then, we turn to the Standard Normal Distribution in Appendix A to find that $z = 1.645$ leaves 5 percent in one tail to guarantee a 95-percent service level. The safety

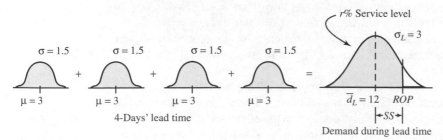

FIGURE 14.8 Demand during lead time.

stock that is required to ensure the desired service level is calculated using equation (11):

$$SS = z_r \sigma \sqrt{LT}$$
$$= (1.645)(1.5)\sqrt{4}$$
$$= 5$$

Using equation (8), we find the reorder point for RMP to be

$$ROP = SS + d_L$$
$$= 5 + 12$$
$$= 17$$

INVENTORY CONTROL SYSTEMS

Many different inventory control systems are used in actual practice. They differ in the methods for determining the order quantity and when a replenishment order should be made. We shall restrict our discussion here to two of the most common inventory control systems: the continuous review system (Q,r), and the periodic review system (i.e., order-up-to). In all inventory control systems, two questions must be answered: (1) When should an order be placed? and (2) What size is the order quantity? Because inventory control systems face uncertainty in demand, we will find that when one of these questions is answered using a fixed value, the answer to the other must accommodate the uncertainty in demand.

Continuous Review System

Figure 14.9 depicts inventory balances for the continuous review system. The inventory level decreases in a variable fashion because of uncertainty in demand until it reaches a predetermined trigger level, the reorder point *ROP*. When the inventory balance reaches the *ROP*, an order for replenishment is placed with the vendor. For this inventory system, the order quantity *EOQ* is fixed (i.e., *EOQ* units always are ordered each time an order is placed). An example of this "two bin" system is the Hallmark greeting card stand that has a reorder card, containing the stock number, placed near the back of the card display to remind the retailer to reorder the item before the remaining cards are sold.

From the time the reorder point is reached until the replenishment is received, the inventory level continues to decline. Generally, there will be some inventory remaining just before the replenishment is received. The average inventory balance just when the replenishment arrives is the safety stock level *SS*. This inventory is maintained to protect against stockouts that might result from unusually high levels of demand and/or longer-than-expected replenishment lead time. On occasion, however, a stockout does occur. For this system, unsatisfied demand during the lead time period is backordered until the replenishment order is received, in which case the backordered items are set aside and the remaining part of the *EOQ* placed in stock.

Note that for the continuous review system, the order quantity is fixed, but the cycle time between orders varies. A computerized information system using bar codes for each SKU can track inventory balances continuously to indicate when the reorder point is reached. Retailers like Wal-Mart use *point-of-sale (POS)* cash registers to record up-to-the-minute status of stock levels, with an end-of-day report on all items that have

FIGURE 14.9 Continuous review system (*Q, r*).

reached their reorder points. In many cases, the purchase order is generated automatically by the computer and sent to the vendor or, in the case of Wal-Mart, to its distribution center for the next shipment.

Again, the parameter equations for the continuous review system are

$$EOQ = \sqrt{\frac{2\,DS}{H}}$$

$$ROP = SS + \mu LT$$

$$SS = z_r \sigma \sqrt{LT}$$

Periodic Review System

Figure 14.10 depicts inventory balances for the periodic review system. Orders for replenishment are placed after a fixed review period *RP* has elapsed. The order quantity varies and is calculated to be that needed to bring the total inventory (i.e., on-hand plus on-order) up to some predetermined target inventory level *TIL*. Note that occasional backorders can occur with this system, just as with the continuous review system. With the periodic review system, the order quantity varies in response to the demand rate, whereas the cycle time between orders is fixed.

To determine the fixed-review period, first calculate an *EOQ*; then divide the resulting value by the average daily demand to arrive at an expected cycle time. The resulting review period thus balances the holding and ordering costs to achieve a minimum total incremental cost for the system.

The periodic review system generally is used when orders for many different SKUs are consolidated for replenishment from a distributor or regional warehouse that resupplies on a periodic basis (e.g., restocking a convenience store once a week).

FIGURE 14.10 Periodic review system (order-up-to).

The parameter equations for the periodic review system are noted below, where the daily demand has a mean of μ and a standard deviation of ρ. Note that exposure to a stockout for the periodic review system is the review period plus the lead time (i.e., $RP + LT$) instead of just the lead time (LT) as in the continuous review system. Thus, carrying extra inventory is the cost that is paid for lack of continuous information on the inventory status.

$$RP = EOQ/\mu \tag{12}$$

$$TIL = SS + \mu(RP + LT) \tag{13}$$

$$SS = z_r\sigma\sqrt{RP + LT} \tag{14}$$

Example 14.5. Rocky Mountain Power—Periodic Review System

Recall from Example 14.4 that for inventory item SKU 1341, the glass insulator, daily demand is distributed normally, with mean, $\mu = 3$ and standard deviation $\sigma = 1.5$. In Example 14.1, the EOQ was calculated to be 100 units. The replenishment lead time has been a constant 4 days. Again, because SKU 1341 is an important item for utility line maintenance, it is company policy to achieve a 95-percent service level for such items. If a periodic review system is selected to control glass insulator inventory, what are the recommended review period, target inventory level, and safety stock?

Using equation (12), the review period $RP = 100/3 = 33$ days, or approximately once each month. The safety stock is calculated using equation (14):

$$SS = z_r\sigma\sqrt{RP + LT} = (1.645)(1.5)\sqrt{33 + 4} = 15$$

The target inventory level is determined using equation (13):

$$TIL = SS + \mu(RP + LT) = 15 + 3(33 + 4) = 126$$

Thus, once every month the inventory of SKU 1341 on hand is noted with an order placed for an amount that is equal to the difference between that inventory and the target level of 126 units.

The ABCs of Inventory Control

Usually, a few inventory items or SKUs account for most of the inventory value as measured by dollar volume (i.e., demand multiplied by item cost). Thus, we must pay close attention to these few items that control most of the inventory value. The 80-20 rule, or Pareto analysis, introduced in Chapter 3, "Service Quality," is useful for inventory classification. The ABC classification system, shown graphically in Figure 14.11, often is used to organize SKUs into three groups depending on their value. The A class typically contains about 20 percent of inventory items but accounts for 80 percent of dollar volume. These significant items need close attention. At the other extreme are the insignificant class C items, which usually represent 50 percent of inventory items but account for only about 5 percent of the dollar volume. In the middle is class B, which represents 30 percent of items and 15 percent of the dollar volume. Before an inventory control system is decided on, an ABC classification usually is undertaken. Selecting the appropriate inventory control system should be based on the significance of the inventory items.

Table 14.4 shows inventory items for a discount electronics store arranged in order of decreasing dollar volume to achieve an ABC classification. In this case, two items (i.e., computers and entertainment centers) comprise 20 percent of SKUs and account for 74 percent of the total dollar volume. These are the few costly A items that require special managerial attention, because they represent a significant sales opportunity loss if they are out of stock. Intensive computer monitoring of inventory levels as found in the continuous review system should be used for these items.

As is common, 50 percent of the items account for a small percentage of the dollar volume inventory value (in this case, 10 percent). These are the inexpensive C items

FIGURE 14.11 ABC classification of inventory items.

TABLE 14.4

INVENTORY ITEMS LISTED IN DESCENDING ORDER OF DOLLAR VOLUME

Inventory item	Unit cost ($)	Monthly sales (units)	Dollar volume ($)	Percent of dollar volume	Percent of SKUs	Class
Computers	3000	50	150,000	74	20	A
Entertainment centers	2500	30	75,000			
Television sets	400	60	24,000			
Refrigerators	1000	15	15,000	16	30	B
Monitors	200	50	10,000			
Stereos	150	60	9,000			
Cameras	200	40	8,000			
Software	50	100	5,000	10	50	C
Computer disks	5	1000	5,000			
CDs	20	200	4,000			
Totals			305,000	100	100	

and can be managed in a more casual fashion, because a stockout does not represent a serious loss of revenue. For these items, a periodic review system might be used. The review period can be relatively long as well, which results in infrequent orders for large quantities of low-value items.

The three B items are not so costly as to require special managerial attention, but they are not so cheap that they can be overstocked. Either a continuous review or a periodic review system could be used to manage these items.

SINGLE-PERIOD MODEL FOR PERISHABLE GOODS

Businesses sometimes accumulate an inventory in anticipation of future sales that will occur during a short period of time, after which the unsold items are drastically reduced in value. Retail examples include Christmas trees, fresh pastries, fresh fruit and vegetables, magazines, and newspapers. Given some data on past sales experience, the question to answer is how much to stock? If too small, the order quantity results in the possibility of lost sales. If the order quantity is too large, however, unsold stock represents a lost investment that may have minimal salvage value.

This decision on how much to stock will be illustrated using the classic "news vendor problem" (albeit a rather expensive newspaper). First, we begin with some notation, then follow with a distribution of expected sales including $P(D < Q)$:

D = newspapers demanded
Q = newspapers stocked
P = selling price of newspaper, $10
C = cost of newspaper, $4
S = salvage value of newspaper, $2
C_u = unit contribution from sale, $P - C$ = $6 (opportunity cost of *under*estimating demand)
C_o = unit loss from not selling, $C - S$ = $2 (cost of *over*estimating demand)
$P(D < Q)$ = probability of not selling all newspapers stocked
$P(D > Q)$ = probability of selling all newspapers stocked

D	Frequency	p(D)	Q	P(D < Q)
2	1	.028	2	.000
3	2	.055	3	.028
4	3	.083	4	.083
5	4	.111	5	.166
6	5	.139	6	.277
7	6	.167	7	.416
8	5	.139	8	.583
9	4	.111	9	.722
10	3	.083	10	.838
11	2	.055	11	.916
12	1	.028	12	.971

Expected Value Analysis

A payoff table is constructed to account for the financial result of each combination of actual newspapers demanded and stock level selected (for convenience, we will limit Q to values between 6 and 10). Using the probability of newspapers demanded, an expected profit will be calculated for each column of the payoff table (i.e., stock level Q). The stock level that yields the maximum expected profit will best balance the opportunity cost of lost sales and cost of investment in unsold newspapers. The payoff table is best constructed beginning with the upper left-hand cell. For cell ($D = 2$, $Q = 6$), we have the following financial result:

Sales:	2($10)	=	$20
Salvage:	(6 − 2)($2)	=	8
Total revenue:			$28
Less cost:	6($4)	=	−24
Profit:			$ 4

Note that as one moves across the rows, the profit decreases by $(S - C) = 2 - 4 = -\$2$, because one more unsold newspaper must be salvaged. As one moves down the columns, the profit increases by $(P - S) = 10 - 2 = \$8$, because one more unsalvaged unit now is sold. This increase in profit continues until the diagonal, where $D = Q$ is reached, after which the profit remains the same as all available stock is sold and additional demand is not being satisfied.

The expected profit for each stock level Q from 6 to 10 is calculated and shown at the bottom of the table on page 425. Expected profit for $Q = 6$ is calculated by multiplying the probability of demand $p(D)$ in the first column by each payoff in column three under $Q = 6$:

$$\text{Expected profit (for } Q = 6) =$$

$$.028(4) + .055(12) + .083(20) + \cdots + .055(36) + .028(36) = \$31.54$$

For this example, a stock of nine newspapers ($Q^* = 9$) will maximize expected profit at $35.99 per period.

		Stock Q				
$p(D)$	D	6	7	8	9	10
.028	2	4	2	0	−2	−4
.055	3	12	10	8	6	4
.083	4	20	18	16	14	12
.111	5	28	26	24	22	20
.139	6	36	34	32	30	28
.167	7	36	42	40	38	36
.139	8	36	42	48	46	44
.111	9	36	42	48	54	52
.083	10	36	42	48	54	60
.055	11	36	42	48	54	60
.028	12	36	42	48	54	60
Expected profit:		$31.54	$34.43	$35.77	$35.99	$35.33

Marginal Analysis

Another approach to the news vendor problem uses an economic principle called *marginal analysis*. The argument is that the news vendor should continue increasing the stock (size of Q) until the expected revenue on the last unit stocked just exceeds the expected loss on the last sale. From this principle, we can derive a very useful probability called the *critical fractile:*

$$E(\text{revenue on last sale}) \geq E(\text{loss on last sale})$$

$$P(\text{revenue})(\text{unit revenue}) \geq P(\text{loss})(\text{unit loss})$$

$$P(D \geq Q)\, C_u \geq P(D < Q)\, C_o$$

$$[1 - P(D < Q)]\, C_u \geq P(D < Q)\, C_o$$

$$P(D < Q) \leq \frac{C_u}{C_u + C_o} \tag{15}$$

where

C_u = unit contribution from newspaper sale (opportunity cost of *under*estimating demand)

C_o = unit loss from not selling newspaper (cost of *over*estimating demand)

D = demand

Q = newspapers stocked

Using equation (15), we find $P(D < Q) \leq 6/(6 + 2) \leq .75$. Thus, stock $Q = 9$, because as Figure 14.12 shows, the newspaper demand from 2 through 8 sums to a cumulative probability of 0.722. Looking back at the expected profit line in the payoff table, we find confirmation of the marginal analysis principle. Each time we increase Q, beginning with a value of 6 in our abbreviated table, there is a corresponding increase in profit up to the value of 9, after which profit decreases with the 10th unit, creating an expected loss of $0.66.

FIGURE 14.12 Critical fractile for the news vendor problem.

RETAIL DISCOUNTING MODEL

Even with the best planning, attempting to anticipate customer demand has its risks. The sleeveless shirt that seemed to be such a great fashion statement at the Las Vegas trade show just did not catch on in Peoria. Such "dogs" end up on the shelf for months, collecting dust and depriving the retailer of shelf space for displaying new items that might sell faster. Discounting them means a loss of some profit margin, and besides, what should be an appropriate discount? In any event, the retailer surely would never sell them below cost. This dilemma can be resolved by determining the break-even discount price that will clear the inventory of "dogs" in short order and, thus, generate capital to invest in good stock that will turn rapidly. In retailing, profit is a function of mark-up multiplied by turnover. The following terms will be used for determining the discount price:

S = current selling price

D = discount price

P = profit margin on cost (the percent mark-up as a decimal)

Y = average number of years to sell entire stock of "dogs" at current price (total number of years to clear stock divided by 2)

N = *inventory turns,* that is, the number of times good stock turns over during the year

The break-even discount price will be found by equating the loss per item to the gain from investing the revenue that is obtained in good stock:

$$\text{Loss per item} = \text{Gain from revenue}$$

$$S - D = D(PNY)$$

Thus, the discount price is

$$D = \frac{S}{(1 + PNY)} \tag{16}$$

Example 14.6. Sportstown

The Titanium Princess Terminator tennis racket has not been selling well, perhaps because of its poor weight distribution. It is well made, however, and retails at $29.95 with a 40-percent mark-up on cost. Only one sale was made last year, and there were 10 rackets remaining in stock. More popular rackets were selling at a rate of 25 per year.

The percent mark-up on cost as a decimal is $P = 0.40$, with a selling price $S = \$29.95$. With current sales of one per year, the average number of years to clear the stock of 10 rackets is $Y = 10/2 = 5$. If these "dogs" were good rackets, then $25/10 = 2.5$ lots would sell per year; thus, $N = 2.5$. Using equation (16), the discount price is:

$$D = \frac{29.95}{[1 + (0.40)(2.5)(5)]}$$

$$= \frac{29.95}{6}$$

$$= \$4.99$$

Thus, the 10 tennis rackets should be discounted immediately to sell at a price of $4.99 each. Note that we will take an opportunity loss of $(S - D) = (\$29.95 - \$4.99) = \$24.96$ per item; however, the $4.99 will be placed immediately in fast-moving stock. The $4.99 will be marked up by 40 percent and, thus, return $2.00 each time a good racket is sold, $(0.40)(\$4.99)$. Good stock, however, turns over 2.5 times a year, compared with a "dog" that sells one item per year and, thus, makes $2.5(\$2.00) = \$5.00$ a year. Because it will take 5 years on average to clear out the "dogs," the total revenue gain from reinvestment of profits is $5(\$5.00) = \$25.00$.

In other words, we can either hold the "dogs" and eventually sell all of them at $29.95, or we can sell them all immediately at $4.99, put the money (i.e., $50.00) into good stock, and regain our losses in 5 years. Note that the discount price results in a breakeven in which no money is made, and we need not discount to that extreme low level. Because the wholesale price was $29.95/1.4 = $21.39, we might wish to discount the rackets initially to a price of $19.95. If the rackets sell quickly, we will make money even though the selling price is below cost, because the money tied up in inventory now is moving.

SUMMARY

Inventory management can influence significantly the success of an organization. For some organizations, the extent to which their objectives are achieved is affected by the inventory system they adopt. Good inventory management is characterized by concern for inventory holding costs, inventory ordering costs, shortage costs, and the purchase price of the items. Further, the lead time for replenishment and the appropriate service level should be considered.

Because of the widespread use of bar coding, keeping track of inventory using computers is common practice. This simplifies the manipulations of large amounts of data relevant to inventory decisions. We looked at methods of forecasting demand for services in Chapter 10 because inventory is the price a business pays for lack of information.

BOX 14.1

Service Benchmark
WHERE PARTS ARE THE WHOLE

Replacement auto parts companies live and die by their inventories. A full-line distributor carries more than 100,000 individual parts, and even a local retailer may have 10,000. Many distributors and retailers—caught between having enough parts and having too many—are asking computers to do their counting and restocking. Other industries rely on computerized inventory systems too, but few have to sort out the same number and range of items as companies that sell replacement parts.

Even in the computer age, many distributors manage their inventories by instinct and memory, guided by inventory cards attached to the parts. The results of such unsophisticated systems are apparent when the parts industry goes into a downturn. "Because distributors traditionally have been mom-and-pop types of businesses, we have seen a number go out of business anytime there is a shock to the system, like a mild winter," said Gurudutt M. Baliga, an automotive analyst with McDonald & Company Securities.

Analysts credit Genuine Parts Company with taking the industry into the computer age. Most of the 6,000 retailers, or jobbers, that buy parts from Genuine are connected by computer to one of the company's NAPA distribution warehouses. Every time a jobber sells an item, the sale is logged on a computer at the warehouse. The computer updates a list of parts to be delivered the next day to replenish the jobber's stock. Genuine Parts encourages mechanics to use rugged laptop computers to order parts electronically without leaving their service bays.

Genuine is not the only parts company to employ computers. Individual auto parts stores use computers to monitor inventories and other large distributors like Carquest Inc. also have tried to link retail stores directly with warehouses. But analysts say Genuine's system is the most successful.

"Genuine is sophisticated in the way they examine each local market and structure the inventory accordingly," said Mr. Baliga. "If they expected the wiper blade inventory to turn over three times at a particular store, and it only turned once, they send out a team of people to understand why."

Source: New York Times, September 2, 1990, p. F4(N).

KEY TERMS AND DEFINITIONS

Backorder a demand that is not satisfied immediately because of a stockout but is satisfied later because the customer is willing to wait until the replenishment order arrives to take delivery.

Critical fractile the cumulative probability that demand will be less than the stock level that guarantees marginal revenue just exceeds the marginal cost of the last item stocked.

Economic order quantity (*EOQ*) the reorder quantity that minimizes the total incremental cost of holding inventory and the cost of ordering replenishments.

Electronic data interchange (EDI) a computerized exchange of data between organizations that eliminates paper-based documents.

Inventory turns the number of times an inventory stock is sold per year, calculated by dividing annual demand by the average inventory held.

Point-of-sale (POS) online linking of sales transactions, using computerized cash registers, bar-code scanners, or credit-card readers, to a central computer allowing immediate updating of sales, inventory, and pricing information.

Reorder point (*ROP*) level of inventory both on hand and on order when a reorder of a fixed quantity is made.

Replenishment lead time the time, usually in days, from an order being placed with a vendor to the delivery being made.

Safety stock inventory held in excess of expected demand during lead time to satisfy a desired service level.

Service level the probability that demand will be satisfied during replenishment lead time.

SOLVED PROBLEMS

1. Continuous Review (Q, r) System

Problem Statement

A resort hotel is planning to install a computerized inventory system to manage the complementary guest toilet items such as soap and shampoo. The daily usage rate for bars of soap appears to be distributed normally, with mean $\mu = 16$ and standard deviation $\sigma = 3$. Once an order is placed, it takes a full week before delivery is made. The effort to place an order and receive the shipment is approximately one hour's time for a staff person who is paid $10 per hour. The opportunity cost of capital is 20 percent per year. A bar of soap is valued at approximately $0.25. The hotel is concerned about stockouts of such a basic item and, thus, desires a 94-percent service level. Recommend an order quantity (Q) and reorder point (r) for a continuous review system.

Solution

First, calculate the value of Q using equation (3) for the parameters below:

$$D = (16)(365) = 5840 \text{ per year}$$

$$S = 10$$

$$H = IC = (0.20)(0.25) = 0.05$$

$$EOQ = \sqrt{\frac{2DS}{H}} = \sqrt{\frac{2(5840)(10)}{0.05}} = 1528.4 \cong 1500$$

Second, determine the demand during lead-time distribution using equations (9) and (10):

$$d_L = \mu(LT) = (16)(7) = 112$$

$$\sigma_L = \sigma\sqrt{LT} = 3\sqrt{7} = 7.94 \cong 8$$

Third, calculate the safety stock using equation (11), and find the z value in Appendix A with .06 probability in one tail:

$$SS = z_r\sigma\sqrt{LT} = (1.555)(8) = 12.44 \cong 13 \text{ (round up to be conservative)}$$

Finally, the reorder point is the sum of the safety stock and the mean demand during lead-time:

$$ROP = SS + d_L = 13 + 112 = 125$$

2. Periodic Review (Order-Up-To) System

Problem Statement

The resort hotel manager was not interested in continuously monitoring the usage of complementary toilet items, which he felt were better classified as low-value C items. Thus, he requested that a periodic review system be used. Recommend a review period and target inventory level for a system with a 94-percent service level.

Solution

First, calculate the review period using equation (12) based on the *EOQ* from problem 1:

$$RP = EOQ/\mu = 1500/16 = 93.75 \text{ days (or every 3 months)}$$

Second, calculate the safety stock using equation (14):

$$SS = z_r\sigma\sqrt{RT + LT} = (1.555)(3)\sqrt{94 + 7} = 46.9 \cong 47 \text{ units}$$

Finally, calculate the target inventory level using equation (13):

$$TIL = SS + \mu(RP + LT) = 47\ (16)(94 + 7) = 1663 \text{ units}$$

3. Perishable Goods

Problem Statement

A commuter airline prides itself on customer service, with features such as providing its morning passengers with a copy of *The Wall Street Journal*. The paper cost $1.50 per issue on subscription. The newsstand price is $2.50. What size subscription should be ordered if a small plane with only six seats has experienced the demand distribution below:

Passengers	2	3	4	5	6
Probability	.1	.2	.2	.3	.2

Solution

First, prepare a $P(D < Q)$ distribution as shown:

Q	2	3	4	5	6
P(D < Q)	0	.1	.3	.5	.8

Second, identify the cost of underestimating demand as $C_u = \$2.50$, the cost of buying a newsstand paper for the passenger without one.

Third, identify the cost of overestimating demand as $C_o = \$1.50$, the cost of a paper not used.

Finally, using equation (15), we determine the critical fractile $P(D < Q) \leq C_u/(C_u + C_o) \leq 2.5/(2.5 + 1.5) \leq 0.625$. Thus, buy a five-paper subscription to *The Wall Street Journal*.

TOPICS FOR DISCUSSION

1. Discuss the functions of inventory for different organizations in the distribution system (i.e., manufacturing, suppliers, distributors, and retailers).
2. How would one find values for inventory management costs?
3. Compare and contrast a continuous review inventory system with a periodic review inventory system.
4. Discuss how information technology can help to create a competitive advantage through inventory management.
5. How valid are the assumptions for the simple *EOQ* model?
6. In general, how is a service level determined for most inventory items?
7. Some noninventory items (e.g., seats on an aircraft) have the same characteristics as inventories. What inventory model would apply?

EXERCISES

14.1. Annual demand for the notebook binders that Ted's Stationery Shop sells is 10,000 units. Ted operates his business on a 200-workday year. The unit cost of a binder is $2, and the cost of placing an order with his supplier is $0.40. The cost of carrying a binder in stock for one year is 10 percent of its value.

    a. What should the *EOQ* be?

    b. How many orders are placed per year?

    c. How many working days elapse between reorders?

14.2. Deep Six Seafood, a restaurant that is open 360 days a year, specializes in fresh Maine lobsters at a cost of $10 each. Air freight charges have increased significantly, and it now costs Deep Six $48 to place an order. Because the lobsters are shipped live in a saltwater tub, the order cost is not affected by order sizes. The cost to keep a lobster alive until needed runs about $0.02 per day. The demand for lobsters during the 1-day lead time is as follows:

Lead-time demand	Probability
0	.05
1	.10
2	.20
3	.30
4	.20
5	.10
6	.05

    a. Deep Six would like to reconsider its order size. What would you recommend as an *EOQ*?

    b. The Maine distributor is willing to give Deep Six a $0.50 discount on each lobster if orders are placed in lots of 360 each. Should Deep Six accept this offer?

    c. If Deep Six insists on maintaining a safety stock of 2 lobsters, what is the service level?

14.3. Dutch Farms imports cheese by the case from Holland for distribution to its Texas retail outlets. During the year (360 days), Dutch Farms sells 1080 cases of cheese. Because of spoilage, Dutch Farms estimates that it costs the firm $6 per year to store a case of cheese. The cost to place an order runs about $10. The desired service level is 98 percent. The demand for cheese during the 1-day lead time is shown below.

Lead-time demand (cases)	Probability
0	.02
1	.08
2	.20
3	.40
4	.20
5	.08
6	.02

    a. Calculate the *EOQ* for Dutch Farms.

    b. How many cases should Dutch Farms hold as safety stock against stockouts?

    c. Dutch Farms owns a refrigerated warehouse with a capacity of 500 square feet. If each case of cheese requires 10 square feet and must be refrigerated, how much per year could Dutch Farms afford to spend on renting additional space?

14.4. The local distributor for Macho Heavy Beer is reconsidering its inventory policy now that only kegs will be sold. The sales forecast for next year (200 days) is 600 kegs. The cost to store a keg of Macho in a refrigerated warehouse is approximately $3 per year. Placing an order with the factory costs about $4. The demand for Macho during the 1-day lead time is

Lead-time demand (kegs)	Probability
0	.03
1	.12
2	.20
3	.30
4	.20
5	.12
6	.03

    a. Recommend an *EOQ* for Macho Heavy Beer.

    b. If orders are placed in carload lots of 200 kegs, the brewery is willing to give the local distributor a $0.25 discount on the wholesale price of each keg. Based on analysis of total variable inventory costs, is this offer attractive?

    c. What is the recommended safety stock if Macho decides on an 85-percent service level?

14.5. Books-to-Go, Inc., has a recurring problem of clearing its shelves of hardcover books once the publisher releases the paperback edition. These books take up shelf space, and the sales are slow. More important, however, they tie up capital with which to buy new bestsellers. Typically, hardcover bestsellers initially retail for $39.95 and have sales of approximately 30 per month during the introductory period. Once the paperback becomes available, hardcover sales plummet to approximately 3 per month. The mark-up on bestsellers is 50 percent of cost.

    a. If the paperback version sells for $12.95 and 15 hardbacks are in stock, recommend a discount price for the hardcover version.

    b. Explain why the discount price is not influenced by the number of hardcovers in stock.

14.6. Spanish Interiors imports ceramic floor tiles from Mexico with various patterns in anticipation of contractor needs. These tiles usually are ordered a year before delivery, and the production run for each tile pattern requires a separate setup. Therefore, the orders must be large to defray the setup cost. Because orders are made far in advance of customer needs, the company must guess what the contractors will like and order patterns in anticipation of these demands. Occasionally, tile patterns fall out of favor, and Spanish Interiors is stuck with slow-moving stock. The mark-up is 30 percent of the tile cost, and the inventory usually turns over about three times per year. There are two slow-moving tile patterns in stock that management estimates will take 2 years each to clear. The sunburst pattern currently retails for $0.70 per square and the saguaro cactus pattern for $1.05 per square. Calculate the lowest discount price for each pattern that will clear the stock quickly.

14.7. Monthly demand for an inventory item is a normally distributed random variable with a mean of 20 units and a variance of 4. Demand follows this distribution every month, 12 months a year. When inventory reaches a predetermined level, an order for replenishment is placed. The fixed ordering cost is $60 per order. The items cost $4 per unit, and the annual inventory holding cost is 25 percent of the average value of the inventory. The replenishment lead time is exactly 4 months.

    a. Determine the *EOQ*.

    b. Assume that a 10-percent "all units" discount will be given if the order quantity is greater than or equal to 100 units. What order quantity would you recommend with this offer?

    c. Determine the necessary reorder point and safety stock to achieve a 90-percent service level.

14.8. The daily demand for an item is distributed normally, with a mean of 5 and a variance of 2. The cost to place an order is $10, and the carrying charge per day is estimated at 10 percent of the inventory value. The supplier has offered the following purchase plan:

$$\text{Cost per unit} = \begin{cases} \$15 \text{ if} & Q < 10 \\ \$14 \text{ if} & 10 \le Q < 50 \\ \$12 \text{ if} & Q \ge 50 \end{cases}$$

    a. Recommend an optimal order quantity that will minimize the total inventory costs of ordering and holding plus the purchase cost of the units. Although it is not necessary, you may assume 360 days a year.

    b. Determine the reorder point and safety stock that will achieve a 95-percent service level given a constant 2-day delivery lead time. Assume daily demand is an independent variable.

14.9. River City Cement Co. maintains an inventory of lime that is purchased from a local supplier. River City uses an average of 200,000 pounds of lime annually in its manufacturing operations (assume 50 operating weeks per year). The lime is purchased from the supplier at a cost of $0.10 per pound. The inventory holding cost is 30 percent of the average value of the inventory, and the cost of placing an order for replenishment is estimated to be $12 per order.

    a. Assume that River City orders 10,000 pounds of lime every time it places an order for replenishment. What is the average annual cost of maintaining the inventory?

    b. Determine the *EOQ*. If the forecast of annual demand is 10 percent less than actual, how much "extra" is River City paying annually because of an inaccurate forecast of demand (note that this means actual demand for lime averages 220,000 pounds)?

    c. Assume that the supplier offers River City a 10-percent "all units" discount if the order quantity is 13,000 pounds or more. Also, assume that annual demand for lime averages 200,000 pounds. What is the best order quantity?

14.10. A popular item stocked by the Fair Deal Department Store has an annual demand of 600 units. The cost to purchase these units from the supplier is $20 per unit and $12 to prepare the purchase order. The annual inventory holding cost is 20 percent of the purchase cost. The manager tries to maintain the probability of stockout at 5 percent or less. Lead time demand is uniform, between 30 and 70 (i.e., the probability of lead time is $1/41 = .0244$ for demand $= 30, 31, \ldots , 70$).

    a. Calculate the *EOQ*.

    b. Calculate the reorder point.

    c. Calculate the safety stock.

    d. If we purchase 80 units or more, the unit purchase cost is reduced to $19. Calculate the *EOQ* for this quantity discount case.

14.11. The Supermart Store is about to place an order for Valentine's Day candy. The candy can be bought for $1.40 per box, and it is sold for $2.90 per box up to Valentine's Day. After Valentine's Day, any remaining boxes are sold for $1.00 each. All surplus candy can be sold at this reduced price. Demand at the regular retail price is a random variable with the following discrete probability distribution:

Demand (boxes)	Probability
8	.15
9	.15
10	.30
11	.30
12	.10

    a. Determine the expected demand for boxes of candy at the regular retail price.

    b. Determine the optimal number of boxes to stock using the critical fractile approach.

    c. What is the expected profit for your order in **b**?

14.12. Suppose the XYZ Company, which has an annual demand of 12,000 units per year, order cost of $25, and annual holding cost per unit of $0.50, decides to operate with a planned shortage inventory policy with the backorder cost estimated as $5 per unit per year.

    a. Determine the *EOQ*.

    b. Determine the maximum number of backorders.

    c. Determine the maximum inventory level.

    d. Determine the cycle time in workdays (assume 250 workdays per year).

    e. Determine the total inventory cost per year.

14.13. The A & M Hobby Shop carries a line of radio-controlled model racing cars. Demand for these cars is assumed to be a constant rate of 40 cars per month. The cars cost $60 each, and ordering costs are approximately $15 per order regardless of the order size. Inventory carrying costs are 20 percent annually.

   a. Determine the *EOQ* and total annual costs under the assumption that no backorders are permitted.

   b. Using a $45-per-unit-per-year backorder cost, determine the minimum cost inventory policy and total annual cost.

   c. What is the maximum number of days a customer would have to wait for a backorder under the policy in part **b**? Assume the Hobby Shop is open for business 300 days per year.

   d. Would you recommend a no-backorder or a backorder inventory policy for this product? Explain.

   e. If the lead time is 6 days, what is the reorder point in terms of on-hand inventory for both the no-backorder and the backorder inventory policies?

14.14. The J & B Card Shop sells calendars with different coral reef pictures shown for each month. The once-a-year order for each year's calendar arrives in September. From past experience, the September-to-July demand for these calendars can be approximated by a normal distribution with mean of 500 and standard deviation of 120. The calendars cost $1.50 each, and J & B sells them for $3 each.

   a. If J & B throws out all unsold calendars at the end of July (i.e., salvage value is zero), how many calendars should be ordered?

   b. If J & B reduces the calendar price to $1 at the end of July and can sell all surplus calendars at this price, how many calendars should be ordered?

14.15. The Gilbert Air Conditioning Company is considering purchase of a special shipment of portable air conditioners from Japan. Each unit will cost Gilbert $80 and be sold for $125. Gilbert does not want to carry over surplus air conditioners to the following year. Thus, all surplus units will be sold to a wholesaler who has agreed to take them for $50 per unit. Given the probability distribution for air conditioners shown below, recommend an order quantity and the anticipated profit using expected value analysis:

Demand	Estimated probability
0	.30
1	.35
2	.20
3	.10
4	.05

14.16. To limit dependence on imported oil, the Four Corners Power Company has decided to cover a fixed part of the regional demand for electricity by using coal. The annual demand for coal is estimated to be 500,000 tons, which are used uniformly throughout the year. The coal can be strip-mined near the power-generating plant and delivered with a setup requiring 2 days for a cost of $2,000 per mining run. Holding coal in inventory costs approximately $3.00 per ton per year.

   a. Determine the economic order quantity for coal assuming 250 workdays per year.

   b. Assume the daily demand for coal is distributed normally, with mean of 2,000 tons and standard deviation of 500 tons. What quantity should be set as safety stock to guarantee a 99-percent service level?

   c. If the coal were mined in quantities of 50,000 tons per order, a savings of $0.01 per ton could be passed along to the power company. Should Four Corners Power Company reconsider its coal production quantity as calculated in **a**?

   d. What would be the basis for determining the cost of a coal stockout for Four Corners Power Company?

14.17. A wholesaler encounters a constant demand of 200 cases of one brand and box size of soap flakes per week from his retail accounts. He obtains the soap flakes from the manufacturer at $10 per case after paying the transportation costs. The average cost of each order placed is $5, and he computes his inventory carrying charges as 20 percent of the average inventory value on hand over a 1-year period.

   a. Compute the *EOQ* for this product.
   b. Assuming a constant lead time of 5 days for this product, what is the minimum re-order point that will allow the wholesaler to provide 100-percent customer service? Assume 5 operating days per week.
   c. Determine the wholesaler's total cost per year for this product.
   d. The manufacturer offers the wholesaler a quantity discount of $1 per case for purchasing in quantities of 400 cases or more. Should the wholesaler take advantage of this quantity discount?

14.18. Leapycar Tire is interested in carrying insufficient numbers of budget tires deliberately. If a customer finds a budget tire is not available, a salesperson will try to sell a more expensive substitute tire, but if this strategy fails, the customer is placed on a waiting list and notified when the next order arrives from the distributor. Leapyear Tire wishes to design an ordering system that will allow backorders to accumulate to a number approximately one-tenth the size of the replenishment order quantity at the time the delivery arrives from the distributor. The cost to hold a tire in stock for a year is $2 and the cost to place an order with the distributor is $9.

   a. What is the implied cost of backordering a customer?
   b. What would be the recommended order quantity for a 195HR14 tire with an annual demand of 1,000?

Elysian Cycles[3]

Located in a major southwestern U.S. city, Elysian Cycles (EC) is a wholesale distributor of bicycles and bicycle parts. Its primary retail outlets are located in eight cities within a 400-mile radius of the distribution center. These retail outlets generally depend on receiving orders for additional stock within two days after notifying the distribution center (if the stock is available). The company's management feels this is a valuable marketing tool that aids its survival in a highly competitive industry.

EC distributes a wide variety of finished bicycles, but all are based on five different frame designs, each of which may be available in several sizes. Table 14.5 gives a breakdown of product options that are available to the retail outlets.

TABLE 14.5

PRICES AND OPTIONS OF AVAILABLE BICYCLES

Frame style	Available sizes, in.	Number of gears	Suggested list price
A	18, 21, 23	3	$ 99.95
B	18, 21, 23	10	124.95
C	18, 21, 23, 24.5	10	169.95
D	21, 23, 24.5	10	219.95
E	21, 23, 24.5	10 or 15	349.95

EC receives these different styles from a single manufacturer overseas, and shipments may take as long as four weeks from the time an order is made by telephone or telex. Including the costs of communication, paperwork, and customs clearance, EC estimates that it incurs a cost of $65 each time an order is placed. The cost per bicycle is roughly 60 percent of the suggested list price for any of the styles available.

Demand for these bicycles is somewhat seasonal in nature, being heavier in spring and early summer and tapering off through fall and winter (except for a heavy surge in the six weeks before Christmas). A breakdown of the previous year's business with the retail outlets usually forms the basis for EC's yearly operations plan. A growth factor (either positive or negative) is used to refine further the demand estimate by reflecting the upcoming yearly market. By developing a yearly plan and updating it when appropriate, EC can establish a reasonable basis for obtaining any necessary financing from the bank. Last year's monthly demand for the different bicycle styles that EC distributes is shown in Table 14.6.

TABLE 14.6

MONTHLY BICYCLE DEMAND

Month	Frame style A	B	C	D	E	Total
January	0	3	5	2	0	10
February	2	8	10	3	1	24
March	4	15	21	12	2	54
April	4	35	40	21	3	103
May	3	43	65	37	3	151
June	3	27	41	18	2	91
July	2	13	26	11	1	53
August	1	10	16	9	1	37
September	1	9	11	7	1	29
October	1	8	10	7	2	28
November	2	15	19	12	3	51
December	3	30	33	19	4	89
Total	26	216	297	158	23	720

Because of the increasing popularity of bicycles for recreational purposes and for supplanting some automobile usage, EC believes that its market may grow by as much as 25 percent in the upcoming year. There have been years when the full amount of expected growth did not materialize, however, so EC has decided to base its plan on a more conservative 15-percent growth factor to allow for variations in consumer buying habits and to ensure that it is not excessively overstocked if the expected market does not occur. Holding costs that are associated with inventory of any bicycle style are estimated to be about 0.75 percent of the unit cost of a bicycle per month.

Assignment Develop an inventory control plan for EC to use as the basis for its upcoming annual plan. Justify your reasons for choosing a particular type (or combination of types) of inventory system(s). On the basis of your particular plan, specify the safety stock requirements if EC institutes a policy of maintaining a 95-percent service level.

SELECTED BIBLIOGRAPHY

CHIANG, W., J. A. FITZSIMMONS, Z. HUANG, and S. X. Li: "A Game-Theoretic Approach to Quantity Discount Problems," *Decision Sciences,* vol. 25, no. 1, January–February 1994, pp. 153–168.

TEDLOW, RICHARD S.: *New and Improved: The Story of Mass Marketing in America,* Harvard Business School, Boston, 1996.

VOLLMANN, T. E., W. L. BERRY, and D. C. WHYBARK: *Manufacturing Planning and Control Systems,* 4th ed., Irwin, Burr Ridge, Ill., 1997.

ENDNOTES

1. $dTC_p/dQ = -DS/Q^2 + H/2 = 0$, thus $Q^2 = 2DS/H$ and $Q^* = \sqrt{2DS/H}$.

2. Taking the partial derivative of equation (5) with respect to K yields $-2H(Q - K)/2Q + 2BK/2Q$, which is set $= 0$ and solved for $K^* = Q[H/(H + B)]$. Note that $Q - K = Q[B/(H + B)]$ and substituting for K in (5) yields a $TC_b = DS/Q + H[BQ/(H + B)]^2/2Q + B[HQ/(H + B)]^2/2Q$. Taking the partial derivative with respect to Q yields $-DS/Q^2 + HB^2/2(H + B)^2 + BH^2/2(H + B)^2$, which is set $= 0$ and solved for $Q^* = \sqrt{2DS(H + B)/HB}$.

3. Prepared by James H. Vance under the supervision of Professor James A. Fitzsimmons.

Service Supply Chain Management

Learning Objectives

After completing this chapter, you should be able to:

1. Discuss the analogy between the supply chain for physical goods and the service chain for mobile workers.

2. Discuss the unique challenges of service chain management such as bidirectional optimization, perishability, and knowledge management.

3. Classify the purchase of a business service into one of six categories based on the focus of the service and the importance of the service.

4. Discuss the implications of purchasing a business service from each of the six categories of the taxonomy.

5. Prepare a route for a mobile worker using the Clarke-Wright algorithm.

Supply chain management is a total systems approach to delivering manufactured products to the end customer. Using information technology to coordinate all elements of the supply chain from parts suppliers to retailers achieves a level of integration that is a competitive advantage not available in traditional logistics systems.

Consider, for example, the decision of Hewlett-Packard to manufacture a generic DeskJet printer and allow distributors the option to localize the printer by adding the proper manuals and power cords. The result was a significant reduction of finished goods inventory because demand was then consolidated into one generic printer, which eliminated the need for separate inventories for each country. This postponement strategy also produced unexpected savings in shipping costs because generic printers can be packed more densely.[1]

Service supply chain management is an analogous systems approach that is especially suitable for delivering mobile services such as parcel delivery, cable installation, and home health care. The key elements that distinguish service supply chain management from supply chain management are bidirectional optimization, perishability, and simultaneous management of both capacity and demand.

In service chain management, technology innovations such as the Internet and wide-area wireless connectivity make it possible to incorporate the customer into a service company's knowledge management strategy in new ways. The dynamic availability of individual customer requirements and preferences and the ability to associate them with cost and optimization strategies of the enterprise in "real time" provide a new dimension to the knowledge management strategy of service companies.

CHAPTER PREVIEW

Supply chain management for manufactured goods is discussed first to appreciate the benefits obtained from taking a total systems view of the value chain from product design to after-sale customer service. Information technology has been the driving force behind the ability to coordinate the many interrelated activities commonly performed by independent companies. Service chain management is seen as analogous to the physical supply chain, in particular, for services delivered by mobile servers. Finally, a discussion of the purchase of business services is motivated by a classification scheme that highlights the special considerations in the purchase decision.

SUPPLY CHAIN MANAGEMENT

Shortened product life cycles and increasing globalization of markets require a total systems view of the entire supply chain. Many high-tech products now are almost obsolete when introduced, so making manufacturing capacity plans, agreeing on production schedules, and setting inventory stocking levels are challenges because no historical sales data are available. Poor planning can result either in lost sales opportunities or in expensive end-of-life inventory write-offs. Competitive pressures require firms to think in global terms when seeking out suppliers and locating manufacturing operations. For example, a personal computer may have subassemblies manufactured in the United States with parts supplied from Asia, and final assembly-to-order near customers in Europe.

The challenge of supply chain management is to balance the requirements of reliable and prompt customer delivery with manufacturing and inventory costs. Supply chain modeling enables managers to evaluate which options will provide the greatest improvement in customer satisfaction at reasonable costs. The supply chain is modeled as a network that captures the relationship between asset costs (i.e., inventory and capital equipment) and the time domain characteristics of customer service (i.e., responsiveness and reliability in customer delivery).

A comprehensive total systems view that incorporates the interactions among the participants will facilitate a collaborative search for effective measures to meet customer demands. Unreliable deliveries either increase inventory investments in safety stocks or result in unsatisfied customers and lost sales. Using a model to manage the supply chain can lead to reduced costs and higher levels of customer service. Success, however, is only achieved with the formation of effective partnerships and cooperation among participants throughout the entire supply chain.

Network Model

The physical goods supply chain can be viewed as a network of value-adding material-processing stages each defined with supply input, material transformation, and demand output. As in Figure 15.1, these stages (suppliers, manufacturing, distribution, retailing, and recycling) are connected with arrows depicting the flow of material with inventory stocks between each stage. Information transfer in the opposite direction is shown as dashed lines and includes activities by suppliers, process and product design, and customer service. The manufacturing stage represents the traditional operation where raw material arrives from external suppliers; the material is transformed in some manner to add value, creating an inventory of finished goods. The other downstream stages such as distribution and retailing also add value to the materials. For example, materials arriving by truck at a distribution center are unloaded, sorted, or consolidated

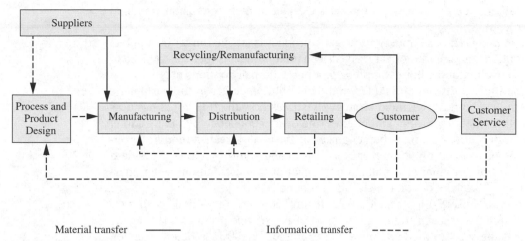

FIGURE 15.1 Supply chain for physical goods.

for delivery to retailers, and possibly customized for the region by including manuals in the appropriate language.

Managing Uncertainty

Managing a supply chain would be straightforward except for the uncertainty arising from three sources: supplier delivery performance, manufacturing reliability, and customer demand. Inventory is used as insurance in this uncertain world. To meet customer service level objectives (e.g., experience stockouts less than 5 percent of the time), a little extra material or safety stocks are held so that customer deliveries can be made when something goes wrong in an upstream process.

Any number of events can cause variability in supplier on-time deliveries: storms delaying a shipment, quality problems, machine failure, or late arrival of raw material supply. Over time, a distribution of delivery performance punctuality can be established for each supplier and used in purchasing negotiations, because the more reliable a supplier is, the smaller the safety stock of materials required to protect the downstream operation. Manufacturing reliability is influenced by the same problems facing suppliers and, also, by internal scheduling delays caused by several products competing for shared resources (e.g., overhead crane in a machine shop). The overall uncertainty is captured by a historical probability distribution of on-time performance. Customer demand variability is the most difficult factor to determine. However, with short product life cycles, there is little time to build historical demand distributions. Market research and past experience with similar products can be used to predict future demand distributions.

Supply Chain Strategic Planning

Strategic initiatives can lessen the impact of uncertainty and thus improve customer service. For example, implementation of total quality control techniques such as statistical process control can improve manufacturing reliability. More dependable transportation modes can be investigated, also. Changes in product design can allow the manufacturing operations to stock uncompleted products and postpone the final customization, thus increasing responsiveness to customer orders. Recall the example of

Hewlett-Packard and the manufacture of generic Deskjet printers for customization at the distributor level.

Product postponement is a strategy in which a product is stocked in an incomplete generic form until a customer order is received. The final product is then customized to the customer's specifications. For example, a product with many options may have the options designed into software and added at the distribution center in the customer's geographic region. The postponement strategy illustrates how the functional business areas of marketing, manufacturing, and engineering design cooperate by taking a total systems view of the supply chain. When engineering designers create a modular product that can be customized by adding options, and manufacturing makes a standard generic product allowing final customization to occur at the distribution center, marketing can then sell the benefits of a customized product.

Fast-food restaurants are often considered as manufacturing-in-the-field because facilitating goods represent a significant component of the service package and thus the physical goods supply chain model applies. For example, Taco Bell adopted a version of the postponement strategy when it decided to remove the kitchen from the retail store. This strategy, discussed in Example 15.1, moves some production away from the customer by postponing final assembly until an order is received.

Example 15.1. Taco Bell and the K-Minus Decision

The physical goods supply chain found in manufacturing is analogous to the service supply chain for Taco Bell. The first stage consists of the natural resources supplied from agriculture (e.g., meat, vegetables, spices, and grain). These ingredients are purchased in bulk and held at regional distribution centers for supply to the retail stores. Because final demand is so difficult to forecast, considerable waste food resulted at the retail stores. Removing the kitchen from the retail store to a central location allowed for consolidation of demand and reduction of waste. The production process at the retail store is changed from make-to-order to assemble-to-order. Response to customer orders has improved—wait times are shorter and the facility is cleaner and more spacious.

Using information technology to track the movement of goods from factory to retailer, product firms like Hewlett-Packard and Frito-Lay (see the Service Benchmark at the end of the chapter) have gained a high level of connectivity and transparency in their respective logistic systems. Table 15.1 displays many of the benefits these firms have realized by considering the before and after elements of the business. Real cost savings have accrued to both consumers and producers because the flexibility to service customer demands has increased without carrying excessive inventory stocks.

The common feature of the supply chain paradigm illustrated by Hewlett-Packard and Frito-Lay is the integration of the customer with factory operations (i.e., becoming more like a service). Dell Computer, however, is one of the most "service-like" goods producers in the market today. The Dell-direct business model incorporates the customer into the production process, taking on a major characteristic of service production. Dell links the order entry process (i.e., customer requirements and preferences) using their Internet website directly with the process of production at or before the moment that actual computer assembly takes place. This ability allows Dell to use capital much more efficiently than competitors do because no inventory of finished product is held in anticipation of demand.

TABLE 15.1

THE IMPACT OF PHYSICAL GOODS SUPPLY CHAIN MANAGEMENT

Element or link	Before	After
Channel structure	Functional silos	Process orientation
Channel relationships	Independent/competitive; many competing suppliers and distributors	Interdependent; a few select suppliers and distributors as partners
Channel integration	Vertical (own the channel to integrate)	Virtual (IT and other mechanisms permit integration without ownership)
Flow of goods	Push	Pull
Flow of information (upstream)	Pull, incomplete, partial, manual; encumbered by numerous human links in the chain; slow, on the order of weeks or months; most recent downstream demand data and production schedules not available	Push, planned, appropriate, automated; high level of connectivity and transparency for all players in the chain; fast, in some cases instantaneous; access to most recent downstream demand data and production schedules
Flow of information (downstream)	Little or no product-tracking information	Product tracking (almost) real-time; advance shipping notices
Business processes	Predominantly in-house; locally optimized for efficiency	In-house for key processes, others outsourced for flexibility; integrated and synchronized to match supply with demand
Demand management	Reactive forecasting used for capacity planning; segmented	Proactive management to remove volatility; customer relationship management
Capacity management	Defined by specialization of labor and use of special-purpose equipment	Flexible using automation and cross-trained workforce
Inventory	High; used as a buffer against uncertainty and lack of information; *bullwhip effect* common	Low; information connectivity reduces inventory buffers due to transparency; delayed differentiation used more effectively to risk pool and reduce inventory further; better positioning of inventory further up the supply chain
Production	Inflexible; long lead times; dominated by material requirements planning (MRP); push; build-to-stock	Flexible; lead time reduction; pull (e.g., just-in-time); mass customization (products based on common components positioned at the right location in the supply chain to meet customer lead times); build-to-order
Distribution	Traditional warehousing network; extend MRP to distribution: distribution requirements planning; push	Pull ideas extended to distribution in such programs as quick response, continuous replenishment; vendor-managed inventory; distribution centers and cross docking; direct delivery more feasible
Product design	Product designed without input from manufacturing or distribution	Greater emphasis on designed for manufacturing and supply chain management
Pricing	Strong emphasis on promotional pricing	Greater emphasis on fixed pricing Everyday low pricing (EDLP)
International operations	Multinational (separate business in each country)	Global (single business with global sourcing)

SERVICE CHAIN MANAGEMENT

We have noted that service chains, unlike physical goods supply chains, often involve the customer as an active participant in the production process. Recent advances in information technology (e.g., the Internet, global positioning satellites, and wide-area wireless networks) involve the customer in a very direct fashion. This involvement creates opportunities for companies to create competitive advantages by leveraging new knowledge management strategies that are built around and include the customer. These strategies provide the opportunity to improve the quality of services while lowering the cost to provide the services.

Stages of the service chain for mobile workers who deliver service to the customer are analogous to those found in the physical goods supply chain as shown in Figure 15.2. Service chain management follows the supply chain paradigm conceptually, but the approach to and relative importance of each component are different.

Conversion

Conversion, or creating value for the customer in manufactured goods, is located in the factory; for mobile servers conversion usually occurs at a customer site. In manufacturing, production rarely involves the customer actively; in services the customer often is a coproducer. In the physical goods supply chain, conversion occurs early in the process and in the service chain it occurs late in the process. Finally, a typical factory will focus on a limited number of standard products, but a mobile service worker generally has considerable discretion and will be expected to customize the service to the customer's needs (e.g., home health nursing). These conversion process differences are important distinctions between the production of goods and services, and they have implications for the strategies used to optimize operations.

Distribution

Manufacturing value is associated with strategies to have products available on the retail store shelf at the time a customer reaches out to make a purchase. The nature and character of the product are determined at the time of assembly and the product attributes are relatively fixed. Distribution logistics and delivery of goods are a relatively low-cost component of most manufactured items.

For mobile service delivery, the nature and character of the service is usually determined close to the time of delivery. Distribution (i.e., the routing and scheduling of

FIGURE 15.2 Service chain for mobile workers.

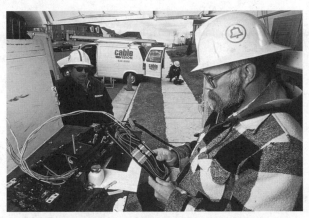

Dynamic routing of mobile servers avoids unproductive travel time.

mobile worker deliveries) essentially occurs before production and is a relatively high cost component of service. This reversal of the distribution–production relationship gives a significantly enhanced importance and value to the role of distribution for mobile service providers. Traditional inventory stocking and demand anticipation strategies of manufacturing are impossible for service providers. The productive capacity of a mobile service worker cannot be placed into inventory for distribution at a later time.

For services provided by mobile workers, however, worker "distribution" comes before production so, therefore, all information from forecasting, current demand, and knowledge management systems can be applied up to the last minute to optimize the service. The result is systemwide optimization that must occur "in real time" in the overall delivery process as opposed to manufacturing with longer time horizons.

Knowledge Management

Knowledge management is a strategy to organize and use available information, experience, and expertise to create a competitive advantage for a business. Technology innovations enable a near-instantaneous inclusion of customer requirements and preferences into the knowledge management strategy of service companies.

Each customer has unique expectations, wants, needs, preferences and desires. These factors are the basis for buying decisions, the perception of quality, the chance for repeat business, and the value of branding. These value parameters are traditionally a function of marketing and provide the specifications for the design of the service products. A firm with the capability to accommodate a specific customer's requirements and preferences as a regular part of the production process will have an improved competitive position.

Mobile Workers

Because they work out in the field with no direct supervision, mobile workers are knowledge workers who have considerable discretion to perform a wide range of services. For example, a gas utility worker can turn on gas, turn off gas, check for leaks, do routine maintenance, replace old equipment, read meters, and convey information. Mobile workers in the business of home health care have hundreds of possible service components such as measuring physiologic parameters, assessing functional abilities, and performing therapeutic procedures.

The effectiveness of these workers depends upon their ability to be at the right place, at the right time, with the right customer, with the right supplies, and at the right cost. Service chain management incorporates the requirements and preferences of customers into models that minimize the overall cost of service production. Call centers, the Internet, wide-area wireless network mobile connectivity, and geographical information systems are now enabling systemwide cost optimization. Integrating customer requirements, preferences, and location with service provider location, skills, training, and availability creates the opportunity to do "real-time" scheduling, dispatching, documentation, and billing.

SOURCES OF VALUE IN SERVICE CHAIN MANAGEMENT

Three primary value components of service chain management are bidirectional optimization, management of productive capacity, and management of perishability.

Bidirectional Optimization

Bidirectional optimization implies the possibility of doing what is best from the customer's perspective while doing the best for the service enterprise. In service production, customers often "coproduce" the service. Direct customer involvement facilitates bidirectional optimization, a simultaneous optimization of both supply and demand for the service. This translates into providing a highly individualized service for the customer that is very cost-effective for the organization. Service chain management of the mobile workforce offers, for the first time, a system to accomplish this with regularity, a feat that paper-based systems have rarely accomplished.

For mobile service, a "time window" is reserved for each customer to be available for a service worker to perform the requested service. Customers see generous time windows as a major inconvenience that wastes their time for the benefit of an inefficient service provider. Typically, managers of mobile workforces ask customers to be available for extended time windows (i.e., between noon and 5:00 P.M.) because routes, customer sequencing, and frequent service provider job status updates are not built into a functionally integrated information system. Service chain management uses forecasting data to construct an initial daily plan for each worker. It then offers customers several appointment choices based on a pre-optimized calculation of an optimized solution for the whole group of service workers in a defined geographic area. The calculation of the optimized solution considers customer preferences and service requirements (i.e., language, worker skills, worker licensing, and supplies on the vehicle) along with geographical information such as where the service workers will be just prior and just after a particular customer's appointment.

Management of Productive Capacity

A primary consideration of *productive capacity* for mobile workers is the amount of time spent between jobs, which correlates with the distance between jobs. Because value is created predominantly during the time that the mobile worker is at the customer site, time spent traveling between customer sites is lost productive capacity. This creates an opportunity to increase greatly the productive capacity of the workforce by better management of the service chain resulting in more cumulative time for workers to be with customers. Strategies to improve productive capacity of the service worker include transfer, replacement, and embellishment.

Transfer   *Transfer* is an approach to make knowledge available to customers so that value can be transferred with very low cost. One example is a web-based, frequently-asked-questions (FAQ) database. This information-transfer tool can be used instead of more expensive human resources and is available at all hours. For example, patients can access disease-specific areas of a website and obtain information about side effects of medicines, explanations of symptoms, or procedures to follow.

Replacement   *Replacement* is a strategy of substituting technology for human resources. Blood pressure measurement is one example. For patients needing blood pressure measurements three times daily, an automated measurement system might be substituted for a nurse visit. A digital blood pressure measurement device is easy for patients to use and it costs less than a single visit from a home health care nurse.

Embellishment   *Embellishment* of customer skills to enable self-service is a third strategy to enhance the productive capacity of the home health care system. Teaching a patient or family member to change a surgical dressing is appropriate in some circumstances. This embellishment of customer skills requires additional nursing time initially, but significantly decreases the subsequent use of nursing resources if, for example, a wound is chronic and requires daily changes for an extended period of time. In such a scenario, a nurse might check the healing wound every three days instead of daily, resulting in a 66-percent decrease in the amount of nursing time required to care for the patient.

Management of Perishability

Management of *perishability* is the approach used in service chain management to minimize the negative impact of idle time on the productive capacity of the distributed service workforce. The productive capacity of a service worker is limited to the time he or she is at the customer site with the right tools and skills and knowledge of the customer's requirements and preferences.

For the mobile workforce, managing perishability has two foci. The first is a time allocation system that offers time windows to customers based on "best use" of workers. In service chain management systems that use dynamic schedule optimization software, schedules are constructed and revised up until the very last possible moment before dispatch of a worker to a job. Service systems with no communication infrastructure are limited to creating a fixed schedule for each mobile worker at the beginning of the workday. Service systems with mobile data communications, however, may produce "real-time" schedules so that a worker learns of the next assignment only after completing the current job. The dynamic allocation of jobs among workers minimizes idle (i.e., perishable) time.

Managing perishability also involves the process of training, refining, and extending skills and capabilities of workers. When potential idle time of workers is identified and directed to training activities, productive capacity can be prospectively reclaimed. This service inventory hedging strategy benefits the firm by directing skill-enhancing activities into idle time slots, which makes the worker available during the time when traditional training efforts otherwise would have consumed productive capacity. The mobile worker with mobile data communication tools can obtain modular, computer-based training, certification, and testing material "online" (using the mobile data terminal of the service vehicle), thereby maximizing this hedging strategy.

Table 15.2 captures many of the benefits service firms with mobile workers have realized by considering the before and after elements of the business.

TABLE 15.2

THE IMPACT OF SERVICE CHAIN MANAGEMENT

Element or link	Before	After
Channel structure	Functional silos	Process orientation
Service recipient	Passive	Active as a coproducer
Channel integration	Vertical (own the channel to integrate)	Virtual (IT and other mechanism permit integration without ownership)
Flow of service	Available waiting for demand	Activated upon demand
Flow of information (upstream)	Pull: manual reporting of demand data results in delayed management response	Push: high level of connectivity and transparency with fast or instantaneous access to most recent demand data
Flow of information (downstream)	Little or no knowledge of resource deployment	Real-time tracking and dispatching
Business processes	Predominantly in-house; locally optimized for efficiency	In-house for key processes, others outsourced for flexibility; integrated and synchronized to match supply with demand
Demand management	Limited to use of appointments and reservations	Proactive, involving customer in scheduling to achieve bidirectional optimization
Capacity management	Limited to use of part-time employees	Creative use of cross-trained employees, outsourcing, and customer self-service
Facilitating goods	High; in anticipation of demand	Lower; owing to process transparency
Service delivery	Inflexible; standardized and impersonal	Flexible; personable with customization possible
Routing and scheduling	Static; fixed daily schedules	Dynamic; based on system connectivity and process visibility
New service design	Marketing initiatives based on firm's perception of customer needs	Virtual value chain design with customer database information driving new services
Pricing	Fixed	Variable; yield management promotes off-peak demand and avoids idle capacity
International operations	Focus on domestic market	Global reach with Internet

PURCHASING BUSINESS SERVICES

The traditional purchase process model is diagrammed in Figure 15.3 and consists of need identification, information search, vendor selection, and performance evaluation.

When the purchase of services is compared to that of goods, however, we find a more complex process with different risks to the buyer. Services are less tangible, making the evaluation of the vendor difficult to measure and the specification of the service

FIGURE 15.3 Purchasing process.

desired less precise. Furthermore, it is difficult to judge if the services being delivered are meeting expectations, because they are not subject to close scrutiny. For example, how does one know if the contractor supplying plant security is being effective? Material goods can be inspected upon delivery, but this opportunity does not exist for purchased services.

The purchase process is complicated also by the need to satisfy a larger number of affected personnel. Contracted services such as travel booking, janitorial services, and food services are examples that affect all employees personally, not in the detached way that material goods acquired for use in the production process are viewed.

Business services often need to be customized to meet an organization's needs, especially in the case of services in support of the manufacturing process. Business services also tend to be more technological in nature than consumer services because of the greater complexity of organizational needs.

The decision process might also differ depending upon the service to be purchased. For example, the purchase of computer software must involve the active participation of the end users and the final selection will be based upon many attributes that are difficult to quantify, such as user friendliness. The purchase of waste disposal service, however, can be handled in a routine manner with cost being one important criterion. Because of the legal liability associated with waste disposal, the selection of a responsible vendor with knowledge and experience with your industrial waste is important. For this reason, we develop a classification of services to assist in the purchase process.

Classification of Business Services

Business services are often classified according to degree of tangibility. The degree of tangibility describes the extent to which the service has physically measurable output properties. Some services such as janitorial or laundry are highly tangible and have well-defined and measurable output. Other services such as public relations or advertising have output that is significantly less measurable and more difficult to define.

Differentiating services on the basis of tangibility does indicate the potential level of difficulty faced by the purchaser, but the degree of tangibility fails to provide the purchaser with sufficient information to assist in the service purchase decision. Thus, the focus of the business service (property, people, and process) is used as the principal dimension for the taxonomy. The degree of service tangibility will be an attribute to be considered when purchasing service in each of these categories. In general, however, service tangibility will decrease as the focus of the service moves from property to people to process.

A second dimension representing the criticality or importance of the service to the buying firm must be considered in the purchase decision. The importance of the service is considered either high or low depending upon the relationship of the service to the firm's core business activity. Services important to the core business will attract higher-level management involvement in the purchase decision, because the fit with corporate goals is critical and involves substantial exposure to risk if failure occurs. This is obvious for sensitive areas such as product testing, medical care, public relations, and advertising. Other services such as laundry, waste disposal, plant security, and travel booking might be considered less important to a firm's core business.

Considering a service as low in importance is a relative viewpoint, however. For example, the uniforms of personnel working in clean rooms of semiconductor manufacturers must be laundered under exacting conditions to avoid introducing contamination into the manufacturing process. Thus, a particular firm, based on its own circumstances, might modify the classification of a service according to importance.

Table 15.3 shows a six-cell matrix of this two-way classification. Each cell has a descriptive title for the business service category, that is, facility support, equipment support, employee support, employee development, facilitator, and professional.

IMPLICATIONS FOR PURCHASE DECISIONS

The purchasing considerations for each category of business service are found in Table 15.4 grouped by the focus of the service.

Facility Support Service (Property/Low Importance)

Services in the facility support category can be treated like the purchase of goods. Tight specifications can be prepared and vendor selection is then based on low bid. Even though the purchase of such services is straightforward, an interested person in the organization must be responsible for evaluating the performance of the service delivered with particular attention to quality and timeliness. For example, because of the higher level of tangibility, it is possible to measure performance on the basis of a before–after comparison (e.g., dirty-to-clean laundry or broken-to-repaired equipment).

TABLE 15.3

TAXONOMY FOR PURCHASING BUSINESS SERVICES

		Importance of service	
		Low	**High**
Focus of service	**Property**	**Facility support:** • Laundry • Janitorial • Waste disposal	**Equipment support:** • Repairs • Maintenance • Product testing
	People	**Employment support:** • Food service • Plant security • Temporary personnel	**Employee development:** • Training • Education • Medical care
	Process	**Facilitator:** • Bookkeeping • Travel booking • Packaged software	**Professional:** • Advertising • Public relations • Legal

TABLE 15.4

PURCHASING CONSIDERATIONS

Focus on property

Facility support service

- Low cost
- Identification of responsible party to evaluate performance
- Writing of precise specifications

Equipment support service

- Experience and reputation of vendor
- Availability of vendor for emergency response
- Designation of person to make service call and to check that service is satisfactory

Focus on people

Employee support service

- Vendor clients contacted for references
- Specifications prepared with end-user input
- Performance evaluated on a periodic basis

Employee development service

- Experience with particular industry important
- Involvement of high levels of management in vendor identification and selection
- Vendor clients contacted for references
- Employees used to evaluate vendor performance

Focus on process

Facilitator service

- Knowledge of alternate vendors important
- Involvement of end user in vendor identification
- References or third-party evaluations useful
- Detailed specifications written by user

Professional service

- Involvement of high-level management in vendor identification and selection
- High importance of reputation and experience
- Performance evaluation by top management

Purchasers place greater importance on price when evaluating less critical services and on quality for more critical services. Many noncritical services such as janitorial, food service, and bookkeeping can be considered as commodity services with price driving the purchase decision.

Equipment Support Service (Property/High Importance)

Equipment support services create an additional problem because the vendor should be located close enough to provide emergency service. Someone in the organization must be identified in the service contract as the person with the authority to request calls for emergency service. Because of the critical nature of maintenance and repair of industrial equipment or product testing, potential vendors should be limited to those with experience in the purchaser's industry. Vendor reputation and references are important selection criteria. In addition to quality of work performed, the performance evaluation will include an assessment of communication problems and dependability.

Employee Support Service (People/Low Importance)

For services that serve people, user input is important in defining the specifications for the service. Requests for employee support service usually originate from a functional department (e.g., a request for temporary personnel) and, thus, the need specification will be developed with their input. Evaluation of the service provided should be made periodically by the same department and is a condition for contract renewal. The process of vendor selection should include obtaining references from vendor clients, a common practice with temporary help service.

Employee Development (People/High Importance)

Employee development service requests also originate within a functional department and usually involve the Personnel Department or a higher level of management. Employee development is an important investment in the firm's human capital that requires expertise to guide the purchase of the service. For example, changing the health insurance carrier for a firm's employees has many ramifications and vendor selection is not a trivial decision. High levels of management must be involved in developing the need specifications and vendor selection. Outside expertise often is sought and vendor reputation and experience with the particular industry are important considerations. Employees affected by the service also can be useful in the evaluation process.

Facilitator Service (Process/Low Importance)

The least tangible classification of business service deals with activities of an information processing nature that support the organization's mission or process. The facilitator service involves routine information processing such as bookkeeping and travel booking. End users should be able to write detailed need specifications and identify possible vendors. For example, the selection of a travel agency benefits from employee inputs about ancillary services (e.g., credit card payment). Published reviews (e.g., critiques of word processing software) or other sources of comparison among vendors are useful in identifying possible sources and selecting appropriate criteria.

When decision criteria are not well formulated, purchasers look for cues in the environment. In this case the final selection is more likely to be made on the basis of secondary considerations. For example, when selecting from several travel agencies that are all reputable and that provide the same basic service of booking travel, the final choice may be decided on the basis of ancillary services offered, such as delivery of tickets and monthly billing rather than payment at the time of purchase. Another secondary consideration involves the interpersonal relationship between the supplier and the buyer.

Professional Service (Process/High Importance)

Because professional service has significant impact on the strategic future of the organization, top management must be involved from the very beginning. The process starts with need identification and proceeds through all stages of the purchase process including, most importantly, performance evaluation. Trust in the supplier is a primary factor, so vendor reputation and experience might be the only important selection criteria. As customization increases, the delivery of a service such as consulting, public relations, or employee training is more likely to be extended over a period of time. As a result, the evaluation of the supplier's performance will necessarily be delayed.

BOX 15.1

Service Benchmark
FRITO-LAY PUTS HAND-HELD COMPUTERS IN THE FIELD

Frito-Lay Inc., the $4.9 billion snack-food division of Pepsico Inc. that is based in Plano, Texas, took the prize in the category of business and related services for its work with hand-held computers. The company's 10,000 sales representatives use them to sell more than 100 different brand-name products to more than 400,000 retail stores.

Using the bricklike Fujitsu computer, which replaced conventional paper forms, each route representative can send detailed sales and inventory information back to Frito-Lay headquarters each day. The computers keep track of prices, special promotions for each store, information on stale or returned products and other details. A printer in each delivery truck allows the sales representative to give the store manager a comprehensive receipt and invoice.

At the end of each day, instead of spreading paper receipts on the kitchen table and reaching for the calculator, pencil and aspirin, the sales representative simply hooks the Fujitsu to a telephone and sends the data to Frito-Lay's headquarters. The data are collected, compiled, and distilled. "We pick up every sale of every bag made to every customer every day," said Charles S. Feld, vice president of management information services for Frito-Lay. This information is then relayed to Frito-Lay's manufacturing and distribution centers as a "real-time" inventory system.

"The result is that we can keep fresh products moving through the system continuously," Mr. Feld said. "Having the right product in the right place at the right time is really critical to us." The daily sales data are also used to develop market strategies.

. . . The company spends about $2,500 to equip each of the 10,000 route salespeople with the Fujitsu computer and a printer for the delivery truck. And Mr. Feld and his team spent more than 18 months developing the software for the central system and for the system that returns the information to manufacturing and distribution centers.

Even so, Mr. Feld said, the system "paid for itself well within a year, and it has paid for itself more than once." A Frito-Lay spokesman said the company saved more than $40 million in its first year from reduced paperwork, reduced losses from stale products and route consolidation.

Mr. Feld said the company was now investigating systems that would hook directly into a customer's computer, handling accounts payable and receivables, and allowing store managers to assess which Frito-Lay products are most profitable.

Source: Reprinted with permission from Peter H. Lewis, "Looking beyond Innovation, an Award for Results," *New York Times,* Sunday, June 23, 1991, p 8.

SUMMARY

A systems view of the supply chain is necessary to account for the significant interactions among all the participants from suppliers, to manufacturing, to the retail customer. The supply chain is modeled as a network of material processing stages buffered by inventory stocks. Uncertainty arises from three sources: supplier delivery performance, manufacturing reliability, and customer demand.

A strategy of postponement, in which a partially completed product is held until a customer order is received, illustrates the possibility for innovation when all supply chain participants cooperate and take an enlarged systems view.

Service chain management for mobile workers is a system that has similarities with the supply chain management systems of the manufacturing sector, but is distinguished by the unique character of services. Bidirectional optimization and the management of productive capacity and perishability are three important parts of the service chain management system. Service chain management systems incorporate customers into the knowledge management strategy of service companies that have mobile workforces and greatly enhance the value and quality of the services produced.

KEY TERMS AND DEFINITIONS

Bidirectional optimization occurs when the service provider and the customer agree on the time a service should be delivered, taking into account the needs of both parties.

Bullwhip effect a phenomenon observed in physical supply chains that occurs when a variation in final demand is propagated up the supply chain in ever-increasing amplitude.

Embellishment of customer skills to enable self-service is a strategy to enhance productive capacity.

Perishability results from the inability to inventory service worker productive capacity and thus lost capacity occurs during periods of idleness.

Productive capacity measured by the worker-hours available to serve customers. Strategies to improve productive capacity include transfer, replacement, and embellishment.

Product postponement stocking a product in a generic or incomplete form until a customer's order is received and then finishing to the customer's specifications.

Replacement a strategy to substitute self-serve technology for customer use in lieu of personal attention.

Transfer an approach to make knowledge available to customers at low cost.

TOPICS FOR DISCUSSION

1. What are some possible disadvantages associated with the product postponement strategy?
2. Discuss the similarities and differences in the product postponement strategy used by Hewlett-Packard and Taco Bell?
3. Can the service chain model for mobile workers be applied to services in general?
4. Speculate on the effect that the Internet will have on the process of business-to-business purchase of services?

Peapod—Smart Shopping for Busy People[2]

Hidden among the myriad of Internet sites is a potential time saver, Peapod®—Smart shopping for busy people®. Peapod uses interactive technology to change the traditional grocery shopping experience. Market research from Andersen Consulting indicates that 42 percent of shoppers want to order groceries from home. So Thomas and Andrew Parkinson went online in 1989 with Peapod, a virtual supermarket shopping and delivery service. Starting with a customer base of 400 families in Evanston, Illinois, Peapod is now a multistate delivery service with more than 71,000 customers in areas such as Boston, Chicago, San Francisco, and Houston.

MARKET ANALYSIS

Studies indicate that the market potential for online grocery shopping is positive. Consumers consider grocery shopping a waste of time, and rank it the least desired household activity. Marketing surveys by Consumer Direct Cooperative (1997) have shown that 65 percent of consumers are frustrated with the traditional grocery shopping experience and 41 percent claim to be dissatisfied with checkout. Consumers are interested in home delivery of groceries, with 47 percent saying it would make shopping easier. Moreover, given the rise in electronic commerce and the increasing number of personal computers in homes, entrepreneurs are looking for ways to offer a personal shopping service on the Internet. Andersen Consulting estimates the market size for online grocery shopping to be 15 million to 20 million households by the year 2005.

ONLINE SHOPPING VERSUS TRADITIONAL SHOPPING

The findings of market analyses are leading companies to eliminate the negative aspects of grocery shopping and to make grocery shopping a more efficient activity. However, advantages and disadvantages exist between the traditional shopping experience of going to the grocery store and the online grocery shopping service as shown in Table 15.5. Some important aspects of the traditional experience include interacting with people, product sampling, and stimulating the senses of vision, touch, smell, taste (e.g., product samples), and sounds that influence buying decisions. Despite traditional grocery shopping advantages, customer dissatisfaction with grocery shopping opens up opportunities for companies such as Peapod.

TABLE 15.5

COMPARISON OF ONLINE AND TRADITIONAL GROCERY SHOPPING

	Online shopping	Traditional shopping
Advantages	It is convenient It saves time Impulse buying is reduced	Five senses influence buying You get exactly what you want Coupons are claimed immediately Memory is triggered You get to sample products You interact with people You are exposed to new items
Disadvantages	There may be computer problems or download problems You have less control (price, selection) You may forget items There is a delivery fee	It is time consuming There are parking and waiting lines You need to carry groceries home You are subject to impulse buying Personal safety is a concern

PEAPOD'S BUSINESS MODEL

The Parkinsons' vision for Peapod includes the following three goals:

1. Improve people's lives by bringing interactive grocery shopping to a broader consumer market.
2. Lead the world in providing local interactive grocery shopping services.
3. Amaze and delight each customer.

Peapod's strategy is to offer customized services on a mass basis by leveraging the wide reach of the Internet. Peapod targets the well-educated, technically savvy, dual-income family and builds market credibility by aligning with one grocery store chain in each of its markets. Customers can place orders via phone, fax, or Internet, although the Internet is the company's main focus. The company generates revenue on a per-order basis and through membership fees. The price structure for Peapod's services is shown in Table 15.6. To meet their goals, the Parkinsons have made significant investments in information systems. Although fewer than 1 percent of consumers purchase groceries online and the company has yet to realize any profits, management is committed to channeling resources toward information technology in the hope that Peapod will reap future success.

Peapod was initially a DOS-based system with graphics. In 1995, however, the company introduced a new version of software on a Windows platform with pictures of various products. Customer data, such as name, address, and previous shopping lists, are stored in databases for customers to use when placing orders in the future. Peapod's back office is linked to the mainframe of its partner supermarket to provide customers instantly with stock-keeping unit (SKU) identification numbers and prices.

Online customers have access to all the items in the grocery store and they can compile grocery lists by category, item, brand, or on-sale items. This feature allows customers to create their own virtual grocery aisles. Within each category, the list can be sorted alphabetically by brand, nutritional value, size, cost per ounce, or price. The customer also is permitted to give specific instructions, such as "substitution okay," for each of the selected items. After consumers have finished shopping, they click "done" and the order is sent to Peapod. Consumers also must choose a delivery time within 30-minute and 90-minute windows. The Peapod personal shopper then picks the items from the grocer's shelves, calculates the total, and stores the groceries in a central location at appropriate temperature, until a different Peapod employee delivers them.

Table 15.7 presents Peapod's financial summary for 1996–1997. Despite many local competitors such as Streamline and Hannaford's HomeRuns, Peapod remains the preeminent national grocery shopping online service in the United States.

Questions

1. Where are opportunities for bidirectional optimization at Peapod?
2. How can Peapod manage service perishability?
3. How can Peapod manage productive capacity?
4. Suggest reasons why Peapod has not yet become profitable.

TABLE 15.6

PEAPOD'S PRICING STRUCTURE

	Monthly fee	Per-order charge
Residential	$4.95–$6.95	$4.95-$6.95 plus 5% of value of order
Commercial	None	$9.95 plus 9% of value of order

TABLE 15.7

PEAPOD'S FINANCIAL SUMMARY

Income statement (in thousands and unaudited)

	Three months ended December 31		Year ended December 31	
	1997	**1996**	**1997**	**1996**
Revenues				
Grocery sales, net of returns	$13,885	$7,188	$43,487	$22,015
Member and retailer services	3,534	1,939	13,898	6,088
Interactive marketing services	617	384	2,222	1,069
Total revenues	$18,036	$9,511	$59,607	$29,172
Costs and expenses				
Cost of groceries sold	13,885	7,188	43,487	22,015
Grocery operations	5,163	2,889	17,496	8,141
General and administrative	485	786	4,129	2,919
Marketing and selling	2,591	1,641	6,514	3,984
System development/maintenance	639	348	1,696	1,492
Depreciation and amortization	278	209	1,234	651
Total costs and expenses	$23,041	$13,061	$74,556	$39,202
Operating income	(5,005)	(3,550)	(14,949)	(10,030)
Other income (expense)				
Interest income	842	175	2,052	537
Interest expense	(25)	(18)	(83)	(73)
Net income	$(4,188)	$(3,393)	$(12,980)	$(9,566)

Balance sheet data (in thousands and unaudited)

	Year Ended December 31	
	1997	**1996**
Cash and cash equivalents	$ 62,876	$ 13,039
Working capital	52,350	7,356
Total assets	69,110	16,528
Long-term obligations	701	340
Total stockholders' equity	54,802	8,403

Operating data

	Year Ended December 31	
	1997	**1996**
Members	71,500	33,300
Orders (for the year ended)	396,600	201,100
Number of markets	8	4
Households in service area	6,488,000	3,581,000

Chapter 15 Supplement
Vehicle Routing

When services require travel to the customer's location, a method to develop vehicle routes quickly that minimizes time and distance traveled is an important consideration. An algorithm to perform this task will be developed and illustrated here.

On a typical Saturday, a college student may need to accomplish several tasks: work out at the gym, do some research in the library, go to the laundromat, and stop at a food market. Assuming no constraints on when these tasks may be done, the student faces no great obstacle in developing an itinerary that will require the least amount of time and distance traveled. The solution is straightforward and can be formulated in one's head.

Many services likewise must develop itineraries, but in these cases, the solutions may not be as obvious as the college student's. Examples range from Federal Express's ground transportation pickup and delivery routes to bread deliveries at your local supermarket to a telephone repairperson's route each day. Clearly, these cases require a useful tool to determine acceptable routing and scheduling without a great deal of hassle.

Enter G. Clarke and J. W. Wright, who developed the Clarke-Wright (C-W) algorithm to schedule vehicles operating from a central depot and serving several outlying points.[3] In practice, the C-W algorithm is applied to a problem through a series of iterations until an acceptable solution is obtained. Practical applications of the algorithm may not necessarily be optimal, but the short amount of time and the ease with which it can be applied to problems that are not elementary and straightforward make it an extremely useful tool. The logic of this algorithm, which involves a savings concept, serves as the basis for the more sophisticated techniques available in many commercial software programs.

The C-W savings concept considers the savings that can be realized by linking pairs of "delivery" points in a system that is composed of a central depot serving the outlying sites. As a very simple example, consider Bridgette's Bagel Bakery. Bridgette bakes her bagels during downtime at her brother Bernie's Beaucoup Bistro. Then she must transport her bagels to two sidewalk concession stands that are run by her sisters, Bernadette and Louise. Each stand is located 5 miles from the Bistro, but the stands themselves are 6 miles apart. The layout may be represented graphically as follows:

In this situation, the C-W algorithm first looks at the cost of driving from the bakery to one concession and back to the bakery, and then driving to the second concession and back to the bakery. Therefore, the total cost is equal to the sum of the costs (in miles) of driving from 0 to 1 and returning ($2C_{01}$) and driving from 0 to 2 and returning ($2C_{02}$), or

$$\text{Total cost} = 2C_{01} + 2C_{02}$$

Bridgette's total cost for following this route is 2×5 (miles) $+ 2 \times 5$ (miles), or 20 miles.

The C-W algorithm next considers the savings that can be realized by driving from the bakery to one concession, then to the second concession, and finally back to the bakery. This route saves Bridgette the cost of one trip from concession 1 back to the bakery and of one trip from the bakery to concession 2, but it adds the cost of the trip from concession 1 to concession 2. The net savings S_{ij} gained by linking any two locations i and j into the same route is expressed as

$$S_{ij} = C_{0i} + C_{0j} - C_{ij}$$

Bridgette would realize a net savings of 4 miles from linking the two concessions by creating one trip from the bakery to concession 1 and then traveling to concession 2 and returning to the bakery.

$$S_{12} = C_{01} + C_{02} - C_{12}$$
$$= 5 + 5 - 6 = 4$$

Admittedly, this example can be solved easily by inspection, and it does not require a sophisticated heuristic. Even so, it does serve as a convenient illustration of the savings concept that forms the basis of the C-W algorithm.

Using the C-W Algorithm Unconstrained

Application of the C-W algorithm to a less obvious situation proceeds through five steps, which will be described as we put them to work helping Bridgette, who is expanding her bagel service to four concessions in outlying areas. The distances related to each of these concessions and the bakery are given in Exhibit 15.1.

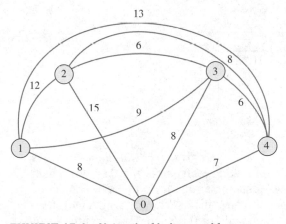

EXHIBIT 15.1 Network of bakery and four concessions with distances in miles.

1. *Construct a shortest-distance half-matrix (i.e., the matrix will contain the shortest distance between each pair of sites, including the starting location). A half-matrix is sufficient for this use because travel distance or time is the same in both directions.* The shortest-distance half-matrix for Bridgette's bakery and the four outlying concessions is shown in Exhibit 15.2. (*Note:* For very large problems, the shortest distances may not be obvious. In these cases, computer software to make these calculations is available.)

2. *Develop an initial allocation of one round-trip to each destination.* Note in the diagram below that each concession is linked to the bakery by double lines with directional arrows. Four round-trips are represented.

		Concessions			
		1	2	3	4
Bakery	0	8	15	8	7
Concessions	1		12	9	13
	2			6	8
	3				6

EXHIBIT 15.2 Shortest-distance half-matrix: miles between bakery and concessions.

3. *Calculate the net savings for each pair of outlying locations, and enter them in a net savings half-matrix.* These net savings for each pair of outlying locations are calculated using the equation for S_{ij}, just as we did in Bridgette's initial problem. In this example, the net savings from linking concessions 1 and 2 is $8 + 15 - 12 = 11$. Similar calculations are made for each of the other possible pairs, and the values then are entered into a net savings half-matrix, as shown in Exhibit 15.3.

		Concessions			
		1	2	3	4
Bakery	0	. . .	. . .	. . .	. . .
Concessions	1		11	7	2
	2			17	14
	3				9

EXHIBIT 15.3 Net savings between all concession pairs.

4. *Enter values for a special trip indicator* T *into appropriate cells of the net savings half-matrix.* Our net savings calculation for linking each pair is based on how much is saved relative to the cost of the vehicle making a round-trip to each member of the pair. We will add to our net savings half-matrix the indicator *T*, which will show if two locations in question—for example, *i* and *j* or 0 (which represents the point of origin) and *j*—are directly linked. *T* may have one of three values, as given below:

   a. $T = 2$ when a vehicle travels from the point of origin (Bridgette's bakery in our example) to location *j* (concession 1, 2, 3, or 4 in our example) and then returns. This is designated as $T_{0j} = 2$ and will appear only in the first row of the half-matrix. The appropriate value of *T* is entered into the net savings half-matrix and circled to distinguish it from the savings value. Remember, $T = 2$ indicates a *round-trip.*

b. $T = 1$ when a vehicle travels *one way directly* between two locations i and j. This is designated as $T_{ij} = 1$ and can appear anywhere in the half-matrix. Remember, $T = 1$ indicates a *one-way trip*.

c. $T = 0$ when a vehicle does *not* travel *directly* between two particular locations i and j. Accordingly, this is designated as $T_{ij} = 0$. Remember, $T = 0$ indicates that *no trip* is made between that pair of locations.

By convention, the $T = 0$ value is not entered; a cell without a T value of 1 or 2 noted in the matrix is understood to have a $T = 0$. It is important to recognize that for each location x, the sum of the T values in column x plus the sum of the T values in row x must equal 2 (i.e., a vehicle must arrive and depart for every location served).

Exhibit 15.4*a* shows Bridgette's net savings half-matrix for her four new concessions, with the appropriate T value of 2 listed in the cells representing round-trips between the bakery and each concession location. Note that the directional lines on the graphical depiction of this initial solution indicate a round-trip to each location.

Routes

EXHIBIT 15.4*a* Initial solution.

5. *Identify the cell in the net savings half-matrix that contains the maximum net savings.* If the maximum net savings occurs in cell (i, j) in the half-matrix, then locations i and j can be linked if, and only if, the following conditions are met:

a. T_{0i} and T_{0j} must be greater than zero.

b. Locations i and j are not already on the same route or loop.

c. Linking locations i and j does not violate any system constraints, which will be discussed later.

If all three conditions are met, set $T_{ij} = 1$. In Bridgette's case, cell (2, 3) has the highest net savings (i.e., 17). T_{02} and T_{03} are each greater than zero, locations 2 and 3 are not already on the same route, and at present, there are no constraints to linking locations 2 and 3. Thus, all conditions are met, and we may enter a T value of 1 in cell (2, 3), as shown in Exhibit 15.4*b*. This $T_{23} = 1$ in the cell indicates a *one-way trip* between concessions 2 and 3. At the same time that we have established the one-way trip between locations 2 and 3, we have eliminated a one-way trip from location 2 back to the bakery (0) and another one-way trip from the bakery to location 3. Therefore, it is necessary to reduce the $T = 2$ values in cells (0, 2) and (0, 3) to $T = 1$ in each. Exhibit 15.4*b* shows the appropriate T values for this new iteration, and the graphical depiction indicates the three new one-way routes.

EXHIBIT 15.4b   First iteration.

Routes: First trip: 0–1–0
          Second trip: 0–2–3–0
          Third trip: 0–4–0

If any one of the conditions—5a, 5b, or 5c—is not met, then identify the cell with the next highest savings and repeat step 5. If necessary, repeat this inspection until you have identified the cell with the highest savings that satisfies all three conditions, and set its T value equal to 1 (remember to reduce the appropriate $T = 2$ or $T = 1$ values in row 0). If no cell meets the conditions, then the algorithm ends. (The algorithm also ends when all locations are linked together on a single route, which we will discover as we proceed with Bridgette's problem.)

This first application of the C-W algorithm has saved Bridgette 17 miles, but still more savings can be realized by subjecting her data to another iteration of step 5. Looking again at Exhibit 15.4b, we can identify cell (2, 4) as having the next highest net savings value (i.e., 14). T_{02} and T_{04} are each greater than zero, locations 2 and 4 are not on the same route at present, and there are no constraints against having locations 2 and 4 on the same route. Therefore, we can link these two locations. Enter $T = 1$ in cell (2, 4), and reduce each of the T values in cells (0, 2) and (0, 4) by one trip, as shown in Exhibit 15.4c. Note in the graphical depiction that the trips from the bakery to concession 2 and from concession 4 back to the bakery have been eliminated, thus requiring an adjustment of the directional arrows.

EXHIBIT 15.4c   Second iteration.

Routes: First trip: 0–1–0
          Second trip:
          0–4–2–3–0

Is further improvement possible? The next highest net savings is 11, found in cell (1, 2). In this situation, T_{01} is greater than zero, but T_{02} is not. Therefore, linking these two locations would violate condition 5a. Moving on, cell (3, 4) has the next highest net savings. The T_{03} and T_{04} values are each greater than zero, but concessions 3 and 4 are already on the same route, which violates condition 5b. Therefore, we must look at the next highest net savings, which is 7, in cell (1, 3). Here, T_{01} and T_{03} are each greater than zero, concessions 1 and 3 are not already on the same route, and no constraints exist. Therefore, we may link these two locations. We enter $T = 1$ in cell (1, 3) and reduce the T values in cells $(0, 1)$ and $(0, 3)$ by 1 each, as shown in Exhibit 15.4d. We have removed one trip between the bakery and concession 1 and one trip from concession 3 to the bakery. The directional arrows suggest that a counterclockwise route be used, but our assumption of equal time or distance traveling in either direction would permit the final route to be traversed in either direction.

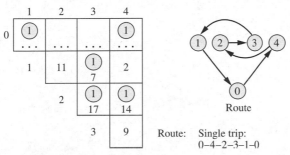

EXHIBIT 15.4d Final solution.

Using the C-W Algorithm with Constraints

Suppose that business booms and Bridgette decides to supply four new franchise operations, and that these franchises are located according to the schematic shown in Exhibit 15.5. Unfortunately, Bridgette cannot carry enough bagels in her Blue Bagel Beamer to supply all the new locations on a single route such as the one we constructed in the previous section. Each franchise requires 500 bagels per day, and she can transport a maximum of 1000 bagels per trip. How can we use the C-W algorithm to solve Bridgette's problem? In general, the introduction of a constraint such as Bridgette's capacity limit or a delivery time window does not alter the method of applying the algorithm. We need only account for the constraint so it does not violate step 5c.

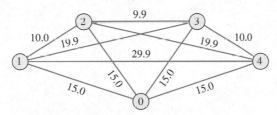

EXHIBIT 15.5 Network representation of a single bakery and four concessions.

In the present example, our first step again is to construct a shortest-distance half-matrix containing the distance between each pair of locations, as shown in Exhibit 15.6.

		1	2	3	4
Bakery	0	15.0	15.0	15.0	15.0
	1		10.0	19.9	29.9
	2			9.9	19.9
	3				10.0

EXHIBIT 15.6 Shortest-distance half-matrix: miles between pairs of locations.

Next, we construct the net savings half-matrix and enter the appropriate $T = 2$ values for the initial solution, as shown in Exhibit 15.7a. (Note that we have not included graphical depictions of the individual trips and their directional arrows in this example, although some readers may find it helpful to add such sketches.)

	1	2	3	4
Bakery 0	②···	②···	②···	②···
1		20.0	10.1	0.1
2			20.1	10.1
3				20.0

Routes: First trip: 0–1–0
Second trip: 0–2–0
Third trip: 0–3–0
Fourth trip: 0–4–0

EXHIBIT 15.7a   Initial solution.

Note that cell (2, 3) has the largest net savings and satisfies all the conditions under step 5 of the C-W algorithm. Therefore, we can link locations 2 and 3. Enter the $T = 1$ value in cell (2, 3) and reduce the T values in cells (0, 2) and (0, 3) to 1, as shown in Exhibit 15.7b.

	1	2	3	4
Bakery 0	②···	①···	①···	②···
1		20.0	10.1	0.1
2			① 20.1	10.1
3				20.0

Routes: First trip: 0–1–0
Second trip: 0–2–3–0
Third trip: 0–4–0

EXHIBIT 15.7b   First iteration.

The route just established from the bakery to franchise 2 to franchise 3 and back to the bakery (0—2—3—0) cannot have any more links added, because additional links would exceed Bridgette's capacity (a violation of condition 5c). Therefore, we must eliminate the following links: (1, 2), (1, 3), (2, 4), and (3, 4). The only link that remains possible is between locations 1 and 4. Adding the $T = 1$ value to cell (1, 4) and reducing the T values in cells (0, 1) and (0, 4) yields the final solution, as shown in Exhibit 15.7c.

	1	2	3	4
Bakery 0	①···	①···	①···	①···
1		20.0	10.1	① 0.1
2			① 20.1	10.1
3				20.0

Routes: First trip: 0–2–3–0
Second trip: 0–1–4–0

EXHIBIT 15.7c   Final solution.

Exhibit 15.8 shows the final routes that we constructed. The total mileage to be driven is 99.8; however, Exhibit 15.9 shows an alternate route devised from inspection that does the job in only 80 miles!

Total distance = 99.8 miles

EXHIBIT 15.8 Final routes developed.

Total distance = 80 miles

EXHIBIT 15.9 Optimal solution.

As noted earlier, the C-W algorithm does not guarantee an optimal solution every time. In fact, in this simple case, the solution with the algorithm is approximately 25 percent poorer than the optimal solution. In general, however, the algorithm is highly effective, yielding very acceptable results that, when combined with its simplicity of use, make it a very useful tool for developing vehicle routes.

Use of a "Minimal Technology Routing System"

Bartholdi et al. have reported using a very clever, manual method for routing vehicles that deliver Meals on Wheels (MOW) for Senior Citizens Services, Inc., in Atlanta, Georgia.[4] This program involved delivering a very large number of lunches to people located in a widely dispersed pattern within the city. This alone could daunt the most intrepid vehicle scheduler, but consider an added complication: the clientele being served were incapacitated, mostly by age and/or illness, which resulted in a high turnover of clients and, accordingly, in routes that had to be changed. Moreover, the sponsoring organization did not have the funding for sophisticated computers or skilled people to operate them. In fact, at the time of this study, one person was responsible for all administrative aspects of the program.

So MOW needed a way of routing and scheduling that could accommodate the following constraints:

1. A large and frequently changing clientele made necessary the ability to add and remove both clients and locations easily.
2. It was necessary to allot the delivery work equally, because meals were delivered by four drivers who were paid by the hour and each was anxious to have his or her fair share of the work.
3. The program had to be utilized without computer support.
4. The program had to be utilized by an "unskilled" scheduler.

Very simply, the solution was first to assign each location on a grid of the Atlanta city map a θ (theta) value. This part was done by the researchers using a traveling-salesperson heuristic based on a "space-filling curve" concept. The resulting θ map would form a reference sheet for the MOW manager to use in scheduling the routes and vehicles. Next, two Rolodex cards were made for each client; the client's cards contained his or her name and address and the θ value of that address. One card was inserted in one Rolodex alphabetically, and the other was filed in a second Rolodex according to increasing values of θ.

Using the system was an exercise in elegance and simplicity. First, the θ file, which was organized according to θ location, was manually divided into four relatively equal parts, and each part was assigned to one delivery person. Accommodating changes in clientele was equally easy. As a person was removed from the service, his or her card was pulled from the alphabetical file, the θ value was noted, and the corresponding card was pulled from the θ file. This automatically updated the route. Similarly, when a client was added to the service, his or her cards were added to the files, and again, the routing was automatically updated. In practice, this system proved to work exceedingly well.

Obviously, many methods exist to facilitate vehicle routing and scheduling, and it would not be possible to explore each and every one in this space. We have, however, looked at one of the most widely used methods, the Clarke-Wright algorithm, and at another method that is charming in its simplicity and usefulness.

SOLVED PROBLEMS

1. Unconstrained Route

Problem Statement

A cable TV installer has the new accounts shown on the map below to visit today for hook-up. Her office is located at node 0 with distances shown in miles between all places she must visit. What route will minimize her total distance traveled to visit each account and return to the office at the end of her workday?

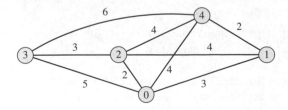

Solution

Step 1: Prepare shortest distance matrix

	1	2	3	4
0	3	2	5	4
1		4	7	2
2			3	4
3				6

Step 2: Prepare savings matrix using the expression $S_{ij} = C_{0i} + C_{0j} - C_{ij}$

	1	2	3	4
0	...	...	...	...
1		1	1	5
2			4	2
3				3

Step 3: Look for the largest savings (5), and connect accounts 1 and 4, creating the routes shown below:

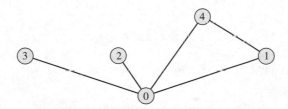

Step 4: Look for the next largest savings (4), and connect accounts 2 and 3, creating the routes shown below:

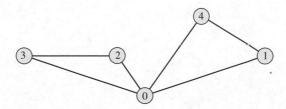

Step 5: Look for the next largest savings (3), and connect accounts 3 and 4, creating the final single route shown below with total travel distance of 16 miles:

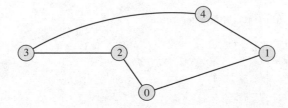

2. Route Constrained by Time Window

Problem Statement

For the cable TV installer, assume that the even-numbered accounts (2, 4) must be accomplished in the morning and the odd-numbered accounts (1, 3) in the afternoon.

Solution

Step 1: Using the savings matrix above, connect accounts 2 and 4, creating the route shown below. If more than two accounts had existed, we would find the largest savings and proceed to build a route with even-numbered accounts.

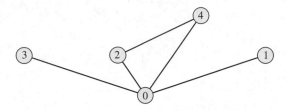

Step 2: Look for the largest savings (5), and connect accounts 1 and 4, creating the routes shown below:

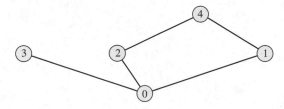

Step 3: Connect accounts 3 and 1, creating the final single route with total distance of 20 miles shown below. Note that accounts 3 and 2 could not be connected, because the resulting route would leave accounts 2 and 4 in the middle of a route, violating the time window.

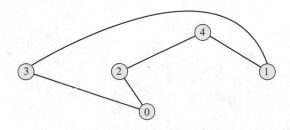

EXERCISES

15.1. For the following net savings matrix, find the recommended route.

	1	2	3	4
0	...	...	...	...
1		3	2	5
2			7	9
3				8

15.2. For the following net savings matrix, find the recommended route.

	1	2	3	4
0	...	...	...	...
	1	2	4	3
		2	5	7
			3	2

15.3. The *New York Times* delivery service has customers at four apartments in the northwest part of town. Recommend an efficient route given the shortest-distance matrix in miles below for travel from the distribution center to and between the apartments.

	1	2	3	4
0	6	7	9	8
	1	12	13	12
		2	8	9
			3	14

15.4. A florist has received orders to deliver flowers to four office buildings. The matrix below contains the shortest distance in miles between the florist's shop and the offices. Construct a net savings matrix and recommend a route to minimize the distance traveled.

	1	2	3	4
0	6	6	9	8
	1	7	11	12
		2	5	9
			3	10

15.5. The Lone Star Beer distributor makes deliveries to four taverns from a central warehouse, as shown in the figure below. Distances are given in miles.
  a. Construct a shortest-route matrix for travel between all pairs of locations.
  b. Construct a net savings matrix.
  c. Recommend a delivery route to minimize the distance traveled.

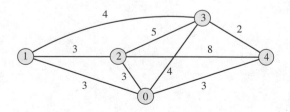

15.6 A university is planning to serve four off-campus apartments with a shuttle bus service. Given the net savings matrix below, recommend a bus route that minimizes the distance traveled.

	1	2	3	4
0	...	...	...	...
1		9	14	2
2			16	7
3				11

15.7. Wal-Mart has five distribution centers and one central warehouse. Below are the distances between all nodes (0 = warehouse). Construct the net savings matrix for this problem, and determine a route to minimize the distance traveled to serve all five distribution centers.

0-1	10 mi	1-2	7 mi	2-4	20 mi
0-2	10 mi	1-3	16 mi	2-5	19 mi
0-3	14 mi	1-4	13 mi	3-4	6 mi
0-4	12 mi	1-5	8 mi	3-5	18 mi
0-5	13 mi	2-3	5 mi	4-5	6 mi

15.8. The city refuse collection department uses a fleet of small trucks that collect trash around the city and make periodic deliveries to four staging sites. Currently, two dump trucks transport the trash from these staging sites to an incinerator. One truck is assigned to service sites 1 and 2 and the other to sites 3 and 4. The network in the figure below gives the miles between the staging sites and the incinerator, which is shown as node 0.

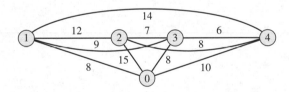

a. What is the cost per day to operate this two-truck system if gasoline is $1.50 per gallon and the trucks average 5 miles per gallon and make 10 trips to each staging site per day? Truck drivers are paid $80 per day.

b. A proposal has been made to purchase one large diesel truck with enough capacity to visit all four staging sites during one trip. What should be its route to minimize the distance traveled?

c. If diesel fuel costs $1 per gallon and the truck averages 10 miles per gallon, determine the daily savings in operating costs.

The Daley Monthly Car Pool[5]

Alice Daley, owner and publisher of the local periodical *The Daley Monthly,* has a staff of six writers. Currently, employees drive in each morning from their homes, as shown in the figure below:

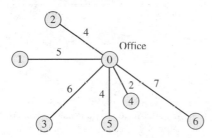

Because of increasing gasoline prices, however, the employees have approached Ms. Daley with a suggestion to use the company's nine-passenger van for a car pool. In considering this idea, Ms. Daley collected the additional data shown below on mileage between all pairs of employee locations.

1-2	2 mi	2-3	5 mi	3-5	5 mi
1-3	4 mi	2-4	6 mi	3-6	10 mi
1-4	6 mi	2-5	7 mi	4-5	3 mi
1-5	6 mi	2-6	11 mi	4-6	5 mi
1-6	12 mi	3-4	6 mi	5-6	5 mi

An alternative to using the company van is using an economy car. A compact car can hold only three pas-sengers, however, so it would require two trips. Even so, the average of 26 miles per gallon for the compact car compared with 12 miles per gallon for the van makes this option worth considering, particularly when gasoline is averaging 90 cents per gallon.

One final consideration is traffic congestion. The average possible speed is 30 miles per hour before 8 A.M. and 15 miles per hour between 8 and 9 A.M.

Questions

1. What is the total cost of gasoline per day under the current arrangement of employees driving their own cars? Assume that fuel economy is 10 miles per gallon.
2. Find the least costly route for a car pool using the nine-passenger van. What would be the cost of gasoline per day for this arrangement?
3. What time would the van need to leave the office to return with all employees by 8 A.M.? By 9 A.M.?
4. If the employee living at location 6 offered to keep the van overnight, how is the route changed? To use the C-W algorithm, what must we now consider to be the origin?
5. If the compact car were used, what routes would you recommend to minimize the gasoline expense? What would the daily cost of gasoline be for this proposal?
6. At what time would the compact car need to leave the office to begin its pickups to be finished by 8 A.M.? By 9 A.M.?
7. Would your routes be modified if the employees living at locations 2 and 5 volunteered to use their compact cars and left from home to begin pickups?
8. What advantages and disadvantages are there to starting work at 8 A.M.?

Airport Services, Inc.[6]

Airport Services, Inc., is planning to implement a remote shuttle service among five terminals and the Port Welkin Airport. Mr. Kelly Mist has been given the task of developing the route and service schedules for the proposed operation to be used in the franchise application to the Port Welkin City Council. Mrs. Janet Rush, Mr. Mist's supervisor, asks him to create schedules with low operating costs for each round-trip. Mrs. Rush states that with the locations currently in mind for terminal sites, Airport Services may have to run five buses, one between each terminal and the airport. She is hopeful, however, that fewer buses can be used.

Assignments

1. Mr. Mist is given the following information on which his analysis must be based:

   Average operating cost: $0.455 per kilometer

   Average operating speed: 60 kilometers per hour

   Average layover time per stop: 9 minutes

   From a city map, he develops a distance matrix for all proposed service locations, designating the airport as site 0. All distances are given in kilometers.

	1	2	3	4	5
0	10	4	5	5	7
1		7	11	15	6
2			8	9	8
3				6	4
4					9

Using the Clarke-Wright algorithm, recommend the best routing schedule under Mrs. Rush's least-cost objective.

2. Mrs. Rush's initial reaction to Mr. Mist's work is very favorable; however, she has just been informed by the mayor that Port Welkin will require each bus to have a round-trip time (to and from the airport) of 40 minutes or less, excluding the loading and unloading time at the airport only. Although Mrs. Rush realizes that this will offer the shuttle users faster service, she is sure that it will cost the company more money.

   Develop a new routing schedule that will meet this new time constraint yet still keep Airport Services's costs low.

3. The Port Welkin City Council awarded Airport Services a shuttle franchise on the basis of Mr. Mist's latest routing plan, and Mrs. Rush feels that initiation of the service has gone about as well as could be expected. Mr. Mist informs her that they are experiencing a recurring shortage of capacity at terminal 3; that is, there are more people boarding the bus than there are seats available.

Mrs. Rush decides to seek a solution that meets the franchise conditions but does not require people to stand or use any more vehicles, even though the operating costs may rise slightly. Mr. Mist has analyzed the normal average boarding and alighting volumes at each remote terminal, as shown below. Also, he knows that Airport Services is using 48-passenger vehicles, which usually are full when leaving the airport on a multistop route.

Terminal	Avg. no. boarding	Avg. no. alighting
1	28	30
2	20	18
3	18	14
4	21	26
5	30	32

Develop a routing schedule that will incorporate the additional capacity constraint. How does this final solution compare with the previous two solutions regarding operating costs and round-trip time?

SELECTED BIBLIOGRAPHY

DAVIS, TOM: "Effective Supply Chain Management," *Sloan Management Review,* vol. 34, no. 4, Summer 1993, pp. 35–46.

FEARON, H. E., and W. A. BALES: Purchasing Nontraditional Goods and Services, National Association of Purchasing Management, 1995.

FITZSIMMONS, J. A., J. NOH, and E. THEIS: "Purchasing Business Services," *Journal of Business and Industrial Marketing,* vol. 13, nos. 4/5, 1998, pp. 370–380.

GRAW, L. H., and D. M. MAPLES: *Service Purchasing,* Van Nostrand Reinhold, New York, 1994.

JACKSON, R. W., P. D. COOPER, L. A. NEIDELL, and D. A. LUNSFORD: "An Empirical Investigation of the Differences in Goods and Services as Perceived by Organizational Buyers," *Industrial Marketing Management,* vol. 24, 1995, pp. 99–108.

LEE, HAU L., and BRENT CARTER: "Hewlett-Packard Gains Control of Inventory and Service through Design for Localization," *Interfaces,* vol. 23, no. 4, July–August 1993, pp. 1–11.

STANK, T. P., T. J. GOLDSBY, and S. K. VICKERY: "Effect of Service Supplier Performance on Satisfaction and Loyalty of Store Managers in the Fast-Food Industry," *Journal of Operations Management,* vol. 17, no. 4, June 1999, pp. 429–448.

ENDNOTES

1. Tom Davis, "Effective Supply Chain Management," *Sloan Management Review,* vol. 34, no. 4, Summer 1993, pp. 42–43.
2. Prepared by Naomi Chen, Vashti Forbes, and Regina Lucas under the supervision of Professor James A. Fitzsimmons.
3. G. Clarke and J. W. Wright, "Scheduling of Vehicles from a Central Depot to a Number of Delivery Points," *Operations Research,* vol. 12, no. 4, July–August 1964, pp. 568–581.
4. Adapted from J. J. Bartholdi III, L. K. Platzman, R. L. Collins, and W. H. Warden III, "A Minimal Technology Routing System for Meals on Wheels," *Interfaces,* vol. 13, no. 3, June 1983, pp. 1–8.
5. Prepared by Roland Bressler and Raymond Matthews under the supervision of Professor James A. Fitzsimmons.
6. Prepared by James Vance under the supervision of Professor James A. Fitzsimmons.

CHAPTER SIXTEEN

Managing Service Projects

Learning Objectives

After completing this chapter, you should be able to:

1. Describe the characteristics of a project and its management challenges.
2. Illustrate the use of a Gantt chart and discuss its limitations.
3. Construct a project network.
4. Perform critical path analysis on a project network.
5. Allocate limited resources to a project.
6. Crash activities to reduce the project completion time.
7. Analyze a project with uncertain activity times to determine the project completion distribution.
8. Monitor a project for time, cost, and schedule variance using an earned value chart.
9. Discuss reasons why projects fail to meet performance, time, and cost objectives.

Projects can vary widely in their complexity, resource requirements, time needed for completion, and risk. Consider, for example, projects that might be undertaken by a passenger airline: opening a new route, overhauling an aircraft, implementing a new marketing strategy, installing a new data processing system, purchasing a new fleet of aircraft, changing in-flight service, and installing a new inventory control system. In this age of time-based competition, successful project management can bring new products to the marketplace sooner, thereby preempting rivals and capturing market share. For example, in the construction industry, Lehrer McGovern Bovis became famous for its construction management services by achieving significant time savings when it used an overlapping phased design-construction process in which the foundation was poured before the final drawings were completed.

The risks that are inherent in a project can threaten the survival of a company. For example, failure to complete a project on time can bankrupt a small construction firm when the contract includes a penalty cost for delay. The potential risks and rewards associated with a project are factors that enter into building a project team, selecting a project leader, and developing a strategy for successful completion of the project.

CHAPTER PREVIEW

The chapter begins with an overview of the nature of projects and the challenges facing the project manager. Project planning begins with a work breakdown schedule and formation of a project team. Traditional bar-chart methods for project scheduling are then presented and discussed. We also introduce the concept of a project network and describe and illustrate methods of analysis. Microsoft Project for Windows is used to illustrate the ease and power of project management software. Project planning issues, such as dealing with resource constraints, activity crashing, and incorporating uncertainty, are explored. Techniques for monitoring projects to achieve objectives for time, cost, and performance conclude the chapter.

THE NATURE OF PROJECT MANAGEMENT

Characteristics of Projects

A *project* can be thought of as the allocation of resources directed toward a specific objective following a planned, organized approach. Project management is concerned with planning, scheduling, and controlling project activities to achieve timely project completion within budget and meeting performance expectations. Project management is a challenge because the three objectives (i.e., cost, time, and performance) are in conflict. More time could enhance performance or quality, for example, but a contractual due date would be sacrificed and costs would exceed budget.

All projects have the following characteristics in common:

1. *Purpose.* The project is usually a one-time activity with clear objectives. An exception, for example, would include the periodic maintenance that airlines perform on their aircraft.
2. *Life cycle.* Each project follows a life cycle of tasks that include project conception, selection of the project to pursue, planning, scheduling, monitoring, control of project activities, and, finally, project termination.
3. *Interdependencies.* Projects involve many activities that must be performed in a specified sequence. The sequence generally is dictated by technological or strategic considerations. For large-scale projects, such as Boeing's development of the 777 aircraft, many partners require extensive coordination.
4. *Uniqueness.* Usually each project has novel features that require customized managerial attention. Many project elements, however, are common and learning can be transferred.
5. *Conflict.* Many stakeholders (e.g., client, parent organization, project team, partners, and functional areas) have conflicting objectives. Thus, projects involve a substantial commitment of resources and management attention during the life of the project.

Project Management Process

Organizations initiate projects for a variety of reasons, such as constructing a new facility, introducing a new service, or performing a consulting engagement. All of these reasons are catalysts that lead to the inception of a project. The management functions of planning, scheduling, and controlling are actively pursued from project conception to termination.

Planning   A project begins with a clearly defined statement of work and objectives agreed upon by all parties. This statement is a written description of the objectives, and it contains a tentative schedule that specifies start and completion dates and a proposed budget. The project scope is divided and subdivided into work packages. An aid to planning is the development of a *work breakdown structure* (WBS), which is a hierarchical tree or indented outline of the tasks required to achieve the objective. A WBS begins with the end objective and successively subdivides work into manageable components such as tasks, subtasks, and work elements. Consider the WBS shown in

1.0 Move the hospital (Project)
    1.1 Move patients (Task)
        1.1.1 Arrange for ambulance (Subtask)
            1.1.1.1 Prepare patients for the move (Work element)
            1.1.1.2 Box patients' personal effects (Work element)
    1.2 Move furniture
        1.2.1 Contract with moving company
                    •
                    •
                    •

FIGURE 16.1 Work breakdown structure.

Figure 16.1, the project of moving a hospital across town to a new location. The project (or program if it is multiyear) is defined as "move the hospital." One task is "move patients." A subtask is "arrange for ambulance transportation." A work element is "prepare patients for the move." The detailed project definition provided by the WBS helps identify the skills and responsibilities that are necessary to achieve the project goals, and it also provides a framework for budgeting.

Scheduling   Scheduling begins with time and cost estimates for each work element or activity and a determination of the precedence relationships between activities. A project network diagram is prepared to provide a visual picture of the project schedule. Project management is then used to determine the start and finish dates for each activity in the project. Allocation of resources to specific activities also is planned at this time, a process that can influence the project duration and cost.

Controlling   The final project schedule becomes the basis upon which the project is implemented and monitored for progress against intermediate completion steps (called milestones). Expenditures against the budget also can be tracked using the project schedule. Controlling is concerned with making sure that all aspects of project implementation are carried out according to both time and budget. If some goals are not met, the schedule and plan are revised as necessary to ensure that project objectives are achieved.

Selecting the Project Manager

Managing a project requires special skills because the objectives of time, cost, and performance are conflicting. The following attributes of candidates should be considered:

- *Credibility*—the technical and administrative experience.
- *Sensitivity*—political and interpersonal conflict resolution skills.
- *Ability to handle stress*—ability to manage multiple objectives within uncertain environment.
- *Leadership*—ability to communicate goal attainment with integrity and enthusiasm.

Building the Project Team

It takes time to build personal relationships that result in accepting differences, being open to disagreement, and enjoying participation in activities together. In projects, people who have never worked together often are assigned to the same team. This group of individuals must develop into an effective team to achieve the project objective. B. W. Tuckman has defined four sequential stages of team development: forming, storming, norming, and performing.[1]

Forming   Forming is the phase when team members get acquainted, similar to the early "courting" phase of a relationship. Team members usually have positive expectations and are eager to get started but are unsure of their roles in the team. Feelings characteristic of this stage include excitement, anticipation, suspicion, anxiety, and hesitancy. The project manager needs to provide direction and structure. During orientation sessions, the project objective, scope of work, schedule, and team operating procedures must be communicated clearly. Discussing the team's make-up and pointing out complementary skills and expertise will help resolve anxiety about roles to be played by the members. To ensure buy-in, it is important to involve the team in developing the project plans.

Storming   In this stage, work begins in earnest and reality sets in, although it does not necessarily match expectations. Team members become dissatisfied with both project constraints and dependence on the direction and authority of the project manager. Conflict emerges, tension increases, and morale is low during this stage. The storming stage is characterized by feelings of frustration, anger, and hostility. The project manager needs to achieve agreement on methods for handling and resolving conflict. This is the time for the project manager to provide an understanding and supportive environment. Dissatisfaction and conflict must be addressed to avoid future dysfunctional behavior.

Norming   After passing through the storming stage, project team cohesion begins to develop and the operating environment is accepted. Control and decision making are transferred from the project manager to the project team. A feeling of camaraderie emerges as trust develops and team members share information and confide in one another. Personal friendships may develop that reach beyond the work environment. The project manager takes on a supportive role and recognizes the progress made by the team. Work performance and productivity accelerate during this phase.

Performing   In the final stage, the team is highly committed and eager to achieve the project objectives. Confidence is high and a sense of unity and pride in team accomplishments emerges. The team feels fully empowered, and members frequently collaborate to solve problems and help with implementation. During this stage, the project manager fully delegates responsibility and authority to the team but monitors its progress with respect to performance, budget, and schedule. If actual progress falls behind, the project manager facilitates and supports the development and implementation of corrective action. Finally, the project manager is in a position to mentor and support the professional development of people working on the project.

Principles of Effective Project Management

General guidelines have evolved from experience in managing projects. Some principles to keep in mind include the following:

1. Direct people individually and as a team.
2. Reinforce the excitement of the project.
3. Keep everyone informed.
4. Build agreements that vitalize team members (i.e., manage healthy conflict).

5. Empower yourself and team members.

6. Encourage risk taking and creativity.

The importance of projects has attracted much attention in recent times and has yielded techniques to help managers. Our discussion begins with Gantt charts and concludes with personal computer software used to analyze projects that are modeled as networks.

TECHNIQUES FOR PROJECT MANAGEMENT

Gantt Project Charts

Developed by Henry Gantt in 1916, a *Gantt chart* is used to determine the timing of individual activities in a project. This chart plots a time line for each activity against a *calendar*. Gantt charts are a useful tool for portraying visually the schedule of activities and monitoring the progress of a project against its plan.

The first step in using a Gantt chart is to break down the project into discrete activities. "Discrete" means that each activity has a distinct beginning and end. After the project has been decomposed into its activities, the sequence of those activities is determined. This task is easier said than done, however. Usually, there are several possible strategies for carrying out a project, and it may not be obvious which one is best. The skill of the project manager, along with the input of other people interested in the project, ultimately determines the sequence that is adopted. A Gantt chart also requires time estimates for each activity. The durations of the activities are assumed to be deterministic and known, which means that we presume to know exactly how long each activity will take. Of course, this is not realistic, but it does provide estimates that are helpful for managing a project.

Example 16.1. Servicing a Boeing 747

Λ Gantt chart can be used to schedule a periodic or repetitive project, because the sequence of activities is well understood and past experience has determined how long each activity takes. Consider the required activities in a routine, 50-minute layover of a Boeing 747 passenger aircraft. Figure 16.2 is a Gantt chart that displays each activity with a horizontal bar indicating its duration in minutes and the scheduled beginning and ending times. Many activities, such as galley servicing, can be accomplished concurrently with others, because the corresponding horizontal bars overlap each other and, thus, are scheduled to be performed during the same time period. For lavatory servicing, however, the aft, center, and forward sections are serviced in sequence, not concurrently. This chart can be used to determine the labor and equipment resources that are required to complete the project on time. Once under way, activities that fall behind schedule can be noted by drawing a vertical line representing the current time and noting which activities have not finished as scheduled and, consequently, need attention to get back on schedule and finish the project in 50 minutes.

A Critique of Gantt Charts

Gantt charts have several appealing features that account for their continued acceptance. They are visual, easy to construct, and easy to understand. More important, however, they result in forced planning. To construct a chart, the project manager is compelled to think in detail about activity scheduling and resource requirements.

Despite their appealing features, Gantt charts are inadequate for large-scale, complex projects. In particular, they do not show clearly the interdependence of activities.

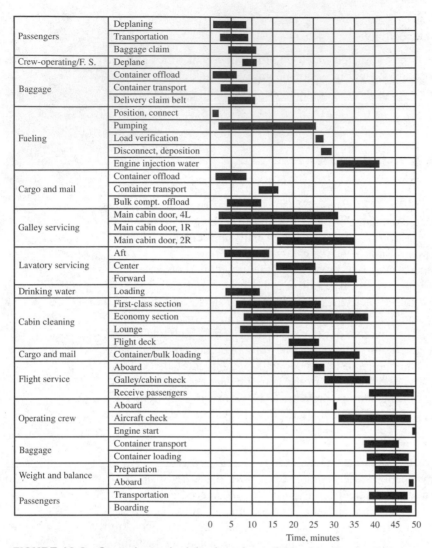

FIGURE 16.2 **Gantt chart schedule of service activities for a Boeing 747.**

For example, in Figure 16.2, galley servicing that uses the main cabin door 2R is delayed, because access to this door is blocked by cargo and mail operations. Consequently, it is difficult to evaluate the effects of changes in project implementation that may result from activity delays or changes in sequence. These charts also do not give any indication about the relative importance of individual activities in completing the project on schedule (i.e., which activities can be delayed without delaying the entire project). Therefore, because the relative importance of individual activities is the basis for allocating resources and managerial attention, Gantt charts are too ineffective and cumbersome to use with large, complicated projects. Consequently, network-based techniques were developed specifically to overcome the deficiencies of Gantt charts.

Constructing a Project Network

A network consists of a set of circles called nodes and also a set of arrows. The arrows connect the nodes to give a visual presentation of the sequence of activities. In one method, known as *activity on node* (AON), the nodes represent project activities, whereas the arrows indicate the activity sequence. In the second method, known as *activity on arrow* (AOA), the arrows represent project activities. The nodes are *events,* which are the starts or completions of activities. An event takes place at an instant of time, whereas an activity takes place over an interval of time. The AON and AOA methods are equally good, but, over time, the AON has become more popular. It is very straightforward to draw, and it does not need a dummy activity artifact such as that found in AOA diagrams. Both diagrams will be illustrated here, but all critical path analyses will use the AON convention, which we will call a *PERT chart* (the accepted name given to project management diagrams).

A key assumption underlying critical path analysis is that an activity cannot begin until *all* immediate predecessor activities are completed. Also, a PERT chart generally has a single node that indicates the project beginning and a single node that indicates the project end. PERT charts are *connected* and *acyclic*. "Connected" means that it is possible to get to any network node by following arrows leaving the start node. "Acyclic" means that the sequence of activities progresses without interruption from the start node to the end node without looping around in circles.

Example 16.2. Tennis Tournament—Project Network

Planning a tennis tournament is an opportunity to use project management. The goal is to hold a successful weekend tournament at a future date, and preparations for the tournament require that all activities be identified. We also need to estimate the durations of these activities and note any constraints in sequence or precedence. Table 16.1 lists the activities that are required for the tournament along with their precedence requirements and durations.

Figure 16.3 shows an AOA project network for the tennis tournament. Note the use of three dummy activities (i.e., the broken arrows) to ensure that activity precedence is not violated. For example, the dummy activity joining nodes 3 and 7 ensures that activity F follows the completion of both activity C and activity B. Dummy activities do not consume time but are included only to maintain the proper activity sequence. The length of an activity arrow has no meaning, although each activity is subscripted to note its duration. Nodes are numbered according to a convention: the node at the arrow head must have a larger number than the node at the tail to indicate the direction of the activity. For example, if the arrow representing the dummy activity that joins nodes 3

TABLE 16.1

TENNIS TOURNAMENT ACTIVITIES

Activity description	Code	Immediate predecessor	Estimated duration (days)
Negotiate for location	A	—	2
Contact seeded players	B	—	8
Plan promotion	C	A	3
Locate officials	D	C	2
Send RSVP invitations	E	C	10
Sign player contracts	F	B,C	4
Purchase balls and trophies	G	D	4
Negotiate catering	H	E,F	1
Prepare location	I	E,G	3
Tournament	J	H,I	2

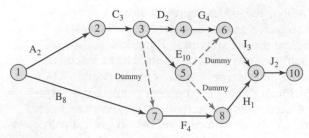

FIGURE 16.3 AOA network for tennis tournament.

and 7 were reversed (i.e., pointing to node 3 instead of node 7), then the precedence interpretation would change (i.e., activity D would follow activity B, which is not correct). Preparing an AOA network requires much care and is prone to errors.

Figure 16.4 is a PERT chart (AON network) of the same tennis tournament project. In this case, arrows represent the sequence of activities, and nodes represent the activities themselves. Preparing a PERT chart is a simple matter of drawing nodes in approximate sequence from beginning to end and joining the nodes with arrows in the appropriate direction. Sometimes a start or finish node is added, as in the tennis tournament example. It should be clear that the AOA and AON networks describe the same sequence of activities.

Critical Path Method

The *critical path method (CPM)* is an approach to determine the start and finish dates for individual activities in a project. A result of this method is the identification of a *critical path,* or unbroken chain of activities from the start to the end of the project. A delay in the starting time of any critical path activity results in a delay in the project completion time. Because of their importance for completing the project, *critical activities* receive top priority in the allocation of resources and managerial effort. In the spirit of *management by exception,* the critical activities are the exceptions that need close scrutiny.

CPM involves some simple calculations, and Table 16.2 lists the notations that are used in this analysis. Note that we have not indicated how the expected activity duration t is determined. In many cases, these values are assumed to be deterministic (i.e., constants) and are based on expert judgment and past experience. In other cases, the expected durations are assumed to be the arithmetic means of known probability distributions. We shall discuss the deterministic case first and treat probability distributions later.

CPM involves calculating early times (ES and EF), late times (LS and LF), and a slack time (TS). Early times are calculated for each activity beginning with the first ac-

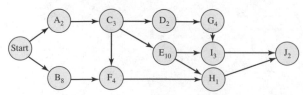

FIGURE 16.4 PERT chart (AON network) for tennis tournament.

TABLE 16.2

NOTATION FOR CRITICAL PATH METHOD

Item	Symbol	Definition
Expected activity duration	t	The expected duration of an activity
Early start	ES	The earliest time an activity can begin if all previous activities are begun at their earliest times
Early finish	EF	The earliest time an activity can be completed if it is started at its early start time
Late start	LS	The latest time an activity can begin without delaying the completion of the project
Late finish	LF	The latest time an activity can be completed if it is started at its latest start time
Total slack	TS	The amount of time an activity can be delayed without delaying the completion of the project

---

tivity and moving successively forward through the network to the final activity. Thus, the early times (ES and EF) are calculated by a *forward pass* through the project. The early start for the first activity is set equal to zero, and the early times for a particular activity are calculated as:

$$ES = EF_{predecessor} \qquad (1)$$

$$EF = ES + t \qquad (2)$$

Note that $EF_{predecessor}$ is the early finish of an immediately preceding activity and that t is the duration of the activity under consideration. When there are several immediate *predecessors,* the one with the *largest* early finish time is used. The early finish for the last activity is the early finish for the project as a whole.

Late times (LS and LF) are calculated for each activity, beginning with the last activity in the network and moving successively backward through the network to the first activity. The late times thus are calculated by a *backward pass* through the project. By convention, the late finish for the last activity is set equal to the early finish (i.e., $LF = EF$). If a project completion date is known, then this date can be used as the late finish for the last activity. For any particular activity, the late times are calculated as follows:

$$LF = LS_{successor} \qquad (3)$$

$$LS = LF - t \qquad (4)$$

Note that $LS_{successor}$ is the late start of an immediately succeeding activity. When there are several immediate *successors,* the one with the *smallest* late start is used.

Slack times are determined from the early and late times. Total slack (TS) for an activity can be calculated in either of two equivalent ways:

$$TS = LF - EF \qquad \text{or} \qquad (5)$$

$$TS = LS - ES \qquad (6)$$

Slack is one of the most important aspects of critical path analysis. Activities that have zero slack are critical, meaning that they cannot be delayed without also delaying the project completion time. When displayed on a Gantt chart, the set of critical activities always forms a complete and unbroken path from the initial node to the completion node of the network. Such a path is referred to as the *critical path;* in terms of duration time, this is the longest path in the network. A project network has *at least* one critical path, and it could have two or more.

Example 16.3. Tennis Tournament—Critical Path Analysis

The PERT chart of the tennis tournament is shown in Figure 16.5. Each node is labeled with the activity code, and the duration is a subscript. Next to each node is a cross to be filled in with the activity schedule times, which are calculated as shown below (note that t represents the activity time):

$$TS = LS - ES$$

$$
\begin{array}{c|c}
ES = EF_{predecessor} & EF = ES + t \\
\hline
LS = LF - t & LF = LS_{successor}
\end{array}
$$

Early times are calculated beginning with the "start" node (i.e., forward pass) and are recorded in the top row of the cross for each activity, after which we see that the project will take 20 days to complete (i.e., EF for the last activity). Note that we need to be especially careful to select the predecessor with the *largest EF* as the time for the ES of the activity in question, which occurs when more than one arrow comes into a node (i.e., activities E and F converge on node H). Because no single activity begins the project, an artificial activity or "start" node is created with a duration of zero. Using this convention, we have a single "start" and a single "finish" node for the project. (Artificial "finish" nodes are used when a project does not have a single concluding activity.)

Figure 16.6 shows the completed critical path analysis. Note that per convention, the late finish for the last activity is set equal to 20 days. This value is the starting point for calculating late times (i.e., backward pass), which are entered into the bottom row of the cross for each activity. Again, we must use caution to select the successor with the *smallest LS* as the time for the LF of the activity in question, which occurs when more than one arrow departs from a node (i.e., activities D, E, and F following node C).

The critical activities have zero slack, which is easily seen as the difference between ES and LS or between EF and LF; thus, these activities have no scheduling flexibility. The critical path is defined by the critical activities A-C-E-I-J. As shown in Figure 16.7, the critical path represents the unbroken line of activities from beginning to end

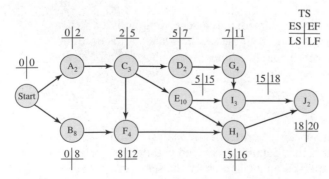

FIGURE 16.5 PERT chart for tennis tournament with early time calculations.

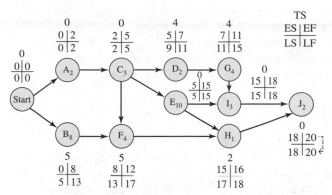

FIGURE 16.6 Completed critical path analysis for tennis tournament.

of the project. Any delay in activities on this path will delay the completion of the project beyond the 20 days.

Figure 16.7 is a modified activity-on-arrow PERT chart (recall Figure 16.3), without dummy arrows, on which each activity is plotted with an arrow equal to its duration in days and scheduled to begin at its early start date. The dotted lines following activities G, F, and H represent slack on noncritical paths. This figure provides a visual picture of a project schedule. For example, activity G has 4 days of total slack. The start of this activity can be delayed, or its duration may take longer than expected, up to a total of 4 days without affecting the project completion time. Note that the 5 days of total slack for activities B and F include the 2 days of total slack of activity H. Thus, if used to its maximum limit, total slack for an activity can drive a following activity to

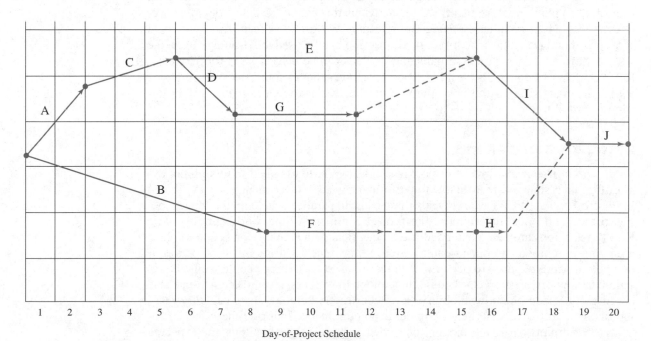

Day-of-Project Schedule

FIGURE 16.7 PERT early start schedule for tennis tournament.

become critical. For example, if the start of activity F were delayed 5 days until the beginning of day 14, then activity H must be accomplished on day 18 with no slack available. Activity F could be delayed 3 days, however, without affecting the *ES* of the following activity (i.e., H). The length of the dotted lines immediately following activities F, G, and H represent what is called *free slack,* because these delays have no effect on the early start of following activities.

Microsoft Project for Windows Analysis

The tennis tournament also can be analyzed using the software program Microsoft Project for Windows. Data are entered using the Gantt chart format shown in Figure 16.8, and a calendar is included noting the dates and days in the week. Each activity's duration and precedence relationship are entered, creating an early start schedule after the last activity has been entered. The critical path is identified by the cross-hatched bars of the critical activities on the Gantt chart. Note these critical activities are bars that begin immediately after each other and, together, add up to the 20-day project duration, excluding weekend days (i.e., Saturday and Sunday) because, in this example, no work is accomplished on the weekend. The program does not break the bar of an activity for the weekend, however, and continues uninterrupted from Friday to the following Monday (see activities 2 and 5).

A Microsoft Project for Windows PERT chart is shown in Figure 16.9. The critical path is shown with darkened boxes and heavy arrows. Corresponding to the Gantt chart, the scheduled start (i.e., beginning of day) and scheduled finish (i.e., end of day) dates are noted for each activity under the activity ID number. The days of duration for each activity also are noted. For example, the first activity, "Negotiate for Location," which requires 2 days to accomplish, begins at the start of day 1/11/95 and finishes at the end of day 1/12/95.

Of what value is the information provided by critical path analysis? First, we know which activities likely will determine the project completion time if everything goes according to plan. We have identified the activities that cannot be delayed and, consequently, require more intense managerial attention. We also have identified noncritical activities that have some scheduling flexibility and can be used to advantage (e.g., the 4 slack days needed to purchase balls and trophies can be used to shop for bargains). Related to this, of course, is the allocation of resources. For example, workers might be shifted from activities with slack time to critical activities to reduce the risk of a project overrun or to make up for delays.

RESOURCE CONSTRAINTS

To this point in our analysis of project networks, we have assumed (although not explicitly) that resources are available to perform many activities concurrently. As shown in Figure 16.9, our PERT chart reveals three paths in parallel, with only the longest being critical and, thus, determining the project completion time. For example, while RSVP invitations are being extended (i.e., the critical path activity), balls and trophies are being purchased and player contracts are being signed. During this time period, if one person were required to perform each task, then at least three people would be required to support our project schedule. In addition to workers, resource constraints also could include equipment availability (e.g., construction crane), shared facility (e.g., laboratory), and specialists (e.g., computer programmers). Ignoring the effect of resource constraints can result in a project schedule being infeasible; thus, the expected project completion date would be unattainable.

FIGURE 16.8 Microsoft Project for Windows Gantt chart.

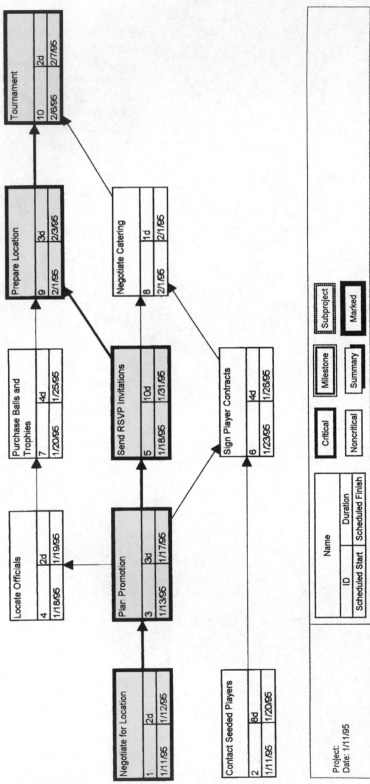

FIGURE 16.9 Microsoft Project for Windows PERT chart.

Returning to the tennis tournament example, an early start Gantt chart is shown in Figure 16.10. An early start schedule is created simply by starting each activity at its early start time (i.e., every line is drawn as far left as possible). In Figure 16.10, the critical path activities are drawn with a heavy line, indicating that the scheduling of these activities cannot be changed if we wish to complete the project in 20 days. The noncritical path activities (i.e., those with slack) are drawn with a light line, indicating that flexibility exists in their schedules. Assuming that one person is required to perform each activity, we have added a "Personnel Required" row at the bottom to indicate the staffing levels for each day in the project. As shown, the scheduled use of resources varies greatly, from one person during the last 4 days to 3 people during the 6th through 11th days.

Using the scheduling flexibility of the noncritical activities, the resource-leveled schedule shown in Figure 16.11 can be created. Note that all the noncritical activities except B have delayed start dates, with activities F and H starting on their late start dates. If only two persons are available to arrange this tournament, however, then the project duration must be extended by 1 day, because our leveled schedule shows that three persons are required on day 14. As might be expected, resource constraints result in stretching out the completion time of a project.

ACTIVITY CRASHING

Construction projects often are undertaken with target completion dates that are important to the client. For example, consider the construction of a student dormitory at a university. If the project is not ready for occupancy by the last week of August, then a serious disruption would occur. At one university, students were housed temporarily in local hotels at the contractor's expense. For this reason, construction contracts often contain clauses to reward early project completion or to penalize a project overrun.

Figure 16.12 shows the costs for a hypothetical project as a function of project duration. As would be expected, the indirect costs of renting equipment, supervision, and insurance increase with project duration. The opportunity cost curve reflects the contractual bonus for early completion (shown as a negative cost) and penalties for overrun. The direct cost of labor is related inversely to project time, because finishing a project in a hurry requires applying more labor than normal to critical path activities to speed up their completion. Adding all these costs results in a convex total cost curve that identifies a minimum-cost project duration from the vantage point of the contractor. Note that the contractor's minimum cost duration may not necessarily coincide with the client's target completion date. Therefore, how could such a discrepancy be resolved?

Example 16.4. Tennis Tournament—Activity Crashing
Although our tennis tournament is not a construction project, we will use it for illustrating the activity crashing analysis because all the preliminary critical path analysis has been done. An activity is considered to be "crashed" when it is completed in less time than is normal by applying additional labor or equipment. For example, using a normal two-person painting crew, the interior of a home can be completed in 4 days; however, a crew of four painters could "crash" the job in 2 days. This information for time and cost of each tennis tournament activity is shown in Table 16.3. The last column of this table contains a calculation called "expedite-cost." Figure 16.13 illustrates the cost-time trade-off for activity E. The slope of the line joining the crash point to the normal point yields the cost per day to expedite the activity assuming a constant rate of

Day-of-project schedule

ID	Activity	Days	1	2	3	4	5	6	7	8	9	10	11	12	13	14	15	16	17	18	19	20
A	Negotiate for location	2																				
B	Contact seeded players	8																				
C	Plan promotion	3																				
D	Locate officials	2																				
E	Send RSVP invitations	10																				
F	Sign player contracts	4																				
G	Purchase balls and trophies	4																				
H	Negotiate catering	1																				
I	Prepare location	3																				
J	Tournament	2																				
	Personnel required		2	2	2	2	2	3	3	3	3	3	3	2	1	1	1	2	1	1	1	1

Critical path activities
Activities with slack

FIGURE 16.10   Early start Gantt chart.

Day-of-project schedule

ID	Activity	Days	1	2	3	4	5	6	7	8	9	10	11	12	13	14	15	16	17	18	19	20
A	Negotiate for location	2	██	██																		
B	Contact seeded players	8	█	█	█	█	█	█	█	█												
C	Plan promotion	3			██	██	██															
D	Locate officials	2									█	█										
E	Send RSVP invitations	10						██	██	██	██	██	██	██	██	██	██					
F	Sign player contracts	4														█	█	█	█			
G	Purchase balls and trophies	4											█	█	█	█						
H	Negotiate catering	1																		█		
I	Prepare location	3																██	██	██		
J	Tournament	2																			██	██
	Personnel required		2	2	2	2	2	2	2	2	2	2	2	2	2	3	2	2	2	2	1	1

██ Critical path activities
— Activities with slack

FIGURE 16.11 Resource-leveled schedule.

FIGURE 16.12 Costs for hypothetical project.

TABLE 16.3

COST-TIME ESTIMATES FOR TENNIS TOURNAMENT

Activity	Time estimate (days)		Direct cost ($)		Expedite-cost slope ($/day)
	Normal	Crash	Normal	Crash	
A	2	1	5	15	10
B	8	6	22	30	4
C	3	2	10	13	3
D	2	1	11	17	6
E	10	6	20	40	5
F	4	3	8	15	7
G	4	3	9	10	1
H	1	1	10	10	—
I	3	2	8	10	2
J	2	1	<u>12</u>	20	8
			115		

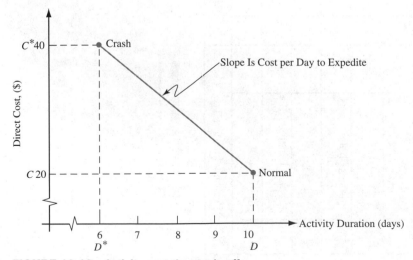

FIGURE 16.13 Activity cost-time trade-off.

cost increase. The values for the expedite-cost slope are calculated using equation (7), which is a ratio of the difference in cost (crash − normal) divided by the difference in duration (normal − crash), yielding an expedite-cost per day.

$$S = \frac{C^* - C}{D - D^*} \tag{7}$$

where C = activity cost (* for crash cost)

D = activity duration (* for crash duration)

In performing the complete analysis that results in a total cost determination for various project durations, schedules for indirect costs and opportunity costs are required. Table 16.4 shows the indirect cost schedule, ranging from \$45 to \$13, and the opportunity costs, ranging from \$8 to −\$8. The analysis begins with the first row showing the normal project duration and costs (the direct cost of 115 came from Table 16.3). The project duration is incrementally reduced 1 day at a time by crashing an activity on the critical path. Using the expedite-cost as a guide, the critical activity with the least expedite-cost is selected (e.g., for the critical path A-C-E-I-J, we find that activity I costs only \$2 to crash 1 day).

Table 16.5 is used to keep track of changes in *all* project paths as we reduce the time of activities on the critical path(s). Note that we have given activity I an asterisk, because it cannot be crashed further (i.e., only 1 day was available) and, thus, is no longer a candidate for crashing. In Table 16.5 under the I* column, we have the revised path durations for the project and find that path A-C-E-I-J, with a duration of 19 days, remains the only critical path. We next turn to activity C to crash for 1 day, followed by crashing activity E for 3 straight days until we create two critical paths of 15 days' duration. With both path A-C-E-I-J and path B-F-H-J being critical, any reduction in project duration must reduce the duration of each path simultaneously. Candidates include selecting activity E on one path and B on the other, at a combined cost of \$9, or selecting activity J, which is common to both paths, at a cost of \$8. As seen in Table 16.5, further crashing involves multiple critical paths. Once the project duration reaches 12 days, it cannot be reduced further in duration, because critical path A-C-E-I-J now contains all activities with an asterisk (i.e., no candidates remain to be crashed). From Table 16.4, however, we see that a project duration of 15 days reaches a minimum total cost. This duration would be acceptable to the client, because a bonus of \$2 is received if the project is completed in 15 days.

TABLE 16.4

TOTAL COST CALCULATIONS

Project duration	Activity crashed	Direct cost $	Indirect cost $	Opportunity cost $	Total cost $
20	Normal	115	45	8	168
19	I*	117	41	6	164
18	C*	120	37	4	161
17	E	125	33	2	160
16	E	130	29	0	159
15	E	135	25	−2	158
14	J*	143	21	−4	160
13	E*, B	152	17	−6	163
12	A*, B*	166	13	−8	171

TABLE 16.5

PROJECT PATH DURATIONS FOLLOWING CRASHING

Project paths	Normal duration	Duration after crashing activity							
		I*	C*	E	E	E	J*	E*, B	A*, B*
A-C-D-G-I-J	16	15	14	14	14	14	13	13	12
A-C-E-I-J	20	19	18	17	16	15	14	13	12
A-C-E-H-J	18	18	17	16	15	14	13	12	11
A-C-F-H-J	12	12	11	11	11	11	10	10	9
B-F-H-J	15	15	15	15	15	15	14	13	12

The crashing procedure can be summarized as

1. Calculate the expedite-cost for each activity using equation (7).
2. List all the paths in the project network and their normal duration.
3. Crash by 1 day the least costly (i.e., minimum expedite-cost) activity on the critical path or the least costly combination of activities on common critical paths. Record the cost of the crashed schedule.
4. Update the duration for each path in the project network.
5. If an activity has reached its crash time, note with an asterisk and do not consider it as a further candidate.
6. If a critical path contains activities all noted with an asterisk, STOP; otherwise, GO to 3.

INCORPORATING UNCERTAINTY IN ACTIVITY TIMES

In Example 16.4, we assumed that activity duration t was a constant. For many situations, however, this assumption is not practical because of the uncertainties involved in carrying out the activities. These durations generally are random variables that have associated probability distributions. Therefore, we do not know in advance the exact durations of all activities; consequently, we cannot determine the exact completion time of the project.

Estimating Activity Duration Distributions

To this point in our analysis, we have assumed that activity durations are known with certainty. However, for projects requiring creativity and experimentation (e.g., staging a Broadway play) or construction projects in adverse locations (e.g., the Alaska crude-oil pipeline), activity durations are random variables. Figure 16.14 shows a typical Beta distribution that is commonly used to describe the duration of uncertain activities. This distribution captures the "skewness" in the distribution of activity duration that is likely to have a mean that is greater than the mode. Further, the Beta distribution can be approximated by simple formulas that require only three critical time estimates:

1. *Optimistic time* (*A*). This is the duration of an activity if no complications or problems occur. As a rule of thumb, there should be about a 1 percent chance of the actual duration being less than *A*.
2. *Most likely time* (*M*). This is the duration that is most likely to occur. In statistical terms, *M* is the modal value.

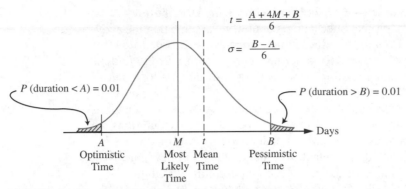

FIGURE 16.14 Beta distribution of activity duration.

3. *Pessimistic time (B).* This is the duration of an activity if extraordinary problems arise. As a rule of thumb, there should be about a 1 percent chance of the actual duration ever exceeding B.

Using these three time estimates, the following formulas can be used to calculate the mean and the variance of each activity distribution. The formula for the mean is a weighted average, with the modal value being given a weight of four:

$$t = (A + 4M + B)/6 \qquad (8)$$

Recall that our definitions of optimistic and pessimistic times stipulate that 98 percent of the distribution should be contained within the range $A - B$. Thus, the standard deviation formula assumes that the optimistic time A and the pessimistic time B are six standard deviations apart.

$$\sigma = (B - A)/6 \qquad (9)$$

The activity variance, which we will use in calculating the project completion time distribution, becomes

$$\sigma^2 = (B - A)^2/36 \qquad (10)$$

Project Completion Time Distribution

Because each activity has a distribution, the project itself will have a completion time distribution that is based on the path of longest duration. The steps involved in the analysis are

1. For every activity, obtain estimates of A, M, and B.
2. Use equation (8) to calculate the expected activity durations, and perform critical path analysis using the expected activity durations t.
3. The expected project completion time T is assumed to be the sum of the expected durations of activities on the critical path.
4. The variance of project completion time σ_T^2 is assumed to be the sum of the variances of activities on the critical path. These variances are calculated by means of equation (10).
5. The project completion time is assumed to be distributed normally.[2]
6. Probabilities regarding project completion time can be determined from standard normal tables. (*See* Appendix A, "Areas of a Standard Normal Distribution.")

Example 16.5. Tennis Tournament—Project Completion Time Distribution

We revisit the tennis tournament project once again, but now we assume that the activity durations are uncertain and obtain the three time estimates as recorded in Table 16.6. Because the tennis facility is booked for other matches, you are asked to find the probability of finishing the tournament within 24 days of initiating negotiations (i.e., of completing the entire project).

The variances and expected activity durations are calculated by means of equations (8) and (10) and are given in Table 16.6. Note that the expected activity durations are identical to the values that were used in the critical path analysis performed in Example 16.3. Thus, the critical path A-C-E-I-J, which was identified earlier in Figure 16.5, will be the focus of our determination of the project completion time distribution.

We would expect the sum of activity durations on this path to take 20 days and, thus, to determine the expected project completion time T. The variance of project completion time is calculated by summing the variances that are associated with the critical activities. This yields

$$\sigma_T^2 = 4/36 + 4/36 + 144/36 + 36/36 + 0 = 188/36 = 5.2$$

We can now use T and σ_T^2 to determine the probability of finishing the project within 24 days. The Z value for the standard normal deviate is calculated using equation (11):

$$Z = \frac{X - \mu}{\sigma} \tag{11}$$

Thus, for the tennis tournament:

$$Z = \frac{X - \mu}{\sigma} = \frac{24 - T}{\sigma_T} = \frac{24 - 20}{\sqrt{5.2}} = 1.75$$

From the standard normal table with $Z = 1.75$, we find the probability of completing the project within 24 days to be approximately 0.96. Figure 16.15 shows the normal distribution of the project completion time with a 0.04 probability of exceeding 24 days' duration.

A Critique of the Project Completion Time Analysis

The key assumption underlying our analysis leading to a project completion time distribution is that the critical path as calculated from expected activity durations will ac-

TABLE 16.6

VARIANCES AND EXPECTED ACTIVITY DURATIONS

Activity	Time estimates A	M	B	Variance, σ^2	Expected duration, t
A	1	2	3	4/36	2
B	5	8	11	36/36	8
C	2	3	4	4/36	3
D	1	2	3	4/36	2
E	6	9	18	144/36	10
F	2	4	6	16/36	4
G	1	3	11	100/36	4
H	1	1	1	0	1
I	2	2	8	36/36	3
J	2	2	2	0	2

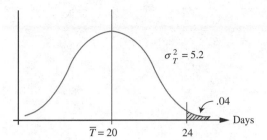

FIGURE 16.15 Project completion time distribution.

tually be the true critical path. This is a critical assumption because it suggests that we know the critical path before all the uncertain activities have been completed. In reality, the critical path itself is a random variable that is not known for certain until the project is completed. We know that the duration of the critical path is uncertain and has a probability distribution associated with it; likewise, the durations of other paths are uncertain. Consequently, it is possible for a path with an expected duration of less than the critical path to become the realized critical path because activities on this path have taken much longer than expected. The net effect is that a path not identified as being critical could determine project completion. Thus, estimates of expected completion time and variance of completion time for the project are biased when they are based only on the single critical path. For the variance, the bias can be either on the high or the low side, but the expected project completion time is always biased optimistically. That is, the true expected completion time is always greater than or equal to the estimate.

A simple guideline can assist in giving a feel for the accuracy of these estimates: if the expected duration of the critical path is much longer than that of any other path, then the estimates likely will be good. In this case, the critical path very likely will actually determine the project completion time. If the project network contains noncritical paths with very little total slack time, however, these paths may well affect project completion time. This situation is called *merge node bias*. That is, the project completion node has several paths coming into it, any one of which could be the critical path that determines the project completion time. In our analysis, only the most likely path is assumed to be critical; thus, our project completion time distribution is biased optimistically because other near critical paths are ignored. Example 16.6 illustrates the effect on the probability of completing a project when a near-critical path contains an activity with a large variance.

Example 16.6. Tennis Tournament—Merge Node Bias

A few days into the project, we discover that the purchase of balls and a trophy (i.e., activity G) may take longer than expected, with revised estimates of $A = 2$, $M = 3$, and $B = 28$. What effect does this have on the probability of completing the project in 24 days?

First, we recalculate the expected duration and variance of activity G using equations (8) and (10) and find that $t = 7$ and $\sigma^2 = 676/36$. Recall from Figure 16.7 that activity G initially had a 4-day expected duration and total slack of 4 days. Thus, with a revised duration of 7 days, activity G still is noncritical, with a $TS = 1$. The large variance of activity G, however, will have an impact on the likelihood of this path A-C-D-G-I-J becoming critical. A completion time distribution can be determined for this near-critical path in the following manner:

Near-critical path	t	σ^2
A	2	4/36
C	3	4/36
D	2	4/36
G	7	676/36
I	3	36/36
J	2	0
	$T = 19$	$\sigma_T^2 = 724/36 = 20$

We now can use T and σ_T^2 of the near-critical path to determine the probability of finishing the project within 24 days. The Z value for the standard normal deviate is calculated using equation (11):

$$Z = \frac{X - \mu}{\sigma} = \frac{24 - T}{\sigma_T} = \frac{24 - 19}{\sqrt{20}} = 1.12$$

Referring to the standard normal table with $Z = 1.12$, we find that the probability of completing the project within 24 days is approximately 0.87. The completion time distribution for this near-critical path is shown in Figure 16.16. Thus, a near-critical path with a high variance activity should not be ignored, because, in fact, such a path may become critical and delay the project completion time. Computer simulation is an approach to determine the project completion time distribution more accurately.[3]

PROBLEMS WITH IMPLEMENTING CRITICAL PATH ANALYSIS

The mechanics of critical path analysis make the use of network models appear to be deceptively simple. After all, the calculations are straightforward. Network analysis does not resolve all the problems inherent in project management, however. Two major concerns are developing the project network and eliciting time estimates for activities.

The project network indicates the sequence in which activities are to be performed. For most projects, several different strategies may be adopted. The technological factors along with the influences of people who are concerned with the project generally determine which strategy is selected. As the project is implemented, the project network is subject to review and possible revision, which may be needed because some activities get off schedule or resources may not be available when needed.

Reviewing and revising the project network can be very time-consuming. The individuals involved with the project must be consulted about anticipated changes. The

FIGURE 16.16 Near-critical path completion time distribution.

process of reviewing and revising the project network is an ongoing process that is made easier with the use of computer software.

The second concern in using network models is eliciting time estimates for activities. Obviously, poor estimates would impact the accuracy of project planning. Resident experts often are sought out for their experience in past projects. It is difficult to get good time estimates, however, because people disagree and consensus may be difficult to achieve.

Another problem is that of bias introduced into estimates of activity durations. For example, an individual actually may expect to carry out an activity in 8 days but gives an estimate of 10 days. Thus, the individual provides a few days' leeway by padding the estimate. To avoid these problems, a database of actual times on past projects could be developed to provide time estimates for common activities. For example, painting the walls of a room could be estimated based on the time per square foot from past experience.

MONITORING PROJECTS

Dealing with uncertainty is the hallmark of project management. The original plans and expectations are seldom realized, because projects often are pioneering endeavors. Monitoring progress against plans is an important activity for the project manager because early detection of problems can lead to corrections in time to avoid failure. Table 16.7 contains examples of unexpected problems in the areas of cost, time, and performance.

Earned Value Chart

Project management tools, such as the project network diagram, are designed to be visual in nature, because they quickly can communicate project status to clients and team members. The earned value chart shown in Figure 16.17 is an effective method of visualizing the project status regarding the objectives of time and costs. The solid line represents the scheduled cost expenditures (i.e., baseline) as a function of time. The dashed actual cost line in this example is drawn above the planned cost expenditure line to illustrate a project that is exceeding cost estimates for work accomplished. The thin solid line below the planned cost expenditure line represents the value of work completed.

TABLE 16.7

SOURCES OF UNEXPECTED PROBLEMS

Cost	Time	Performance
• Difficulties require more resources	• There were delays owing to technical difficulties	• Unexpected technical problems arise
• Scope of work increases	• Initial time estimates were optimistic	• Insufficient resources are available
• Initial bids or estimates were too low	• Task sequencing was incorrect	• Insurmountable technical difficulties occur
• Reporting was poor or untimely	• Required resources were not available as needed	• Quality or reliability problems occur
• Budgeting was inadequate	• Necessary preceding tasks were incomplete	• Client requires changes in specifications
• Corrective control was not exercised in time	• There were client-generated changes	• Complications arise with functional areas
• There were price changes of inputs	• There were unforeseen government regulations	• A technological breakthrough occurs

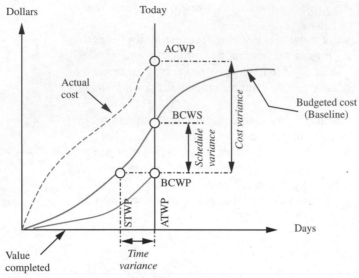

FIGURE 16.17 Earned value chart.

Three sources of variance are shown on the earned value chart: time, cost, and schedule. Because this project is running over budget and behind schedule, all three variances are negative. Note that negative variances indicate problems that need immediate attention. When using project management software like Microsoft Project to monitor project progress, the earned value report is generated automatically. The variances are defined as

Time variance = STWP−ATWP
    STWP = Scheduled time for work performed
    ATWP = Actual time used for work performed

Cost variance = BCWP−ACWP
    BCWP = Budgeted cost for work performed
    ACWP = Actual cost of work performed

Schedule variance = BCWP−BCWS
    BCWP = Budgeted cost of work performed
    BCWS = Budgeted cost of work scheduled to be performed to date

Project Termination

All projects are not successful and termination can occur in several ways. Upon completion of a project, however, the preparation of a project history report can become a learning document for improvement in managing future projects. Methods of project termination include

Extinction: Successfully completed or killed.

Addition: Successful project becomes institutionalized as part of parent organization.

Integration: Successful project is dismantled and distributed throughout parent organization.

Starvation: Slow death by budget cuts.

Project History Report

The project history report documents the project experience and provides opportunities to learn from mistakes and success. A history report should include

Project performance: Comparison of proposal with termination evaluation.

Administrative performance: Comments on effective and ineffective practices.

Organizational structure: How good was it?

Project and administrative teams: Confidential assessment of team members.

Techniques of project management: Seek recommendations for improvement.

SUMMARY

Managers of organizations typically are immersed in the detailed operations of ongoing projects. They also are responsible for generating new projects. The vitality of an organization can be seen in the way projects are conceived and carried out. For dynamic organizations, project management has important dimensions that involve planning, scheduling, and controlling the activities necessary to carry out a project successfully.

For small uncomplicated projects, Gantt charts are useful for assisting project managers. But for large projects that involve many interdependent activities, Gantt charts are cumbersome. Network techniques, such as CPM and PERT, were developed as tools for aiding managers of complex projects. Most network techniques use a similar methodology known as critical path analysis. PERT specifically addresses the problem of uncertain activity duration. It allows the manager to make probability statements with regard to meeting project objectives.

Network techniques are very important tools for project management. They indicate the activities that are likely to affect project completion. They also facilitate the evaluation of changes in project implementation. Furthermore, advances are being made with regard to the accuracy and efficiency of network approaches. These advances, in conjunction with the availability of faster and cheaper computer resources, will make network techniques even more valuable to service operations managers.

KEY TERMS AND DEFINITIONS

Calendars specifications of the days and hours that resources such as people and equipment are available for work.

Critical activities activities on the critical path that, if delayed, would result in the delay of the project as a whole.

Critical path the sequence of activities in a project that has the longest duration, thus defining the project completion time.

Critical path method (CPM) the process for determining the start and finish dates for individual activities, thus creating the *critical path* for the project.

Gantt chart a graphical representation of the project schedule containing horizontal bars for each activity with the length of the bars corresponding to the duration of the activity.

PERT chart a graphical representation of the relationship between activities using arrows to show precedence and nodes for activity descriptions.

Predecessor an activity that must precede another activity.

Project a collection of related activities or steps that are performed in a specified sequence for the purpose of meeting a defined, nonroutine goal.

Successor an activity that follows another activity.

Work breakdown structure a family-tree subdivision of the effort that is required to achieve the project objective.

BOX 16.1

Service Benchmark
PROJECT MANAGEMENT SOFTWARE IN USE

The project manager's job has been made easier with the use of computer software that goes beyond the planning and scheduling of activities, as illustrated by Microsoft Project for Windows, to the motivation and management of people. In the effort of getting a project finished on time, many managers are so consumed in daily tasks that they may forget to manage the project employees. A new software program called Managepro for Windows does just that. It reminds the executive that there are important management issues that go beyond deadlines.

"In today's corporation you see a rapidly expanding scope of management, or span of control, and the result is that you wind up with a manager being responsible for more and more people," said Kerry N. Diehl, a general manager at a large Eastern electric utility that he asked not be named. "Unless you can come up with a good tool or mechanism for controlling and delegating projects and activities, you end up spending more time trying to figure out what you gave to whom than you do actually managing."

For Mr. Diehl, that tool is Managepro for Windows, which pairs people management with project management. A dash of philosophy and psychology, in the form of an expert system that offers online advice, is tossed in for good measure. The combination is powerful and effective. Managepro for Windows should not be confused with simpler project management software, which helps executives set goals and timetables for a given work activity. And indeed it can be quite helpful at planning most common business tasks.

But Managepro for Windows prefers to call itself a new type of software: goal and people management. That reflects how it works: separate but integrated sets of operations, one for goals and one for people. As a manager, you set the goal and assign tasks toward reaching that goal to various people. You want to know how the project is going, and that means keeping track of how the people are doing.

"I use it to track projects, due dates, and the people who are responsible," said Stacey Richardson, manager of management information systems at the Ridge Tahoe, a time-sharing condominium resort in South Lake Tahoe, Nevada. "And then you can get your reports out either on project information, showing progress on all the steps, or a completely different view, showing all the steps that have to be taken by a given individual."

The goals part of the software helps managers define, as specifically as possible, the broad company goals. Examples might be to reduce shipping errors to less than 1 percent by June 15, or to double sales in Minnesota by the end of the year. The goals are listed on a scoreboard similar to a spreadsheet showing for each one a description of the deadline, the person or teams responsible for achieving the goal, and an indicator for how the project is going—whether it is on track, behind schedule, or critical.

The goals are listed in what is commonly known as a collapsed outline form. If the manager wants more information—Why is our shipping project behind schedule?—she clicks on that item to reveal greater levels of detail: Aha! Linda in the shipping department was going to report by April 1 on alternative shipping services. She's behind schedule.

Now the manager can shift to the people dimension—finding out, for example, whether Linda has a pattern of missing deadlines and might benefit from more oversight of interim progress. A series of buttons on screen can be clicked to summon information for each employee: goals, progress, feedback, review, recognition, development, commitment, calendar, details, and notes. The information is kept confidential with a simple password protection scheme.

"It's a manager's dream come true," said Randy Dugger, who manages work station local area network support for Tandem Computers Inc. of Cupertino, California. "Before Managepro, you typically had to write down all this information in some word processing file, and you'd print it out and put the paper in the employee's file," he said. "It was all paper tracking, searching through files to find the right piece of information. With Managepro, everything concerning your project is two or three clicks away. "I keep track of everything concerning my employees, the good messages as well as the bad, as well as counseling sessions. Everything is fully documented. I can print out a report and use it during the employee review process."

BOX 16.1 (CONTINUED)

Another button on screen, the supervisor, offers experts' wisdom on human relations management. How does a manager help nurture and develop the skills of workers? How does she become a more effective manager? How do managers deal with workers who are not doing their assigned jobs, or those who do the jobs but wreak havoc along the way?

The Managepro adviser notes that some employees are like war canoes, getting from point A to point B swiftly and without a ripple. Others are like garbage scows: They get there eventually, but they are noisy and smelly and leave an oil slick. "The people in Department X tell me they don't ever want to work with you again because of your aggressive behavior," the adviser says as an example of how to pilot a garbage scow. "Fix that relationship in the 60 days left in this project so that they tell me they look forward to working with you again."

Managepro also may remind the manager that it's time to reward a promising employee with a pair of tickets to a ballgame or dinner for two.

"It does come with what is basically a human resources philosophy behind it," said Mr. Diehl, the utility manager. "By taking the broader look, not just being a task manager but addressing the ideas of employee evaluation and the issues of compensation and recognition, it provides a much-needed dimension to project management. It's not that people don't think of it, but the software helps as a reminder."

Mr. Dugger of Tandem said: "I wouldn't say that it has changed my management style. It's just made my job a lot easier. The nice thing is that you can use as much or as little of it as you want. It doesn't force you to use the whole thing all at once. You can grow into it."

Source: Adapted from Peter H. Lewis, "Pairing People Management with Project Management," *New York Times,* April 11, 1993, p. 12.

SOLVED PROBLEMS

1. Critical Path Analysis

Problem Statement

You have been asked to head a special project team at McDonald's to bring out a new breakfast item called the McWaffle. You have prepared the network diagram below showing the necessary activities with their expected times in days. Calculate the scheduling times *ES*, *LS*, *EF*, and *LF*, and slack time *TS* for each activity. What are the critical path and project duration?

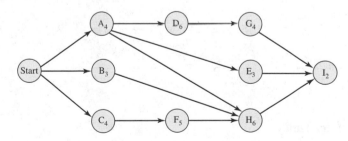

Solution

Activity	Time	Forward pass		Backward pass		TS = LS − ES
		ES	EF	LF	LS	
A	4	0	4	5	1	1
B	3	0	3	9	6	6
C	4	0	4	4	0	0
D	6	4	10	11	5	1
E	3	4	7	15	12	8
F	5	4	9	9	4	0
G	4	10	14	15	11	1
H	6	9	15	15	9	0
I	2	15	17	17	15	0

The critical path activities are C, F, H, and I, because *TS* = 0 in each case. The project duration is 17 days, the sum of the critical path activity times.

2. Activity Crashing

Problem Statement

For the network above, assume that an activity's daily expedite-cost in dollars per day is equal to the activity's time (e.g., the cost to reduce the activity time of H by one day is $6). Further, assume that each activity may be crashed only 1 day. What activities should be crashed to reduce the project duration by 3 days at least cost?

Solution

In the table below, the circled numbers represent the project duration, starting with 17 days. After activity C is crashed, two paths become critical; thus, two activities must be crashed (one on each path) to achieve a 14-day project duration.

Project path	Normal time	Activities crashed		
		I	C	F&A or F&G
A-D-G-I	16	15	(15)	(14)
A-E-I	9	8	8	8 or 7
A-H-I	12	11	11	11 or 10
B-H-I	11	10	10	10
C-F-H-I	(17)	(16)	(15)	(14)

3. Incorporating Uncertainty in Activity Times

Problem Statement

Assume the McWaffle project above contained some uncertain activity times as shown below. Calculate the mean and variance of all activities, and determine the probability of completing the project within 20 days without crashing any activities.

Solution

First, calculate the mean and variance for each activity using equations (8) and (10):

Activity	A	M	B	Mean	Variance
A	3	4	5	4	4/36
B	3	3	3	3	0
C	3	4	5	4	4/36
D	4	6	8	6	16/36
E	2	3	4	3	4/36
F	2	4	12	5	100/36
G	3	4	5	4	4/36
H	4	5	12	6	64/36
I	2	2	2	2	0

Second, determine the critical path. This calculation yields activity means that are identical to those of the original problem statement. Thus, the critical path is C-F-H-I, with an expected time of $T = 17$ days. The variance of the project completion time is the sum of the critical activity variances. This yields $\sigma_T^2 = 4/36 + 100/36 + 64/36 + 0 = 168/36 = 4.67$. Using equation (11), we calculate the Z value for a project completion within 20 days:

$$Z = \frac{X - \mu}{\sigma} = \frac{20 - T}{\sigma_T} = \frac{20 - 17}{\sqrt{4.67}} = 1.39$$

Using Appendix A, "Areas of a Standard Normal Distribution," we find a probability of $0.5 + 0.4177 = 0.9177$, or approximately a 92-percent chance of competing the project within 20 days.

TOPICS FOR DISCUSSION

1. Give an example that demonstrates the trade-off inherent in projects among cost, time, and performance.
2. Illustrate the four stages of team building from your own experience.
3. Are Gantt charts still viable project management tools? Explain.
4. Explain why the PERT estimate of expected project duration is always optimistic. Can we get any feel for the magnitude of the bias?
5. What purpose does a project history report serve?
6. Discuss the differences among time variance, cost variance, and schedule variance.

EXERCISES

16.1. An electric utility is planning its annual project of shutting down one of its steam boilers for maintenance and repair. An analysis of this project has identified the following principal activities and their expected times and relationships.

Activity	Time, days	Immediate predecessor
A	4	—
B	3	—
C	4	—
D	6	A
E	3	A
F	5	C
G	4	D
H	6	A,B,F
I	2	E,G,H

a. Prepare a project network diagram.

b. Calculate the scheduling times and total slack for each activity.

c. List the critical path activities and project duration.

d. Assuming that one worker is required for each activity, prepare a resource-leveled schedule. What is the maximum number of workers required to finish the project on time?

16.2. A consulting firm is planning a reengineering project for a client. The following activities and time estimates have been identified:

Activity	Time, days	Immediate predecessor
A	1	—
B	2	—
C	2	—
D	2	A,B
E	4	A,C
F	1	C
G	4	D
H	8	G,E,F

a. Draw a project network diagram.

b. Calculate the scheduling times and total slack for each activity.

c. List the critical path activities and project duration.

d. Assuming that one worker is required for each activity, prepare a resource-leveled schedule. What is the maximum number of workers required to finish the project on time?

16.3. Slippery Rock College is planning a basketball tournament. The following information has been collected on each activity in the project:

Activity	Time, days	Immediate predecessor	Description
A	3	—	Select teams
B	5	A	Mail out invitations
C	10	—	Arrange accommodations
D	3	B,C	Plan promotion
E	5	B,C	Print tickets
F	10	E	Sell tickets
G	8	C	Complete arrangements
H	3	G	Develop schedules
I	2	D,H	Practice
J	3	F,I	Conduct tournament

a. Draw a network diagram of this project, and label the activities and events.

b. Calculate the total slack and scheduling times for all activities. What is the critical path?

c. When should team selection begin if the tournament is scheduled to start on the morning of December 27? (Include Saturday and Sunday as working days.)

16.4. A simple network consisting of four activities has the following network diagram:

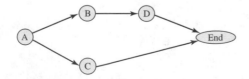

The cost/time relationships for the activities are

Activity	Minimum time, weeks	Maximum time, weeks	Cost/time relationship ($1000)
A	5	10	100 − (3 × activity time)
B	5	10	100 − (2 × activity time)
C	10	30	100 − (2 × activity time)
D	10	15	100 − (5 × activity time)

For example, if completed in 5 weeks, activity A would require $85,000, and if completed in 10 weeks, it would require $70,000.

a. What would be the minimum cost of completing this project in 20 weeks?

b. If the desired completion date is 33 weeks and the profit markup is 20 percent above cost, what should be the bid price for this project?

16.5. The following project network and table provide the normal times and costs as well as the crash times and costs for the activities required to complete a project. Crash the completion time to the minimum level.

Activity	Normal time, weeks	Cost	Crash time, weeks	Cost
A	4	$2500	2	$6000
B	5	4000	4	5000
C	2	3000	1	5000
D	2	2000	1	3000
E	6	3000	4	4000
F	3	2000	1	5000
G	1	2000	1	2000

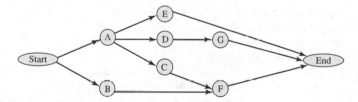

16.6. A construction firm has been commissioned to renew a portion of the Alaska crude-oil pipeline that has fallen into a state of disrepair. The project activities with the estimated times and their relationships are

Activity	Code	Time, days	Immediate predecessor
Assemble crew for job	A	10	—
Build inventory with old line	B	28	—
Measure and sketch old line	C	2	A
Develop materials list	D	1	C
Erect scaffolding	E	2	D
Procure pipe	F	30	D
Procure valves	G	45	D
Deactivate old line	H	1	B,D
Remove old line	I	6	E,H
Prefabricate new line	J	5	F
Place valves	K	1	E,G,H
Place new pipe	L	6	I,J
Weld pipe	M	2	L
Connect valves	N	1	K,M
Insulate	O	4	K,M
Pressure test	P	1	N
Remove scaffolding	Q	1	N,O
Clean up	R	1	P,Q

a. Prepare a project network.
b. List the critical path activities and the expected project duration.
c. Determine the scheduling times and total slack for all activities.
d. In the contract, a bonus of $100,000 per day will be paid for each day the project is completed earlier than its expected duration. Evaluate the following alternatives to shorten the project duration and then make a recommendation:
  1. Crash activity B by 4 days at a cost of $100,000.
  2. Crash activity G by 1 day at a cost of $50,000.
  3. Crash activity O by 2 days at a cost of $150,000.
  4. Crash activity O by 2 days by drawing resources from activity N, thereby extending the time of N by 2 days.

16.7. The following activities have been identified by a consulting firm that is developing an information system for an insurance firm to make a transition to a "paperless" organization:

		Activity duration, months		
Activity	Immediate predecessor	Optimistic	Most likely	Pessimistic
A	—	4	6	8
B	—	1	2	3
C	A	4	4	4
D	A	4	5	6
E	B	7	10	16
F	B	8	9	10
G	C	2	2	2
H	D,E,G	2	3	7
I	F	1	3	11

a. Draw the project network showing the activities with their expected times.
b. What is the critical path and the expected duration of the project?
c. What is the probability of completing the project within 2 years?

16.8. The following activities are required for completing a project:

		Activity duration, days		
Activity	Immediate predecessor	Optimistic	Most likely	Pessimistic
A	—	3	6	15
B	—	2	5	14
C	A	6	12	30
D	A	2	5	8
E	C	5	11	17
F	D	3	6	15
G	B	3	9	27
H	E,F	1	4	7
I	G	4	19	28
J	H,I	1	1	1

a. Draw a network diagram of this project showing the activities and their expected duration times.
b. What is the critical path and the expected completion time of the project?
c. What is the probability of completing the project in 41 days or less?

16.9. The project network and table below show the expected number of weeks to complete a series of activities and the corresponding variances:

Activity	Expected duration, weeks	Variance, weeks
A	5	1
B	10	2
C	4	1
D	7	1
E	6	2
F	8	1
G	4	2
H	3	1
I	5	1
J	7	2
K	8	3

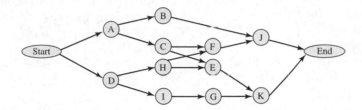

    a. Determine the critical path and the earliest expected completion time.

    b. What is the probability of completing the project in 24 weeks or less?

16.10. You have been asked to plan the following covert operation for the AIC:

Activity	Immediate predecessor	Activity duration, days		
		Optimistic	**Most likely**	**Pessimistic**
A	—	1	2	3
B	A	3	3	3
C	B	4	6	8
D	A	2	8	8
E	A	6	9	12
F	D,C	4	7	10
G	D	10	10	16
H	D,E	4	5	6
I	F,G,H	2	2	2

    a. Draw a network diagram for this project.

    b. Calculate the expected time and variance for each activity.

    c. Determine the critical path and the expected project completion time.

    d. What is the probability of the project taking more than 25 days to complete?

Info-Systems, Inc.

Info-Systems is a rapidly growing firm that specializes in information systems consulting. In the past, its projects have been relatively short term and not required extensive project scheduling or close management surveillance. Recently, however, Info-Systems was awarded a contract to develop and implement a large inventory system for a manufacturing firm.

During the initial proposal study, Info-Systems determined that the manufacturing firm's current hardware configuration was inadequate to meet its long-term needs, and new general hardware specifications were developed. Therefore, as part of its assignment, Info-Systems is to perform a vendor evaluation and selection for this new hardware. The initial study also proposed that the system would comprise a combination of batch and online processing and estimated a minimum of 1 year for completion.

Info-Systems plans to divide the project into four major areas involving the activities to support: (1) hardware selection and installation, (2) batch processing development, (3) online processing development, and (4) conversion from the old system to the new one. Further, it feels the use of a project management system would be very beneficial in providing a more definitive estimate of the probable project completion, in controlling the project once it is under way, and in assigning personnel to the project at the appropriate times. Therefore, Info-Systems has assigned several of its senior staff to develop a detailed task list, which is presented below:

Tasks		Work duration, days	Immediate predecessor
A.	Evaluate and select hardware.	30	—
B.	Develop batch processing system requirements (e.g., data definition, transaction volume).	60	—
C.	Develop online processing requirements (e.g., volume response times).	40	—
D.	Define specific hardware requirements; order and receive	100	A,B,C
E.	Design report layouts for batch system.	30	B
F.	Design input forms for batch system.	20	E
G.	Design screen layouts for online system.	25	C
H.	Design file layouts.	20	F,G
I.	Prepare program specifications for *daily* batch cycle.	30	H
J.	Prepare program specifications for *weekly* batch cycle.	20	H
K.	Prepare program specifications for *monthly* batch cycle.	15	H
L.	Prepare program specifications for online processing.	20	H
M.	Install and test new hardware.	15	D
N.	Code programs for *daily* batch cycle.	20	I
O.	Code programs for *weekly* batch cycle.	15	J
P.	Code programs for *monthly* batch cycle.	10	K
Q.	Code programs for online cycle.	18	L
R.	Document batch system.	35	I,J,K
S.	Document online system.	25	L
T.	Test *daily* cycle.	20	M,N
U.	Test *weekly* cycle.	15	M,O
V.	Test *monthly* cycle.	12	M,P
W.	Test online processing.	15	M,Q
X.	Test total system.	20	T,U,V,W
Y.	Design conversion requirements, programs, and files.	30	H
Z.	Prepare conversion programs.	20	Y
AA.	Test conversion programs.	15	Z
BB.	Run actual conversion.	3	X,AA
CC.	Operate system in parallel and train users.	60	R,S,BB
DD.	Gain user acceptance.	5	CC
EE.	Implement production system.	5	DD

Questions

1. Using Microsoft Project for Windows, prepare a network and identify the critical path activities, the expected project duration, and scheduling times for all activities.
2. The elapsed time for delivery of the hardware is estimated at 90 days. Would the project completion time be affected if delivery of the hardware were delayed by 30 days? Would the critical path change?
3. Using the original network and critical path, what strategies could management consider to complete the project on time if activity B were delayed by several weeks?

Whittier County Hospital

After some 50 years at its present location, Whittier County Hospital is preparing to move into a new building sometime in the near future, when construction and outfitting are completed. The hospital's board of directors has appointed a special management committee to control the entire procedure, including coordination with outside agencies as well as internal departments. As a first step in its mission, the committee wishes to develop a base of information that will be used to (1) establish an initial sketch plan for proceeding through the detailed planning and moving phases and (2) provide a fundamental management and scheduling tool for day-to-day operations during the transition period.

The management staff believes that a PERT analysis of a sketch plan would be very helpful to the committee's understanding of the moving process, so it begins to develop a network of activities and duration estimates for the task. After consultation with the general contractor at the building site, it is estimated that completion of construction and checking the newly installed equipment likely will take 50 more days, with 40 and 60 days being the optimistic and pessimistic estimates, respectively. At this point the structure will be vacated by the contractor and turned over to the board.

Before this occurs, however, a detailed plan of action for each hospital department must be drawn up for approval by the Move Committee (as it is formally known). The staff estimates this will take at least 10 days, perhaps as many as 20 days, and most likely 15 days to develop and secure approval.

Once the detailed plan has received an initial go-ahead, the staff will have a number of activities to perform before a trial run and subsequent evaluation of the plan are made:

1. Develop and distribute an information newsletter to all hospital employees outlining the general procedures, with specific procedures attached for each department; it is estimated that this will take at least 3, probably 4, and at most, 7 days.
2. Develop information and generate media coverage for the upcoming events; this is estimated to take at least (and probably) 2 days, and 3 days at most.
3. Negotiate with local EMS and private ambulance services for transferring the patients; this is estimated to take at least 10, probably 14, and at most, 20 days.
4. Negotiate with professional moving companies for transferring equipment, records, and supplies; this is estimated to take at least 4, probably 5, and at most, 8 days.
5. Coordinate the procedures with, and determine the responsibilities of, the local police and fire departments; this is estimated to take at least 3, probably 5, and at most, 10 days.
6. Coordinate the admissions and exchange procedures during the transition period with other hospitals in the surrounding area; this is estimated to take at least 2, probably 3, and at most, 5 days.

Once the construction and equipment checkout is completed, the new facility must be cleaned thoroughly by hospital staff before the actual move so that it will conform to the required levels for such institutions. Also, after the contractor vacates the premises, the employees can be oriented to the layout and workings of the new building. Because this orientation process is very important, the management staff wants to ensure that it begins after the newsletter is distributed and that it is completed before the trial run of the move. The staff estimates that cleaning and orientation can occur at the same time without problems. Cleaning will take at least 2, probably 3, and at most, 5 days; the employee orientation will take at least 4, probably 5, and at most, 7 days.

Although the actual trial run will take only 1 day, the entire activity, including evaluation, is estimated to need at least (and most likely) 3 days, with 5 days at most if serious problems are encountered. Once this step is finished, coordination of final plans and schedules with the patient and equipment carriers, local agencies, and area hospitals should take 2 days (3 at most). Finally, the completed schedules and procedures will be discussed in each department throughout the hospital on the day before moving day, and this discussion is expected to run the entire day because of the normal work schedules and tasks that all employees will be maintaining.

For the moving day, the staff has broken the entire process into seven different activities for the sketch plan:

	Activity duration, days		
Activity	**Optimistic**	**Most likely**	**Pessimistic**
Administration, accounting, and business office	0.25	0.5	1.0
Library and medical/personnel records	0.25	0.5	0.75
Laboratory and purchasing/stores	0.3	0.8	1.0
Housekeeping and food services	0.5	0.75	1.3
Other equipment and supplies that must move same day as patients	0.8	1.0	1.2
Patients	0.4	1.0	1.0
Other equipment and supplies (noncritical) that will be moved after patients	1.0	2.0	2.5

The staff feel confident that basic operations will be fully under way at the new location once the first six activities are complete, and this is the critical goal established by the hospital's board of directors. The new location, of course, will not be fully operational until the remaining, noncritical equipment and supplies are moved.

Questions

1. Assume that you are part of the management staff whose task is to develop this sketch plan. Using Microsoft Project for Windows, develop the PERT network as outlined above, identify the critical path, and determine the expected time to reach basic operational status at the new facility.

2. The board of directors has said that it would like to try to move on a Sunday to minimize interference with weekday traffic. If there are Sundays that fall 46, 53, 60, 67, and 74 days from now, determine the probability (using a normal distribution) of reaching basic operational status at the new location on the two Sundays that are closest to the expected time you calculated previously.

3. Briefly assess the potential problems you see in applying critical path analysis to the sketch plan for moving Whittier County Hospital.

SELECTED BIBLIOGRAPHY

BRANCH, M. A.: "Where Do Wal-Marts Come From?" *Progressive Architecture,* vol. 9, 1993, pp. 66–69.

BRASSARD, MICHAEL, and DIANE RITTER: *The Memory Jogger II,* GOAL/QPC, Methuen, Mass., 1994.

CLELAND, DAVID I.: "The Age of Project Management," *Project Management Journal,* vol. 22, no. 1, March 1991, pp. 19–24.

FERSKO-WEISS, HENRY,: "Project Management Software Gets a Grip on Usability," *PC Magazine,* July 1992, pp. 323–369.

GOLDRATT, ELIYAHU M.: *Critical Chain,* The North River Press, Great Barrington, Mass., 1997.

GRAY, CLIFFORD F., and ERIK W. LARSON: *Project Management,* Irwin/McGraw-Hill, Burr Ridge, IL, 2000.

KATZENBACH, JON R., and DOUGLAS K. SMITH, *The Wisdom of Teams,* HarperBusiness, New York, 1994.

LIENTZ, BENNET P., and KATHRYN P. REA: *Project Management for the 21st Century,* Academic Press, San Diego, Calif., 1995.

MEREDITH, JACK R., and SAMUEL J. MANTEL JR.: *Project Management,* 3rd ed., Wiley, New York, 1995.

RANDOLPH, W. A., and BARRY Z. POSNER: "What Every Manager Needs to Know about Project Management," *Sloan Management Review,* Summer 1988, pp. 65–73.

ENDNOTES

1. B. W. Tuckman, "Developmental Sequence in Small Groups," *Psychological Bulletin,* vol. 63, 1965, pp. 384–399.
2. This assumption is based on the Central Limit Theorem from statistics, which states that the sum of many independent random variables is a random variable that tends to be distributed normally. In this case, the project completion time is the sum of the individual durations of activities on the critical path.
3. R. M. Van Slyke, "Monte Carlo Methods and the PERT Problem," *Operations Research,* vol. 11, no. 5, September–October 1963, pp. 839–860.

CHAPTER SEVENTEEN

Linear Programming Applications in Services

Learning Objectives

After completing this chapter, you should be able to:

1. Describe the features of constrained optimization models.
2. Formulate linear programming models for computer solution.
3. Use graphics to solve a two-variable linear programming model, and explain the nature of sensitivity analysis.
4. Use Excel Solver to solve a linear programming model, and interpret the results, including the sensitivity analysis.
5. Formulate a goal programming model and interpret the solution.

Linear programming (LP) is a general computer-based modeling tool for making resource allocation decisions that transcend all aspects of service operations management. Linear programming is not computer programming; it refers to planning that uses mathematical models consisting of linear expressions.

A model is a selective abstraction of reality. Modeling is an art, because judgments are made when selecting the important features of reality for the problem at hand. Modeling also is a science, however, because data are collected to measure the relationship between decision variables, objectives desired, and resources available. The process of identifying decision variables and clarifying objectives imposes a discipline that is useful in itself.

Use of models such as LP springs from a belief that the decision-making process can be enhanced by applying the scientific method. Scientists study nature and conduct controlled experiments to understand better the phenomena of interest. Decision models are the laboratory of managers who are interested in testing the outcomes of decisions before their actual implementation. In this way, potential disasters may be avoided, and the decision-making process may be improved through a better understanding of the environment.

CHAPTER PREVIEW

This chapter emphasizes the art of formulating LP models and interpreting computer output. The mathematical details involved in solving an LP model are not discussed. The availability of computer programs to solve such models is extensive, and users need not be concerned about the mechanics of how optimal solutions are found any more than one need know the theory of the internal combustion engine to drive an automobile. The chapter concludes with a discussion of an extension of LP called goal programming, which is useful when one is dealing with the multiple objectives that often are present in service decision making. We begin by discussing the concept of an optimum solution to a constrained model.

CONSTRAINED OPTIMIZATION MODELS

Each day, we are faced with making decisions in which our potential set of alternatives is restricted by money, time, physical limitations, or some other element. For example, suppose we wish to buy a car, we can qualify for a $10,000 loan, and we want a vehicle with an EPA rating of at least 30 miles per gallon. The set of possible cars is constrained by time, budget, and mileage performance. These constraints are restrictions that reduce the allowable set of solutions to our problem. Thus, constraints actually help us to make decisions by limiting our search for a solution to cars that meet the stipulated requirements.

If economy were our goal, we could measure this by calculating the cost per mile for each car that meets our constraints. The car with the lowest cost-per-mile value would be considered the optimum solution to our constrained decision problem.

Constrained optimization problems are common to service operations. For example, a potential location for a service facility is constrained by the available sites. Scheduling telephone operators is constrained by variations in demand for the service and by the personnel policies regarding split shifts.

Linear programming models are a special class of constrained optimization models. In LP, all relationships are expressed as linear functions, and all LP models have the following algebraic form:

Maximize (or minimize)
$$c_1 x_1 + c_2 x_2 + \cdots + c_n x_n$$

subject to
$$a_{11} x_1 + a_{12} x_2 + \cdots + a_{1n} x_n \begin{cases} \leq \\ = \\ \geq \end{cases} b_1$$

$$a_{21} x_1 + a_{22} x_2 + \cdots + a_{2n} x_n \begin{cases} \leq \\ = \\ \geq \end{cases} b_2$$

$$\vdots$$

$$a_{m1} x_1 + a_{m2} x_2 + \cdots + a_{mn} x_n \begin{cases} \leq \\ = \\ \geq \end{cases} b_m$$

and nonnegativity constraints
$$x_1, x_2, \ldots, x_n \geq 0$$

Note that each system constraint is limited to only one of the conditions $\leq$ or $=$ or $\geq$ (strictly $>$ or $<$ is not permitted). This problem structure contains the following characteristics:

1. *Decision variables.* The variables $x_1, x_2, \ldots, x_n$ are called decision variables, which take on real values greater than or equal to zero. These variables represent actions

the decision maker can take, such as assigning ten telephone operators to the Tuesday afternoon shift.

2. *Objective function.* The function $c_1x_1 + c_2x_2 + \cdots + c_nx_n$ is called the objective function, which is either maximized (e.g., profits) or minimized (e.g., costs) depending on the nature of the coefficients $c_1,c_2, \ldots ,c_n$. The problem states that this function is made as large or as small as possible provided that a system of constraints is met.

3. *Constraint functions.* As numerical values are assigned to the decision variables $x_1,x_2, \ldots ,x_n$ to influence the objective function, these values also are assigned to each constraint function. The model requires that numerical values be assigned such that no constraint is violated. The numbers $b_1,b_2, \ldots ,b_m$ taken together are called the *right-hand sides* (RHS). These numbers indirectly limit the possible values of the decision variables. For example, these RHS values could be resource constraints, such as total worker hours available.

4. *Parameters.* The coefficients in the objective function and the RHS values are parameters. Parameters are entities whose values remain fixed during the problem solution but could be changed later. Examples are unit profit contributions for the objective-function coefficients and the availability of resources for the RHS values.

5. *Constants.* The coefficients $a_{11},a_{12}, \ldots ,a_{1n}$ represent the consumption of the first RHS resource per unit of each decision variable. These coefficients reflect a constant rate of resource use (e.g., the ounces of beef required to make a hamburger).

Example 17.1. Stereo Warehouse

The retail outlet of Stereo Warehouse, a discount audio-components store, is planning a special clearance sale. The showroom has 400 square feet of floor space available for displaying this week's specials, a model X receiver and series Y speakers. Each receiver has a wholesale cost of $100, requires 2 square feet of display space, and will sell for $150. The wholesale cost for a pair of speakers is $50; the pair requires 4 square feet of display space and will sell for $70. The budget for stocking the stereo items is $8,000. The sales potential for the receiver is considered to be no more than 60 units; however, the budget-priced speakers appear to have an unlimited appeal. The store manager, desiring to maximize gross profit, must decide how many receivers and speakers to stock.

This problem can be formulated as an LP problem in the following manner:

Let x = number of receivers to stock
y = number of speakers to stock

Maximize	$50x + 20y$	gross profit
subject to	$2x + 4y \leq 400$	floor space
	$100x + 50y \leq 8000$	budget
	$x \leq 60$	sales limit
	$x, y \geq 0$	

The decision variables x and y appear in both the objective function and the constraint functions to ensure that the optimum solution does not violate resource limits. The objective is to maximize gross profit, which represents the difference between the selling price and the wholesale cost for each receiver and speaker sold. Thus, the objective becomes maximize $(150 - 100)x + (70 - 50)y$, or $50x + 20y$. The first two constraints account for resources that cannot be exceeded (i.e., available floor space and budget dollars). Thus, the 400 square feet of floor space represent a less-than-or-equal-to constraint, with each receiver occupying 2 square feet and each speaker occupying 4 square feet. Likewise, the $8,000 budget is consumed by the expenditure of $100 for each receiver and $50 for each pair of speakers stocked. Finally, the sale of receivers is limited to 60 units.

The solution to this problem will increase the values of x and y until some, but not necessarily all, of the resources are depleted. The solution to the Stereo Warehouse example is deferred until a later section.

Before leaving the topic of constrained optimization models, a few caveats are in order. When a constrained optimization model is solved, the solution is called optimal, meaning that the best values for the decision variables have been found. This so-called optimal solution, however, is optimal relative to the model but may not be optimal in reality. Recall that the model is only an abstraction and cannot include all the elements of reality. There can be a vast difference between the optimal solution of the model and what finally is implemented by the decision maker for reasons ranging from political considerations to personal preference. An optimal site selection for company headquarters could be vetoed by the corporate president, who refuses to live in the selected city. When used with care, however, LP models provide an excellent vehicle to structure a problem in explicit detail for all to see and question. Constraints can be modified, added, or eliminated, and objective functions can be changed. Further, the cost of pursuing a nonoptimal solution can be determined.

Next, we discuss the art of formulating LP models and consider examples of classic LP model structures as applied to services.

FORMULATING LINEAR PROGRAMMING MODELS

The ability to recognize a potential LP problem and to structure it for computer solution is an art that is acquired from experience. Some exposure to examples of classical forms of LP models can help, however. For example, recognizing that a problem is like the classical "diet problem" suggests the likely mathematical structure that will evolve, and experience with formulating LP problems suggests that the following strategy can be helpful:

1. Draw a diagram or construct a table showing the relationships in the problem, including the parameters and constraints.
2. Identify and invent symbolic notation for the decision variables.
3. State the objective in words.
4. Express each constraint in words, identify the RHS values, and note the direction of the inequality.
5. Write the complete model in algebraic form. Begin with the objective function; then list the right-hand sides, followed by the inequality signs; and finish by filling in the left-hand algebraic expressions for each constraint.
6. Note the nonnegativity conditions for the decision variables.
7. Using possible solutions, test the problem for internal consistency and completeness.

These guidelines are followed in formulating the example problems.

Diet Problem

This class of problems is illustrated by the selection of various food items for a meal that meets certain nutritional requirements. Given that each item selected contributes to the nutritional requirements at different rates, the objective is to identify the food and amounts that minimize costs.

Example 17.2. Lakeview Hospital

The dietitian at Lakeview Hospital is preparing a special milkshake as a "treat" for pediatric care patients recovering from surgery. The dietitian wants to ensure that the level of cholesterol will not exceed 175 units and the level of saturated fat 150 units. The protein content should be at least 200 units, and the calorie content should exceed 100 units. The dietitian has selected three possible ingredients: an egg custard base, ice cream, and butterscotch-flavored syrup. One unit of the egg custard base costs 15 cents and contributes 50 units of cholesterol, no fat, 70 units of protein, and 30 calories. One unit of ice cream costs 25 cents and contributes 150 units of cholesterol, 100 units of fat, 10 units of protein, and 80 calories. One unit of butterscotch-flavored syrup costs 10 cents and contributes 90 units of cholesterol, 50 units of fat, no protein, and 200 calories. How many units of each ingredient should be included in the milkshake if costs are to be minimized?

The information from the problem statement is organized and displayed in Table 17.1.

The problem suggests the following decision variables:

Let E = units of egg custard base in the shake
C = units of ice cream in the shake
S = units of butterscotch syrup in the shake

The object is to minimize the total cost of the milkshake. Table 17.1 identifies the constraints as a cholesterol content less than or equal to 175 units, fat content less than or equal to 150 units, protein content equal to or more than 200 units, and calorie content equal to or more than 100 units. The algebraic expression of the model then becomes:

$$
\begin{array}{lll}
\text{Minimize} & 0.15E + 0.25C + 0.10S & \\
\text{subject to} & 50E + 150C + 90S \leq 175 & \text{cholesterol} \\
& 100C + 50S \leq 150 & \text{fat} \\
& 70E + 10C \geq 200 & \text{protein} \\
& 30E + 80C + 200S \geq 100 & \text{calories} \\
& E, C, S \geq 0 &
\end{array}
$$

TABLE 17.1

LAKEVIEW HOSPITAL DIET PROBLEM

Units of nutritional element per unit of ingredient

Nutritional element	Egg custard	Ice cream	Syrup	Nutritional requirement
Cholesterol	50	150	90	≤ 175
Fat	0	100	50	≤ 150
Protein	70	10	0	≥ 200
Calories	30	80	200	≥ 100
Cost per unit, cents	15	25	10	

Note that as formulated, the problem could yield a solution using egg custard base alone (i.e., $E = 3.5$, $C = 0$, and $S = 0$). Because such a solution would hardly be considered a milkshake, additional constraints should be added to the problem that preclude this from occurring.

Shift-Scheduling Problem

This problem arises when an operation must be staffed for a period of time during which the requirements for service vary. The objective is to schedule staff assignments to meet the requirements during that period using the minimum number of people.

Example 17.3. Gotham City Police Patrol

Unable to hire new police officers because of budget limitations, the Gotham City police commissioner is trying to utilize the force better. The minimum requirements for police patrols on weekdays are

Period	Time	Patrol officers, minimum
1	Midnight–4 A.M.	6
2	4–8 A.M.	4
3	8–Noon	14
4	12–4 P.M.	8
5	4–8 P.M.	12
6	8–Midnight	16

Patrol officers are assigned in pairs to a patrol car, and they work an 8-hour shift. Currently, patrol officers report for duty at midnight, 8 A.M., and 4 P.M. The commissioner believes that better use of officers could be achieved if they also were permitted to report for duty at 4 A.M., noon, and 8 P.M. Of course, this might require some officers to switch partners after 4 hours of duty. How many officers should report for their 8-hour shifts at each of the six reporting times? The assignments must minimize the total number of officers yet still meet the minimum staffing requirements.

The shaded areas in Figure 17.1 show the periods of overstaffing that result from the current practice of officers reporting for 8-hour shifts at three reporting times (i.e., $x_1 = 6$, $x_3 = 14$, and $x_5 = 16$).

The decision variables for the staffing problem are defined as:

Let x_i = number of officers scheduled to report at reporting time i for
$\quad i = 1, 2, 3, 4, 5, 6$

The problem is directed at minimizing the total number of patrol officers, with constraints on the minimum number required for each 4-hour time interval during the day. The algebraic expression of the model also accounts for the implied constraint that once an officer reports for duty, he or she remains on duty for a complete 8-hour shift.

$$
\begin{aligned}
\text{Minimize} \quad & x_1 + x_2 + x_3 + x_4 + x_5 + x_6 \\
\text{subject to} \quad & x_1 \qquad\qquad\qquad\quad + x_6 \geq 6 \qquad \text{period 1} \\
& x_1 + x_2 \qquad\qquad\qquad \geq 4 \qquad \text{period 2} \\
& \qquad x_2 + x_3 \qquad\qquad \geq 14 \quad \text{period 3} \\
& \qquad\qquad x_3 + x_4 \qquad\quad \geq 8 \qquad \text{period 4} \\
& \qquad\qquad\qquad x_4 + x_5 \quad \geq 12 \quad \text{period 5} \\
& \qquad\qquad\qquad\qquad x_5 + x_6 \geq 16 \quad \text{period 6}
\end{aligned}
$$

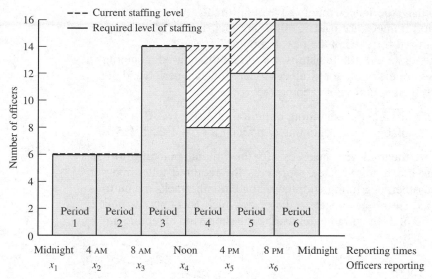

FIGURE 17.1 Gotham City Police shift-scheduling problem.

Note that each decision variable appears in exactly two constraints to account for the 8-hour shift. For example, officers reporting at 4 A.M. (i.e., x_2) contribute to the staffing requirements for both the second and third period, because each period is 4 hours in duration. Because we are dealing with numbers of patrol officers, the decision variables must be restricted to integer values. Fortunately, because of the problem structure, the LP solution will be integer. In general, however, such a solution yields nonnegative real (integer or fractional) numbers.

Workforce-Planning Problem

Employee turnover is common among service occupations; for example, bank tellers and airline attendants often leave their jobs. Further, new employees require a training period before they are ready to meet the public. The level of staff that is required also varies in response to changes in consumer demand, such as during summer or holiday vacation periods for airlines. Workforce planning involves identifying when and how many people to recruit to meet future staffing requirements and replace employees who leave. The objective is to meet staff requirements in a dynamic setting at a minimum personnel cost.

Example 17.4. Last National Drive-In Bank

Last National Bank must decide how many new tellers to hire and train over the next 6 months. The teller requirements, expressed as the number of teller-hours needed, are 1500 in January, 1800 in February, 1600 in March, 2000 in April, 1800 in May, and 2200 in June. One month of training is necessary before a teller can be assigned to duty; thus, tellers must be hired 1 month before they actually are needed. Also, each trainee requires 80 hours of simulated job experience, supervised by a regular teller, during the month of training. Hence, for each trainee, 80 fewer hours are available from a regular teller. Each experienced teller works 160 hours per month, whether he or she is needed or not. Last National has 12 experienced tellers available at the beginning of January. Past experience has shown that by the end of each month, approximately 10 percent of the experienced tellers have quit. Regular tellers receive a salary of $600 per month, and trainees are paid $300 during their month of training. How many tellers should be hired for each of the next 6 months?

Figure 17.2 captures the essential relationships for this time-phased planning model. The decision variables are the number of trainees to hire for each period and the number of tellers available at the beginning of each period.

Let T_t = number of trainees hired at the beginning of period t for $t = 1, 2, 3, 4, 5, 6$
A_t = number of tellers available at the beginning of period t for $t = 1, 2, 3, 4, 5, 6$

The objective is to minimize the total personnel costs for the 6-month planning horizon. Two sets of constraints are required. One represents the required teller-hours for each of the 6 months; the other, beginning with the second month, tracks the number of available tellers carried from one month to the next, which accounts for new hires and employee turnover. The following model uses some shorthand algebraic notations:

$$\text{Minimize} \sum_{t=1}^{6} (600A_t + 300T_t)$$

$$
\begin{array}{lll}
\text{subject to} & 160\,A_1 - 80\,T_1 \geq 1500 & \text{January} \\
& 160\,A_2 - 80\,T_2 \geq 1800 & \text{February} \\
& 160\,A_3 - 80\,T_3 \geq 1600 & \text{March} \\
& 160\,A_4 - 80\,T_4 \geq 2000 & \text{April} \\
& 160\,A_5 - 80\,T_5 \geq 1800 & \text{May} \\
& 160\,A_6 - 80\,T_6 \geq 2200 & \text{June} \\
& A_1 = 12 & \\
& 0.9A_{t-1} + T_{t-1} - A_t = 0 & \text{for } t = 2, 3, 4, 5, 6 \\
& A_t, T_t \geq 0 \text{ and integer for } t = 1,2,3,4,5,6 &
\end{array}
$$

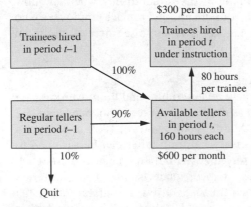

FIGURE 17.2 Monthly teller transition diagram.

Note that when this model is used, only the value for January hiring is of immediate interest. The trainee hires for the other months can be treated as estimates for now. Before the start of February, the model is run again, with the requirements for January dropped and the July requirements added. In this manner, each hiring decision is based on a 6-month projected requirement plan, which permits a gradual adjustment in the size of the workforce. Also, as in the police patrol example, the decision variables must be restricted to integers. Unfortunately, this problem structure does not necessarily yield integer results. This problem illustrates a special class of LP models called *integer programming,* which requires a special computer code that guarantees integer results.

Transportation Problem

Transportation problems are a special class of LP models called networks. The problem structure also ensures an integer solution. The problem essentially is one of shipping goods from origins, or supply points, to destinations, or demand points. Each destination has a particular demand and each origin a particular supply. The number of origins need not equal the number of destinations. To facilitate a solution, a dummy origin or destination is added to balance the total demand and supply. Given a unit cost for shipping between each origin and destination pair, the objective is to minimize the total shipping cost. This problem structure also arises in nontransportation situations, such as when assigning personnel to jobs.

Example 17.5. Lease-a-Lemon Car Rental

Lease-a-Lemon Car Rental has discovered an imbalance in the distribution of rental cars within its northeast territory. The following surpluses exist: 26 cars in New York, 43 in Washington, and 31 in Cleveland. Shortages include 32 cars in Pittsburgh, 28 in Buffalo, and 26 in Philadelphia. The distance in miles to transfer a car between each city is

	Pittsburgh	Buffalo	Philadelphia
New York	439	396	91
Washington	296	434	133
Cleveland	131	184	479

Develop a plan to redistribute the cars at a minimum cost on the basis of a transportation charge of $1 per mile.

Figure 17.3 is a network representation of the problem, with origin nodes showing a positive supply and destination nodes a negative demand. The supply and demand are balanced with the addition of a dummy destination node showing a -14 (i.e., 86 $-$ 100) demand. The dummy represents cars not redistributed and, thus, has unit transportation costs of zero. Decision variables are the numbers of cars sent from the supply cities to the demand cities, including the dummy destination.

The objective is to minimize the total redistribution cost. Two sets of constraints are required: one limiting the supply from each origin and the other limiting the demand at each destination. All the constraints will be equalities because supply and demand are balanced.

FIGURE 17.3 Lease-a-Lemon car redistribution network.

Let x_{ij} = number of cars sent from city i to city j for $i = 1, 2, 3$ and $j = 1, 2, 3, 4$

Minimize $439x_{11} + 396x_{12} + \cdots + 479x_{33} + 0x_{34}$

subject to

$$
\begin{aligned}
x_{11} + x_{12} + x_{13} + x_{14} &&&= 26 \\
x_{21} + x_{22} + x_{23} + x_{24} &&&= 43 \\
x_{31} + x_{32} + x_{33} + x_{34} &= 31 \\
x_{11} \quad\quad + x_{21} \quad\quad + x_{31} &&&= 32 \\
x_{12} \quad\quad + x_{22} \quad\quad + x_{32} &&&= 28 \\
x_{13} \quad\quad + x_{23} \quad\quad + x_{33} &&&= 26 \\
x_{14} \quad\quad + x_{24} \quad\quad + x_{34} &= 14 \\
x_{ij} \geq 0 \quad \text{for all } i, j
\end{aligned}
$$

Note the characteristic structure of the constraints that is common to all transportation problems. This structure and appearance of only coefficients of 1 in the constraint equations assure an integer solution.

OPTIMAL SOLUTIONS AND COMPUTER ANALYSIS

The Stereo Warehouse problem (Example 17.1) is used to illustrate graphically the nature of LP models and their solutions. Because this problem has only the two decision variables x and y, we can draw a picture of the model and see how an optimal solution is achieved. This geometric representation of the model also is used to explain the computer-generated solution.

Graphical Solution of Linear Programming Models

Recall the formulation of the Stereo Warehouse model, in which x and y represent the number of receivers and speakers to be stocked. In this formulation, Z represents the value of the objective function.

$$
\begin{array}{llll}
\text{Maximize} & Z = 50x + 20y & & \text{gross profit} \\
\text{subject to} & 2x + 4y \leq 400 & & \text{floor space} \\
& 100x + 50y \leq 8000 & & \text{budget} \\
& x \leq 60 & & \text{sales limit} \\
& x, y \geq 0 & & \text{nonnegativity}
\end{array}
$$

The set of inequalities or constraints defines a region of permissible values for x and y. Note that letting $x = 0$ and $y = 0$ satisfies all the inequalities, as it should, because that is the "do-nothing" alternative. Our interest, however, is in finding the best, or optimal, values of x and y that maximize the objective function. For a two-variable problem, the permissible, or *feasible,* region can be identified if we plot each constraint inequality. The procedure for drawing the feasible region is

1. Assign one variable to the x axis and the other to the y axis.
2. Note that the nonnegativity constraints on the variables limit the feasible region to the first quadrant (i.e., upper right-hand corner).
3. Temporarily change each inequality constraint to an equality.
4. Plot each constraint as an equation using the x and y intercepts (i.e., assume that $x = 0$ and solve for the y intercept, repeat for $y = 0$ to find the x intercept, then draw a straight line joining these two axis intercepts). If $(0, 0)$ happens to be a solution of the equation (e.g., $2x - 3y = 0$), however, then another arbitrary point must be selected and the line drawn from that point through the origin.
5. Identify the feasible side of the inequality. This can be accomplished by substituting $x = 0$ and $y = 0$ into the inequality constraint, unless $(0, 0)$ happens to be on the line, in which case some other arbitrary point must be selected. If the inequality is satisfied, then the side containing $x = 0$ and $y = 0$ should be shaded; otherwise, the opposite side of the line is shaded (i.e., it represents a feasible region).
6. Note that each constraint further reduces the feasible region into a geometric figure called a *convex polygon* (i.e., from inside the space looking outward, all the corners point outward).

This procedure is followed for Stereo Warehouse to create the feasible region, as shown in Figure 17.4. Note for the first constraint that the x intercept ($y = 0$) is $400/2 = 200$ and the y intercept ($x = 0$) is $400/4 = 100$. Also note that the test point $x = 0$, $y = 0$ satisfies all three constraints; thus, the shaded area is either below or to the left of each constraint. Further, note that any point (i.e., combination of x and y values) within the feasible region simultaneously satisfies all three constraints and the nonnegativity condition.

The optimal solution to the problem now can be found graphically. Recall that the objective is to make Z as large as possible provided that the values of x and y are in the feasible region. If we let Z take on a trial value (e.g., 2000), then we can plot Z as a straight line using the intercept approach. For $Z = 2000$, the x intercept ($y = 0$) is $2000/50 = 40$ and the y intercept ($x = 0$) is $400/4 = 100$. Figure 17.5 shows the objective function $Z = 2000$ plotted on the graph of the feasible region. As the value of Z is increased to 3000, 3600, and, finally, 3800, the objective function moves out from

FIGURE 17.4 Stereo Warehouse feasible region.

the origin in parallel lines, or contours. The maximum value of $Z = 3800$ occurs at point C (i.e., $x = 60$, $y = 40$), a corner of the polygon. If Z moves out any further, no point on the contour line will be common to the feasible region, and we have just demonstrated an axiom of LP. An optimal solution to an LP model always will occur at a corner, or *extreme point*, of the feasible region. In the special case in which the slope of the objective function is identical to the slope of a constraint, the optimal solution also will include any point between the extreme points along the constraint line.

Linear Programming Model in Standard Form

Realizing that an optimal solution will be found at an extreme point reduces our search for a feasible region to a finite set of points. Further, each extreme point is defined as the simultaneous solution of a pair of constraints that are stated as equations.

A formal way of restating an inequality constraint as an equation in LP models is accomplished with the use of a *slack,* or *surplus,* variable. For constraints of the $\le$ variety, a nonnegative slack (i.e., resources not used) variable is added to the left-hand side. For example, the Stereo Warehouse floor-space constraint would be restated as

$$2x + 4y + s_1 = 400$$

The slack variable s_1 would represent available floor space not used by the receivers and speakers stocked. For constraints of the $\ge$ variety, a nonnegative surplus (i.e., results produced in excess of requirements) variable is subtracted from the left-hand side. For example, in the Gotham City Police Patrol problem, the first-period patrol officer requirement would be restated as

$$x_1 + x_6 - s_1 = 6$$

FIGURE 17.5 Stereo Warehouse optimal solution.

In this case, the surplus variable s_1 would represent the number of patrol officers assigned to the first period in excess of the requirement of six officers. Note that the subscript number for the slack or surplus variable corresponds to the constraint number.

The Stereo Warehouse model can be reformulated using the following slack variables:

Let s_1 = square feet of floor space not used
s_2 = dollars of budget not allocated
s_3 = number of receivers that could have been sold

Maximize $Z = 50x + 20y$

subject to
$$2x + 4y + s_1 \qquad\qquad = 400 \qquad \text{(constraint 1)}$$
$$100x + 50y \quad + s_2 \qquad = 8000 \qquad \text{(constraint 2)}$$
$$x \qquad\qquad\qquad + s_3 = 60 \qquad \text{(constraint 3)}$$
$$x, y, s_1, s_2, s_3 \geq 0$$

The Stereo Warehouse problem is solved by examining each extreme point, identified by the letters A, B, C, D, and E in Figure 17.5. Table 17.2 contains the analysis of these extreme points. At each extreme point, variables with positive values are labeled as *basic* and variables with zero values as *nonbasic*. Note that the number of basic variables equals the number of constraints in the problem. This result always is true for LP

TABLE 17.2

STEREO WAREHOUSE EXTREME-POINT SOLUTIONS

Extreme point	Nonbasic variables	Basic variables	Variable value	Objective-function value Z
A	x, y	s_1	400	0
		s_2	8000	
		s_3	60	
B	s_3, y	s_1	280	3000
		s_2	2000	
		x	60	
C	s_3, s_2	s_1	120	3800
		y	40	
		x	60	
D	s_1, s_2	s_3	20	3600
		y	80	
		x	40	
E	s_1, x	s_3	60	2000
		y	100	
		s_2	3000	

problems, except for the special case in which a basic variable also is zero-valued (a situation that is referred to as a *degenerate solution*). Also, note that when a slack variable is nonbasic, its corresponding constraint is binding (i.e., all the resource is used).

The computer solution of LP problems evaluates the extreme points in a systematic way. This procedure is called the *simplex algorithm.* In our Stereo Warehouse example, the simplex algorithm starts at point A, proceeds to extreme point B (because variable x contributes more than variable y does to the objective function), and stops at extreme point C (the optimum). The algorithm is able to identify optimality; thus, all the extreme points need not be examined. Details of the simplex algorithm are not discussed here, but they can be found in any management science textbook (See Selected Bibliography).

Computer Analysis and Interpretation

The following illustrations of computer input and output reports result from using Excel Solver 7.0 for personal computers.

The computer input for the Stereo Warehouse example shown in Table 17.3 is an illustration of the Excel Add-ins Solver feature provided by Paul A. Jensen.[1]

The computer solution and sensitivity report for the Stereo Warehouse problem is shown in Table 17.4. Each decision variable x and y and the slack variable s_1 have a nonzero solution value. The zero values for s_2 and s_3 indicate that these are nonbasic variables; thus, the corresponding constraints are binding.

The *shadow price* shown in the sensitivity table has an important managerial interpretation. Recall that a nonbasic slack variable means that the corresponding constraint is binding at optimality. For the Stereo Warehouse problem, the budget constraint of $8000 (corresponding slack variable s_2) and limit of 60 units for receiver sales (corresponding slack variable s_3) are restricting the profit to a maximum of $3800. The floor-space constraint is no problem, because at optimality, 120 square feet (value of s_1) of the available 400 square feet is not being used. If profits are to be increased, more of

---

TABLE 17.3

FORMULATION OF THE STEREO WAREHOUSE PROBLEM IN MICROSOFT® EXCEL 7.0 USING LINEAR PROGRAMMING ADD-INS SOLVER

Linear Model

Name:	Stereo
Type:	LP
No. Var.:	2
Int. Var.:	0
No. Con.:	3
Nonlinear:	0

Objective Value
0

			1	2
Variables	Num.		X	Y
Model	Name			
0	Values		0	0
2	Linear Obj. Coef.		50	20
TRUE	Lower Bounds		0	0
TRUE	Upper Bounds		99999	99999

				Constraint Bounds		
TRUE	Constraints					
TRUE	Num.	Name	Value	Lower	Upper	Constraint Coefficients
100	1	Floor	0	0	400	2	4
	2	Budget	0	0	8000	100	50
	3	Sales	0	0	60	1	0

---

the limiting resources must be obtained. The shadow price of $10 associated with the slack variable s_3 represents the increase in the objective-function value if one more receiver could be sold. Note that if the limit on receiver sales is increased by 1, the budget constraint and limit on x sales define the new extreme point:

$$100x + 50y = 8000$$

$$x = 61$$

The solution of these simultaneous equations yields $x = 61$ and $y = 38$. Substituting these values into the objective function provides a revised profit of $3810, which is an increase of $10. A similar analysis explains the $0.40 increase in the objective-function value if the RHS of the budget constraint is increased by $1 to $8001 and the limit on x remains at 60 (the solution becomes $x = 60$ and $y = 40.02$).

The shadow price represents the imputed price of a unit of the limited resource. Shadow prices can be used by managers to decide on the value of securing more resources. For example, if money can be borrowed for less than 40 cents on the dollar during the period of the sale, the difference will become additional profit.

Most computer programs use the convention that if a unit increase in the RHS value improves the objective function (i.e., increases it for maximization or decreases it for minimization), then the shadow price is positive and represents the amount of objective-function change. In some problems, however, increasing an RHS could result in impairing the objective function. For example, if the protein constraint in the Lakeview Hospital diet problem were increased, then contrary to the minimization desired, the objective function could increase. The shadow price would be negative for this constraint if it were binding at optimality.

Finally, note that the shadow price of a resource in excess (corresponding slack variable is basic) is considered to be zero. In the Stereo Warehouse problem, the value to the manager of securing additional floor space is zero, because not all the available floor space is being used.

TABLE 17.4

MICROSOFT® EXCEL 7.0 SOLUTION AND SENSITIVITY REPORT FOR STEREO WAREHOUSE

Target Cell (Max)

Cell	Name	Original Value	Final Value
H5	Stereo_Obj	0	3800

Changing Cells

Cell	Name	Final Value	Reduced Cost	Objective Coefficient	Allowable Increase	Allowable Decrease
G8	Values X	60	0	50	1E+30	10
H8	Values Y	40	0	20	5	20

Constraints

Cell	Name	Final Value	Shadow Price	Constraint R.H. Side	Allowable Increase	Allowable Decrease
D14	Floor Value	280	0	400	1E+30	120
D15	Budget Value	8000	0.4	8000	1500	2000
D16	Sales Value	60	10	60	20	20
D14	Floor Value	280	0	0	280	1E+30
D15	Budget Value	8000	0	0	8000	1E+30
D16	Sales Value	60	0	0	60	1E+30

SENSITIVITY ANALYSIS

What happens to the optimal solution of an LP problem if the values of the model parameters change? This question is of great interest to a decision maker in an uncertain environment. The sensitivity of a solution regarding the objective-function coefficients is discussed first, and then constraint RHS ranging is analyzed.

Objective-Function Coefficient Ranges

The permissible range of each objective-function coefficient is shown in the "changing cells" portion of Table 17.4. The y-variable coefficient may range from a low of 0 to a high of 25; the x-variable coefficient may range from 40 to infinity. Within these ranges, the optimal solution remains at extreme point C, as shown by Figure 17.6, in which the objective-function slope changes with different coefficient values and essentially pivots about extreme point C.

Note that with a y coefficient of 0, the objective function lies along the line segment BC of constraint 3. When the y coefficient is 25, the objective function lies along the line segment DC, which is parallel to constraint 2. Note also that if the coefficient of y exceeds 25, the optimal solution moves to the extreme point D. A similar analysis can be made for the x objective-function coefficient. The decision maker must be cautioned that the range for each coefficient is limited to changing one parameter at a time while holding all others fixed. Further, the value of the objective function changes as these coefficients are changed.

FIGURE 17.6 Stereo Warehouse objective-function coefficient ranging.

Right-Hand-Side Ranging

The allowable RHS range for each constraint is shown in the "constraints" portion of Table 17.4. The RHS for the budget constraint ranges from 6000 to 9500; the RHS for the sales constraint ranges from 40 to 80. Within these ranges, the optimal solution contains the same basic variables s_1, x, and y. The values of these variables as well as the objective-function value will change. It should be noted that the shadow price for each resource applies only within these ranges. For example, recall that the shadow price for constraint 3 is a $10-per-unit increase in the RHS. Note that the objective-function value increases from $3800 to $4000 when the RHS increases from 60 to 80 [i.e., $(80 - 60)(10) = 200$]. Likewise, the objective-function value is reduced by $200 when the RHS of constraint 3 decreases from 60 to 40.

Note in Figure 17.7 what happens graphically when the RHS of constraint 3 is changed. As the RHS increases, the extreme point C moves along the line segment CI until it becomes coincident with I at RHS = 80. The values of the basic variables at extreme point I are $s_1 = 240$, $x = 80$, and $y = 0$. This is a degenerate solution, because variable $y = 0$ but it still remains in the basis.

If the RHS of constraint 3 is reduced, the extreme point C moves along the line segment CD until it becomes coincident with D at RHS = 40. The values of the basic variables at extreme point D are $s_1 = 0$, $x = 40$, and $y = 80$. This is a degenerate solution, because variable $s_1 = 0$ but it still remains in the basis. A similar analysis for binding constraint 2 can be made to show the movement of extreme point C along the line segment BII as the RHS is changed from 6000 to 9500.

FIGURE 17.7 Stereo Warehouse right-hand-side ranging.

The concept that the resource shadow price is limited to the RHS range is important in *postoptimality analysis.* For example, in the Stereo Warehouse problem, suppose that additional money can be obtained at a cost that is less than the shadow price of 40 cents per dollar. The question of how much to obtain at this price is answered by the RHS range on the budget constraint. Secure $9500 − $8000, or $1500 in additional financing to maximize profits. The same caution raised earlier, however, about treating the sensitivity analysis as being limited to changing one parameter at a time while holding all others fixed is true for RHS ranging.

GOAL PROGRAMMING

Linear programming models allow for only one objective, and all constraints must be met absolutely. Many problems, however, particularly in the public sector, have multiple objectives in different units of measure. This makes construction of a consolidated single objective difficult, if not impossible. For example, an emergency ambulance system could have the following objectives:

1. Maintain an average response time of approximately 4 minutes.
2. Ensure that 90 percent of all calls receive aid in less than 10 minutes.
3. Try not to exceed a budget of $100,000 per year.
4. Allocate calls to ambulance crews in an equitable manner.

Goal programming is a variation of LP that permits multiple and conflicting goals with different dimensions. Multiple goals are rank-ordered and treated as *preemptive priorities.* In the solution procedure, higher-ranked goals are not sacrificed to achieve lower-ranked goals. The solution approach is equivalent to solving a series of nested LP problems in which higher-ranked goals become constraints on lower-ranked goals.

While LP optimizes a single objective, goal programming minimizes deviations from goals. This solution approach is known as *satisficing,* because not all goals necessarily will be met. Instead, the goals will be achieved as closely as possible.

The objective function will contain only deviational variables (i.e., plus or minus deviations from goals), which also can be given *deviational weights* to distinguish relative importance within a priority level. The objective always is to minimize the sum of the deviations at each priority level, with consideration being given to the hierarchy of preemptive priorities. All constraints are stated as equalities and contain both plus and minus deviational variables in addition to decision variables. To illustrate a goal programming model, the Stereo Warehouse example is reformulated as a goal program.

Example 17.6. Stereo Warehouse as a Goal Program

Let x = number of receivers to stock

y = number of speakers to stock

d_1^- = amount by which profit falls short of $999,999

d_1^+ = amount by which profit exceeds $999,999

d_2^- = amount by which floor space used falls short of 400 square feet

d_2^+ = amount by which floor space used exceeds 400 square feet

d_3^- = amount by which budget falls short of $8000

d_3^+ = amount by which budget exceeds $8000

d_4^- = amount by which sales of receivers fall short of 60

d_4^+ = amount by which sales of receivers exceed 60

P_k = priority level with rank k

Minimize $$Z = P_1 d_4^+ + P_2(d_1^- + 2d_3^+) + P_3(d_2^- + d_2^+)$$

subject to

$$50x + 20y + d_1^- - d_1^+ = 99{,}999 \qquad \text{profit goal}$$

$$2x + 4y + d_2^- - d_2^+ = 400 \qquad \text{floor-space goal}$$

$$100x + 50y + d_3^- - d_3^+ = 8000 \qquad \text{budget goal}$$

$$x + d_4^- - d_4^+ = 60 \qquad \text{sales-limit goal}$$

$$x, y, d_1^-, d_1^+, d_2^-, d_2^+, d_3^-, d_3^+, d_4^-, d_4^+ \geq 0$$

This formulation has translated the profit objective into a goal at the second priority level. Note that only d_1^- is included in the objective function to be minimized. Minimizing d_1^-, which is the underachievement of the goal, forces the profit to approach 99,999, a large number far in excess of expected profit. The floor space used for display now becomes a third priority, in which both deviational variables are minimized. In other words, we want to use approximately 400 square feet. The goal programming model permits a previous absolute constraint on available space to be treated as a more realistic approximate requirement. Exceeding the budget is to be avoided, so only d_3^+ is found in the objective function. The deviational weight of 2 indicates that meeting the budget is twice as important as maximizing profit. Finally, exceeding the sales limit of 60 receivers is found at the first priority. This illustrates how system or physical constraints are treated in goal programming. Thus, the typical LP absolute constraints, such as $\leq$ or $\geq$, have their appropriate deviational variable at the first priority level. The goal hierarchy ensures that no solution will violate these system constraints.

TABLE 17.5

GOAL PROGRAMMING FORMULATION FOR STEREO WAREHOUSE

Linear Model

			Name:	Stereo
Type:	LP
No. Var.:	10
Int. Var.:	0
No. Con.:	4

Objective Value: 0

Model	Variables	Num. Name	Nonlinear: 0	1 X	2 Y	3 DM1	4 DM2	5 DM3	6 DM4	7 DP1	8 DP2	9 DP3	10 DP4
0		Values		0	0	0	0	0	0	0	0	0	0
10		Linear Obj. Coef.		0	0	100	1	0	0	0	1	200	1000
TRUE		Lower Bounds		0	0	0	0	0	0	0	0	0	0
TRUE		Upper Bounds		99999	99999	99999	99999	99999	99999	99999	99999	99999	99999

	Constraints			Constraint Bounds									
TRUE	Num.	Name	Value	Lower	Upper	Constraint Coefficients							
FALSE	1	Profit	0	99999	99999	50	20	1	0	0	0	-1	0	0	0
100	2	Floor	0	400	400	2	4	0	1	0	0	0	-1	0	0
	3	Budget	0	8000	8000	100	50	0	0	1	0	0	0	-1	0
	4	Sales	0	60	60	1	0	0	0	0	1	0	0	0	-1

Table 17.5 shows the Excel formulation for the Stereo Warehouse goal programming model. To ensure that the goal hierarchy is not violated, priority ranks have been given increasingly large weights (i.e., $P_1 = 1000$, $P_2 = 100$, and $P_3 = 1$). The variables labeled DM represent underachievement deviations (d^-) and the variables labeled DP represent overachievement deviations (d^+).

The goal-programming solution to the Stereo Warehouse example is found in Table 17.6. Note that the values for the decision variables x and y are identical to the values in the previous LP solution. When the value for DM1 is subtracted from its RHS of 99,999, the profit is found to be $3800, as before. The deviational variable DM2 takes on a value of 120, indicating the underachievement of our goal to use approximately 400 square feet of floor space. Our budget of $8000 is completely exhausted, because DP3 = 0. The deviational variable DM4 is zero, as is required to achieve the constraint on receiver sales. In summary, all goals are met, except for the desire to utilize 400 square feet of floor space. The objective-function value is of little consequence, because it simply is the sum of all the weighted deviations. Unfortunately, the shadow prices are of no interest in this case, because the objective function has no economic meaning.

TABLE 17.6

**MICROSOFT® EXCEL 7.0 GOAL PROGRAMMING SOLUTION
AND SENSITIVITY REPORT FOR STEREO WAREHOUSE**

Target Cell (Min)

Cell	Name	Original Value	Final Value
H5	Stereo_Goal_Obj	0	9620020

Changing Cells

Cell	Name	Final Value	Reduced Cost	Objective Coefficient	Allowable Increase	Allowable Decrease
G8	Values X	60	0	0	994	6
H8	Values Y	40	0	0	3	497
I8	Values DM1	96199	0	100	0.6	99.4
J8	Values DM2	120	0	1	165.6666667	1
K8	Values DM3	0	40.08	0	1E+30	40.08
L8	Values DM4	0	994	0	1E+30	994
M8	Values DP1	0	100	0	1E+30	100
N8	Values DP2	0	2	1	1E+30	2
O8	Values DP3	0	159.92	200	1E+30	159.92
P8	Values DP4	0	6	1000	1E+30	6

Constraints

Cell	Name	Final Value	Shadow Price	Constraint R.H. Side	Allowable Increase	Allowable Decrease
D14	Profit Value	99999	0	99999	1E+30	0
D15	Floor Value	400	0	400	1E+30	0
D16	Budget Value	8000	-40.08	8000	1500	0
D17	Sales Value	60	994	60	20	0
D14	Profit Value	99999	100	99999	0	96199
D15	Floor Value	400	1	400	0	120
D16	Budget Value	8000	0	8000	0	1E+30
D17	Sales Value	60	0	60	0	1E+30

Service Benchmark

AN ANALYSIS OF ALTERNATIVE LOCATIONS AND SERVICE AREAS OF AMERICAN RED CROSS BLOOD FACILITIES

The blood service of the American Red Cross (ARC) is divided into a number of regions. Each region has responsibility for blood collection, testing, and distribution. The mid-Atlantic ARC region has responsibility for most of Virginia and northeastern North Carolina.

The ARC collects, tests, and sells blood throughout the mid-Atlantic region, except in the immediate vicinity of Richmond. It owns and operates facilities for collecting, testing, and distributing blood. The mid-Atlantic region of ARC has three facilities, each performing some of these functions. They are located in Norfolk and Charlottesville, Virginia, and in Greenville, North Carolina. Currently, the Norfolk and Greenville facilities both collect and distribute blood in their assigned areas, while Charlottesville only collects. The Norfolk facility does all the testing.

The ARC uses site-specific drives to collect the blood. The three fixed facilities send out vans (called "mobiles") to collect blood at various sites. These mobiles generally carry the necessary equipment and staff and stay at one site all day. All collections are arranged by entities called chapters. There are a number of chapters responsible for collection sites in each county within a facility's area. Each chapter has an established collection goal, which determines the number of collections and the assigned resources. Blood is also collected from walk-in donors at the fixed facilities.

Nightly "shuttles" from Greenville and Charlottesville transport the blood collected each day to be tested at Norfolk. ARC is not interested in duplicating or relocating the testing facility because it has invested heavily in specialized equipment.

After the blood is tested, the Norfolk and Greenville facilities distribute it to regional hospitals and medical centers, which are ARC's main customers. The number of distributions to customers remains fairly constant except in emergency situations. Typically, volunteer drivers make three deliveries a week to each customer.

To remain competitive and reduce costs, the mid-Atlantic ARC assessed its entire system to explore alternatives for its major activities. Its managers considered relocating the Charlottesville facility to the Richmond area with the goal of attracting new customers and collection sites. However, before making a final decision, they wanted to understand the financial implications.

DECISION ALTERNATIVES FOR COLLECTIONS

To evaluate the feasibility of opening a collection facility in the Richmond area, three location decision alternatives were generated:

1. Retain the three existing collection facilities, Norfolk, Greenville, and Charlottesville, without expanding into Richmond.
2. Close the Charlottesville collection facility and open a new collection facility in Richmond. Retain the existing collection facilities in Norfolk and Greenville.
3. Retain the Charlottesville collection facility and open a new collection facility in Richmond. Consider Norfolk, Greenville, Charlottesville, and Richmond facilities for collections.

For each of these location alternatives, three allocation scenarios were used to analyze the financial implications:

A. Retain the current allocation of resources and allocation of collection sites to facilities. Using this scenario with alternative 1 creates a "do nothing" or baseline case.
B. Within the existing resource constraints, optimize the allocation of collection sites to facilities.
C. Remove the resource constraints and optimize the allocation of collection sites among facilities. This scenario could cause some shifting of both collection sites and resources among facilities, resulting in the biggest change from the current structure.

DECISION ALTERNATIVES FOR DISTRIBUTION

Two location decision alternatives were developed to evaluate the feasibility of opening a distribution facility in the Richmond area:

4. Retain the two existing distribution facilities in Norfolk and Greenville, without expansion into Richmond.
5. Open a new facility in Richmond for distributions. Retain distribution facilities in Norfolk and Greenville.

BOX 17.1 (CONTINUED)

Two allocation scenarios were proposed to analyze the financial implications:

D. Retain the current allocation of customers to facilities. Using this scenario with alternative 1 creates a "do nothing" or baseline case.

E. Optimize the allocation of customers to facilities.

INTEGER PROGRAMMING MODELS

Based on this framework, the integer programming models shown here were developed. In each case the objective was to minimize transportation costs for each combination of alternative and scenario for collection decisions and distribution decisions. The number of variables and constraints for each model varied depending upon the alternative and scenario being considered.

Collection Model

The model is formulated as follows:

$$\text{Min} \sum_{i=1}^{m} \sum_{j=1}^{n} x_{ij}D_{ij}$$

subject to

$$\sum_{i=1}^{m} \sum_{j=1}^{n} x_{ij}y_{ij} < A_i$$

$$\sum_{i=1}^{m} \sum_{j=1}^{n} x_{ij}w_{ij} < B_i$$

$$\sum_{i=1}^{m} \sum_{j=1}^{n} x_{ij}z_{ij} \le C_i$$

$$\sum_{i=1}^{m} \sum_{j=1}^{n} x_{ij} = 1$$

where

m = number of facilities

n = number of chapters

$$x_{ij} = \begin{cases} 1 & \text{if chapter } j \text{ is assigned facility } i \\ 0 & \text{if not} \end{cases}$$

D_{ij} = distance between facility i and chapter j

y_j = number of operations required for chapter j

A_i = total number of operations facility i can conduct

w_j = the pints of blood chapter j needs to collect

B_i = total pints of blood facility i can collect

z_j = number of staff chapter j requires

C_i = total number of staff available at facility i

Distribution Model

The model is formulated as follows:

$$\text{Min} \sum_{i=1}^{m} \sum_{j=1}^{n} x'_{ij}D'_{ij}$$

subject to

$$\text{Min} \sum_{i=1}^{m} \sum_{j=1}^{n} x'_{ij} = 1$$

where

m = number of facilities

n = number of customers

D'_{ij} = distance between facility i and chapter j

$$x_{ij} = \begin{cases} 1 & \text{if customer } j \text{ is assigned facilty } i \\ 0 & \text{if not} \end{cases}$$

BOX 17.1 (CONTINUED)

ANALYSIS OF RESULTS FOR COLLECTION MODELS

The results of the collection models were quite surprising. Comparison of retaining the current collection facilities, Norfolk, Greenville, and Charlottesville (alternative 1) and relocating Charlottesville to Richmond (alternative 2) provides an unexpected result: opening a collection facility in Richmond causes increased transportation costs under all three scenarios. The reason that the move to Richmond does not immediately generate savings is that a number of the existing collection sites are very close to Charlottesville. However, retaining Charlottesville and opening a new facility in Richmond for collections (alternative 3, scenario C) provides noticeable savings in transportation costs. This is because Charlottesville can still serve most of its collection sites while the Richmond facility can incorporate some of Norfolk's and Greenville's collection sites. From examining these three alternatives, ARC should keep Charlottesville as a collection facility and open a new collection facility in Richmond, as shown in the table below.

| | Scenario A | Scenario B | Scenario C |
	Retain current capacity and allocations of collection sites	Retain current capacity but optimize allocation of collection sites	Remove capacity constraints and optimize allocation of collection sites
Alternative 1 Norfolk Greenville Charlottesville	$207,437	$197,984	$197,984
Alternative 2 Norfolk Greenville Richmond	$237,514	$215,187	$214,294
Alternative 3 Norfolk Greenville Charlottesville Richmond	—	—	$173,254

ANALYSIS OF RESULTS FOR DISTRIBUTION MODELS

The ARC should consider opening a distribution facility in Richmond and realize transportation cost savings. Even without a facility in Richmond, it could still reduce distribution costs by reallocating its customers between the current Norfolk and Greenville facilities, as shown in the table below.

| | Scenario D | Scenario E |
	Retain current allocations of customers to facilities	Optimize allocation of customers to facilities
Alternative 4 Norfolk Greenville	$128,016	$125,568
Alternative 5 Norfolk Greenville Richmond	—	$95,904

Source: Adapted from D. A. Jacobs, M. N. Silan, and B. A. Clemson, "An Analysis of Alternative Locations and Service Areas of American Red Cross Blood Facilities," *Interfaces,* vol. 26, no. 3, May–June 1996, pp. 40–50.

SUMMARY

Linear programming is one of the most popular computer-based modeling techniques available to the modern service operations manager. The power of LP to find optimal solutions and conduct sensitivity analyses is invaluable to the decision maker. Further, the structure of the constrained optimization model fits well with the real world of the service operations manager.

The art of formulating LP models is developed through examples and practice using a systematic approach. Many examples of LP models illustrate the general problem-solving nature of LP. We find that the discipline of formulating LP models helps decision makers to clarify objectives and to identify resource constraints.

The procedure for solving LP models was demonstrated by use of graphics. Because no one solves real LP models by hand, interpretation of computer solutions was stressed. Again, using graphics, the concepts of shadow prices and sensitivity analysis were demonstrated. Because many service operations managers are faced with multiple objectives, the concept of goal programming was introduced. With goal programming, the manager attempts to satisfy goals rather than to optimize a single objective.

KEY TERMS AND DEFINITIONS

Basic variables variables that solve a set of constraint equations when a set of nonbasic variables are set to zero.

Convex polygon the geometric figure defined by the set of constraint functions stipulating the feasible region of possible solutions.

Degenerate solution an occasion when a basic variable also is zero-valued.

Deviational weights weights given to goals within a priority level to show their relative importance.

Extreme point any corner of a convex polygon in which at least one point will define the optimal solution that maximizes (or minimizes) the objective function.

Goal programming a variation of linear programming that is useful when dealing with multiple objectives.

Objective function an algebraic statement measuring the performance of a system when decision variables take on values.

Postoptimality analysis use of the shadow prices of limited resources and their right-hand-side ranging to evaluate the opportunities for investment in more resources.

Preemptive priorities a condition in goal programming where higher-ranked goals are not sacrificed to achieve lower-ranked goals.

Shadow price an opportunity cost (or imputed price) assigned to a limited resource.

Simplex algorithm a systematic procedure to evaluate the extreme points in search of an optimal solution.

SOLVED PROBLEMS

1. Formulating a Linear Programming Model

Problem Statement

Moonstruck Country Store packages and sells three blends of coffee labeled (A)maretto, (B)reakfast blend, and (C)hicory, at prices of $2.60, $2.50, and $2.30 per pound, respectively. The blends are made from two coffee beans, Colombian and Mexican. The percentage of Colombian beans in blends A, B, and C is 80 percent, 50 percent, and 30 percent, respectively, with the remaining percentage being Mexican beans. At present, Moonstruck has an inventory of 20 pounds of Colombian beans purchased at 90 cents per pound and 30 pounds of Mexican beans purchased at 50 cents per pound. The roasting and packaging cost for all three brands is $1.20 per pound. Formulate a linear programming model to determine the pounds of each brand to mix that will maximize profits.

Solution

First, formulate the objective function by determining the profit per pound for each blend using the following relationship:

Profit per pound = Selling price − Packaging cost − Colombian bean cost as
percentage − Mexican bean cost as percentage

$$\text{Max } Z = [2.60 - 1.20 - (0.8)(0.9) - (0.2)(0.5)] \text{ A} + [2.50 - 1.20 - (0.5)(0.9) - (0.5)(0.5)] \text{ B} + [2.30 - 1.20 - (0.3)(0.9) - (0.7)(0.5)] \text{ C}$$

$$= 0.58 \text{ A} + 0.60 \text{ B} + 0.48 \text{ C}$$

Second, formulate the constraints:

$$0.8 \text{ A} + 0.5 \text{ B} + 0.3 \text{ C} \le 20 \qquad \text{Colombian bean inventory}$$

$$0.2 \text{ A} + .05 \text{ B} + 0.7 \text{ C} \le 30 \qquad \text{Mexican bean inventory}$$

$$\text{A, B, C} \ge 0$$

2. Computer Solution and Interpretation of Results

Problem Statement

Use Excel Solver to find the optimal product mix and to perform postoptimality analysis.

Solution

From Table 17.7, we find that the optimal solution yields a profit of $27 with a product mix of 25 pounds of (B)reakfast blend and 25 pounds of (C)hicory blend. Note that with two constraints, only two variables can be basic; thus, it is not optimal to produce all three blends.

Considering the objective-function coefficient sensitivity, we see that the (A)maretto blend will be produced only if the unit profit contribution exceeds 78 cents (or a selling price of $2.80). The shadow prices indicate that we are overpaying for Mexican beans, because they are worth only 30 cents per pound in our solution but we paid 50 cents per pound.

TOPICS FOR DISCUSSION

1. Give some everyday examples of constrained optimization problems.
2. How can the validity of LP models be evaluated?
3. Interpret the meaning of the opportunity cost for a nonbasic decision variable that did not appear in the LP solution.
4. Explain graphically what has happened when a degenerate solution occurs in an LP problem.

TABLE 17.7

MOONSTRUCK FORMULATION, SOLUTION, AND SENSITIVITY REPORT USING MICROSOFT® EXCEL 7.0

Linear Model

			Name:	Moonstruck				
			Type:	LP				
			No. Var.:	3				
			Int. Var.:	0		Objective Value		
			No. Con.:	2		0		
	Variables	Num.	Nonlinear:	0		1	2	3
Model		Name				A	B	C
0		Values				0	0	0
3		Linear Obj. Coef.				0.58	0.6	0.48
TRUE		Lower Bounds				0	0	0
TRUE		Upper Bounds				99999	99999	99999
TRUE	Constraints			Constraint Bounds				
TRUE	Num.	Name	Value	Lower	Upper	Constraint Coefficients		
100	1	Col	0	0	20	0.8	0.5	0.3
	2	Mex	0	0	30	0.2	0.5	0.7

Target Cell (Max)

Cell	Name	Original Value	Final Value
H5	Moonstruck_Obj	0	27

Changing Cells

Cell	Name	Final Value	Reduced Cost	Objective Coefficient	Allowable Increase	Allowable Decrease
G8	Values A	0	-0.2	0.58	0.2	1E+30
H8	Values B	25	0	0.6	0.2	0.08
I8	Values C	25	0	0.48	0.133333333	0.12

Constraints

Cell	Name	Final Value	Shadow Price	Constraint R.H. Side	Allowable Increase	Allowable Decrease
D14	Col Value	20	0.9	20	10	7.142857143
D15	Mex Value	30	0.3	30	16.66666667	10
D14	Col Value	20	0	0	20	1E+30
D15	Mex Value	30	0	0	30	1E+30

5. Using Figure 17.6, analyze the x objective-function coefficient that ranges from a value of 40 to infinity.
6. Using Figure 17.7, explain what happens to the LP solution as the RHS of binding constraint 2 ranges from $6000 to $9500.
7. Linear programming is a special case of goal programming. Explain.
8. What are some limitations to the use of LP?

EXERCISES

17.1. The Economy Cab Company wants to mix two fuels (A and B) for its taxicabs to minimize operating costs. The company needs at least 3000 gallons to operate its cabs next month. There are only 2000 gallons of fuel A available, but fuel B is unlimited in supply. The mixed fuel must have an octane rating of at least 80.

When fuels are mixed, the amount of the fuel that is obtained equals the sum of the amounts put in, assuming that no spillage or evaporation occurs. The resulting octane rating is the average of the individual octane ratings, weighted in proportion to the respective volumes. Fuel A costs 20 cents per gallon and has an octane rating of 90; fuel B costs 10 cents per gallon and has an octane rating of 75.

   a. Formulate this blending problem (a variation on the diet problem) as an LP model to minimize the cost of the blended fuel.

   b. Using the graphical method, determine the amount of each fuel that is required for an optimum blend.

17.2 Springdale has been ordered by a federal district court to desegregate its school system. The city is divided into seven school districts and is served by three elementary, one junior high, and one high school. The table here gives the distance from each district to each elementary school and the number of both minority and white children in each district. Ideally, minorities should represent 40 percent of enrollment in each elementary school. Achieving perfect desegregation is not practical, however, so the school board is willing to settle for a percentage of minorities in each school that is not less than 30 percent or more than 50 percent. Each school has a capacity of 400 students. Formulate an LP model to minimize the total number of student miles traveled by bus. Do not solve.

	Distance to school, miles			Numbers in district	
District	A	B	C	Minorities	Whites
1	10	18	32	90	40
2	0	25	38	110	20
3	20	13	24	50	60
4	8	22	33	70	70
5	35	0	16	40	130
6	26	14	24	30	120
7	38	7	0	10	160
Total				400	600

17.3 The computer input for the Lakeview Hospital example is shown in Table 17.8, with E, C, and S defined as units of egg custard base, ice cream, and butterscotch syrup. The results of the computer solutions are given in Table 17.9.

   a. What is the cost of the special milkshake?

   b. How many units of each ingredient are required for this minimum-cost shake? If you feel that this mixture is unacceptable, suggest a constraint that would guarantee an acceptable milkshake.

   c. What would be the cost of including one unit of ice cream in the mixture? Explain why this cost is less than 25 cents.

   d. What is the cholesterol, fat, protein, and calorie content of this milkshake?

   e. What are the ranges of acceptable unit costs for the egg custard base and butterscotch syrup for the computer solution to remain optimal?

   f. What would the milkshake cost if the protein requirement were increased to its RHS limit?

   g. Why are there no upper limits on the requirements for cholesterol and fat?

TABLE 17.8

MICROSOFT® EXCEL 7.0 FORMULATION FOR LAKEVIEW HOSPITAL

Linear Model

Name:	Lakeview		
Type:	LP		
No. Var.:	3		
Int. Var.:	0		
No. Con.:	4		
Nonlinear:	0		

Objective Value: 0

Model	Variables	Num. Name		1	2	3
				E	C	S
0		Values		0	0	0
3		Linear Obj. Coef.		0.15	0.25	0.1
TRUE		Lower Bounds		0	0	0
TRUE		Upper Bounds		99999	99999	99999
TRUE	Constraints					
TRUE	Num.	Name	Value			
100						

Constraints				Constraint Bounds		Constraint Coefficients		
Num.	Name	Value		Lower	Upper			
1	Chol	0		0	175	50	150	90
2	Fat	0		0	150	0	100	50
3	Protein	0		200	99999	70	10	0
4	Calories	0		100	99999	30	80	200

TABLE 17.9

MICROSOFT® EXCEL 7.0 SOLUTION AND SENSITIVITY REPORT FOR LAKEVIEW HOSPITAL

Target Cell (Min)

Cell	Name	Original Value	Final Value
H5	Lakeview_Obj	0	0.435714286

Changing Cells

Cell	Name	Final Value	Reduced Cost	Objective Coefficient	Allowable Increase	Allowable Decrease
G8	Values E	2.857142857	0	0.15	1.335	0.135
H8	Values C	0	0.190714286	0.25	1E+30	0.190714286
I8	Values S	0.071428571	0	0.1	0.503773585	0.1

Constraints

Cell	Name	Final Value	Shadow Price	Constraint R.H. Side	Allowable Increase	Allowable Decrease
D14	Chol Value	149.2857143	0	175	1E+30	25.714285714
D15	Fat Value	3.571428571	0	150	1E+30	146.4285714
D16	Protein Value	200	0	99999	1E+30	99799
D17	Calories Value	100	0	99999	1E+30	99899
D14	Chol Value	149.2857143	0	0	149.2857143	1E+30
D15	Fat Value	3.571428571	0	0	3.571428571	1E+30
D16	Protein Value	200	0.001928571	200	33.33333333	200
D17	Calories Value	100	0.0005	100	57.14285714	14.28571429

TABLE 17.10

MICROSOFT® EXCEL 7.0 FORMULATION FOR GOTHAM CITY

Linear Model

Name: Gotham_City
Type: LP
No. Var.: 6
Int. Var.: 0
No. Con.: 6
Nonlinear: 0

Objective Value: 0

Model	Variables	Num. Name		1	2	3	4	5	6
0				X 1	X 2	X 3	X 4	X 5	X 6
6		Values		0	0	0	0	0	0
TRUE		Linear Obj. Coef.		1	1	1	1	1	1
TRUE		Lower Bounds		0	0	0	0	0	0
TRUE		Upper Bounds		99999	99999	99999	99999	99999	99999
FALSE									
100									

Constraints Num.	Name	Value	Constraint Bounds Lower	Upper	Constraint Coefficients					
1	Period 1	0	6	99999	1	0	0	0	0	1
2	Period 2	0	4	99999	1	1	0	0	0	0
3	Period 3	0	14	99999	0	1	1	0	0	0
4	Period 4	0	8	99999	0	0	1	1	0	0
5	Period 5	0	12	99999	0	0	0	1	1	0
6	Period 6	0	16	99999	0	0	0	0	1	1

17.4. The computer input for the Gotham City Police Patrol example is shown in Table 17.10, with x_j defined as the number of patrol officers reporting for duty at the beginning of period j. The results of the computer solution are given in Table 17.11.

   a. How many patrol officers are required to meet the staffing requirements? Is this solution an improvement over the current practice of officers reporting at only three times during the day?

   b. In what period is there an excess of officers? As the police commissioner, how could you make full use of their time?

   c. Using Figure 17.1, sketch the results of this optimum staffing schedule.

   d. What does the reduced cost of zero for variable x_4 suggest?

   e. A police officer, unhappy about reporting for duty at midnight, suggests the following schedule: $x_1 = 0$, $x_2 = 8$, $x_3 = 6$, $x_4 = 2$, $x_5 = 10$, and $x_6 = 6$. Show that this schedule is both feasible and optimal.

17.5. The computer input for the Last National Drive-In Bank example is shown in Table 17.12, with A_j and T_j representing the number of tellers available and trainees hired at the beginning of period j. The results of the computer solution are given in Table 17.13.

   a. The solution did not result in integer values as required. On the basis of the fractional solution, how many trainees would you recommend be hired in each of the coming six periods?

   b. Is your recommendation in part **a** feasible?

   c. Why are you not surprised to find that T_6 is nonbasic?

   d. How much overstaffing results from your solution?

   e. Explain why this LP formulation cannot be solved as an integer program.

17.6. The computer input for the Lease-a-Lemon Car Rental example is shown in Table 17.14, with x_{ij} representing the number of cars to send from city i to city j. The results of the computer solution are given in Table 17.15.

   a. What is the recommended schedule of car movements?

   b. Is this solution degenerate?

17.7. A certain company is planning to introduce a new product that will be promoted by specially trained agents. The new-product campaign will be guided by the following considerations: (1) the training session for special agents should be as close to 20 working days as possible; (2) sales during the first quarter, it is hoped, will be near 5 million units; and (3) under no circumstances can training costs exceed $600,000. Write the objective

TABLE 17.11

MICROSOFT® EXCEL 7.0 SOLUTION AND SENSITIVITY REPORT FOR GOTHAM CITY

Target Cell (Min)

Cell	Name	Original Value	Final Value
H5	Gotham_City_Obj	0	32

Changing Cells

Cell	Name	Final Value	Reduced Cost	Objective Coefficient	Allowable Increase	Allowable Decrease
G8	Values X 1	2	0	1	0	1
H8	Values X 2	6	0	1	0	0
I8	Values X 3	8	0	1	0	0
J8	Values X 4	0	0	1	1E+30	0
K8	Values X 5	12	0	1	0	1
L8	Values X 6	4	0	1	1	0

Constraints

Cell	Name	Final Value	Shadow Price	Constraint R.H. Side	Allowable Increase	Allowable Decrease
D14	Period 1 Value	6	0	99999	1E+30	99993
D15	Period 2 Value	8	0	99999	1E+30	99991
D16	Period 3 Value	14	0	99999	1E+30	99985
D17	Period 4 Value	8	0	99999	1E+30	99991
D18	Period 5 Value	12	0	99999	1E+30	99987
D19	Period 6 Value	16	0	99999	1E+30	99983
D14	Period 1 Value	6	1	6	99991	2
D15	Period 2 Value	8	0	4	4	1E+30
D16	Period 3 Value	14	1	14	99985	4
D17	Period 4 Value	8	0	8	4	8
D18	Period 5 Value	12	1	12	4	2
D19	Period 6 Value	16	0	16	2	4

function and constraints if the sales target is considered to be twice as important as the training time target. The training cost is $20,000 per day, and each day of training will produce 150,000 units of sales during the first quarter. The decision to be made concerns the number of days that should be spent training sales agents.

Let x = the number of days devoted to training. Define other variables as necessary and formulate a goal-programming model.

17.8. Tennis World carries three lines of its Toe-brand tennis racket: the Student, the Weekender, and the Professional. The more expensive the line, the greater the markup, but the more expensive lines also require more floor space for increasingly elaborate displays. Pertinent data can be summarized as

Tennis racket	Cost per racket to Tennis World, $	Tennis World markup, %	Display space per racket, ft²
Student	10	10	1
Weekender	15	20	2
Professional	30	50	5

TABLE 17.12

MICROSOFT® EXCEL 7.0 FORMULATION FOR LAST NATIONAL BANK

Linear Model

Name: National_Bank
Type: LP
No. Var.: 12
Int. Var.: 0
No. Con.: 12
Nonlinear: 0

Objective Value
0

Model	Variables Num. Name						A1	A2	A3	A4	A5	A6	T1	T2	T3	T4	T5	T6
							1	2	3	4	5	6	7	8	9	10	11	12
0	Values						0	0	0	0	0	0	0	0	0	0	0	0
12	Linear Obj. Coef.						600	600	600	600	600	600	300	300	300	300	300	300
TRUE	Lower Bounds						0	0	0	0	0	0	0	0	0	0	0	0
TRUE	Upper Bounds						99999	99999	99999	99999	99999	99999	99999	99999	99999	99999	99999	99999

	Constraints Num.	Name	Value	Constraint Bounds Lower	Upper	Constraint Coefficients											
TRUE																	
FALSE	1	Jan	0	1500	99999	160	0	0	0	0	0	-80	0	0	0	0	0
100	2	Feb	0	1800	99999	0	160	0	0	0	0	0	-80	0	0	0	0
	3	Mar	0	1600	99999	0	0	160	0	0	0	0	0	-80	0	0	0
	4	Apr	0	2000	99999	0	0	0	160	0	0	0	0	0	-80	0	0
	5	May	0	1800	99999	0	0	0	0	160	0	0	0	0	0	-80	0
	6	June	0	2200	99999	0	0	0	0	0	160	0	0	0	0	0	-80
	7	Initial A	0	12	12	1	0	0	0	0	0	0	0	0	0	0	0
	8	Feb-A	0	0	0	0.9	-1	0	0	0	0	1	0	0	0	0	0
	9	Mar-A	0	0	0	0	0.9	-1	0	0	0	0	1	0	0	0	0
	10	Apr-A	0	0	0	0	0	0.9	-1	0	0	0	0	1	0	0	0
	11	May-A	0	0	0	0	0	0	0.9	-1	0	0	0	0	1	0	0
	12	June-A	0	0	0	0	0	0	0	0.9	-1	0	0	0	0	1	0

In deciding on the optimal merchandising plan, the manager states the following goals in order of preference: (1) avoid overrunning the purchasing budget of $2000, (2) achieve a gross margin (i.e., the sum of markups for each racket) of at least $500, (3) avoid using more than 300 square feet of floor space for displays, and (4) ensure that the entire purchasing budget is spent. Formulate a goal-programming model to determine the number of each type of tennis racket to stock. Recall the following retailing relationship: selling price = cost + (markup) (cost).

TABLE 17.13

MICROSOFT® EXCEL 7.0 SOLUTION AND SENSITIVITY REPORT FOR LAST NATIONAL BANK

Target Cell (Min)

Cell	Name	Original Value	Final Value
H5	National_Bank_Obj	0	46865.35692

Changing Cells

Cell	Name	Final Value	Reduced Cost	Objective Coefficient	Allowable Increase	Allowable Decrease
G8	Values A1	12	0	600	1E+30	330
H8	Values A2	11.67432039	0	600	1E+30	630
I8	Values A3	11.35552913	0	600	1E+30	847.2413793
J8	Values A4	12.93103448	0	600	1E+30	922.1521998
K8	Values A5	12.5	0	600	1E+30	947.9835172
L8	Values A6	13.75	0	600	1E+30	1226.890868
M8	Values T1	0.87432039	0	300	366.6666667	300
N8	Values T2	0.848640781	0	300	700	750
O8	Values T3	2.711058264	0	300	941.3793103	858.6206897
P8	Values T4	0.862068966	0	300	1024.613555	896.0760999
Q8	Values T5	2.5	0	300	1053.315019	908.9917586
R8	Values T6	0	913.445434	300	1E+30	913.445434

Constraints

Cell	Name	Final Value	Shadow Price	Constraint R.H. Side	Allowable Increase	Allowable Decrease
D14	Jan Value	1850.054369	0	99999	1E+30	98148.94563
D15	Feb Value	1800	0	99999	1E+30	98199
D16	Mar Value	1600	0	99999	1E+30	98399
D17	Apr Value	2000	0	99999	1E+30	97999
D18	May Value	1800	0	99999	1E+30	98199
D19	June Value	2200	0	99999	1E+30	97799
D20	Initial A Value	12	0	12	1E+30	0
D21	Feb-A Value	2.33147E-15	0	0	1E+30	0
D22	Mar-A Value	2.77556E-15	0	0	1E+30	0
D23	Apr-A Value	-3.10862E-15	0	0	1E+30	0
D24	May-A Value	3.44169E-15	0	0	1E+30	0
D25	June-A Value	0	0	0	1E+30	0
D14	Jan Value	1850.054369	0	1500	350.0543688	1E+30
D15	Feb Value	1800	2.715517241	1800	218.7607346	202.8423306
D16	Mar Value	1600	3.651902497	1600	698.8505747	285.4827586
D17	Apr Value	2000	3.974793964	2000	222.2222222	827.9
D18	May Value	1800	4.08613585	1800	644.4444444	290
D19	June Value	2200	7.668067925	2200	49517.3608	580
D20	Initial A Value	12	330	12	0	1.508855038
D21	Feb-A Value	2.33147E-15	300	0	0	0.87432039
D22	Mar-A Value	2.77556E-15	517.2413793	0	0	1.230529132
D23	Apr-A Value	-3.10862E-15	592.1521998	0	0	3.568534483
D24	May-A Value	3.44169E-15	617.9835172	0	0	1.25
D25	June-A Value	0	626.890868	0	0	3.625

TABLE 17.14

MICROSOFT® EXCEL 7.0 FORMULATION FOR LEASE-A-LEMON

Linear Model

Name: Lease_A_Lemon
Type: LP
No. Var.: 12
Int. Var.: 0
No. Con.: 7
Nonlinear: 0

Objective Value
0

Model	Variables	Num. Name				1 X 11	2 X12	3 X13	4 X 14	5 X21	6 X22	7 X 23	8 X24	9 X31	10 X 32	11 X 33	12 X 34
0		Values				0	0	0	0	0	0	0	0	0	0	0	0
12		Linear Obj. Coef.				439	396	91	0	296	434	133	0	131	184	479	0
TRUE		Lower Bounds				0	0	0	0	0	0	0	0	0	0	0	0
TRUE		Upper Bounds				99999	99999	99999	99999	99999	99999	99999	99999	99999	99999	99999	99999

	Constraints			Constraint Bounds		Constraint Coefficients											
TRUE	Num.	Name	Value	Lower	Upper												
FALSE																	
100	1	NYC	0	26	26	1	1	1	1	0	0	0	0	0	0	0	0
	2	DC	0	43	43	0	0	0	0	1	1	1	1	0	0	0	0
	3	Clev	0	31	31	0	0	0	0	0	0	0	0	1	1	1	1
	4	Pitt	0	32	32	1	0	0	0	1	0	0	0	1	0	0	0
	5	Buff	0	28	28	0	1	0	0	0	1	0	0	0	1	0	0
	6	Phil	0	26	26	0	0	1	0	0	0	1	0	0	0	1	0
	7	Dummy	0	14	14	0	0	0	1	0	0	0	1	0	0	0	1

TABLE 17.15

MICROSOFT® EXCEL 7.0 SOLUTION AND SENSITIVITY REPORT FOR LEASE-A-LEMON

Target Cell (Min)

Cell	Name	Original Value	Final Value
H5	Lease_A_Lemon_Obj	0	16495

Changing Cells

Cell	Name	Final Value	Reduced Cost	Objective Coefficient	Allowable Increase	Allowable Decrease
G8	Values X 11	0	143	439	1E+30	143
H8	Values X12	0	47	396	1E+30	47
I8	Values X13	26	0	91	42	1E+30
J8	Values X 14	0	0	0	47	42
K8	Values X21	29	0	296	47	74
L8	Values X22	0	85	434	1E+30	85
M8	Values X 23	0	42	133	1E+30	42
N8	Values X24	14	0	0	42	47
O8	Values X31	3	0	131	74	47
P8	Values X 32	28	0	184	47	184
Q8	Values X 33	0	553	479	1E+30	553
R8	Values X 34	0	165	0	1E+30	165

Constraints

Cell	Name	Final Value	Shadow Price	Constraint R.H. Side	Allowable Increase	Allowable Decrease
D14	NYC Value	26	0	26	1E+30	0
D15	DC Value	43	0	43	1E+30	0
D16	Clev Value	31	0	31	1E+30	0
D17	Pitt Value	32	0	32	1E+30	0
D18	Buff Value	28	0	28	1E+30	0
D19	Phil Value	26	-74	26	0	0
D20	Dummy Value	14	-165	14	0	0
D14	NYC Value	26	165	26	0	0
D15	DC Value	43	165	43	0	0
D16	Clev Value	31	0	31	0	1E+30
D17	Pitt Value	32	131	32	0	0
D18	Buff Value	28	184	28	0	0
D19	Phil Value	26	0	26	0	1E+30
D20	Dummy Value	14	0	14	0	1E+30

Munich Delicatessen

Among the most popular items served by the Munich Delicatessen is its bratwurst. This sausage is based on an original Old World recipe combining beef, chicken, lamb, and assorted spices in a pure animal casing. By U.S. Department of Agriculture regulations, the Munich Deli must display on the sausage label certain content information and adhere to those content specifications in the processing and packaging of the sausage. Because of the popularity of its bratwurst, Munich Deli can sell all the bratwurst it can make. Potential variability of the costs of the major ingredients, however, causes a continuing problem for the processing manager, who must determine the amount of each ingredient to mix into the sausage.

Bratwurst is prepared in 100-pound batches. According to the label, which cannot be altered except through a lengthy and costly procedure, each batch consists of at least 30-percent lamb by weight, with no specific requirement on beef or chicken. Moreover, the label indicates that each batch, by weight, is at most 24-percent fat, at least 12-percent protein, and at most 64-percent water and other ingredients. It can be reasonably assumed that the spices and casing add an insignificant amount to the total sausage weight and almost nothing in terms of the elements being controlled.

A recent Department of Agriculture study has shown that the major ingredients in bratwurst contain the label-controlled elements in the following proportions:

	Percentage of weight		
Element	Beef	Chicken	Lamb
Fat	20	15	25
Protein	20	15	15
Water and others	60	70	60

Currently, the costs of the principal ingredients are $1.00, $0.50, and $0.70 per pound for beef, chicken, and lamb, respectively. At these costs, there seem to be unlimited supplies. Thus, the processing manager at Munich Deli must decide how much of each principal ingredient to mix into each batch of bratwurst to meet the labeling requirements at the lowest cost.

A preliminary analysis suggests that this decision problem can be formulated as an LP model, with

x_1 = number of pounds of beef per batch
x_2 = number of pounds of chicken per batch
x_3 = number of pounds of lamb per batch

Formulate this problem as an LP problem and solve.

Questions

1. Suppose that the early, unseasonably cold weather reduces the production of lamb and that the price for new supplies rises to 85 cents per pound. What effect will this situation have on the optimum contents of the sausage found originally? What effect will this situation have on Munich Deli's production costs for each batch of bratwurst?

2. The Department of Agriculture is considering the adoption of new regulations that would restrict the water content in all sausage. For what range of water-content values would Munich Deli continue to use the same ingredients in its sausage as in the original optimum (i.e., the same basic variables)?

3. Suppose that a meat supplier advises Munich Deli of the availability of veal tongues. The original recipe for bratwurst reveals that veal tongues could be used, and, technically, this ingredient already is covered on the sausage label under the generic category "beef and beef by-products." Unlike the regular beef originally considered, these tongues are 30-percent fat, 15-percent protein, and 55-percent water, all by weight. The meat supplier is willing to sell Munich Deli these tongues for $0.40 per pound. Should this new ingredient be included in the optimal sausage composition? Why?

Sequoia Airlines

Sequoia Airlines is a well-established regional airline serving California, Nevada, Arizona, and Utah. Sequoia competes against much larger carriers in this regional market, and its management feels that the price, frequency of flight service, ability to meet schedules, baggage handling, and image projected by its flight attendants are the most important marketing factors that airline passengers consider when deciding to use a particular carrier.

In each of these areas, Sequoia is attaining its desired objectives. Maintaining its flight-attendant staff at desired levels has been difficult in the past, however, and many times, it has had to ask flight attendants to work overtime because of worker shortages. This has resulted in excessive personnel costs and some morale problems among the attendants. One reason for these worker shortages is a higher-than-industry-average turnover rate resulting from experienced attendants being hired away by other airlines. This is not totally due to morale problems; that cause seems to become important only during seasonal peak-demand periods, when shortages are particularly bad. By interviewing the existing personnel, Sequoia has discovered that competing regional carriers (whose training programs are not as highly developed) have been hiring away from Sequoia a significant proportion of its staff by offering slightly higher direct salaries, attractive indirect benefit packages, and guarantees of a minimum number of flying hours in off-peak demand periods.

As a beginning, Sequoia's management has asked for a 6-month hiring and training analysis of the flight-attendant staff requirements beginning next month (July). An investigation of the operations schedule indicates that 14,000 attendant-hours are needed in July, 16,000 in August, 13,000 in September, 12,000 in October, 18,000 in November, and 20,000 in December. Sequoia's training program for new personnel requires an entire month of classroom preparation before they are assigned to regular flight service. As junior flight attendants, they remain on probationary status for 1 additional month. Periodically, there is some personnel movement from the working flight attendant staff to the staff that supervises the training of new employees. Figure 17.8 shows the relationships and percentages of interstaff movements.

When no personnel shortages occur, each junior flight attendant normally works an average of 140 hours per month and is paid a salary of $1050 during the probationary period. During the training period, each new employee is paid $750. Experienced flight attendants receive an average salary of $1400 per month and work an average of 125 hours per month. Each instructor receives a salary of $1500 per month.

The poorly kept secret of Sequoia's personalized training program is that the number of trainees is limited to no more than five per instructor. Instructors not needed in a particular month (i.e., surplus) may be used as flight attendants. To ensure a high level of quality in flight service, Sequoia requires that the proportion of junior flight attendant hours not exceed 25 percent of any month's total (i.e., junior plus experienced) attendant-hours.

In May, Sequoia hired 10 new employees to enter the training program, and this month, it hired 10 more. At the beginning of June, there were 120 experienced flight attendants and six instructors on Sequoia's staff.

FIGURE 17.8   Sequoia Airlines flight-attendant flows.

Let T_t = number of trainees hired at the beginning of period t, with $t = 1, 2, 3, 4, 5, 6$

J_t = number of junior flight attendants available at the beginning of period t, with $t = 1, 2, 3, 4, 5, 6$

F_t = number of experienced flight attendants available at the beginning of period t, with $t = 1, 2, 3, 4, 5, 6$

I_t = number of instructors available at the beginning of period t, with $t = 1, 2, 3, 4, 5, 6$

S_t = number of surplus instructors available as flight attendants at the beginning of period t, with $t = 1, 2, 3, 4, 5, 6$

Questions

1. For the forecast period (i.e., July–December), determine the number of new trainees who must be hired at the beginning of each month so that total personnel costs for the flight-attendant staff and training program are minimized. Formulate the problem as an LP model and solve.

2. How would you deal with the noninteger results?

3. Discuss how you would use the LP model to make your hiring decision for the next six months.

SELECTED BIBLIOGRAPHY

Anderson, D. R., D. J. Sweeney, and T. A. Williams: *An Introduction to Management Science,* 7th ed., West Publishing Co., New York, 1994.

Chang, Yih-Long: *WinQSB,* John Wiley, New York, 1998.

Jensen, Paul A.: *Operations Research Add-ins for Microsoft Excel,* Operations Research Group, Dept. of Mechanical Engineering, University of Texas at Austin, 1996.

Microsoft® Excel 2000, Microsoft Corporation, Redmond, Wash., 1999.

ENDNOTE

1. Paul A. Jensen, *Operations Research Add-ins for Microsoft Excel,* Operations Research Group, Department of Mechanical Engineering, University of Texas at Austin, June 1996.

PART FOUR

TOWARD
WORLD-CLASS SERVICE

Competition in services has become global, as Federal Express discovered during its attempt to expand overseas. The danger of services following the decline in competitiveness that has been experienced by manufacturing is possible, because no market is isolated in today's global economy. A service firm can reach, and sustain, a competitive position by promoting a culture of continuous improvement in productivity and quality. In this regard, the application of Deming's philosophy of continuous service process improvement is explored. A technique called *data envelopment analysis (DEA)* will be used to measure productivity of a service unit as the ratio of resource inputs to service outputs.

Service expansion strategies can be described in the context of being multisite or multiservice. The traditional multisite service expansion strategy of franchising is explored, with a discussion of the issues that arise between franchisee and franchiser. For services considering multinational expansion, additional considerations such as cultural transferability and host-government policies arise.

Productivity and Quality Improvement

Learning Objectives

After completing this chapter, you should be able to:

1. Categorize a service firm according to its stage of competitiveness.
2. Discuss the analogous roles that inventory plays in manufacturing and queuing plays in services.
3. Discuss the organizational implications of following a strategy of continuous improvement.
4. Perform a walk-through audit (WtA).
5. Lead a plan-do-check-act (PDCA) process improvement initiative.
6. Use quality tools for analysis and problem solving.
7. Discuss the corporate programs available for quality improvement.
8. Conduct a data envelopment analysis (DEA).

Changing demographics and the anticipated future labor shortage will force services to become more productivity-conscious. Consider the labor-saving ideas that have been incorporated by the new Sleep Inn chain to reduce the labor costs of operating a hotel unit. For example, clothes washers and dryers are located behind the front desk, so the night clerk can load and unload laundry while on duty. To help reduce house-keeping chores, nightstands are bolted to the wall so that maids need not vacuum around legs, and the shower stall is round to prevent dirt from collecting in corners. In addition, the computerized electronic security system has eliminated room keys: guests use their own credit cards to enter their rooms. Also, to reduce energy costs, heat or air-conditioning is turned on or off automatically when the guest checks in or out. In addition, the computer records the time that maids spend cleaning each room. Thus, creative facility design, effective use of labor, and innovative use of computers can have a major impact on increasing service productivity.[1]

CHAPTER PREVIEW

The focus of this chapter is on continuous improvement (CI) in service organizations using productivity and quality initiatives. World-class service firms are noted by their commitment to ongoing improvement in customer service and, thus, raising the bar of excellence for the industry. Continuous improvement is a way of thinking that needs to be incorporated into a firm's culture.

By way of an analogy, queue reduction in services and inventory reduction in manufacturing using the just-in-time (JIT) philosophy are shown as powerful motivators for process improvement. A proactive customer survey called a walk-through audit is presented as a diagnostic tool for discovering areas that need improvement.

The Deming philosophy of continuous improvement is captured in the plan-do-check-act (PDCA) cycle. Quality tools for analysis and problem solving are described and illustrated using an example in the airline industry. Corporatewide quality improvement initiatives are explored, including global standards captured in ISO 9000.

Finally, a linear programming model referred to as data envelopment analysis (DEA) is introduced as a method of measuring the efficiency of service delivery units. The comparative analysis of unit performance using DEA provides an opportunity to promote continuous improvement through shared learning.

We begin our discussion by exploring the customer value equation that puts quality and productivity improvement in the context of all the elements important to customers.

CUSTOMER VALUE EQUATION[2]

The value of a service from a customer's perspective can be captured in the following equation:

$$\text{Value} = \frac{\text{Results produced for the customer} + \text{Process quality}}{\text{Price to the customer} + \text{Costs of acquiring the service}}$$

Results Produced for the Customer

Customers do not seek out a service any more than buy a product for no reason. The purchase of the service must result in addressing a need. Even though a restaurant's environment might be pleasant and service courteous, the meal must be satisfying. Some services such as buying gasoline for an automobile, however, are serving a maintenance function that customers would avoid if possible.

Process Quality

The way a service is delivered is often as important as the results produced for the customer. Consider the convenience of shopping for a book on the Internet compared to the effort of buying at a local bookstore. Because the customer is a participant in the service delivery, improvements in process quality must be acceptable to customers. The postal service, for example, requires new housing developments to install neighborhood postal boxes instead of offering door-to-door delivery in order to provide more timely delivery at lower cost. Needing a key to open their box will now inconvenience customers, but security of their mail is assured.

Price to the Customer

Continuous improvement efforts should have a payoff in both improved quality and lower costs as the postal example illustrates. There is no reason to believe a trade-off exists between cost and quality. Achieving more consistency in service quality should yield lower costs, because customer perceptions are more aligned with expectations. Customers also become easier and less expensive to serve because their participation adds value in self-service activities (e.g., ordering a ticket on the Web saves the airline six dollars).

Cost of Acquiring the Service

Often service firms make the mistake of thinking that customers are interested only in price when the cost of acquiring the service may be of equal importance. Convenience has value to customers, a fact not lost on Internet retailers such as Amazon.com. When shipping costs are included, books ordered on the Internet may cost more than the trip to the local store, but the hassle is avoided. Finding ways to lower the acquisition cost for customers should be considered a competitive strategy.

The customer value equation puts in perspective the various elements and opportunities for competitive process improvement. A focus on initiatives to improve quality and productivity should not ignore the other elements of acquisition cost and results produced for the customer.

Next we consider a framework that categorizes service firms according to their level of competitiveness with respect to key operational dimensions, all of which are sources of productivity and quality innovations.

STAGES IN SERVICE FIRM COMPETITIVENESS[3]

If a service firm is to remain competitive, continual improvement in productivity and quality must be part of its strategy and corporate culture. The framework shown in Table 18.1 was developed by Chase and Hayes to describe the role of operations in the strategic development of service firms. This framework also is useful as an illustration of the many sources of productivity and quality improvement (i.e., new technology is only one source). In addition, the framework provides a way to measure and evaluate a firm's progress in the development of its service delivery system. It organizes service firms into four different stages of development according to their competitiveness in service delivery, and for each stage, the management practices and attitudes of the firm are compared across key operational dimensions.

It should be noted that services need not start at stage 1, but during their life cycle, they could revert to stage 1 out of neglect. For example, one might argue that Federal Express began service as a stage 3 competitor because of its innovative hub-and-spoke network concept, whereby all sorting is accomplished at the single Memphis hub (thus guaranteeing overnight delivery).

Available for Service

Some service firms—and, often, government services in particular—fall into this category because they view operations as a necessary evil to be performed at minimum cost. There is little motivation to seek improvements in quality because the customers often have no alternatives. Workers require direct supervision because of their limited skills and the potential for poor performance that results from minimal investment in training. Investment in new technology is avoided until it is necessary for survival (e.g., consider the long-overdue adoption of Doppler radar by the Federal Aviation Administration for air traffic control). These firms are essentially noncompetitive, and they only exist in this stage until they are challenged by competition.

Journeyman

After maintaining a sheltered existence in stage 1, a service firm may face competition and, thus, may be forced to reevaluate its delivery system. Operations managers then must adopt industry practices to maintain parity with its new competitors and avoid a significant loss of market share. For example, if all successful airlines used the same

TABLE 18.1

FOUR STAGES OF SERVICE FIRM COMPETITIVENESS

	1. Available for service	2. Journeyman	3. Distinctive competence achieved	4. World-class service delivery
	Customers patronize service firm for reasons other than performance.	Customers neither seek out nor avoid the firm.	Customers seek out the firm on the basis of its sustained reputation for meeting customer expectations.	The company's name is synonymous with service excellence. Its service doesn't just satisfy customers; it *delights* them and thereby expands customer expectations to levels its competitors are unable to fulfill.
	Operations is reactive, at best.	Operations functions in a mediocre, uninspired fashion.	Operations continually excels, reinforced by personnel management and systems that support an intense customer focus.	Operations is a quick learner and fast innovator; it masters every step of the service delivery process and provides capabilities that are superior to competitors.
Service quality	Is subsidiary to cost, highly variable.	Meets some customer expectations; consistent on one or two key dimensions.	Exceeds customer expectations; consistent on multiple dimensions.	Raises customer expectations and seeks challenges; improves continuously.
Back office	Counting room.	Contributes to service, plays an important role in the total service, is given attention, but is still a separate role.	Is equally valued with front office; plays integral role.	Is proactive, develops its own capabilities, and generates opportunities.
Customer	Unspecified, to be satisfied at minimum cost.	A market segment whose basic needs are understood.	A collection of individuals whose variation in needs is understood.	A source of stimulation, ideas, and opportunity.
Introduction of new technology	When necessary for survival under duress.	When justified by cost savings.	When promises to enhance service.	Source of first-mover advantages, creating ability to do things your competitors can't do.
Workforce	Negative constraint.	Efficient resource; disciplined; follows procedures.	Permitted to select among alternative procedures.	Innovative; creates procedures.
First-line management	Controls workers.	Controls the process.	Listens to customers; coaches and facilitates workers.	Is listened to by top management as a source of new ideas. Mentors workers to enhance their career growth.

Source: Reprinted from "Operations' Role in Service Firm Competitiveness," by R. B. Chase and R. H. Hayes, *Sloan Management Review,* vol. 33, no. 1, Fall 1991, p. 17, by permission of publisher. Copyright © 1991 by the Sloan Management Review Association. All rights reserved.

kind of plane, then a fledgling airline just entering the market also might be inclined to use that same aircraft. The contribution of operations in this hypothetical situation becomes competitive-neutral, because all the firms in the industry have adopted similar practices and even look like each other (because they have purchased equipment from the same supplier).

When firms do not compete on operations effectiveness, they often are creative in competing along other dimensions (e.g., breadth of product line, peripheral services, advertising). The workforce is disciplined to follow standard procedures and is not expected to take any initiative when unusual circumstances arise. These firms have not yet recognized the potential contribution of operations to a firm's competitiveness.

Distinctive Competence Achieved

Firms in stage 3 are fortunate to have senior managers with a vision of what creates value for the customer and who understand the role that operations managers must play in delivering the service. For example, Jan Carlzon, CEO of Scandinavian Airlines (SAS), realized that recapturing the business-traveler market, which had been lost to aggressive competition, required improving on-time departure performance. To achieve this goal, he had to provide a leadership role that fostered operations innovations, which then would improve the delivery system.

Operations managers are the typical advocates of total quality management (TQM) in their firms and take the lead in instituting service guarantees, worker empowerment, and service-enhancing technologies. Workers in these organizations often are cross-trained and encouraged to take the initiative when necessary to achieve operational goals that are stated clearly (e.g., overnight delivery for Federal Express). Firms in this category implement management strategies to achieve the corporate vision and, thereby, differentiate themselves from their competition.

World-Class Service Delivery

Not satisfied with just meeting customer expectations, world-class firms expand on these expectations to levels that competitors find difficult to meet. Management is proactive in promoting higher standards of performance and identifying new business opportunities by listening to customers. World-class service firms such as Disney, Marriott, and American Airlines define the quality standards by which others are judged.

New technology no longer is viewed only as a means to reduce costs; it is considered to be a competitive advantage that is not easily duplicated. For example, Federal Express developed COSMOS (*C*ustomer *O*perations *S*ervice *M*aster *O*n-line *S*ystem) to provide a system that tracks packages from pickup to delivery. Customers can call at any time and receive information on the exact location of their packages. This system also can be used to tell a driver en route to make customer pickups.

Working at a world-class firm is considered to be something special, and employees are encouraged to identify with the firm and its mission. For example, a Disney trash collector is considered to be a "cast member" who helps visitors to enjoy the experience.

Sustaining superior performance throughout the delivery system is a major challenge. Duplicating the service at multiple sites, however, and in particular overseas, is the true test of a world-class competitor.

MAKING CONTINUAL IMPROVEMENT A COMPETITIVE STRATEGY[4]

The history of economic development has been based on learning from experience and then applying this knowledge to improve productivity. For example, Henry Ford is credited with discovering the revolutionary concept of the moving assembly line, on which material is moved past workstations in a factory; however, this idea could have originated from an agricultural analogy, in which equipment is moved through stationary fields for planting and harvesting. This analogy also could be extended to service firms, in which customers are moved to or through a process at a fixed facility. Thus, with proper translation, it is possible for a productivity improvement in one sector of the economy to be useful in another.

For the past decade, we all have been students of the Japanese manufacturing philosophy. First, we observed the use of the *kanban* card and concluded that this novel method of shop-floor control must be the secret of success. Further study revealed the emphasis on inventory reduction, however, and we coined the phrase *just-in-time (JIT)* to describe the process of production with zero inventories. Our understanding of JIT led to an appreciation of its effect on quality improvement. Then, to our surprise, we discovered a method of organizing production that yielded high-quality products at low cost. This realization shattered our long-held assumption of a trade-off between quality and cost. The production function itself now has become a strategic competitive weapon. The success of Japanese penetration into foreign markets proves the effectiveness of this competitive strategy.

Identifying inventory as undesirable because it hides mistakes and decouples workers allows us to see its most serious fault. With inventory buffers, management and, more important, workers are not motivated to engage in problem solving. When inventory is reduced, problems no longer can be buried or sent to a rework area; instead, they must be faced immediately by the workers themselves. A manufacturing culture is established in which everyone is responsible for process and quality improvement. Reliance on a staff of industrial and manufacturing engineers to provide ideas for process improvements is not necessary; instead, the workers dealing with the process on a daily basis are asked to use their minds as well as their hands.

The concept of making continual improvements in the production process is central to a firm's competitive strength and a nation's productive growth. Approximately 70 percent of the gross national product of the world's leading economic nations is generated by the service sector; thus, an ethic of productivity improvement for services is imperative to assure future prosperity.

Inventory and Waiting Line Analogy

In *manufacturing,* the focus of attention is on *material* resources. JIT views idle material resources or inventory as an "evil" to be eliminated, or at least reduced. In *services,* the focus of our attention is on *human* resources. The "evils" to be eliminated or reduced in this case are customer waiting lines and idle staff. Thus, an analogy between inventory in manufacturing and waiting lines in services can be made.

As Table 18.2 shows, inventory and waiting lines share some common features. The cost of a customer waiting in line is a forgone opportunity, which generally is difficult to quantify. Unlike investment in inventory, which can be quantified in financial terms, the cost of keeping customers waiting for service is subjective, but it can be very high. For example, one business executive who was kept waiting in his doctor's office sued the physician for lost time—and won the case. Thus, real costs can be associated with customer waiting, the most important being loss of future business. Storing inventory requires space and the associated investment in a protective facility. Waiting lines also create the need for otherwise unproductive space, which, in addition, should be attractively furnished. Banks have been known to devote one-half of their expensive real estate to drive-in banking facilities, with most of the area being used for a driveway.

TABLE 18.2

INVENTORY AND WAITING LINE ANALOGY

Feature	Inventory	Waiting line
Costs	Opportunity cost of capital	Opportunity cost of time
Space	Warehouse	Waiting area
Quality	Poor quality hidden	Negative impression
Decoupling	Promotes independence of production stages	Allows division of labor and specialization
Utilization	Work in process keeps machines busy	Waiting customers keep servers busy
Coordination	Detailed scheduling not necessary	Avoids matching supply and demand

Inventory is an excellent place to hide poor quality. The intangibility of services makes it difficult for customers to judge quality. Thus, they use surrogates such as the length of time they are kept waiting in line to evaluate service performance. As noted in Chapter 11, "Managing Waiting Lines," excessive waiting can be considered psychological punishment, and the significant negative impression that it creates is difficult for the service to overcome.

Waiting lines also perform some of the same functions in the management of services that inventory did for manufacturing before the advent of JIT. For years, the decoupling function of inventory has been used to simplify the management of production operations. Work-in-process inventory allows management to divide the production process into independent departments, or stages, that can be managed in a decentralized fashion, with supervisors and other work leaders having centralized production control. Waiting lines serve a similar decoupling function by permitting division of labor and specialization. For example, lines for a commercial teller at a bank cannot be served by idle retail tellers or, heaven forbid, by a loan officer. Thus, management is able to create different job classifications and pay according to the skills that are required, with high-customer-contact tellers being paid entry-level wages. This division of labor has its price in loss of flexibility to respond to customer demands.

In manufacturing, work-in-process inventory traditionally has been used to reduce, or even eliminate, machine or operator idle time. Keeping an inventory of inputs before an operation would ensure high labor and equipment utilization. Waiting customers are used in a similar role to keep service personnel busy and under pressure to work at a productive rate. The U.S. Post Office is notorious for employing this strategy as a cost-saving measure, but physicians also keep their waiting rooms full to avoid being idle themselves. In job shops, the level of inventory is quite high, which reflects the complex nature of coordinating the operation. Detailed scheduling of the operation as a whole is impossible, and inventory is used to decentralize the scheduling and allow individual machine centers to focus on selecting jobs from their queue. For service managers, waiting lines are used to store excess demand when it is impossible to adjust service capacity. Restaurants traditionally have used the bar as a holding area for customers who walk in without reservations.

The presence of excessive inventory in a factory or of long waiting lines at a service is an indictment of poor management. This reliance on idle resources (i.e., queues of people or material) to create a smooth operation reveals a lazy management that is unwilling to assume the responsibility of continual process and quality improvement. Organizations without such a competitive operations strategy will be handicapped in the marketplace.

Continual Improvement as Part of the Service Organization Culture

How can continual improvement in productivity and quality be made a part of the service organization culture? What is needed is a clear and visible signal that problem solving is required. An excessively long waiting line of customers or idle servers is an obvious indication that the service is not being deployed effectively. Depending on the circumstance, a variety of responses are possible:

- Ask back-office personnel to come forward and open additional service stations in parallel. For example, have platform personnel at a bank open additional teller windows.
- Ask back-office personnel to assist in performing the service. For example, have stockers assist checkout clerks in bagging groceries in a supermarket.

In response to periods of front-office idleness, customer-contact personnel can help in the back office. For example, in banking, tellers can help to prepare customer account statements for mailing. For a supermarket, checkout clerks can help to stock shelves during slow periods. In general, the response is a redeployment of personnel to serve the customer better while maintaining high utilization of human resources.

What can be learned from these experiences to improve the service process? If customer queues develop at the same time each day, then redeployment can be instituted before the lines form instead of in reaction to them. Other ideas could follow, such as instituting an express lane during these busy periods or having the manager preapprove checks to avoid delays. Ideas should flow naturally, because service employees themselves are service customers and know instinctively what solutions should guarantee reasonable results. In banking, instead of opening express lanes, a better approach might be to staff special desks for the time-consuming services (e.g., selling traveler's checks and CDs). A host or hostess, or even a sign, could direct arriving customers to the appropriate server. In this way, the large number of short transactions is expedited and the congestion eliminated quickly. Customers with minor requests, and who often are in a hurry, will be served promptly. Customers with more demanding requirements usually are more willing to wait, because the ratio of service time to wait time meets their expectations.

This example illustrates the need for improved real-time communication among personnel. In the JIT environment, this is accomplished by use of cards (the Japanese term is kanban) and other simple devices. We are convinced that service employees can create innovative methods to alert coworkers to changing levels of customer demands and, thus, to initiate the necessary redeployment of resources. The resulting interconnectedness will promote a team approach to customer service.

A major distinction between the traditional manufacturing organization and JIT is the source (i.e., direction) of production control. Traditionally, work was released to the first stage of the production process and then *pushed* through the plant from one station to the next. In the JIT system, production orders originate at the final assembly station, and work is *pulled* from the upstream stages as needed. Thus, the entire production system becomes interconnected, and work focuses on meeting the final demand. Each workstation is both a customer for upstream stations and a server for downstream stations. The result is a chain of workers acting as one team. For services, the process flow is seldom as well-defined as that in manufacturing; thus, there is a greater need for an innovative communication linkage between servers. In services, upstream stations such as the receptionist are the first to experience customer demand, unlike the situation in JIT manufacturing (where work is pulled by the final assembly station from upstream stations). Thus, these stations are in a position to provide advance warning to downstream stations to prepare for arriving customers. Ideally, when a customer enters a service system, a "greeter" identifies the particular needs and uses an internal communication system (i.e., kanban) to alert the downstream service providers. Just as in the JIT manufacturing system, the customer "pulls" resources into play as they are needed.

Examples of this approach already exist. When a long line develops at a Burger King or Wendy's, a service person walks up the line and takes orders to speed the transaction time at the counter and, possibly, to deter customer reneging. At a motor vehicle license and registration office, a greeter is stationed just inside the entry to provide customers with forms and directions to the appropriate service counter. The most comprehensive example is found at The Limited retail clothing stores. Sales trends are collected immediately by electronic cash registers and sent directly to the huge Columbus, Ohio, warehouse for distribution; at the same time, factory orders are placed worldwide on the basis of demand, which is being monitored in real time.

The customer automatically becomes the focus of attention when service employees redeploy their efforts to reduce the waiting lines. Thus, even if new ways to improve service are not immediately discovered, at least the customer is aware that special efforts are being made on her or his behalf.

Management Implications

Allowing service employees the discretion to react to customer waiting lines in creative ways has many implications for management. Table 18.3 compares the work environment and dimensions of organizational structure for traditional and world-class service organizations.

We begin with the assumption that a service organization operates as an open system in its environment. This does not suggest that some back-room activities cannot be treated as a buffered core (i.e., isolated from direct customer contact). For the customer-contact personnel, however, we premise their job design on the need for flexibility. Adam Smith's concept of "division of labor," although appropriate for the closed systems in manufacturing, can be counterproductive in an open service environment, in which servers are in direct contact with customers. Flexibility for service

TABLE 18.3

ORGANIZATIONAL STRUCTURE AND WORK ENVIRONMENT OF TRADITIONAL AND WORLD-CLASS SERVICE ORGANIZATIONS

Dimension	Traditional	World-class
System assumption	Closed system	Open system
Job design premise	Division of labor	Flexibility
Structure	Rigid	Fluid
Relation to others	Individual	Team player
Employee orientation	Task	Customer
Management	Supervisor	Coach and facilitator
Technology	Replace human effort	Assist service delivery
Information	Efficiency	Effectiveness

jobs means cross-training, with the ability either to step in and perform another's task or to help facilitate the activities of another employee. Cross-training implies an increased organizational commitment to its personnel and, thus, a change in attitude about the desirability of high turnover and use of minimum-wage labor. This should translate into improved employee relations, because workers are treated with the same respect as the customers.

The organizational structure must be fluid to permit the redeployment of all personnel to meet fluctuations in customer demand. On occasion, back-office personnel must share the task of serving customers directly. If restrictive union work rules such as those found in manufacturing were applied to services, however, they would prevent realization of the competitive advantage of this operations strategy of fluidity. With this strategy, working as a team becomes the norm, and attention is focused on serving the customer instead of simply completing a task. In addition, the role of management changes from that of a traditional supervisor or checker to a coach and team builder.

Technology becomes more important as a method to assist delivery of the service rather than to replace human contact. An exception to this approach is the promotion of self-service through devices such as automated teller machines or airline ticket machines. For example, Southwest Airlines offers a free cocktail to customers who use their credit cards to purchase tickets at a self-service machine. This role of the customer as participant in the service process to increase productivity is an important feature of services, and computerized information processing will play a central role in high-tech, high-touch service delivery systems. The creative use of information is central to the effective delivery of a service by acting as the kanban to permit prepositioning of service delivery activities in a "pull" work-scheduling environment.

It is interesting to note the implications of a service "pull" philosophy that is based on corporate flexibility and real-time information processing, as well as the implications of the traditional mass-marketing "push" philosophy practiced by most manufacturers (e.g., automobile firms). In a service "pull" environment, the operations function becomes critical instead of being taken for granted as in the "push" environment, in which marketing is critical. With the exception of some group services such as lectures, sports events, or the theater, services are not batched; instead, they are performed on the individual. Thus, there is no set-up as in manufacturing. Consequently, a service "pull" system can be implemented with ease. Customer experience with service "pull" systems will provide the incentive for manufacturers to adopt a more service-oriented approach. Eventually, we should witness the transformation from a *push* economy to a *pull* economy.

WALK-THROUGH AUDIT

Delivery of a service should conform to customers' expectations from the beginning to the end of the experience. Because the customer is a participant in the service process, his or her impressions of the service quality are influenced by many observations. An environmental audit can be a proactive management tool for the systematic evaluation of a customer's view of the service provided. A *walk-through audit* (WtA) is a customer-focused survey to uncover areas for improvement.

Fitzsimmons and Maurer developed such a walk-through audit for full-service sit-down restaurants.[5] The audit consisted of 42 questions spanning the restaurant dining experience. The questions begin with approaching the restaurant from the parking area, then walking into the restaurant and being greeted, waiting for a table, being seated, ordering and receiving food and drinks, and finally receiving the check and paying the bill. The questions include nine categories of variables: (1) maintenance items, (2) person-to-person service, (3) waiting, (4) table and place settings, (5) ambiance, (6) food presentation, (7) check presentation, (8) promotion and suggestive selling, and (9) tipping. Thus, the entire customer experience is traced from beginning to end. Unlike the brief and overall customer satisfaction survey as shown in Figure 18.1, the WtA is focused on the details of the service delivery process in an effort to uncover actionable items for improvement.

Designing a Walk-through Audit

The first step in designing a WtA is the preparation of a flowchart of customer interactions with the service system. A WtA for the Helsinki Museum of Art and Design is shown in Figure 18.2. Observe that the questionnaire is divided into five major service delivery process sections (i.e., ticketing, information, experience, facilities, and satisfaction). Within each section a number of statements are made concerning observations that a customer would make (e.g., signs give clear information about exhibits' locations). A five point Likert scale is used to gauge customer perceptions (i.e., 1 = strongly disagree to 5 = strongly agree). As this WtA illustrates, other questions of interest to management are included such as "Where did you hear about the event" to gauge the effectiveness of advertising. It is also useful to leave a final section for "comments" that may provide customer insights not anticipated in the questions asked. To avoid overwhelming the customer, the WtA should be limited to two pages printed back-to-back.

The WtA can be administered in several ways (e.g., mail, telephone interview, in person) but the most effective method is in person immediately following the service experience. Rewarding the customer with a gift certificate or money off on a return visit has significantly increased participation. Survey design issues such as sample size and stratifying the sample to poll all customer segments should be considered. The Selected Bibliography at the end of the chapter lists books that have information on this subject.

As Your Guest, I Would Like to Tell You . . .

_____

_____

_____

_____

	Great	Good	Fair	Poor
Food quality				
Service speed				
Service attentiveness				
Cleanliness				
Atmosphere				

Name_____

Address _____

City _____ State _____ Zip _____

Phone _____ Date _____

FIGURE 18.1 Restaurant satisfaction survey.

Hello, we are from the Helsinki School of Economics and Business Administration and we are conducting a survey to find out, what do people think about the service experience when visiting this museum. Please answer the following questions.

All information in this questionnaire is strictly confidential!

1. **Was it easy getting to the Museum?** ❏ Yes ❏ No
2. **Are the Museum's opening hours acceptable?** ❏ Yes ❏ No
3. **Did you arrive alone or with others?** ❏ Alone ❏ Others Number in Party: _____
4. **Where did you hear about this event:** [Check all that apply]

❏ Newspaper	❏ Internet
❏ Magazine	❏ Friends or relatives
❏ Tourist/City guide	❏ Passing by
❏ Radio	❏ Other: (Specify) _____

5. **Did you come here to see**
   ❏ Brooching It Diplomacy
   ❏ Wine—Nectar of Gods
   ❏ The Holy Cross
   ❏ The permanent exhibition
   ❏ All exhibitions
6. **Which of the following facilities did you visit?** ❏ Cafeteria ❏ Gift shop ❏ Restrooms
7. **How many hours did you spend in the museum?** _____ hours

8. Ticketing	Strongly Disagree	Disagree	Not Sure	Agree	Strongly Agree
a. It is easy to find information about ticket prices.	1	2	3	4	5
b. The ticket price is a good value for the money.	1	2	3	4	5
c. You did not spend too much time by waiting in the ticket line.	1	2	3	4	5
d. You would like to purchase tickets ahead of time, via phone or Internet.	1	2	3	4	5

9. Information	Strongly Disagree	Disagree	Not Sure	Agree	Strongly Agree
a. Signs gave clear information about exhibits' locations.	1	2	3	4	5
b. After arriving at the exhibition, you found adequate information about the exhibition(s).	1	2	3	4	5
c. The information provided was in your language.	1	2	3	4	5
d. Guide services were available.	1	2	3	4	5
e. There was enough information about the objects.	1	2	3	4	5
f. The explanations provided on the objects were clear.	1	2	3	4	5
g. You would like to see a variety of media (video, etc.) providing explanations.	1	2	3	4	5
h. You would like to have access to self-guided material such as a cassette player.	1	2	3	4	5
i. You would like to have more information about the process for creating the objects.	1	2	3	4	5
j. You would like to learn more when visiting exhibits.	1	2	3	4	5
k. It was easy to get additional information from the staff.	1	2	3	4	5
l. The staff helping you was friendly.	1	2	3	4	5

10. The experience	Strongly Disagree	Disagree	Not Sure	Agree	Strongly Agree
a. There was a clear path in which you were guided through the exhibition.	1	2	3	4	5
b. There was enough room to move around the exhibits.	1	2	3	4	5
c. Lighting was adequate.	1	2	3	4	5
d. There was pleasant background music.	1	2	3	4	5
e. The background sounds were pleasant.	1	2	3	4	5
f. The objects on display were adequately spaced apart.	1	2	3	4	5
g. There is enough opportunity for interaction with the displayed objects.	1	2	3	4	5
h. Touching, smelling, and hearing make the experience memorable.	1	2	3	4	5
i. You would also like to touch the material.	1	2	3	4	5

11. Facilities	Strongly Disagree	Disagree	Not Sure	Agree	Strongly Agree
a. There were clear signs giving information about the facilities.	1	2	3	4	5
b. The toilettes were easily accessible.	1	2	3	4	5
c. The toilettes were clean.	1	2	3	4	5
d. The food was of good quality.	1	2	3	4	5
e. There was enough variety of food and beverages.	1	2	3	4	5
f. The food was of good value for the money.	1	2	3	4	5
g. Smoking should be allowed in the restaurant.	1	2	3	4	5
h. The selection of gifts (including books) met your needs.	1	2	3	4	5
i. The gifts were of good value for the money.	1	2	3	4	5

12. Satisfaction	Strongly Disagree	Disagree	Not Sure	Agree	Strongly Agree
a. The services met my needs.	1	2	3	4	5
b. I found the overall service outstanding.	1	2	3	4	5
c. I am likely to use this service again.	1	2	3	4	5
d. I would recommend this museum to my friend.	1	2	3	4	5
e. Could we improve the service to better meet your expectations?	1	2	3	4	5

13. Comments

_____

_____

_____

FIGURE 18.2 Walk-through audit for Helsinki Museum of Art and Design. (Prepared by Eivor Biese, Lauren Dwyre, Mikes Koulianos, and Tina Hyvonen under the supervision of Professor James A. Fitzsimmons.)

Implications for Management

The walk-through audit is an opportunity to evaluate the service experience from a customer's perspective, because customers often become aware of cues the owners and managers might have overlooked. There is no inherently superior service design. There are, instead, designs that are consistent and that provide a signal to customers about the service they can expect. Providing tangibility in a service involves giving the customer verbal, environmental, sensory, and service cues that define the service for the customer and encourage repeat visits.

THE WALK-THROUGH AUDIT AS A DIAGNOSTIC INSTRUMENT

The walk-through audit can be a useful diagnostic instrument for management to evaluate the gaps in perception between customers and managers of the service delivery system. Customers visit a site less frequently than do managers and, thus, are more sensitive to subtle changes (e.g., peeling paint or worn rugs) than are managers who see the facility every day and who are likely to overlook gradual deterioration of the supporting facility. The quality of customer service also can deteriorate and be less noticeable to employees as well as managers.

To test this use of a WtA, the same Helsinki Museum of Art and Design audit that was given to customers was also given to the managers and employees. The responses for each item on the audit were averaged for the three groups and are shown in Figure 18.3. This figure highlights the gaps in service perceptions among management, employees, and customers. Some of the gaps are not surprising, such as "There was

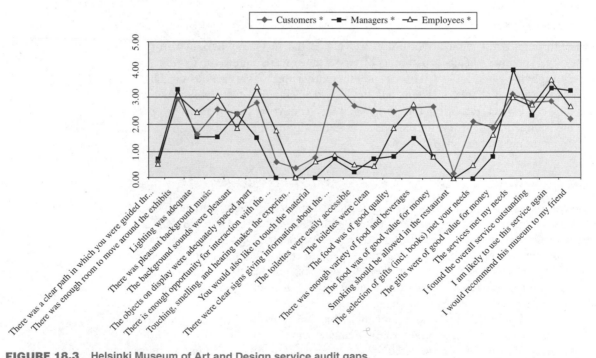

FIGURE 18.3 Helsinki Museum of Art and Design service audit gaps.
(Prepared by Eivor Biese, Lauren Dwyre, Mikes Koulianos, and Tina Hyvonen under the supervision of Professor James A. Fitzsimmons.)

enough information about the objects," because the employees are quite familiar with the exhibits. Other gaps suggest some improvements are in order; for example, "It was easy to get additional information from the staff" and "The staff helping you are friendly." It is interesting to note where management and employee perceptions deviated, such as "The explanations provided on the objects were clear" and "There is enough opportunity for interaction with the displayed objects." In both cases, employees were more in agreement with the statements than customers were and management agreed least.

QUALITY AND PRODUCTIVITY IMPROVEMENT PROCESS

Foundations of Continuous Improvement

Continuous improvement is based on the teachings and philosophy of W. Edwards Deming. Deming is credited with helping Japanese industry recover from WWII and pursue a strategy of exporting goods of high quality at affordable prices. This combination of quality and low cost was thought impossible because people took for granted that quality was only achieved at high cost. The foundations of Deming's teachings consisted of three principles:

1. *Customer satisfaction.* Focusing on satisfying customers' needs should be paramount in workers' minds. This requires an attitude of putting the customer first and a belief that this principle is the object of one's work.
2. *Management by facts.* To encourage scientific thinking, objective data must be collected and presented to management for decision making. This approach requires formal data gathering and statistical analysis of the data by the quality-improvement teams.
3. *Respect for people.* A companywide quality-improvement program assumes that all employees have a capacity for self-motivation and for creative thought. Employees are given support, and their ideas are solicited in an environment of mutual respect.

Plan-Do-Check-Act (PDCA) Cycle[6]

Deming's approach to quality emphasizes that checking or inspecting for quality is just one stage in the quality-improvement process. Deming's approach, represented by a wheel, consists of four steps: *plan,* select and analyze the problem; *do,* implement the solution; *check* the results of the change; and *act* to standardize the solution and reflect on the learning. As shown in Figure 18.4, the Deming wheel is a repetitive cycle with quality improvements resulting from continuous incremental turns of the wheel.

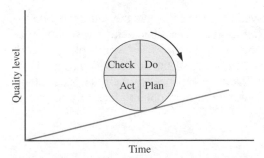

FIGURE 18.4 Deming's quality-improvement wheel.

Plan. Planning begins with the selection of the problem. Problems will appear as changes to important customer indicators, such as rate of defections or complaints. Narrow the project focus and describe the improvement opportunity. The current process is documented, perhaps with a flowchart, and data are collected. The possible causes are brainstormed and, using data, agreement is reached on the root cause(s). Develop an action plan that includes a workable solution, measures of success, and the implementation targets agreed upon.

Do. Implement the solution or process change perhaps on a trial basis. Monitor the implementation plan by collecting data on performance measures and noting progress against milestones.

Check. Review and evaluate the result of the change. Check that the solution is having the intended effect and note any unforeseen consequences.

Act. Reflect and act on learning from the experience. If successful, the process changes are standardized and communicated to all involved workers with training in the new methods as needed. In some cases this could include external participants such as customers and suppliers. Celebrate the success and repeat the PDCA cycle on another problem.

Problem Solving

A systematic approach to solving problems is central to a worker-empowered program of continuous improvement in quality and productivity. The principal objective of continuous improvement is eliminating the cause of problems so they do not recur. A problem-solving approach based on Deming's PDCA cycle is described in Table 18.4.

QUALITY TOOLS FOR ANALYSIS AND PROBLEM SOLVING[7]

Quality improvement teams use many tools in the PDCA process. The tools aid in data analysis and provide a foundation for decision making. In the following section, eight tools are described with an example application to a problem that Midway Airlines faced. Midway Airlines, a regional carrier, serves business travelers from a hub at the Midway Airport in Chicago. The hub-and-spoke network requires on-time departures to avoid delays that would compromise the efficient transfer of passengers during their multileg journeys. Midway has been monitoring departure delays and finds its systemwide on-time performance has deteriorated, causing irritation among its business passengers. The quality tools are presented next in the sequence in which they would be used in the problem-solving process.

Check Sheet

A check sheet is a historical record of observations and represents the source of data to begin the analysis and problem identification. Originally a check sheet was simply a sheet of paper listing potential problems, and each day workers would place check marks in the appropriate column to tally the frequency of occurrence. Today, data on problem frequency are entered online in an Excel spreadsheet to facilitate data interpretation. Figure 18.5 is an Excel spreadsheet record of problems faced by Midway during the prior year.

Run Chart

A run chart tracks change in an important process variable over time to detect trends, shifts, or cycles in performance. Run charts are easy to interpret and useful in predict-

TABLE 18.4

PROBLEM-SOLVING STEPS IN THE PDCA CYCLE

Step 1 Recognizing the Problem and Establishing Priorities
During the recognition stage, the problem is outlined by management in very general terms based on information from many sources.

Step 2 Forming Quality Improvement Teams
An interdisciplinary team of individuals close to the problem is created and given a mandate to address the problem. Management involvement sets the team focus and shows buy-in on finding a solution that will be implemented.

Step 3 Defining the Problem
The team first must define the problem and its scope clearly. Pareto analysis often can point to significant areas to investigate.

Step 4 Developing Performance Measures
The effect of changes on the process can be verified only by taking before and after measures of performance.

Step 5 Analyzing the Problem/Process
Flowcharting the process is often the first step at this stage to get a full understanding of all the intricacies involved. Information gathered at this stage will help determine potential solutions.

Step 6 Determining Possible Causes
The cause-and-effect diagram is particularly helpful in identifying possible causes of the problem. The team can use the diagram to brainstorm ideas for the root cause. In a brainstorming session the team members are encouraged to throw out ideas without comment from the other members. Absolutely no arguing, criticism, or evaluation of ideas is allowed during this session, which is devoted to generating possible causes. After the possible causes are identified, data are organized using check sheets, scatter diagrams, histograms, and run charts to discover the root cause.

Step 7 Selecting and Implementing the Solution
This is the most exciting stage, but temptation to propose solutions immediately must be curtailed. The criteria for selecting a solution include focus on the root cause, prevention of problem recurrence, cost-effectiveness, and timeliness.

Step 8 Evaluating the Solution: The Follow-up
Once the solution has been implemented and time has passed, the process is checked to verify that the problem has been solved. Run charts are useful for comparing prior data with current performance.

Step 9 Ensuring Permanence
New methods need to be established and workers must be trained. Control charts can be used to monitor the process to ensure that the process remains stable.

Step 10 Continuous Improvement
As the Deming wheel in Figure 18.4 suggests, quality and productivity are ramped up only with repetitions of the PDCA cycle. Once a problem is solved, another opportunity is identified for a new round of improvement analysis.

Source: From D. C. S. Summers, *Quality,* 2nd ed., Prentice-Hall, Upper Saddle River, N.J., 2000, pp. 64–109.

ing trends. Teams can use run charts to compare a performance measure before and after implementation of a solution. As shown in Figure 18.6, Midway has been experiencing a steady increase in the number of departure delays.

Histogram

A histogram presents data collected over a period of time as a frequency distribution in bar-chart form. Using the chart command in Excel, data from the check sheet can be presented visually to obtain a sense of the distribution. Unusual features become obvious, such as lack of symmetry, or skewness. A distribution with two peaks, or bimodal, suggests that two distributions with different means underlie the data. For airlines, a bimodal distribution of departure delays could be explained by a seasonality effect based

Month	Problem area				
	Lost luggage	Departure delay	Mechanical	Overbooked	Other
January	1	2	3	3	1
February	3	3	0	1	0
March	2	5	3	2	3
April	5	4	4	0	2
May	4	7	2	3	0
June	3	8	1	1	1
July	6	6	3	0	2
August	7	9	0	3	0
September	4	7	3	0	2
October	3	11	2	3	0
November	2	10	1	0	0
December	4	12	2	0	1
Total	44	84	24	16	12

FIGURE 18.5 Excel check sheet.

upon weather conditions. In Figure 18.7 we selected "lost luggage" for our histogram. Note that the distribution is not symmetrical but skewed toward the fewer occurrences.

Pareto Chart

A *Pareto chart* orders problems by their relative frequency in a descending bar graph to focus efforts on the problem that offers the greatest potential improvement. Vilfredo Pareto, a 19th century Italian economist, observed that relatively few factors usually

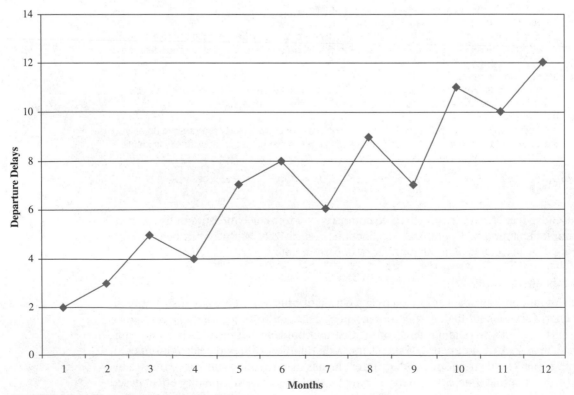

FIGURE 18.6 Run chart of departure delays.

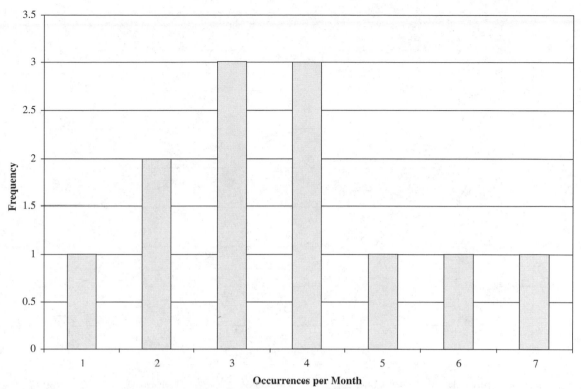

FIGURE 18.7 Histogram of lost luggage.

account for a large percentage of the total cases (e.g., 80 percent of a country's wealth resides with 20 percent of its citizens). This principle, know as the *80/20 rule,* has been observed in many situations. For example, 80 percent of a retailer's sales are generated by 20 percent of the customers. Figure 18.8 presents the total number of problem occurrences for the year as a Pareto chart to identify "departure delay" as the most serious customer-related problem to address.

Flowchart

Flowcharts are a visual representation of the process and help team members identify points where problems might occur or intervention points for solution. Flowcharting conventions use diamonds to represent decision points, rectangles for activities, and ovals for beginning and ending points. All symbols are connected with arrows to represent the sequence of activities. In Figure 18.9 we provide a flowchart of the process at the departure gate to capture possible sources of delay, such as customers attempting to board with oversized luggage.

Cause-and-Effect Diagram

Cause-and-effect analysis offers a structured approach for a team to identify, explore, and display graphically, in increasing detail, all of the possible causes related to a problem in order to discover the root cause. The cause-and-effect diagram is also known as a *fishbone chart,* owing to its skeletal shape, or an Ishikawa chart, named after its originator. Figure 18.10 contains a cause-and-effect diagram for departure delays. The construction of the chart begins with the problem at the head and traces the major categories of causes back along the spine. For services, categories such as information,

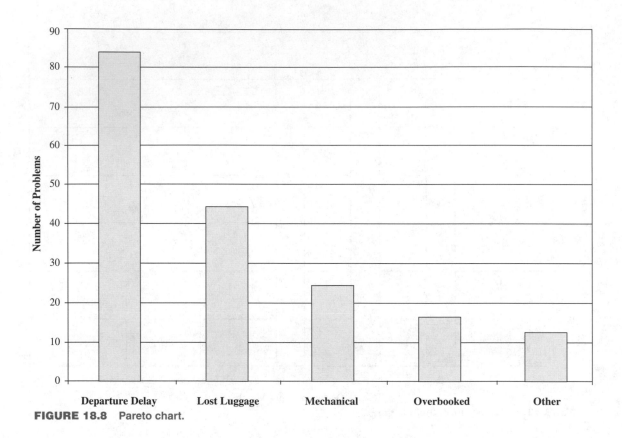

FIGURE 18.8 Pareto chart.

customers, material, procedures, personnel, and equipment are typical. Using the brainstorming technique, the detailed causes are filled in under each category and sub-category. Often causes are uncovered by asking the *who, what, where, when, why,* and *how* questions. The fishbone chart now can be used to eliminate the causes of delayed departure through a process of discussion and consensus; the remaining possibilities are targeted for additional data gathering.

Table 18.5, for example, shows a Pareto chart of the possible causes. Note that approximately 88 percent of the departure delays are accounted for by four root causes. Finally, fishbone charts become records of cause-and-effect relationships and often are posted in work areas for consultation.

Scatter Diagram

A scatter diagram visually shows the relationship between two variables. Plotting possible-cause variables against the problem can identify where a strong correlation exists (i.e., scatter points form a tight trend line). As shown in Figure 18.11, the scatter diagram of late passengers versus departure delays confirms the identification of a root cause.

Acceptance of late passengers, thus, was shown to be the major root cause of departure delays. Because gate agents were anxious to avoid antagonizing latecomers, they delayed flight departures, and, consequently, inconvenienced punctual passengers. As a solution, Midway established and advertised a policy of on-time departures that would be implemented by refusing late passengers to board even if the plane is still at the gate. After passengers realized that Midway was serious, the incidence of late ar-

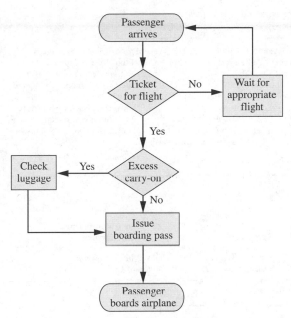

FIGURE 18.9 Flowchart at departure gate.

rivals declined significantly. Other causes of delay (e.g., waiting for pushback or fueling) were then addressed.

Control Chart

Control charts, a topic in Chapter 3, "Service Quality," are used to monitor a process. As shown in Figure 18.12, a control chart shows when a process is out of control (i.e., the plot did not remain within the boundaries during the prior year). After the problem solution is implemented, the control chart is a check that the process is under control (e.g., percentage of on-time departures remains above 90 percent with a target of 95 percent). For the current year, the process is in control and the solution appears permanent.

PROGRAMS FOR ORGANIZATIONAL QUALITY IMPROVEMENT

Service quality begins with people. All our measurements to detect nonconformance by means of statistically based control charts do not produce a quality service; instead, quality begins with the development of positive attitudes among all people in the organization. How is this accomplished? Positive attitudes can be fostered through a coordinated program that begins with employee selection and progresses through training, initial job assignments, and other aspects of career advancements. To avoid complacency, an ongoing quality-improvement program is required. These programs emphasize preventing poor quality, taking personal responsibility for quality, and building an attitude that quality can be made certain.

Personnel Programs for Quality Assurance

Multisite service firms face special problems of maintaining consistent service across all units. For example, customers expect the same service from a hotel unit in Chicago

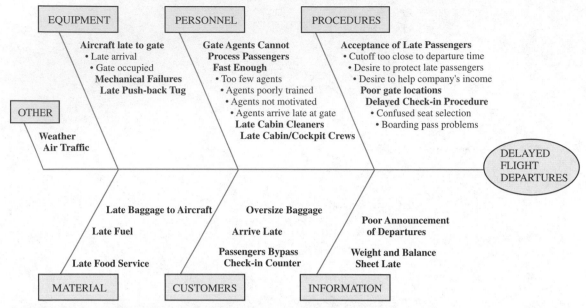

FIGURE 18.10 Cause-and-effect diagram for delayed flight departures.

that they found previously in a New Orleans unit of the same chain. In fact, the idea of "finding no surprises" is used as a marketing feature.

G. M. Hostage[8] believes the success of Marriott Corporation results in part from personnel programs that stress training, standards of performance, career development, and rewards. He finds that service quality is enhanced by the attitude a company takes toward its employees. The following eight programs have been the most effective:

1. *Individual development.* Using programmed instruction manuals, new management trainees acquire the skills and technical knowledge that are needed for the entry-level position of assistant manager. For a geographically dispersed organization, these manuals ensure that job skills are taught in a consistent manner.
2. *Management training.* Management personnel through the middle levels attend one management development session each year. A variety of professional management topics are addressed in 2- and 3-day seminars that are attended by lower-level managers from various operating divisions.
3. *Human resources planning.* The kinds of people who will be needed to fill key company positions in the coming years are identified, and an inventory of good prospects is created for future promotion. A key element of the plan is periodic performance review of all management personnel.

TABLE 18.5

PARETO ANALYSIS OF FLIGHT DEPARTURE DELAY CAUSES

Cause	Percentage of incidents	Cumulative percentage
Late passengers	53.3	53.3
Waiting for pushback	15.0	68.3
Waiting for fuel	11.3	79.6
Late weight and balance sheet	8.7	88.3

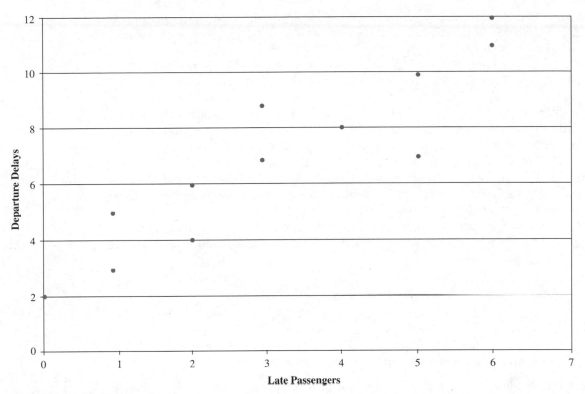

FIGURE 18.11 Scatter diagram.

4. *Standards of performance.* A set of booklets was developed to instruct employees in how to conduct themselves when dealing with guests and, in some cases, even in how to speak. The *Marriott Bellman* stresses how to make a guest feel welcome and special. The *Switchboard Operator* tells in detail how to speak with a guest and handle a variety of specific situations. The *Housekeeper* tells precisely how a room is to be made up, right down to the detail of placing the wrapped soap bar on the proper corner of the washbasin with the label upright. In many cases, booklets are

FIGURE 18.12 Control chart of Midway departure delays.

accompanied by an audiovisual film or a videotape to demonstrate proper procedures. Adherence to these standards is checked by random visits from a flying squad of inspectors.

5. *Career progression.* A job-advancement program with a ladder of positions of increasing skill and responsibility gives employees the opportunity to grow with the company.

6. *Opinion surveys.* An annual rank-and-file opinion survey is conducted by trained personnel at each unit. Subsequently, the results are discussed at a meeting. This survey has acted as an early warning system to head off the build-up of unfavorable attitudes.

7. *Fair treatment.* Employees are provided with a handbook of company expectations and obligations to its personnel. The formal grievance procedure includes access to an ombudsperson to help resolve difficulties.

8. *Profit sharing.* A profit-sharing plan recognizes that employees are responsible for much of the company's success and that they deserve more than just a paycheck for their efforts.

Quality-Improvement Program to Achieve Zero Defects

Philip Crosby, a former vice president for quality at ITT and now a sought-after quality-management consultant, advocates a 14-step zero-defects quality-improvement program.[9] His program has been implemented at a number of service firms, such as the Paul Revere Insurance Company, and has the following 14 sequential steps:

1. *Management commitment.* The need for quality improvement first is discussed with members of management to gain their commitment. This raises the level of visibility and concern for quality at the highest levels, and it ensures everyone's cooperation.

2. *Quality-improvement team.* Representatives from each department are selected to form a team that runs the quality-improvement program, which ensures each department's participation.

3. *Quality measurement.* The status of quality throughout the organization is audited. This requires that quality measurements be reviewed and established where they do not exist. Once quality becomes measurable, an objective evaluation is made to identify nonconformance and to monitor corrective action. Developing quality measures for services is a difficult task, but it represents an opportunity for worker participation. Service personnel most often respond with enthusiasm and pride when asked to identify quality measures for their work.

4. *Cost-of-quality evaluation.* To avoid any bias in the calculations, the comptroller's office identifies the cost of quality, which is composed of items such as litigation, rework, engineering changes, and inspection labor. Measuring the cost of quality provides an indication of where corrective action will be profitable for an organization.

5. *Quality awareness.* The cost of poor quality is communicated to supervisors and employees through the use of booklets, films, and posters. This helps to change attitudes about quality by providing visible evidence of the concern for quality improvement.

6. *Corrective action.* A systematic process of facing problems, talking about them, and resolving them on a regular basis is needed. The habit of identifying quality problems and correcting them at the local level is encouraged.

7. *Establishment of a zero-defects program.* Three or four members of the team are selected to investigate the zero-defects concept and to implement the program.

The committee should understand the literal meaning of the phrase *zero defects*. The idea that everyone should do his or her work right the first time must be communicated to all employees.

8. *Supervisor training.* A formal orientation is conducted for all levels of management to enable them to explain the program to their people.

9. *Zero-defects day.* An event is created that employees can recognize as a turning point in the organization's attitude toward quality. From this day on, zero defects will be the performance standard for the organization.

10. *Goal setting.* Employees are encouraged to think in terms of establishing improvement goals for themselves and their groups. Supervisors should help their employees to set specific and measurable goals.

11. *Error-cause removal.* People are asked to describe on a simple, 1-page form any problem that keeps them from performing error-free work. The appropriate department is asked to respond to the problem expeditiously.

12. *Recognition.* Award programs are established to recognize those employees who meet their goals. With genuine recognition of performance, continued support for the program will result.

13. *Quality councils.* The quality professionals are brought together on a regular basis to discuss actions that are necessary to improve the program.

14. *Do it over again.* A typical program takes more than 1 year, and, by then, employee turnover necessitates a new educational effort. Such repetition makes the program a permanent part of the organization.

Deming's 14-Point Program

W. Edwards Deming generally is credited with initiating the highly successful Japanese quality revolution. In Deming's view, management was responsible for 85 percent of all quality problems and, therefore, had to provide the leadership in changing the systems and processes that created them. Management needed to refocus attention on meeting customer needs and on continuous improvement to stay ahead of the competition. His philosophy is captured in a 14-point program:[10]

1. *Create constancy of purpose for improvements of product and service.* Management must stop its preoccupation solely with the next quarter and build for the future. Innovation in all areas of business should be expected.

2. *Adopt the new philosophy.* Refuse to allow commonly accepted poor levels of work, delays, and lax service.

3. *Cease dependence on mass inspection.* Inspection comes too late and is costly. Instead, focus on improving the process itself.

4. *End the practice of awarding business on price tag alone.* The purchasing department should buy on the basis of statistical evidence of quality, not on the basis of price. Reduce the number of vendors, and reward high-quality suppliers with long-term contracts.

5. *Constantly and forever improve the system of production and service.* Search continually for problems in the system, and seek ways of improvement. Waste must be reduced and quality improved in every business activity, both front office and back office.

6. *Institute modern methods of training on the job.* Restructure training to define acceptable levels of work. Use statistical methods to evaluate training.

7. *Institute modern methods of supervising.* Focus supervision on helping workers to do a better job. Provide the tools and techniques to promote pride in one's work.

8. *Drive out fear.* Eliminate fear by encouraging the communication of problems and expression of ideas.

9. *Break down barriers between departments.* Encourage problem solving through teamwork and use of quality-control circles.

10. *Eliminate numerical goals for the workforce.* Goals, slogans, and posters cajoling workers to increase productivity should be eliminated. Such exhortations cause worker resentment, because most of the necessary changes are outside their control.

11. *Eliminate work standards and numerical quotas.* Production quotas focus on quantity, and they guarantee poor quality in their attainment. Quality goals such as an acceptable percentage of defective items do not motivate workers toward improvement. Use statistical methods for continuing improvement of quality and productivity.

12. *Remove barriers that hinder hourly workers.* Workers need feedback on the quality of their work. All barriers to pride in one's work must be removed.

13. *Institute a vigorous program of education and training.* Because of changes in technology and turnover of personnel, all employees need continual training and retraining. All training must include basic statistical techniques.

14. *Create a structure in top management that will push every day on the above 13 points.* Clearly define management's permanent commitment to continuous improvement in both quality and productivity.

Malcolm Baldrige National Quality Award

The Malcolm Baldrige National Quality Award was created by Congress on August 20, 1987. The award is named for Malcolm Baldrige, who served as Secretary of Commerce from 1981 until his death in a rodeo accident in 1987. The award is given annually to recognize U.S. companies that excel in quality achievement and management. There are three eligibility categories for the award: manufacturing companies, service companies, and small businesses.

Each company participating in the award process submits an application, which includes an Award Examination; sample examination items and point values are listed in Figure 18.13. Note the heavy emphasis on "business results" and "customer focus and satisfaction." The Award Examination is designed not only to serve as a reliable basis for making awards but also to permit a diagnosis of the applicant's overall quality management. All applicants receive feedback prepared by teams of U.S. quality experts. Because of this quality-audit aspect of the award, Motorola requires all its vendors to apply for the award.

ISO 9000

ISO 9000 is a series of quality standards defined by the International Standards Organization (ISO), which is a consortium of virtually all the world's industrialized nations. The most difficult standard to attain is ISO 9001, which provides quality standards for organizations that design, produce, service, and install products. ISO 9002 is similar but applies to organizations that do not perform design and service activities. Service firms fall under ISO 9003. Information about the quality standard program series is contained in ISO 9004.

Documentation of processes and consistent performance are the key features of ISO standards. ISO 9000 seeks to achieve this by requiring that businesses implement a three-component cycle:

1. *Planning.* Activities affecting quality must be planned to ensure that goals, authority, and responsibility are both defined and understood.

1998 CRITERIA FOR PERFORMANCE EXCELLENCE—ITEM LISTING

1998 Categories/Items	Point Values
1 Leadership	**110**
1.1 Leadership System	.80
1.2 Company Responsibility and Citizenship	.30
2 Strategic Planning	**80**
2.1 Strategy Development Process	.40
2.2 Company Strategy	.40
3 Customer and Market Focus	**80**
3.1 Customer and Market Knowledge	.40
3.2 Customer Satisfaction and Relationship Enhancement	.40
4 Information and Analysis	**80**
4.1 Selection and Use of Information and Data	.25
4.2 Selection and Use of Comparative Information and Data	.15
4.3 Analysis and Review of Company Performance	.40
5 Human Resource Focus	**100**
5.1 Work Systems	.40
5.2 Employee Education, Training, and Development	.30
5.3 Employee Well-Being and Satisfaction	.30
6 Process Management	**100**
6.1 Management of Product and Service Processes	.60
6.2 Management of Support Processes	.20
6.3 Management of Supplier and Partnering Processes	.20
7 Business Results	**450**
7.1 Customer Satisfaction Results	.125
7.2 Financial and Market Results	.125
7.3 Human Resource Results	.50
7.4 Supplier and Partner Results	.25
7.5 Company-Specific Results	.125
TOTAL POINTS	**1000**

FIGURE 18.13 Malcolm Baldrige National Quality Award criteria.

2. *Control.* Activities affecting quality must be controlled to ensure that specified requirements at all levels are met, problems are anticipated and averted, and corrective actions are planned and carried out.
3. *Documentation.* Activities affecting quality must be documented to ensure an understanding of quality objectives and methods, smooth interaction within the organization, feedback for the planning cycle, and to serve as objective evidence of quality system performance.

The motivation for considering ISO 9000 arises from the fact that the European Economic Community has adopted this certification as a requirement for doing business in the member countries. Many companies follow and implement the ISO 9000 quality standards for reasons other than compulsory requirements, however. Companies have found that the very process of implementing the standard and the benefits from quality improvement are significant enough to justify this effort.

Benchmarking

The measure of the quality of a firm's performance can be made by comparison with the performance of other companies known for being "best in class," which is a process known as *benchmarking*. For example, Singapore Airlines has a reputation for outstanding cabin service, Federal Express for consistent overnight delivery, Hampton Inns for clean rooms, and Nordstrom's department store for attentive salespersons. For every quality dimension, some firm has earned the reputation for being "best in class" and, thus, is a benchmark for comparison. Benchmarking, however, involves more than comparing statistics. It also includes visiting the leading firm to learn firsthand how management has achieved such outstanding performance. For obvious proprietary reasons, this often requires going outside one's own field. Some manufacturers, for example, have visited the pit stops at automobile races to learn methods of reducing the time for production-line changeovers. Others have visited Domino's Pizza to understand how it delivers customized products within 30 minutes.

For a typical example, consider an electronics company seeking to improve its purchasing function. This company formed a study team that visited Ford to learn how it reduced the number of its suppliers, talked with Toyota about vendor relationships, and observed the buying process at Reliance Electric. The team returned with quantifiable measures that benchmarked the superior performance of these leading firms and with knowledge of how these gains were accomplished.

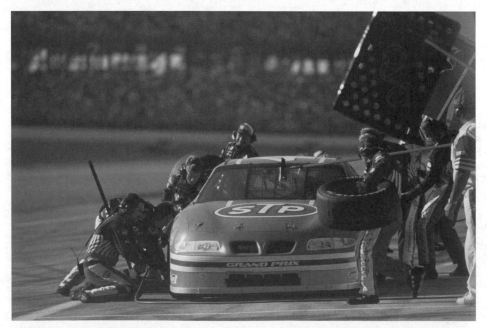

Airlines have learned to reduce turnaround time at the gate by observing the teamwork at automobile racetracks. © Kevin Fleming/CORBIS

Service Benchmark

SHOPPERS ACT AS THEIR OWN CASHIERS AT SOME STORES

Your shopping cart is loaded with bread and toilet paper and eggplant, and you're ready for the checkout line.

Instead of looking for the speediest checker, you head toward the lane with only a computer screen and an empty bag. You scan your groceries, bag them, and pay with a bank card.

If you stick an unscanned bottle of antacid into your bag, a face comes on the computer screen and points out your—ahem—mistake.

This scenario is being played out throughout the country at grocery and drug stores experimenting with self-service checkout.

"The customer feels it's faster because they walk up and do the scanning themselves," said Jonathan Hayward, vice president and chief engineer at Stores Automated Systems, Inc., in Bristol, which recently introduced a self-scan checkout system.

Stores can save money by replacing some cashiers, even though a flesh-and-blood clerk must be stationed at the junction of three checkout lanes to assist shoppers using SASI's system, Hayward said.

Rite Aid, the drugstore chain with 2,771 stores in 21 states and Washington, D.C., is testing SASI's new system, eXPRESS, at two Philadelphia-area stores this summer.

A sensitive scale under the customer's bag detects any unscanned items. Customers using coupons or paying with cash still need the help of the clerk, as will anyone who bags an unscanned item.

"We are a very convenience-oriented chain, and this is basically one additional possible service that we could provide to assist in the convenience of our shoppers," Rite Aid spokesman Craig Muckle said.

After a six-month test, Rite Aid will decide whether to place the system in other stores.

Several grocery chains have been experimenting with self-scanning stations produced by Optimal Robotics of Plattsburgh, N.Y. Store employees monitoring the checkouts over a closed-circuit television are available to help any customers stymied by the system, U-Scan Express.

Joanne Gage, spokeswoman for Price Chopper of Schenectady, N.Y., said the company has made modifications to Optimal's system while testing it at a Clifton Park, N.Y., grocery the past three years.

"It's used more like an express lane. People tend not to use it for big orders . . ." she said. "There are some customers that never want to use it."

Shoplifting has not been a problem, said Gage, who called the system foolproof.

"There is some supervision. There is a person there who helps to identify produce. One person can man four stations, so it's a great labor-saving device," she said.

Price Chopper will install the system in one store but has no plans to expand to its 90 other groceries.

A Lakewood, Ohio, Finast supermarket has been testing a hand-held scanner, the Personal Shopper System, which allows shoppers approved by the store to register their selections as they roll their carts through the aisles.

The store initially tested the portable scanners with 100 shoppers, has extended it to 300, and plans to have 1,000 customers using the system by the end of summer, according to Nancy Tully, spokeswoman for scanner developer Symbol Technologies Inc. of Holtsville, N.Y.

The portable scanner, first used in the Netherlands, has been installed in 24 stores in a British chain that plans to introduce it to 36 more markets this summer. Another dozen U.S. grocery and discount stores are planning to test the system as well, Tully said.

When customers return their scanners, they receive a bar-coded ticket that they take to the clerk in a special express lane.

The portable system costs $200,000 to $300,000. Grocers report shoppers are spending more and shoplifting has declined, said Tully.

Wendell Young III, president of United Food and Commercial Workers Union Local 1776 in Philadelphia, said he was more concerned about the effect the machines will have on employees.

BOX 18.1 (CONTINUED)

"One person handling three machines, especially in a food store, it's just not humanly possible. I don't see it working because so far it hasn't worked. I don't see it's going to be revolutionary and replace people," Young said.

Young said customers still want personal interaction with a clerk.

"It's like being served a beer by a robot in a pub," he said.

Source: Dinah Wisenberg Brin, "Shoppers Act as Their Own Cashiers at Some Stores," *Austin American Statesman,* August 12, 1996, p. D3.

SUMMARY

Quality and productivity improvement address two of the elements of the customer value equation and represent strategic moves in advancing a service firm toward world-class status. Making continual improvement a competitive strategy was explored by considering an analogy between JIT in manufacturing and reduction of queues in services.

The discussion of approaches to quality and productivity improvement began with the walk-through-audit survey instrument. Such a questionnaire can uncover customers' lack of appreciation for specific aspects of the service delivery process. The Deming continuous improvement process is a repetition of a plan-do-check-act cycle. Eight quality analysis tools were illustrated using the example of a commuter airline struggling with flight departure delays. Several corporatewide quality initiatives were explored.

In Chapter 19 we will consider another challenge that services face in the global market—growth and expansion.

KEY TERMS AND DEFINITIONS

Benchmarking the practice of comparing one's performance with that of other firms that are known as "best in class."

Cause-and-effect analysis a process using an Ishikawa chart shaped like a fishbone to trace back possible causes of a service quality problem.

Data envelopment analysis (DEA) the use of a linear programming model to identify efficient and inefficient units in a multisite service operation.

Just-in-time (JIT) a production process that emphasizes operating with minimal levels of inventory and a resulting attention to quality.

Kanban the Japanese term for a card used to communicate the specifications for material or parts from an upstream or prior station in an assembly process.

Pareto chart arrangement of data so that causes of a problem are ordered in descending frequency of occurrence in order to highlight the most likely cause.

Walk-through audit a process-oriented questionnaire given to customers and managers to evaluate the perception of the customer service experience.

TOPICS FOR DISCUSSION

1. Could firms in the "world-class service delivery" stage of competitiveness be described as "learning organizations"?
2. Contrast the philosophies of "continuous improvement" and "process reengineering." Is there a role for both points of view in service firms?
3. Compare the philosophies of Deming (i.e., 14-point) and Crosby (i.e., zero defects) as revealed by their programs for quality improvement.
4. What are the limitations of "benchmarking"?

The Museum of Art and Design[11]

The Museum of Art and Design is a small privately owned museum located in the center of Helsinki, Finland. It occupies a beautiful three-story 19th century building that used to be a school. It specializes in design and industrial art. The museum was founded in the early 20th century and its original goal was to educate the public about design. During the big era of Finnish design in the 1950s, the museum focused on Finnish design. Recently, however, the museum has become more outward looking and frequently organizes international exhibits. Last spring, for example, the museum brought the Dalai Lama to Finland for a big Tibet exhibit. The museum themes bridge both the past and the future.

The museum produces its own exhibits and hosts exhibits from other museums, both foreign and Finnish. It strives to have three or four major exhibits per year, in addition to devoting space to a number of smaller exhibits and its own private collection. The museum has a private café and a gift shop owned by the museum foundation. Customers include professional design people as well as lay people. The typical museum visitor was a middle-aged woman, but the increased cultural emphasis has been attracting a wider audience. Recently, after the building had undergone significant renovation, the new managing director hired a communications manager. The museum had never had a public relations person before. The advertising that was done in this year alone equaled the amount of advertising that had been done in the past 20 years. As a result of the new effort to increase the visibility of the museum, and the popular Tibet exhibit, the museum had a record number of visitors—more than 100,000 people. Only 5 of Finland's 1,000 museums attracted that many people.

The museum is privately owned by a foundation, but does receive 60 percent of its budget from government funding. Forty percent of its budget is derived from operating revenues. In addition to admission tickets sold, other revenue comes from the café, the gift shop, and events that the museum organizes in connection with exhibits. Lectures on wine and wine-tasting evenings, for example, were offered

in conjunction with an exhibit on wines. The museum also has a closed society called Friends of the Museum, which provides the museum with funding to buy more objects for its private collection. The museum's major competition comes from the specialist museums: Design Forum, the University of Design Museum, and the Finnish National Museum, which is going to open a new museum of ethnography in Helsinki.

WALK-THROUGH AUDIT

A walk-though audit (WtA) of the Museum of Art and Design was conducted by a team of students from the MBA program at the Helsinki School of Economics and Business Administration. The WtA is a survey questionnaire used to evaluate a service from the perspective of the customer's experience. The same survey is also given to managers and staff to identify "gaps" between the perceptions of managers and customers. The WtA is used as a diagnostic tool to uncover misconceptions in the perceptions of what customers are experiencing during the service delivery process.

The team interviewed four members of the museum staff and then prepared a questionnaire for visitors to fill out. Thirty-two visitors responded to the questionnaire, shown in Figure 18.2. Museum management and contact personnel (i.e., primarily guides) filled out the same questionnaire, responding as if they were customers. The team did a statistical analysis of the questionnaire results to identify gaps between museum personnel's (i.e., both management and contact personnel) perceptions of the services offered and visitors' perceptions.

GAP ANALYSIS

On the basis of the questionnaire responses, the team found several categories of gaps between the museum personnel's perceptions and visitors' perceptions. The gaps were related to how visitors heard of the exhibits, information, experience, whether or not visitors come alone, and facilities. A graph showing the gaps was presented in Figure 18.3 earlier in this chapter.

Awareness of Exhibits

Visitors to the museum obtained information about exhibits primarily from newspapers, but also from magazines and by word of mouth. Management, however, thought newspapers played a smaller role in creating awareness but they were accurate about the influence of magazines. Management also thought word of mouth was significantly more important than it was and that the radio was a more important source of information than it was.

Information

Two types of gaps related to information were identified. The first gap concerns the museum management and contact personnel who believe that visitors are highly aware of their services. The management and contact personnel also believed they were an easy source of information for customers. The visitors, however, did not agree. This gap might exist because the contact personnel do not perceive that visitors would have any problem identifying or having contact with them.

In the second gap management was more critical in its assessment of clarity and adequacy of information and explanations about exhibited objects. The visitors in turn were more positive about these issues. Visitors did not seem to have an interest in self-guided material (e.g., headphones), but the museum staff thought that it might be worthwhile to look into the possibility of having such material. We might conclude that visitors may have a preference for human contact.

Experience

Visitors appreciated the multidimensional aspects of exhibits, such as music, but managers underestimated how much the visitors noticed and appreciated them. Contact personnel were more in touch than management with visitors' views on the spacing of displays. Both the visitors and the museum staff were not sure about experimenting with new experiences, such as those involving the senses, having more interactions, and demonstrating processes. Perhaps this factor is explained by lack of familiarity with these types of interaction.

Visitor Habits

The museum staff believed that visitors came alone more often than they did. In fact, a large number came in twos or threes. Museum staff also had a different perception of visitors' interests in exhibit offerings. Even though the management thought most visitors went to all of the exhibits, only 38 percent of the visitors saw all the exhibits. The remaining visitors came for one of the main exhibits and did not spend time at the others. The permanent exhibit received the smallest number of visitors (i.e., 13 percent including three foreign visitors). We might conclude that each exhibit attracts different visitors.

Facilities

Visitors generally had a more favorable opinion of the facilities than did the museum management and personnel. Specifically, visitors rated food value, gift selection, signage, and cleanliness of restrooms favorably. Perhaps the expectations of visitors were not as high as museum management and personnel thought.

Language

Museum managers and contact personnel are aware that information is presented primarily in Finnish and Swedish. Of the 32 visitors surveyed, only three were nonnative speakers and, therefore, the majority did not identify language as a problem area. During the summer tourist season, more visitors would probably identify the limitations of information that is available only in Finnish or Swedish.

Questions

1. Critique the WtA gap analysis. Could there be other explanations for the gaps?
2. Make recommendations for closing the gaps found in the WtA.
3. How can the servicescape help in self-selecting customers and employees?

Mega Bytes Restaurant[12]

Mega Bytes is a restaurant that caters to business travelers and has a self-service breakfast buffet. To measure customer satisfaction, the manager constructs a survey and distributes it to diners during a three-month period. The results, as summarized by the Pareto chart in Figure 18.14, indicate that the restaurant's major problem is customers waiting too long to be seated.

A team of employees is formed to work on resolving this problem. The team members decide to use the Seven-Step Method (SSM), which is a structured approach to problem solving and process improvement originally developed by Joiner Associates, Inc., of Madison, Wisconsin. The SSM leads a team through a logical sequence of steps that force a thorough analysis of the problem, its potential causes, and its possible solutions. The structure imposed by the SSM helps the team to focus on the correct issues and avoid diffusing its energy on tangential or counterproductive efforts. The SSM is directed at analytic rather than enumerative studies. In general, analytic studies are interested in cause and effect and in making predictions, whereas enumerative studies are focused on an existing population.

The steps in this method are shown in Table 18.6 and applied here to the case of Mega Bytes:

Step 1: Define the project. The results of the Mega Bytes survey indicate that customers wait too long to be seated. Most customers are business travelers who want to be served promptly or an opportunity to discuss business during their meal. The team considers several questions such as "When does the wait start? When does it end? How is it measured?" and then arrives at an operational definition of the problem it must solve as "waiting to be seated."

Step 2: Study the current situation. The team collects baseline data and plots them as shown in Figure 18.15. At the same time, a flowchart for seating a party is developed, and the team also diagrams the floor plan of Mega Bytes as shown in Figure 18.16.

The baseline data indicate that the percentage of people who must wait is higher early in the week than it is late in the week. This finding is to be expected, however, because most Mega Bytes customers are business travelers. The size of the party does not appear to be a factor, and no surprises were found when a histogram of the number of people waiting in excess of one minute was plotted against the time of the morning: more people wait during the busy hours than during the slow hours.

The reason for the waiting, however, is interesting. Most people are kept waiting either because no table is available or no table in the area of their preference is available. Customers seldom have to wait because a host or hostess is not available to seat them or others in their party have not yet arrived. At this point, it would be easy to jump to the conclusion that the problem could be solved just by adding more staff early in the week and during the busy hours.

FIGURE 18.14 Pareto chart of complaints.
(*Source:* Reprinted with permission from M. Gaudard, R. Coates, and L. Freeman, "Accelerating Improvement," *Quality Progress,* vol. 24, no. 10, October 1991, p. 83.)

FIGURE 18.15 Run chart of percent of customers waiting more than one minute to be seated.
(*Source:* Reprinted with permission from M. Gaudard, R. Coates, and L. Freeman, "Accelerating Improvement," *Quality Progress,* vol. 24, no. 10, October 1991, p. 83.)

FIGURE 18.16 Restaurant floor plan.
(*Source:* Reprinted with permission from M. Gaudard, R. Coates, and L. Freeman, "Accelerating Improvement," *Quality Progress,* vol. 24, no. 10, October 1991, p. 83.)

The team members decide, however, that they need additional information on why these tables are not available and how seating preferences affect the waiting time. Subsequent data indicate that "unavailable" tables usually are unavailable because they need to be cleared, not because they are occupied by diners. The data also show that most people who wait have a preference for the nonsmoking section.

Step 3: Analyze the potential causes. A cause-and-effect diagram is constructed for "why tables are

not cleared quickly," as shown in Figure 18.17. The team concludes that the most likely cause of both problems (i.e., uncleared tables and waiting for nonsmoking tables) may be attributed to the distance between the tables and the kitchen and, perhaps, to the current ratio of smoking-to-nonsmoking tables.

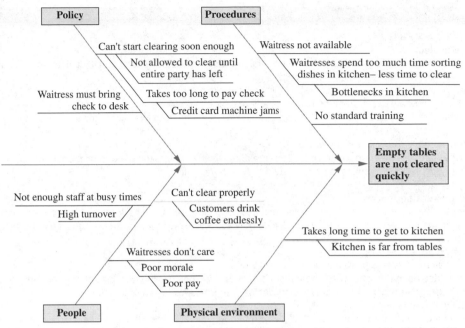

FIGURE 18.17 **Cause-and-effect diagram describing why tables are not cleared quickly.**
(*Source:* Reprinted with permission from M. Gaudard, R. Coates, and L. Freeman, "Accelerating Improvement," *Quality Progress,* vol. 24, no. 10, October 1991, p. 84.)

Step 4: Implement a solution. The team develops a list of possible solutions. Because the team cannot verify its conclusion by controlling variables, it chooses a solution that can be tested easily: set up temporary work stations in the nonsmoking area. No other changes are made, and data on the percentage of people now waiting longer than one minute to be seated are collected.

Step 5: Check the results. The team analyzes the results of data collected for one month in step 4 of the study. As Figure 18.18 shows, the improvement is dramatic.

Step 6: Standardize the improvement. The temporary work stations are replaced with permanent ones.

Step 7: Establish future plans. The team decides to address the next highest bar in the Pareto chart of customer complaints: that the buffet table is not well organized.

FIGURE 18.18 **Run chart of percent of customers waiting more than one minute to be seated after implementation of solution.**
(*Source:* Reprinted with permission from M. Gaudard, R. Coates, and L. Free-man, "Accelerating Improvement," *Quality Progress,* vol. 24, no. 10, October 1991, p. 85.)

TABLE 18.6

THE SEVEN-STEP METHOD

Step 1 Define the project.

1. Define the problem in terms of a gap between what is and what should be. (For example, "Customers report an excessive number of errors. The team's objective is to reduce the number of errors.")
2. Document why it is important to be working on this particular problem:
   - Explain how you know it is a problem, providing any data you might have that support this.
   - List the customer's key quality characteristics. State how closing the gap will benefit the customer in terms of these characteristics.
3. Determine what data you will use to measure progress:
   - Decide what data you will use to provide a baseline against which improvement can be measured.
   - Develop any operational definitions you will need to collect the data.

Step 2 Study the current situation.

1. Collect the baseline data and plot them. (Sometimes historical data can be used for this purpose.) A run chart or control chart is usually used to exhibit baseline data. Decide how you will exhibit these data on the run chart. Decide how you will label your axes.
2. Develop flowcharts of the processes.
3. Provide any helpful sketches or visual aids.
4. Identify any variables that might have a bearing on the problem. Consider the variables of what, where, to what extent, and who. Data will be gathered on these variables to localize the problem.
5. Design data collection instruments.
6. Collect the data and summarize what you have learned about the variables' effects on the problem.
7. Determine what additional information would be helpful at this time. Repeat substeps 2 through 7 until there is no additional information that would be helpful at this time.

Step 3 Analyze the potential causes.

1. Determine potential causes of the current conditions:
   - Use the data collected in step 2 and the experience of the people who work in the process to identify conditions that might lead to the problem.
   - Construct cause-and-effect diagrams for these conditions of interest.
   - Decide on most likely causes by checking against the data from step 2 and the experience of the people working in the process.
2. Determine whether more data are needed. If so, repeat substeps 2 through 7 of step 2.
3. If possible, verify the causes through observation or by directly controlling variables.

Step 4 Implement a solution.

1. Develop a list of solutions to be considered. Be creative.
2. Decide which solutions should be tried:
   - Carefully assess the feasibility of each solution, the likelihood of success, and potential adverse consequences.
   - Clearly indicate why you are choosing a particular solution.
3. Determine how the preferred solution will be implemented. Will there be a pilot project? Who will be responsible for the implementation? Who will train those involved?
4. Implement the preferred solution.

Step 5 Check the results.

1. Determine whether the actions in step 4 were effective:
   - Collect more data on the baseline measure from step 1.
   - Collect any other data related to the conditions at the start that might be relevant.
   - Analyze the results. Determine whether the solution tested was effective. Repeat prior steps as necessary.
2. Describe any deviations from the plan and what was learned.

Step 6 Standardize the improvement.

1. Institutionalize the improvement:
   - Develop a strategy for institutionalizing the improvement and assign responsibilities.
   - Implement the strategy and check to see that it has been successful.
2. Determine whether the improvement should be applied elsewhere and plan for its implementation.

TABLE 18.6 (CONTINUED)

Step 7 Establish future plans.
1. Determine your plans for the future:
   - Decide whether the gap should be narrowed further and, if so, how another project should be approached and who should be involved.
   - Identify related problems that should be addressed.
2. Summarize what you learned about the project team experience and make recommendations for future project teams.

Source: Reprinted with permission from M. Gaudard, R. Coates, and L. Freeman, "Accelerating Improvement," *Quality Progress,* vol. 24, no. 10, October 1991, p. 82.

The authors of the article on which our Mega Bytes case is based report that managers who used SSM in various situations found the method's focus and restraint to be valuable because it provided organization, logic, and thoroughness. The managers also were impressed with the method's use of data instead of opinions, and they credited this factor with reducing territorial squabbles and promoting both cooperation and trust among team members.

While very valuable, SSM does entail some difficulties. For example, project teams have found several concepts in the first two steps very difficult to formulate. In particular, a team may have trouble developing a problem statement, because the tendency is to frame a solution as a problem. In the case of Mega Bytes, the team had to avoid identifying the problem as "There are too few servers," "There aren't enough tables," or "The servers need to work faster." The real problem was identified correctly as "The customers must wait too long."

Another concept that has been difficult for study teams is localization, which is a process of focusing on smaller and smaller vital pieces of the problem. This concept initially proved difficult because team members had not yet internalized the idea that improvement should be driven by customer requirements.

Some study teams have experienced an assortment of other difficulties. Occasionally, team members could not see the benefit of collecting data accurately, or they did not understand how baseline data would be used to validate a solution. Some members had trouble keeping an open mind and, consequently, resisted investigating the effects of variables they felt to be irrelevant. In some cases, members had to learn new skills, such as how to obtain information in a nonthreatening way from workers in the system. Finally, organizational problems such as arranging meeting times and getting support from coworkers had to be resolved as well.

Questions
1. How is SSM different from Deming's PDCA cycle?
2. Prepare a cause-and-effect or fishbone diagram for a problem such as "Why customers have long waits for coffee." Your fishbone diagram should be similar to that in Figure 18.17, using the main sources of cause: policy, procedure, people, and physical environment.
3. How would you resolve the difficulties that study teams have experienced when applying SSM?

Chapter 18 Supplement
Data Envelopment Analysis (DEA)

How can corporate management evaluate the productivity of a fast-food outlet, a branch bank, a health clinic, or an elementary school? The difficulties in measuring productivity are threefold. First, what are the appropriate inputs to the system (e.g., labor hours, material dollars) and the measures of those inputs? Second, what are the appropriate outputs of the system (e.g., checks cashed, certificate of deposits) and the measures of those outputs? Third, what are the appropriate ways of measuring the relationship between these inputs and outputs?

Measuring Service Productivity

The measure of an organization's productivity, if viewed from an engineering perspective, is similar to the measure of a system's efficiency. It can be stated as a ratio of outputs to inputs (e.g., miles per gallon for an automobile).

To evaluate the operational efficiency of a branch bank, for example, an accounting ratio such as cost per teller transaction might be used. A branch with a high ratio in comparison with those of other branches would be considered less efficient, but the higher ratio could result from a more complex mix of transactions. For example, a branch opening new accounts and selling CDs would require more time per transaction than another branch engaged only in simple transactions such as accepting deposits and cashing checks. The problem with using simple ratios is that the mix of outputs is not considered explicitly. This same criticism also can be made concerning the mix of inputs. For example, some branches may have automated teller machines in addition to live tellers, and this use of technology could affect the cost per teller transaction.

Broad-based measures such as profitability or return on investment are highly relevant as overall performance measures, but they are not sufficient to evaluate the operating efficiency of a service unit. For instance, one could not conclude that a profitable branch bank is necessarily efficient in its use of personnel and other inputs. A higher-than-average proportion of revenue-generating transactions could be the explanation rather than the cost-efficient use of resources.

The DEA Model

Fortunately, a technique has been developed with the ability to compare the efficiency of multiple service units that provide similar services by explicitly considering their use of multiple inputs (i.e., resources) to produce multiple outputs (i.e., services). The technique, which is referred to as *data envelopment analysis (DEA),* circumvents the need to develop standard costs for each service, because it can incorporate multiple inputs and multiple outputs into both the numerator and the denominator of the efficiency ratio without the need for conversion to a common dollar basis. Thus, the DEA measure of efficiency explicitly accounts for the mix of inputs and outputs and, consequently, is more comprehensive and reliable than a set of operating ratios or profit measures.

DEA is a linear programming model that attempts to maximize a service unit's efficiency, expressed as a ratio of outputs to inputs, by comparing a particular unit's efficiency with the performance of a group of similar service units that are delivering the same service. In the process, some units achieve 100-percent efficiency and are referred to as the *relatively efficient units,* whereas other units with efficiency ratings of less than 100 percent are referred to as *inefficient units.*

Corporate management thus can use DEA to compare a group of service units to identify relatively inefficient units, measure the magnitude of the inefficiencies, and by comparing the inefficient with the efficient ones, discover ways to reduce those inefficiencies.

The DEA linear programming model is formulated according to Charnes, Cooper, and Rhodes, and is referred to as the CCR Model.[13]

Definition of Variables   Let E_k, with $k = 1, 2, \ldots, K$, be the efficiency ratio of unit k, where K is the total number of units being evaluated.

Let u_j, with $j = 1, 2, \ldots, M$, be a coefficient for output j, where M is the total number of output types considered. The variable u_j is a measure of the relative decrease in efficiency with each unit reduction of output value.

Let v_i, with $i = 1, 2, \ldots, N$, be a coefficient for input i, where N is the total number of input types considered. The variable v_i is a measure of the relative increase in efficiency with each unit reduction of input value.

Let O_{jk} be the number of observed units of output j generated by service unit k during one time period.

Let I_{ik} be the number of actual units of input i used by service unit k during one time period.

Objective Function   The objective is to find the set of coefficient u's associated with each output and of v's associated with each input that will give the service unit being evaluated the highest possible efficiency.

$$\max E_e = \frac{u_1 O_{1e} + u_2 O_{2e} + \cdots + u_M O_{Me}}{v_1 I_{1e} + v_2 I_{2e} + \cdots + v_N I_{Ne}} \tag{1}$$

where e is the index of the unit being evaluated.

This function is subject to the constraint that when the same set of input and output coefficients (u_j's and v_i's) is applied to all other service units being compared, no service unit will exceed 100-percent efficiency or a ratio of 1.0.

Constraints

$$\frac{u_1 O_{1k} + u_2 O_{2k} + \cdots + u_M O_{Mk}}{v_1 I_{1k} + v_2 I_{2k} + \cdots + v_N I_{Nk}} \leq 1.0 \qquad k = 1, 2, \ldots, K \tag{2}$$

where all coefficient values are positive and nonzero.

To solve this fractional linear programming model using standard linear programming software requires a reformulation. Note that both the objective function and all constraints are ratios rather than linear functions. The objective function in equation (1) is restated as a linear function by arbitrarily scaling the inputs for the unit under evaluation to a sum of 1.0.

$$\max E_e = u_1 O_{1e} + u_2 O_{2e} + \cdots + u_M O_{Me} \tag{3}$$

subject to the constraint that

$$v_1 I_{1e} + v_2 I_{2e} + \cdots + v_N I_{Ne} = 1 \tag{4}$$

For each service unit, the constraints in equation (2) are similarly reformulated:

$$u_1 O_{1k} + u_2 O_{2k} + \cdots + u_M O_{Mk} - (v_1 I_{1k} + v_2 I_{2k} + \cdots + v_N I_{Nk}) \leq 0 \qquad k = 1, 2, \ldots, K \tag{5}$$

where

$$u_j \geq 0 \qquad j = 1, 2, \cdots, M$$
$$v_i \geq 0 \qquad i = 1, 2, \cdots, N$$

A question of sample size often is raised concerning the number of service units that are required compared with the number of input and output variables selected in the analysis. The following relationship relating the number of service units K used in the analysis and the number of input N and output M types being considered is based on empirical findings and the experience of DEA practitioners:

$$K \geq 2(N + M) \tag{6}$$

TABLE 18.7

SUMMARY OF OUTPUTS AND INPUTS FOR BURGER PALACE

Service unit	Meals sold	Labor-hours	Material dollars
1	100	2	200
2	100	4	150
3	100	4	100
4	100	6	100
5	100	8	80
6	100	10	50

Example 18.1: Burger Palace

An innovative drive-in-only burger chain has established six units in several different cities. Each unit is located in a strip shopping center parking lot. Only a standard meal consisting of a burger, fries, and a drink is available. Management has decided to use DEA to improve productivity by identifying which units are using their resources most efficiently and then sharing their experience and knowledge with the less efficient locations. Table 18.7 summarizes data for two inputs: labor-hours and material dollars consumed during a typical lunch-hour period to generate an output of 100 meals sold. Normally, output will vary among the service units, but in this example, we have made the outputs equal to allow for a graphical presentation of the units' productivity. As Figure 18.19 shows, service units S_1, S_3, and S_6 have been joined to form an efficient-production frontier of alternative methods of using labor-hours and material resources to generate 100 meals. As can be seen, these efficient units have defined an envelope that contains all the inefficient units—thus the reason for calling the process "data envelopment analysis."

For this simple example, we can identify efficient units by inspection and see the excess inputs being used by inefficient units (e.g., S_2 would be as efficient as S_3 if it used $50 less in materials). To gain an understanding of DEA, however, we will proceed to formulate the linear programming problems for each unit, then solve each of them to determine efficiency ratings and other information.

FIGURE 18.19 Productivity frontier of Burger Palace.

We begin by illustrating the LP formulation for the first service unit, S_1, using equations (3), (4), and (5).

$$\max E(S_1) = u_1 100$$

subject to

$$u_1 100 - v_1 2 \ - v_2 200 \leq 0$$
$$u_1 100 - v_1 4 \ - v_2 150 \leq 0$$
$$u_1 100 - v_1 4 \ - v_2 100 \leq 0$$
$$u_1 100 - v_1 6 \ - v_2 100 \leq 0$$
$$u_1 100 - v_1 8 \ - v_2 80 \ \leq 0$$
$$u_1 100 - v_1 10 - v_2 50 \ \leq 0$$
$$v_1 2 + v_2 200 = 1$$
$$u_1, v_1, v_2 \geq 0$$

Similar linear programming problems are formulated (or, better yet, the S_1 linear programming problem is edited) and solved for the other service units by substituting the appropriate output function for the objective function and substituting the appropriate input function for the last constraint. Constraints 1 through 6, which restrict all units to no more than 100-percent efficiency, remain the same in all problems.

This set of six linear programming problems was solved with Excel Solver 7.0 in fewer than five minutes by editing the data file between each run. Because the output is 100 meals for all units, only the last constraint must be edited by substituting the appropriate labor and material input values from Table 18.7 for the unit being evaluated.

The data file for unit 1 of Burger Palace using a linear programming Excel add-in is shown in Figure 18.20. The linear programming results for each unit are shown in Table 18.8 and summarized in Table 18.9.

In Table 18.9, we find that DEA has identified the same units shown as being efficient in Figure 18.19. Units S_2, S_4, and S_5 all are inefficient in varying degrees. Also shown in Table 18.9 and associated with each inefficient unit is an *efficiency reference set*. Each inefficient unit will have a set of efficient units associated with it that defines its productivity. As Figure 18.19 shows for inefficient unit S_4, the efficient units S_3 and S_6 have been joined with a line defining the efficiency frontier. A dashed line drawn

Linear Model

Name:	Unit 1
Type:	LP
No. Var.:	3
Int. Var.:	0
No. Con.:	7
Nonlinear:	0

Objective Value
0

Model	Variables Num. Name					1	2	3
						u1	v1	v2
0	Values					0	0	0
3	Linear Obj. Coef.					100	0	0
TRUE	Lower Bounds					0	0	0
TRUE	Upper Bounds					99999	99999	99999

	Constraints			Constraint Bounds		Constraint Coefficients		
TRUE	Num.	Name	Value	Lower	Upper			
100	1	Unit 1	0	-99999	0	100	-2	-200
	2	Unit 2	0	-99999	0	100	-4	-150
	3	Unit 3	0	-99999	0	100	-4	-100
	4	Unit 4	0	-99999	0	100	-6	-100
	5	Unit 5	0	-99999	0	100	-8	-80
	6	Unit 6	0	-99999	0	100	-10	-50
	7	Inputs	0	1	1	0	2	200

FIGURE 18.20 Excel data file for DEA analysis of Burger Palace unit 1.

from the origin to inefficient unit S_4 cuts through this frontier and, thus, defines unit S_4 as inefficient. In Table 18.9, the value in parentheses that is associated with each member of the efficiency reference set (i.e., .7778 for S_3 and .2222 for S_6) represents the relative weight assigned to that efficient unit in calculating the efficiency rating for S_4. These relative weights are the shadow prices that are associated with the respective efficient-unit constraints in the linear programming solution. (Note in Table 18.8 that for unit 4, these weights appear as opportunity costs for S_3 and S_6.)

The values for v_1 and v_2 that are associated with the inputs of labor-hours and materials, respectively, measure the relative increase in efficiency with each unit reduction of input value. For unit S_4, each unit decrease in labor-hours results in an efficiency increase of 0.0555. For unit S_4 to become efficient, it must increase its efficiency rating by 0.111 points. This can be accomplished by reducing labor used by 2 hours (i.e.,

TABLE 18.8

LP SOLUTIONS FOR DEA STUDY OF BURGER PALACE

| Summarized results for unit 1 | | | | | | | Page : 1 |

Variables		Solutions	Opportunity costs	Variables		Solutions	Opportunity costs
No.	Names			No.	Names		
1	U1	+1.0000000	0	6	S3	0	0
2	V1	+.16666667	0	7	S4	+33.333336	0
3	V2	+.00333333	0	8	S5	+60.000000	0
4	S1	0	+1.0000000	9	S6	+83.333336	0
5	S2	+16.666670	0	10	A7	0	+100.00000

Maximized objective function = 100   Iterations = 4

| Summarized results for unit 2 | | | | | | | Page : 1 |

Variables		Solutions	Opportunity costs	Variables		Solutions	Opportunity costs
No.	Names			No.	Names		
1	U1	+.85714287	0	6	S3	0	+.71428573
2	V1	+.14285715	0	7	S4	+28.571430	0
3	V2	+.00285714	0	8	S5	+51.428574	0
4	S1	0	+.28571430	9	S6	+71.428574	0
5	S2	+14.285717	0	10	A7	0	+85.714287

Maximized objective function = 85.71429   Iterations = 4

| Summarized results for unit 3 | | | | | | | Page : 1 |

Variables		Solutions	Opportunity costs	Variables		Solutions	Opportunity costs
No.	Names			No.	Names		
1	U1	+1.0000000	0	6	S3	0	+1.0000000
2	V1	+.06250000	0	7	S4	+12.500000	0
3	V2	+.00750000	0	8	S5	+10.000001	0
4	S1	+62.500000	0	9	S6	0	0
5	S2	+37.500008	0	10	A7	0	+100.00000

Maximized objective function = 100   Iterations = 3

TABLE 18.8 (CONTINUED)

Summarized results for unit 4							Page : 1

No.	Names	Solutions	Opportunity costs	No.	Names	Solutions	Opportunity costs
1	U1	+.88888890	0	6	S3	0	+.77777779
2	V1	+.05555556	0	7	S4	+11.111112	0
3	V2	+.00666667	0	8	S5	+8.8888893	0
4	S1	+55.555553	0	9	S6	0	+.22222224
5	S2	+33.333340	0	10	A7	0	+88.888885

Maximized objective function = 88.88889   Iterations = 3

Summarized results for unit 5							Page : 1

No.	Names	Solutions	Opportunity costs	No.	Names	Solutions	Opportunity costs
1	U1	+.90909088	0	6	S3	0	+.45454547
2	V1	+.05681818	0	7	S4	+11.363637	0
3	V2	+.00681818	0	8	S5	+9.0909100	0
4	S1	+56.818180	0	9	S6	0	+.54545450
5	S2	+34.090916	0	10	A7	0	+90.909088

Maximized objective function = 90.90909   Iterations = 4

Summarized results for unit 6							Page : 1

No.	Names	Solutions	Opportunity costs	No.	Names	Solutions	Opportunity costs
1	U1	+1.0000000	0	6	S3	0	0
2	V1	+.06250000	0	7	S4	+12.500000	0
3	V2	+.00750000	0	8	S5	+10.000001	0
4	S1	+62.500000	0	9	S6	0	+1.0000000
5	S2	+37.500008	0	10	A7	0	+100.00000

Maximized objective function = 100   Iterations = 4

TABLE 18.9

SUMMARY OF DEA RESULTS

Service unit	Efficiency rating (E)	Efficiency reference set	Relative labor-hour value (v_1)	Relative material value (v_2)
S_1	1.000	N.A.	0.1667	0.0033
S_2	0.857	S_1 (0.2857) S_3 (0.7143)	0.1428	0.0028
S_3	1.000	N.A.	0.0625	0.0075
S_4	0.889	S_3 (0.7778) S_6 (0.2222)	0.0555	0.0067
S_5	0.901	S_3 (0.4545) S_6 (0.5454)	0.0568	0.0068
S_6	1.000	N.A.	0.0625	0.0075

TABLE 18.10

CALCULATION OF EXCESS INPUTS USED BY UNIT S_4

Outputs and inputs	Reference set		Composite reference unit C	S_4	Excess inputs used
	S_3	S_6			
Meals	$(0.7778) \times 100 + (0.2222) \times 100 =$		100	100	0
Labor-hours	$(0.7778) \times \quad 4 + (0.2222) \times \quad 10 =$		5.3	6	0.7
Material ($)	$(0.7778) \times 100 + (0.2222) \times \quad 50 =$		88.9	100	11.1

2 hours $\times$ 0.0555 = 0.111). Note that with this reduction in labor-hours, unit S_4 becomes identical to efficient unit S_3. An alternative approach would be a reduction in materials used by \$16.57 (i.e., 0.111/0.0067 = 16.57). Any linear combination of these two measures also would move unit S_4 to the productivity frontier defined by the line segment joining efficient units S_3 and S_6.

Table 18.10 contains the calculations for a hypothetical unit C, which is a composite reference unit defined by the weighted inputs of the reference set S_3 and S_6. As Figure 18.19 shows, this composite unit C is located at the intersection of the productivity frontier and the dashed line drawn from the origin to unit S_4. Thus, compared with this reference unit C, inefficient unit S_4 is using excess inputs in the amounts of 0.7 labor-hour and 11.1 material dollars.

DEA offers many opportunities for an inefficient unit to become efficient regarding its reference set of efficient units. In practice, management would choose a particular approach on the basis of an evaluation of its cost, practicality, and feasibility; however, the motivation for change is clear (i.e., other units actually are able to achieve similar outputs with fewer resources).

DEA and Strategic Planning

When combined with profitability, DEA efficiency analysis can be useful in strategic planning for services that are delivered through multiple sites (e.g., hotel chains). Figure 18.21 presents a matrix of four possibilities that arise from combining efficiency and profitability.

FIGURE 18.21 DEA strategic matrix.

Considering the top-left quadrant of this matrix (i.e., underperforming potential stars) reveals that units operating at a high profit may be operating inefficiently and, thus, have unrealized potential. Comparing these with similar efficient units could suggest measures that would lead to even greater profit through more efficient operations.

Star performers can be found in the top-right quadrant (i.e., benchmark group). These efficient units also are highly profitable and, thus, serve as examples for others to emulate in both operations efficiency and marketing success in generating high revenues.

The lower-right quadrant (i.e., candidates for divestiture) contains efficient but unprofitable units. These units are limited in profit potential, perhaps because of a poor location, and should be sold to generate capital for expansion in new territories.

It is not clear which strategy to employ with the lower-left quadrant units (i.e., problem branches). If profit potential is limited, investments in efficient operations might lead to a future candidate for divestiture.

EXERCISES

18.1. For the Burger Palace example, perform a complete analysis of efficiency improvement alternatives for unit S_2, including determination of a composite reference unit.

18.2. For the Burger Palace example, perform a complete analysis of efficiency improvement alternatives for unit S_5, including determination of a composite reference unit.

18.3. For the Burger Palace example, what is the effect of removing an inefficient unit from the analysis (e.g., S_2)?

18.4. For the Burger Palace example, what is the effect of removing an efficient unit from the analysis (e.g., S_6)?

CASE

Mid-Atlantic Bus Lines

Mid-Atlantic Bus Lines was founded by a group of managers from Trailways when that company was acquired by Greyhound. They launched a first-class, express bus service operating between the major coastal cities from Philadelphia, Pennsylvania, to Jacksonville, Florida. By hiring laid-off Trailways drivers and leasing buses, they established franchises in each city with local entrepreneurs, who were given the right to operate a Mid-Atlantic bus terminal. A percentage of the passenger ticket sales and freight sales would be kept by the terminal operator to cover his or her costs and profit.

After several months of operation, some franchisees complained about inadequate profits and threatened to close their terminals. Because other franchisees were pleased with their experiences, however, a study of all terminal operations in the system was undertaken. The information in Table 18.11 was collected over several weeks and represents a typical day's operation.

TABLE 18.11

OUTPUTS AND INPUTS FOR MID-ATLANTIC BUS LINES

Bus depot	City served	Ticket sales	Freight sales	Labor-hours	Facility dollars
1	Philadelphia, Pa.	700	300	40	500
2	Baltimore, Md.	300	600	50	500
3	Washington, D.C.	200	700	50	400
4	Richmond, Va.	400	600	50	500
5	Raleigh, N.C.	500	400	40	400
6	Charleston, S.C.	500	500	50	500
7	Savannah, Ga.	800	500	40	600
8	Jacksonville, Fla.	300	200	30	400

Questions

1. Use DEA to identify efficient and inefficient terminal operations. Formulate the problem as a linear programming model, and solve using computer software such as Excel Solver that permits input file editing between runs.
2. Using the appropriate reference set of efficient terminals, make recommendations for changes in resource inputs for each inefficient terminal.
3. What recommendations would you have for the one seriously inefficient terminal in regard to increasing its outputs?
4. Discuss any shortcomings in the application of DEA to Mid-Atlantic Bus Lines.

SELECTED BIBLIOGRAPHY

BANKER, RAJIV D., A. CHARNES, and W. W. COOPER: "Some Models for Estimating Technical and Scale Inefficiencies in Data Envelopment Analysis," *Management Science,* vol. 30, no. 9, September 1984, pp. 1078–1092. (The "BCC" Model)

CHARNES, A., W. W. COOPER, and E. RHODES: "Measuring the Efficiency of Decision Making Units," *European Journal of Operations Research,* vol. 2, no. 6, November 1978, pp. 429–444. (The "CCR" Model)

DESSLER, GARY, and D. L. FARROW: "Implementing a Successful Quality Improvement Programme in a Service Company: Winning the Deming Prize," *International Journal of Service Industry Management,* vol. 1, no. 2, 1990, pp. 45–53.

FREI, FRANCIS X., and PATRICK T. HARKER: "Measuring the Efficiency of Service Delivery Processes: An Application to Retail Banking," *Journal of Service Research,* vol. 1, no. 4, May 1999, pp. 300–312.

KUPERS, WENDEIN: "Phenomenology of Embodied Productivity in Services," *International Journal of Service Industry Management,* vol. 9, no. 4, 1998, pp. 337–358.

MAULL, ROGER, and STEPHEN CHILDE: "Business Process Re-engineering: An Example from the Banking Sector," *International Journal of Service Industry Management,* vol. 5, no. 3, 1994, pp. 26–34.

MCLAUGHLIN, CURTIS P., and SYDNEY COFFY: "Measuring Productivity in Services," *International Journal of Service Industry Management,* vol. 1, no. 1, 1990, pp. 46–64.

MEHRA, S., and R. A. INMAN: "JIT Implementation within a Service Industry: A Case Study," *International Journal of Service Industry Management,* vol. 1, no. 3, 1990, pp. 53–61.

METTERS, RICHARD D., FRANCES X. FREI, and VICENTE A. VARGAS: "Measurement of Multiple Sites in Service Firms with Data Envelopment Analysis," *Production and Operations Management,* vol. 8, no. 3, Fall 1999, pp. 264–281.

NACHUM, LILACH: "The Productivity of Intangible Factors of Production: Some Measurement Issues Applied to Swedish Management Consulting Firms," *Journal of Service Research,* vol. 2, no. 2, November 1999, pp. 123–137.

NARASIMHAN, R., and J. JAYARAM: "Reengineering Service Operations: A Longitudinal Case Study," *Journal of Operations Management,* vol. 17, no. 1, December 1998, pp. 7–22.

SHERMAN, DAVID H., and GEORGE LADINA: "Managing Bank Productivity Using Data Envelopment Analysis (DEA)," *Interfaces,* vol. 25, no. 2, March–April 1995, pp. 60–73.

VUORINEN, ISMO, RAIJA JARVINEN, and UOLEVI LEHTINEN: "Content and Measurement of Productivity in the Service Sector: A Conceptual Analysis with an Illustrative Case from the Insurance Business," *International Journal of Service Industry Management,* vol. 9, no. 4, 1998, pp. 377–396.

ENDNOTES

1. From David Wessel, "With Labor Scarce, Service Firms Strive to Raise Productivity," *The Wall Street Journal,* June 1, 1989, p. 1.

2. J. L. Heskett, W. E. Sasser, Jr., and L. A. Schlesinger, *The Service Profit Chain,* Free Press, New York, 1997, pp. 40–42.

3. Adapted from R. B. Chase and R. H. Hayes, "Operations' Role in Service Firm Competitiveness," *Sloan Management Review,* vol. 33, no. 1, Fall 1991, pp. 15–26.

4. From James A. Fitzsimmons, "Making Continual Improvement a Competitive Strategy for Service Firms," *Service Management Effectiveness,* Bowen, Chase, Cummings and Associates, Jossey-Bass Publishers, San Francisco, 1990, pp. 284–295.

5. J. A. Fitzsimmons and G. B. Maurer, "Walk-Through-Audit to Improve Restaurant Performance," *Cornell HRA Quarterly,* February 1991, pp. 95–99.

6. From Michael Brassard and Diane Ritter, *The Memory Jogger II,* GOAL/QPC, Methuen, Mass., 1994, pp. 115–131.

7. From D. Daryl Wyckoff, "New Tools for Achieving Service Quality," *Cornell HRA Quarterly,* vol. 25, no. 3, November 1984, pp. 78–91.

8. G. M. Hostage, "Quality Control in a Service Business," *Harvard Business Review,* vol. 53, no. 4, July–August 1975, pp. 98–106.

9. Philip B. Crosby, *Quality Is Free: The Art of Making Quality Certain,* McGraw-Hill, New York, 1979.

10. W. Edwards Deming, *Quality, Productivity, and Competitive Position,* MIT Center for Advanced Engineering Study, Cambridge, Mass., 1982.

11. Prepared by Eivor Biese, Lauren Dwyre, Mikes Koulianos, and Tina Hyvonen under the supervision of Professor James A. Fitzsimmons.

12. Reprinted and selectively adapted with permission from M. Gaudard, R. Coates, and L. Freeman, "Accelerating Improvement," *Quality Progress,* vol. 24, no. 10, October 1991, pp. 81–88.

13. A. Charnes, W. W. Cooper, and E. Rhodes, "Measuring the Efficiency of Decision Making Units," *European Journal of Operations Research,* November 1978, pp. 429–444.

CHAPTER NINETEEN

Growth and Expansion

Learning Objectives

After completing this chapter, you should be able to:

1. Identify the expansion strategy that a service firm is using.
2. Discuss the nature of franchising from the franchiser and the franchisee points of view.
3. Discuss the factors to be considered in multinational development.
4. Describe and contrast the global service strategies.

In June 1991, a guest and an employee were found electrocuted by a faulty underwater light in the swimming pool of a Days Inn in Orange, Texas.[1] This tragic incident is part of the story of a once-successful motel chain that was taken over in a leveraged buyout in 1984. Cecil B. Day founded the chain in 1970 and operated it for years on the principle of strict adherence to exacting standards of excellence. A high-minded man, Day prohibited the sale of alcohol on his properties, kept a chaplain on call 24 hours a day at each unit, and established a security department that was the envy of the industry. To maintain standards and consistency, the company owned at least half of its motels and granted franchises sparingly, rejecting more than 90 percent of applicants.

Twenty-two years after its founding, Days Inn does not own a single motel. After the 1984 leveraged buyout, Days Inn became an organization that merely sells its sign and its reservation and marketing services—and claims to be the fastest-growing motel chain. Franchise revenue became all that mattered, with each inn paying Days Inn 6 to 10 percent of its sales revenue. Lack of attention to the properties has resulted in stained walls, worn furniture, and broken air conditioners. More important, guests now appear to be at some risk from lax security and deferred maintenance, as illustrated by the electrocution incident.

Unlike competitors that require a new franchisee to build an inn from the ground up to exacting specifications, the post-takeover Days Inn would erect its sign on a franchisee's existing property and ask for compliance later. This practice has resulted in inconsistent quality throughout the chain. Note that a major selling point of most motel chains is consistent quality, and Days Inn's willingness to accept any existing motel as part of its chain has not been lost on Red Roof Inns, which advertises that its competition has "no two . . . alike" while touting its own inns as being corporate-owned and -operated. By selling off all company-owned units, Days Inn also deviated from accepted franchising practice. Without daily involvement in operations, a franchiser generally is believed to be less effective in dealing with franchisee problems. Former company insiders and industry experts point to Days Inn as an example of the dangers of rapid franchising.

CHAPTER PREVIEW

This chapter begins with a look at service growth and expansion in the context of multisite and multiservice expansion strategies. Using these dimensions, we put services into four classifications: focused service, focused network, clustered service, and diversified network.

Franchising can be an effective multisite expansion strategy for a well-defined service concept. We will explore benefits to the franchisee and responsibilities of the franchiser in an organizational arrangement held together by a contract.

Because our world has become "borderless," service expansion no longer can end with development of the domestic market alone. Expansion overseas presents unique challenges, however, such as the cultural transferability of the service and discriminatory practices of foreign governments to protect their own domestic services from competition.

GROWTH AND EXPANSION STRATEGIES

The expectation of an entrepreneurial innovation is initial acceptance of the service concept followed by increasing customer demand. The need to expand a successful innovative service often is thrust on the owner by the pressure of market potential and the desire to protect the service concept from competitors through building barriers to entry. To understand better the various ways in which a firm can expand its concept, consider Figure 19.1, which shows the fundamental expansion strategies that are available to service firms. We shall explore each of these strategies in turn with a discussion of the risks involved and the implications for management.

Focused Service

Typically, a service innovation begins at a single location with an initial service concept. This initial service concept usually is a well-defined vision focused on delivering a new and unique service. For example, Fred Smith's vision for Federal Express was use of a single hub-and-spoke network to guarantee overnight delivery of packages.

Success leads to increased demand, which requires capacity expansion at the site. Typically, the facility is expanded and personnel added.

The successful firm also will attract competition and need to build a preferred position among as many customers as possible in the local market area. Adding peripheral services is one approach to penetrating the market or holding market share against the competition. Examples of peripheral services for a restaurant would include a salad bar

	Single Service	**Multiservice**
Single Location	*Focused service:* • Dental practice • Retail store • Family restaurant	*Clustered service:* • Stanford University • Mayo Clinic • USAA Insurance
Multisite	*Focused network:* • Federal Express • McDonald's • Red Roof Inns	*Diversified network:* • Nations Bank • American Express • Arthur Andersen

FIGURE 19.1 Multisite and multiservice expansion strategies.

or drive-through window. The core service for a successful restaurant, however, usually is excellent cuisine.

Risks that are associated with a single service location include being captive to the future economic growth of that area and being vulnerable to competition that can move in and capture market share. Management and control of the enterprise, however, are much simpler than in any of the other growth strategies.

Many examples of successful focused services exist. Consider fine restaurants in particular, such as Chez Panisse in Berkeley or Antoine's in New Orleans. A *focused service* often is limited to a single site because of talented personnel, such as an award-winning chef or a nationally recognized heart surgeon. If the site is a key element of the service, such as a sheltered cove for a marina, it may not be duplicated easily elsewhere.

Focused Network

A service firm that must be readily accessible to customers (e.g., a fast-food restaurant) must consider adding sites to achieve significant growth. For firms such as McDonald's, a *focused network* allows management to maintain control, which ensures consistency of service across all locations. For services such as Federal Express and other transportation or communications firms, the existence of a network is required merely to enable the service to function. Also, an entrepreneurial firm that has a successful, well-defined service concept and wants to reach a mass market can prevent imitation from competitors by capturing premium locations in different geographic areas.

The service concept must be well focused, however, thus being easy to replicate with rigorous control of service quality and costs. Frequently, the "cookie-cutter" concept of replicating service units is employed in facility construction, operating manuals, and personnel training. Franchising often is used to achieve the objective of rapid growth, with investment capital from franchisees and the motivation of independent operators. A more complete discussion of franchising is found later in this chapter.

For a single site, the founder is physically present to manage the firm's resources, market the service, train personnel, and ensure the integrity of the service concept. Especially in the beginning, expansion can occur on an incremental basis. Initially, as the number of locations grows, managerial control slowly shifts from being informal to being formal so that the owner can control operations effectively even though he or she is absent from the additional sites.

Managing a network of service locations requires different management skills, however, and it involves the challenges of using sophisticated communications and control. Above all, the service concept must be rationalized and communicated to unit managers and staff, who then must execute the service consistently on a daily basis. Much planning must precede a multisite expansion, such as preparing training and operations manuals, branding the concept, and launching a national marketing effort.

Service growth using the multisite strategy is very attractive because of its ability to reach the mass market quickly, but the risks of overexpansion and loss of control have resulted in many failures. Even so, the miles of "franchise rows" that are found in almost every city attest to the success of delivering a focused service through a multisite network.

Finally, having multiple sites in different geographic locations reduces the financial risk to the firm from severe, localized economic downturns. A longitudinal study of occupancy at La Quinta Motor Inns during the 1980s dramatically illustrates the benefit of geographic risk containment. Founded in Texas, La Quinta Motor Inns became a major presence in the state, with inns in all the major Texas cities by 1980. During the oil and gas boom of the early 1980s, La Quinta began an expansion strategy of following the exploration activity into the oil-producing states of Colorado, Louisiana, Oklahoma, and Wyoming. When the oil and gas boom ended in the mid-1980s, the occupancy of many of the new inns, and even some of the inns in Texas, plummeted. A financial disaster for the firm was avoided, however, because other La Quinta inns that were not associated with the oil and gas industry continued to prosper.[2]

Clustered Service

Service firms with large fixed facilities often decide to grow by diversifying the service they offer. For example, during the 1970s, many small colleges expanded into four-year regional universities to accommodate the increasing demand for a university degree. Another example is United Services Automobile Association (USAA), which originally was founded to provide automobile insurance for military officers by direct mail. Located in San Antonio, Texas, USAA now is a major employer, and the physical facility is situated in a campus-like setting of several acres. Today, the services offered by USAA have been expanded to include banking, mutual funds, auto and homeowners' insurance, travel services, and a buying service. Large medical complexes such as the Mayo Clinic, M.D. Anderson, and Massachusetts General Hospital are examples of classic multiservice, single-site facilities, or *clustered service*. All these examples share the common feature that their service market is not defined by their location. For some, such as medical centers and colleges, customers are willing to travel to the service location and spend considerable time at the facility (even years in the case of college students). For others, such as USAA, travel is unnecessary, because business is conducted without the need for physical interaction with a customer.

A major risk of service diversification is potential loss of focus and neglect of the core service. For example, a ski resort may decide to use idle facilities during the summer by attracting conference business; however, the accommodations, food, and beverage facilities that are suitable for skiers may be inadequate for hosting such meetings. One saving grace in this situation is that at least the different market segments are separated by the seasons. Facility management becomes extremely complex when an attempt is made to serve more than one market segment concurrently. For example, hotels serving both tourists and business customers may have difficulty satisfying both markets.

To avoid losing focus, a strategy of "concentric diversification" has been advocated.[3] Concentric diversification limits expansion to services with synergistic logic around the core service. The evolution of the convenience store is an excellent example. Beginning with a limited selection of convenience items that could be purchased in a hurry, these stores have added self-serve gasoline, video rentals, an automatic car wash, and self-serve microwave lunches. Concentric diversification creates economies of scale, because the additional services require only marginal increases in variable costs (e.g., no additional cashier is needed).

Diversified Network

Service firms that grow through acquisition often find themselves combining both the multisite and the multiservice strategies. Several years ago, United Airlines acquired hotels and car-rental agencies in the belief that sufficient synergy existed through use of its Apollo reservation system to direct the traveling customer to its several businesses. Anticipated revenues never materialized, however, so United sold off the peripheral services and returned to its core airline business. Managing a *diversified network* is a very complex task, as United Airlines and many other firms have learned.

Success more often is realized when the services are offered under one brand name that establishes a broad marketing image. American Express has been particularly successful managing a global service network that offers financial and travel services with real synergy.

FRANCHISING

Franchising is an alternative to expanding through use of internally generated profits or by seeking funds in the capital markets. Franchising is a common vehicle, however, for replicating a service geographically by attracting investors who become independent owner-operators bound by a contractual agreement. For multisite services, incorporation of conformance quality into the service concept has been the hallmark of the franchising agreement. The franchiser guarantees a consistent service, because the concept is standardized in design, operation, and pricing. Just as they make no distinction between products of the same brand, customers expect identical service from any franchise outlet. All outlets benefit from this consistency in service, because customers develop a brand loyalty that is not bound by geography. For example, a U.S. tourist in Germany is treated to a McDonald's french fries, burger, and Coke meal that is identical to that served in San Francisco, Tokyo, and, now, Moscow.

The Nature of Franchising

The International Franchise Association defines franchising as a system by which a firm (i.e., the franchiser) grants to others (i.e., the franchisees) the right and license (i.e., franchise) to sell a product or service and, possibly, use the business system developed by the firm.

The franchisee owns the business through payment of a franchise fee and purchase of the facility and equipment, and he or she assumes responsibility for all normal operating activities, including hiring employees, making daily decisions, and determining local advertising. The initial investment will vary depending on capital requirements. For example, an H & R Block franchise may cost only $5000, but a McDonald's franchise could require $500,000. The service franchisee usually is granted an exclusive right or license to deliver the service in a specific market region to protect the franchisee against dilution of sales from other franchisees of the same brand. For example, Hardee's, a fast-food restaurant, agrees not to license another Hardee's franchisee within $1\frac{1}{2}$ miles of existing locations.

The franchiser retains the right to dictate conditions. Standard operating procedures must be followed. Materials must be purchased from either the franchiser or an approved supplier. No deviation from the product line is permitted, training sessions must be attended, and continuing royalty fees (e.g., 4 percent of gross sales for Wendy's) must be paid.

Benefits to the Franchisee

As a franchisee, the owner relinquishes some personal independence and control in return for a relationship based on the expectation of greater gains through group membership. The franchisee is given the opportunity to own a small business that carries a lower-than-normal risk of failure because of the identification with an established service brand. Membership in the franchiser organization also includes many additional benefits.

What city is this? Franchising has been criticized for homogenizing the American landscape. © David Barber / PhotoEdit

Management Training   Before opening a new outlet, many franchisers provide an extensive training program. For example, McDonald's franchisees must spend two weeks at Hamburger University in suburban Chicago learning the McDonald's way of food preparation and customer service. This training accomplishes two objectives. First, the franchisee becomes prepared to operate a business profitably; second, McDonald's ensures that its procedures will be followed to guarantee consistency across units. Subsequent training often is offered through videotapes and traveling consultants.

Brand Name   The franchisee gains immediate customer recognition from the nationally known and advertised brand name. The result is more-immediate increased customer draw; thus, the break-even point is reached sooner than in a traditional new-business venture.

National Advertising   Although the franchisee usually must contribute approximately 1 percent of gross sales to the franchiser for national advertising, the results benefit all operations. Further, for businesses such as fast-food restaurants and motels in particular, a significant proportion of sales is to customers arriving from outside the immediate geographic region.

Acquisition of a Proven Business   Traditionally, independent owners face a high rate of failure, which a franchisee can expect to avoid. The franchiser has a track record of selecting appropriate sites, operating a reliable accounting system, and, most important, delivering a service concept that already is accepted by the public.

Economies of Scale   As a member of the franchiser network, the franchisee benefits from centralized purchasing and savings on the cost of materials and equipment that are unavailable to an independent owner.

Issues for the Franchiser

Franchising is an alternative to internally generated expansion for a firm seeking to develop a focused network of geographically dispersed units. Franchising allows the firm to expand rapidly with minimal capital requirements by selling the business concept to prospective entrepreneurs. Thus, franchising relies heavily on the motivation of investor-owners, and it allows the firm to grow without the cost of developing key managers. Of course, the process of screening potential franchisees must go beyond the minimum requirement of simply having the necessary capital. For example, Benihana of Tokyo found that many early franchisees were unqualified to manage an authentic Japanese-theme restaurant.

Other issues include decisions on the degree of franchisee autonomy, the nature of the franchise contract, and a process for conflict resolution.

Franchisee Autonomy   A franchisee's autonomy is the amount of freedom that is permitted in the operation of the unit. The degree of autonomy is a function of the extent of operations programming dictated in the franchise contract and of the success of "branding" the national advertising achieves.

The extent of operations programming is important to guarantee compliance with uniform standards of quality and service throughout the entire chain. If some franchisees were allowed to operate at substandard levels, the image of the entire chain would suffer, as occurred in the Days Inn example. A highly programmed operation might include

1. Franchiser specifications such as day-to-day operating procedures, site selection, facility design, accounting system, supplies used and their sources, pricing, and menu items for the restaurant.
2. Frequent inspections of the facility.
3. The right to repurchase the outlet for noncompliance.

Branding reinforces operations programming by establishing rather clear customer expectations from which it is difficult for the individual franchisee to deviate. In addition, successful branding should lead to a greater profit potential, reduced risk, and a more sought-after investment opportunity.

Franchise Contract   Control and power tend to concentrate in the hands of the franchiser, and this raises questions concerning the relationship between franchiser and franchisee as well as the misuse of power. The franchise contract is the vehicle for providing this relationship on a continuing basis. Very often, these contracts include specific obligations on the part of the franchisee but are ambiguous regarding the responsibilities of the franchiser, and, often, no attention is given to the rights of the franchisee. For example, litigation has arisen from contract stipulations regarding establishment of the resale value of the franchise and binding agreements requiring the purchase of supplies from the franchiser.

The objective in writing franchise contracts should be to avoid future litigation that might prevent a cooperative relationship from developing. Franchise contracts should be prepared to protect both parties and preserve the competitive strength of the entire franchise organization.

Conflict Resolution   An intelligent and fair franchise contract will be the most effective means to reduce potential conflict. Conflict frequently arises, however, over the following issues because of differing objectives of the franchiser and franchisee:

1. How should fees be established and profits distributed?
2. When should franchisee facilities be upgraded, and how are the costs to be shared?
3. How far should the franchiser go in saturating a single market area with outlets?

The franchise system is a superorganization requiring interorganizational management. Thus, a critical task of the franchiser is the development of policy and procedures to handle conflict before it becomes divisive and impairs the entire system.

MULTINATIONAL DEVELOPMENT

Because its customers increasingly wanted to send packages to Europe and Asia, Federal Express decided in 1988 to duplicate its service overseas, and these overseas operations have been drawing red ink ever since, resulting in a first-ever quarterly operating loss for the company in 1991. Unfortunately, Federal Express arrived well after the competition, DHL and TNT, which, having imitated the Federal Express concept in the late 1970s, had been providing express service to this region for about a decade. Also, Federal Express was unprepared for the government regulations and bureaucratic red tape that are used to protect established firms. For example, it took three years to get permission from Japan to make direct flights from the Memphis hub to Tokyo, a key link in the overseas system. Just days before that service was to begin, however, Federal Express was notified that no packages weighing more than 70 pounds could pass through Tokyo; this was a provision to protect local transport businesses.

The company's obsession with tight central control also contributed to the problems. Until recently, all shipping bills were printed in English, and the cutoff time for package pickups was 5 P.M., as is the practice in the United States. The Spanish, however, typically work until 8 P.M. after a lengthy midday break. Federal Express now is relaxing its go-it-alone, centralized-control method of business that has been successful in the United States. Pickup times, weight standards, and technology now will vary from country to country, and joint ventures with local firms are being sought to handle deliveries and marketing.[4]

Another issue is the frequent lack of supporting infrastructure, something we take for granted in the United States, in some foreign countries. For example, the opening of the first McDonald's in Moscow required substantial supplier development. Management not only had to build a commissary to prepare all products for the restaurant but also had to show farmers how to plant and harvest the crops that were needed (e.g., potatoes and lettuce).

The Nature of the Borderless World[5]

Kenichi Ohmae, who has written extensively on strategic management, argues that we now live in a borderless world, where customers worldwide are aware of the best products and services and expect to purchase them with no concern over their national origin. In his strategic view, all firms compete in an interlinked world economy, and to be effective, they must balance the five C's of strategic planning: *c*ustomers, *c*ompetitors, *c*ompany, *c*urrency, and *c*ountry.

Customers   When people vote with their pocketbooks, they are interested in quality, price, design, value, and personal appeal. Brand labels such as the "golden arches" are spreading all over the world, and news of performance is hard to suppress. The availability of information, particularly in the industrialized "Triad" markets of North America, Europe, and Japan, has empowered customers and stimulated competition.

Competitors   Nothing stays proprietary for long. Equipment and software vendors supply their products and services to a wide range of customers, and the result is rapid dispersion of the technology available to all firms. Two factors, time and being the first mover, now have become more critical as elements of strategy. Further, a single firm cannot be on the cutting edge of all technologies. Thus, operating globally means operating with partners, a lesson that Federal Express has learned.

Company   Automation during the recent past has moved firms from a variable-cost to a fixed-cost environment. Management focus thus has changed from boosting profits by reducing material and labor costs to increasing sales to cover fixed costs. This is particularly true for many service firms (e.g., airlines and communications businesses), which to a large extent are fixed-cost activities with huge investments in facilities and equipment. The search for a larger market has driven these firms toward globalization.

The nature of a firm's corporate culture, however, may determine how effectively its service will travel overseas. The domestic success of Federal Express was built on a go-it-alone attitude, on rewards for nonunion employees who propose cost-cutting ideas, and on direct access to the CEO, Fred Smith, with any complaints. In contrast, UPS, which works with a union labor force and strict work standards, has moved overseas with fewer problems.

Currency   Global companies have tried to neutralize their exposure to fluctuating currency exchange rates by matching costs to revenues and becoming strong in all regions of the Triad so that if one region is negative, it may be offset by others that are positive. Companies also have employed international finance techniques such as hedging and options. Thus, to become currency-neutral, a firm is forced into global expansion.

Country   Having a strong presence in all Triad regions provides additional strategic benefits beyond currency considerations. First, as noted, exposure to economic downturns in one region may be offset by operations in other economies. Second, selling in your competitor's domestic market neutralizes that competitor's option to employ a strategy of using excessive profits earned in a protected domestic market for expansion overseas. For example, with government cooperation, Japanese companies have exploited this strategy and recently been criticized for this by their trading partners.

Only truly global companies, however, can achieve "global localization" (a term coined by Akio Morita of Sony) and, thereby, be accepted as a local company while maintaining the benefits of worldwide operations. To reach this level, a firm must become close to the customers in the foreign country and accommodate their unique service needs. For fast-food restaurants, discovering the drinking and eating habits of the host country is critical for success; thus, instead of expecting the Germans to enjoy a Big Mac with a Coke, McDonald's added beer to the menu. Permitting local management to modify the service within limits to accommodate local tastes should be encouraged, even at the risk of introducing some inconsistency across locations. An extreme example is Mr. Donut's in Japan, which changed everything about its product and service except the logo.

Considerations in Planning Multinational Operations[6]

In true services, which exclude receipts and payments on investments and government transactions, the United States has been maintaining a trade surplus for the past 20 years. Leadership in "knowledge-based" services such as software, telecommunications, and information services has proved to be very mobile. Not all services travel equally well, however, and considerations of cultural transferability, network development, and host-government policy must be considered.

Cultural Transferability   Commercial banking would seem to be culturally neutral, because financial needs and associated business transactions are relatively homogeneous worldwide. Of course, the exception is the Middle East, where paying interest on a loan is not recognized by the Muslim faith; thus, banks must adjust by creating service charges that include, but do not mention, interest costs. Customer services also are faced with the obvious language barrier and behavioral customs that might affect the service delivery (e.g., the need for nonsmoking areas in U.S. restaurants).

In food service, however, the desire often is to emulate the cultural experience of a foreign land. The success of Benihana of Tokyo in the United States partly results from creating the illusion of a Japanese dining experience while still serving familiar food. Likewise, for many non-Americans, eating at McDonald's and drinking a Coke is an opportunity to experience something "American."

Network Development   As in the case of Federal Express, many service firms reluctantly expand into global operations, forced by the desires of their customers. In the

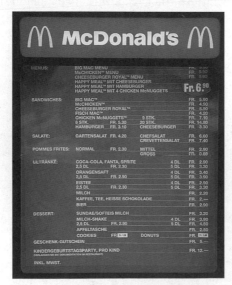

When a successful business in one country expands to another country, it often modifies some features of the service package to accommodate the local culture. © Susan Van Ettew / PhotoEdit

case of VISA and MasterCard, customers expected to be able to use their credit cards wherever they traveled. In both cases, the original concept was designed for a domestic market, but the customers eventually insisted on a global network. Maintaining operations control and standards of quality becomes difficult, however, because staffing usually is accomplished with nationals of the host country and, thus, entails inherent language and cultural differences.

Host-Government Policy   Governments around the world have played a significant role in restricting the growth of multinational services. This includes, but is not limited to, making it difficult to repatriate funds (i.e., to take profits out of the host country). Discrimination has taken a number of creative forms, such as banning the sale of insurance by foreign firms, giving preferential treatment to local shippers, placing restrictions on the international flow of information, and creating delays in the processing of licensing agreements. A major reason for this situation is the continuing refusal of countries (with the exception of the United States) to recognize the importance of services in international trade.

   In November 1982, for the first time, trade barriers on services were placed on the agenda at a meeting of the General Agreement on Tariffs and Trade (GATT), a group of 88 trading nations that for decades has been establishing codes of conduct for trading goods. In 1993, the GATT agreement considering financial services was held hostage by several Asian countries that wished to protect their domestic firms from global competition. For example, Korea prohibits outright foreigners selling mutual funds to local investors, and Japan requires a multiyear application process with no clear objective criteria for approval.[7] In 1994, the Uruguay round of trade negotiations produced new rules to help liberalize trade in services such as tourism.

GLOBAL SERVICE STRATEGIES[8]

Firms and industries must pay attention to the need for global competitive strategies for their services. The biggest factor in a service operations globalization decision should be whether it fits with the firm's global strategy. The service company that responds to heightened competition will look very different from its predecessors. Because it will be focused strategically, it will have an efficient delivery system, a high-quality product, and a flexible cost structure.

   Five basic globalization strategies can be identified: (1) multicountry expansion, (2) importing customers, (3) following your customers, (4) service unbundling, and (5) beating the clock. These strategies are not all mutually exclusive, however. One can think of a number of ways to combine strategies (e.g., combining multicountry expansion with beating the clock).

   Table 19.1 shows how each globalization strategy is affected by the globalization factors faced by multinational service firms. Using this table, managers can consider how these factors affect the implementation of various candidate strategies and their likelihood of success for a specific business in a target country or region. Table 19.1 also summarizes key opportunities and potential problems that each globalization factor contributes to each global service strategy. The service strategy and management implications for service globalization are discussed, beginning with the multicountry expansion strategy.

TABLE 19.1

CONSIDERATIONS IN SELECTING A GLOBAL SERVICE STRATEGY

Globalization factors	Global service strategies				
	Multicountry expansion	Importing customers	Following your customers	Service unbundling	Beating the clock
Customer contact	Train local workers	Develop foreign language and cultural sensitivity skills	Develop foreign customers	Specialize in front- or back-office service components	Provide extended hours of service
Customization	Usually a standard service	Strategic opportunity	Reprototype locally	Meet segments' needs better	More need for reliability and coordination
Complexity	Usually routine	Strategic opportunity	Modify operations	Opportunity for focus	Time compression
Information intensity	Satellite network	On-site advantage	Move experienced managers	May require heavy capital investments	Exploit opportunity
Cultural adaptation	Modify service	Accommodate foreign guests	Could be necessary to achieve scale	Manage worker diversity	Common language necessary
Labor intensity	Reduced labor costs	Increased labor costs	Hire local personnel	Reduced labor costs	Reduced labor costs
Other	Government restrictions	Logistics management	Inadequate infrastructure	Merchandise unbundled component	Capital investments

Source: Adapted from Curtis P. McLaughlin and James A. Fitzsimmons, "Strategies for Globalizing Service Operations," *International Journal of Service Industry Management,* vol. 7, no. 4, 1996, pp. 45–59.

Multicountry Expansion

Multisite expansion commonly has been accomplished using franchising to attract investors and a "cookie-cutter" approach to clone the service rapidly in multiple locations. This expansion strategy is necessary when the service market is defined by the need for customers to travel physically to the service facility. Exporting a successful service to another country without modification, however, can capitalize on selling "a country's cultural experience," as illustrated by the success of McDonald's in Europe, and especially by its experience in Moscow. Cultural adaptation often requires some modification of the service concept, however, as seen in the availability of beer in German McDonald's. Federal Express faced a different cultural adaptation problem in Spain, where the standard 5:00 P.M. pickup was not workable because of the midday siesta and business hours extending into the evening.

Many strategic issues are involved in moving a service operation out and around the world, or *multicountry expansion.* Duplicating a service worldwide is best accomplished when routine services are involved, such as in the example of McDonald's. The customer contact or front-office operations require sensitivity to the local culture, however. The best approach would appear to be hiring and training locals to handle that part of the process in consultation with those who know the approaches that have been successful in other countries.

With the exception of professional services, customization and complexity are not important issues considering the routine nature of many multisite consumer services (e.g., fast foods). Information intensity is not an important consideration either, but managing a global network of service sites might require communications by satellite.

Cultural adaptation, however, is a major issue in service design. Should it be centralized or managed country by country? These questions were addressed by Kentucky Fried Chicken, as noted by the following quote explaining the situation in the late 1960s with which successive sets of professional managers at Heublein and RJ Reynolds (now RJR Nabisco Holdings Corporation) struggled for another 20 years:[9]

> The country managers were like Roman governors sent to govern distant provinces with nothing more than an exhortation to maintain Rome's imperial power and reputation. Few had any operating expertise, they were offered little staff support and the only attention paid to operations was Colonel Sanders' personal efforts to maintain the quality of his original product. Each country manager was on his own to make a success of his venture, and most had to learn the business from scratch.

Unfortunately, the corporate staff seemed to have had little to offer, except to try making the foreign operation conform to the U.S. template. After all, the raison d'être of franchising collapses in the face of local cultural adaptation. The country managers were well aware, however, that the cookie-cutter approach also would not work.

Importing Customers

For the multiservice single-site strategy to be successful internationally, customers must be willing to travel a long distance and stay for an extended time, or telecommunications must be substituted for physical travel. Many services such as prestigious colleges and universities, medical centers (e.g., Mayo Clinic), and tourist attractions (e.g., Disney World) meet these stipulations. Because of a unique tourist attraction at a particular location (e.g., Mt. Crested Butte in Colorado), a service evolves that is focused on that attraction, such as catering to skiers in the winter and mountain bikers in the summer. Rather than exporting the service as in a multisite strategy, the multiservice strategy involves *importing customers*.

A service that decides to retain its location and attract customers from around the world will be faced with developing the foreign-language skill and cultural sensitivity of its customer-contact employees. It may have to pay more to get those skills. The unique features of the location (e.g., tourist attraction or reputation of service personnel) will dictate the selection of this strategy. Differentiation will occur through customization and complexity of the service, and transportation infrastructure and logistics management will be required to accommodate the visiting customers. For example, the Netherlands island of Bonaire, off the coast of Venezuela, caters to scuba divers and is served once a week by a direct KLM flight from Amsterdam.

Following Your Customers

Many service companies open offices overseas not to serve the local markets but to follow their corporate clients overseas and continue to serve them. Attracting local business may require modifications in the service package, however, as well as employment of people who are familiar with local business practices.

To implement the strategy to *follow your customer,* one of the largest business-travel agencies has formed partnerships in almost every area of the world. Its corporate customers want their people served adequately wherever they go. For example, the local representative on the Arabian peninsula was able to extricate travelers from Kuwait during the Iraqi invasion.

Just as law firms expanded into multiple cities to align themselves with their corporate accounts, service companies are pushed to operate in the same countries as their clients. The truly global company wants and demands truly global service from its travel agents, auditors, consultants, and others.

The weakness of this strategy for a company already committed to overseas operations is that it ignores the vast markets represented by the rapidly growing middle classes of many countries. It also leaves the companies that serve these populations free to grow without competition until they reach sufficient quality and scale to become a threat internationally.

Usually, the sales volume that is available from visitors or expatriates in a foreign country is small. This leaves the service manager with interesting choices—should I design my service to follow my customers and their needs, design it to adapt to the local culture, or make a compromise between the two and hope to straddle them both successfully? Everything that operations managers know about services would seem to argue against the likelihood of a successful straddle. Therefore, managers have interesting focus and scale issues to contend with in terms of whether to serve expatriates and visitors or cater to local customers. Where expatriate markets are small and the local market requires considerable adaptation, partnering with local organizations would seem to be an attractive alternative. Even when a new service prototype is not needed for the front office, it may be necessary to adapt operations to the local environment and bring in experienced and flexible managers to make the transplantation work in the face of local infrastructure and social system complexities.

Service Unbundling

Service unbundling involves separating pieces of the value-added chain and focusing on those parts not requiring face-to-face interactions. Discount brokerage is an example: the routinized market transaction activities in the back office are separated from customized professional advising activities and made into a distinct and viable business. When creating global service operations, unbundling can lead to many of the benefits of a focused strategy being achieved.

Complexity seems to be less and less of a problem as managers find more and more ways of unbundling service components and moving those that are information-intensive globally. In the long run, complexity probably will prove to be no more of a barrier to globalization in services than it has been in manufacturing. Many countries have large pools of unemployed and underemployed educated persons, many of whom have high levels of technical training. They are looking for any level of work but readily adapt to higher levels, especially those who have quantitative skills.

All managers should be aware of the distinction between the physical and the informational parts of a process, and they should recognize that today, the informational work can be done almost anywhere in the world. New overseas operations may offer opportunities to install prototype reengineered systems without concern for existing capital investments and employee work rules or habits. This phenomenon is important, for example, in international banking, in which newcomers have major advantages over existing, and often overstaffed, domestic financial services firms. This is especially true for new competitors in countries where automation may have taken place to offset inflationary uncertainties but labor laws or syndicates have restricted downsizing.

Labor intensity often is a factor in choices that are made concerning the globalization of services, but it is not always the same labor-intensity issue that the operations management literature has emphasized. Labor intensity has tended to be associated with customer contact. Managers should examine the labor intensity of an operation when considering alternatives for globalization, but they also should study the interaction of labor intensity with information intensity.

If management chooses to unbundle the service and focus on only part of the former value-added chain, then the customer segments involved will have to accept the new service concept. The unbundled operations must meet those segments better than before, which may require heavy capital investments in information processing and telecommunications facilities to upgrade and enhance the service globally.

Beating the Clock

Beating the clock describes the competitive advantages gained from the fact that one can bypass the constraints of the clock and domestic time zones, including time-based domestic work rules and regulations. Companies in the United States long have known that combining the demand from multiple time zones could improve the productivity of reservation clerks and telemarketers. Quarterdeck, a California software company, provides technical support to its more easterly U.S. customers by transferring their early morning telephone inquiries to Quarterdeck's European technical support center in Ireland. The advantage derives from supplying service to East Coast customers at hours when the California office would be closed. The advantage of being able to give 24-hour service despite local work norms or government regulations on market closings has helped to produce the true globalization of securities markets.

Projects can be expedited by taking advantage of coordinated activities around the globe. For example, a North Carolina bank is having its loan record systems expanded and reprogrammed by an Indian firm. Indian personnel in the United States communicate daily with programmers in India via satellite. The bank management is delighted because the work goes quickly as workers at the Indian site do programming for one-half of the clock and workers at the North Carolina site do testing and debugging during the other half.

The advantages from time compression of the software development process are not likely to go unnoticed in a number of settings. Time-based competition is a widely accepted strategy in manufacturing. In the real-time world of services, there is every reason to expect new innovations to use the speed of light to beat the clock around the world and gain a competitive advantage.

Managers should look at their service processes to find ways in which electronic means can be used to beat the clock. Once these are identified, managers should begin to develop either offensive or defensive strategies. This analysis should include consideration of the potential impact of time-zone shifts on marketing, operations, or human resource aspects of the service. Can such shifts (1) result in economies of operation, (2) provide better access for foreign and domestic customers, (3) support time-based competition in operations, or (4) add to the creativity available in the process without slowing it down? Defensive strategies would involve forming strategic alliances in other time zones. Offensive activities might involve moving to or modifying operations in nondomestic time zones to tap new markets or improve existing ones to beat the competition by beating the clock.

The need for greater reliability and coordination among locations and time zones may require substantial additional investments in training, methods of operation, and telecommunications. Telecommunications certainly will be necessary to make the shift in location transparent to the customer and to realize the full value from the time advantage.

BOX 19.1

Service Benchmark

BIG MACS TO GO: AMERICA'S CONTRIBUTION TO ASIAN CULTURE: HOW TO WAIT IN LINE AND EAT STANDING UP

I once asked my 5-year-old son, who has grown up largely in Tokyo, about his favorite Japanese foods. Gregory thought for a moment and decided on rice balls and McDonald's.

It makes perfect sense to think of Big Macs as Japanese food, since McDonald's is a much more important part of his life in Japan than it is when we are on vacation in America. In particular, given the cramped homes in which most Japanese live, when his Japanese friends have birthdays, the most common place to hold parties is McDonald's.

Golden Arches East is a fascinating study that explores issues of globalization by focusing on McDonald's in five Asian economies, and it comes to conclusions that Gregory would approve of. In many countries McDonald's has been absorbed by local communities and become assimilated, so that it is no longer thought of as a foreign restaurant and in some ways no longer functions as one.

At a time when academics regularly write impenetrably about abstruse irrelevancies, this book is engaging and arises from straightforward questions: how do countries react to McDonald's, and what does the interaction say about those nations? This book, edited by James L. Watson, a distinguished China scholar and professor of anthropology at Harvard University, was a terrific idea, and the authors pull it off very well. Separate scholars look at McDonald's in Hong Kong, China, Taiwan, South Korea, and Japan.

The inquiry is not trivial. McDonald's has had an enormous impact in Asia, affecting manners and mores and the way people live. Ten percent of the beef sold in Japan is in McDonald's hamburgers, and the daily lives of most Japanese people have been shaped more by McDonald's than the State Department.

The most fascinating aspect of this study is its exploration of how McDonald's changed Asia. While America may envision itself as a global beacon for democracy and free markets, this book suggests that the most powerful American influences in East Asia are more mundane.

Take toilets. Bathrooms in Hong Kong restaurants used to range from the merely dirty to the wrenchingly disgusting. And then McDonald's rode into town, in 1975, with bathrooms that offered a novelty—cleanliness. Perhaps the impact is exaggerated, but this book credits McDonald's for helping to raise standards of cleanliness in public rest rooms in Hong Kong.

Likewise, the concept of waiting in line was an alien one in Hong Kong in the old days, and the battle to get on a bus or to get to a cash register was usually like a rugby scrum. Then McDonald's, aghast at the chaos, rigorously imposed lines at its restaurants. The result, many Hong Kong natives think, was that McDonald's helped spread the concept of waiting in line throughout the territory.

Japan's mores have been changing for decades, as an extremely formal country has become steadily more casual, and McDonald's may be a catalyst in that process. Japan has an ancient taboo against *tachigui,* or standing while eating, but this is breaking down, and this book suggests that part of the reason is the spread of McDonald's—whose first outlet in Japan did not have any seats at all.

In China, restaurants traditionally have been maelstroms of loud conversations and bones strewn on the floor. But according to this book, customers at McDonald's outlets in China spoke in lower tones than in other restaurants and were careful not to spit or throw rubbish on the ground: "People in McDonald's were, on the whole, more self-restrained and polite toward one another. One possible explanation for this difference is that the symbolic meaning . . . of the new food, along with customers' willingness to accept the exotic culture associated with fast food, has affected people's table manners in particular and social behavior in general."

All this may amount to American cultural imperialism. But it is hard to imagine even the most passionate nationalist in Asia denouncing American exports like courtesy or clean toilets.

Source: Nicholas D. Kristof, *New York Times,* March 22, 1998, book review of *Golden Arches East: McDonald's in East Asia,* edited by James L. Watson, Stanford University Press, Stanford, Calif., 1998.

SUMMARY

A successful service innovation can grow in two fundamental ways: (1) duplication of the service in different geographic locations with a multisite strategy of becoming a "focused network" or (2) incorporation of different services at the original site using a multiservice strategy, thereby becoming a "clustered service." Although it is not necessarily a desirable objective, some mature service firms combine both strategies and become a "diversified network."

Franchising has become the most common method to implement a multisite strategy in a very rapid manner, using capital that is furnished by investor-owners. Franchising is attractive to prospective entrepreneurs because of the many advantages of buying into a proven concept, but most important, the risk of failure is diminished.

We now live in a "borderless world," with information on products and services available to customers worldwide. For many services, a global presence no longer is an option but a necessity if they wish to continue to serve their customers. Overseas expansion has its risks and challenges depending on the cultural transferability of the service, network development in a foreign land, and government discrimination against foreign services.

KEY TERMS AND DEFINITIONS

Beating the clock using service locations around the globe to achieve 24-hour service availability.

Clustered service a situation in which many services are offered at a single location (e.g., a hospital).

Diversified network a situation in which many services are offered at multiple locations (e.g., branch banks).

Focused network a single service offered at multiple sites, often by use of franchising (e.g., a motel chain).

Focused service a single service offered at a single location (e.g., a family restaurant).

Follow your customers a concept involving expansion overseas to service existing customers who already have established multinational operations.

Franchising a method of duplicating a service concept by attracting investors who become owner-operators bound by a contractual agreement to offer the service in a consistent manner.

Importing customers an approach to growth that attracts customers to an existing site rather than building sites overseas.

Multicountry expansion a growth strategy in which a service is replicated in more than one country using a franchising formula with little adaptation to the local culture.

Service unbundling a separation of the front- and back-office activities to permit a focused strategy, such as outsourcing the back-office activities to an offshore site.

TOPICS FOR DISCUSSION

1. For service firms, how does the operations strategy differ from the marketing strategy?
2. Is the competitive role of operations more important for a service firm than a manufacturing firm?
3. Do you agree that the effect of learning and experience on total unit cost (i.e., the learning curve) has not been demonstrated in a service situation?
4. Manufacturing firms often grow through product innovation. Are there examples of service firms that practice the equivalent strategy?
5. What is your assessment of the multinational competition in services?

Goodwill Industries International, Inc.[10]

"Every time you donate to Goodwill, you give someone the power to change his or her life by getting a job . . . Who knew the shirt you wore last year could turn into a job for someone?"

—*Helping! Magazine*, a publication of Goodwill Industries International Inc., Winter 1998

COMPANY BACKGROUND

Goodwill Industries of Central Texas was founded in 1958 to help people with disabilities lead productive lives. The startup was composed of a staff of four who managed a small retail operation and a Vocational Services Center. Today, Goodwill Industries generates $20 million in gross revenue with 11 retail stores, 25 donation sites, four departments, and 500 employees during peak employment. Sales have continued to rise as the organization has experienced a 20 percent growth in revenue during 1996 and 1997. Exhibit 19.1 presents a graph of revenue and headcount growth.

Goodwill Industries of Central Texas is a nonprofit organization that is independently run and operated, but is affiliated with Goodwill Industries International Inc. (GIII), an organization that helps individual Goodwills with resource issues, national marketing campaigns, executive search information, and federal legislative lobbying. Currently, there are 184 Goodwills in North America and 237 Goodwills throughout the world—each focused on the same mission.

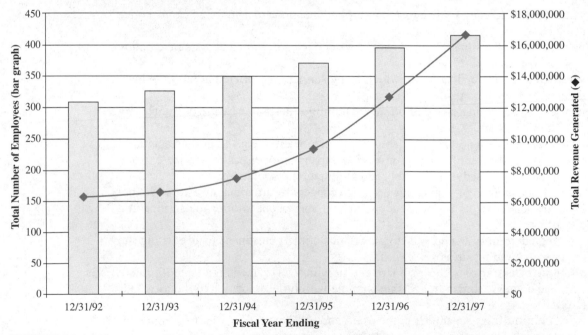

EXHIBIT 19.1 Revenue and headcount growth.

DONATIONS TO DOLLARS

Goodwill Industries operates primarily through the generosity of people and businesses in the local community. The Donated Goods department generates the greatest source of its revenue. The organization relies heavily on donations of used clothing, housewares, electronics, sporting goods, and any other salable items in order to generate the revenue necessary to provide its services. Indeed, the sale of donated goods is expected to generate about $12 million in 1998, while the total budget for the organization in 1998 is $18 million. Exhibit 19.2 displays actual 1997 revenue by source, a distribution typical of the past several years.

THE CHALLENGE AHEAD

Executive management recognizes the emergence of an increasingly competitive marketplace in the thrift arena. This fact is forcing the organization to change the way it does business. Recently there has been increasing pressure for the stores to perform better and better each year despite much stiffer competition for employees and donations. As a result, some retail locations failed to meet store revenue goals. To compound the problem, employee turnover at Goodwill reached as high as 160 percent in some stores during 1997, and local unemployment rates were near 2.5 percent. The mission of Goodwill is to help people find meaningful employment, but when a person is hired as an employee of Retail Operations, the organization tries to retain that person to help create a stable and highly qualified workforce.

THE COMPETITION

Goodwill is faced with competition on two fronts—competition for donations and competition for the sale of those donations. Until a few years ago, Good-will Industries had little competition for its primary raw material—donated used goods. People donated to Goodwill because there was no other outlet except the trash pile. The Salvation Army emerged as a competitor, but for a long time the Salvation Army and Goodwill were the only shows in town. That began to change, however, with the emergence and popularity of consignment stores and "mom and pop" thrift stores. People began to have more choices as to where to donate or sell their used items. These small operations not only eat up potential donations, but also they increase the competition for sales as well. The thrift dollar has become much more competitive in the late 1990s.

There is also an emerging threat from for-profit thrift (FPT) stores, such as Thrift Town, that actively solicit used goods from the same population as Goodwill. Thrift Town is a subsidiary of TGV, a publicly held company whose business plan calls for international expansion by the end of the decade. TGV has completed extensive market research to determine where local nonprofits are weak and is moving into those areas as part of its growth strategy.

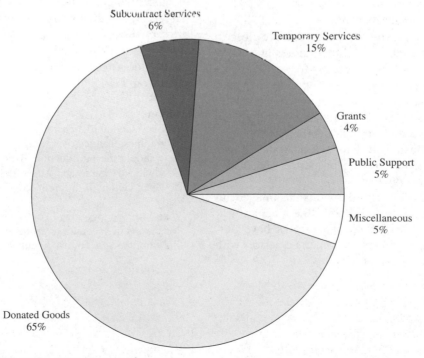

EXHIBIT 19.2   1997 sources of revenue.

Despite the increase in local competition, however, the retail operations of Goodwill Industries International, Inc. grew by 20 percent in 1997. Two new stores were opened and significant expansions were started on two others in 1997. Goodwill Industries International Inc. has an explicit strategy to expand its operations by opening and operating new locations throughout the 15-county territory for which it is responsible. A 20 percent growth in revenue is expected each of the next three years.

WHAT HAS SUSTAINED GROWTH?

Goodwill has developed a unique strategy for competing in the broader local retail market. It has chosen not to compete head-to-head with other retailers for the traditional holiday (i.e., Christmas season) spending dollar. Instead, it has chosen to create a niche for itself by marketing Halloween costumes and decorations. Stores are decorated in Halloween themes and employees are encouraged to come to work in costumes. About 45 percent of the annual advertising budget is geared toward Halloween promotions. This strategy seems to be working, because October accounts for almost 30 percent of retail revenue for the year. On the other hand, this also means that a bad financial Halloween could mean a bad year for the organization.

Goodwill Industries has relied on its ability to open stores in high-traffic locations that are close to the population that donates to their stores and shops in them. There is no formal process for searching for new locations. The decision is left up to the management of the retail operations after visiting potential locations. Goodwill recently built its first store from the ground up in a developing suburban community. This was a significant shift from a long-standing philosophy of leasing or buying properties that had a history of being productive.

Finally, Goodwill has tried to polish its image with the public by trying to look more like a department store than like a thrift shop. The stores have purchased new fixtures and spruced up the exteriors with new signs and paint. Greater care is being taken to ensure that dressing rooms are cleaned regularly and that donation drop-off sites look appealing and clean. The transportation department has recently painted its trucks with the Goodwill logo and the phrase "those jeans you donated just got someone a job."

CUSTOMER ISSUES

A frequent criticism from the public is the difficulty they have in donating to the organization. At one time Goodwill offered a donation pickup service but stopped doing it because of too much difficulty coordinating pickups at homes. The organization also is concerned with the amount of "trash" that the home pickup workers had to deal with. At present, donors must transport to the nearest donation site. This policy went into effect in 1995 but people are still unaware of the change, possibly because they have infrequent contact with Goodwill. Most home pickups were usually for furniture or garage sale remnants that may only bring that donor into contact with Goodwill every five or six years.

Another area of customer concern is Goodwill's retail policy of "all sales are final." Customers complain that they may purchase an item that works during testing at a store but fails to operate at home. The "all sales final" policy means that it is impossible to get a refund, but the manager is empowered to offer a store exchange. These exchanges rarely occur. Part of the reason for the policy is that it is difficult to prove that the items being returned were previously purchased from Goodwill.

Questions

1. Who are Goodwill's customers and how have their demographics changed over time?
2. How should the introduction of for-profit thrifts affect Goodwill's decisions about the role of customer service?
3. How can Goodwill differentiate itself from the competition?
4. Visit http://shopgoodwill.com/ where Goodwill auctions items of special interest and discuss why this online store has great profit potential.

CASE

Federal Express: Tiger International Acquisition[11]

What has become one of America's great success stories began operations almost two decades ago in Memphis, Tennessee. At that time, those who knew of Fred Smith's idea did not realize that his small company was about to revolutionize the air-cargo industry.

In 1972, the Civil Aeronautics Board ruled that operators flying aircraft with an "all-up" weight of less than 75,000 pounds could be classified as an "air taxi" and would not be required to obtain a certificate of "public convenience and necessity" to operate. This made it possible for Federal Express (FedEx) to penetrate the heavily entrenched air-freight industry. FedEx ordered a fleet of 33 Dassault Falcon fan-jets in 1972 and commenced operations a year later. On April 17, 1973, the company delivered 18 packages, becoming the first to offer nationwide overnight delivery.

One of FedEx's fundamental principles was use of the hub-and-spoke system, in which all packages were flown to Memphis first, sorted during the night, and then shipped to their destinations the following morning. This system allowed FedEx to serve a large number of cities with a minimum number of aircraft. It also provided tight control and efficiency of ground operations and soon became increasingly important as package-tracking systems were installed.

During the first two years of operations, FedEx lost money, but revenues surpassed the $5 billion mark in fiscal year 1989, partly because of the acquisition of Tiger International.

As Table 19.2 shows, FedEx began global expansion in 1984, when it purchased Gelco International. FedEx followed that expansion with its first scheduled flight to Europe in 1985, and it established a European headquarters in Brussels, Belgium, that same year.

TABLE 19.2

FEDERAL EXPRESS CORPORATION TIMELINE

1973	Began service with Falcon fan-jets to 25 cities from Memphis in April.
1977	Air-cargo industry deregulated.
1978	Purchased its first Boeing 727 and became a publicly held corporation.
1980	Took delivery of first McDonnell Douglas DC10 and implemented computerized tracking system.
1981	Introduced Overnight Letter, a lower-cost document service. Opened greatly expanded Superhub in Memphis.
1982	Shortened overnight delivery commitment to 10:30 A.M. in all major markets.
1983	Opened first Business Service Center. Became first company to achieve annual revenues of $1 billion in ten years.
1984	Purchased Gelco International and made first scheduled trans-Atlantic flight to Europe. Established European headquarters in Brussels.
1986	Enhanced tracking and informational capabilities with introduction of SuperTracker. Acquired Lex Wilkinson Ltd. of United Kingdom and Cansica of Canada.
1987	Acquired Indianapolis hub. Was granted exclusive small-cargo route to Japan.
1988	Scheduled first trans-Pacific flight to Japan. Acquired nine offshore transportation companies. Announced plan to purchase Tiger International.
1989	Completed purchase of Tiger International and merged Flying Tigers into system, becoming the world's largest full-service all-cargo airline.

Domestic operations were expanded as well. In 1986, regional hubs were established in Oakland, California, and in Newark, New Jersey. In 1987, a sorting facility was opened in Indianapolis, and Honolulu was chosen for the Far East headquarters. That same year, FedEx was granted the rights to a small-cargo route to Japan, and the following year the company was making regularly scheduled flights to Asia.

International expansion did not result in immediate international success, however. In Asia, its planes were flying at half their capacity because of treaty restrictions, and a lack of back-up planes in its South American operations jeopardized guaranteed delivery when regular aircraft were grounded. Even worse, many managers of the companies acquired in Europe had quit.

As a solution to these international bottlenecks, FedEx made a dramatic move in December of 1988, announcing plans to purchase Tiger International, the parent company of Flying Tigers, the world's largest heavy-cargo airline. The purchase price was about $880 million.

This action catapulted FedEx to the forefront of the international cargo market, giving it landing rights in 21 additional countries; however, the addition of Tigers was not without challenges. For example, the leveraged acquisition more than doubled FedEx's long-term debt, to approximately $2 billion. Moreover, FedEx had bought into the business of delivering heavy cargo, much of which was not sent overnight, which represented a significant departure from FedEx's traditional market niche. One of the largest dilemmas facing FedEx following the merger was how to integrate the two workforces.

MAJOR PLAYERS IN THE DOMESTIC AIR-CARGO INDUSTRY

Federal Express is the nation's largest overnight carrier, with more than 40 percent of the domestic market. United Parcel Service (UPS), Emery Air Freight, Airborne Express, DHL (an international carrier based in Brussels), and a few other carriers account for the remaining market share. FedEx had revenues of $3.9 billion and a net income of $188 million in 1988.[12] FedEx had lost approximately $74 million on its international business since 1985, however, prompting the carrier to purchase Tiger International. That acquisition, which gained U.S. government approval on January 31, 1989, gave FedEx a strong entry position into heavy cargo as well as access to 21 additional countries.

Price wars, which began with UPS's entry into the overnight business, have decreased FedEx's revenues per package by 15 percent since 1984. Another setback to FedEx was its $350 million loss on Zapmail, which it dropped in 1986. A document transmission service that relayed information via satellite, Zapmail was quickly made obsolete by facsimile machines.

FedEx does offer its customers several other benefits not matched by its competitors, however. For example, it offers a 1-hour "on-call" pickup service, and through use of its database information system, COSMOS, FedEx guarantees that it can locate any package in its possession within 30 minutes. FedEx has found that this type of customer security helps to ensure continued growth.[13]

THE NATURE OF THE COMPETITION

The air-cargo industry has undergone a series of mergers resulting from the recent price wars that rocked the industry. Also, marketing alliances have been formed between domestic and foreign carriers to take better advantage of international trade and to create new routes and services (e.g., package tracking).

When UPS entered the overnight-package market in 1982, competition rose substantially, starting the series of price wars that have hurt all air-cargo players. FedEx's average revenue per package declined by 30.3 percent between 1983 and 1988.

Fortunately, it appears that the price-cutting strategy may have finally run its course. When UPS, which created the price wars, announced another price cut in October of 1988, its competitors refused to follow, and in January 1993, UPS announced its first price increase in almost six years, a 5-percent increase in charges for next-day service. Several factors such as continued overcapacity, low switching costs, and high exit barriers, however, will continue to make the air-cargo industry extremely competitive.

CONCLUSIONS ON THE AIR-CARGO ENVIRONMENT

Although the situation may be improving, intraindustry competition and rivalry remain the main deterrent to the air-cargo industry. With overcapacity in the industry, firms, desperate to fill planes, continue to realize declining yields on the packages they ship.

Moreover, passenger airlines are reentering the air-cargo market with increased vigor, which also does not help the capacity situation. All these factors are leading current players to consolidate their operations in hope of achieving increased economies of scale.

Technology is acting as both friend and foe of the air-cargo industry. Facsimile machines have carved a large niche from the overnight-document segment; on the other hand, improved databases are enabling companies to provide their clients with another valuable service: improved tracking information on the status of important shipments.

Until now, the large number of shippers has enabled buyers to enjoy low rates, but because of their wide dispersion, buyers are not able to control effectively the air-cargo companies. Likewise, air-cargo companies continue to have an advantage over their suppliers. The ability to purchase older planes keeps firms less dependent on aircraft manufacturers, and a large, unskilled labor pool helps to keep hub labor costs down. A lack of available airport facilities, however, presents a serious problem to the commercial air-freight industry. Not only is the lack of landing slots a problem in the United States, but acquiring government-controlled access to crowded international hubs can present a formidable challenge.

WORLDWIDE DISTRIBUTION

As the globe continues to shrink and economies grow more interdependent, customers are demanding new services to facilitate revamped production processes. One of the most publicized is the just-in-time (JIT) system that many U.S. firms have borrowed from their Japanese competitors. JIT systems argue for elimination of the traditional inventory stockpiles common to manufacturing, including the raw material, work-in-process, and finished-goods inventories. Without question, such a scheme relies on having the right part at the right place at the right time.

Air express has been able to play a reliable role in delivering these needed materials on time. FedEx and its competitors have succeeded in contracting with manufacturers to supply the needed logistical expertise to support its JIT framework. Essentially, the planes have become flying warehouses. As this area grows, the Tiger addition to FedEx should reap large yields with its ability to handle the heavier shipments that are associated with international manufacturing.

For example, an increasing amount of parts made in Asia are being shipped to the United States for final assembly.

POWERSHIP

To facilitate further penetration into a customer's business, FedEx developed Powership, which is a program that locates terminals on a client's premises and, thus, enables FedEx to stay abreast of the firm's needs. In simplifying the daily shipping process, an automated program tracks shipments, provides pricing information, and prints invoices. Such a device helps to eliminate the administrative need of reconciling manifests with invoices. Currently, more than 7,000 of FedEx's highest-volume customers are integrated into the Powership system.

At Federal Express, customer automation is expected to play an increasingly significant role. By tying technological innovations with reliable on-time delivery, FedEx is achieving its goal of getting closer to the customer.

CORPORATE CULTURE

Many believe that FedEx could not have grown to its current magnitude had it been forced to deal with the added pressure of negotiating with a unionized workforce. FedEx has never employed organized labor, although attempts at unionization have been made. In 1976, the International Association of Machinists and Aerospace Workers tried to organize the company's mechanics, who rejected the offer. Likewise, FedEx's pilots rejected an offer by the Airline Pilots Association during that same period. In 1978, the Teamsters attempted to organize the hub sorters but could not get enough signatures for a vote.

Despite an admirable human resource track record, the outlook for FedEx to continue its past performance is hazy. Because of the Tiger International acquisition, FedEx had to merge the unionized Flying Tigers workforce with its own union-free environment. Previously, the willingness of FedEx workers to go above and beyond in performing their duties had given the company a marked advantage over UPS, the nation's largest employer of United Brotherhood of Teamsters members. As the FedEx–Tiger merger progressed, however, many questions remained to be answered.

ACQUISITION OF TIGER INTERNATIONAL

In December 1988, FedEx announced its intent to purchase Flying Tigers, and in early 1989, more than 40 years of air-cargo experience were merged with FedEx. Besides giving FedEx entry into an additional 21 nations, the Tigers merger possessed several other advantages for the aggressive company. Almost overnight, FedEx became owner of the world's largest full-service, all-cargo airline, nearly three times the size of its nearest competitor. Because FedEx could use this large fleet on its newly acquired routes, it no longer would be forced into the position of contracting out to other freight carriers in markets not served previously.

The addition of heavy freight to the FedEx service mix was viewed as a boost to its traditional express package–delivery business. The merger fit in neatly with the company's plans to focus on the higher-margin box business while shifting away from document service. During the preceding two years, box shipments had increased by 53 percent, generating as much as 80 percent of revenues and an estimated 90 percent of profits.

On the downside, as noted earlier, the $2 billion debt that was incurred by the merger and the capital intensiveness of the heavy-cargo business made the company more vulnerable to economic swings. Although the merger meshed well into its plans, FedEx still was a newcomer to the heavy-cargo market.

Another hurdle was that many premerger Flying Tigers customers were competitors that used Tigers to reach markets where they, like FedEx, had no service or could not establish service.

Finally, FedEx had to integrate the 6,500 unionized Tigers workers into a union-free company. Although Flying Tigers was founded with much the same type of entrepreneurial spirit that was cherished at Federal Express, the carrier had seen its workforce become members of organized labor early in its existence.

At the time of the merger, the Tigers union ties were severed. FedEx promised to find positions for all employees, but critics felt that the union background of Tigers workers would dilute the corporate culture at Federal Express. Whether FedEx could continue its success story appeared to hinge on its ability to impart its way of life to the Tigers workers, not vice versa.

Questions

1. Describe the growth strategy of Federal Express. How has this strategy differed from those of its competitors?
2. What risks are involved in the acquisition of Tiger International?
3. In addition to the question of merging FedEx and Flying Tigers pilots, what other problems could be anticipated in accomplishing this merger?
4. Suggest a plan of action that Fred Smith could have used to address the potential acquisition problems given in your answer to the previous question.

SELECTED BIBLIOGRAPHY

CHASE, R. B., and R. H. HAYES: "Operations' Role in Service Firm Competitiveness," *Sloan Management Review,* vol. 33, no. 1, Fall 1991, pp. 15–26.

DONTHU, NAVEEN, and BOONGHEE YOO: "Cultural Influences on Service Quality Expectations," *Journal of Service Research,* vol. 1, no. 2, November 1998, pp. 178–186.

HAYWOOD-FARMER, J., and J. GARCELON: "The Theoretical Issues Propagated by International Trade in Services," *Operations Management Review,* vol. 9, no. 1, 1992, pp. 18–27.

——— and J. NOLLET: "Growth and Strategy," *Services PLUS,* G. Morin Publisher Ltd., Boucherville, Quebec, Canada, 1991, chap. 8, pp. 119–136.

HESKETT, J. L.: "The Multinational Development of Service Industries," *Managing in the Service Economy,* Harvard Business School Press, Boston, 1986, chap. 8, pp. 135–152.

JOHNSON, MICHAEL D., ANDREAS HERRMANN, and FRANK HUBER: "Growth Through Product-Sharing Services," *Journal of Service Research,* vol. 1, no. 2, November 1998, pp. 167–177.

MCLAUGHLIN, C. P., and J. A. FITZSIMMONS: "Strategies for Globalizing Service Operations," *International Journal of Service Industry Management,* vol. 7, no. 4, 1996, pp. 45–59.

OHMAE, KENICHI: *The Borderless World,* Harper Business, New York, 1990.

ENDNOTES

1. From Kevin Helliker, "How a Motel Chain Lost Its Moorings after 1980's Buy-Out," *The Wall Street Journal,* May 26, 1992, p. 1.
2. S. E. Kimes and J. A. Fitzsimmons, "Selecting Profitable Hotel Sites at La Quinta Motor Inns," *Interfaces,* vol. 20, no. 2, March 1990, pp. 12–20.
3. M. Carman and Eric Langeard, "Growth Strategies for Service Firms," *Strategic Management Journal,* vol. 1, no. 1, January–March 1980, p. 19.
4. From Daniel Pearl, "Federal Express Finds Its Pioneering Formula Falls Flat Overseas," *The Wall Street Journal,* April 15, 1991, p. 1.
5. From Kenichi Ohmae, *The Borderless World,* Harper Business, New York, 1990, p. 19.
6. From James L. Heskett, "The Multinational Development of Service Industries," *Managing in the Service Economy,* Harvard Business School Press, Boston, 1986, chap. 8, pp. 140–152.
7. From Robert C. Pozen, "Is America Being Shut Out Again?" *New York Times,* January 10, 1993, p. 13.
8. From Curtis P. McLaughlin and James A. Fitzsimmons, "Strategies for Globalizing Service Operations," *International Journal of Service Industry Management,* vol. 7, no. 4, 1996, pp. 45–59.
9. Kentucky Fried Chicken (Japan) Limited, case no. 9-387-043, Harvard Business School, Boston, 1993, p. 1.
10. Prepared by Steve Callahan, Cindy Gage, and Kathleen Woodhouse under the supervision of Professor James A. Fitzsimmons.
11. Prepared by Garland Wilkinson under the supervision of Professor James A. Fitzsimmons.
12. Dean Foust, "Mr. Smith Goes Global," *Business Week,* February 13, 1989, pp. 66–72.
13. David A. Clancy, "Air Cargo Takes Off," *Transportation and Distribution,* January 1989, pp. 32–36.

Areas of a Standard Normal Distribution

An entry in the table is the area under the curve that is between $z = 0$ and a positive value of z. The area in the tail is found by subtracting the table entry from 0.5. Areas for negative values of z are obtained by symmetry.

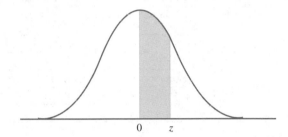

z	0.00	0.01	0.02	0.03	0.04	0.05	0.06	0.07	0.08	0.09
0.0	0.0000	0.0040	0.0080	0.0120	0.0160	0.0199	0.0239	0.0279	0.0319	0.0359
0.1	0.0398	0.0438	0.0478	0.0517	0.0557	0.0596	0.0636	0.0675	0.0714	0.0753
0.2	0.0793	0.0832	0.0871	0.0910	0.0948	0.0987	0.1026	0.1064	0.1103	0.1141
0.3	0.1179	0.1217	0.1255	0.1293	0.1331	0.1368	0.1406	0.1443	0.1480	0.1517
0.4	0.1554	0.1591	0.1628	0.1664	0.1700	0.1736	0.1772	0.1808	0.1844	0.1879
0.5	0.1915	0.1950	0.1985	0.2019	0.2054	0.2088	0.2123	0.2157	0.2190	0.2224
0.6	0.2257	0.2291	0.2324	0.2357	0.2389	0.2422	0.2454	0.2486	0.2517	0.2549
0.7	0.2580	0.2611	0.2642	0.2673	0.2703	0.2734	0.2764	0.2794	0.2823	0.2852
0.8	0.2881	0.2910	0.2939	0.2967	0.2995	0.3023	0.3051	0.3078	0.3106	0.3133
0.9	0.3159	0.3186	0.3212	0.3238	0.3264	0.3289	0.3315	0.3340	0.3365	0.3389
1.0	0.3413	0.3438	0.3461	0.3485	0.3508	0.3531	0.3554	0.3577	0.3599	0.3621
1.1	0.3643	0.3665	0.3686	0.3708	0.3729	0.3749	0.3770	0.3790	0.3810	0.3830
1.2	0.3849	0.3869	0.3888	0.3907	0.3925	0.3944	0.3962	0.3980	0.3997	0.4015
1.3	0.4032	0.4049	0.4066	0.4082	0.4099	0.4115	0.4131	0.4147	0.4162	0.4177
1.4	0.4192	0.4207	0.4222	0.4236	0.4251	0.4265	0.4279	0.4292	0.4306	0.4319
1.5	0.4332	0.4345	0.4357	0.4370	0.4382	0.4394	0.4406	0.4418	0.4429	0.4441
1.6	0.4452	0.4463	0.4474	0.4484	0.4495	0.4505	0.4515	0.4525	0.4535	0.4545
1.7	0.4554	0.4564	0.4573	0.4582	0.4591	0.4599	0.4608	0.4616	0.4625	0.4633
1.8	0.4641	0.4649	0.4656	0.4664	0.4671	0.4678	0.4686	0.4693	0.4699	0.4706
1.9	0.4713	0.4719	0.4726	0.4732	0.4738	0.4744	0.4750	0.4756	0.4761	0.4767
2.0	0.4772	0.4778	0.4783	0.4788	0.4793	0.4798	0.4803	0.4808	0.4812	0.4817
2.1	0.4821	0.4826	0.4830	0.4834	0.4838	0.4842	0.4846	0.4850	0.4854	0.4857
2.2	0.4861	0.4864	0.4868	0.4871	0.4875	0.4878	0.4881	0.4884	0.4887	0.4890
2.3	0.4893	0.4896	0.4898	0.4901	0.4904	0.4906	0.4909	0.4911	0.4913	0.4916
2.4	0.4918	0.4920	0.4922	0.4925	0.4927	0.4929	0.4931	0.4932	0.4934	0.4936
2.5	0.4938	0.4940	0.4941	0.4943	0.4945	0.4946	0.4948	0.4949	0.4951	0.4952
2.6	0.4953	0.4955	0.4956	0.4957	0.4959	0.4960	0.4961	0.4962	0.4963	0.4964
2.7	0.4965	0.4966	0.4967	0.4968	0.4969	0.4970	0.4971	0.4972	0.4973	0.4974
2.8	0.4974	0.4975	0.4976	0.4977	0.4977	0.4978	0.4979	0.4979	0.4980	0.4981
2.9	0.4981	0.4982	0.4982	0.4983	0.4984	0.4984	0.4985	0.4985	0.4986	0.4986
3.0	0.4987	0.4987	0.4987	0.4988	0.4988	0.4989	0.4989	0.4989	0.4990	0.4990

Source: Donald H. Sanders, A. Franklin Murph, and Robert J. Eng, *Statistics—A Fresh Approach,* McGraw-Hill Book Company, New York, 1976.

Uniformly Distributed Random Numbers [0,1]

0.06785	0.39867	0.90588	0.17801
0.81075	0.87641	0.67964	0.43877
0.98544	0.51653	0.44093	0.79428
0.31479	0.75057	0.28248	0.26863
0.12484	0.88287	0.78805	0.00907
0.23882	0.82137	0.51759	0.24723
0.23897	0.93060	0.94078	0.44676
0.40374	0.57000	0.33415	0.90000
0.73622	0.85896	0.36825	0.31500
0.36952	0.39367	0.09426	0.79517
0.14510	0.05047	0.01535	0.46997
0.12719	0.35159	0.55903	0.01268
0.99407	0.53816	0.64881	0.64309
0.32694	0.57237	0.74242	0.68045
0.42780	0.54704	0.63281	0.92243
0.00633	0.87197	0.90597	0.95629
0.38490	0.27804	0.06567	0.49591
0.22363	0.96354	0.25298	0.88459
0.54105	0.62235	0.93190	0.66122
0.31786	0.84724	0.04084	0.98260
0.47556	0.38855	0.52135	0.34085
0.70850	0.55051	0.86505	0.21192
0.64791	0.89438	0.83997	0.00898
0.21424	0.34592	0.77920	0.16675
0.77524	0.41976	0.08429	0.71506

Values of L_q for the *M/M/c* Queuing Model

ρ	$c = 1$	$c = 2$	$c = 3$	$c = 4$	$c = 5$	$c = 6$	$c = 7$	$c = 8$
0.15	0.026	0.001						
0.20	0.050	0.002						
0.25	0.083	0.004						
0.30	0.129	0.007						
0.35	0.188	0.011						
0.40	0.267	0.017						
0.45	0.368	0.024	0.002					
0.50	0.500	0.033	0.003					
0.55	0.672	0.045	0.004					
0.60	0.900	0.059	0.006					
0.65	1.207	0.077	0.008					
0.70	1.633	0.098	0.011					
0.75	2.250	0.123	0.015					
0.80	3.200	0.152	0.019					
0.85	4.817	0.187	0.024	0.003				
0.90	8.100	0.229	0.030	0.004				
0.95	18.050	0.277	0.037	0.005				
1.0		0.333	0.045	0.007				
1.1		0.477	0.066	0.011				
1.2		0.675	0.094	0.016	0.003			
1.3		0.951	0.130	0.023	0.004			
1.4		1.345	0.177	0.032	0.006			
1.5		1.929	0.237	0.045	0.009			
1.6		2.844	0.313	0.060	0.012			
1.7		4.426	0.409	0.080	0.017			
1.8		7.674	0.532	0.105	0.023			
1.9		17.587	0.688	0.136	0.030	0.007		
2.0			0.889	0.174	0.040	0.009		
2.1			1.149	0.220	0.052	0.012		
2.2			1.491	0.277	0.066	0.016		
2.3			1.951	0.346	0.084	0.021		
2.4			2.589	0.431	0.105	0.027	0.007	
2.5			3.511	0.533	0.130	0.034	0.009	
2.6			4.933	0.658	0.161	0.043	0.011	
2.7			7.354	0.811	0.198	0.053	0.014	
2.8			12.273	1.000	0.241	0.066	0.018	
2.9			27.193	1.234	0.293	0.081	0.023	
3.0				1.528	0.354	0.099	0.028	0.008
3.1				1.902	0.427	0.120	0.035	0.010
3.2				2.386	0.513	0.145	0.043	0.012
3.3				3.027	0.615	0.174	0.052	0.015
3.4				3.906	0.737	0.209	0.063	0.019
3.5				5.165	0.882	0.248	0.076	0.023
3.6				7.090	1.055	0.295	0.091	0.028

ρ	$c = 1$	$c = 2$	$c = 3$	$c = 4$	$c = 5$	$c = 6$	$c = 7$	$c = 8$
3.7				10.347	1.265	0.349	0.109	0.034
3.8				16.937	1.519	0.412	0.129	0.041
3.9				36.859	1.830	0.485	0.153	0.050
4.0					2.216	0.570	0.180	0.059
4.1					2.703	0.668	0.212	0.070
4.2					3.327	0.784	0.248	0.083
4.3					4.149	0.919	0.289	0.097
4.4					5.268	1.078	0.337	0.114
4.5					6.862	1.265	0.391	0.133
4.6					9.289	1.487	0.453	0.156
4.7					13.382	1.752	0.525	0.181
4.8					21.641	2.071	0.607	0.209
4.9					46.566	2.459	0.702	0.242
5.0						2.938	0.810	0.279
5.1						3.536	0.936	0.321
5.2						4.301	1.081	0.368
5.3						5.303	1.249	0.422
5.4						6.661	1.444	0.483
5.5						8.590	1.674	0.553
5.6						11.519	1.944	0.631
5.7						16.446	2.264	0.721
5.8						26.373	2.648	0.823
5.9						56.300	3.113	0.939
6.0							3.683	1.071
6.1							4.394	1.222
6.2							5.298	1.397
6.3							6.480	1.598
6.4							8.077	1.831
6.5							10.341	2.102
6.6							13.770	2.420
6.7							19.532	2.796
6.8							31.127	3.245
6.9							66.055	3.786
7.0								4.447
7.1								5.270
7.2								6.314
7.3								7.675
7.4								9.511
7.5								12.109
7.6								16.039
7.7								22.636
7.8								35.898
7.9								75.827

Equations for Selected Queuing Models

Definition of Symbols

n = number of customers in the system

λ = [lambda] mean arrival rate (e.g., customer arrivals per hour)

μ = [mu] mean service rate per busy server (e.g., service capacity in customers per hour)

ρ = [rho] traffic intensity

N = maximum number of customers allowed in the system

c = number of servers

P_n = probability of exactly n customers in the system

L_s = mean number of customers in the system

L_q = mean number of customers in queue

L_b = mean number of customers in queue for a busy system

W_s = mean time customer spends in the system

W_q = mean time customer spends in the queue

W_b = mean time customer spends in queue for a busy system

I. Standard *M/M*/1 Model ($0 < \rho < 1.0$)

$$P_0 = 1 - \rho \tag{I.1}$$

$$P(n \geq k) = \rho^k \tag{I.2}$$

$$P_n = P_0\rho^n \tag{I.3}$$

$$L_s = \frac{\lambda}{\mu - \lambda} \tag{I.4}$$

$$L_q = \frac{\rho\lambda}{\mu - \lambda} \tag{I.5}$$

$$L_b = \frac{\lambda}{\mu - \lambda} \tag{I.6}$$

$$W_s = \frac{1}{\mu - \lambda} \tag{I.7}$$

$$W_q = \frac{\rho}{\mu - \lambda} \tag{I.8}$$

$$W_b = \frac{1}{\mu - \lambda} \tag{I.9}$$

II. Standard *M*/*M*/*c* Model ($0 < \rho < c$)

$$P_0 = \frac{1}{\left(\sum_{i=0}^{c-1} \frac{\rho^i}{i!} \right) + \frac{\rho^c}{c!(1 - \rho/c)}} \tag{II.1}$$

$$P_n = \begin{cases} \dfrac{\rho^n}{n!} P_0 & \text{for } 0 \le n \le c \\[2ex] \dfrac{\rho^n}{c! c^{n-c}} P_0 & \text{for } n \ge c \end{cases} \tag{II.2}$$

$$P(n \ge c) = \frac{\rho^c \mu c}{c!(\mu c - \lambda)} P_0 \tag{II.3}$$

$$L_s = \frac{\rho^{c+1}}{(c-1)!(c-\rho)^2} P_0 + \rho \tag{II.4}$$

$$L_q = L_s - \rho \tag{II.5}$$

$$L_b = \frac{L_q}{P(n \ge c)} \tag{II.6}$$

$$W_s = \frac{L_q}{\lambda} + \frac{1}{\mu} \tag{II.7}$$

$$W_q = \frac{L_q}{\lambda} \tag{II.8}$$

$$W_b = \frac{W_q}{P(n \ge c)} \tag{II.9}$$

III. Standard *M*/*G*/1 Model (*V*(*t*) = service time variance)

$$L_s = L_q + \rho \tag{III.1}$$

$$L_q = \frac{\rho^2 + \lambda^2 V(t)}{2(1 - \rho)} \tag{III.2}$$

$$W_s = \frac{L_s}{\lambda} \tag{III.3}$$

$$W_b = \frac{L_q}{\lambda} \tag{III.4}$$

IV. Self-Service $M/G/\infty$ Model ($e = 2.718$, the base of natural logarithms)

$$P_n = \frac{e^{-\rho}}{n!}\rho^n \qquad \text{for } n \geq 0 \tag{IV.1}$$

$$L_s = \rho \tag{IV.2}$$

$$W_s = \frac{1}{\mu} \tag{IV.3}$$

V. Finite-Queue $M/M/1$ Model

$$P_0 = \begin{cases} \dfrac{1-\rho}{1-\rho^{N+1}} & \text{for } \lambda \neq \mu \\[3mm] \dfrac{1}{N+1} & \text{for } \lambda = \mu \end{cases} \tag{V.1}$$

$$P(n > 0) = 1 - P_0 \tag{V.2}$$

$$P_n = P_0\rho^n \quad \text{for } n \leq N \tag{V.3}$$

$$L_s = \begin{cases} \dfrac{\rho}{1-\rho} - \dfrac{(N+1)\rho^{N+1}}{1-\rho^{N+1}} & \text{for } \lambda \neq \mu \\[3mm] \dfrac{N}{2} & \text{for } \lambda \neq \mu \end{cases} \tag{V.4}$$

$$L_q = L_s - (1 - P_0) \tag{V.5}$$

$$L_b = \frac{L_q}{1 - P_0} \tag{V.6}$$

$$W_s = \frac{L_q}{\lambda(1 - P_N)} + \frac{1}{\mu} \tag{V.7}$$

$$W_q = W_s - \frac{1}{\mu} \tag{V.8}$$

$$W_b = \frac{W_q}{1 - P_0} \tag{V.9}$$

VI. Finite-Queue $M/M/c$ Model

$$P_0 = \frac{1}{\left(\displaystyle\sum_{i=0}^{c} \frac{\rho^i}{i!}\right) + \left(\dfrac{1}{c!}\right)\left(\displaystyle\sum_{i=c+1}^{N} \frac{\rho^i}{c^{i-c}}\right)} \tag{VI.1}$$

$$P_n = \begin{cases} \dfrac{\rho^n}{n!}\, P_0 & \text{for } 0 \leq n \leq c \\[3mm] \dfrac{\rho^n}{c!\,c^{n-c}}\, P_0 & \text{for } c \leq n \leq N \end{cases} \qquad\qquad \text{(VI.2)}$$

$$P(n \geq c) = 1 - P_0 \sum_{i=0}^{c-1} \frac{\rho^i}{i!} \qquad\qquad \text{(VI.3)}$$

$$L_s = \frac{P_0 \rho^{c+1}}{(c-1)!(c-\rho)^2}\left[1 - \left(\frac{\rho}{c}\right)^{N-c} - (N-c)\left(\frac{\rho}{c}\right)^{N-c}\left(1 - \frac{\rho}{c}\right)\right] + \rho(1 - P_N) \qquad \text{(VI.4)}$$

$$L_q = L_s - \rho(1 - P_N) \qquad\qquad \text{(VI.5)}$$

$$L_b = \frac{L_q}{P(n \geq c)} \qquad\qquad \text{(VI.6)}$$

$$W_s = \frac{L_q}{\lambda(1 - P_N)} + \frac{1}{\mu} \qquad\qquad \text{(VI.7)}$$

$$W_q = W_s - \frac{1}{\mu} \qquad\qquad \text{(VI.8)}$$

$$W_b = \frac{W_q}{P(n \geq c)} \qquad\qquad \text{(VI.9)}$$

SUBJECT INDEX